The Road to Disunion

Secessionists Triumphant
1854–1861

By William W. Freehling

Prelude to Civil War: The Nullification Controversy
in South Carolina, 1816–1836

Willie Lee Rose, Slavery and Freedom (Editor)

Secession Debated: Georgia's Showdown in 1860
(Editor, with Craig M. Simpson)

The Reintegration of American History: Slavery and the Civil War

The South vs. The South: How Anti-Confederate Southerners
Shaped the Course of the Civil War

THE ROAD TO DISUNION

Volume I: Secessionists at Bay, 1776–1854
Volume II: Secessionists Triumphant, 1854–1861

The Road to Disunion

VOLUME II

Secessionists Triumphant
1854–1861

WILLIAM W. FREEHLING

OXFORD

UNIVERSITY PRESS

2007

OXFORD
UNIVERSITY PRESS

Oxford University Press, Inc., publishes works that further
Oxford University's objective of excellence
in research, scholarship, and education.

Oxford   New York
Auckland   Cape Town   Dar es Salaam   Hong Kong   Karachi
Kuala Lumpur   Madrid   Melbourne   Mexico City   Nairobi
New Delhi   Shanghai   Taipei   Toronto

With offices in
Argentina   Austria   Brazil   Chile   Czech Republic   France   Greece
Guatemala   Hungary   Italy   Japan   Poland   Portugal   Singapore
South Korea   Switzerland   Thailand   Turkey   Ukraine   Vietnam

Copyright © 2007 by William W. Freehling

Published by Oxford University Press, Inc.
198 Madison Avenue, New York, NY 10016
www.oup.com

ISBN 978-0-19-505815-4

Oxford is a registered trademark of Oxford University Press

The Library of Congress has catalogued Volume I as follows:
Freehling, William W., 1935–
The road to disunion / William W. Freehling
p. cm.
Contents: v. 1. Secessionists at bay, 1776–1854
ISBN 0-19-505814-3 (v. 1)
1. United States—History—Civil War, 1861–1865—Causes
2. Secession. 3. Southern States—Politics and
government—1775–1865. 4. United States—Politics and
government—1815–1861. I. Title.
E468.9.F84   1990
973.7'11—dc20   89-26511   CIP

1 3 5 7 9 8 6 4 2
Printed in the United States of America
on acid-free paper

Again and again

for

Alison

and in memory

of

Sheldon Meyer

Contents

Illustrations, x

Maps, xi

Preface, xii

Prologue: Yancey's Rage, 1

PART I BETTER ECONOMIC TIMES GENERATE WORSE DEMOCRATIC DILEMMAS, 7

    1. Democracy and Despotism, 1776–1854: *Road,* Volume I, Revisited, 9

    2. Economic Bonanza, 1850–1860, 19

PART II THE CLIMACTIC IDEOLOGICAL FRUSTRATIONS, 25

    3. James Henry Hammond and the Unsolvable Proslavery Puzzle, 27

    4. The Three Imperfect Solutions, 35

    5. The Puzzling Future and the Infuriating Scapegoats, 48

PART III THE CLIMACTIC POLITICAL FRUSTRATIONS, 59

    6. Bleeding Kansas and Bloody Sumner, 61

    7. The Scattering of the Ex-Whigs, 85

    8. James Buchanan's Precarious Election, 97

9. The President-Elect as the Dred Scotts' Judge, 109

10. The Climactic Kansas Crisis, 123

11. Caribbean Delusions, 145

12. Reopening the African Slave Trade, 168

13. Reenslaving Free Blacks, 185

PART IV   JOHN BROWN AND THREE OTHER MEN
          COINCIDENTALLY NAMED JOHN, 203

14. John Brown and Violent Invasion, 205

15. John G. Fee and Religious Invasion, 222

16. John Underwood and Economic Invasion, 236

17. John Clark and Political Invasion, 246

PART V   THE ELECTION OF 1860, 269

18. Yancey's Lethal Abstraction, 271

19. The Democracy's Charleston Convention, 288

20. The Democracy's Baltimore Convention, 309

21. Suspicious Southerners and Lincoln's Election, 323

PART VI   SOUTH CAROLINA DARES, 343

22. The State's Rights Justification, 345

23. The Motivation, 352

24. The Tactics and Tacticians, 375

25. The Triumph, 395

    Coda: Did the Coincidence Change History? 423

PART VII   LOWER SOUTH LANDSLIDE, UPPER
           SOUTH STALEMATE, 427

26. Alexander Stephens's Fleeting Moment, 429

    Coda: Did Stephens's and Hammond's Personalities
    Change History? 442

27. Southwestern Separatists' Tactics and Messages, 445

28. Compromise Rejected, 463

29. Military Explosions, 476

30. Snowball Rolling, 490

31. Upper South Stalemate, 499

32. Stalemate—and the South—Shattered, 517

    Coda: *How* Did Slavery Cause the Civil War? 531

Abbreviations Used in Notes, 535

Notes, 537

Index, 587

Illustrations

Compiled with the help of Erik Alexander

William Lowndes Yancey and Nathan Beman, 5

David Atchison and Stephen A. Douglas, 63

Preston Brooks, Charles Sumner, and a Brooks/Sumner Drawing, 83

James Buchanan and Howell Cobb, 106

Harriet and Dred Scott and Roger B. Taney, 120

Charleston Harbor and New Orleans Harbor, 156

Natchez's Monmouth and Dunleith, 164

The Harpers Ferry Environs, 211

Gentle John Brown and Violent John Brown, 216

John Brown and Henry Wise, 218

John G. Fee and Cassius Clay, 228

Jefferson Davis and Albert Gallatin Brown, 277

A Charleston Single House, a Charleston Double House, and a Charleston Spiked Fence, 358

John Townsend, Robert Gourdin, Andrew Magrath, and Robert Barnwell Rhett, Sr., 392–93

James and Mary Chesnut, 397

The Younger James Hammond and the Older James Hammond, 417

David Flavel Jamison and a South Carolina Palmetto Tree, 423

Alexander Stephens and Stephens's Liberty Hall, 434

The Unfinished Capitol Building, John Crittenden,
and Robert Toombs, 473

James Holcombe and George Randolph, 510

Edmund Ruffin, Fort Sumter Bombarded, and
Fort Sumter Devastated, 522–523

Maps

by David Fuller

The Three Souths and the Border North, 1860, 2
The Kansas/Missouri Battleground, 66
The New Orleans Dream of Empire, 146
The Maryland Reenslavement Controversy, 192
The Harpers Ferry Environs, 210
South Carolina's Key Railroads During the Secession Crisis, 407
The Virginia Regions, 1860, 505
Forts Sumter and Pickens, 518

Preface

In this second and concluding volume of my southern *Road to Disunion,* Northerners sometimes step front and center, to illuminate provokers, targets, and effects of southern defenders' rage. But by usually focusing on aggressively defensive Southerners, I seek to resurrect their pre–Civil War political saga, one of America's most important and mysterious epics.

The importance lies in the illumination of colliding democratic and despotic governing systems. The Old South combined dictatorship over blacks with republicanism for whites, supposedly cleanly severed by an All-Mighty Color Line. But to preserve dictatorial dominion over blacks, the slaveholding minority sometimes trenched on majoritarian government for whites, in the nation as well as in their section.

These preventative strikes leached much of the mystery from Yankees' antisouthern responses. Northerners called the militant slavocracy the Slave Power, meaning that those with autocratic power over blacks also deployed undemocratic power over whites. Most Yankees hardly embraced blacks or abolitionists. Yet racist Northerners would fight the Slave Power to the death to preserve their white men's majoritarian rights.[1] More mysterious is why Southerners risked a potentially suicidal rebellion against Northerners who disclaimed any intention of forcing abolition on southern states.

My explanation emphasizes that problems inside southern culture nurtured both fury at any outside criticism and determination to prevent antislavery democratic discourse from seeping anywhere near despots' doors. The internal travail and its external consequences become clearest in widest perspective. Thus my first volume of *Road,* published a decade and a half ago, traced the democratic-despotic section's political traumas from the American Revolution through the 1854 passage of the Kansas-Nebraska Act. This sequel moves from that law's bloody Kansas aftermath to the Civil War's first blood. As the war nears, my narrative slows, to detail the spectacles that started with John Brown's raid and ended with Fort Sumter's surrender. My slimmer epilogue volume, *The South vs. The South*, published a half decade ago, traces my *Road to Disunion* themes from Fort Sumter through the war.[2]

In this book, as in *The South vs. The South* and as in my previous *Road* volume, widening southern divisions between regions, races, and classes frustrated attempts to forge a single civilization.[3] To bridge potentially corrosive differences, late antebellum Southerners deployed ever more intriguing proslavery ideologies and ever more zany political crusades. Because these initiatives failed, the secessionist faction of white Southerners considered President-elect Lincoln an immediate menace to their imperfectly consolidated regime. Most Southerners at first retorted that secessionists exaggerated the immediate threat and rushed to revolution prematurely. Yet disunionists strained, struggled, and ultimately secured a southern majority, not least to preclude any Republican Party attempt for a majority inside the most exposed southern states.

The minority of the minority's stretch illuminated the tension that exists between majority will and minority power whenever democracy exists—and the deeper difficulty of a democratic resolution when a despotic social institution thrives. A wider understanding of why our peaceful democratic processes failed at home may temper overconfidence that American republicanism will always work abroad. Furthermore, slaveholders' intolerance for contrary opinion devastated our House Divided; and a broader awareness of that historical lesson may spare democracies from some cries that disagreement proves disloyalty.

Once again in this volume, I resist academics' tendency to maximize multicultural social history and to minimize mainstream political history. Four million blacks' emancipation, for example, a central social history event, becomes unintelligible without establishment white males' political (and military) history. Instead of dismissing mainstream political history, social history must deeply inform it. Thus the nature of masters' dictatorship over blacks compelled their partial closure of republicanism for whites. Furthermore, the nature of slaves' resistances propelled their uninvited (and important) intrusions into white men's political upheavals.

I here also resist academic historians' tendency to maximize abstract analysis and to minimize dramatic writing. I write stories about striking individuals and fetching places for deeper reasons than to make history intelligible beyond the academy (although historical lessons are too important to be restricted to fellow professors). Where many academic historians dismiss epic stories as old-fashioned fluff, I believe that classic tales of headline events, when retold from fresh angles, help sort out the culture's underlying forces.

To take a prime example from the following narrative, a current historical wisdom alleges that southern planters thought they needed fresh land in new U.S. territories to endure economically. Thus the slavocracy supposedly rose in revolution against President-elect Lincoln's threatened containment of Slave Power territorial expansions. Some parts of that abstraction illuminate some of the disunionists, some of the time (and many mainstream southern political leaders, before secessionist times).

But right after Lincoln's election, as in the nullification and gag rule controversies of the 1830s, the first precipitators of secession, the South Carolina extremists, usually tepidly if at all desired territorial expansion. So too, the most important territorial expansionists, the New Orleans urban imperialists, usually tepidly if at all desired secession. Moreover, neither the critical South Carolina disunionists nor the pivotal New Orleans Caribbean expansionists primarily craved agricultural profits from virgin terrain.

Instead, South Carolina reactionaries primarily sought to shield their uniquely old-fashioned, aristocratic republican political system (and their uniquely top-heavy slavery system) from new-fashioned American egalitarian democracy. So too, when territorial controversies became consuming, slaveholders' desire to protect their vulnerable peripheral areas from a neighbor's open democratic processes dictated which territories became most controversial. Sometimes the feared contagion of liberty involved British antislavery influence on the Texas Republic, sometimes Spanish "Africanization" of Cuba, sometimes Yankee free soilers' capture of Kansas (bordering on enslaved Missouri), sometimes ungagged abolitionist debate in Congress, sometimes Lincoln's bid to build a Southern Republican Party in the Border South. But always the clashing necessities of open democracy for whites and closed despotism over blacks strained the national republic toward the breaking point.[4]

Yet this narrative will fail if it only succeeds in substituting one theory about the impersonal causes of the Civil War for another. The following history shows that personal emotions exploded past impersonal drives, often uniting otherwise divided southern whites in rage against Yankees' condemnations. Portraits of angry confrontations, not dissections of abstruse concepts, best lead to empathy with insulted combatants. Moreover, a dissection of detached forces, barren of accidents or coincidences or personalities, erases too much of the human condition.

One of this narrative's climactic episodes illustrates the phenomenon. At South Carolina disunionists' critical moment, the impact of unexpected leaders, fleeting conspiracies, and one incredible coincidence boosted jittery secessionists over the top. The collision of despotic and democratic imperatives likely would have yielded disunion in other ways and/or at other times, if other characters or alternate contingencies had exerted sway. The odds against averting military combat in 1861 were large. The odds against avoiding some kind of civil war, at some moment, were larger. The odds against abolishing slavery without bloodshed were larger still.

But as gamblers forget at their peril, unanticipated quirks of character and luck can slightly divert the most relentless forces. Changes in how, where, and when a war commences can also condition the course of the war. Analysts of epics large and small thus must illuminate both the relentless forces and the little deflections. In that spirit, I offer this exploration and portrait of how secession actually triumphed, in the eccentric ways and at the memorable places and during the suspenseful moments when extremists strove to sever one of the world's greatest republics. At the intersection of the colorlessly impersonal and the colorfully personal came the climactic fractures, and there I most cherish the storytelling style.

My narrative style has changed more than my analysis during the fifteen years since I wrote Volume I. The aging process has sustained my taste for characters, locations, and confrontations. But I have lost some zest for nicknames, imaginary conversations, and plays on words.

Changes in the Old South rather than in its intrigued historian compelled a stress on different background materials in the two volumes. Slaveholders' attempts at social control, whether over contrary blacks or whites, had to be spotlighted in Volume I, for these social dynamics conditioned southern politics from the beginning. In contrast, proslavery theorists had to star in this volume, for their intellectual gymnastics matured very late (not in the 1830s, as is commonly supposed). Since each volume omits background information that clarifies its political saga, and because earlier and later political stories illuminate each other, the whole narrative becomes clearest when readers experience both halves. But once again in this volume, I have strived to make half the epic stand on its own, this time featuring the crowning episodes on the road to disunion.

During the half century and more since Avery Craven wrote the last synthesis of the South's course to secession, many fellow academics have discovered additional pieces of the story. Some discoverers have been my friends during our shared decades of exploration, including Jean Baker, Ira Berlin, Dave Bowman, Bill Cooper, Dan Crofts, David Brion Davis, Charles Dew, Ron Formisano, George Fredrickson, Betsey Fox-Genovese, Gene Genovese, Jack Greene, Mike Holt, Chaz Joyner, Gary Kornblith, Bill Miller, Willie Lee Rose, Anne Scott, Craig Simpson, Ken Stampp, Mark Summers, Steve Weisenburger, Joel Williamson, and Bert Wyatt-Brown. I believe that we have together enriched U.S. slavery studies and that each of us has been the more successful because we have been together. I know hundreds of other fine scholars mostly or only through their illuminating work. As my endnotes reveal, I have borrowed from them often, with admiration and gratitude.

I am also grateful to the Horace Rackham Fund of the University of Michigan, to the National Endowment for the Humanities, and to the Guggenheim Foundation, for financing my study of the many documents discovered since Professor Craven's researches. I am equally indebted to the American Antiquarian Society, to the University of Kentucky, and to my fine new professional home, the Virginia Foundation for the Humanities at the University of Virginia, for aid, comfort, and inspiration while writing this volume. My narrative would have been less effective without Sheldon Meyer's editing and David Fuller's maps. But all professional debts pale compared to my obligations to Alison, who creates even finer adventures than this labor of love.

William W. Freehling
Charlottesville, Virginia
Christmas Day 2006

The Road to Disunion

Secessionists Triumphant
1854–1861

Prologue: Yancey's Rage

By the middle of the 1850s, William Lowndes Yancey and fellow secessionists had suffered through two decades as a cornered minority. During this exasperating time, Yancey perhaps dreamed that he would someday help prod half the South out of the Union. But the stymied Alabama extremist probably never imagined that he would surrender to a reluctant secessionist, when secession remained only half accomplished.

Yancey's abdication occurred in Montgomery, Alabama, provisional capital of the Southern Confederacy. The capitulation transpired on February 17, 1861, eve of Jefferson Davis's inauguration as president of the half-formed nation. Yancey introduced Davis, who had opposed secession as late as December 1860, by declaring that "the man and the hour have met." The extremist thereby bet his revolution on a National Democratic Party moderate. Such opponents of extremism had long kept revolutionaries at bay in the South.[1]

Mainstream politicians' leverage inside the South began with their leverage inside the nation's majority party. For a quarter century, the Democratic Party's southern establishment in Washington had secured many proslavery protections. With the Union featuring minority bulwarks, why gamble on disunion?

And why doubly gamble on reckless leaders? Revolutionary hotheads had long been called "fire-eaters." With their fiery rhetoric, they sought to incinerate the Union, whatever the risks. The less agitated southern majority craved cooler rulers, especially during nervous revolutionary times. Even in South Carolina, the most disunionist state, cautious revolutionaries had to drive an outraged Robert Barnwell Rhett into the shadows before uneasy squires would dare disunion.

Yancey, unlike Rhett, scored a revolutionary coup before succumbing to less revolutionary leaders. The subtle Alabamian, unlike the inflexible South Carolinian, saw how to turn mainstream Democrats' middle ground into extremist terrain. At the National Democratic Party's 1860 convention, Yancey used one of Jefferson Davis's watered-down proslavery crusades to strain the party past the breaking point, realizing that Davis's compromised southern extremism might be too uncompromising for northern moderates to swallow. So too, in February 1861, Yancey prayed that President-elect Davis, reluctant rebel, could lure hesitant Southerners into revolution. With such leery revolutionaries directing the revolution, Rhett answered, fire-eaters "will only have changed masters."[2]

But in early 1861, Yancey knew that fire-eaters could not master the revolution. South Carolina's initial strike had provoked only the southernmost slaveholding states into rebellion. This so-called Lower South included South Carolina, Florida, Georgia, Alabama, Mississippi, Louisiana, and Texas. Only in these seven secessionist states did cotton reign as king, slaves comprise almost half the population, and enslaved blacks outnumber free blacks more than fifty to one.

Twice as many white Southerners resided in the less torrid, less enslaved, less secessionist Upper South, comprised of Border South and Middle South

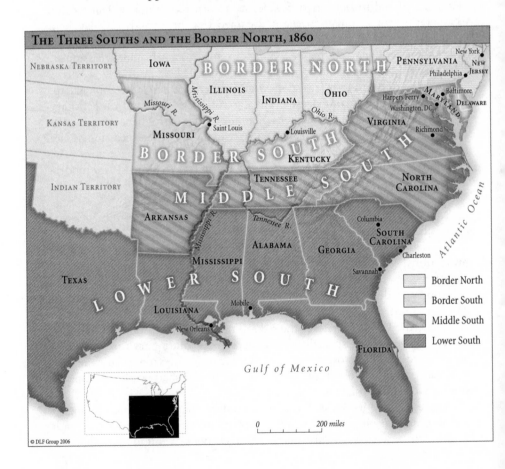

THE THREE SOUTHS AND THE BORDER NORTH, 1860

tiers of states. When Yancey conceded the disunion revolution to Davis, two weeks before Abraham Lincoln's March 4 inauguration as president of the United States, the Middle South shunned the Lower South's republic, and the Border South had even less use for the revolution. The borderland tier of southern states, located closest to the North, included Delaware, Maryland, Kentucky, and Missouri. Here, the relatively few slaveholders almost never grew cotton. Here, seven of eight residents were white, while one of five blacks was free. Here, Yankee-style cities, immigrants, and industries were far more important than in the Lower South.

The four states of the Middle South (Virginia, North Carolina, Tennessee, and Arkansas) lay between Lower and Border Souths. These Middle South states contained aspects of the colliding southern cultures above and below them. Middle South fence sitters might rally behind a Lower South moderate such as Jefferson Davis. But the Middle South shunned extremists, even an ultra like Yancey who sometimes found judiciousness useful.

Yancey looked more like a judicious moderate than a fanatical extremist.[3] Small in height, he was large in girth and fat of face. His half-closed eyes gave him a drowsy appearance. Under his double chin, his bow ties flopped in puffy ribbons. Over his slumped posture, his suits crumpled in disarray. Since inflamed nerves tormented his ribs and spine, he hardly moved as he spoke. Because he had no front teeth, his soft voice barely sounded distinct. How could such a motionless drawler arouse the sleepy to fury?

Because both Yancey's legend and his vocabulary screamed that Yankees' libels demanded stinging retorts. According to the perhaps apocryphal legend, Yancey began storming at northern insulters as an undergraduate. He then allegedly hurled a pickle barrel through a window at Williams College. The Massachusetts college supposedly disciplined the southern native, whose aunt called him a youth of "wild notions, who never could rest in one place two months at a time."[4]

The wild youth belied his genial façade again, a few years later, when he gunned down his wife's uncle after an obscure affront. Still later, Yancey would end his career sprawled on the floor of the Southern Confederacy's Senate, blood spurting from his face, after a fellow senator slit him with a jagged ink container. Whether he insulted or suffered insult, whether pickle barrels or inkwells or bullets augmented wounding words, Yancey, the fire-eaters' most apparently becalmed orator and sometimes most disciplined tactician, always verged on reckless rage.

Northern abolitionists especially enraged the Alabamian. The South's self-proclaimed paternalists, according to abolitionist sneers, presided not over Christian hearths but over anti-Christian sewers. Slaveholders supposedly gutted black families by selling children from parents and parents from each other. The tyrants also allegedly trashed family life, white and black, by raping their female property.

American Slavery as It Is, Testimony of a Thousand Witnesses dwelled on these abominations. In this best-selling American book (beside the Bible) until *Uncle Tom's Cabin,* the American Antislavery Society called slaveholders "as dead to their slaves' domestic" agony as if serviles "were cattle." In planters' houses, testified a Connecticut visitor, "I could distinguish the family resemblance in the slaves who waited upon the table." Female slaves commonly "have white children," and "little or nothing is ever said about it." According to another Connecticut traveler, slaves "lived in a state of promiscuous concubinage." Their "master said he took pains to breed from his best stock—the whiter the progeny, the higher they could sell for house servants." A borderite added that "brothers and sisters, husbands and wives, are *torn* asunder." In every *"neighborhood, . . . village or road,"* one observes "the sad procession of manacled outcasts, whose mournful countenances tell that they are exiled by *force* from ALL THAT THEIR HEARTS HOLD DEAR."[5]

By charging that slaveholders broke domestic hearts, abolitionists assaulted the slavocracy where it claimed to be most virtuous. Southerners entitled slavery the Domestic Institution. The title asserted that slaveholding patriarchs treated all lesser humans, whether children or wives or slaves, as esteemed family members. Yankee capitalists, according to slaveholders' familial logic, had no familial compulsion about firing their employees or divorcing their wives. And now these antifamilial hypocrites cursed Southerners as family breakers!

As William L. Yancey grew up, he closely observed a hypocrite who severed a family. Yancey's father died when the lad was three years old. The proud, penniless Yancey clan faced a bleak future. But soon had appeared the ancient South Carolina family's self-proclaimed savior. The Reverend Mr. Nathan Beman, a migrant from the North, taught at Mt. Zion Academy in Georgia. This zealot married the widowed Mrs. Yancey when William was seven.

Beman scorned one possession of his new family. The preacher sold the ex–Mrs. Yancey's three slaves, a mother and two infants. The black family brought $700. A year later, Beman moved his white family to Troy, New York. There, Yancey's stepfather demanded that the national General Assembly of the Presbyterian Church resolve that "selling . . . a human being as property, is in the sight of God, a heinous sin."[6]

Yancey recalled more than the moralist who pocketed $700 for indulging in heinous sin. Up in Troy, after Yancey's mother defended slavery as morally decent, Beman banned her allegedly indecent opinion from his presence. He possibly beat her physically. He assuredly abused her verbally and sometimes nailed her in her room. She still called the Domestic Institution virtuous. Beman responded that her reconciliation of "the pure system of Jesus Christ" with "the abomination of slavery" was "a complete failure."[7] Beman sent the Christian failure down to the barbarous South, for a year and a half of reconsideration.

The exiled wife sought to bury "the hatchet" by "dividing the blame equally between us." I would be "a fool or a knave," Beman answered, to admit "any part of the blame." Instead, "all our difficulties have commenced with yourself." His "sole object has been to save your reputation and [the] character and standing of my family, in a Christian community." Since Satan had forever blinded her to virtue, this "once beloved but fallen woman . . . must stay at the South and keep quiet," so "that the disgrace and turmoil occasioned by your conduct may die away."[8]

When Mrs. Beman instead came back to Troy, her spouse barred her at the door. Yancey's mother spent the rest of her life wandering between other people's homes, ever battling Beman to see their daughter. As she eked out a miserable subsistence, her condemner spent part of his pulpit time castigating slave sellers who smashed black homes.

To reemphasize his self-proclaimed moral ascendancy, Nathan Beman savored a pulpit that made him seem taller; and he was a huge man, with a tough square face, a stern expression, and spectacles that magnified his frowning eyes.[9] When accused of sinning by selling his wife's three slaves, he dismissed the insinuation. He had merely swept the unchristian filth from his Christian home.

Had he then been wrong to sweep his wife from her home? Of course not, he thundered. "I shall never keep house" with a servant of Lucifer "a day while life lasts."[10] Could the South reconcile white democracy and black slavery? Of course not, Beman snarled. That "brotherhood" resembled "an alliance between Jerusalem and Sodom," or "a friendly league between an archangel and Lucifer," or "the consummation of nuptials . . . between

William Lowndes Yancey (left), looking like the opposite of a ferocious southern fire-eater, and his stepfather, Nathan Beman (right), looking just like an imperious northern critic. Courtesy of the Library of Congress (Yancey) and the Archives and Special Collections, Rensselaer Polytechnic Institute, Troy, New York (Beman).

heaven and hell." The slaveholders' "loathsome . . . political hypocrisy" would make "Benedict Arnold . . . blush" and "would lead Judas Iscariot to cast down thirty pieces of silver and go hang himself."[11]

Not for a hundred pieces of gold could William Lowndes Yancey tolerate such slurs from such frauds. Whenever righteous Yankees heaped ridicule on Southerners, Yancey poured contempt right back. No American egalitarian could abide a critic's better-than-thou posture. Nor could a slaveholder tolerate being labeled as scum. That epitaph only fit slaves.

With whites being called morally filthier than slaves, Yancey the orator, that stationary drawler, needed no gestures, no screams to play on Southerners' prickly rectitude. In the South and in the North too, this genial fanatic softly demanded that Southerners must be treated as Yankees' equal. "Do not destroy our self respect; do not overtax our manliness," Yancey warned citizens of Syracuse, New York (under 100 miles from Beman in Troy). Do not "walk in a field and tread on a caterpillar," he cautioned Boston abolitionists, or "the poor creature will turn on your boot and try to sting you."[12]

By insisting that Southerners turn on stinging moral enslavers, disunionists had long hoped to escape from confinement at the edge of southern politics. For years, Yancey had prayed that Southerners' fury at Yankee maligners would someday defeat the compromising Jefferson Davises, propel uncompromising revolutionaries to power, fuse one South out of many subregions and classes, and burn the Nathan Bemans in a firestorm of revenge. But the prewar question always remained, whether in mid-1854 or in early 1861: Could most Southerners' hatred of northern critics overcome their love of Union, their dread of disunion, their divisions from each other, and their distrust of the fire-eaters?

PART I

BETTER ECONOMIC
TIMES GENERATE WORSE
DEMOCRATIC DILEMMAS

During the first two decades of the slavery controversy, 1835–54, the huge majority of Southerners believed that the William L. Yanceys counterproductively exaggerated the South's peril. Then, in the mid- and late 1850s, a more respectable minority of Southerners believed that the secessionists offered a productive escape from imminent danger. Yet at the very time more Southerners saw themselves as disastrously afflicted politically, their economic afflictions largely lifted. Why should a sunnier economic outlook have coincided with a stormier political mood?

In part because the South's stormiest disunionists, the South Carolina aristocrats, enjoyed less of the brighter economic prospects. In part because southern prosperity elsewhere widened the section's provoking divisions: not only between contracting South Carolinians and expanding Southwesterners but also between slaveholders and nonslaveholders, between black belt and white belt areas, between the Lower South and the Border South. Meanwhile, at the very time that southern divisions widened, northern antagonism swelled. Never had the minority of masters in the South, or the minority of Southerners in the Union, or the minority of South Carolinians in the master class felt so vulnerable, defending an unrepublican institution inside republican government.

CHAPTER 1

Democracy and Despotism, 1776–1854: *Road*, Volume I, Revisited

As in *Road to Disunion,* Volume I, let us focus on the immersion of the world's most powerful slaveholders in the world's most advanced republic, for that phenomenon most paved the southern road to disunion.[1] From the moment that road began amidst the American Revolution, republican ideology and government posed special threats to despotism's antirepublican essence. Yet the American republican system also lent special protections to an aggressively defensive slavocracy. The dialectic between extra threats and extra protection tipped toward slaveholder safety until the mid-1850s. Then the balance shifted, at the very time the slavocracy's internal divisions widened.

– 1 –

Where republican rule over whites required free speech and the consent to be governed, dominion over blacks invited dictatorial compulsions and the coercion of the nonconsenting. The slaveholders needed an All-Mighty Color Line to keep such irreconcilable regimes severed. But the color line leaked. Whites freed some blacks. Some citizens became so-called poor white trash— trashier than slaves. Some masters used supposedly inferior blacks to direct their slaves. Many enslavers inhibited white antislavery debate, lest the enslaved—or the citizens—challenge despotism's compatibility with democracy. At their most undemocratic, white censors deployed lynch mobs, anticipating the most savage postwar South's terrorizing.

Yet the democrat in the slaveholder resisted physical violence against white citizens. Rather than impose lynch law, the establishment preferred nonviolent pressure to conform, especially the accusation that hesitation about proslavery tactics revealed softness on slavery. Every four years in presidential campaigns and whenever agitation about slavery threatened, southern politics featured loyalty finger pointing. Accusations of "traitor" became rife and politically lethal.[2]

9

The slaveholding democrat found the relentless brutalizer of slaves as repulsive as the relentless lyncher of citizens. Masters preferred to control their slaves with familial kindness, Christmas presents, and soothing concessions (especially the granting of private garden plots). Slaves, mastering their job of wrenching maximum concessions from would-be paternalists, often played the role that slaveholders desired. They pretended to love their patriarch and to consent, just like citizens, to his supposedly fatherly dominion.

Sometimes, pretense edged toward reality, among both the charade's would-be "fathers" and its would-be "boys." The ideal master's most revealing word for the ideal servile was not "boy," not even "Sambo," but "Cuffee." Just cuff a childish black, declared the condescending word, and he will become that alleged impossibility, the consenting slave.

But most often, Cuffee's and Massa's role slipped, belied by duplicity on both sides of the color line. Dubious paternalists regularly faced exasperating slaves' lies, misunderstood orders, slovenly work, and dark glances. Occasionally pretenses altogether disappeared. In the nineteenth century, massive slave revolts almost never ripped apart the Massa-Cuffee charade. The last slave revolt, Nat Turner's in 1831, came to seem ages ago. But individual slaves who ambushed masters were not as rare. Individual slave runaways were not rare at all, especially in the South closest to the North.

Thus Massa faced the impossible, indispensable task of discovering whether Cuffee's act of consent was true blue. The underling here taught the superior that life was a charade, that professions of loyalty must be scrutinized, and that affectations of friendship must be doubted. Cuffee's lessons bore painfully on loyalty politics among whites. Southern politicians' extravagant professions of love for slavery might be a charade. As for northern declarations of true-blue friendship, who could trust a Yankee con man after experiencing Cuffee, the ultimate pretender? To live with Cuffee was to disbelieve the world out there. Thus did the master form the slave and the slave form the master, and the two together generate a hothouse culture, too dictatorial to be comfortably democratic.

– 2 –

The discomforts of 1860 took centuries to become consuming. Early English migrants to future United States areas comfortably planted slavery inside the most republican (for white men) New World society, for almost no one yet considered slavery a problem. Seventeenth-century British republicans, the most advanced in the Old World, came in far larger numbers, compared to nonwhite native or imported peoples, than did white European colonists to other New World slavocracies. With their late eighteenth-century Declaration of Independence, and especially its announcement that all men are created equal, this most republican concentration of ex-Europeans theoretically gave equal rights to all humans, whatever their race, sex, or economic position.

Then the compatibility of despotism and democracy became a widely perceived problem.

Black slavery pockmarked all thirteen of England's revolting colonies in 1776. Indeed slavery's contagion spread in an odd New World direction: away from North America's most tropical habitats. True, in 1776, slavery already massed thickest in the constricted Georgia and especially South Carolina coastal swampland. Here, dense concentrations of slaves tilled rice and a rare, silklike fleece called Sea Island cotton. Here, an especially top-heavy social structure lent an especially intractable aristocratic mentality to the slaveholder as republican.

But rice and Sea Island cotton only flourished within a few dozen miles of the Atlantic Ocean. Few eighteenth-century entrepreneurs could envision a staple to grow in the thousands of miles west of the coastal swamps. At first, capitalists considered the Lower South too far north to grow the lush South American money crops, coffee and sugar. The Lower South also seemed too far south to grow the Upper South's crucial cash crop, tobacco.

With white capitalists considering the Lower South's western expanse relatively unpromising in 1776, three times more slaves grew tobacco and grains in the Middle South's Virginia and in the Border South's Maryland than toiled in Georgia and South Carolina. Furthermore, many more slaves grew grains in Pennsylvania, New Jersey, and New York than inhabited all Lower South areas west of the U.S. coastal jungles. With slavery also a New England legality and reality, the institution was as national as the American Revolution. Slavery also posed the greatest national embarrassment to those who would build a nation atop the Declaration's foundations.

The more northern of the original thirteen states, by striking against the embarrassment, first indicated slavery's special peril in republican America. But the qualified nature of the first strike also indicated slavery's special strength in this especially republican (for white men) culture. Pennsylvania scored the (auspiciously blunted) first strike. The state's legislature passed the New World's first antislavery law in 1780. This pathbreaking edict, however, liberated only blacks born after the enactment and only after the afterborn reached twenty-eight years of age. The law indirectly consigned all slaves born before 1780 to permanent thralldom. The edict also freed no slave until a third of a century after the American Revolution.

Blacks' prospects in the largest northern slave state, New York, remained still bleaker. New York's legislature, acting two decades after Pennsylvania's, also freed only the afterborn and only after they reached adulthood. This legislation, intended to liberate no one until a half century after the American Revolution, ultimately failed to free a third of its intended belated beneficiaries. Many New York masters sold slaves down South, into permanent enslavement, before emancipating birthdays. In 1827, New Yorkers freed their last remaining slave. Then New Jersey still had 2200 and Pennsylvania 400 slaves.

Northern slavery persisted partly because natural rights to property countered natural rights to liberty. Northern slaveholders fought to delay or to circumvent seizure of their (human) property. Their persistence helped delay an uncompromising northern attack on southern slavery. Finally in 1831, a whopping fifty-five years after the Declaration of Independence and four years after New York became altogether free soil, Massachusetts's William Lloyd Garrison used his new *Liberator* to pledge all-out attack on U.S. slavery. True to Garrison's pledge, the growth rate of northern abolition led the New World for a decade. But after this auspicious beginning, U.S. abolitionists hit a wall around 1840. No more than 2 percent of prewar Yankee voters ever demanded that slavery be wiped out of southern states.

Once again, republican ideology proved to be a two-edged antislavery sword. While slaves' natural right to liberty sharpened thrusts for emancipation, slaveholders' natural right to property blunted emancipators' parries. Furthermore, the Garrisonian army, where white women and blacks fought alongside white men, violated the no-trespass sign of American republicanism: Only white men shall govern. Garrisonians' female agitators enraged male chauvinists, who believed that women must only speak in the home. Black agitators also infuriated white supremacists, who believed that the supposedly inferior race must only assume menial positions.

Worse still for U.S. abolitionists, most Northerners equated American republicanism with (white men's) Union. Thus Southerners, by threatening to break up the Union, aroused Northerners against abolitionists' pleas for liberty. Furthermore, few Yankees wanted liberated blacks in their neighborhood. They hoped to deport freedmen to Africa, just as Native Americans had been exiled to western reservations. Then all Americans would be liberated—and lily-white. This pervasive racism heaped crushing burdens atop the Garrisonians' drive to liberate all humans.

The burden afflicted the national Congress as much as state legislatures. The first generation of national congressmen, impelled in part by the Declaration's ideology, helped ease the national institution into a southern peculiarity. The congressional Northwest Ordinance of 1787 barred future slaves from five future midwestern states. Then the national government abolished the African slave trade in 1807. Slaveholders stood proscribed from taking or importing new slaves into half the nation's territory and from importing overseas slaves.

Yet if the first national leaders helped corner an underpopulated slavocracy, they also helped arm slaveholder defenses. While the congressmen of 1787 banned new slaves from entering the northwestern territories, they emancipated no slave already on the ground. The result: Persisting Illinois slaveholders led an ominous, albeit failed, drive to perpetuate the system in the 1820s. The Founders also expanded the white men's republic southward, without ensuring that only free republicans could enter. The result: Slaveholders enslaved the national republic's vast new tropical empire. President Thomas Jefferson's Louisiana Purchase and President James Monroe's Florida purchase added a Slave Power colossus to the United States: the future states of Louisiana, Florida, Arkansas, Missouri, and parts of Mississippi and Alabama.

A late eighteenth-century invention enabled the Founding Fathers' new Lower South empire to become the nineteenth-century slavocracy's new core. In the 1790s, Eli Whitney and others invented cotton gins to process a more common, crude product than Sea Island cotton: short-staple cotton fiber. Slave labor then became profitable in the previously apparently useless Lower South areas west of the Atlantic coast swamps, including upcountry South Carolina, Georgia, Mississippi, Louisiana, Alabama, Florida, and after annexation in 1845, Texas. Meanwhile, short-staple cotton cultivation also triumphed in the Middle South's western Tennessee and Arkansas. Furthermore, a lush sugar empire belatedly flourished in the Lower South's Louisiana. No longer did slavery's base swell northward, in Virginia and Maryland tobacco belts. No longer did only the Georgia and South Carolina coastal swamps nurture a Lower South core of slaveholders.

The slaveholding establishment had to become thinner northward to become thicker southward. After the federal government closed the overseas slave trade, Lower South slaveholders could not legally import Africans. Instead, black laborers, some 875,000 of them from 1800 to 1860, drained to the newer South from the older South: from South Carolina, from Virginia, and especially from the Border South.[3] While slaves had been 25 percent of the Border South population in 1790, they comprised only 13 percent in 1860, compared to 32 percent in the Middle South and to 47 percent in the Lower South. While in 1790, 21 percent of southern slaves had lived in the Lower South, 59 percent resided in the area in 1860. After this sea change in the slaveholders' geographical base, could the Slave Power's expanding power in new tropical habitats sufficiently offset its shrinking power in old northern bastions? It was a classic question in human affairs: whether a shrinking, unconsolidated periphery could do in an expanding, consolidated core.[4] In this case, much depended on whether Border South slaveholders, now located at North American slavery's most northern outposts, could cling to their regime more interminably than had the hard-fighting, belatedly extinguished New York and Illinois slavocracies. Few questions better defined the road to disunion—or the path to Appomattox.

– 3 –

In the most northern South, no Border South state emulated Pennsylvania's or New York's emancipation edicts, although Delaware came close and every border state legislature debated the possibility. More often, border masters manumitted some slaves. Slaveholder expediency augmented antislavery principle. Borderland blacks, compared to blacks deeper in the South, could more easily dash onto northern free soil. That reality led some border masters to grant eventual freedom, if slaves accepted temporary enslavement.

In this "semislavery" system, owners bribed slaves against gambling on flight by promising to grant manumission after a term (usually seven years) of loyal labor. The advantage for the slave: certain eventual freedom rather than the uncertainties of flight, perhaps capture, and then assuredly awful punishment. The advantage for the master: profitable interim labor rather than the peril of an investment tomorrow vanished.[5] The disadvantage for the whole South: partial erosion of slavery in the borderlands.

By 1850, erosion had proceeded furthest in the eastern borderlands. At midcentury, 89 percent of Delaware blacks and 45 percent of Maryland blacks were free. Manumission occurred far less often in the western borderlands. At midcentury, only 3 percent of Missouri blacks and 5 percent of Kentucky blacks enjoyed freedom. Still, Kentucky contained five times more white nonslaveholding than slaveholding families, and Missouri six times more. Borderland slavery's erosion could deepen if Border South investors more swiftly cashed in their exposed human property in Lower South auctions, as had so many New Yorkers.

Nothing would sour borderland slave investors faster than a rash of slave runaways. The peril again showed how blacks conditioned whites. Just as Cuffees turned slaveholders into highly suspicious agitators, so runaways turned proslavery politicians into champions of an iron curtain between the most exposed South and the more libertarian North. From 1836 through 1854, the increasingly demanding southern minority won many border consolidations, over the protests of an increasingly awakened northern majority.

Majoritarian government often yields minority control, especially when committed minorities face sleepy majorities. But U.S. republicanism handed the slaveholders extra power to combat any Yankee majority. Since the racist northern majority cared more about white men's Union than about republicanism for nonwhites, slaveholders' threat of disunion could secure national protections for slavery. The National Democratic Party lent slaveholders' threats added leverage. Democrats usually won national elections. They almost always ran strongest in the South, especially in the deepest South. So the minority section wielded the power base of the majority party. When Southern Democrats threatened to quit the party unless northern allies supported a proslavery law, enough Northern Democrats tended to give in, not only to save their republic but also to save their party.

The U.S. Constitution augmented the minority's leverage. The Constitution's so-called three-fifths clause added three out of every five nonvoting slaves to a state's number of voting citizens, when determining the state's proportion of members in the House of Representatives. So the South in 1860, with 29 percent of the nation's voting citizens, elected 38 percent of the House. Moreover, each state elected two senators. Since northern states outnumbered southern states by only two, the southern 29 percent of the American white population elected 47 percent of the U.S. Senate in 1860. In addition, each state received one member of the Electoral College, the body electing the president, for each senator and congressman. So the South's three in ten white Americans elected four of ten Electoral College voters. As an added bonus, disproportionate southern control over the White House and Congress yielded disproportionate control over the Supreme Court. All this extra power, beyond one citizen, one vote, inspired the North's most loaded political term, Slave Power, meaning that slaveholders possessed arguably unrepublican power over whites as well as over blacks.

The U.S. constitutional amendment process guarded the Slave Power's power. As William Lloyd Garrison conceded, the federal government would need a constitutional amendment to abolish slavery. Three-fourths of existing states had to approve constitutional amendments. In 1860, the nation contained seventeen free labor states and fifteen slave states. If all fifteen slave states perpetually rejected antislavery, only a Union swollen to sixty states, forty-five of them free labor states, could have forced abolition upon the South. In some future century, the Union might balloon to sixty states. No such gargantuan swelling could be imagined in the mid-nineteenth century.

Thus an antislavery constitutional amendment required some southern consent. If the four Border South states had consented to emancipation, slaveholders would have been sliced to eleven states and free laborers boosted to twenty-one. Subsequently, if twelve more free labor states had been admitted to the Union, the free labor states' three-fourths majority of a forty-four-state Union could have imposed emancipation on the minority. The forty-fourth state would be admitted to the Union in 1890, two years after Brazil, the last New World slaveholding nation, abolished the institution. That possible road to an emancipating constitutional amendment could be imagined in 1860.

If the slaveholders had lost the four Border South states, they would have lost control of Congress long before they lost the power to kill constitutional amendments. Several key antebellum slaveholder victories, especially the annexation of Texas in 1845, required an almost unanimous southern congressional contingent. That necessity left U.S. slaveholders only as politically strong as their weakest link—their Border South hinterland area, where more slaves ran toward the North, where more slaveholders sold slaves toward the deepest South, and where by 1850 the percentage of slaveowning families had sunk to under 12 percent of total white families.

Nonslaveholding majorities commanded not just the Border South but also most southern areas. Only one-third of all citizens, Southwide, owned slaves. But wherever whites extensively owned blacks, in a so-called black belt area, the regime locally, like the slaveholders nationally, exerted far more power than its minority of numbers indicated.

In black belt neighborhoods, defined here as communities with populations 25 percent or more enslaved, rich and poor whites worshipped at the same churches, cherished the same family circles, relished the same political parties, and nurtured the same crops (with a squire often helping rednecks by ginning their cotton or buying their foodstuffs or loaning them small sums). Here, all whites helped control blacks, whether by voting for orthodox candidates or by expelling abolitionist meddlers or by lashing disobedient slaves when serving on nightly patrols. Here, all whites who helped enchain blacks stormed at Yankees who damned slavery perpetuators. Rednecks and neighboring squires also shared responsibility to perpetuate paternalism in their homes, whether by directing supposedly inferior blacks or by governing supposedly inferior wives and children. In plantation neighborhoods, slaveless whites, while only aspiring to be slaveholders, already savored some of slaveholders' sexist and racist power.

Whites' nineteenth-century egalitarian republican ideology also fused rich and poor in a black belt area. The poorest citizen relished his white skin, which allegedly made him the equal of all white males and superior to all blacks. Proudly equal plebeians could not bear holier-than-thou Yankees, with their posture of moral superiority to all who helped enslave blacks. Nor could rednecks tolerate any abolitionist effort to raise black slaves to the level of white citizens. Egalitarianism, the great reason why some colorblind Yankees opposed slavery, was also the great reason why racist whites massed to keep blacks ground under.

The most superficial question about the Old South is why nonslaveholders in black belts supported slaveholders. The better question is why any nonslaveholder who lived among numerous blacks would want the despised other lower class freed. The psychological wages of being a white man were too treasured among poor whites, and the sting of abolitionists' lordly presumption too wounding, and the fear of competing with free blacks too rife, for a turn against the slaveholders to be inviting in the black belt.

Possibilities of a yeoman resistance to slaveholders increased wherever few slaveholders or slaves or blacks resided. The section's areas with 5 percent or less slaves, here called the white belt South, stretched past its Border South core to cover the most mountainous sections of the Middle South, including western Virginia and eastern Tennessee, and of the Lower South, including northern Georgia and northern Alabama. Here, white belt nonslaveholders lacked black belt nonslaveholders' reasons for proslavery zealotry. Here, few rednecks knew blacks to loathe and to police. Here, few yeomen encountered slaveholders to visit and to emulate. Here, whites usually cared more about preserving the Union than about preserving slavery. Here, most citizens, like most Northerners, would have preferred to rid the nation of slavery, if they could also rid America of blacks and retain the Union of whites. And in this white belt borderland between the black belt South and the free labor North, few whites lamented that the slave drain continued to thin blacks out of their area and to thicken the institution in the most southern South, repeating the turtle-slow erosion of slavery in the most southern North between 1776 and 1830.

– 4 –

Concern about pressure on the most exposed parts of the South precipitated every successful southern deployment of national leverage, always aimed at shutting down democratic agitation where yeomen and Cuffees might wish to be free of the Slave Power. In the gag rule debates, 1835–44, Southerners sought to silence congressional discussion of slavery in Washington, D.C., itself neighboring the Border South. When Secretary of State Abel P. Upshur first precipitated the Texas annexation issue, the Virginian sought to seal off English agitators from the relatively lightly enslaved (for a Lower South region) Texas Republic and thus from the U.S. slavocracy's southwest border. When Senator James Mason of Virginia precipitated the Fugitive Slave Controversy in 1850, he sought to stop the hemorrhage of slaves from his state's (and the South's) northwestern extremity. When Senator David R. Atchinson of Missouri precipitated the Kansas-Nebraska Act, he sought to solidify the institution on his Border South state's western flank.

After each proposal to fortify hinterland slaveholders against democratic agitation, some southern leaders doubted that the proposed remedy could shore up the slavocracy's peripheral areas. Other leaders saw more hope. But always disagreement over the practicality of the proposed undemocratic consolidation gave way to fury that some Yankees called the proposal—and the proposing slavocracy—barbaric. So what always began as a Southerner's calculated (if arguably futile) strategy to protect the hinterlands always turned into a touchy civilization's enraged spree of self-justification.

Then few black belt Southerners dared turn away from the border's call to the colors; the deserter would be labeled a traitor during the next election campaign. In their competition to prove that their professions of loyalty to slavery were true blue, both Southern Democrats and Southern Whigs demanded that northern party allies support border fortifications. Northern Whigs, with their party's base in the North, always labeled such demands undemocratic blackmail. In contrast, most Northern Democrats, with their party's base in the South, usually appeased the slaveholders.

The National Democratic Party's proslavery laws, protecting slavery in the Union, kept restless disunionists at bay in the South. The Democracy's proslavery laws also weakened Southern Whigs. Southern Democrats derided their partisan foes as traitors to slavery, allied with Yankee defamers who rejected national protections of slavery. After the Democracy's midcentury proslavery laws, first Lower South Whigs, then Upper South Whigs, could no longer risk their political vulnerability. The Whigs were finished as one of the two great national parties.

The surviving National Democratic Party faced severe northern trouble. Yankee appeasers of the slavocracy had been willing to protect slavery, in order to save the Union and the party. But the minority's demands for protection increasingly endangered majoritarian Union. Majority acquiescence in minority demands prevented white men from debating in Congress, then forced white men to return alleged fugitive slaves to slavery without the protection of jury trials, and then led to an antirepublican government in Kansas. So the South's prime appeasers, the Northern Democrats, faced murderous political charges that they had helped white Southerners to enslave white

Northerners. Thus did the issue of republicanism swerve from liberty for blacks, where Yankee abolitionists successfully awakened only so many whites to a colorblind consciousness, to liberty for whites, where no Yankee racist needed a raised conscious.

With Yankees ever more determined to save white republicanism by containing Slave Power aggressiveness, ever more Southerners looked more favorably at disunion. Here again, American republicanism lent the slaveholders extra potency and extra trouble. The Declaration of Independence's basis—a people's right to withdraw their consent to be governed—seemed to make secession theoretically legitimate. But another of republicanism's foundations—that the losers must obey ballot box winners—ill supported a minority's attempt to withdraw consent from an electoral verdict.

If Lower South states opted for disunion, especially after the slaveholders lost a national election, Middle and Border South states would have to decide between protecting the elected majority's right to rule and protecting the departing minority's right to withdraw consent. Their decision would be critical, for as in Congress, southern unity would be mandatory. If a third or more of the South stayed with the North, disunionists' chances in a civil war would plummet. So whether in or out of the Union, the southern core in tropical climes remained dependent on the southern periphery in northern climes. And southern border folk continued to insist on protecting slavery only *in* the Union, not in a seceded southern republic.

But could slavery, particularly at the South's exposed edges, be forever protected inside the national government? That question pressed harder after the Kansas-Nebraska Act, when many more Northern Democrats disavowed any further Slave Power demand for protection. And at this very moment when the slaveholders' national leverage narrowed, a changing southern economy widened the slavocracy's internal divisions, and especially augmented the split between Border and Lower Souths.

CHAPTER 2

Economic Bonanza, 1850–1860

Since revolutionaries must risk life, fortune, and honor, only a plight perceived to be horrendous inspires the gamble. The perceived prerevolutionary horror may take many forms: threats to one's life, one's family, one's reputation, one's psyche, one's religion, one's sacred rights. But economic travail provides the most common goad to revolution.

In only one respect, albeit a crucial one, did economic crisis cause the disunion revolution. Those exceptions to everything normally southern, South Carolina's exceptionally secessionist aristocrats, often faced exceptional economic affliction in the 1850s. Southerners everywhere else usually enjoyed a decade of economic boom. Yet prosperity had its unsettling aspect. Better economic times helped worsen southern social divisions, thereby threatening King Cotton's suddenly well-heeled army of fanciers.

– 1 –

Like most capitalists, slaveholders tended to do better or worse depending on the era, the locale, and the enterprise. Because they exported staple crops, their fortunes fluctuated according to national and world economic conditions. Two American banking panics, first in 1819 and then in 1837, each ushered in more than a decade of dismal markets for southern agricultural producers. For a few years in the mid-1830s, southern farmers enjoyed better prices. Otherwise, agrarian life after 1820 featured exhausting struggles with poor markets, lashing storms, and pressing bankers.

Battles began in the tobacco-exporting Upper South and especially in Virginia. Eighteenth-century Virginia tobacco planters ranked among the wealthiest Americans. Then, late in the century, the Virginia Dynasty's leaders' economic power shrank while their political power swelled. The George Washingtons, James Madisons, Thomas Jeffersons, and James Monroes watched prices for their tobacco sink, thanks to worldwide overproduction.

19

Their tobacco yields also sank, thanks to depleted soil. In response, many Virginians moved west, to virgin soil beyond their declining commonwealth. As for stalwarts who loyally remained in debilitated Virginia, they had to retrench, diversify crops, fertilize soils, and sell some slaves. A limping economic endurance ensued.

More financial problems haunted coastal South Carolina, eighteenth-century domain of aristocrats even richer than the Virginians. Off the South Carolina coast, gentlemen's slaves usually planted Sea Island cotton. That luxurious fiber, while normally commanding lucrative returns, periodically suffered from erratic prices and savage hurricanes. Storms also occasionally decimated the main business on South Carolina's coastal mainland, rice production. The unsteady weather helps explain why rice planters, who until the 1850s enjoyed tolerably steady prices and yields, had been economically stressed since the Panic of 1819.

Poor managerial practices compounded rice planters' economic difficulty. Since South Carolina coastal swamps spawned malarial mosquitoes, rich men often fled the area in the April–October growing season. Absentees seldom efficiently managed intricate rice operations. Inefficient plantations seldom sufficiently financed six-month vacations.

South Carolina planters of the coarser short-staple cotton, situated above the sickly coastal swamps on the rolling hills of the piedmont, had long been better managers, yet more imperiled entrepreneurs. South Carolina's healthy upcountry habitat yielded less planter absenteeism and therefore more intensive slaveholder direction than did the state's dank lowcountry. But upcountry producers of crude cotton, compared to lowcountry producers of rice and Sea Island cotton, suffered from worse prices and yields during the period from 1820 to 1850. Upcountry South Carolina, America's first short-staple cotton kingdom, had also been the first to exhaust its soil. In the 1820s and early 1830s, then again in the late 1830s and 1840s, when poor cotton prices compounded poor yields, South Carolinians by the tens of thousands deserted their state. South Carolina, home of the South's densest concentration of blacks and thickest concentration of disunionist reactionaries, thus became the only Lower South state to lose population.

Deserters from South Carolina often brought disunion aspirations to that great land of hustle: the lush river valleys of Alabama, Mississippi, Louisiana, Texas, and Arkansas. In the virgin Southwest but not in aging South Carolina, booming yields compensated for lagging prices. Thus a cotton planter's contest against the elements had usually seemed narrowly winnable. During the terrible depression of the early 1840s, however, the entire Cotton Kingdom seemed imperiled. In that dismal period, difficulties also afflicted producers of the South's subsidiary exports, including hemp growers in Missouri, sugar planters in Louisiana, and tobacco farmers in Virginia.

Smaller farmers suffered fewer anxieties. Slaveless yeomen farmers, when living in the cotton belt, sometimes grew and sold a few bales. More often, they exclusively cultivated food for their families. Beyond the plantation regions, particularly up in mountain habitats, fluctuating worldwide markets even less afflicted self-sufficient yeomen.

Fear of the plantation South's market vulnerability climaxed in 1844 when Mississippi's U.S. Senator Robert J. Walker urged that Texas must be annexed to the United States. Virgin Texas acres, Walker argued, would give hard-pressed planters a safety valve for superfluous blacks. Without Texas's safety valve, Walker gloomed, multiplying and starving black barbarians would inundate the South. Southern entrepreneurs bought into Walker's dismal vision. With that shudder at racial and economic claustrophobia, rich and poor brought to climax their thirty years of struggle, struggle, struggle.

– 2 –

Then, at midcentury, struggle largely vanished. Cotton prices, sugar prices, tobacco prices shot up, despite extravagant increases in crop production. The big southern cash crop, short-staple cotton, which had sold for some $74,000,000 a year in the 1840s, sold for some $169,000,000 yearly in the 1850s. In the four years before the Civil War, the crop yearly averaged some $207,000,000 in value, almost three times more than the average figure a decade earlier.[1] So too, in the 1850s compared to the 1840s, the Sea Island cotton crop increased 200 percent in value, the sugar crop 150 percent, and the tobacco crop 67 percent.[2] In comfortable contrast, the southern cost of living during the 1850s eased up less than 33 percent.[3]

Only those politically crucial gentlemen, South Carolina rice planters, still suffered under dreary economic skies. These squires' debts had multiplied faster than their assets even in the 1820s, when rice yields and prices had remained more immune than cotton figures from the worldwide economic downturn. In the 1850s, rice planters' immunity from market caprices and soil exhaustion ended. Meanwhile, their absentee mismanagement continued. Rice prices increased 6 percent during the 1850s, not beginning to offset the 24 percent decline in rice produced. The average yearly worth of the crop dived from some $2,500,000 in the 1840s to some $1,900,000 in the 1850s. In the year of secession, the value of these incensed gentlemen's exports plunged under $1,400,000, an all-time low. The lowcountry's careful entrepreneurs could still profit with rice production. But care became all the more necessary.[4]

While economic disaster honed a new edge on many South Carolina coastal squires' desire for disunion, entrepreneurs elsewhere sought a fortune rather than a revolution. Southerners developed almost 30,000,000 previously untouched acres during the 1850s, increasing the land under cultivation by over a third. Southern farmland doubled in value during the decade;[5] southern railroad lines more than tripled in length;[6] and southern industrial receipts swelled 66 percent.[7] Compared to the North, the South remained poorly developed industrially and ill connected by railroads. But in the late 1850s, the rate of new development in Dixie surpassed Yankee standards.

In one area, the South set records that Yankees scorned. The price of slaves took off in the 1850s. The average price for a Lower South slave, after hovering around $925 from 1830 to 1850, averaged $1240 in 1851–55 and $1658 in 1856–60, a 79 percent rise in the South's largest capital investment.[8] After the national Panic of 1857, when the North fell into prolonged depression and the South quickly recovered, Southerners gloated about getting rich quicker than money-mad Yankees.[9]

That fresh swaggering exemplified the new tone in the newest South. Vanished from the Lower South, except from aging South Carolina, were gloomings about stagnating profits, superfluous slaves, and a diseased economy trapped without a safety valve. Omnipresent were visions of new beginnings, of expanding slave empires, even, in some quarters, of importing fresh Africans. What a time this was, in the land where cotton became, almost overnight, a very wealthy king.

– 3 –

But the true American monarch remained King Numbers, with that sovereign's potential dominion over King Cotton. Since the North possessed more citizens than the South, and the South more nonslaveholders than slaveholders, the slaveholders needed double minority dominion: over sectional and national majorities. Unless southern nonslaveholders cared more about preserving slavery and/or about defying the Yankees than about anything else, other priorities—to the Union, to peace, to prosperity—could bend poor folks' allegiance. Then nonslaveholder nonzeal could yield congressional compromises on slavery or civil war collaboration with Yankee armies.

Unfortunately for the slavocracy's southerly core areas, the better economic times of the 1850s nudged the northerly peripheral areas toward becoming more culturally Yankee. One fact was paramount: Slaves grew dramatically more expensive, almost twice as expensive in 1860 as in 1850. One result was omnipresent: Slaveless farmers could not often afford $1600 slaves, while big planters could profitably pay the price. One consequence was troublesome: The relative proportion of slaveholders to nonslaveholders shrank fastest in slaveholders' least committed spot, the Border South.

In the whole South during the presecession decade, slaveholding families sank from 43 percent to 37 percent of all southern white families. Meanwhile, the number of white families owning twenty or more slaves boomed six times faster than the number owning one to four slaves. While large slaveholders' holdings grew faster, white belt areas grew whiter. Slaves generated profits faster in Lower South tropical cotton and sugar kingdoms than on Upper South tobacco or grain farms. Fugitive slaves also escaped easiest from the border areas, where slave labor generated smallest profits. So during the 1850s, Border South masters sold some 53,000 slaves and Middle South masters some 84,000 to Lower South capitalists.[10]

As blacks drained out of the more northern South, white immigrants from foreign nations poured in. Between 1850 and 1860, the Border South attracted some 142,000 foreign immigrants, almost three times more laborers than the blacks it lost. Meanwhile, the Middle South gained some 31,000 foreign immigrants, over one-third of the blacks it lost.[11] The resulting percentage of slaveowning white families dropped in the Middle South from 30 percent to 25 percent and plunged in the Border South from 23 percent to 16 percent. If nonslaveholder percentages continued to plummet at those rates, the most northern South, within a decade or two, would have the same relatively paltry proportion of slaves, circa 5 percent, as the colonial North had had in 1776, when the area had begun its fifty-year creep toward abolishing slavery.

In one key way, the 1860 Border South was already too Yankee. By 1860, the Border South contained some 419,000 immigrants and free blacks, compared to barely more slaves—some 429,000. In 1860, Maryland contained almost as many foreign immigrants (some 77,000) as it contained free blacks (some 84,000) or slaves (some 87,000). In 1860, Missouri contained 40 percent more foreign immigrants than slaves. The Lower South, in contrast, contained almost fourteen times more slaves than foreign immigrants. As the Border South slowly became less dependent on slave labor and more dependent on immigrant and free black workers, the Lower South became a blacker, more enslaved society—and a culture where higher slave prices made slaveless white yeomen and tenants increasingly less likely to become slaveholders.

While the economic boom drained more slaves from the most northern to the most southern South, South Carolina lost its people at a more alarming pace than ever. Some 7000 whites and 70,000 slaves trooped from South Carolina to the virgin Southwest during the 1850s. The hemorrhage somewhat afflicted upcountry South Carolina cotton planters. These squires' better times, while a relief from previous awful times, could not match booming times on the Lower South frontier. But the stagnating coastal rice fields pressed more people out of debilitated South Carolina. Charleston, mecca of the rice gentry, lost a third of its slaves, with foreign immigrants replacing enslaved laborers. Charleston, to the alarm of its crusty aristocracy, was becoming, of all things, a little like a Yankee free labor city.[12]

Here, as usual, Charlestonians took southern apprehensions to an abnormal extreme. But whether in Charleston, Mobile, or New Orleans, southern cities displayed a new normality: cheap immigrant wage earners replacing expensive black slaves.[13] So too, not only the contracting South Carolina lowcountry but also the prosperous Upper South tobacco kingdoms extensively dispatched slaves to southwestern cotton and sugar lands. The Southwest, that most prosperous Southland, grew ever more confident, ever more black with slaves, and ever more alienated from the increasingly Yankee-like northern South and the increasingly afflicted Charleston environs.

Such differential prosperity somewhat aided the disunionists. The Lower South area most falling behind, South Carolina, had the classic economic desperation to start a revolution. The Lower South area most marching ahead, the lush Southwest, had the classic economic confidence to consider war winnable, if South Carolina should start one. How, after all, could the North whip the South in a civil war, when Southerners had routed Northerners at Yankees' own game, getting rich quick? Meanwhile the declining South Carolinians and the ascending Southwesterners, together the core of the plantation South, harbored a cultural center's classic concern about its periphery. The Border South, while still containing 400,000 slaves and very few abolitionists, was drifting toward becoming more a periphery of the North. Why not strike for a southern nation when the Border South periphery might still go along— and before South Carolinians lost the nerve to do any striking at all?

In part because the National Democratic Party still existed and might still protect the slavocracy in the Union. Moreover, in the midst of their newly discovered prosperity, most Southerners, whether inside or outside the Democracy, preferred to get rich quick inside the Union. The ever more Yankee Border South demonstrated especial loathing for disunion.

How could all these increasingly different folk be rallied behind a dangerous revolution? Worse, how could slaveholders forge a single world when their great weapon of social control over blacks, coercive terror, could not generate universal white conformity? Lower South planters could, did, lynch some dissenters in their neighborhoods. But the southern core areas could not invade their peripheral areas, to lynch uncommitted or heretical Border South citizens.

So forging a single southern culture had to begin the democratic way, with fashioning an ideology and building a consensus. All Southerners had to consider slavery a blessing—and dearer than any other blessing. But what proslavery idea could unify the South's ideological superstructure, with the civilization's material substructure more divided than ever?

PART II

THE CLIMACTIC

IDEOLOGICAL FRUSTRATIONS

According to a pivotal conventional historical wisdom, one generation after Thomas Jefferson and other southern Founding Fathers called slavery a necessary evil (and only necessary until blacks could be removed from the United States), proslavery writers convinced all Southerners that slavery was a positive good (and should never be removed). The Virginia legislature's two-week debate in 1832 allegedly marked the last southern consideration of antislavery. Thereafter, nothing was supposedly left to discuss, for everyone celebrated slavery's glory.

This misconception errs in every essential. The necessary-evil argument remained widely believed in the Upper South. The dream of eventually removing blacks (and thus making the evil unnecessary) continued to thrive, including in the most advanced Upper South proslavery polemics. Important Upper South legislative discussions of slavery came after the Virginia 1832 debate. The most sophisticated Lower South intellectuals never completely mastered the proslavery puzzle. The ideological shortfall made political solutions to southern divisions seem all the more necessary.

The frustrating problem, ideologically no less than politically, was to reconcile unlimited slaveholder power with limited republican power. Attempts at ideological reconciliation took three colliding forms, based on class, race, and religion. Each received preliminary elaboration in the 1830s. All gained more polish in the 1850s. None swept all minds and hearts before the Civil War.

Some Southerners still emerged with fresh excitement about a better understood mission. Others gloomed about persistently intractable problems. Others hoped that slavery could be improved and then might wither away. In their climactic proslavery arguments, late antebellum Southerners still disagreed about why and whether the institution was a blessing—and about whether slavery could be reformed and/or eventually ended.

CHAPTER 3

James Henry Hammond and the Unsolvable Proslavery Puzzle

After William Lloyd Garrison inaugurated his *Liberator* (1831), slaveholders desired a better defense than the necessity of an evil. By the mid-1840s, new arguments for slavery's glory dodged the republican case for slavery's shame: that masters possessed absolute power, and absolute power corrupts absolutely.

This first wave of proslavery writers severed a paternalist's absolute power to uplift inferiors inside private homes from a republic's restricted power to regulate equals outside private gates. Some 1830–45 polemicists claimed that by cleaving unlimited household rule from limited governmental rule, they had converted every southern republican to domestic absolutism. South Carolina's James Henry Hammond proclaimed victory especially grandiosely. Yet Hammond demonstrated, in his published theory and in his domestic life, that pre-1845 proslavery writers had not reconciled republican and absolute power, whether inside or outside the home.

– 1 –

The clash between antislavery Northerners and proslavery Southerners often centered on domestic hearths. Southerners called slavery the *Domestic* Institution. Slave labor under caring paternalists inside domestic sanctuaries, they affirmed, beat free labor exploitation under uncaring employers beyond the home. Your homes, retorted Yankees, are bespattered brothels, not caring sanctuaries. You fornicate with your slaves and thus further dirty unchristian households.

Yankees wielded sexual slurs so self-righteously, so scornfully, and so pornographically that they could sound like anti-Catholic voyeurs, spinning tales of righteous priests abed with virginal nuns. "The slave States," intoned George Bourne in an 1837 pamphlet published in Boston, "are one vast brothel," featuring "incests, polygamy, adultery, and other uncleanness."

When the supposedly Christian master "forces" his slave, "she dare not complain."

To illustrate the sufferer, Bourne told of a "nearly white" slave. Her master's son compelled "her, whenever he pleased," to share "his bed." The servile "could not appeal to her master for protection, for he was guilty of like practices." This "pious . . . victim of the brutal lust of a dissolute young man" had "no prospect before her" except "being again and again polluted, whenever his unbridled passions should dictate."[1]

Southerners called the charge irrelevant sensationalism. How many southern Christians, after all, degenerated into sexual monsters? Quantities of grotesqueness, answered abolitionists, are irrelevant. A few masters' sexual selfishness illustrated all masters' license to be brutes. In addition to sexually exploiting slaves, owners sold black families apart, prevented slaves from reading the Bible, and brutally lashed their serviles. A Christian republic must check and balance fallen man's power to devastate natural rights, in the home no less than in the government.

Englishmen no less than New Englanders pressed this plea. In 1845, James Henry Hammond, recently governor of South Carolina, answered the grand old man of the English antislavery movement, Thomas Clarkson. The South Carolinian's swiftly published *Letters to Clarkson* summarized the first wave of proslavery writing.

Hammond denied that slaveholders alone possessed absolute power. Unrestrained employers could fire or underpay powerless employees. Undernourishment ensued during free labor society's boom times and unemployment in bad times. In all times, poor folks' "illicit sexual intercourse" prevailed "from an early period of life." If England's Thomas Clarkson wished to protect impoverished laborers and hapless females, he should elevate his society's so-called free laborers to the condition of "our slaves." He would then accomplish "a most glorious act of *emancipation*."[2]

Slavery emancipated free laborers from devastation, explained Hammond, because owners loved their things as fondly as they loved themselves. Thus the self-interested patriarch selflessly fed and protected his purchased people. The selfless slaveholder also ensured republican stability. In nonslaveholding republics, demagogues rallied "ignorant and poor free laborers" to seize employers' property. In the free labor North, "a fearful crisis in republican institutions" will explode "at no remote period." Slaveholder republicanism prevented such explosions. Because slaves, "the poorest and most ignorant" half of the population, could not vote, slavery provided the "foundation of every well-designed and durable" republic.[3]

Hammond here dared a political minefield. The colorblind case for enslaving all lower classes repelled the very class a slaveholding minority needed to rally, the southern white nonslaveholding majority. So Hammond, like almost all southern proslavery writers, aborted the colorblind argument before he had half developed it. After he swerved, in the conventional fashion, from slavery for all laborers to bondage for exclusively black laborers, he reiterated that vulnerable inferiors needed disinterested protectors. But he now declared that race, not class, doomed inferiors to haplessness. Without white masters' paternalistic protection, Hammond warned, biologically inferior blacks, loving sleep above all and "sensual excitements of all kinds *when awake,*" would first snooze, then wander, then plunder, then murder, then be exterminated or reenslaved.[4]

This argument for exclusively *black* slavery better suited whites' tastes. But Hammond's racist appeal belied southern facts. Some planters trusted black drivers more than white overseers to supervise their plantations. Many Border South masters manumitted trusted black slaves, especially in Delaware and Maryland. These Southerners needed scientific evidence that seemingly superior blacks were really inferior.

Hammond offered biblical instead of biological proof. In the Old Testament, he argued, Hebrews often practiced slavery. In the New Testament, Christ never denounced servitude.

The argument invited the retort that Christ loathed the selfish spirit. Abolitionists, stressing the spirit of Christianity, denied that slaveholders' selfishness guaranteed selflessness. Rather, self-interest impelled masters to sell slaves, to deny blacks the Bible, to lash them into hard labor, and to despoil them sexually. Enslavers, concluded abolitionists, not employers, exemplified the selfish individualist, that antithesis of selfless Christ.

The charge, like the abolitionist's brothel terminology, laid bare the republican and Christian essence of the matter: Did masters' self-interest sufficiently check and balance their unlimited power to be brutes? Hammond answered that abolitionists' absolute liberty to be Jacobinical, not slaveholders' absolute power to be abominable, caused any southern brutality. Hammond regretted that "the slave is not allowed to read his Bible," but "the sin rests upon the abolitionists." Because of their unchecked agitation, slaves would read Scripture not as "a book of hope, and love, and peace, but of despair, hatred, and blood."[5]

Since antislavery fanatics "aim at loosening all ties between master and slave," continued Hammond, we must somewhat "abandon our efforts to attach them to us, and control them through their affections and pride. We have to rely more and more on the power of fear." While frightful discipline "is painful to us," "we should be ineffably stupid" to allow our domestic servants to "read your writings" and "cut our throats!"[6]

Hammond answered abolitionists' most distressing charge—unchecked sexual exploitation—with another castigation of Yankees' unlicensed liberty. Antislavery perverts, regretted Hammond, had absolute freedom to publish pornographic fantasies. Sexually frustrated Yankees imagined that "licentiousness . . . necessarily arises from slavery." But "such irregularities" as interracial sex and the resulting mulattoes occur "here, for the most part, in the cities." Urban nonslaveholders or "natives of the North or foreigners" were the "chief offenders." As "decided proof" of masters' "continence," Hammond called the "proportion" of mulattoes "infinitely small, and out of the towns next to nothing."

Hammond inquired why female abolitionists, "learned old maids" all, would "linger with such an insatiable relish" on planters' next to no "scandalous stories." Only one explanation could occur "to even the most charitable mind. . . . Ladies of eminent virtue," by their "delight to dwell" on "ridiculously false" charges, reveal that "rage without" which "betrays the fires within." So too, Yankee clergymen, by condemning plantations as brothels,

> Compound for sins they are inclined to
> By damning those they have no mind to.[7]

This savage tone contrasted with Hammond's serene conclusion. The South Carolinian thanked abolitionists for Southerners' "perfect ease of conscience." Before "abolition agitation," many Southerners saw a "duty . . . to get rid of slavery." But external attack compelled internal reconsideration. Southerners emerged with the "*universal conviction* that in holding slaves, we violate no law of God,—inflict no injustice on any of his creatures."[8] In the year 1845, exulted James Henry Hammond, conversion to proslavery had been totally accomplished, and the Slave South had become a monolith perfected.

– 2 –

So limited an argument could hardly score so unlimited a triumph. By deviating to slavery for only blacks, Hammond surrendered his colorblind case for enslaving all laborers. By never demonstrating blacks' inferiority, the South Carolinian built no foundation for racist slavery. By charging that abolitionists caused slaveholders' unchristian brutality, Hammond conceded that southern brutes existed. By sneering that only Yankee virgins and clergymen would dwell on planters' "next to no" sexual brutalizations, he created the suspicion that the gentleman protested too much.

Hammond's private papers confirm the suspicion. Hammond the polemicist called all blacks inferior to all whites. But Hammond the planter called his black driver superior to his white overseer. "I wish you to consult" my driver "on all occasions," he wrote his overseer, "& in all matters of doubt take his opinion wh. [which] you will generally find supported by good reasons."[9]

Again, where Hammond the theorist declared that selfishness impelled masters to uplift underlings benevolently, Hammond the practitioner subjected his initial slaves to a "year of severity which cost me infinite pain" to "subdue" them.[10] While Hammond's subsequent lashings decreased, his sexual exploitations accelerated. Six years before writing the *Letters to Clarkson*, Hammond purchased eighteen-year-old Sally Johnson and her one-year-old daughter, Louisa. The new owner enjoyed Sally—and later Louisa—as his bedmate(s). Hammond's son shared these enjoyments. Hammond's wife, upon discovering that her husband had turned her home into a bordello, demanded that the absolutist end the outrage. Hammond refused. His wife then left home for half a decade.[11]

Louisa and Sally bore Hammond's—and/or his son's—half-white children. Hammond kept his two mistresses and their children in a separate slave cabin, without a black male resident. Hammond's deployment of absolute power thus precluded two black marriages and smashed his white family.

This antidomestic chapter in the history of the Domestic Institution told no tale of romantic love transcending class and racial barriers. "My love," conceded Hammond, "has been either lustful or purely platonic." No wife could be "purer, more high minded, and devoted" than his. But her purity could not satisfy "his appetites."[12]

The slave women who satisfied Hammond's "appetites" could not, he regretted, satisfy his "tastes." His most distasteful problems involved his half-white children. In an 1856 letter to his legitimate son, Harry, Hammond declared that his—or were they Harry's?—illegitimate children must not be freed. "It would be cruelty to them. Nor would I like that any but my own blood should own as Slaves my own blood." James Hammond implored Harry not to allow "any of my children or possible children [to] be slaves of Strangers. Slavery *in the family* will be their happiest earthly condition."[13]

Despite his antifamilial sexual sprees, Hammond here sincerely extolled familial slavery. Even blacks who possessed half his own genes, he thought, still needed a white paternalist's protection. Because James Henry Hammond truly believed in paternalists' absolute power, he writhed the more when abolitionists pointed out its antipaternal outrages. His apologetics—most proslavery arguments—brewed pride and shame into a polemic saturated with hate.

Perhaps Hammond spewed out especially hateful hypocrisy about abolitionist "clergymen and virgins" because his debauchery obliterated his central point about the Slave South: That selfishness drove slaveholders to be selfless. Supposedly benevolent despots have always hailed that position. The absolutist, allegedly possessing everything, allegedly can gain nothing by exploiting his subjects. But Hammond gained sexual pleasure by exploiting his slaves, even if he risked his good name and his good wife. He betrayed his highest interest by indulging his lowest appetites. No wonder republicans deny that absolutists will be selfless.

Sexually, Hammond was an exceptionally selfish absolutist. But his very exceptionalness confirmed abolitionists' point. The licentious slaveholder was not the norm, just the most spectacular illustration that self-interest hardly guaranteed disinterestedness. In the very letter to his son that proved Hammond's uncommon sexual grotesqueness, he also exposed a more common slaveholder selfishness. By pleading with his white son to retain ownership of half white slaves, he conceded that economically pressed heirs often self-ishly sold servants, despite paternalism's selfless code. As another slaveholder lamented, nothing could prevent the *"possibility"* that favorite servants might be sold away from their spouses and children. Even if "a good owner inherited a slave family," the deceased could not "answer for" the heir's "life—and the thousand accidents which befall property."[14]

Nor could Hammond, even while living, altogether answer for his mulatto children's treatment. After his slave Louisa alleged that Hammond had sired her son Henderson, the master decided to keep Henderson "in the family." But Henderson's "wild & daring spirit" and "propensity for petty theft" disrupted Hammond's Big House. So the patriarch dispatched his perhaps son from his not-so-happy South Carolina home.

After being apprenticed to a Georgian, the unhappy Henderson unsuccessfully ran away. In retaliation, Henderson's supervisor strung up Hammond's maybe son by the feet, with the mulatto's shoulders barely touching the ground and his arms bound behind his back. Hammond, although distressed enough to investigate, dared not intervene. What else could he do with the not-so-black "boy" who must not come "home"?[15] His question raised another: Could every Southerner believe that absolute power had been reconciled with domestic happiness and Christian republicanism?

– 3 –

No way, as Hammond once again confessed in private. In 1848, upon reading a Border South minister's supposedly proslavery tract, the South Carolinian privately termed the author *"utterly* opposed to slavery." The Border South divine, Hammond pointed out, believed that Southerners would abolish slavery in "a moment if they could get rid of " blacks. Worse, the author hoped that African colonization would rid America of blacks, "and that is being three-fourths abolitionist in my estimation." The softheart's "views are these of the [Border South] regions" where he "was reared." There, "the march of events will ere long abolish the institution entirely."[16]

In 1847, some Charlestonians, seeking to preclude borderland abolition, asked Hammond to help establish a proslavery newspaper. Hammond refused. He "feared that a large proportion of slaveholders, who in every emergency will unite with us" against Yankee invasion, "would refuse to unite with us in sustaining an organ that supported slavery as a blessing to be preserved, when they are well known to regard it as an *evil*, which they one day hope to get rid of. The consequences of an *open* and *avowed* division . . . among the slaveholders on this vital point might be serious."[17] And this was the man who two years earlier had publicly pronounced Southerners "universally" converted to slavery's permanent blessings.

The private rather than the public Hammond properly diagnosed the persisting variety of southern opinions. Proslavery writers in the 1850s often admitted that, *Letters to Clarkson* to the contrary, most southern conversions had occurred since 1845. Until "the last few years," Virginia's George Fitzhugh conceded in 1856, most apologists declared *Negro* slavery to be "justifiable" only because racially "exceptional." Others, "by far the greater number," called even Negro slavery "wrong in principle, and looked forward to gradual emancipation." Only "very recently" had Southerners "taken stronger and bolder grounds." Fitzhugh's favorite Virginia proslavery writer, George Frederick Holmes, agreed that only "in recent years" had "an entire revulsion of feelings and judgment" alleviated "troubled" consciences and "speculative" doubts.[18]

Yet pleas to relieve doubts persisted. In 1851, an admirer of Iverson Brookes, a prominent South Carolina proslavery minister, offered to subsidize the cleric's pamphlet, written to combat Kentuckians' prayer for abolition. Brookes's admirer feared that northern "fanaticism" might infect "the consciences of the weak minded good Christian people of the South, upon the question of *Right*."[19]

A year later, a conscience-stricken Georgian wrote the Reverend James Henley Thornwell, South Carolina's leading proslavery theologian, confessing a "very difficult" time forming "a settled opinion" on "correct principles." According to the unsettled Georgian, "every man who conscientiously believes slavery to be wrong" must use "whatever influence he may possess against it." Furthermore, every man who conscientiously believes "it to be right" must "defend and advocate it." Could Thornwell "satisfy my mind?"[20]

The most important Virginia proslavery cleric of the 1850s aspired to satisfy unsettled minds. In 1856, the Reverend Dr. William A. Smith, president of Randolph-Macon College, published his classroom *Lectures on the Philosophy and Practice of Slavery*. "A secret suspicion of the morality of African slavery in the South," regretted Smith, troubled "many of our best citizens." Too many slaveholders harbored the "private but painful suspicion" that something must be "wrong in the principle of domestic slavery."[21] That suspicion extended beyond slaveholders. Smith's greatest "difficulty," he privately wrote the governor of Virginia in 1857, was "to get the ear of the white laborer," of whom "nine-tenths" would abolish slavery "tomorrow," if they could "vote the slaves out of the state."[22]

George Sawyer, a Louisiana lawyer, who published his *Southern Institutes* in 1859, also regretted that "thousands" of Southerners "blindly acknowledge" slavery as "*a great moral and political evil*." Such "consciousness of wrong gives a faint heart and a craven resolve to the bravest soldier." The South could never achieve "breathless frenzy and indomitable zeal" until all her sons understood "the true character and spirit of our institutions."[23] Fourteen years after James Hammond's *Letters to Clarkson,* a year before the South rose in rebellion, the George Sawyers still faced enervating suspicions that unlimited power might be anti-Christian and antirepublican.

– 4 –

Three questions bedeviled every post-Hammond attempt to reconcile republican and absolute power: Did colorblind theorists dare argue that *white* lower classes should be enslaved? Could racist polemicists prove all blacks' inferiority to all whites? And what could deter absolute masters from violating the spirit of Christianity?

Answering these questions required transcending James Hammond's effort—indeed transforming southern society. Hammond had retreated from his argument that republics must enslave all laborers of all colors. But if braver theorists insisted on the colorblind position, southern white free laborers would have to be enslaved. Again, the retreating Hammond had stopped short of proving blacks' inferiority. But if racial theorists advanced to scientific proof of blacks' biological hopelessness, a quarter-million southern free blacks would have to be reenslaved.

Whether future proslavery writers sanctified a transformed Domestic Institution on a racial or on a colorblind basis, the spirit of Christianity might require limits on anti-Christian selfishness. Even if Christ had never decried absolute power, He surely would have denounced Hammond's sexual absolutism. Preachers would have to convince absolutists that only selfless paternalism served their God, their families, and their interests. If religious persuasion failed, southern legislatures would have to ban perversions of the Christian spirit.

But limits on masters, while rescuing the spirit of Christianity and of republicanism, would abolish unlimited power. Once again, perfecting a Christian republican's defense of absolute power would require the world defended to be transformed. In the wake of the *Letters to Clarkson,* the puzzle of absolute versus republican power remained unsolved—and disconcerting either to put together or to leave in pieces.

CHAPTER 4

The Three Imperfect Solutions

In the 1850s, advanced proslavery sophisticates based their arguments on three conceptions of human inferiority. Virginia's George Fitzhugh emphasized economic helplessness. He sought colorblind protection of all lower-class laborers, white or black. Alabama's Dr. Josiah Nott stressed racial incapacity. He urged protective dominion over all blacks, slave or free. South Carolina's Reverend James Henley Thornwell underlined Christian depravity. He craved evangelical cleansing of all sinners, masters or slaves. Late antebellum Southerners thus enjoyed several soothing reconciliations of despotic government over inferiors and democratic government for equals. But all arguments fell frustratingly short of compelling universal proslavery belief.

– 1 –

To the delight of southern warriors who loved to defend by attacking, colorblind proslavery theorists decried Yankee free labor as economically exploitative and politically disastrous. By giving laborers the ballot but no other protection against exploitation, Northerners invited an electoral revolution against the exploiters. After the revolution of the rabble would come the lawlessness of the mob.

Yet this satisfying assault on northern sins remained forbidden fruit. The majority of southern citizens, nonslaveholding lovers of egalitarianism and despisers of blacks, would never vote to reduce themselves to black slavery. Only in the oldest and crustiest South, in coastal South Carolina and in pockets of tidewater Virginia, did the colorblind natural outcome of slaveholding hauteur (and unnaturally nonracist way to rally all whites) dominate the climactic proslavery argument—and usually only in a few sentences or in a short pamphlet. Only tidewater Virginia's George Fitzhugh wrote book-length pleas for enslaving all lower classes.[1]

Fitzhugh could not have been a more merry or a more savage polemicist.

35

The Virginian tore into abolitionists (alias "communists") and capitalists (alias "cannibals"). He then invited his insulted foes to be his amused correspondents.

A ferocious fanatic, to be so amiable, needed serenity about his superiority. Fitzhugh cockily belonged. He was after all a Fitzhugh, that great name in the oldest Virginia. This latest offspring of two centuries of bluebloods lived "in a rickety old mansion, situated on the fag-end of a once noble estate."[2] His slim form, slicked-back hair, Roman nose, and patriarchal profile seemed at odds with his well-used apparel.[3] But nothing was shabby about his link to a First Family or his pride in eastern Virginia's ancient patriarchy. George Fitzhugh confidently challenged northern rich men to ignore his case for enslaving poor men, urging them even to cherish his delightful (of if you will, horrifying) colorblind slogans.

Fitzhugh's were the eye-catching slogans of the journalist. Because he had inherited everything except cash, he struggled to keep his fag-end of the old estate. To scrape for dollars, he practiced freelance political journalism and its nineteenth-century Siamese twin, chasing political patronage. To sell occasional pieces, he wrote explosive prose. Thereafter, he collected his zany explosions in a book, usually without revision, even when his verbal strikes devastated each other. The amusement of reading his fireworks in the newspapers evolved into the sport of reading his roller-coaster books—and the fun of imagining George Fitzhugh chuckling at his own daffy somersaults on colorblind slavery.

George Fitzhugh's very title pages assaulted free labor capitalism with soundbites. *Sociology for the South, or the Failure of Free Society* (1854) was followed by *Cannibals All! or, Slaves Without Masters* (1857). The titles announced that defense of "mere negro slavery" was mankind's "most absurdly untenable proposition."[4] If only blacks should be enslaved, why did Southerners enslave whites? According to southern law, masters owned their female slaves' children. According to southern practice, generation after generation of enslaved women, after sleeping with white men, produced whiter and whiter offspring, still legally enslaved. "Men with as white skins as any of us" were "held in slavery in every state of the South."[5]

White-skinned slaves also pervaded Scripture. If only blacks should be bondsmen, God was a sinner. By His "express command," Hebrews enslaved whites. Greeks and Romans also enslaved whites. Fitzhugh would rather chuck "the negroes than the Bible" and the ancients.[6]

The Virginian would also rather chuck the Negro than abandon the colorblind principle of slavery: "The will of the superior controls and directs the will and action of the inferior." Superiors' controlling willpower, Fitzhugh claimed, made slavery peculiar not to the mere South or the mere Negro but universal, in every nation, in every family, in every factory. "Nine tenths of government was slavery, even in (so called) free societies. Married women, children, sailors, soldiers, wards, apprentices, etc., are not governed by law, but by the will of superiors."[7]

Fitzhugh contrasted the universality of superiors' overweening willfulness, alias slavery, with the rarity of responsible dominators, alias southern slaveholders. Northern employers, unlike southern masters, felt obligated only to protect their profits. The resulting dreadful wages and horrendous unemployment showed that "man, isolated and individualized, is a devil."[8]

Satanic Yankees considered slavery the ultimate restraint on their beloved individualism. But attacks on the ultimate restraint would widen into attacks on all restraints. If slaves should be free of protective masters, wives should be free of protective husbands, children free of protective parents, parishioners free of protective preachers, and the governed free of protective governors.

Then all superiors would be free to savage all inferiors. Previously protected inferiors would also be free today, before tomorrow succumbing to a nonprotective exploiter. "A social revolution certainly impends throughout free society, and that revolution, directed at first against negro slavery, now proposes to destroy" all protectors, "all religion, all government, and all private property."[9]

Fitzhugh satirized proponents of abolishing slavery, alias proponents of abolishing all protective hierarchies, as a "small squad" of "half-starved, half-naked Frenchmen, and Infidel Germans, flanked by a crowd of unsexed women and free negroes," screaming "give us liberty or give us death!" Only an individual's liberty to be selfish is "recognized by philosophers, abolitionists, wise women, free lovers, geologists, free negroes, agrarians, anarchists, Jeffersonians, spiritualists, Millerites, Mormons, Chartists, fishwomen, proletariats, cannibals, sans culottes, red republicans, black ditto, and Yankees!" The "real abolitionists" are "socialists of the darkest dye, . . . anti-marriage . . . anti-chastity. . . . Indeed sir, half the North is partially insane, worse than France during the Reign of Terror."[10]

Fitzhugh pitted the mercies of southern hierarchies against the mendacities of northern individualism. Especially in the southern family, self-serving patriarchs promoted "their own well-being, by kindness to their inferiors." Wife and children, when happy, made the head of the family merrier. Selfishness also made the merry protector lovingly kind "to his horse and his cattle, which are useful to him," and to "his dog, which is of no use. He loves them because they are his."[11]

Slaves were also his. The domestic "affection which all men feel for what belongs to them, and for what is dependent on them," thus became "nature's magna carta, which shields, protects, and provides for wives, children, and slaves."[12] This slaveholding mentality fostered layer upon hierarchical layer of southern schools, churches, families, and governments, all featuring beneficent protection of grateful dependents. In the antihierarchical North, in contrast, the supposedly "free" laborer now—and soon the wife and the child—stood shiveringly liberated from protectors.

The question was thus stark: Should inferiors be liberated to be crushed? Or should superiors be enshrined to protect inferiors? "One set of ideas," soared Fitzhugh, "will govern . . . the civilized world. Slavery will everywhere be abolished or everywhere reinstituted." He was "quite as intent on abolishing Free Society," he told the abolitionists, "as you are on abolishing slavery."[13]

So was Fitzhugh intent on enslaving all American laborers, North and South, black and white? The Virginian ever renounced that inescapable—and inescapably politically disastrous—outcome of his flight beyond the mere Negro. Again and again, he sped right back to merely Negro slavery—*in America.*

In crowded Europe, Fitzhugh explained, factory workers found starvation wages inescapable. But in underpopulated America, starving laborers could "escape to the West, and become proprietors."[14] Fitzhugh here anticipated Frederick Jackson Turner's "safety valve" argument. Turner, the renowned late nineteenth- and early twentieth-century historian of the frontier, would declare that virgin western lands freed the New World from Old World exploitation, economic and political.

Fitzhugh, a half century before Turner, cheered that the poorest Americans, when "out of employment or starving," could "emigrate to the great West," there to become well-fed farmers. By making oppression intolerable, eastern capitalists "drive population westward, prevent its excessive accumulation on the Atlantic, . . . and open up the desert spots of the earth for the residences of man." In "very new and sparsely settled countries" such as America, wage slavery would remain "the greatest of human blessings, . . . until the Northwest is peopled."[15]

But how long *until* the Northwest would be crowded and the Northeast enslaved? In his first book, Fitzhugh declared that "until" meant "soon." The flood of immigrants to the North, he wrote in *Sociology for the South*, made "the situation of the laborer at the North as precarious as in Europe."[16] But later, in *Cannibals All*, Fitzhugh declared that since America had "vast unsettled territories, . . . many centuries may elapse" before nature's nation would need to abolish free labor. The more Fitzhugh thought about it, the more the centuries multiplied. "Thousands of years may elapse," he declared in *De Bow's Review*, before all lands "between the Atlantic and Pacific are settled and monopolized, and a refluent population is pouring back on the East." Why "anticipate evils that may never happen?" The North's situation, applauded the North's severest critic, was "natural, healthful, and progressive."[17]

That stunning admission apparently made southern slavery indefensible. If no black should be enslaved merely because he was a Negro, and if no dependent laborer should be enslaved when he could become an independent farmer, black laborers should be freed to light out for the territories. In the vast, sparsely peopled southwestern domain of Texas, Arkansas, and Mississippi, free blacks could be productive pioneers.

To escape that colorblind heresy, Fitzhugh clutched color-infested orthodoxy. In *Sociology for the South,* the Virginian called blacks' "freedom but the wild and vicious license of the fox, the wolf, or the hawk." Peculiarly "negro slavery would be changed immediately to some form of peonage, serfdom, or villenage, if the negroes were sufficiently intelligent and provident to manage a farm." But the Negro was "a child, and must be governed as a child."[18]

Fitzhugh reiterated in *Cannibals All* that "the negro has neither energy nor enterprise." His "improvident habits" turn "liberty" into "a curse to himself, and a greater curse to the society around him." As Fitzhugh summed up his surrender to merely black slavery, "no sane man in America proposes to make slaves of white men." But "as well send monkeys to settle, reclaim and cultivate the far West, as free negroes. . . . Even in America, negroes should be slaves."[19]

With this journey straight away and then straight back to mere Negro slavery, Fitzhugh completed a rollicking Grand Tour. His passage away from racist slavery exposed northern capitalism's colorblind inequities, to the delight of Yankee-hating southern reactionaries. His pilgrimage back to racial enslavement exposed American freedom's color-infested qualifications, to the delight of black-hating southern rednecks. Yet Fitzhugh, like James Hammond, came back to the saving racial bunker without proving the racial inferiority. With that omission, Fitzhugh's wild ride through the intellectual universe shot past its tracks. Only proslavery racists could produce that prayed-for universal southern belief, and only if their biological proof could prevent the colorblind conclusion that blacks should go west, young man, go west, in order to share the American individualistic glory.

– 2 –

With his famed "cornerstone" speech, Alexander Stephens displayed how superficially easily race-based theory could stop Fitzhugh's class-based spin. The "foundation" and "cornerstone" of our Southern Confederacy, declared Stephens shortly after assuming the new nation's vice presidency in 1861, "rests upon the great truth that the Negro is not equal to the white man, that slavery—subordination to the superior race—is his natural or normal condition." Our master "idea," added William L. Yancey, is that every "white man is the equal of every other white man. The second idea is that the negro is the inferior race."[20]

Exponents of the master idea often concurred with George Fitzhugh that Yankee employers ruthlessly exploited white employees. Then they insisted that no white should be owned or employed. Only blacks should be dependent laborers. Only the South allegedly spared whites from menial labor.

James Henry Hammond made the point famously in his "mudsill" outburst to the U.S. Senate on March 4, 1858. As architects use the words, "sill" denotes a structure's lowest part. A "mudsill" bottom portion sinks into the mud. As Hammond used housing structure to illuminate social structure, a "mudsill" class must "do the menial duties" and "perform the drudgery of life." By turning whites into mudsills, Northerners have abolished only the "*name*" slavery. "Your whole hireling class of manual laborers" is indeed free—free to beg on your streets. Our enslaved black mudsills, in contrast, display "no starving, no begging, no want of employment."

Having crept up Fitzhugh's path, the Hammond of the late 1850s seemed poised to leap to higher ground: to argue that since employed mudsills suffered more than owned mudsills, white employees should be owned. Hammond instead glided down the racial path in the next sentence: "We do not think that whites should be slaves either by law or necessity." No white should do mudsill work, whether as an employee or as a slave. All mudsills should be "black, of another and inferior race"—and enslaved. Otherwise, Hammond warned Northerners, your white mudsills, turning on exploitative employers, will leave "your society . . . reconstituted, your government overthrown, your property divided."[21]

South Carolina's Congressman Laurence Keitt reinforced Senator Hammond's warning. "In every quarter of the world, save in the South," declared Representative Keitt, exploited and exploiters are of the same race. Demagogues then enflame the downtrodden. In the South's saving version of republican government, however, the distinction is "between races, and not classes." Here "the superior race" rules an "inferior" race of noncitizens, "content with its position and destiny." "The destruction of African slavery," soared Laurence Keitt, "would be the destruction of republicanism."[22]

Yet Keitt knew as well as Fitzhugh and Hammond that white menials pervaded the southern as well as the northern social structure and everywhere could vote. The ideological strain yielded the most absurd element in the proslavery argument. The scorching southern sun, so the nonsense ran, prevented whites from manual labor! "The white man cannot stand the climate," William L. Yancey exclaimed, but "the negro can." While overseers "seek shelter under a tree or an umbrella," blacks "look the sun in the eye without flinching." James De Bow added that "outside the tropics, the negro will not and cannot labor. Inside of them, the white man perishes if he attempts it. White field labor does exist in parts of the South, it is true, but so is cotton grown in Boston green-houses"![23]

Whites laboring under the southern sun as rare as cotton grown in Boston! Instead of that preposterous version of racism, racial proslavery required evidence of blacks' inferiority. Physicians claimed special expertise in blacks' supposed biological depravity. Louisiana's Samuel Cartwright, for example, asserted that his black patients' brains were a ninth or tenth the size of his white patients'. Since all men had equal quantities of nerves, fewer nerves in undersized brains meant more nerves "to the senses." Thus blacks cherished "sensuality, at the expense of intellectuality."

Blacks' "profuse distribution of nervous matter to the stomach, liver, and genital organs would make the Ethiopian race entirely unmanageable," continued Dr. Cartwright, except that their profuse chest nerves crowded out their lung tissue. Blacks' insufficient lungs consumed insufficient oxygen.

This "defective hematosis," plus "a deficiency of cerebral matter," caused "indolence and apathy," along with "that debasement of mind, which has rendered the people of Africa unable to take care of themselves."

Blacks' biological diseases, Dr. Cartwright diagnosed, included both "Drapetomania," an unquenchable propensity toward fleeing, and "Dysaesthesia," an insatiable appetite for sloth. To cure the maladies, masters must lash and lash, so blacks' "molasses-like" blood would move less sluggishly and pick up more oxygen.[24] In this popular rendition, Dr. Cartwright turned physical coercion into a physician's miracle drug.

While Cartwright's provincial cure satisfied snickering rednecks, sophisticates preferred Josiah Nott's cosmopolitan theory. The Notts had long been among America's most cultivated families. Josiah Nott's father, Abraham Nott, was of a First Family of Connecticut. Both father and son, like ancestors for a century, had been educated at Yale. But where previous Notts became scholarly New England preachers after graduation, Abraham Nott became a scholarly South Carolina lawyer, a large slaveholder, and chief judge of his adopted state's highest court.

His son Josiah brought the family's ancestral love of scholarship to the services of southern slavery. After graduating from South Carolina College, Josiah Nott studied medicine in New York, Philadelphia, and Paris before marrying a South Carolina blueblood and migrating to Mobile, Alabama. There he settled down to his life's work: using advanced science to improve worldwide medical practice, to cure southern patients, and to defend the slavocracy.[25]

Nott's rumpled clothes and long beard suggested a detached scholar. His warm smile suggested that his scholarship had been pursued for his patients' benefit. His research benefited patients far beyond his own. His first publication translated a French physician's book. His subsequent essays publicized his discoveries of needles to remove eye cataracts, splints to cure compound fractures, and gorgets for bladder surgery.

But this cosmopolitan physician's inventive gadgetry and international theory could not cure the local scourge, yellow fever. That plague decimated New Orleans and Mobile, brutally in the 1840s, then horrendously in 1853, when half of the two Gulf cities' population sickened and a fifth of the afflicted perished.[26] According to local lore, yellow fever came from a miasma in the air. But those who breathed the air inside sickrooms, Nott noticed, remained as healthy as those outside. Nor could Nott abide the conventional sickroom cure: draining supposedly miasmic blood from weak patients.

One day, while despairing over his futility, this seeker exploded that "I'm damned if I don't believe it's bugs."[27] Had Nott guessed that mosquitoes were the murderous bugs, he would have gained fame as a magnificent healer rather than as a frustrated racist. But instead of mosquitoes, he speculated that almost invisible bugs spread the pestilence.

At this moment of his almost breakthrough, mosquitoes swarmed over his sleeping children. In the summer of 1853, one of his offspring caught yellow fever, then two, three, four. All suffered through the killing cycle: first raging temperatures, then icy, yellowed skin, then expelling crystal clear vomit, then emitting blackened fluids. Within seven days, a quartet of Josiah Nott's beloved children expired. Having failed to protect his dependents, the anguished scientist covered their graves with a cast-iron replica of the family's watchdog.

The hapless watchman, having known too agonizingly little to secure his children's survival, clung the harder to what he thought he knew best: the biological requirements for southern survival. The grief-stricken workaholic labored day and night to demonstrate that the diseased Negro had been created unequal and must be kept separate. Otherwise, plagues more lethal than yellow fever would exterminate more southern families than his own.

Nott's first article on the subject flourished a Fitzhugh-like soundbite of a title: "The Mulatto a Hybrid—probable extermination of the two races if the Whites and Blacks are allowed to intermarry." In arguing for total biological separation, Nott wielded the newest rage among advanced biological scientists, the doctrine of polygenesis. Polygenesists held that, the Book of Genesis to the contrary, separate races did not spring from a single pair of humans, residing in the Garden of Eden. Instead, separate races originated in separate areas. The tale of Adam and Eve was a nonscientific myth. Scientific truth demanded that slavery ensure permanent separation of separately created races.

Nott the polygenesist, like Nott the physician, worked within a transatlantic community of empiricists. Samuel G. Morton, a Philadelphia physician and the polygenesis movement's leader, possessed the world's most famous collection of skulls. In his masterpiece, *Crania Americana* (1839), Morton argued that blacks' skulls displayed smaller brain areas.[28]

Morton's followers included not only Josiah Nott but also George Gliddon, an English-born expert on ancient Egypt, E. G. Squire, a New York specialist on ancient Indians, and Louis Agassiz, a Swiss native and Harvard professor who compared human environments. These scholars separately concluded that immense differences in skull types, climatic zones, and ancient civilizations must have evolved in more than a mere 6000 years (the time then assumed to have transpired since Adam and Eve). God may have created a single human pair many more than 6000 years ago. More likely, God created pairs of humans, at different times and in different places.

In the four years after his children's decimation, Nott, the only Southerner in the international group, labored feverishly to publish two collaborative, gorgeously illustrated polygenesist tomes, *Types of Mankind* (1854) and *Indigenous Races of the Earth* (1857). In addition to the exhausting task of editing these two volumes, Nott wearily expanded his studies of mulattoes. The physician grew ever more persuaded that his brown patients, compared to whites and blacks, sickened more easily and reproduced less successfully. Just as horse and ass mated to produce the sterile mule, he argued, so a white and black union yielded the less fertile mulatto. Put "a hundred white men and one hundred black women" on an isolated island, Nott predicted, and "they would in time become extinct." Thus to prevent the suicide of both races, slavery must ensure separation of whites and blacks.[29]

Yet by bolstering the proslavery argument with anti-Genesis science, Nott seemed blasphemous to many proslavery Christians. Most southern Christians believed that the Word alone must command. To interpret Genesis was to tamper with God. Polygenesists especially tampered with the Word, for they disputed God's account of His creation.

Nott's writings spread infidelity about more than Genesis. The physician saw "no evidence" that "any influence of civilization" could uplift inferior races' "physical" and "consequently their moral character." Masters or reverends, when preaching Christian salvation to slaves, wasted their time. Africans, because cursed with fewer brains, could never comprehend the white man's cultivated religion.[30]

In Nott's hands, blacks' biological inferiority, supposedly the reason why the unfortunates needed paternalistic direction, instead made paternalism impossible. Nott's cultivated drift, no less than Cartright's crude sneers, invited contempt for blacks, barbaric lashing rather than Christian instruction, contemptuous willingness to break up families of blacks who were supposedly too brutish to care. The "predominance of the animal propensity," declared George Sawyer, "predisposes" blacks to "moral insensibility, intellectual stupidity, indolence, and gluttony." A black aspires "to satiate his appetite, then to lounge, sleep, sweat, and steam in the sun, like the moping alligator upon his log." Blacks would like nothing better, claimed Daniel R. Hundley, than to resort "again to toad-eating and cannibalism," reproducing "on the shores of the New World, a second Africa, all except the lions and elephants."[31]

Josiah Nott shuddered at such crudity. But his vision of slavery was itself shuddering. He clung to the horror of enslavement of black barbarians only to avoid the greater horror of biological suicide, just as he worked himself to exhaustion with his polygenesis obsession lest he go mad over his children's deaths. This grieving physician understandably told an English visitor that "he detests slavery, but he does not see what could be done."[32] With that admission, Nott's proslavery racism looked as trapped as Fitzhugh's colorblind theory.

George Fitzhugh saw that his own escape required overturning Josiah Nott's form of racism. "You must not think I consider our form of society perfect," he wrote with his usual astonishing private candor to his arch public enemy, William Lloyd Garrison. Southern servitude "might be the best practical form, if the negroes were only white and straight haired, for then domestic affection would come into full play to correct those evils, which difference of race and that diabolical theory of the Types of Mankind, seem only to aggravate."[33] Just as Fitzhugh needed the "mere negro" to dodge his admission that American lower classes need not be enslaved, so racists needed a humane

Christianity to escape Nott's admission that blacks remained too disgusting to be uplifted and slavery too repulsive to be cherished.

– 3 –

John Bachman, a Lutheran minister and professor of natural history at South Carolina's College of Charleston led the evangelical detour around Nott and the polygenesists. Bachman's masterpiece, *The Unity of the Human Race* (1850), reconciled science and Genesis by urging that a single human creation eventually spawned multiple races. Instead of degrading blacks into "a different species, incapable of receiving the truths of Christianity," paternalists must take "a race of men, stamped with inferiority," and "elevate their moral characters, instruct them in the duties they owe to their Creator, and give them the consolations and hopes of a future life." Then these "members of our household" and "playmates of our family" will be seen not as small-skulled barbarians but as members of "the whole human family," bound in "universal dependence and brotherhood" to Jesus Christ.[34]

To transform slavery into a brotherhood of Christ, evangelists had to convince not only polygenesists to accept the brotherhood of man but also unlimited masters to accept Christian limits. Proslavery preachers, who wrote more defenses of slavery than secular Southerners, joined antislavery polemicists in describing masters as screaming too much, lashing too hard, smashing slave marriages too often, and barring too many slaves from hearing or reading the Gospel. Yet such anti-Christian absolutism, proslavery preachers shot back at abolitionists, hardly required that unlimited power be abolished. Instead, absolutists must be taught to use their absolute power to fulfill the Christian spirit.

South Carolina's James Henley Thornwell, leader of this movement to reform and thus better defend the upper class, was to the lower class born.[35] His impoverished father died when Thornwell was eight. The frightened son, standing over his father's corpse, wondered aloud, "*What will mother do? What will become of us?*"[36] The tableau paralleled the scene of Josiah Nott standing over his children's corpses, despairing that southern health would further sicken unless masters clung to racial barricades. Thornwell's forebodings also prefigured the stance of George Fitzhugh standing before his dilapidated ancestral mansion, fearing that Yankee individualists would smash ancient hierarchies.

All three intellectuals feared a world of predators and victims, with weaker individuals slaughtered in the chaos. That would remain Thornwell's image of England and the North. But the fatherless boy found South Carolina to be something mercifully else: a society of hierarchy, of roles and responsibilities, of the strong protecting the weak. The family provided the first southern defense against savage individualism. Thornwell's first protector, a cousin, epitomized the ideal. He provided the bereaved clan with a nearby cabin.

The southern hierarchy for protecting orphans radiated out from the family to the school. A teacher replaced the cousin as the boy's provider. Then Thornwell's teenage reputation as a prodigy captured the attention of a prominent attorney, William H. Robbins. Robbins unofficially adopted Thornwell, treated the adolescent as a younger brother, and moved his ward's spare bed to the foot of his commodious bedstead.

The ensuing familial drama prefigured Thornwell's lifelong crusade to transform unjustifiable secular tyranny into sanctified Christian slavery. Robbins wanted Thornwell to become a lawyer—to become just like him. The teenager instead aspired to be a clergyman. The patriarch, conceived the dependent, used overwhelming power unconscionably, preventing a powerless ward from spreading the Word.

Thornwell, trembling to confront his erring patriarch, wrote a letter. Robbins found the epistle under his plate at tea. "I am incapable of speaking to you on the delicate subject without tears," the paternalist read. Why must the ward "bid farewell, with great heaviness of heart, to a beloved patron, who kindly clothed me when naked, fed me when hungry, and, above all, has much labored to dispel ignorance from my mind"? Because Thornwell could not "reconcile my conscience to the practice of the Law." He must become a theologian, for "the glory of God and the good of men."[37]

Robbins found Thornwell huddled on the porch, weeping. Embracing the would-be cleric, the guardian agreed that the ward must become a minister. Thornwell had passed the critical moment in his journey away from dependence. He now strode toward the independence of the evangelist who would teach wayward masters how to be benevolent Christians.

South Carolina's institutions propelled the ex-orphan upward to instruct the slaveholders. After undergraduate triumphs at South Carolina College, Thornwell taught at Cheraw Preparatory Academy, then trained for the Presbyterian ministry. After serving remote South Carolina upcountry congregations, he accepted prominent pulpits in Columbia and Charleston, then the presidency of South Carolina College, and then his favorite post, a chair at the Columbia (South Carolina) Theological Seminary. His rise showed that rich planters embraced poor nonslaveholders who espoused slaveholder convictions. Thornwell aspired for more. He would improve slaveholders' convictions. *If* he could reform all patriarchs the way he had reformed William Robbins, slavery would become a road to Christ for all races and all classes.

By emphasizing that *if,* Thornwell demonstrated that the biblical facts did not alone make slavery universally justifiable. Southern preachers endlessly pointed out that in the Old Testament, many Hebrews held slaves; and in the New Testament, Christ and His disciples never cried shame. Since man must follow the Word literally, biblical history's literal facts apparently sanctified subsequent slavery.

But abolitionists emphasized that the Word handed down more than a past history. Scripture also provided a guide to how present life ought to be lived. No matter how many pre-Christians or early Christians practiced slavery, modern slavery must exude the spirit of Christianity.

Thornwell and fellow preachers agreed. The spirit-of-Christianity issue, they also concurred, hinged on the Golden Rule and on the ethic of sanctified masters: "Masters, give unto your servants that which is just and equal, knowing that ye also have a Master in Heaven." As abolitionists parsed that biblical injunction, masters must give slaves the same equality and justice that slaveholders would want, if they were enslaved. Masters, if slaves, would want to be free. This abolitionist reading of the Golden Rule could lead to the abolition not just of slavery but of all distinctions between mankind, all hierarchies, all institutions. All inferiors, after all, would prefer to be equals.

Proslavery preachers answered that God created inferiors, superiors, and hierarchies because He hardly wished all humankind to be the same. His Golden Rule scarcely insisted that unless masters wished to be slaves, they must abolish slavery. The Word instead instructed us to "treat our slaves as we should" wish to "be treated, if we were slaves" and if we were inferior in intelligence and willpower.[38] God would then not want us to be freed, to compete against our superiors. He would want His superiors to guarantee our "just and equal" material sustenance and access to Christ.

Thornwell prized spiritual access more than material sustenance. The injustice of denying slaves their daily bread "is nothing to the injustice of defrauding them of that bread which cometh down from Heaven." Slaveholders defrauded blacks when they barred evangelicals from bringing Christianity to the quarters. Masters also debased bondsmen when their slave sales divided Christian families. After such anti-Christian travesties, slavery lost its divine sanction as "the state in which the African is most effectively trained to the moral end of his being."

Christian paternalists, emphasized Thornwell, must ensure that ex-Africans learned and practiced Christianity. Then slavery, although a "natural evil" and sprung "from the nature of man as sinful and the nature of society as disordered," would provide effective "punishment" for Adam's "crime." Considering "the diversities in moral position, which sin has been the means of entailing upon the [black] race," ran Thornwell's revealingly guarded conclusion, "we may be justified in affirming that, relatively to some persons and to some times, slavery may be a good, or to speak more accurately, a condition, though founded in a curse, from which the Providence of God extracts a blessing."

Thornwell did not here win the biblical argument for the slaveholders, any more than he won the argument by showing that Hebrews held slaves. Rather, he showed slaveholders how to win the spirit-of-Christianity argument. When masters failed to be Christian paternalists—when they whipped harshly or severed black marriages or barred the Word from the quarters—when they, in short, used absolute power to defy Christ's injunctions, they failed to give their servants that which is just and equal. Then southern preachers must condemn sinning absolutists. When too many masters sinned, preachers must condemn slavery itself. But when masters dispensed mild punishment and kept black families intact and suffused the quarters with the Word, they would rout the abolitionists as exemplars of the Christian spirit.

Fortunately for proslavery preachers' equanimity, ever more masters during the 1845–60 period treated their slaves as Christian paternalists should. Revivalists converted ever more blacks, as masters allowed ever more preachers into the quarters. But had revivalists converted enough masters and slaves to prove that absolute power served the spirit of Christianity? Or did too many masters still sell slave mates from each other and prevent too many slaves from hearing or reading the Word?

The queries tortured James Henley Thornwell. For all his worldly success, this thin, frail, retiring scholar, with his drooping eye, ever present cigar, and violent coughs, exuded a haunted air, akin to Josiah Nott's. Just as Alabama's medical leader dwelled on children who perished without protection from yellow fever, so South Carolina's theological leader dwelled on blacks who perished without inspiration from the Word. To forsake the hapless slave who shuddered at the unchristian master would be to betray his own defining moment, when he had been the hapless orphan who shuddered to confront his unchristian patron.

Whenever trouble beset the South, Thornwell conceived that God signaled His anger with slavery's unchristian shortcomings. On the eve of the Civil War, Thornwell, fearing chaos and anarchy, momentarily felt that slavery must be at least partially abolished, before God devastated His unholy people. As Thornwell summed up the conditional that put his nerves on edge, the Bible provided *"the true impregnable position of the Christian Slaveholder,"* but "only when he obeys its directions as well as employs its sanctions. Our rights are there established, but it is always in connection with our duties; if we neglect the one, we cannot make good the other."[39]

If. Once again those two little letters performed the big work in reconciling unlimited absolute power with limited republican power. Just as colorblind theorists required rescue from George Fitzhugh's exaltation that no U.S. mudsills need be enslaved, and just as racist theorists required redemption from Josiah Nott's exclamation that no black could be saved, so preachers required delivery from sinning masters who defiled the spirit of Christianity.

CHAPTER 5

The Puzzling Future
and the Infuriating Scapegoats

Theoretically, political reform could have supplied the proslavery puzzle's missing piece. If southern states had imposed Christian limits on limitless authoritarians, democracy and dictatorship might have been eased toward reconciliation. But democratic reform requires open discussion. Slaveholders could not calmly debate internal corrections, they reiterated, while outside agitators advertised their supposed monstrosities.

Southerners may have sincerely believed that Yankee scapegoats inhibited slavery's improvement. Defensive zealots rarely consider internal reform while a hated enemy screams about appalling perversions. Still, to credit the sincerity is not to accept the diagnosis. Even if outside agitators had been silenced, unlimited dictators would have been squeamish about discussing or accepting democratic limits. Authoritarians' gingerly discussions about a reformist future reveal a culture at a frustrating crossroads— and enraged about scapegoats who supposedly precluded reconciliation of the unreconcilable.

– 1 –

Thomas R. R. Cobb, an evangelical zealot who codified Georgia's laws, called limits on masters "of exceeding nicety and difficulty." Laws, "if possible," should prevent the "wanton separation of . . . husband and wife." But "to fasten upon a master . . . a vicious, corrupt negro, sowing discord and dissatisfaction," would make slaveholding "a curse." Cobb hoped the state would prevent bankruptcy sales from separating families. But to go "farther, the lawgiver . . . requires . . . all the deliberation and wisdom of . . . Christian philanthropy."[1]

George Fitzhugh wished to go farther, despite his published declaration that unlimited power guaranteed selfless paternalism. Fitzhugh had asked why selfish patriarchs would devastate their own family and their own possessions.

James Hammond's cuckolded wife and pair of slave mistresses could have answered Fitzhugh. The Virginian scarcely needed their instruction. After bragging about his ancient family in his most revealing *De Bow's Review* essay, Fitzhugh condemned less scrupulous families. The head of the family, Fitzhugh regretted, "is often deficient in temper, in wisdom, in morals, and in religion." Although he "corrupts . . . and oppresses" his household, no "law" exists "to check or correct his misrule." We now call popes fallible. Yet we transfer "infallibility from the Vatican to the cottage." The "crying defect in modern social organization," concluded this two-paragraph outburst against uncontrolled patriarchs, is "the want" of "family supervision and control from without."[2]

Brilliantly said—and never again publicly said so bluntly. In his other public writing, Fitzhugh only warily and infrequently criticized unlimited domestic power, and only under the cover of contempt for Yankee critics. "Domestic slavery," he would occasionally concede, "has its imperfections." We should "correct such as can be corrected, and we would do so if the abolitionists would let us alone."[3]

Privately, Fitzhugh was more candid. "I assure you, Sir, I see great evils in Slavery," he whispered, "but in a controversial work I ought not to admit them." The Virginian added that "black slavery" is "an odious thing," and "liable to great abuses." Harriet Beecher Stowe's *Uncle Tom's Cabin* was "right" concerning the "bitter treatment of slaves. . . . Law, Religion, and Public Opinion should be invoked to punish and correct those abusers." He differed "widely with slaveholders generally as to the proper treatment of slaves—I think they [the slaves] should be educated, and that the Law should compel masters to feed and clothe them well and to treat them humanely."[4]

While George Fitzhugh knew that selfishness did not alone prevent familial abuse, James Henley Thornwell doubted that preachers alone could preclude patriarchal selfishness. Like Fitzhugh, Thornwell wanted state governments to preserve slaves' families and their right to read the Bible. Only "adequate protection," as "defined by law and enforced by penalties," could preserve "the real rights of the slave."[5]

In 1847, Thornwell chaired a committee of the South Carolina Presbyterian Synod, charged with petitioning the state for slaves' adequate protection. "We shall probably recommend," he privately wrote, "that a law may be enacted, to protect the family relations of the slave; and that the disgraceful statute, which prevents them from learning to read, may be repealed."[6] But Thornwell never publicly called the existing statute "disgraceful." Nor did he publicly protest when the South Carolina legislature ignored his petition.

In the mid-1850s, some Virginians and North Carolinians, bolder than Fitzhugh and Thornwell, developed statewide petition campaigns, demanding that state legislatures restrain masters. The petitions, sometimes signed by over a hundred would-be reformers, urged the legislature to prohibit slave sales from breaking up families and to require slaves to be taught to read and write. Without these restraints on absolute power, wrote the petitioners, masters would brutalize "the race to a degree that should cause even our self-ish interests to shudder." State legislatures instead shuddered at discussing checks on absolute authority, at the moment when northern abolitionists called unbounded power ungodly. The petitioners' request, lamented a sympathizer, is alleged to be too "exceedingly nice & *delicate*" to "be agitated at so critical a time."[7]

Several years after slaveholders silenced this delicate debate, South Carolina Episcopalians reopened the subject. In early 1859, Christopher G. Memminger, the prominent Charleston lawyer and future Confederate secretary of the treasury, chaired the Committee on Marriage of Servants for the state's Episcopalian Convention. Memminger's committee report called "absolute authority . . . wise and expedient." But the statewide church must awaken absolutists' "conscience" against shattering slave marriages.[8]

Memminger, opposing regulation, urged only a religious awakening. Still, cries of "heresy" greeted his report. The Episcopalian Convention swiftly tabled the subject. One anonymous Charleston newspaper correspondent protested that this "morbid intolerance of the discussion of slavery" remained the Slave South's "greatest weakness." Discussion could only be legitimately smothered if we have "no evils" or if "we are afraid or unable to reform them."[9]

Memminger's "damnable heresy," answered the *Charleston Standard*, demanded imprisonment, not discussion. A church convention must keep unholy hands off masters' holy power. As for the supposed sin of selling children from parents, a black sold away weeps "more from grief at parting with the white children of the family than the black."[10]

Memminger scorned that dubiously Christian verdict. The next year, he again asked the South Carolina Episcopalian Convention to condemn sales that severed Christian families. Memminger called debate on an institution's defects perfectly safe, as long as no debater wanted to level the defective institution. Colonel John Phillips, a prominent Charlestonian, retorted that discussion would bring out the wrecking crews.

Even in South Carolina, worried Phillips, "the anxiety to free slaves" remained as "great as it was many years ago." While less "loose" public talk now occurred, softhearts "often" consulted lawyers about "how the law may be defeated, by leaving slaves free" in last wills and testaments. Should such wanderers "be told that they shall make no contract, except what the Church authorizes?" Should a slave be invited "to ask his master to stand by the law" of the Church convention? And "if you commence in the Church, where is it to end?"[11]

Calling discussion of these questions "fraught with mischief," Phillips insisted that the subject be retabled. The convention concurred. The *Charleston Courier's* editor, a member of the Memminger committee, issued one last feeble protest: "A Carolinian should scorn to acknowledge" that a godly "institution . . . has anything to fear from free, full, and unreserved discussion."[12]

– 2 –

The only southern book that unreservedly discussed state limitations of masters contained murky disguises. Perhaps young Henry Hughes of Mississippi deliberately developed camouflaging jargon, lest his book be damned as heresy. Or perhaps personal confusions impelled the dreamy misfit's foggy rhetoric. Whatever the reason, Mississippi's most fascinating neurotic found the obscuring language to come right out with the state regulation heresy.

Henry Hughes's unpublished adolescent diary reveals a lonely, tormented, and rich young gentleman. Hughes aspired for control over his sexual urges and over the universe; "I would be statesman & soldier, master & servant: a despot," he told his diary. "Almighty God, let me be a despot." And how would this son of a slaveholding despot use his despotic power? "The chief aim of my life," answers his diary, "shall be to unite the great powers of earth in one Republic." He would then "reform the system of human laws and human philosophy." He would finally "abolish slavery."[13]

The unlimited despot who would forge a worldwide limited republic and use it to abolish masters' unlimited power! That adolescent vision impelled Hughes, as a young adult, toward republican limits on absolute power. At age twenty-five, Hughes publicized his panacea in *Treatise on Sociology* (1854). With this book, Hughes joined George Fitzhugh as the first American to use "sociology" in a book's title.

Where Fitzhugh usually publicly omitted his hope that republics would restrain uncurbed masters, Hughes's language disguised the hope. In Hughes's opaque terminology, a "warrantor" (the guarantor of social health) must "warranty" (guarantee) that all "warrantees" (those who receive a guarantee) will live decently. Hughes's jargon foreshadowed modern automobile terminology. Just as the car manufacturer (the warrantor) guarantees (issues a warranty) that the warrantee (the purchaser) has received an adequate vehicle, so a warrantor's guarantee of laborers' adequate treatment must be "unvarying, positive, absolute, and unconditional."

In a free labor society, Hughes lamented, neither governments nor employers warrant employees' welfare. A free labor society thus becomes "a live murder machine. It is organized homicide." It "is atrocious. It is revolting. It is supreme and horrible."[14]

Most proslavery writers, when discoursing in this colorblind vein, called slave labor far from horrible, because masters, unlike employers, guaranteed laborers a decent life. Hughes insisted instead that southern "governments," not masters, must guarantee subsistence and order. The *government's* role would be obscured because a "capitalist" (Hughes's word for slaveholder) would ostensibly govern the slave. But the state, the "supreme warrantor," should allow the "capitalist," its "deputy warrantor," to control slaves only if the "agent" carried out the state's guarantee of subsistence and order.[15]

The state as supervisor, Hughes insisted, must allow its agent no "power to punish" slaves, "except after a trial or hearing," and "no power to separate families," except when separation "is essential to the subsistence of all," and no "power to separate mothers and children under the age of ten years," without exception. Whenever an "agent" violated the state's warrant, the "supreme warrantor" must fine or jail its deputy warrantor. If the state's corrected "agent" then defied the state's guarantees, the state must force the irresponsible master to sell his slaves to a more responsible "capitalist." Servants guaranteed a stable tomorrow, Hughes affirmed, "are not slaves. They are warrantees. . . . They are insured." They are guaranteed a "chicken in every man's pot."[16]

Just as Hughes wished southern government to warrant a chicken for every slave, so he wanted northern government to warrant a meal for every free laborer. An activist, social welfare government should prevent employers from turning the economy sour, move the unemployed to areas of employment, warrant that employers pay employees decently, and ensure that the unemployable receive unemployment compensation. Labor unions should also act as deputy warrantors, guaranteeing that hard labor will earn fair wages.[17]

Henry Hughes, premodern Southerner, here advocated postmodern capitalism. By urging Big Government and Big Labor to contain Big Capitalists, Hughes anticipated John Kenneth Galbraith and Franklin D. Roosevelt. This nineteenth-century southern racist, however, gave latter-day progressive security a reactionary twist. The North, said Hughes, because largely inhabited by one race, needed only economic warranteeism. But the South, home of two races, also needed racial warrants. The presence of superior and inferior "ethnical" groups, as Hughes called the white and black races, demanded "warranteeism with the ethnical qualification" (Hughes's jargon for *black* slavery) to establish "hygienic order."[18]

Hughes, like Josiah Nott, considered racial mixture a hygienic disaster. "Hybridism is heinous," he shuddered. "Mulattos are monsters." To avoid the monstrous, Hughes, like George Fitzhugh and every other would-be colorblind proslavery writer, ended up defending only racial slavery.[19]

As Hughes summed up American Warranteeism, the North, largely inhabited by only one race, needed only governmental economic warrants. But in the South, two "ethnical" groups with a "hygienic problem" required "WARRANTEEISM WITH THE ETHNICAL QUALIFICATION."[20] Or to put it in mercifully non-Hughes language, blacks must be owned, and the state must regulate the owners.

– 3 –

To step beyond Hughes—to argue that regulated slavery could generate regulated emancipation—demanded even more protective cover than Hughes's cloudy vocabulary. The new disguised heresy, frequent in Upper South polemics but rare in Lower South arguments, built on an old undisguised orthodoxy. In the late eighteenth and early nineteenth centuries, many Upper

South masters had hoped to terminate slavery, if free blacks could be colonized in Africa. But in the 1830s, governments such as Virginia's and Maryland's had barely financed only a little state colonization. South Carolina, by threatening to secede, had stifled debate on funding national colonization. African colonization, the hope of Upper South apologists from Thomas Jefferson to Henry Clay, became an underground political chimera.[21]

It resurfaced as a theological goal. When the colonization dream passed from the most prominent Upper South politicians' hands in the 1830s to the most prominent Upper South preachers' hands in the 1850s, it became vaguer (and thus more politic) in its perceived time to be accomplished. It also became more evangelical (and thus more compelling) in its Christianity to be realized. Now, southern evangelicals would bring ex-Africans to Christ. Later, ex-slaves would bring Christianity to Africa.

In the presecession decade, Virginia's William A. Smith especially celebrated this double triumph. This Methodist preacher and president of Randolph-Macon College described his civilization as still "in a state of great embarrassment" over how to reconcile slavery and liberty. The reconciliation required patience. In blacks' "*present state* of mental imbecility, moral degradation, and physical inferiority, they should be placed under that more decided form of control called domestic slavery."

The Virginia Methodist emphasized "*present state*" because he could not "affirm—nay I do not believe"—that blacks are inferior "in the original structure of their minds." Rather, evangelists' preaching, in the slow "process of time," would "greatly elevate the race" from "ages of barbarous and pagan" African life. Then blacks, converted in America, would "improve the privilege of civil liberty" in Africa. Thus would "Divine Providence" serve "the civilization of the African in America, and the redemption of his fatherland."[22]

The Reverend Mr. Richard Fuller, a wealthy South Carolina planter who became an important Maryland preacher, asked slaveholders for only one concession: "that slavery is not a good thing, and a thing to be perpetuated." Few Southerners, claimed Richard Fuller in 1851, "would hesitate about making this concession." For "the Gospel," cheered the reverend, "is love. This love is now altering the relation between master and slave. It will gradually melt off all servile bonds." Then masters will send freed slaves to Christianize Africa, "the sublimest enterprise which ever employed the wisdom and power of a great empire."[23]

Professor Albert Taylor Bledsoe of the University of Virginia, also in the highest echelons of Upper South proslavery writers, still more mistily called for slavery's eventual termination. In his *Liberty and Slavery* (1856), Professor Bledsoe decried northern abolitionists for proposing that "this frightful mass of degradation" should "be blotted out *at once.*" He was, Bledsoe hedged, "in favor of slavery," so long as blacks "remain unfit for freedom." As to whether southern slaves would become fit for African liberty, he referred his readers to an obscure colonizationist in an out-of-the-way colonization journal (who urged that slaves would become fit colonizers).[24]

Lower South gentlemen seldom publicly agreed that the good of slavery could be temporary. But in a priceless 1852 private letter, the chief justice of the Alabama Supreme Court, E. S. Dargan, asked Virginia's U.S. Senator Robert M. T. Hunter for "your individual opinions or conclusions as to the final result of slavery." Chief Justice Dargan wished to know "when it will terminate" and with "what troubles?" He assumed "that you see it must ultimately end, for to me it is as manifest as any fact can be that still remains in the womb of futurity. This expression of course is confidential, as would be the expression of any opinion of yours."[25]

In the safety of private expression, Stephen Elliott, Episcopalian Bishop of Georgia, boldly asserted that preachers and masters are elevating "the negro population . . . both spiritually and physically; they will soon be our equals as regards morals, and when they become our equals, they can no longer be our slaves." In public, however, Bishop Elliott put that heresy mistily: "We are educating these people as they are educated nowhere else," thereby "working out God's purposes, whose consummation we are quite willing to leave in *His* hands."[26]

Sometimes Lower South preachers called His future plans too cloudy to consider. Southerners must "do what He so clearly defines to be *present* duty," urged Georgia's Charles Colcock Jones, and let *Him* reveal "our future duty." More often, Deep South clergy ambiguously hinted at future emancipation. "We do not see why it might not be perpetual," declared South Carolina's Reverend Thomas Smyth, utilizing a dodging double negative. "Yet we do not see reason to say it will be so." On the next page, he left "it to God to remove, when His time comes."[27]

A Lower South lawyer rather than preacher, Charleston's Edward Pringle, gave the uncertain future theme its most sophisticated treatment. Pringle's underappreciated 1853 pamphlet, *Slavery in the Southern States,* exuded that rarity among fierce provincial polemics: a calm synthesis, grounded in a cosmopolitan's understanding of the human predicament and appealing to the measured sensibility of all men of goodwill.

Like Josiah Nott, Pringle came from a wealthy South Carolina family. Both clans had long featured South Carolina insiders but had moved inside from outside regions—the Notts from Connecticut and the Pringles from Scotland. Both the latest heirs enjoyed New England higher educations, Josiah Nott at Yale and Edward Pringle at Harvard. Both savored transatlantic intellectual connections, Nott in the polygenesis movement and Pringle from two postgraduate years in London and Paris. Both left South Carolina to pursue nonslaveholding professions, Nott as a Mobile physician and Pringle as a San Francisco lawyer. Both published their proslavery masterpieces outside the South, Nott in Philadelphia and Pringle in Cambridge, Massachusetts.

But where Josiah Nott's cosmopolitan science advertised provincial racism, Edward Pringle's *Slavery in the Southern States* exuded cultivated poise. Instead of castigating Yankee abolitionists as intolerable meddlers, the

South Carolinian dryly noted that to preach at "distant" communities "is very cheap philanthropy,—the cheaper in proportion to the distance. The feeling of self-satisfaction exists without the necessity of personal sacrifice." So too, instead of proclaiming slavery a divine institution, Pringle regretted that Yankees' emphasis on slavery's "exaggerated horrors" had interfered with southern "calmness of judgment on many points of slavery." Slaveholders must renounce "a war of recrimination," where victory goes "not to the strongest, but to the most vulgar." We must remember that slavery, like "all social systems," contains "many errors." Only "time, and caution, and serious thought can correct" our defects. Southerners must be true to the most "splendid career, intellectually speaking": that of a slaveholder "who is thoroughly awakened to the difficulty of his position."[28]

In some ways, continued Pringle, slaveholders displayed "a solemn sense of responsibility." Blacks' food, clothing, shelter, and medicine abounded. So too, churches multiplied "every day for the simple worship of the negro." Still, Pringle gloomed that slave sellers caused "the destruction of family ties . . . more than is necessary."[29]

Moreover, the question of "how far slavery will prove conducive or antagonistic to the development of" Christian slaves remained unanswered, "for the South has not put forth her strength in her task of regeneration." Both "the difficulties of this whole subject" and the "bitterness caused by the fanatics at the North" had made Southerners "fearful," neglectful, "oversensitive." Many slaves could not hear the Gospel, and still fewer slaves could read the Bible. Erring slaveholders reminded Pringle of English capitalists, who also "feared to touch . . . the question of the poor and their education, . . . lest a wrong step might involve inextricable ruin."[30]

Would slaveholders ultimately outperform employers in providing "the great mass of laboring men" with "intellectual or religious education"? Upon the answer to "this question," wrote Pringle, "depends the future of slavery." Pringle admitted that enslavement, perhaps more than employment, encouraged dependency and discouraged literacy. Still, he thought that slaveholders possessed one advantage over employers: The southern patriarch has "always before him the effects of his act." He "will be moved to pity by the sight of the misery that is caused by his thoughtlessness or violence." In contrast, the employee, because "out of view" of the employer, arouses no "conscience," no "duty," no "responsibility."[31]

Edward Pringle here touched hands with George Fitzhugh; slave labor, not free labor, better ensured conscientious superiors. Then why not enslave white laborers? Pringle answered in the manner of Fitzhugh: America has no "excess of labor," the "great problem of the day in older countries."[32] Yet despite America's excess of virgin land, Pringle joined Fitzhugh in concurring with Josiah Nott and Samuel Cartwright: Hapless blacks still must be enslaved.

Unlike convinced racists such as Nott and Cartwright, however, Pringle remained uncertain why blacks were now hapless. Future scientists, he speculated, might disprove black innate inferiority and "place the two races" on an equal "level." Now, however, blacks were inferior, whether because of heredity or environment. So now, the slaveholder must uplift blacks, not "brush the slave away from his path, as the white man in America has done the Indian."[33]

How far could the black be uplifted? Again, Pringle wondered. Perhaps as those who rate a black "lowest suppose," he must always be "driven to unwilling labor." Or perhaps, as whites who rate a black highest suppose, he "is destined to rise to an equality with the white man, and to break the fetters which bind him." Perhaps some freedmen would assume "the noble mission" of civilizing Africa.

Pringle could "not forejudge" these issues. He could hold only "this for certain": that "amidst all the perplexities and uncertainties which shroud the future," slavery, to be moral, must serve "a great purpose for the negro." Blacks' "dependence" must inspire more slaveholders "to teach and to elevate." Then mankind would applaud "an institution, which, if it disappears because of an increased energy and higher character in the blacks, will have had its day of usefulness, as the source of that energy and that elevation of character."[34]

Edward Pringle's sophistication, candor, and stylistic ease showed how far the proslavery argument had advanced in the mere seven years since James Hammond's coarse outburst to Thomas Clarkson. Muted was the siege mentality, the defensive hysteria, the hypocrisy of describing slaveholders' sexual transgressions as Yankee do-gooders' fantasy. Slaveholders emerged, in Pringle's synthesis, as improving although imperfect patriarchs, kinder to their workers than Old World capitalists, uplifting their blacks better than Yankee racists, showering Christ's Word on blacks more promisingly than white missionaries to Africa, and perhaps someday developing the best sort of paternalism: the one that prepares children to grow up and leave home.

During the Civil War, an unforgettable tableau illustrated the most mature proslavery polemicists' fresh self-assurance. The star this time, Virginia's Reverend Thornton Stringfellow, seemed to have been born to believe in southern paternalism. His father was a wealthy slaveholder. His first wife's dowry included many bondsmen. The double inheritance lent Stringfellow a steward's mentality. To him much was given. Of him much was expected. He would give back by training slaves and slaveholders to fulfill Christ's plan for saving Africa.[35]

Our Lord, the Reverend Mr. Stringfellow emphasized in one of the most important Upper South proslavery books published in the 1850s, "singled out the greatest slaveholders of that age, as the objects of his special favor." Then as now, the institution furnished "great opportunities to exercise grace and glorify God," whenever "its duties are faithfully discharged." In our times, "it has brought within the range of gospel influence, millions of Ham's descendants among ourselves, who but for this institution, would have sunk down to eternal ruin." Slaveholders "did not seek or desire the responsibility, and the onerous burden, of civilizing and christianizing these degraded savages." But once the Lord brought the heathen to us for instruction, we could not cease accomplishing His work "if we would—and ought not, if we could." We can "put an end to African slavery," Stringfellow concluded, only when "God opens a door to make *its termination a blessing, and not a curse.* When He does that, slavery in this Union will end."[36]

During the Civil War, Yankee troops carried their war to end disunion inside Stringfellow's house. When he first beheld the muddy invaders, the preacher wondered if God had deserted him. Then he realized what the Lord must desire. Ungodly bullets having failed, God's steward must repel Satan's monsters with the holy truth. Stringfellow strode to his library. He found his proslavery book. He marched back to the invaders. He thrust his book at them.[37] See, the gesture said, I am right, you are wrong; you must read my words and flee. There was a convert's—a converter's—faith that paternalists marched against the infidel.

– 4 –

Like Thornton Stringfellow, the Southerners of the 1850s did not mindlessly regurgitate a stale faith that had been perfected twenty years agone. These pilgrims enjoyed a lately refurbished justification. The colorblind polemics of the George Fitzhughs generated deeper conviction that Yankee free labor capitalism exuded rank individualism. The racist polemics of the Josiah Notts and Samuel Cartwrights spread firmer belief that biologically depraved blacks needed patriarchal direction. The holy polemics of the James Henley Thornwells inculcated biblical faith that slavery per se was no sin, only a calling to serve Christ's future design.

But frustration accompanied exhilaration, for slaveholders' limitless authority to defy the Word undermined secular as well as biblical justifications. Allegedly, slavery lifted Northerners over Southerners in perfecting the home. But if uncurbed masters savaged households, black and white, no claim for southern domestic superiority could pass muster. Again, slavery supposedly raised the South over the North in establishing social hierarchies that restrained irresponsible individualists. But if unrestrained despots deployed unchristian rule, the Southerner would be America's ugliest individualist.

Ugly imperfections made Yankee critics doubly insufferable. Outside agitators not only sneered at proslavery's advances. The fiends also allegedly inhibited the further advances that would end the theoretical frustration.

Furthermore, an incompletely justified black belt faith offered nothing to white belt folk. In the spottily enslaved hinterlands of the slavocracy's northern peripheral areas, racists thanked the Lord that blacks were largely another South's problem. Nor did the torrid South's case for unperfected paternalism convince the many patriarchs in coolish Delaware and Maryland, who congratulated themselves on perfecting a paternalism that taught blacks to be freedmen. Nor did the orderly, productive work of the freed black proletariat in the upper Chesapeake, a hundred thousand liberated laborers strong and more numerous than the area's slaves, further the case that Maryland and Delaware must move backward toward the Lower South's social order (though, as we will see, a fascinating rearguard crusade sought exactly that).

The omnipresence of unconvinced Border South voters, together with the greater danger that borderland slaves would flee, made a free and open democratic debate over slavery seem especially menacing in the South's northern peripheral areas. There, outnumbered reactionaries (lamely) sought to close down challenges to the regime. The hinterland slavocracy also (lamely) strived in Congress to keep further antislavery challenges from seeping over the Mason-Dixon line from the borderland North. Black belt congressmen always rushed to defend white belt closures.

But whatever happened to their half-open outposts, proslavery apostles inside slavery's core would not tolerate Yankees' insults, not when slaveholders felt more godly than the insulters, not when the insults brushed the sore places, not when the ugliest sores allegedly could not be cured while fanatics ranted. So slavery's partially thwarted ideological defenders massed politically, to charge at northern defamers. They thereby invited still more frustrations.

PART III

THE CLIMACTIC

POLITICAL FRUSTRATIONS

Southern political adventures from the Kansas-Nebraska Act (May 1854) to John Brown's Raid (October 1859) resembled the proverbial dog chasing its tail. Round and round the slaveholders went, seeking protections abroad and consolidations at home. Whether in pursuit of a slave state for Kansas, or a slave empire in the Caribbean, or safeguards from the U.S. Supreme Court, or more slaves from Africa, or the reenslavement of southern free blacks, Southerners mounted spectacular initiatives and scored some apparent victories. But each triumph proved to be empty and/or counterproductive. By the end of the decade, thwarted crusades had honed an angrier edge on a frustrated slavocracy.

CHAPTER 6

Bleeding Kansas and Bloody Sumner

Two related republican traumas began in Washington, D.C., precisely two years apart. On May 22, 1854, Congress finalized the Kansas-Nebraska Act. On May 22, 1856, South Carolina's Congressman Preston Brooks brutalized Massachusetts's Senator Charles Sumner. Bleeding Kansas and bloodied Sumner embodied the same provocation: The defense of despotism over blacks savaged democratic process for whites—including for northern citizens.

– 1 –

In sixty seconds, Brooks's assault on Sumner clarified the antirepublican lesson of a thousand-plus days of post–Kansas-Nebraska Act turmoil. The two republican traumas illuminated the South's two prime hot spots, far apart geographically but like twins in disruptive potential. The flighty Brooks, representative of the Lower South's center of secessionism, demonstrated South Carolina's potential for national havoc, if the edgy state could muster the daring to act. So too, convulsed Missouri, the Border South's most inflammatory locale, demonstrated the borderland's threat to national peace, especially about slavery in the Kansas-Nebraska territories.

In early December 1853, Illinois's U.S. Senator Stephen A. Douglas introduced an allegedly sectionally neutral version of a Kansas-Nebraska bill, opening the area for settlement without saying whether slaveholding settlers could come.[1] Douglas, leader of senatorial Northern Democrats, did not care if slavery entered these territories. He only cared that white settlers in a new area, not far-off congressmen, should decide whether to sustain slavery. Still, he hoped to remain silent about Congress's controversial Missouri Compromise of 1820, prohibiting slaveholding settlers from entering the Kansas/Nebraska terrain (as from entering all Louisiana Purchase territories north of the 36° 30' line).

Missouri's Senator Davy Atchison, champion of western Missouri slave-holders, punctured Douglas's silence. Settlers would have scant chance to decide for slavery in Kansas, Atchison stormed, if the Missouri Compromise had barred slaveholding settlers. Atchison aroused fellow Southern Democrats in his Washington boardinghouse (the so-called F Street Mess) to give slaveholding settlers a detour around the Missouri Compromise prohibition.

Then U.S. Senator Archibald Dixon of Kentucky, a Whig, would not settle for a detour. He insisted that the Douglas bill must erase the prohibition. Southern Democrats wanted no Southern Whig to outflank them on a proslavery initiative. They accordingly pressured Douglas to accept Dixon's repeal of Missouri Compromise emancipation, as it applied to Kansas and Nebraska. Otherwise, Southern Democrats would oppose the Northern Democrat's bill.

Douglas knew that southern opposition meant no congressional act, no territory opened for white settlement, no transcontinental railroad traversing the terrain, and none of the boost to Democratic Party fortunes (and to his own presidential fortunes) that the Illinoisan expected from the law. Besides, by removing the congressional Missouri Compromise prohibition from Kansas-Nebraska, Douglas could restore sovereignty over slavery to the (white) local populace—his own Popular Sovereignty principle. Douglas finally agreed to be Douglas. He rallied half the Northern Democrats behind "his" bill, as Atchison, Dixon, and other Southerners had insisted on revising it, even while protesting that his surrender of the Missouri Compromise prohibition would raise "a hell of a storm" in the North.

The Illinoisan correctly predicted the political weather. "His" bill decimated that sacred Missouri Compromise. It invited slaveholders into U.S. territories where slavery had been barred. It defied the majority section's majority of citizens. It spotlighted how the southern minority section had long controlled national majoritarian decisions—by using its leverage in the Democracy, the nation's majority political party, to press Northern Democrats toward proslavery law. It highlighted how the northern majority could rescue majoritarianism from the minority. Yankee voters must throw out Northern Democrats who appeased the Slave Power.

In the fall of 1854, Yankee voters threw out 84 percent of the northern congressmen who had supported "Douglas's" bill. Still, during congressional debate on the Kansas-Nebraska bill, many Southerners had predicted that after enactment of the law, the political storm would ebb. Insulted gentlemen, went this southern argument, scorned banishment from a territory merely because of their (and slavery's) alleged barbarism. But after the Kansas-Nebraska Act removed the Missouri Compromise insult, continued this widespread southern prophecy, no longer proscribed slaveholders would silently concede icy Kansas (and icier Nebraska) to nonslaveholding settlers. The majority of settlers would decide slavery's fate; the more populated North could send more settlers; and potential slaveholding settlers would prefer the safely enslaved, more tropical, equally virgin acres of Arkansas and Texas. Then exclusively free labor settlers would turn Kansas and Nebraska territories into free states.

U.S. Senator David Atchison (left), frontier ruffian from the Border South's Missouri, who sought to force proslavery salvations on the nation and on U.S. Senator Stephen A. Douglas (right), suave nationalist from the Border North's Illinois. Courtesy of the Library of Congress (Atchison) and the Abraham Lincoln Presidential Library, Springfield, Illinois (Douglas).

But Davy Atchison's countervailing predictions augured a persisting northern storm. When Atchison denounced the original Douglas bill, the western Missourian promised that once given a chance, his constituents would capture Kansas. Atchison delivered on his promise. A tiny minority of Missourians, under Atchison's leadership, grasped territorial Kansas for the Slave Power. Thus did Atchison, the first denouncer of "Douglas's" bill, become the prime post-act provocateur of Bleeding Kansas. Thus did occurrences after the Kansas-Nebraska Act, not the act itself, keep the Yankee storm howling for a thousand days and more.

– 2 –

The persisting controversy repeated the history of the Fugitive Slave Law. In 1850, a border senator, James Mason of northwestern Virginia, first insisted on undemocratic procedures to return slavery runaways to their owners. As with the subsequent Kansas-Nebraska Act, northern outrage might have eased if Southerners had never used the antirepublican procedures. But with fugitive slaves as with Kansas, a relatively few border state citizens provocatively used the law.[2] They thereby turned the initial national wounds into lasting national sores.

This Border South intransigence is curious, for men from the least enslaved, most unionist part of the South initiated, then sustained, the two most Union-shattering slavery controversies of the 1850s. Why? Because wide-open republican procedures threatened the Border South's outposts of slavery more than the Lower South's consolidated sanctums. When antislavery warriors agitated in Yankee communities, located only a few miles from southern communities with few slaves, the flight of blacks toward freedom could increase. White belt nonslaveholders' qualms about slavery could also increase, as could slave sales to the safer Lower South.

Potentially damaged slaveholders comprised only a small minority of the Border South population. Intransigent hotheads comprised only a small minority of border slaveholders. Still, a handful of worried slaveholders, by whipping up resentment of nearby Yankees' interference with the South's business, could precipitate closures of the half-open border. Theirs was the latest demonstration of a great pre–Civil War truth: In a majoritarian democracy, minorities often prevail.

The minority of proslavery warriors located farthest north in the South faced increased trouble in the 1850s. More than ever in the particularly profitable presecession decade, Deep South purchasers drew slaves out of the Border South. More than ever, European and eastern free white laborers surged into border communities that had sold slaves. More than ever, Border South slaveholders' increasingly superfluous slaves had opportunities to flee over southern borders, to the increasingly antisouthern North.

More than citizens in other Border South states, Missourians resided inside a noose of free labor areas. All border slave states encountered a free labor neighbor to their north (Iowa in Missouri's case). But only Missouri faced an additional free labor neighbor to the east (Illinois). Only Missouri might encounter yet another free labor neighbor to the west (Kansas). And only in western Missouri, just across the Missouri River from Kansas, did a Border South state's largest concentration of most embattled slaveholders face a threat just over their border.

Proslavery Missourians also suffered the Border South's largest invasion of Yankee and European migrants. Between 1850 and 1860, the state's white population increased almost 80 percent, a Border South high. The surge reduced Missouri's percentage of slaves to under 10 percent, a Border South low (except for barely enslaved Delaware). In 1850, Missouri contained 15,000 more slaves than foreign immigrants. In 1860, the state contained 45,000 more European immigrants than slaves.

The unusually surrounded and diluted Missouri slaveholder outpost staged an unusually long-lasting debate over slavery during the 1850s. Since the Virginia antislavery debate of 1832, residents of Delaware and Maryland had often discussed whether slavery should end. Kentucky had also staged an extensive debate over terminating slavery in the late 1840s.[3] But in the 1850s, Missouri smashed all Border South records for persistence of slavery debates and success of antislavery politicians.

Increasing percentages of nonslaveholders helped embolden Missouri's antislavery politicians. In the Lower South, the ratio of slaveholder to nonslaveholder families approached one to one. In Missouri from 1850 to 1860, the nonslaveholder majority soared from six to one to eight to one, a surge encouraging to abolitionists. Worse, slavery barely existed in most Missouri locales. By 1860, only seventeen Missouri counties contained over 20 percent slaves, while seventy-seven contained less than 10 percent. Moreover, only three Missouri counties contained over 30 percent slaves, compared to fifty-one (of ninety-four) counties under 3 percent. In St. Louis County, Missouri's most densely populated and most antislavery zone, slaves comprised only 2.28 percent of the population by 1860.

St. Louis City, eastern Missouri's unofficial capital, lay a whole state removed from western Missouri's proslavery bastion. The city's isolated slaveholders battled not only against their paltry numbers and their economic irrelevance but also against a celebrity. Thomas Hart Benton, now in his seventies, had been the most powerful Missourian during the years between 1820 and 1850. In 1850, however, slaveholders, suspecting Benton of softness on slavery, ousted him from the U.S. Senate. In 1852, St. Louis nonslaveholders defiantly returned the alleged heretic to Washington, this time to a seat in the House of Representatives. Subsequently, eastern Missouri nonslaveholders' hero meant to bring his revenge to climax by trouncing western Missouri slaveholders' champion, U.S. Senator Davy Atchison, in the senatorial election of 1855.

During this, his last campaign, the embattled Benton was at his largest in girth and at his angriest in mood. The political colossus, once the duelist who had desperately wounded his latter-day friend Andrew Jackson, always remained the street fighter as the Democracy's best campaigner and the pompous intellectual as rednecks' adored champion. But even more now, Big Bully Benton defended the Union against politicians who agitated for or against slavery. He condemned Davy Atchison's championing of the Kansas-Nebraska Act as a crime against the nation as well as against white Missourians' interests. By irresponsibly agitating for slavery, Benton charged, Atchison caused many potential nonslaveholding migrants to Missouri to veer toward Iowa. The blunderer thus prevented Missouri's full development as a western oasis for whites.

Benton denied that opposing proslavery agitation meant favoring antislavery action. He favored pure nonagitation: no agitation for or against slavery. If Missouri slaveholders hushed, the Union would be saved and white migrants would enrich Missouri. Then no one would notice Missouri's increasingly trifling number of slaveholders.

If we hush, Davy Atchison and his western Missouri supporters responded, Benton will drop his nonagitation disguise. After white migrants engulf Missouri, Bentonians will oppose slavery enough—and encourage enough slaves to run away—so that Missouri slaveholders will sell their endangered property to the Lower South. The ex-slave state will become Benton's dream: western laborers' lily-white mecca.

Benton's vision that nonagitation would make slavery irrelevant, like Atchison's vision that proslavery forces must agitate to survive, gave Missouri's famous senatorial election of 1855 more importance than a partisan brawl.

The contest effectively began a year before the Kansas-Nebraska Act, when Atchison momentarily dropped his previous insistence that Congress open Kansas to slaveholders. His angry western Missouri constituents then warned Atchison to resume their fight or forfeit their support. Atchison promised never again to relent. He and his constituents prayed that their proslavery wave, rising higher the more he campaigned atop it, might drown Thomas Hart Benton and eastern Missouri's antislavery movement before slavery faded from the Border West.[4]

– 3 –

Missouri slaveholders worried not only about Benton's popularity and about Missouri's ever-whitening white belts but also about the lack of proslavery consolidation in their not very black belts. Missouri's center of slavery counties followed the Missouri River, down the state's western (Kansas) border and

then eastward across mid-Missouri. The thin line of Missouri River counties possessed a fat proportion of slaves for Missouri—in the 20 percent range. But a population 20 percent black represented almost a white belt in the Cotton Kingdom. Inside Missouri's grayish black belts, manumission occurred more often than in the Lower South. Border slaveholders also more often allowed slaves to rent out their labor, save some proceeds, and eventually buy a manumission certificate.

In this somewhat freer atmosphere, heretics more easily encouraged slaves to flee. With or without whites' encouragement, blacks grew bolder, and not always with their feet. In the boldest strike during Kansas-Nebraska times, a Missouri slave named Celia, perhaps with the help of George, her black lover, murdered her master (alias, she alleged, her frequent rapist). The assassin(s) then burned up the corpse. White authorities captured and hanged Celia. But George's successful flight from Missouri, and the notorious murder itself, epitomized the way blacks invaded slaveholders' consciousness.[5]

Blacks' impact remains the most overlooked cause of the Civil War. Blacks never voted outside New England. They never served in Congress. But without blacks who sought freedom, no slaves would have been fugitives. Without fugitive slaves, no fugitive slave law crises would have erupted. Without the runaways, western Missouri slaveholders would have been less apprehensive about having free territory on a third, Kansas side.

The Platte County Self-Defensive Association embodied western Missouri slaveholders' retaliation.[6] Slaveholders formed the organization in Weston, across the Missouri River from Kansas, two months after Congress passed the Kansas-Nebraska Act and two days after four Platte County slaves ran away. The founding fathers included U.S. Senator Davy Atchison, Platte County's favorite resident, and ex–state attorney general Benjamin Franklin Stringfellow, Atchison's favorite lieutenant. The association pledged to capture Kansas, to expel free blacks and antislavery whites from Missouri, to try antislavery suspects without judge or jury, and to oust disloyal merchants. Vigilantes also intended to sweep away Thomas Hart Benton and nonagitation. They would turn the most endangered Border South locale into the borderland's base for proslavery agitation.

The Platte County Self-Defensive Association patrolled the northwestern edge of southern Christendom. Its border ruffians were hard-drinking, hard-hating vigilantes. Davy Atchison epitomized their hard-bitten persona. "Bourbon Dave," as he was often called, was a coarse, charismatic frontier brawler, vicious to his enemies and charming to his friends. His crude charm won him numerous elections as U.S. Senate president pro tem (second in command, after the nation's vice president, and thus two heartbeats from the presidency). His face and figure announced a man never to be crossed: hulking frame, powerful visage, with a square chin, a thick nose, a prolonged forehead, and hair commencing far back, then erupting into a thick bush that defied orderly control.[7]

Republican niceties, Platte County rednecks vowed, would not sustain

antislavery in Kansas, or hand Missouri from Atchison to Benton, or allow
blacks to flee. Antirepublican coercions, they believed, must supplement overly
republican laws. No Missouri law, explained Benjamin Franklin Stringfellow,
made "the expression of abolition sentiment . . . a penal offense." No law allowed free blacks to be ousted if they inspired fugitive slaves to flee toward
neighboring northern communities. No law stopped Missourians, white and
black, from trading with abolitionists. No law recognized that "in a slaveholding community, the expression" of antislavery dissent was like "kindling
the torch of the incendiary."[8]

No language better illuminated why an All-Mighty Color Line could not
segregate white liberty from black slavery, not when black men's bloody
chains demanded white men's fettered freedom.[9] No plea better demonstrated why political history and social history could not be severed, not
when an establishment's means of social control demanded political control.[10] As the Platte County Self-Defensive Association expressed the very
core of Missourians' nationally fatal Kansas crusade, unless a system of coercive slavery limited a system of consenting democracy, blacks and whites
"who at heart were against us" would destroy us.

The Platte County Self-Defensive Association struck its first unrepublican
blows not at black fugitives but at white citizens. On July 20, 1854, vigilantes
expelled a Massachusetts native to Iowa. His crime? He supposedly favored a
free soil Kansas. Three days later, patrolmen ousted a white drunkard. The
evidence that he aided fugitives to escape? The testimony of one black (who
could not testify in a legal court).[11]

Their preliminary deportations finished, vigilantes sought their main
prey. The Reverend Mr. Frederick Starr, a New Englander and a Yale graduate, privately aided Missourians who secretly deplored the institution. On
July 29, 1854, the Platte Country Self-Defensive Association "arrested" the
Yankee preacher. They demanded that he confess his private opinions.[12]

Starr savored the public spectacle. After donning white pants, a clean shirt,
and garters, he rounded up his supporters. Then he marched on that supposed
citadel of republicanism, the packed courthouse. Inside, the New Englander
pulled out a huge jackknife, sliced off a six-inch plug of tobacco, jammed it
between his lips, and demanded to know the charges.

Starr had taught slaves to read, slaveholding frontiersmen answered. He
had helped blacks to purchase their freedom. He had ridden beside blacks in
his carriage. Slaveholders would no longer abide his insurrectionary heresy.

Starr's defense featured worse heresy. He followed, said the alleged traitor, Missouri slaveholders' conventional wisdom. Yes, he taught slaves to
read, but only with their masters' permission. Should not masters transform
slaves into better Christians? Did not better Bible readers make better Christians? Should not an imminent freedman be taught Christian uses of liberty?
"My desire was to enable one man, if he should ever get his freedom, to become respectable & useful."

John Vineyard, an owner of recent runaways and Starr's prosecutor, asked if the preacher always had masters' permission. Yes, the New Englander answered. Then you did nothing wrong, Vineyard conceded. G. W. Bayliss chimed in that four of his slaves could read the Bible. The crowd murmured approval.

The preacher pressed his advantage. Yes, he had helped a slave, as the master had requested, to save money toward purchasing freedom. But could not slaves, with masters' permission, work for wages? Could not a master sell a slave to anyone, including to the slave himself? You did right, muttered Vineyard, you did right.

Yes, a black rode beside me, cried the spellbinder. But true-blue Southerners cherished familial dependents. Only Yankees cringed from personal contact with blacks. Mr. Vineyard rides next to his black. Why can't I? Because I am too poor to own slaves?

The audience gasped. A shamefaced Vineyard moved that the association acquit Frederick Starr. Vineyard's surrender carried, with only twenty votes against it. In celebration of his vindication, Starr further explained his views. Manumission, he said, remained masters', not nonslaveholders', business. Native Southerners, not visiting Northerners, must generate southern antislavery opinion. But if insiders wished to free slaves, outsiders could prepare future freedmen and dispatch freed blacks to Africa. "If any man through love, justice, or duty sees fit to free his slave," we will mercifully remove that black "from the competition of the Anglo-Saxon."

That antislavery conclusion provoked Benjamin Franklin Stringfellow to deliver a proslavery harangue that would have done George Fitzhugh proud. Anyone who cheered Frederick Starr, declared Stringfellow, considered slavery "an evil to be borne, not an institution to be defended." Then we should rid "ourselves of such a curse." But the North suffered from a worse curse: free labor. Wage earners would be better off enslaved, for slaveowners bestowed kindly direction, while employers exacted cruel toil.

The courtroom audience gasped. Many rednecks rejoiced to be wage earners. They proudly belonged to no man. They would not be called worse off than blacks. They had come to oust Starr. They left determined to destroy Stringfellow.

In the next few days, Stringfellow frantically buttonholed everyone who would stop, trying to explain his overly orthodox orthodoxy away. Those disloyal to slavery, he said, had misquoted him. He had never said whites should be enslaved. He had always been loyal to his race. He would yet rout the disloyal Starr.[13]

Stringfellow considered his subsequently published *Negro Slavery, No Evil,* an uncompromising rout of Starr's antislavery sentiments. The pamphlet instead showed that the border remained too compromised for proslavery, Lower South style. Once again, Stringfellow proclaimed that free labor capitalism bred inequality and class war. But this time, he discreetly added that racial slavery made all whites equal. This time, he discreetly left unresolved how whites could be equal if a free labor economy generated inequality. This time, he espoused another marvel. This time, he called slavery's territorial expansion the best route to abolition. He thereby repopularized the diffusion argument of Thomas Jefferson, the prince of Upper South apologists for slavery.

Unless slavery diffused over wide areas, Stringfellow explained in the Jeffersonian vein, slaves would be crammed into a suffocating area. Then plantations would become huge, relationships between slaveholders and slaves impersonal, and masters' personal benevolence unlikely. But if slavery spread, claimed the co-founder of the Platte County Self-Defensive Association, slaveholdings would be small, relationships intimate, and benevolence personal. Affection would spring up "between master and slave." The resulting black liberation would come the best way—after preparation, from love, to benefit family friends. Antislavery crusaders, then, should seek to extend slavery!

That view remained common among Missouri proslavery agitators. Stringfellow sounded like Robert H. Miller, editor of the proslavery *Liberty* (Missouri) *Tribune*. Unless you "*go to Kansas now,*" declared Miller, "not only Kansas, but Missouri will be taken." Besides, since the Creator plans "to colonize the African race in their own native land, . . . they should be enlightened and Christianized. This can only be done by enlarging the area of slavery." In other words, the Platte County Self-Defensive Association stood for capturing Kansas to secure Frederick Starr's and Thomas Jefferson's panacea: abolition plus colonization![14]

A Lower South slaveholder, reading incredulously about this ideological capitulation to Jefferson, would have understood why Missouri slaveholders considered their regime vulnerable, especially if neighboring Kansas became free soil. Imagine, forming an association to lynch a Yankee who disapproved of slavery for blacks, and instead almost lynching a Southerner who advocated slavery for all civilizations! Imagine, Stringfellow, the campaigner for George Fitzhugh's anti-Jeffersonian views, surrendering to Thomas Jefferson's vision of ending slavery!

More surrenders followed. The Platte County Self-Defensive Association, after the debacle of Frederick Starr's victory over Benjamin F. Stringfellow, resolved that "those who hate slaveholders have no right to a slaveholder's money." Slaveholders must not trade with disloyal merchants. The association must enforce the extralegal decree.

In response, Weston's commercial establishment formed a countervailing extralegal association. Their association insisted that vigilantes obey the law, that accused heretics be tried in republican courts, that free blacks could remain in Missouri, and that law-abiding merchants or preachers could freely promote goods and ideas. If Stringfellow wished to rout white men's republicanism, he could have civil war here and now.

Once again, Atchison, Stringfellow, and the Platte County Self-Defensive Association retreated. They suspended economic nonintercourse. They postponed extralegal rule. But without antidemocratic vigilantism, how could western Missouri slaveholders survive their loose proslavery ideology and looser slave controls, to say nothing of Benton's nonagitation, Starr's principles, runaway slaves, black Celias and Georges, and especially a wide-open, free soil Kansas neighbor? We must, Atchison and his supporters answered, strike first and hard in Kansas. After securing the neighbor for slavery, we must pour uncompromising proslavery repressions back on our compromised state and neighborhood.

– 4 –

Most antebellum Americans (and most Southerners) doubted that slaveholding Missourians could capture Kansas. The weather and the soil seemed to forbid the institution so far north. Slaveholders could seize slave states down in torrid Gulf of Mexico climes. But up on the icy Kansas plains?!

The question missed a key point: The Kansas plains were as slaveholder friendly as any Border South terrain, including Missouri's. The eastern third of Kansas, where the battle for the territory would be decided, was a lush, undulating prairie, with the same weather and soil that nurtured slavery in western Missouri. The Missouri River, forming the northern third of the Missouri-Kansas border, could enrich slaveholders on the Kansas no less than on the Missouri side. Although the river eventually swerved eastward, to benefit central Missourians, eastern Kansans enjoyed alternate rivers, including the Kansas, Arkansas, Neosho, Osage, and Verdigris. Moreover, by 1854, farmers had worked Missouri's Missouri River Valley for a generation. Kansas's many river valleys contained untouched forests.

No wonder, then, that supporters of slavery who visited eastern Kansas in 1854, expecting to find a climate alien to slaveholders, enjoyed an exhilarating shock. "When I left home," wrote a North Carolinian in December 1854, I saw no "chance of introducing slavery into Kansas." But after touring the territory, "I am fully convinced that slave labor can be . . . profitably employed" on "the rich alluvial bottoms" and "the rich rolling prairie."[15]

Since eastern Kansas offered ideal Border South farming conditions, the territory stripped a big question to its essentials: Could the slavocracy retain even its most fertile Border South outposts, given its shortage of slaves and the North's abundance of free laborers? Even on the richest Border South terrain, neither sugar nor cotton could thrive; and whatever the profitability of a Border South grain or hemp or tobacco plantation, sugar and cotton plantations secured larger fortunes farther south. Yankee neighbors also made slavery riskier. For these reasons, northern and European free laborers had been speeding westward into Missouri, and slaves had been slowly draining southward to the tropics.

If climate doomed slavery in Kansas, in short, the doom would eventually engulf every Border South area. If majorities would decide slavery's fate, proslavery Missourians would have no chance for Kansas, just as the shrinking percentage of slaveholders in Delaware, Maryland, Kentucky, and Missouri had no chance to become a majority. But aggressive border slaveholders had survived nonslaveholder majorities everywhere in the Border South. By condemning their opponents as heretics, and sometimes by adding physical intimidation to verbal coercion, the slaveholding 12 percent of Missouri's population had deterred the passive or indifferent or dissimulating (and bitterly racist) Missouri nonslaveholding majority from liberating blacks.

Atchison's border ruffians also meant to defy the inevitable free labor majority in Kansas. While a long-term slaveholder majority in Kansas looked impossible, a short-term minority takeover looked plausible. Most Yankees had to come from far away in order to settle in Kansas permanently. Missouri slaveholders had only to step over the border and stay only long enough to vote. If slaveholders seized the initial Kansas government, they could be hard to dislodge, whatever the numbers later against them, as they had been in Delaware, Kentucky, Maryland, and Missouri (and as they had been hard to dislodge for half a century in New York, New Jersey, and Pennsylvania).

A month before the Kansas-Nebraska Act passed, a headline-making northern initiative ironically aided proslavery Missourians. On April 26, 1854, the Massachusetts legislature chartered Eli Thayer's Massachusetts Emigrant Aid Society. Thayer aspired to buy presettlement Kansas land cheaply, to lure New Englanders to the plains, and to sell newcomers his lands. The land speculator did not plot to send antislavery gunmen or guns to Kansas. Nor did his society, soon reincorporated as the New England Emigrant Aid Society, ever arm a man. Missourians, however, thought they saw gunslinging, slave-stealing fanatics invading. If antislavery outlaws captured neighboring Kansas, Missouri slaves might flee across the border. Then many Missouri capitalists might cash out their slaves in Lower South slave auctions, making the evil ever more unnecessary up north.[16]

That perception intensified Missouri extremists' determination to capture the initial Kansas governmental apparatus. The perception also increased Missouri moderates' toleration for an Atchisonian capture. Missourians, while divided about whether to ease slavery (and blacks) away, concurred about who should decide such matters. Missourians must decide their own fate. Yankee meddlers must have no part in the decision, especially not with rifles, particularly not if outside fanatics emancipated Missouri by using Kansas bases to steal slave property. The image of New England thieves massing on Missouri's borders, an image that Atchisonians played up for every penny of its vast political worth, gave proslavery extremists a priceless boon.

The shrewd Atchison took every advantage of his heaven-sent (or rather Yankee-sent) opportunity to seize the initiative before Yankees overwhelmed his soon-to-be-outnumbered Missouri border ruffians. "We will have difficulty with the Negro thieves in Kansas," Atchison wrote Jefferson Davis in September 1854, but "our people are resolved to go in and take their '*niggers*' with them." I have publicly advised "squatters in Kansas and the people of Missouri to give a horse thief, robber, or homicide a fair trial, but to hang a Negro thief or Abolitionist, without Judge or Jury." Since "we will shoot, burn, and hang," Atchison assured Davis, the antislavery threat "will be soon over."[17]

In the first Kansas election, called to select a nonvoting delegate to the U.S. Congress in late November 1854, Bourbon Dave taught Missourians how to preclude any antislavery threat. Campaigning in western Missouri rather than in eastern Kansas, he told his constituents that "when you reside within one day's journey of the territory, and when your peace, your quiet, and your property depend upon your action, you can, without an exertion," spend a day in Kansas and "vote in favor of your institutions." Atchison asked for 500 one-day Kansans.[18]

He received more than three times that number. On voting day, some 1700 one-day Kansans cast ballots, as opposed to only 1100 permanent Kansans. The one-day Kansans secured but a bauble: Kansas's nonvoting territorial delegate to Congress. But the next Kansas election would select territorial legislators. In January 1855, Missouri's stalemated U.S. Senate election increased the importance of that Kansas election.

– 5 –

Until the twentieth century, state legislators selected U.S. senators. In January 1855, Missouri legislators balloted on whether to return the Democrats' Davy Atchison to his seat in the U.S. Senate or to replace him with a proslavery Whig, A. W. Doniphan, or with his Democratic Party rival, Thomas Hart Benton. In the prevote debate, Frank Blair, Jr., Benton's chief lieutenant, denied that Bentonians sought to abolish black slavery. Rather, they sought to save white republicanism. All true republicans, emphasized Blair, believe democrats can discuss anything, from whether to rotate crops to whether to use slaves. All true unionists understand that Atchison's proslavery illegalities would smash the national republic. All true entrepreneurs wince that Atchison's antidemocratic repressions will deter free white laborers from the Kansas plains.

All Missourians should hope for a free labor Kansas, continued Blair, because only then would Kansas and Missouri flourish. Compared to slave labor, free labor brought more people, more enterprise, and more profits to an area. Missourians, by controlling Kansans' trade, would boom alongside the free labor neighbor. The economic takeoff would bring still more free laborers to Kansas and Missouri. Still more people would mean still more prosperity. If Atchison's antirepublican coercions prevailed instead, Missouri would receive sparse migrants, enjoy scarce free speech, and achieve scant prosperity.[19]

G. W. Goode answered for the Atchisonians. Are we "to remain a Slave State," asked Goode? Or should we "humbly yield to an insidious influence?" Frank Blair claims to be no abolitionist. Yet he also claims a free labor Kansas would be most prosperous. "As a necessary corollary, he would have Missouri be a Free State," for surely the gentleman favors "the greatest prosperity."

Only an abolitionist, continued Goode, would think that he has "as

much right to discuss the emancipating of our negroes" as to discuss the ro-
tating of our crops. Crops do not run away. No one calls crops an abomination. Blair's freedom of speech meant license to spread the fatal judgment
that slave "property is a curse."

Goode urged agitation against that verdict. If slaveholders who lived "on
the border of Kansas" stand "quietly by, . . . thousands of fanatics and Abolitionists of the North, will hasten hitherto, to aid in the work already begun." Goode conceded that Benton might not share Blair's "designs." Benton's insistence on nonagitation, however, encouraged Missouri slaveholders'
"listlessness." Unless Missourians repudiated listlessness, agitated for slavery, and elected Atchison, antislavery would creep forward.[20]

After the speeches ended, Atchison and the Whigs' A. W. Doniphan each
tallied around 37 percent and Benton around 25 percent of legislators' votes.[21]
On slavery, Doniphan resembled Atchison more than Benton. "A large portion of my worldly wealth consists of slave property," the Whig declared.
Like Atchison, Doniphan lived in western Missouri's Platte County, "in full
view of the fertile plains of Kansas." A free labor Kansas would "force me to
leave my adopted State and seek in some more congenial clime of the sunny
South that protection to my property which I could not enjoy here."[22] But
Doniphan considered Whigs to be slavery's best protectors. So he refused to
throw his votes to Democrats. None of the three candidates could secure the
required 50 percent of the legislators. Atchison's old U.S. Senate seat would
remain empty at least until the next legislative election, in 1857.

Atchison's defeat augured later victory for his principles. Three out of
four legislators voted for Atchison or Doniphan. Neither candidate could
abide a Yankee takeover in Kansas or Benton nonagitation in Missouri. Of
the two proslavery partisans, only Atchison wielded an organization capable
of seizing Kansas. Atchison's faction could end their political frustration in
Missouri by storming inside Kansas voting booths; and Doniphan's votes
proved that Missourians' disgust for neighboring free soiler meddlers spilled
past Atchison's partisans. For the Platte County Self-Defensive Association,
the time had come to strike for Kansas.

Western Missourians struck triumphantly on March 30, 1855, Election
Day for the first Kansas territorial legislature. An early 1855 census of Kansas
territory demonstrated that Missourians comprised almost half of the resident voters. But Atchison refused to stake slavery's chances on rallying an
almost-majority of ex-Missourians in Kansas (some of whom favored Benton, nonagitation, and free soil). Instead, Atchison again campaigned in
western Missouri, to rally one-day Kansans against permanent Kansans.
"Eleven hundred" will come "over from Platte County to vote," he bragged,
"and if that ain't enough, we can send five thousand—enough to kill every
God damned abolitionist in the Territory."[23]

This time, Atchison predicted the right number. On Election Day, 4968
one-day Kansans overwhelmed the 1210 permanent Kansans who voted. The
territorial census showed the extent of the fraud. Only 2905 voters inhabited

the territory! Atchison privately confessed that fewer than one-third of proslavery voters meant to stay in Kansas. "But we are playing for a mighty stake; if we win, we carry slavery to the Pacific Ocean; if we fail, we lose Missouri, Arkansas, and Texas."[24]

The first Kansas territorial legislature, convening on July 2, 1855, consolidated slavery in Kansas and therefore hopefully in Missouri. The new Kansas violations of republicanism barred opponents of slavery from holding office, from speaking for antislavery, and from serving on juries in cases involving slavery. Opponents of the fugitive slave law faced disenfranchisement. Aiders of fugitive slaves faced capital punishment. Opponents of these laws faced imprisonment for at least two years.

The edicts dissolved the question of whether slaveholders could capture the Kansas government. The capture had been accomplished. The new laws, Benjamin Franklin Stringfellow bragged, are "more efficient to protect slave property than any State in the Union" has passed, and they "have already silenced the Abolitionists." Since "Kansas and Missouri have the same latitude, climate, and soil," added Davy Atchison, the neighbors must "have the same institutions." Either Missourians would enslave Kansas or "Missouri must have free institutions."[25]

Cool-headed observers of the ensuing Kansas bloodshed, then and since, have wondered why Kansas settlers created Bleeding Kansas over the slavery issue. The huge majority of settlers, after all, cared much more about land claims and land speculation. But the men who precipitated the crisis in Kansas were largely not settlers in the territory. They were largely one-day Kansans. They cared primarily about slavery's fate where they were settled: in shaky western Missouri.

By crossing the border for a day to consolidate their regime at home, they established a new issue in Kansas territory. The issue no longer involved whether Kansas could legalize enslavement of blacks. The question had become whether Kansans could abide antirepublican repression of whites. Would the white majority allow an unrepublican government to hang them for helping a free black, or to jail them for mounting a republican opposition?

Northern settlers considered tyrannical power over *them* far more important than any land speculation. So too, Missourians in Kansas fought to keep the power they had dearly won. A very natural, very bloody war over white men's republicanism in Kansas loomed, precipitated by very natural one-day warriors from a very exposed slaveholder outpost, who very naturally wondered whether Missouri's slaveholding regime could survive if wide open republican governments assaulted it from yet a third side.

– 6 –

Proslavery momentum, having swept across the border into Kansas, spilled back into Missouri. Nine months before the first Kansas showdown, the

Platte Country Self-Defensive Association had faltered before the Reverend Mr. Frederick Starr. Two weeks after the first Kansas legislative elections, Atchisonians expelled a compatriot of Starr's, George Park, from Missouri.

Park, a Vermonter, had founded the town of Parkville on the Missouri River. The *Parkville Luminary*, Park's newspaper, had condemned Atchisonians' repressions of Kansas white republicanism. On April 14, 1855, the Platte County Self-Defensive Association threw the *Parkville Luminary*'s press into the Missouri River. Border ruffians warned Park and his associate editor that they would be spilled into the same watery grave, if they resided in Missouri three weeks hence. Moreover, if the alleged heretics moved to Kansas, "*we pledge our honor as men* to follow and hang them."[26] Park left for the North. So, within the week, did Frederick Starr.

A month later, the rape of republicanism in the western Missouri/eastern Kansas corridor came to a fetid climax. A gang of twelve seized William Phillips, an alleged antislavery sympathizer, in Leavenworth, Kansas, across the Missouri River and slightly south of Weston, Missouri (the center of the Platte County Self-Defensive Association's agitations). The kidnappers forced their victim across the river. Then they stripped Phillips, shaved his head, smeared him with tar, decorated him with feathers, and hoisted him atop a rail. The vigilantes carted their decked-out prey through the Weston streets while "a number of niggers and boys" banged old pans and rang loud bells. They stopped at the slave auction block near the St. George Hotel. There "an old nigger auctioned him off & bid him in at 3 to 5 cents."[27]

William Phillips finally escaped to the North, where he published a book on the savagery. This white citizen turned into a humiliated black, with blacks assisting in the shaming, excoriated the illusion that black slavery was the best cornerstone for white republicanism. The old amused query, "are you 'sound on the Goose Question,'" exclaimed Phillips, is no laughing matter "in Western Missouri." Did Americans "feel . . . indignation" about enslavement "of the press and of speech in France or Austria"? Well, the "veriest tyrant in Europe *dare* not exercise so fearful and despotic control over opinion."[28]

Just as the previously faltering Platte County Self-Defensive Association caught its despotic stride in Missouri after conquering Kansas, so supporters of Atchison, after faltering in the 1855 legislative election for a U.S. senator, captured not one but both of Missouri's U.S. Senate seats in 1857. Atchison, now too notoriously controversial, stepped aside as candidate, to further his party's victory. In January 1857, Missouri's legislature elected two of his less notorious colleagues, Tristam Polk and James Green, to the U.S. Senate.

Since the politically astute Atchison felt compelled to step aside, most Missourians obviously thought Atchison went too far, in violating republicanism for whites. But since Atchison's adherents prevailed, most Missourians obviously thought that Yankee slave stealers went too far, and at Missouri slaveholders' very door. That southern readiness to see Yankee neighbors as holier-than-thou robbers always gave the South's most provocative defenders a leg up, if they dared to pitch the South into a brawl. Missouri's Atchison had dared—and then had shrewdly stepped aside. Alabama's William L. Yancey would repeat the statecraft in 1860–61.

– 7 –

Seventy-two hours after the Missouri legislature endorsed Atchison's adherents, without electing Atchison, Bentonians shed the camouflage of nonagitation, without Benton's endorsement. On January 16, 1857, the *St. Louis Democrat,* controlled by Frank Blair, Jr., and B. Gratz Brown, declared that Bentonians must now oppose not just proslavery agitation but also slavery itself. The substitution of "free white labor for servile black labor" declared the *Democrat,* would be "wise and lofty statesmanship."[29]

In retaliation, Atchison supporters introduced a resolution in the Missouri legislature, calling emancipation "impolitic, unwise, and unjust." The resolution invited yet another legislative debate on slavery. On February 12, 1857, in the Missouri House of Representatives, B. Gratz Brown accepted the invitation.

Brown was a blueblood from the Kentucky Blue Grass. Both his grandfathers had been U.S. senators. Raised in Frankfort and educated at Lexington's Transylvania University and at Yale, he favored Cassius Clay's gradual emancipation proposal during the Kentucky antislavery debate of 1849. A few months after Kentucky voters rejected Cassius Clay, Brown joined his cousin Frank Blair, Jr., in Missouri. There, hiding his antislavery inclinations, he only agitated, Benton style, against proslavery agitation.

As he shed the nonagitation disguise before the legislature on February 12, 1857, B. Gratz Brown looked to Atchison's followers as incendiary as they thought he sounded. A slender man of middling height, he seemed to swell as one's eye swept up his frame. His head, too large for his body, hinted at intellectual power. His thatch of red hair, towering atop his head, hinted at a Jacobinical intelligence.[30]

He would no longer be driven into hiding, he warned, "by the arraignment, in the cant language of the day," of being disloyal "to the institutions of the State." Were colonial Virginians forever loyal to primogeniture? Were American Revolutionaries eternally loyal to King George? With the cry for perpetual loyalty, "bigots intimidate fools. Loyalty to existing institutions shuts out all reform."

Brown proposed no legislative antislavery reform, for *"there is, sir, already a gradual emancipation act in force in Missouri."* The state census of 1856 showed that even in the twelve most enslaved Missouri River counties, the white population had grown twice as fast as the black since 1851. In the rest of the state, the white population had increased ninety times faster than the slave. This is nonlegislative emancipation "on its largest, proudest, grandest scale—emancipation gathered as a triumph in the forward march of the white race."

Brown applauded freedom's march "not so much for the mere emancipation of the black race" as for "THE EMANCIPATION OF THE WHITE RACE. I seek to emancipate the white man from the yoke of competition with the negro." He also sought to liberate white orators from the dictatorial "spell which has silenced many voices." But silent migration would accomplish almost all the liberating. White migrants' westward surge would drive almost all blacks out of Missouri. That magic moment "is almost upon us." He would then introduce an antislavery law, to free the trifling few slaves remaining. Or as Brown's compatriot, James Gardenhire, put it in yet another legislative debate on slavery eight months later, Missourians would not so much abolish slavery "as simply let it go."[31]

Slaveholders would hardly let slavery go. Nine days after B. Gratz Brown spoke, the legislature approved Atchisonians' resolution against legislative emancipation, 107–12.[32] The 90 percent margin demonstrated Border South slavery's stubborn staying power, even when it was most besieged. Still, Benton's former apostles were not yet seeking legislative emancipation, and Benton himself wanted no part of any siege. Benton called it "the greatest Outrage" that his ex-lieutenants, Blair and Brown, had begun "a new slavery agitation," contrary "to the whole policy of my life, *which has been to keep slavery agitation out of the state.*"[33] Atchison supporters, as it turned out, had been paranoid to suspect Benton but prescient to suspect Blair.

Whatever Benton preferred, his young turks had brought agitation against slavery into the state for the duration. In Missouri's urban centers, the Brown-Blair party's successes appalled proslavery men throughout the South. In the late 1850s, Jefferson City elected James Gardenhire mayor, while St. Louis elected Frank Blair, Jr., to Congress and the equally antislavery John Wimer as mayor. Missouri's persisting slavery debates in the 1850s, unlike Virginia's one-shot affair in 1832, had spawned a permanent southern antislavery party. The new organization controlled 10 percent of the Missouri legislature and over 50 percent of Missouri urban governments. The heretics stood poised to collaborate with a northern antislavery party—poised to become founding fathers of a Southern Republican power base for Abraham Lincoln.

Only an especially obtuse cynic could now think that Davy Atchison's fear of antislavery politicians in Missouri, and thus his agitation in Kansas, had been only a self-serving myth, concocted merely to steal political power. Free laborers' migration into Missouri, the drain of Missouri slaves southward, urban free white laborers' loathing of George Fitzhugh–style colorblind proslavery, some blacks' resistance to slavery (epitomized by George and Celia), the pretenses of Frank Blair, Jr.—all these trends had swelled in Missouri's cities as the Civil War approached. Like borderites who insisted on the Fugitive Slave Law, Atchison supporters gambled that only intense and sometimes undemocratic agitation could seal the slavocracy's borders and deter slavery's slow erosion in the northernmost South. By cajoling some voters, transforming others into one-day Kansans, and intimidating others, Atchison had turned the innervating stalemates of 1854–55 into the exhilarating triumph of 1857. But the triumph deepened resentment of the Slave Power in St. Louis and lesser towns. Furthermore, the rape of Kansas republicanism fanned white republicans' rage at the Slave Power beyond Missouri, in the North and in Kansas itself.

By mid-1856, Yankee migrants to Kansas outnumbered Missouri migrants. Slavery's foes also bore better arms, partly financed by officers of the New England Emigrant Aid Society (the society itself never financed a rifle). As free soiler protests mounted, the Atchison forces countered with the same antidemocratic repression that had expelled Frederick Starr and George Park from Missouri. In a preventative strike on May 20–21, 1856, over 500 proslavery vigilantes, including Davy Atchison's Platte County Rifles, massed against free soilers' Kansas stronghold, the town of Lawrence, some twenty-five miles west of the Missouri border. The proslavery mob battered Lawrence's main hotel, torched the free soil leader's house, and heaved the free soilers' press, the *Herald of Freedom,* into the Kansas River.

On May 23–24, 1856, a northern heralder of freedom retaliated against this so-called Sack of Lawrence. John Brown, the same warrior who would assault Harpers Ferry, Virginia, in 1859, massed six followers, including four of his sons, against slumbering proslavery settlers on the Pottawatomie Creek, some thirty miles south of Lawrence. Brown and his henchman dragged five men from rude log cabins. They shot their victims, slit them open, and mutilated their corpses.

With Brown's celebration of an eye for an eye, the nation's problem was not just that proslavery violence spawned antislavery violence. The worse problem was that more Kansans and more Northerners than John Brown, whatever they thought of black slavery, already preferred civil war to slaveholder repressions of white men's republicanism. Thanks to the aftermath of the Kansas-Nebraska Act that Davy Atchison's followers had spawned, a continuing Kansas crisis loomed huge on the national horizon.

– 8 –

On May 22, 1856, exactly two years after the passage of the Kansas-Nebraska Act, one day after the Sack of Lawrence, and one day before the Pottawatomie Massacre, violence inside the U.S. Senate brought the crisis of white republicanism sharply into focus. When Preston Brooks of South Carolina and the national House of Representatives invaded the U.S. Senate chamber to smash Charles Sumner of Massachusetts into silence and unconsciousness, slaveholders achieved none of Davy Atchison's gains in Missouri. They only popularized a symbol of gutted republicanism in the North. Before Brooks's brutality, most Northerners had considered Charles Sumner an overly learned, overly abusive fanatic. After the brutalizing, Sumner, unable to return to the Senate for two and a half years, silently epitomized white men's right to speak, whether in the U.S. Senate or in Kansas.

Some Southerners, understanding this counterproductive result, wished

Preston Brooks had merely verbally assaulted Charles Sumner or only cuffed the irritant, preferably outside the Senate chambers. But even they believed that the infuriating New Englander had invited a correction.[34] Charles Sumner's speeches on slaveholders' barbarism, researched exhaustively, memorized totally, rehearsed privately before the mirror, were infuriatingly calculated insults.

Sumner delivered his especially insulting oration, "The Crime Against Kansas," to the Senate on May 19 and 20, 1856.[35] The Massachusetts free soiler particularly condemned a trio of senators: Virginia's James Mason, Illinois's Stephen A. Douglas, and South Carolina's Andrew P. Butler. Sumner called Mason, who had inaugurated the Fugitive Slave Controversy of 1850, the exemplar of slave-selling Virginia, "where human beings are bred as cattle." The Massachusetts orator castigated Douglas, who had acceded to southern demands for Missouri Compromise repeal, "as the squire of Slavery, its very Sancho Panza, ready to do all its humiliating offices."

Sumner at least chose his first two targets appropriately, for Mason and Douglas had been centrally responsible for late proslavery laws. They also could defend themselves in the Senate. Poor befuddled Andrew P. Butler, in contrast, had never accomplished much in the Senate. He now remained in South Carolina, unable to control his saliva after a stroke. Yet Sumner mocked the convalescent as discharging "incoherent phrases" and "loose expectoration," whenever he opens "his mouth." To this image of spittle flying aimlessly, Sumner added hints of the South as a brothel. Butler, snarled Sumner, rushed "forward in the very ecstasy of madness," having "chosen a mistress," that "harlot, slavery, . . . to whom he has made his vows, and who, though ugly to others, is always lovely to him."

This humiliating language aroused universal southern rage. Whether Southerners wished to perpetuate slavery or to reform it or to remove it, they loathed officious insulters who called them tyrannical champions of brothels. With his speech, Charles Sumner not only shamed an ailing elder but also touched a raw nerve. By connecting the choice for slavery to a choice for a mistress, he indirectly alluded to masters' supposed ecstasy in the arms of hapless female slaves. The competition was on among Southerners in Washington, D.C., to scream back at his holier-than-thou attitude, even to slap his leering face.

Preston Brooks became the natural Southron to do the honors, since Andrew Butler was his cousin. But less natural—more demanding of explanation—is why Brooks's response went way beyond a tirade, immensely beyond a cuffing. Why did Preston Brooks savage Charles Sumner more horrendously than the southern code of honor required, indeed more terribly than the South Carolinian intended? If Brooks had struck, as he had planned, only a blow or two, wounding Sumner for only a week or two, Northerners would have been less enraged. But the uncontrolled nature of Brooks's rampage, blasting a senator out of Congress for many months, extended the northern outrage, just as the Atchison takeover in Kansas extended Yankees' initial fury at the Kansas-Nebraska Act for a thousand days.

Charles Sumner perhaps psychosomatically extended his illness long after he was physically cured. But Brooks's extended assault would have wrecked anyone's physical health for a few months, extending through the presidential election campaign of 1856. That is when northern furor over the mugging most counted. The question, then, is not only whether the victim extended the recovery but also why the assailant extended the brutalization.

The answer transcends Preston Brooks. The South Carolina congressman's assault was a minute-long spree of relief, following almost a hundred hours of torment, about whether he could summon the nerve to strike at all. Brooks here offered a preview of the convulsive consequences of South Carolinians' repressed rashness. In 1860, after agonized hesitation, the state would finally dare to strike for disunion, in the manner of Brooks's unstoppable rage. Four years earlier, when the irresolute South Carolina congressman at last brought himself to swing the stick, he was too ecstatic to stop. In his desperation to achieve the precipitancy that he shuddered to begin, Charles Sumner's assailant was the essential South Carolinian.

For three decades before the Civil War, most South Carolinians (and few other Southerners) had seen only two choices. They could strike for disunion. Or ultras could allow slavery to fade undramatically from the South. As Brooks explained the choice in Kansas, if the South allows the territory to become "a hireling State, . . . Abolitionism will become" Missouri's "prevailing sentiment. So with Arkansas—so with Upper Texas." Then we should "put our house in order to die by inches." But if Kansas becomes "now a point of honor with the South," the "slavery question" will be "settled, and the rights of the South are safe."[36]

Still, Brooks worried, in the South Carolina manner, that the state's strike would be counterproductive, unless the whole South backed up the precipitators against the wealthier, more populated North. In the Nullification Controversy of 1832–33, South Carolinians had climbed out on a precarious limb, naked of any other state's support. Declaring the national tariff law null and void in their state, nullifiers had promised disunion, if the federal government enforced the nullified tariff. But when all other southern states rejected nullification, nervous precipitators had settled for a compromise.

Ever after, South Carolinians, the Southerners most likely to dare disunion, were scared of their own daring, ashamed of their own fright, and infuriated at those who laughed at their charges and retreats. At midcentury, these reluctant revolutionaries had staged an especially inconsistent performance, hurtling ahead, then tumbling backward from disunion after the Compromise of 1850. Preston Brooks had then been one of the most ardent Carolina revolutionaries—and one of the most reluctant.

When honor came calling again in 1856, Brooks raced out, again and again, to assault Charles Sumner, only to quail, again and again. His problem was partly physical, again mirroring South Carolina's predicament. Just as the North and the rest of the South could turn tiny South Carolina's honorable charge into dishonorable flight, so the stronger Sumner could force the weaker Brooks into contemptible retreat. The virile and handsome Sumner towered over the slight, limping, dissipated Brooks. Yet a South Carolinian must correct the insulting Sumner, Brooks believed, or other Southerners' dishonorable stupor would continue.

Immediately after Brooks heard that Sumner had mocked Butler, the mercurial South Carolinian determined to "avenge the insult."[37] Then the avenger stalled, as had South Carolina so often. Brooks decided to wait for the printed version of Sumner's speech. Upon reading the published oration two days later, Brooks searched for Sumner. Then he aborted the search. That night, he barely slept. Upon rising on May 22, he charged out to intercept Sumner as the insulter walked to the Senate. After hours of storming through Washington streets, Brooks decided his effort would exhaust him. Then the stronger Sumner would prevail. So he again withdrew. Sumner stepped into the Senate, unaware that he was hunted prey.

The harried hunter now waited at the Senate door for his prey to leave the chamber. Sumner stayed at his desk. Brooks entered the chamber. He sat three seats from the senator. A lady watched from the Senate gallery. Brooks asked that she be removed. She stayed. The South Carolinian retreated to the lobby.

Finally, the lady left. Only then did the assailant bellow that he could "stand this thing no longer." Brooks strode into the senatorial chamber. He rushed up to the seated Sumner. Screaming of "a libel on South Carolina, and Mr. Butler, who is a relative of mine," Brooks struck, as he had intended, a light blow with the smaller end of his gold-headed walking stick. Then, liberated at last, the exhilarated revenger could not restrain himself. Again and again, he clubbed Sumner, this time with the thick end of the cane. The wounded Sumner instinctively thrust himself backward and erect, ripping his desk from its moorings, then reeling as consciousness faded. When Sumner started to fall, Brooks caught him, propped him up, then struck again and again with the splintering cane.

John J. Crittenden, the Kentucky successor to Henry Clay's seat, lurched up to the assailant. "Don't kill him," he cried. Laurence Keitt, Brooks's young South Carolina colleague in the House, intercepted Crittenden, raised yet another cane, and screamed, "Let them alone, God damn you." Thus did South Carolina almost brutalize not only Massachusetts, center of free soil extremism, but also Kentucky, center of border compromising.

That preview of the secessionists' double enemy among white men, inside and outside the South during the Civil War, flickered but briefly. Georgia's Senator Robert M. Toombs restrained Keitt from assaulting Crittenden while Brooks smashed the unconscious Sumner to the floor. Then the assailant strode away from the desecrated Senate chamber. He left behind the most vivid imaginable symbol of the North's reaction to the Slave Power. Not even congressional gag rules against discussing slavery, not even unrepublican

SOUTHERN CHIVALRY — ARGUMENT versus CLUB'S.

The slighter Preston Brooks (top left), whose ambush of the stronger Charles Sumner (top right) underlined the question of the decade: Would southern antimajoritarian defenses continue to maul northern majoritarian processes? Courtesy of the Library of Congress (Brooks and Sumner images) and the Library Company of Philadelphia (Brooks/Sumner drawing).

procedures to return fugitive slaves, not even unrepublican laws in Kansas compared symbolically with the senator soaking freedom's chamber with his blood, unable to speak, unable to rise, a free white debater lashed more insufferably than a supposedly trashy slave.

For all this, Preston Brooks received applause, first from Southerners in

Washington, D.C., then in South Carolina. While many Southerners privately thought that, as usual, South Carolina had gone a little too far, most of them publicly castigated Charles Sumner for pushing oratorical insults way too far. Border politicians such as John Crittenden condemned Brooks. But this important exception aside, most Southerners cheered Preston Brooks's silencing of an unbearable Yankee with all the passion of William L. Yancey's loathing for his stepfather. Isolated South Carolinians usually postured, then retreated. But Preston Brooks, tremulously, had finally done it—and had usually won southern huzzahs. It was all another ominous rehearsal for 1860–61.

As echoes of southern applause for Preston Brooks cascaded around an appalled North, so did Charles Sumner's whispered lament, before he lapsed again into unconsciousness: "I could not believe that a thing like this was possible." But the famed Massachusetts poet and essayist Ralph Waldo Emerson better summed up the more extreme Northerners' thought. "I think we must get rid of [black men's] slavery," wrote Emerson, "or we must get rid of [white men's] freedom."[38]

Most northern citizens still doubted that they had to rid the South of black slavery to eliminate Slave Power outrages against Yankee whites. But Bleeding Kansas and bloody Sumner had generated an anti–Slave Power storm that consumed northern political attention as the presidential election of 1856 approached. Yankees' determination to obliterate the Slave Power's antirepublican defenses especially threatened to seal the fate of the dying National Whig Party.

CHAPTER 7

The Scattering of the Ex-Whigs

Although the slavery issue eventually divided both national parties, Whigs split first. During the 1832–52 years, when both parties thrived, Whigs won most often in the North (and especially in the farthest North), while Democrats triumphed most often in the South (and especially in the farthest South). Because of these different power bases, Southern Democrats could wrench slavery concessions from their weaker northern allies, while Southern Whigs could never squeeze slavery safeguards from their stronger northern wing.

As Southern Democrats secured ever more prosouthern laws, Southern Whigs faced ever more dispiriting accusations of remaining "disloyally" in an antisouthern party. In 1852, after the Democracy delivered the Fugitive Slave Law and Northern Whigs screamed in protest, many Lower South Whigs evaded the taint of disloyalty by staying home on Election Day. In 1854, after the National Democratic Party secured the Kansas-Nebraska Act and Yankee Whigs screeched about a Slave Power travesty, Border and Middle South Whigs joined Lower South brethren in searching for alternate allies.[1]

No new Whiggish national alliance could be based on slavery issues, or Southern Democrats' charge of soft on slavery would again be killing. Ex-Whigs' predicament offered another illustration of democracy's and despotism's problematic match. While sporadic lynchings such as William Phillips's horror in Missouri provided the most spectacular evidence that free opinion and coercive tyranny could never be cornerstones for each other, habitual southern accusations of disloyalty more constantly grinded at the national republic (and national party) foundations.

In even the soundest republics, loyalty politics will poison open discourse whenever a foreign enemy threatens. But when the very nature of a prime internal institution forbids dissent, suspicion of secret treason becomes unendingly corrosive. United States slavery for blacks generated omnipresent mistrust of white loyalty for many reasons: because enslaved Cuffees' pretenses raised awareness of human insincerity; because nonslaveholders judiciously hid doubts about slavery; because slaveholders disagreed about whether loyalty to slavery entailed belief in permanent, unlimited, unreformed absolute power. Rampant suspicions made a counteroffensive the only defense against the charge of being soft on slavery. Southern Whigs had to urge that Democrats were softer still and delivered only compromised proslavery goods. Southern Whigs eventually lost that game.

After Whiggery's collapse in 1855, ex–Southern Whigs could only tolerate other political games, if the grand old party was ever to rise again. Ex–Northern Whigs' infatuation with the anti–Slave Power issue, auguring the same old slavery disruptions, thus threatened to cleave Whiggery forever, leaving only the Democracy as a national party. Against that lethal threat to the Union as well as to further national opposition to the Democrats, ex–Southern Whigs desperately sought to interest northern ex-colleagues in any new national issue, based on anything except agitation about slavery.

– 1 –

An alternate northern issue seemed to invite a revived national opposition to the Democracy. Between 1850 and 1854, Northern Whigs faced not only those alleged slaves of the Slave Power, Northern Democrats, but also a new party that denounced European immigrants as slaves of the pope. This so-called nativist movement, dedicated to stopping "disloyal" newcomers from becoming voters anytime soon, flourished amidst the first massive rush of non-English, non-Protestant whites to America. During the 1845–54 decade, some 300,000 Europeans migrated annually to America. By 1854, newcomers comprised about one out of nine Americans. The strangers were overwhelmingly impoverished, Roman Catholic, German or Irish, inexperienced in democratic voting, impressed with papal pronouncements, drawn toward the National Democratic Party—and for all these reasons repugnant to Whiggish Protestants of British ancestry.

Nativist arguments stressed that non-English Catholics, and especially their tyrannical pope, undermined Anglo-American Protestants' moral and religious supremacy. Impoverished newcomers furthermore coveted old-time Americans' jobs. Longtime Americans must bar nouveau Americans from voting and perhaps bar immigrants from the so-called land of opportunity, or else no American opportunity would be safe.

Nativist candidates increasingly flaunted these fresh slogans to attract northern voters from the collapsing Whig Party during the early 1850s. Then the Kansas-Nebraska Act demonstrated that outmoded Whigs offered as little protection against the Slave Power as against immigrants. When the 1854 northern electorate turned out northern congressmen who had voted for the Kansas-Nebraska Act, anti–Slave Power and anti-immigrant appeals both nourished assaults on the Democracy.[2]

As ex–Southern Whigs departed their old party, they prayed that ex–Northern Whigs would abandon anti–Slave Power rhetoric. If the old allies ignored the supposed Slave Power and massed only against immigrants, all that had been lately ghastly for Southern Whigs would turn glorious. The hideous politics of sectional disloyalty would give way to the uplifting politics of national patriotism. A new superpatriotic national party would lure 100 percent Americans to save the republic from papal and foreign control.[3]

In late 1854, this southern prayer emerged as a mysterious, exotic chant. SAM, SAM, SAM went the cry, vote for SAM to make everything right. SAM will save slavery. SAM will fortify the Union. SAM will maul the Democrats.

Who is SAM, who is SAM, who is SAM, went the suspicious response from Southern Democrats, aware that their reinvigorated challengers wielded the glamour of a new secret. As the glamorous mystery spilled out in a hundred political campaigns, it became something yet more seductive: the previously unconsidered cure-all. SAM as quick fix, it turned out, meant S. AM., Southern American, the southern wing of a new antiforeign, newly christened American Party. SAM was a good uncle, an Uncle Sam. Uncle Sam would stop foreign immigrants from destroying American institutions. He would bar newcomers from voting for twenty-one years. Then longtime Americans, united in the American Party, would preserve America for the ages.

To ex–Southern Whigs, SAM's attractions abounded. At a time when ex–Southern Whigs had to disown northern allies who blasted the Slave Power, SAM invited an alliance with Yankees who blasted the immigrants; and immigrant blasting had lately been a winning northern pursuit. So too, at a time when Southerners and Northerners trembled for the Union, the most trembling Southerners could crusade for a reunited America.

All this and protecting slavery, too. At a time when Southern Democrats claimed to provide all the protections of slavery, SAM would provide the best protection yet. Federal law in 1807 had stopped the South from importing black immigrants. Now, nativists had to stop the North from enfranchising white immigrants. The Democratic Party, darling of immigrant voters, would then secure fewer ballots. The antislavery cause, another alleged immigrant treasure, would be weakened. The North, shorn of its swelling immigrant votes, would receive fewer congressional representatives and fewer voters in new territories. Slavery would also be safer in the Border South, for booming numbers of immigrants could no longer vote to expel waning numbers of slaves.

Back in 1787, explained the Alabama Executive Committee of the new American Party, "the non-slaveholding States, in the House of Representatives," possessed "only" a "majority of *five*." The "majority now is fifty-four!!" The Yankee advantage has swelled because "two and a half *millions* of foreigners" have arrived "in this country since the adoption of the Federal Constitution. *Nine-tenths* make their homes in the *non*slaveholding States." There they exhibit "the most ultra opposition to the institutions of the South." Worse, at their present rate of increase, immigrants will add "FORTY ADDITIONAL Representatives" to the northern House majority in ten more years.[4]

The *Savannah Daily Republican* opined that "in a few years more, unless this tide is checked, the South will be completely at the mercy of the
North, and what then will become of our boasted rights, our property, and our
firesides?"[5] As the question emphasized, a southern antiforeign appeal could
take a seductive northern idea, add an alluring southern veneer, fuse a national American Party, and save everything American except the slavery-
obsessed Democratic Party.

– 2 –

Still, for all SAM's potential shrinking of the number of northern voters—
and thus SAM's potential protection of southern voters—foreigners remained, from a Lower South perspective, largely a faraway problem. Immigrants swarmed inside only a few Lower South neighborhoods. In 1860,
immigrants comprised 10 percent of Texas's population (largely Germans
living in West Texas) and 23 percent of Louisiana's peoples (largely foreigners thriving in New Orleans). In these atypical Lower South areas, and especially in New Orleans, nativist passions reached northern-like peaks. But
elsewhere in the Cotton Kingdom, foreigners only comprised around 2 percent of the population. That minuscule figure offered thin nourishment to
Lower South voters who thought they fattened on the Democratic Party's
proslavery legislation.

In much of the Border South, however, the booming influx of immigrants
was fast becoming *the* local concern. Between 1850 and 1860, the immigrant percentage of the Border South population soared from 8.7 percent to
11.7 percent, while the slaves' percentage of the population ebbed from 15.6
percent to 12.7 percent. By 1860, Delaware and Missouri both contained
more immigrants than slaves. Furthermore, Maryland's expanding number
of nonnative whites almost matched the state's declining number of slaves.

Throughout this least southern South, but especially in the cities, immigrants captured many jobs and decided some elections. Here, disenfranchising
foreigners could improve a native voter's life. "Let all sectional disputes and all
discussion of the slave question be laid aside," urged the *Baltimore Clipper*.
"Our future should turn upon . . . whether natives or foreigners shall rule."[6]

This sentiment particularly burned through Maryland, the most promising southern state for a nativist conflagration.[7] True, Missouri harbored a
faster-growing percentage of immigrants. That western outpost of the Border South, however, faced slavery-infested turmoil on its Kansas frontier.
Maryland, in contrast, occupied the Border South's eastern extremity. Here,
far-off Kansas turmoil remained an abstraction. A different turmoil heaved
up in Baltimore, where the South's largest urban immigrant population
resided. Amidst arson-infested Baltimore streets and roaming gangs of so-
called plug uglies, native-born Protestants brawled with Irish and German
Catholics. Upper-class patricians wrung their hands over the chaos.

In their first attempt to quell disorder by disenfranchising immigrants, southern nativists elected the previously unknown Samuel Hinks to be mayor of Baltimore in October 1854. Hinks never campaigned at public rallies. Instead, he addressed secret meetings. Who is Samuel Hinks, and what evil is he plotting, Maryland Democrats asked in dismay. We know nothing, answered Hinks's partisans, thus repeating the nativist motto—Know-Nothings—that swept the North and gave the antiforeigner convulsion its nickname.

In 1855, the Know-Nothing or American Party spread the nativist convulsion from Baltimore across the state, capturing Maryland's legislature and four of its six congressmen. Two years later, Maryland's American Party elected Thomas Hicks governor. Meanwhile, Know-Nothingism sprawled over the Border South, securing Delaware's single congressional seat, six of Kentucky's ten seats, and three of Missouri's seven. With nativists simultaneously seizing five of Tennessee's ten congressional seats, the next question was whether SAM could rout the Democracy throughout the Middle South and then invade the Lower South.

– 3 –

Virginia's gubernatorial election of 1855 decided the question.[8] Antebellum Virginians considered themselves America's preeminent decision makers. During the republic's first forty years, their fabled Virginia Dynasty had handed the nation's presidency to each other. But after James Monroe turned over the White House keys to Massachusetts's John Quincy Adams in 1825, Virginia's magic faded, in everyone's eyes but the Virginians'. The state's fabulous vein of statesmen ran thin after Monroe. Simultaneously, its once lush tobacco-based economy, already shabby in Thomas Jefferson's day, turned as worn as its soil.

Worse, Virginia's attempts at making southern decisions usually produced nondecisions. The divided state drifted on the big question: Could slavery and egalitarian democracy coexist? In 1831–32 after Nat Turner's slave revolt, western Virginia nonslaveholding egalitarians staged a legislative struggle with eastern Virginia elitists over whether slavery, the basis of the gentlemen's bloated political power, should be drained out of the state. In part because of rich men's extra representatives in the legislature, poorer men's legislators could only pass an unhistoric, vaguely antislavery bill, too riddled with conditions to dent the institution. In 1850, disappointed western Virginia nonslaveholders warned those eastern Virginia slaveholders to surrender their undemocratic power over whites, if they wished to retain dictatorial power over blacks. So rich gentlemen, in constitutional convention assembled, reluctantly gave all whites equal governmental power—and then gave slaveowners unequal tax privileges.[9]

But if Virginia never could reconcile slaveholders in its eastern black belt areas with yeomen in its western white belt areas, the state seemed perfectly situated to decide whether nativism could become southern as well as northern stuff. North of this Middle South state lay the Border South, where swarming immigrants and waning slaves made Know-Nothingism a natural contagion. Southward lay the Lower South, where few immigrants and many slaves usually made nativism a strangers' infatuation. Up in Virginia's northwestern extremity, in Wheeling, located as far north as Pittsburgh, Pennsylvania, the almost entirely white residents had as little use for slaves or for reactionary squires as did Pennsylvania Know-Nothing fanciers. But down in Old Virginia black belts, many reactionary planters cherished South Carolina's haughty aristocrats. With all varieties of Southerners contending above and below and inside her borders, Virginia could best judge whether Yankees' anti-immigration prejudice could secure a southern party.

Virginia's most charismatic compromiser starred in the state's uncompromising showdown on nativism. Henry A. Wise, approaching fifty years old as he campaigned in Virginia to contain nativism to the Border South and North, had long used dizzying compromises as a means of acquiring state political power. A bony man with perhaps the South's thinnest, longest face, the frenzied Wise could be unkindly seen, through a Whiggish gentleman's eyes, as a blur without a core. A worshipper of Andrew Jackson, Wise had leapt to become a State's Rights Whig, then tumbled back into the Democratic Party. A slaveholder, prone to attacking his opponents' loyalty to the South, he had hinted that slavery could and should end. Ostensibly a passionate defender of slaveholders' rights to decide slavery questions, Wise had led the drive to empower nonslaveholders in the midcentury Virginia convention. Then he had led the convention's drive to give slaveholders tyranny over tax rates on slaves. Through it all, this self-styled conserver of the establishment had played the rough and hardy egalitarian, shrieking from the hustings and spitting like a small *d* democrat. He had also scoffed at Whig old fogies who decried such demagogues as traitors to Old Virginia's patriarchal tradition.

Wise had in fact traded Old Virginia's eighteenth-century elitist style for the nineteenth century New South's more egalitarian, more Jacksonian modes of defending rich white men. That sea change in southern and American mainstream politics had left reactionaries isolated in the most elderly South. Old-fashioned eastern seaboard oligarchs scorned what they ridiculed as "mobocracy"—especially two demagogic parties staging electioneering circuses in quests for the rabble's votes. Fossils pined for the good old days, when the best men ruled, the poorest men deferred, and all property, including slave property, was safe from the mob. They shuddered at the new southern politics, with its supposedly absurd presumptions that any (white) Tom, Dick, and Harry could equally rule and that supposed equals would never attack the unequally rich. They considered such demagogic nonsense the poison pill of slavery, indeed of civilization itself.

Henry Wise was of the new breed, convinced that defenders of the status quo must use supposedly mobocratic politics to spread the gospel that only race, sex, and age made humans unequal. White male adults, superiors all, must direct blacks, women, and children, inferiors all. But if the superiors who controlled blacks (or wives or children) haughtily sneered at their (white male) equals, the South's nonslaveholding majority, refusing to cower like black slaves, would assault slaveholders' presumption. Defenders of slavery must instead plunge into the muck. They must teach muddy toilers the true (racial) foundation of equality. So Wise incited propertyless whites to see themselves not as propertyless but as white—superior folk with a racial interest in keeping inferior folk enslaved.

Because of all this mobocratic electioneering, Wise became, to fading eastern Virginia reactionaries, the foulest faker who ever pretended to uphold superiors' rights. Edmund Ruffin called Wise "a political liar of the first magnitude." Beverley Tucker characterized this "petted child" as "incapable of grand ideas." Wise's genius consisted of "putting forth petty conceptions with an air of grandeur," thus "giving to mustard seed" the "velocity . . . of a cannon ball."[10]

Velocity was the word for Wise's antinativist campaign for governor in 1855. In an unprecedented dash throughout vast Virginia, the Democratic Party's nominee, decked out in disheveled homespun, sped through 3000 miles in four months, begging his fellows to stop Know-Nothingism at Virginia's gates. For two, three, four hours every night, the supposed commoner stomped and spit and shrieked before his supposed equals, with gaslights flickering at his every tirade and his voice sinking to an exhausted whisper. It was the greatest show since the circus went on tour.

SAM's partisans called the spectacle too disgusting to copy. To oppose Wise for the governorship, nativists nominated Richmond's Thomas Flournoy. This rich lawyer wished to direct poor folk in the manner a gentleman should. The patriarchal ex-Whig scorned Wise's rude pitches to commoners. Instead, Flournoy loftily instructed voters in an acceptance letter. Then he shunned disgusting public meetings.[11]

Flournoy's aristocratic hauteur, standard in the oldest South in the eighteenth century, still saturated old South Carolina and also often survived among Virginia's coastal State's Rights Whigs. Abel P. Upshur, the important secretary of state in Texas annexation times, had been tidewater reactionaries' beau ideal. Now the outmoded crowd cheered Thomas Flournoy's refusal to prostitute himself before the mob. Not even expelling the immigrant pollution from voting booths, they sniffed, justified polluted electioneering.

In 1855, Henry Wise had his best opportunity to teach such contemptuous squires how egalitarian persuasion, not aristocratic hauteur, offered rich men's salvation. Throughout other occasions when Wise orated on the stump for hours, his message grew more mystifying with every sentence. This time, this wonderer about slavery did not have to pretend that the institution was a wonder. Nor did this savior of gentlemen have to pretend that he deferred to commoners. Nor did this squirmer at secession have to pretend that he favored disunion. On nativism, Wise was the sincere rabble-rouser, determined to teach all native white southern males, rich and poor alike, to see Know-Nothings as traitors to American democracy and to southern slavery, too.

I hold in my hand, the political preacher endlessly repeated, the traitors' blue book, befouled with nativists' secret names, passwords, and grips. Why do they maintain this secret mumble jumble? Because they cannot bear a democrat's scrutiny! They defy freedom of religion, by proscribing Catholics. They defy white men's equality, by disenfranchising white immigrants. They defy freedom of speech, by refusing to debate in the open air. "If that is 'Americans ruling America,'" intoned Wise, "I can have nothing to do with it."[12]

Wise called Know-Nothings' secrecy an invitation to antislavery as well as to intolerance. White men who schemed in secret meetings, he demagogically hinted, taught blacks how to plot clandestinely. Discussions of slavery in hidden dens, he sincerely affirmed, allowed wary nonslaveholders to consider abolitionism. Down among Richmond and Norfolk white laborers, he warned, resentful poor men "for ten years have been petitioning the secretary of the navy to forbid the employment of slave labor." Up in the lily-white northwestern panhandle of the state, he exclaimed privately after haranguing the folk, Northwesterners "are *not Virginians*." Because they live on the borders of the North, they can't "hold . . . niggers," and thus "a *white* slave has to clean your boots."[13]

And now who bids to lead Virginia's white boot cleaners, with all their resentment of patronizing squires who called their labor "nigger work"? A disloyal Southerner who preferred free labor to slave labor! Years before, Thomas Flournoy had asserted "*that no country can be prosperous with a slave population.*"[14] That declaration, Wise warned, established Flournoy's softness on slavery. And now SAM's partisans spread Flournoy's unsound opinion in dangerously a-southern places, using dangerously secretive tactics.

More damningly still, Wise claimed that Southern Know-Nothings proved their softness on slavery by allying with antisouthern Northerners. In January 1855, at almost the exact moment when the Virginia Democracy nominated Henry Wise, to stop the Border South's Know-Nothing infatuation from spreading throughout the slaveholding section, the Massachusetts legislature elected the Know-Nothings' Henry Wilson, to spread anti–Slave Power insistences in the U.S. Senate. Wilson, only nominally anti-immigrant, was ferociously anti–Slave Power. For months, both Wise and his newspapers daily highlighted Thomas Flournoy's newly notorious northern ally. "What southern man can sympathize," asked Wise's main newspaper, with a secret order, "whose headquarters are in Massachusetts, and whose whole basis for action there stands upon religious intolerance and antislavery fanaticism?"[15]

Wise's campaign here shrewdly deployed the politics of loyalty against an especially vulnerable candidate. The snobby Thomas Flournoy refused to go public, to explain his supposedly "unsound" opinions. His supporters met only in secret, to discuss heaven knows what opinions. And the whole suspiciously secretive crew stood nakedly guilty of association with the new prince of Northern Know-Nothings, Henry Wilson, worst of anti–Slave Power insulters.

In May 1855, an unprecedented voter turnout demonstrated Wise's rhetorical power. Henry Wise won more votes than any other Virginia campaigner for any office anytime in the nineteenth century. Deeper in the South, Democratic Party chieftains sighed with relief. While immigration was more the Border South's problem, they had worried that the SAM solution could become the whole South's panacea. The nativist program, after all, could disenfranchise millions of Yankee votes. That gambit, far more than an open gate to chilly Kansas, would massively increase the minority South's relative political power. "If Wise is elected," wrote Mississippi's U.S. Senator Albert Gallatin Brown, "we shall have very little trouble in Mississippi." But if the Virginian loses, "the disorder will run like the cholera all over the South."[16]

Yet despite Wise's electioneering advantages and his huge voter turnout, Flournoy received 47 percent of Virginia's vote. Less than 2 percent of Wise voters, by switching sides, could have spread the Border South's nativist gospel to the Middle South. Wise had secured at least that decisive handful by playing the Lower South's political trump card: the charge that secretly antislavery Southerners proved themselves traitors by associating with openly antisouthern Yankees. The moral of Wise's victory: If ex–Northern Whigs allowed ex–Southern Whigs to be incinerated in the loyalty politics of slavery all over again, farewell to Whiggery. But if erring Yankees could be brought right—if the Henry Wilsons would at last forget the Slave Power and excoriate only the immigrants—the Middle and Lower Souths might yet repudiate Virginia's anti–Know-Nothing arbitration.

– 4 –

That was the burden of ex–Southern Whigs' ensuing attempt to forge a sectionally neutral national Know-Nothing Party that could win in Virginia and perhaps points southward. In June 1855, a month after Wise's victory, the national council of the Know-Nothing or American Party met in Philadelphia. The southern councilmen asked their northern brethren to read the election returns. "Fools and fanatics in the Legislature of Massachusetts," a southern nativist ranted, ran "riot during the [Virginia] Canvass"; and Wise partisans "harped upon" their anti-southern "proceedings . . . with the grossest exaggerations." If the blundering Henry Wilsons would replace anti–Slave Power slurs with anti-immigrant blasts, nativism could yet deliver the South, consolidate the North, resurrect National Whiggery, rout the Democracy, and win the presidency in 1856.[17]

In Philadelphia, the American Party's southern councilmen hoped that a possible national victory would entice northern delegates. The anti-immigrant cause, as often as the anti–Slave Power crusade, had driven northern opposition to the Democracy during Whigs' waning years. Reassume your anti-immigrant stance and we will together rule our saved nation, southern delegates promised northern compatriots. But if you continue to veer toward anti–Slave Power slurs, they correctly warned, nothing national, least of all the American Party, will endure.

Just here, Missouri ruffians' seizure of power in Kansas in early 1855 became crucial. If border ruffians' violent takeover of Kansas had not followed the Kansas-Nebraska Act—if western Missourians had peacefully watched more numerous northern settlers make Kansas free soil—then Northerners might have seen the pope rather than the Slave Power as the worst menace to American republicanism. But from the moment one-day Kansans illegitimately seized the territorial government, anti–Slave Power zeal outpaced anti-immigrant frenzy among the Democratic Party's northern opponents. Northern nativists had always considered the Slave Power and the immigrants to be twin reasons why the republic staggered. But after the "monstrous outrages in Kansas," Indiana's prominent ex-Whig Schuler Colfax stormed, "I *cannot* give up my hostility to the extension or encouragement of Slavery, & if the Order requires *that,* I cannot submit." Unless the American Party's Philadelphia national council adopts an anti–Slave Power plank, added Henry Wilson of Massachusetts, I will "blow their party to hell."[18]

In Philadelphia in June 1855, all southern delegates and just enough northern delegates blew Wilson's threat back in his face. The American Party's national council called the existing laws on slavery "final and conclusive." Thus the American Party must dwell only on immigrants. But a majority of northern delegates, led by Henry Wilson, meant to continue dwelling on the Slave Power. They quit the Philadelphia proceedings.

Eight months later, at the national convention of the American Party in (again) Philadelphia, northern delegates returned. But southern delegates hued to the same line: Only the nativist issue, and never the slavery issue, should be agitated. Many disgusted Yankee anti–Slave Power zealots then left again, this time permanently. The remnant of the February 1856 convention nominated ex-president Millard Fillmore of New York. The candidate called for silence on slavery and agitation on nativism, to save the Union and win the White House.

But Northerners stampeded away from Fillmore three months later, after the Sack of Lawrence (Kansas) and the Brooks-Sumner affair. Proslavery "violence," warned the usually restrained *New York Evening Post,* "has now found its way into the Senate chamber," and "violence has carried election after election" in Kansas. Slave Power violence, having engulfed the Senate, will the more "succeed if the people of the free states are as apathetic as the slaveholders are insolent."[19] For Know-Nothings such as Henry Wilson, the Fillmore-led American Party's sectional neutrality in the face of Slave Power outrages had zero appeal compared to the emerging alternative: the blooming Northern Republican Party's slight emphasis on nativism and its heavy stress on containing Slave Power violence.

By failing to rally most ex–Northern Whigs, Millard Fillmore became uninteresting to most ex–Lower South Whigs. A Yankee who could rout the

Northern Democrats on a sectionally neutral nativist program might have been intriguing. But if the North had to be lost anyway, a vigorous proslavery campaign could better combat Lower South Democrats. Fillmore's neutrality on slavery only sufficiently attracted border Southerners, who feared that slavery agitation would imminently blow up the Union—and in the process soak their farms with blood.

The November 1856 election returns demonstrated the American Party's narrowly regional appeal in the South. Fillmore received a competitive 48 percent of Border South voters. He won in Maryland, that prime southern locale of Know-Nothingism. In contrast, only 43 percent of Middle South voters, 41 percent of Lower South voters, and 11 percent of northern voters favored the New Yorker. The American Party, above and below the Border South, had followed the Whig Party to the grave.

The latest national corpse reemphasized that the slavery issue, in its anti–Slave Power form, most provoked the looming Civil War. Whigs' inability to reunite demonstrates the point, for no politicians had suffered more from the slavery issue's contaminations or tried harder to avoid a dread repetition. Nativism, that seductive nonslavery issue, had been wildly popular among the Democracy's northern opponents in the early 1850s. In the mid-1850s, ex–Southern Whigs begged for a party based on only that cause.

But not even southern nativists could escape the lure of the slavery issue's electoral power. Southern Know-Nothings paraded the proslavery appeal of disenfranchising a fat slice of the North's swelling majority. So too, after border ruffians and Preston Brooks struck, Northern Republicans' anti–Slave Power emphasis drowned out anti-immigrant emphases. Once the North's anti–Slave Power contention hardened, no "loyal" ex–Southern Whigs could ally themselves with Yankee insulters.

– 5 –

After Fillmore's American Party became extinct, Lower South opponents of the Democracy had only two choices. Most joined their long-hated enemy, the increasingly prosouthern Democratic Party. But ex–Lower South Whig holdouts continued to assault hateful Democratic tormenters as not prosouthern enough. Without a national party, however, ex-Whig assaulters had no hope of winning national concessions. They could only force Lower South Democrats to demand still more concessions from Northern Democrats. Those endangered Yankees faced political oblivion if they conceded another morsel to the Slave Power. Whiggish Lower South patriarchs, no friends of disunion, had ironically become as destructive of compromise, party, and Union as the secessionists.

In the Border South, in contrast, Fillmore's success gave ex-Whigs a foundation to oppose the Democracy and later the disunionists. In this section where slave populations grew thinner and immigrant populations thicker, the Know-Nothings' successful anti-immigrant formula proved that nonslavery politics could triumph. The stage was set for a (yet again!) new named party, the Opposition Party, to compete on equal terms with National Democratic politicians throughout the Border South in the 1857–60 period.

Thus where the heavily enslaved Lower South's experience with nativism had yielded a largely one-party system, with the hapless ex-Whig remnant in position only to carp at the proslavery Democracy, the lightly enslaved Border South had regenerated a competitive two party system, with the powerful ex-Whig fragment in position to defeat the Democracy. The Lower South and Border South had generated different political institutions, compounding their different social institutions. In 1860, the borderland's powerful surviving ex-Whig partisan organizations would give the region's Unionist Party a leg up in defeating secessionists. But in the Lower South, the uncompetitive ex-Whigs would offer no such institutional bulwarks against disunion.

The more immediate question, during the presidential campaign and election of 1856, was whether the sole surviving national party, the Democracy, could turn back an almost exclusively northern anti–Slave Power movement's bid to elect a president. The further question was whether the Union would survive if the new antisouthern party won. And could even a narrowly victorious Democracy survive any further southern demands for protection of slavery, including any further effort to fortify slavery in the southern borderlands?

CHAPTER 8

James Buchanan's Precarious Election

In 1856, only the Northerners who lived closest to the South could stop the North's anti–Slave Power surge, newly institutionalized in the Republican Party. To stymie the Republicans, James Buchanan, son of the northern borderlands and presidential nominee of the National Democratic Party, needed to combine almost all of the Border North's Electoral College votes with all of the South's. But a coalition tipped so far southward could easily reignite Yankees' hatred for Slave Power defenses. Before Buchanan even started his presidency, his cabinet selections, featuring a southern Camelot, foretold trouble ahead for a Yankee borderite who might not be Yankee enough.

– 1 –

Buchanan's Border North differed from the farther northern states as much as the Border South differed from the Lower South. The Border North, meaning free labor states adjoining slaveholding states, included Iowa, Illinois, Indiana, Ohio, Pennsylvania, and New Jersey. Compared to Yankees who lived farther from the South, and especially New Englanders, Border Northerners voted for Democrats and southern proposals more often. Their southern North attracted fewer New England puritans and more Border Southerners. Among Northerners, they clung to slavery longer, legislated against free blacks more repressively, and would harbor more so-called Copperhead opponents of Lincoln's Civil War. Particularly the Border North's southernmost areas little differed from the Border South's northernmost areas.

James Buchanan grew up in Mercersburg, Pennsylvania, a scant ten miles north of slaveholding Maryland. He prospered as an adult in Lancaster, only another fifteen miles above the slavocracy's border. No other important pre–Civil War Northerner lived closer to the South or befriended so many Southerners.

James Buchanan especially savored Southerners who emotionally resided

97

where he did: on the edge of both sections. The lifelong bachelor's most frequent Washington, D.C. roommate, U.S. Senator William R. King of Alabama, and his most frequent overnight guest in the White House, Secretary of the Treasury Howell Cobb of Georgia, were Lower South titans who detested Lower South extremists. Buchanan's other intimates included a native Northerner who lived in the South (U.S. Senator John Slidell of Louisiana), two native Southerners who lived in the North (U.S. Representative J. Glancy Jones of Pennsylvania and Robert Tyler of Philadelphia), and an Indianian who owned slaves in Kentucky (U.S. Senator Jesse Bright). The president gave his most sensitive office (territorial governor of Kansas) to a native Pennsylvanian who had been a U.S. senator from Mississippi and lately had haunted New York City (Robert J. Walker).

James Buchanan found the line between North and South almost invisible. This Border Northerner had been a slaveholder the Border South way. In 1834, Buchanan bought two female slaves, aged five and twenty-two. He immediately signed their freedom papers, to take effect in seven years (in the case of the twenty-two-year-old) and twenty-three years (in the case of the five-year-old). These blacks, he anticipated, would serve as unpaid household help in the interim.[1]

Buchanan's turtle-slow manumission was vintage Border South practice. By offering a slave freedom tomorrow in exchange for hard work today, border capitalists usually secured a decent profit—and a safer profit than permanent slavery yielded. A permanently enslaved border black, possessing no promise of future freedom to lose, would more likely light out for the nearby North.

Yet temporary slaves' expectation of eventual freedom could whet hunger for freedom sooner. Then blacks might make a dash beyond slavery's border. Such flights could make semislavery's risks outweigh its profits. Then sales of Border South slaves to the Lower South could increase, along with prospects that the fifteen slave states would be sliced to eleven. That specter helped prod borderites to initiate both the Fugitive Slave Law and the Kansas-Nebraska Act and to use the edicts to provoke more crises still.

James Buchanan, gradual emancipator, experienced not only temporary slavery's rewards but also its risks and its nation-shattering riots. The worst riot over semislavery occurred in Buchanan's neighborhood, five years before the Pennsylvanian won the presidency. In 1851, a northern Maryland slaveholder, Edward Gorsuch, rode with his son into the rural hamlet of Christiana, Pennsylvania, located under fifteen miles from Buchanan's Lancaster doorstep. Gorsuch demanded the return of his four runaway slaves, harbored in Christiana structures. His slaves and their rescuers, black and white, instead rained bullets on the intruders. Gorsuch was slain, his son badly wounded, his slaves never returned, and his killers never convicted.[2]

Gorsuch had had a Buchanan-like agreement with his border slaves. He had pledged to free them in some eight years, if they would work hard. But instead of settling for freedom eventually, Gorsuch's slaves gambled on freedom now. They thereby pronounced semislavery insufferable and a semimaster befouled.

James Buchanan loathed the verdict. Border North slave rescuers and Border South fugitive slaves, this border man conceived, decimated property, order, and Union. In contrast, borderland gradual emancipators, Buchanan congratulated himself, followed Christian principles, the genial way. James Buchanan was a northern man with southern principles, if one means a Border North man with Border South principles.

Both sections shared his paternalistic principles. According to proslavery polemicists (and according to an especially dubious current historical wisdom), only the ownership of servants creates paternalism toward dependents. Supposedly, the employer of labor necessarily lacks paternalistic feelings toward his employee. But wealthy Anglo-Americans' caring relationships with hired servants show that paychecks hardly forbid paternalism. Witness the famous upstairs-downstairs relationships in English grand houses, the intimate connections between upper-class Northerners and lifelong servants, and the paternalistic regime in the nineteenth-century Lowell (Massachusetts) Mill.

North or South, England or America, what counted was the caring, not whether the superior paid or owned the inferior. Buchanan's paternalistic, lifelong relationship with his beloved paid housekeeper, Miss Hetty, epitomized the hardly exclusively southern paternalistic ideal.[3] This patriarch, residing an easy two hours' horseback ride from the South, saw himself and his southern friends as equally responsible for their domestic folk, white or black, paid or owned, manumitted someday or always enslaved.

Buchanan thus instinctively understood his southern pals' outrage when abolitionists called them monsters. To hear zealots tell it, Buchanan's southern favorites smashed black families and raped black favorites. But his friends, the Pennsylvanian conceived, would no more sell or sexually assault their family friends than he would fire or violate Miss Hetty. So when Buchanan's roommate William R. King raged in 1837 that, unless Northerners silenced foul-tongued abolitionists, "we will separate from them," the Pennsylvanian credited the threat. Buchanan meant to deter "a catastrophe" that "may come sooner than any of us anticipate."[4]

Like many pre–Civil War aspirants to save the Union, Buchanan's defining act of deterrence came in the Gag Rule Controversy of the 1830s. When petitions to abolish slavery first flooded congressmen's mails, the then most powerful Northern Democrat, New York's Martin Van Buren, offered a compromised way of silencing debate. Van Buren would admit antislavery petitions for congressional consideration, send them to committee, and there bury them.

Buchanan, who lived much closer to the South than did the New Yorker, would instead trash the petitions before they reached committee. But this borderland appeaser stopped short of South Carolina's John C. Calhoun. Calhoun insisted that Congress must not even receive antislavery petitions. In a representative democracy, Buchanan responded, representatives must at least receive constituents' prayers for action. Pennsylvania's U.S. senator would do almost anything to calm rightfully outraged southern friends. But they must allow him to stop slightly short of enraging Border North constituents.[5]

That borderland way to avert civil war informed Buchanan's appeasements of indignant Southerners throughout his ascending career as U.S. representative, U.S. senator, minister to Russia, minister to England, and secretary of state. Despite that superb training for the presidency and despite Buchanan's long-standing sympathy for Southerners, Southern Democrats preferred other candidates for the party's presidential nomination in 1856. Southerners vaguely sensed what the secession crisis would prove: that despite his empathy for Southerners, Buchanan remained narrowly a Yankee. Buchanan seldom read broadening books and traveled for pleasure less. His conversation usually centered on Lancaster enterprise (he was a rich lawyer) and on Pennsylvania politics (he manipulated patronage very successfully).

Buchanan's tastes also betrayed the Yankee puritan. While he was fond of liquor, no one considered him a drunkard. While he was a notorious flirt, no one called him a womanizer. While he gave the merriest presidential parties in decades, he banned cards and dancing from the White House. This wealthy Yankee accounted for every penny and advised southern friends to hoard their every nickel. That brand of Yankee rectitude stopped miles short of looking down on slaveholding. But slaveholders somewhat kept their secrets from (and sometimes privately ridiculed) this slightly judgmental, slightly pompous, slightly humorless, slightly fastidious, slightly ponderous, slightly inflexible white-haired northern materialist.

In early 1856, Southern Democrats most regretted that Buchanan was not President Franklin Pierce or U.S. Senator Stephen A. Douglas.[6] Those Northern Democrats had given slaveholders the Kansas-Nebraska Act, while Buchanan served as minister to England. Most Northern Democrats, however, preferred Buchanan precisely because of the Pennsylvanian's noninvolvement with the Kansas-Nebraska Act. These Yankee politicos feared that Pierce or Douglas would turn 1856 into a repetition of 1854, when northern voters had purged congressional supporters of the Slave Power's favorite law. At the Democratic National Convention, fifteen stalemated ballots proved that Southern Democrats' two preferred Northern Democrats could not be nominated. So Southerners settled for their third choice, the largely asectional James Buchanan.

In his ensuing campaign for the presidency, Buchanan made the nonsectional case he cared most about: saving the Union.[7] By 1856, the Republican Party had emerged from the demise of the Whigs as most ex–Northern Whigs' party of choice. Anti–Slave Power had also emerged as most Republicans' issue of choice. If Republicans won on that insulting issue, the Pennsylvanian believed, resentful Southerners would secede before the president-elect could be inaugurated. Republicans could win without a single southern electoral vote, Buchanan correctly saw, if they swept his own Pennsylvania, a couple of other Border North states, and all states farther northward.

Buchanan also correctly saw that the Border North could best stop the Republicans and that civil war would most batter the borderlands. Maryland and Pennsylvania, he exclaimed, would "suffer more than any other members of the Confederacy." Thus only "the grand and appalling issue of union or disunion should matter."[8]

– 2 –

For Buchanan's issue to matter decisively, at least Border Northerners had to be convinced that the South would secede if a Republican won the 1856 presidential election. But that disunion scenario did not seem then (and does not seem now) altogether certain. True, a prime provoker of secession, southern hatred of Yankee holier-than-thou attitudes, reached scornful heights in 1856, boosted by Republicans' charge of Slave Power barbarism. Still, the towering roadblock to disunion, most Southerners' love of Union and terror of civil war, was also omnipresent, and very obvious to Yankees who considered secessionists but blowhards and Buchanan but a scaremonger. Moreover, Southerners' favorite alternative to disunion, the National Democratic Party, remained alive and well and perhaps still capable of furthering southern rule through the nation's majority party.

The lack of an organized southern effort for supposedly inevitable secession also undermined Buchanan's scary prophecy. In the fall of 1856, secessionists' only visible planning looked abortive. After Virginia's Henry Wise invited eleven fellow southern governors to a mid-October conference in Raleigh, North Carolina, to plot strategy in case Buchanan lost, empty seats dominated the conference table. Only the governor from North Carolina (who opposed disunion and had but to step across the street) and from (where else!) South Carolina came to hear Wise's irresolute gasconade.[9]

If northern voters had been privy to secessionists' private mail in 1856, they would have been even less convinced that revolution loomed ahead. Compared to the conspiratorial correspondence that had occurred in 1850–52 and would occur in 1860–61, disunionists scarcely corresponded, much less plotted, with each other in 1856.[10] Southern extremists expected Buchanan to win, making disunion premature.

With no preexisting revolutionary organization to push the southern majority toward disunion, enough Southerners would have to consider disunion necessary. But if a Republican won the presidency, would the winner necessarily menace slavery? When debate swirled on that question in 1860–61, the elected Republican president, Abraham Lincoln, had a long, clear record of at least moral opposition to slavery. In contrast, John C. Frémont, Republicans' 1856 candidate, had no record on much of anything. Republicans nominated the charismatic "Pathfinder" because of his fabled explorations out west, not because he ever called slavery iniquitous.[11]

With Frémont silent on slavery's morality and offering no antislavery plan, Southerners could only scrutinize the Republican Party's position. Republicans agreed that the Slave Power menaced white men's republicanism outside the South; that the menace must be contained inside the South; and that the Missouri Compromise's containment must be restored. Republicans also concurred on slavery's inequity. Their 1856 platform linked the South's Peculiar Institution with Mormon polygamy as a "a twin relic of barbarism." Republicans here repeated Charles Sumner's slur. By calling slaveholders twins of Mormons who enjoyed several wives, the Republican platform alluded to supposed paternalists who allegedly bedded their slaves. The party's platform pledged to bar the Slave Power from new U.S. territory. Republicans would thus jail the supposed horror inside old southern states, like a rat in a cage. But would they inject antislavery poison inside the imprisoned South?

Republicans seldom answered. Their coalition of racist reactionaries and colorblind radicals, nativists and foreigners, and lower-class Democrats and upper-class Whigs only agreed that the Slave Power must be contained. A march beyond containment might split the alliance before the Slave Power had been imprisoned.

A premature advance also would throw away the Republicans' politically brilliant half-adoption of antislavery. By the mid-1850s, antislavery extremists had convinced most Northerners that slavery was an abomination. That crucial triumph, along with abolitionists' equally crucial provocation of a furiously aggressive southern defensiveness, turned Yankee extremists into indispensable actors in causing the Civil War. But antislavery extremism never conquered the prewar North's racism, or its dread of civil war, or its conviction that forcible intervention inside the South, to emancipate the slaves, would be unconstitutional. To bring antislavery into the antebellum mainstream, a moderate form of the radicalism became mandatory.

Mainstream Republicans' moderating impulse took the form of opposition to the southern zealotry that northern zealots had provoked, while keeping Yankee extremists themselves at arm's length. Moderate Republicans demanded that the Slave Power's defenses must be stopped from polluting white men's republican procedures. But Republicans stopped short of demanding that the federal government impose freedom for blacks on the contained South. By insisting on the immediate end of the Slave Power's supposed enslavement of white citizens, while only vaguely talking about ultimate freedom for black slaves (say in a hundred years, speculated Abraham Lincoln), Republicans played on Northerners' perception that the South's late national proslavery victories fastened shackles on northern whites more infuriatingly than on southern blacks.

When the more radical Republicans occasionally and gingerly explained how they would move from containing the Slave Power to attaining slavery's ultimate extinction (Lincoln never did explain), they usually stressed that Southerners must do the emancipating. Radical Republicans' main postcontainment plan involved using federal patronage to encourage the South's own politicians to build a Southern Republican Party. Then home-grown Southern Republicans might bring forth what Salmon P. Chase called a "vast . . . dormant mass of antislavery feeling at the South."[12]

Yet as Ohio's Chase knew well, a vast antiblack feeling helped keep antislavery feeling dormant, North as well as South and especially in both sections' borderlands. Against that paralyzing racism, Republicans offered only the hope that the federal government would remove freed blacks from America. The colonization strategy recognized that almost all potential Border South Republicans favored removing free blacks from their states, including the Blairs of Missouri and Cassius Clay of Kentucky. As Wisconsin's U.S. Senator James Doolittle explained, colonization of free blacks would help "our friends in Missouri, Maryland, Delaware, Kentucky, and Virginia" to emancipate "and Republicanize these states."[13]

The colonization strategy also helped distinguish radical abolitionists from moderate Republicans. Garrisonian antislavery campaigns assaulted colonizationists as vehemently as slaveholders. These radicals called expelling blacks as repulsive as enslaving the unfortunates.

By embracing supposedly repulsive colonization, Republicans completed the task of drawing the fangs from antislavery radicalism, yet still claiming its moral glory. They sought ultimate freedom from slaveholders for blacks—but immediate freedom from the Slave Power for whites. They favored emancipation in the South—but only if Southerners became the emancipators. They would lure southern emancipators—but only with federal patronage. They would help allay southern racism—but only with freedmen's federal tickets to Africa.

The most secessionist Southerners considered this half endorsement of radical abolitionism nothing short of the whole dread thing. Southern social control demanded that antislavery agitation be silenced, lest slaves or nonslaveholders be exposed to heresy. Now a Southern Republican Party, financed by federal patronage, might pry open the closed society. "Did you ever expect to see the day," Virginia Congressman William O. Goode privately asked a friend, "when the success of a presidential candidate would probably fill every Federal office in the *South*—with a *Free Soiler*?" Goode, a charter member of the F Street Mess that had pressured Stephen A. Douglas on Kansas-Nebraska, would secede rather than allow "Black Republicanism . . . to plant and rear their party in the South." Since "everything must be done to prevent a result so fatal," climaxed Goode, we must teach "our people . . . a proper appreciation of the danger."[14]

A proper appreciation of the Southern Republican menace would have been as crucial to secessionists' success in 1856 as it would become in 1860. All other possible Republican menaces to slavery—abolishing territorial slavery, repealing fugitive slave laws, prohibiting slave sales between slave states, forbidding the institution in federal forts inside slave states—all such new laws would require Republican dominion over both houses of Congress as well over the White House. Republicans had as little chance to win congressional majorities in 1856 as they would in 1860. So southern unionists' prime cry in 1860—that disunion could safely wait until Congress passed an "overt act" against slavery—would have been omnipresent in 1856 and to even more effect, for the National Democratic Party then still existed, to win the next congressional election.

Technically, a Republican president's power to menace slavery by appointing Southern Republicans also required a congressional majority (to approve the appointments). But Congress had never rejected every presidential nomination; and Southerners would have considered any Republican officeholder beholden to the enemy. Nor could Northern Democrats help Southerners stop every appointment, lest they be the more dammed as slaves of the Slave Power. Thus southern unionists almost never protested that Congress would save the South from Republican local appointments. That power a Republican president *would* have, almost everyone assumed. If a president's appointing power inside the South could immediately menace slavery, the unionist case for awaiting congressional "overt acts" would be irrelevant.

But in 1856 as William O. Goode conceded, southern voters still lacked widespread understanding of the Southern Republican danger. Here as everywhere, the secessionists' problem, if Frémont had won in 1856, would have been that the final boosts to disunionism had not yet developed. In early 1860, a major national crisis over Northern Republicans' Southern Republican strategy would advertise the menace. So too, during the 1860 election campaign, Republicans would run an explicitly antislavery (in theory) presidential candidate, the National Democratic Party would split in half, and Lower South governors would commence a conspiratorial correspondence. Even then, securing secession against the wishes of a vast majority of southern whites would become a tense adventure. In 1856, an even tenser escapade would have had to feature even wilder scenes.

Still, the 1856 South contained some wild secessionists, insisting that southern honor and safety required defiance of an elected Republican president. Virginia's U.S. Senator James Mason, for example, pledged that if Frémont won, "one course remains for the South: Immediate, absolute, and eternal separation."[15] No 1856 bet against Mason, yet another powerful resident of the F Street Mess, would have been a sure thing. But four years before Lincoln's election, Buchanan's trouble, as he tried to convince Northerners that only his election could save the Union, remained that disunion, if he lost, looked uncertain.

– 3 –

At the 1856 polls, Buchanan's scaremongering only worked inside and near the South. Democrats won 56 percent of southern popular votes and every southern electoral vote except Know-Nothing Maryland's. In contrast, Buchanan secured only 41 percent of Northerners' ballots (compared to Republicans' 45 percent) and only three of ten northern electoral votes.

In the North no less than in the nation, Buchanan support tilted southward. In the six free labor states bordering on a slave labor state, Democrat's Border North presidential candidate secured 111,000 votes more than Frémont, while losing only Ohio. In the rest of the North, the Republicans secured 239,000 votes more than Buchanan, while losing only California.

The farthest southern sections of Border North states gave Buchanan his saving northern margin. In Pennsylvania, Frémont won all but one of the state's northernmost counties (and two-thirds of the tier's popular votes). But Buchanan won all the state's southernmost counties (again by a two-thirds majority). In the two tiers taken together, Buchanan secured 9000 more votes. So too, Buchanan's overwhelming majorities in southern Illinois gave him more votes than Frémont's overwhelming majorities in northern Illinois. A similar outcome allowed southern Indiana's Buchanan supporters to whip northern Indiana's Frémont supporters. No other national mandate bent further in the sectional minority's direction.

The winner's cabinet appointments furthered the image of a barely northern president, bending toward the South. Buchanan, seeking a more sectionally balanced image, gave his most prestigious post, secretary of state, to Michigan's Lewis Cass. But Cass, in his midseventies and feeling his age, never amounted to much, especially not compared to Buchanan's lively southern appointments.

Four of the seven cabinet posts went to energetic young Southerners. The youthful sports came to be called the Directory. Georgia's Howell Cobb, a third of a century younger than Cass, became Buchanan's secretary of the treasury and the Directory's unofficial prime minister. Cobb, although barely thirty years old in Compromise of 1850 times, had precociously earned national fame by joining Robert Toombs and Alexander Stephens in a conquering Georgia unionist triumvirate. The trio had stopped midcentury secession as cold as Henry Wise would halt the Southern Know-Nothing movement in 1855.

The rotund Cobb wore his southernness lightly (he would free his darkies, he loved to tell Yankees, if only his family friends needed his kindly direction less totally). Cobb also displayed his love of Union ostentatiously, his capacity to dine robustly, and his taste for picky administrative labor ravenously. Buchanan loved the jolly workaholic. A Yankee could trust the Union, breathed the Border Northerner, in such a scrupulous Southerner's neutral hand. But in the Kansas crisis, Buchanan would discover that Cobb, his supposedly saving southern neutral, tipped to the South. Similarly, in the secession crisis, the Directory would discover that the president, their allegedly saving northern neutral, tipped to the North.

Less worthy of the president's trust than Cobb (and far less influential) was the less amiable, less middle-of-the-road, less drudging, less scrupulous secretary of war, Virginia's John Floyd. During the Buchanan years, corruption would befoul Floyd's department. The secretary of war escaped even more public outcry because his most important military act, secretly transferring

President James Buchanan (left), his head cocked at its customary odd angle, as if announcing his atypical Northern Border political leanings—leanings still not ultimately southern enough for the Lower South's Secretary of the Treasury Howell Cobb (right), the president's favorite youthful, jovial southern moderate. Courtesy of the Library of Congress (both images).

thousands of stands of arms from northern to southern armories in case of secession, never became public knowledge.

Buchanan's choice for secretary of the interior, Mississippi's wealthy Jacob Thompson, emitted none of his fiery southernness unless a Yankee moralist damned his ethics. Then Thompson could become one mean antagonist, as the Pennsylvania-born Robert Walker, temporarily a Mississippi resident and U.S. senator, had discovered. But in the cocoon of the Buchanan circle, Thompson delighted the chief executive with his asectional hilarity, with his convivial wife, Kate, and with his talented niece, Miss Wiley. That maiden's snow-white hand on the harp often strummed away Washingtonians' broodings about political clouds.

Along with Tennessee's Aaron Brown, Buchanan's postmaster general and yet another southern grandee fond of sumptuous parties, Jacob Thompson controlled the most important patronage-dispensing departments. The two secretaries filled the federal government's southern posts with proslavery Southrons. They thus demonstrated how much had been gained, in keeping Southern Republicans out of office.

To the Directory's southern political direction, its wives added southern social dominance. Especially Howell Cobb, the epitome of Buchanan's wish for an asouthern salvation of the Union, adored the new southern dominance in Washington parlors. Previously, this man huge in girth, in political power in the House, in material possessions (he owned well over a thousand slaves), and in domestic standing (he was wonderfully married to a Lamar, that southwestern clan oozing with wealth, influence, and respectability)—this man who seemed to have everything had ached for what he did not have. His congressional power, even when he was a Speaker, had fallen short of senatorial, cabinet, and presidential sway. His domestic life had also fallen short of his design. His wife, a potentially sterling asset in Washington society, had relished their plantation Big House too much to accompany Congressman Cobb to muddy Washington very often.

But after Cobb's appointment as secretary of the treasury and his standing as second only to the president in cabinet councils, Mrs. Cobb cherished her role as second most important queen bee in the capital, behind only Harriet Lane, the bachelor president's niece and hostess. Mary Ann Lamar Cobb called Miss Lane "the model of an American girl," the Old Squire "the greatest President we have had since Washington and Jackson," and White House parties "splendid, in spite of the damp air."[16]

Mrs. Cobb's new zest for her husband's humid town sprang the treasury secretary from his cramped boardinghouse. For the then princely sum of $1800 a year, he rented a Washington mansion. The puritanical president, upon glimpsing the extravagant pile, twitted Cobb for displaying too many riches. I'm not rich, responded the secretary. Then your wife must be, smiled Buchanan. The two Cobbs twitted the president right on back for spoiling some Washington fun by barring cards whenever Miss Lane went out to party.[17]

The joshing spread from Buchanan and his southern dominated cabinet to the Southerners who often commanded the U.S. Senate. Buchanan's old comrade, Louisiana's U.S. Senator John Slidell, together with Mississippi's Jefferson Davis, Alabama's Clement C. Clay, Jr., and their spouses, shared the cabinet's festivities. From these rural titans' urban mansions, their favorite slaves carried notes back and forth. A missive from Mary Ann Lamar Cobb, for example, asked Mrs. Clement Clay to "please inform your liege lord that he missed an elegant breakfast this morning." Senator Clay lost out on "beefsteak, mutton chops, sausages, Georgia biscuits," and "*fresh* milk from *our own* cow." A senator would have to "go far, *even* to *Alabama*," teased Mrs. Cobb, "to get a better breakfast." So too, Kate Thompson informed Howell Cobb that "the president says he will dine with me today at 5 o'clock—and you must come and join us, . . . for you cannot get dinner today at the *White House*." As for the bachelor at the center of the Directory's bonhomie, Varina Davis knitted the president some slippers, to remind him "of these who love you."[18]

During Washington's long, hot summers, Buchanan and his loving Directory moved southward, to the cool mountain air of White Sulphur Springs in western Virginia. Headquarters became not the White House but the Old White Hotel (the predecessor to the Greenbrier). There, sixteen hundred guests, mostly Southerners, joined Washington's southern celebrities in whirling around the president. It was all so hearty, so happy, so heartwarming for provincials who had lately been so dammed by the insufferable Charles Sumner.

Their revenge provided yet another deterrent to disunion. Washington's southern potentates had no desire to leave a town that had turned enchanted, not at least until James Buchanan had disappeared. For disunion to achieve full steam while the capital remained under Buchanan's watch, the impetus would have to come from outside the Washington southern establishment that cherished the Old Squire.

Yet southern devotees' delight threatened the Pennsylvanian's presidency. In 1856, Buchanan's northern electoral base had been precarious. To win the White House in 1860, his Republican foes would only have to retain their newly won northern terrain and add a few thousand Border North votes. Any further evidence that the southern minority dominated the majoritarian republic could boost Republicans' almost victorious revolution against Slave Power dominion over the top. Despite the danger, James Buchanan began a stunning prosouthern intervention where no president or president-elect had dared trod, before he even issued his suspect Inaugural Address.

CHAPTER 9

The President-Elect
as the Dred Scotts' Judge

Two weeks before Buchanan's presidency began, the president-elect secretly intervened in U.S. Supreme Court deliberations. The nonjudge urged the judges to eliminate the issue that could destroy his administration (and his nation). His plea arguably shaped the Court's so-called Dred Scott Decision, announced two days after his presidential inauguration. Thus did the Border North moderate, in collaboration with the Court's primarily moderate southern majority, begin a pro-Union administration that would further disunion.

– 1 –

The conventional wisdom about Dred Scott's southern judges eliminates that irony. Their famous—infamous—Supreme Court decision supposedly threw down the proslavery verdict of southern diehards, determined to save slavery at whatever cost to Union.[1] But in reality, these judges sought to save the Union from sectional storms, partly in hopes that pacified slaveholders might incrementally reform and perhaps end absolute power. The majority of the judges would stay in the Union during the Civil War, at whatever cost to slavery.

James Buchanan initiated misconceptions of their decision. In his Inaugural Address, the new president declared that the Court's decision, whatever it turned out to be, would settle the slavery issue forever. Just before Buchanan professed ignorance about what the Court would decide, observers saw him whispering with Chief Justice Roger B. Taney on the inauguration stand.

Forty-eight hours later, Maryland's Taney read the Supreme Court's decision. The five Southern Democratic judges (with one Northern Democratic judge concurring and another not dissenting) ruled that Congress could not constitutionally bar slavery from U.S. territories. The verdict implicitly forbade Buchanan's Republican foes from restoring the Missouri Compromise prohibition of slavery in Kansas and Nebraska territories (and from enacting any other prohibition of territorial slavery). And Buchanan claimed to have had nothing to do with this demolition of his political enemies!

Republicans responded that the Northern Democrats' dissimulating president (elected without a popular majority) had conspiratorially encouraged proslavery, disunionist Democratic judges (elected by no one) to veto the majority section's majority: those 1.3 million citizens who had lately voted for John C. Frémont. The conspiratorial part of Republicans' tale of a disunionist travesty, although sounding like the most preposterous part, was actually the most correct aspect. President-elect Buchanan, while drafting his Inaugural Address, did clandestinely prod jurists toward their decision. Buchanan did secretly learn (slightly incorrectly) about the imminent verdict. He did pretend total unawareness in his Inaugural Address.

But most of the Court's controlling five southern judges no more cherished slavery or savored disunion than did Buchanan. Instead, their so-called Dred Scott Decision meant to save the Union by declaring the future of slavery none of Yankees' or the federal government's business. The judges also hoped that Southerners, once spared northern meddlers' convulsions, would calmly trim or end absolute power.

If the Supreme Court's controlling majority had been proslavery ultras and/or disunionists, they would have betrayed the presidents who had nominated them. Southern Democrats commanded the Court in 1857 because the Democratic Party, with its southern power base, had won five of the previous seven presidential elections. The Democracy's presidents had aspired to stop extremists, North and South, from smashing their party and their Union. Andrew Jackson, father of this Democratic Party statecraft, had appointed three of the five Southern Democrats who ruled the Court in 1857. He had chosen southern moderates who shared his antiabolitionist, antidisunionist position.

Dred Scott's judges, with one exception, demonstrated that President Jackson and his Jacksonian successors had nominated the right antiextremists. The exception, Virginia's Peter Daniel, often threatened disunion. When would the North, asked Daniel in 1851, "ever produce anything that is good and decent?"[2] If Judge Daniel had lived to see Abraham Lincoln elected president (the jurist died six months earlier), he probably would have been that Virginia rarity: instantly for secession.

In 1860–61, all Peter Daniel's southern compatriots on the 1857 Supreme Court would disown knee-jerk disunionism. Although Alabama's John A. Campbell would eventually go along with his Confederate state, he opposed secession so heatedly, sought reunion so ardently, and resigned from the Supreme Court so tardily that his hometown, Mobile, ousted him. Unlike Campbell, Georgia's James Wayne, Tennessee's John Catron, and Maryland's Taney (all Jackson's own appointees) would never secede, from the nation or from the Civil War bench. Wayne and Catron would pay for their perpetual unionism. Their Confederate states would confiscate personal property worth tens of thousands of dollars from both alleged traitors. The town of Nashville would expel Catron, without his ailing wife. Mr. Justice Catron would answer in Andrew Jackson's (and James Buchanan's) spirit: "I have to punish treason, and I will."[3]

According to these eternally pro-Union judges, Yankee holier-than-thous undermined not only Americans' right to own (slave) property but also the requirement of republican Union: that white men must treat each other as equals. Peter Daniel's unionist colleagues agreed with their fire-eating compatriot that the South's condescending critics assume "an insulting exclusiveness or superiority" and denounce us for "a degraded inequality or inferiority." These do-gooders say "in effect to the Southern man, Avaunt! You are not my equal and hence are to be excluded" from America's territories.[4] "We must not suffer ourselves to be depreciated or degraded," added John Campbell. Looking "our calumniators proudly in the face," we must "maintain . . . our equal rank."[5]

Dred Scott's southern judges saw northern calumniators as traitors to black men's no less than white men's interests. Outside meddlers did not know the slaveholding world they would tear apart. They did not understand that a delicate institution must be changed slowly. They did not fathom, wrote Roger B. Taney, that "a general and sudden emancipation would be absolute ruin to the negroes."[6] Yankee fanatics did not comprehend, Alabama's Campbell added, that "we cannot afford to be the subjects of experiment." As blacks' guardians, Southerners "must not yield the destinies of this people to . . . visionaries and unreasonable fanatics; and least of all, to [Yankee] politicians not responsible" to us.[7]

But these judicial guardians, while slapping outsiders' hands off insiders' governance, wondered about unlimited governance over slaves. Peter Daniel, the closest to a defender of black slavery, hired white house servants. James Wayne, whose lowcountry Georgia family had owned huge plantations, retained only nine slaves. He allowed this remnant to hire themselves out, beyond his willpower. So too, John Catron violated his state's law by permitting some of his Tennessee slaves to live like free blacks. John Campbell and Roger B. Taney gradually manumitted almost all their slaves. None of his liberated slaves, wrote the Border South's Chief Justice Taney *at the time of his so-called Dred Scott Decision,* "have disappointed my expectations. . . . They were worthy of freedom; and knew how to use it."[8]

Alabama's John Campbell and Georgia's James Wayne took heresy beyond the Border South's Taney and the Middle South's Catron. The Lower South's two judges wanted public reform to complement private manumissions. In an 1847 *Southern Quarterly Review* article, John Campbell promoted "an important alteration of our law. . . . The connection of husband and wife, and of parent and child are sacred in a Christian community, and should be rendered secure in the laws of a Christian state." Creditors, by "frequently" dividing slave families after bankruptcies, had "greatly deteriorated" blacks' "character and deprived the [master-slave] relation of some of its patriarchal nature."

Campbell urged patriarchs to provide "more abundant supplies of moral and religious instruction" for slaves and "an increase of their mental cultivation." He wished southern legislators to limit masters' use of slave property "as a basis of credit," when pursuing loans, and to forbid the severing of a slave family, "at the pursuit of a creditor." Our laws and practices, declared Justice Campbell, "formed when the blacks were fresh from their native Africa, with gross appetites and brutal habits," have become "the worn out maxims of other ages." We must instead embrace "progress and amelioration," with laws that "steadily and systematically . . . prove that the negro race is susceptible of great improvement."[9]

That plea for state curbs on absolute power made sense from Campbell, an ex-slaveholder who had renounced all power over his slaves. But how could the same man slap down federal curbs on slaveholders' property rights and thus keep the Dred Scotts enslaved? Because none of the Court's southern judges doubted that a *state* could abolish or regulate the institution. All of them deplored *federal* jurisdiction over slavery (and deplored the disunion that overreaching Yankees would provoke). That federal/state distinction underlies the second stunning public document written by Dred Scott's allegedly proslavery judges: Georgia's James Wayne's 1854 address to the American Colonization Society's annual meeting in Washington, D.C.

Heretically (for a Deep South slaveholder), Wayne urged that the federal government, to promote the general welfare, constitutionally could and ethically should send free blacks back to Africa. Southern ultras had long denounced that argument. If the general welfare required blacks to be removed, couldn't the general government free more blacks to remove? Wayne answered that Congress could not seize property but could remove property that owners had renounced. No one called removing free Indians to reservations unconstitutional, Wayne pointed out. Why was removing freed slaves to Africa constitutionally different?!

But would not colonization unconstitutionally promote abolition by encouraging more slaveowners to free more blacks? Here Wayne, in the southern manner, covered heretical opinion with verbal fudge. After achieving federal colonization of free blacks, he would "leave the future to that Providence which guides us in mercy." He mercifully guessed that "the Southwestern States," although now containing few free blacks, "may soon free" larger numbers, "if governments financed removal" of freedmen. That would be the right reform—"reformation with a slow foot."

But about slavery's immorality, the edgy heretic removed the fudge. The Georgia jurist decried proslavery Southerners' "mistaken" religious views as but "pretext for reducing men into slavery." The mistake aside, "communal safety may not permit the dissolution of the evil *all at once*. Rights grow up under such a system, which cannot with justice be *suddenly* taken away." Any "*untimely* interference," especially when "attempted by an *external* intervention, *out of the sovereignty where it exists*," can only produce "bloodshed, massacre, and war." But if judges used "our National Constitution" to keep outsiders' hands off the South, Wayne agreed with Campbell, no longer defensive insiders might slowly meet their philanthropic obligations (emphasis mine).[10]

In 1857, Judge Wayne's four southern colleagues perhaps disagreed with his procolonization philanthropy, although Chief Justice Taney had previously called black removal the right road toward black emancipation. So too, Campbell's compatriots perhaps disagreed with his plea that state governments must curtail masters' absolute power, although these jurists had curtailed their own unlimited dominion. Still, all these Southern Democrats shared the Wayne-Campbell premises. All fretted about perpetual absolute power. All despised outside critics. All believed that presumptuous interference would drive rightfully angry southern egalitarians out of the Union and beyond reconsideration of slavery's permanence. By prohibiting federal tampering with slaveholder property rights, they aspired to build a cocoon of safety, sanity, and serenity, for the Union, for slaveholders' self-respect, and perhaps for the South's own incremental trimming of unlimited power.

– 2 –

Because the majority of these southern jurists hoped to perpetuate the Union, not to perpetuate unreformed slavery, the Court's private deliberations in the so-called Dred Scott Case featured a suspenseful debate about whether to uphold Scott's master in a monumental or unmonumental manner. The Dred Scott Case must be termed so-called because it involved not just Dred Scott's plea for liberty but also his wife's parallel suit and the enslaved couple's mutual plea for their two daughters' freedom. In that famous fabricated title, the Dred Scott Case, Americans turned a slave family into an invisible institution.[11]

Mr. and Mrs. Scott's very visible two cases turned on whether slaves' temporary residence on free terrain ended their bondage, even if they subsequently resided on enslaved terrain. Dred Scott, a Missouri slave, had lived with his master in Illinois, a free state, and in the Wisconsin and Minnesota territories, congressionally liberated Louisiana Purchase areas. In Wisconsin Territory, Scott had met and married his enslaved wife, Harriet.

After the Scotts' master returned his slaves to enslaved Missouri, the black husband and wife separately sued for the family's freedom. After the Missouri Supreme Court decided against the Scott family, the Scotts appealed to the U.S. Supreme Court. In mid-February 1857, after twice hearing public arguments, the nine judges privately conferred on their key question: not whether to keep the Scotts enslaved but whether to rule against the slaves on sweeping or limited grounds.

To keep the Scotts enslaved on the most sweeping grounds, the Court could decree that neither Congress nor a state could constitutionally abolish slave property. To issue a less sweeping but still monumental judgment, the Court could prohibit only *congressional* authority to emancipate in the territories.

To decide for the master on nonmonumental grounds, the jurists could throw out the Scotts' suits, without a word about congressional or state power to emancipate. They could simply uphold the Missouri Supreme Court's verdict, sanctioning the state legislature's decree that once serviles returned to Missouri, temporary residence elsewhere did not free them. The Court could also evade a decision on territorial questions by ruling that no black, including the Scotts, could sue in U.S. courts.

The debate in Supreme Court chambers swiftly eliminated two options and made a third problematic. Only the two northern non-Democrats (one already a Republican and the other soon to become one) wished to free the Scotts. None of the seven Democrats wished to deny that a *state* could emancipate slaves. Since only three jurists definitely denied that blacks could sue in federal courts, a potential majority on this matter remains problematical.[12]

A majority could be surely mustered for only two positions. The Court could advance to an historic judgment: that Congress could not emancipate slaves in national territories. Or the judges could retreat to the less historic position: that Missouri's laws legitimately denied the Scotts' claim to freedom once they had returned from freed territory. All five Southern Democrats preferred the epic decision against congressional emancipation in federal territories. Both Northern Democrats sought the nonepic evasion of that explosive question.

Those numbers could have precluded debate. Had the Court's majority, those five Southern Democrats, wished only to perpetuate slavery's alleged blessings by barring congressional territorial emancipation, they could have issued the ban without listening to the Yankees. But since these Southerners wished to tranquilize the Union by settling the slavery issue, they trembled to issue a solely southern judgment. They feared that if five southern jurists barred congressional territorial emancipation and four northern jurists vehemently dissented, the Union would be further convulsed, not forever calmed.

That fear forced the five Southerners to keep talking to those four Yankees. Perhaps at least the two Northern Democrats would see an historic destiny to save the Union. Then, the five Southerners reasoned, an asectional majority of seven, not a sectional majority of five, could forbid Congress from abolishing slavery in the territories. That apparently more asectional verdict, these southern unionists dreamed, would win national acceptance.

The two Northern Democrats, Samuel Nelson of New York and Robert Grier of Pennsylvania, remained blind to the vision. The two Yankees considered a decision against congressional authority to abolish territorial slavery wildly provocative. They favored a discrete decision: Missouri law must prevail over Missouri slaves.

Sometime during the first week of the debate in chambers, and perhaps on the first day, February 14, 1857, the Southerners surrendered. The seven

Democrats appointed New York's Nelson to write a decision that perpetuated the Scotts' enslavement solely by upholding Missouri law. Thus blacks' right to sue in federal courts, the constitutionality of the Missouri Compromise, and the constitutionality of state or of congressional emancipations—all those explosive issues would be evaded.

But the five Southerners squirmed at their evasion. Although the Court had ostensibly decided, judges kept on furiously talking in chambers, while Samuel Nelson kept on remorselessly writing an evasively narrow decision. As the Southerners became more strident, the Northerners became more irritated. In the increasingly incriminating atmosphere, Southerners thought they heard (maybe did hear) the two northern non-Democrats threaten to write dissenting opinions, upholding congressional abolition in the national territories. If those Yankees laid down antisouthern pronouncements, Southerners, being Southerners, had to issue answers. So the five Southern Democrats edged toward repudiating their surrender, defying the two Northern Democrats, and issuing an exclusively southern verdict against congressional power to emancipate. But they fretted again that a purely southern decision, with no northern jurist concurring, would provoke a northern scream about a Slave Power conspiracy—a reaction fatal to the Union.

– 3 –

At this grim moment, when all options looked dark, Tennessee's John Catron endeavored to bring an unprecedented light into the chambers. Although the two Northern Democrats found southern jurists unconvincing, maybe they would heed their fellow Northern Democrat, the president-elect. If James Buchanan would urge his fellow Pennsylvanian Democrat, Robert Grier, to concur with the southern majority, maybe that stubborn Northern Democrat—and then maybe New York's even more stubborn Samuel Nelson—would cave in.

On February 3, 1857, Buchanan had written the Tennessee unionist, discreetly asking about only the *timing* of the Court's decision. Would the verdict be handed down before his Inaugural Address on March 4? Catron, the most street-smart of the judges and a Buchanan intimate, read between the lines. He discerned that his former roommate's discreet inquiry about timing clothed an indiscreet inquiry about substance. The president-elect wanted to know not only when but *if* the Court would save the new administration and the Union from the issue of slavery in the territories. Would the judges thankfully declare the explosive subject out of bounds, for everyone who exerted federal power? Then the shattering question need never bother President Buchanan.

Catron sent less welcome news. On February 6 and more informatively on February 10, the jurist wrote Buchanan that the Scott cases would be decided February 14, when the judges met in conference. (Actually, February 14 turned out to be not the day of decision but the beginning of over a week of deliberation.) Probably, Catron added, you will not "be helped by the decision in preparing your Inaugural." On "the question of power" over slavery in the territories, the verdict "will settle *nothing*, in my present opinion" (emphasis his).[13]

On February 19, Catron sent more promising but still not definitive news, along with a plea for the president-elect's aid in the still incomplete deliberations. "I *think* you may safely say" in your Inaugural, Catron now calculated, that the "high and independent" Supreme Court will "settle & decide a controversy which has so long and uselessly agitated the country." Catron predicted that the two northern non-Democratic judges would force the "majority of my brethren . . . to this point" (emphasis mine).

Buchanan, as calculating a political operator as his good friend Catron, knew what the judge's "think" meant. The Court's deliberations, while heading the right way, had not yet quite arrived at the promised land. That happy but still unfinalized trend gave importance to Catron's unprecedented appeal. "Will you drop [Robert] Grier a line, saying how necessary it is & how good the opportunity is, to settle the question by an affirmative decision of the Supreme Court, the one way or the other?"

Grier would rule the right way on the question of congressional power in the territories, Catron assured Buchanan, if the president-elect's fellow Pennsylvania Democrat could be convinced to rule on the issue at all. Grier "has been persuaded" to avoid the subject sheerly "for the sake of repose." The president-elect need not indiscreetly beg a Supreme Court justice to decide a particular way. Buchanan need only discreetly suggest that the Court would best serve the Union's "repose" by deciding the matter "one way or the other."

Buchanan, having received Catron's appeal on Friday morning, had his plea in Grier's mailbox the next Monday morning. The haste indicated the president-elect's urgency about the Court's looming decision. Buchanan knew that the issue of slavery in the territories could shatter his fragile administration, party, and nation. How sublime if slavery agitation could be thrown forever out of Congress, not by a transient gag rule this time but by a permanent Supreme Court decree. The Court, Buchanan believed, could best achieve the Union's "repose" not Grier's way, by ducking Supreme Court controversy, but the southern jurists' way, by removing the controversy forever from national deliberations.

Grier answered within hours. With the president-elect calling, a patriot (himself no independent thinker) felt compelled to fall in line. While a controversial decision might not serve the Union's "repose," the mistake, if so it turned out to be, was now Buchanan's. With his election, the president-elect arguably had won the right to make such purely political calls.

Before your letter arrived, Grier wrote Buchanan, Samuel "Nelson & myselff" had refused "to commit ourselves" on "the power of Congress & the validity of the [Missouri] compromise act." Even now, "perhaps Nelson will remain neutral." But Grier had shown Buchanan's letter to Wayne and Taney, and the three of them all now "concur in your view" that "an expression of the opinion of the Court on this troublesome question" would be desirable.

Furthermore, Grier regretted, the Court's two non-Democratic jurists seemed determined to issue their opinion, reaffirming congressional power to emancipate territorial slaves. So the Southern Democrats "feel compelled to express their opinions" against that power. If the Southerners compelled Nelson and himself to decide on the Missouri Compromise, Grier added, the "line of division in the court" must not be between sections. So to secure a nonsectional decision, Grier, Taney, and Wayne, after their conversation about Buchanan's letter, had agreed to go for denying Congress power to cleanse U.S. territories of slavery and to "use our endeavors to get brothers Daniel & Campbell & Catron to do the same."

By the same mail, Buchanan received another letter from Catron, written before Grier's conversion, urging again that Grier must be "*speeded.*" Then, Catron predicted, "whatever you wish may be accomplished." Buchanan, having just read Grier's promise to speed ahead, apparently assumed that all his wishes would now be swiftly accomplished.[14]

The Court speedily accomplished somewhat less than Buchanan wished. Either the day or the day after Grier received Buchanan's letter, the converted Pennsylvania Democrat and the five Southern Democrats met, without Nelson, the unconverted New York Democrat, being told of the meeting.[15] The rump caucus voted, on Wayne's motion, that Taney, not Nelson, should speak for the majority. Taney should stress that the Constitution forbade Congress from abolishing slavery in U.S. territories.

Buchanan had hoped for a further decision: that since Congress could not emancipate, the body created by Congress, a territorial legislature, also could not emancipate. That addendum, Buchanan prayed, would sweep slavery controversies out of the territories as well as out of Congress. What bliss, for a vulnerable president-elect who dreaded further slavery controversies over bloody Kansas Territory.

Chief Justice Taney shared that view of bliss. He eventually placed a few sentences, denying territorial legislatures' right to emancipate, in his final opinion. But the rest of the Court had stopped, at least in chambers, where the Grier-Taney-Wayne conference had planned—with a six-judge majority against congressional emancipation in the territories. Meanwhile, the by-passed Nelson remained silent on this issue, while concurring with the verdict against the Scotts on his own grounds: Missouri law.

Eight days after privately receiving glad tidings from Grier and Catron, the new president publicly declared, in his Inaugural Address, that the question of congressional power over slavery in the territories "legitimately belongs to the Supreme Court of the United States." The Court, Buchanan mistakenly asserted, would also "speedily and finally" settle the question of a territorial legislature's power over slavery. To the Court's "decision, . . . whatever this may be," Buchanan added, I, "in common with all good citizens, . . . shall cheerfully submit."

– 4 –

Two days later came the decision. Most northern citizens did not cheerfully submit. Nor did the northern populace cheerfully believe Buchanan's claim to no prior knowledge of what the Court would decree. But while the president's dissimulation failed to produce public belief in his noninvolvement, the question remains whether Buchanan's secret intervention produced the Supreme Court's verdict. Or to ask the question another way, without the president-elect's intrusion, would the Court have chosen its less provocative option: reaffirming Missouri's law?

The possibility that Buchanan turned around the Court's Scott deliberations hangs on whether Robert Grier would have bowed to the Southern Democrats' desire, without the president-elect's note to his fellow Pennsylvanian, and on whether the southern judges would have declared congressional emancipation unconstitutional, without the Yankee jurist's acquiescence. If Buchanan had not intervened, Grier might have eventually caved in anyway. Alternatively, the southern jurists might have at last dared to move ahead uncomfortably without him. As Grier and Catron both told Buchanan, the recriminations flying around chambers, especially between the Southern Democrats and the northern non-Democrats, were driving the Court in those directions, before the president-elect intervened.

But once before, the Southerners had reluctantly pulled back, when they could not budge Grier or Nelson. Perhaps, after failing again to move Grier, they would have retreated again. If the southern jurists had again decided that going it alone would be counterproductive, perhaps the two northern non-Democrats would have agreed to remain silent on congressional power to emancipate, in exchange for southern agreement to fall silent, too. All those "perhapses" add up to an important possibility. Without James Buchanan's intervention, there might have been no Dred Scott Decision, as contemporaries came to mislabel, to know, and to hate it.

If Buchanan had defended instead of hidden his perhaps crucial clandestine visit to the judicial domain, he probably would have claimed, as would latter-day presidents, that grave national crises require unprecedented presidential responses, even if such actions momentarily transcend the Founding Fathers' checks and balances. Buchanan probably would have added that the long-sought panacea of Supreme Court intervention, to silence a question that would otherwise tear apart the republic, legitimated an executive to step on the Court's terrain, this one time only.

But the unprecedented intervention could be no more legitimate than the assumption that produced it. Buchanan's assumption that the Republican Party would surrender congressional abolition of slavery in the territories, because a Court controlled by Southern Democrats ordered the surrender, was the wildest illusion. So too, the five Southern Democratic jurists' assumption that they could make the issue of slavery in the territories magically vanish, if only one or two Northern Democratic jurists would join their magic act, was delusive fantasy. The lesson of the so-called Dred Scott Decision was neither that proslavery perpetualists decreed nor that fire-eating judges paid no heed to Union. Instead, a distressed imminent president and six jurists shared admiration of perpetual Union, qualms about perpetual and unreformed absolute power, and anxiety about northern antislavery attacks, southern fury, and a crashing republic. They thus developed frantic illusions about a paper panacea that could only feed the sectional flames.

– 5 –

The Court's mode of announcing its verdict was almost as inflammatory as the substance. The provoking appearance of foul play involved not only Buchanan's dissimulation in his Inaugural Address, not only his whispering with Chief Justice Roger B. Taney on the inauguration stand, but also Taney's bearing and logic, when he read the Court's decision on March 6, 1857. The judges had chosen the wrong messenger to convince the nation that their message was right.

The choice of Taney was a natural mistake. The well-known chief justice had led the Court for over a quarter century. Ever since John Marshall's day, the chief justice had written and read the Court's most important decisions. This verdict compared in importance with any of Marshall's.

But however logical the choice of Taney, the Marylander plastered a sour sectional face over a decision meant to produce national smiles. The chief justice, almost eighty years old at this, his most important moment, felt, looked, and acted like a fossil, angry to be discarded. His wife was dead, his children busy, most of his friends perished. The lonely survivor, once a rich lawyer, now struggled on a judge's salary. And for all his sacrifices, had he received the nation's adoration, as had his predecessor, the sainted John Marshall? No way. He was widely respected but seldom cherished. Some Washingtonians even dismissed the fading relic as just another Southerner. That meant to many Yankees just another tyrant.

To the bitter Taney, that distortion epitomized all the misunderstanding lately heaped on his sagging shoulders. He had given his life and fortune to the cause of limited constitutional government. He had freed his slaves from his unlimited governance. And holier-than-thous had the presumption to call *him* tyrant!

With his so-called Dred Scott Decision, the antique threw back every scrap of his scorn. Less than two weeks separated the long-wavering Court's final, late February turnaround and Taney's March 6 announcement. During this overly short period, the aging and feeble chief justice often felt too exhausted to write. When his energy fitfully returned, he scribbled frantically, still drafting up to the minute before he delivered his oral opinion, still redrafting his written opinion for weeks thereafter.

That harried, hurried process of composition left no possibility that this angry Southerner's arguments would calmly distill the Court majority's

Chief Justice Roger B. Taney (left), looking to Northerners and to Harriet and Dred Scott (above) as grimly tyrannical as his proslavery Supreme Court decree sounded. But Taney actually harbored the Maryland unionist and manumission inclinations that worried proslavery perpetualists. Courtesy of *Frank Leslie's Illustrated Newspaper* (the Scotts) and the National Archives (Taney).

opinions. As a result, Taney announced as the Court's judgment some verdicts that no Court majority had accepted in chambers (for example, that blacks could not be citizens). His rationales also made some of the Court majority squirm. So the other southern judges felt compelled to write so-called concurring opinions, which on some points implicitly dissented. Thus the public heard not one pronouncement but clashing voices. The result: doubt about what had been decreed, and why.

Taney also dubiously justified his most critical proposition. To argue that Congress could never abolish slavery in the territories, Taney issued an unnecessarily problematic interpretation of the "due process" words in the U.S. Constitution's Fifth Amendment. That amendment decrees that "no person" shall be deprived of "life, liberty, and property, without due process of law." As abolitionists interpreted this wording, Congress could give black "persons" their "liberty," even if slaveholders thereby were deprived of "property," so long as lawmakers followed a "due process of law." In his dismissive answer, Taney insisted, with scant explanation, that no congressional "process of law" could validate any seizure of any property, for any purpose whatsoever.[16]

Judge Peter Daniel, in his concurring argument, developed the more discreet position that Taney barely mentioned. Slavery, Daniel urged, because the only form of property explicitly mentioned in the Constitution (witness the fugitive slave clause), retained special protections against congressional seizure. But by pushing property protection limitlessly beyond Daniel's limited due process protection, Taney looked all the more to be rationalizing an extremist's prejudice, not defining a majority consensus.

The man who served up this motley argumentative stew looked as distracted as his reasoning. The elderly jurist's skin was slack and sallow, his mouth fixed in a sinister frown, his body wrapped in cloths like a mummy's, his brow shadowed by a descending clump of hair. On March 6, 1857, as the few citizens packed into the tiny Supreme Court chamber strained to hear his words, his voice grew fainter, fainter, then unintelligible. The aged chief seemed the last of some extinct species, squandering his expiring breath in a final defiance of those who dismissed his world as thankfully obsolete.

His reactionary words and his spectral form helped his decision to be misunderstood as fossilized proslavery reaction. But this raging patriarch, still bragging that his own manumitted blacks had proved worthy of freedom, hardly clung to slaves with a death grip. The very great importance of Roger B. Taney was that he could not have flung a more hate-packed decree at the Republicans if he had been a zealot for perpetual enslavement and disunion. So too, the Southerners who made the so-called Dred Scott Decision (and the Border North's president-elect who begged them to save the Union) could not have better greased the nation's slide toward disunion if they had been Slave Power ultras.

In this Supreme Court verdict, as in almost all governmental decisions leading toward the battlefield, the Democratic Party commanded a majority of the decision makers; the South commanded a majority in the party; and southern moderates commanded a majority of the Southerners. These ruling moderate slaveholders always feared that northern extremists would provoke southern extremists to disunion, not least because southern nonultras shared ultras' fury at insulting northern holier-than-thous. So to save the Union, believed many southern foes of disunion, the Union's government must erect walls against provoking meddlers. So too, to hold calm internal debates about reforming slavery, moderates must sustain blockades against inflammatory outsiders. Yet southern moderates' barricades, and especially that mother of all barricades, the so-called Dred Scott Decision, always inspired the same outcry from northern moderates: You can exert foul tyranny over blacks, if you must, but you will not tyrannize over your fellow whites— over *us*.

That was the chorus of Union-smashing voices that shook James Buchanan and his southern Camelot's attempt at a Union-saving administration, but forty-eight hours into its doomed mission. In the late election, the North's Republican majority had said in effect to outraged slaveholders: You are criminally immoral, and we will bar you like lepers from expanding into national territories. Now Dred Scott's southern judges had replied to outraged Republicans: You are criminally foulmouthed, and we hereby ban you from exercising power over slavery in the territories. And at this convulsed moment, with moderates everywhere throwing down gauntlets over who was a pariah, Kansas turmoil swept toward its shattering finale.

CHAPTER 10

The Climactic Kansas Crisis

In 1855, after proslavery Kansas settlers (including one-day settlers) unexpectedly secured an enslaved territory, dreams of an enslaved slave state multiplied. Dreamers knew that if the statehood decision came at the usual time, when 90,000 settlers of all ages, sexes, and colors inhabited a territory, the more numerous Yankees would flood the plains. Then the majority of the maybe 35,000 adult white males would choose a free labor state. But if the strike for statehood came prematurely, say in 1857, Southerners just might be a majority of the maybe 20,000 voters. The 1856–57 campaign for a slave state thus began with Southwide appeals for immediate white male adult migrants.

– 1 –

In 1857, around 5000 newly migrating southern citizens, if added to the 5000 already in Kansas, could match the 10,000 Yankee voters. The 5000 proslavery newcomers could mock every supposed reason why Kansas could never become a slave state. The fact that the North contained millions more whites would become irrelevant. So would the fact that Kansas, at the moment of decision, contained only around 200 slaves and under a hundred slaveholders. Slaves did not vote, and nonslaveholders often voted for slavery.[1] If only one in every 400 voting southern citizens came and brought a proslavery attitude, the unexpected slave territory of 1855 could blossom into a still more unexpected slave state in 1857. Then slaves could safely come.

Emboldened by the surprising possibilities, the South's Kansas devotees ardently sought to attract southern entrepreneurs. The *Charleston Courier* declared that "a negro could . . . sow wheat" in Kansas latitudes "as well as in Tennessee." The *Richmond South* argued that enslaved Missouri, Kentucky, Maryland, Delaware, and most of Virginia and Tennessee all lay "in the same latitude" as Kansas. That Border South latitude, pointed out the *New Orleans Delta*, was "not adjacent to the North Pole."[2]

123

By swarming on the Kansas borderlands, continued pleas for settlers, slaveholders could gain not only profits for themselves but also two new U.S. senators for the South. If a free labor Kansas triumphed, however, the North would gain four senators: Kansas's immediately and Missouri's soon. In 1856–57, prospects for that double defeat mounted. St. Louis free soilers elected Frank Blair, Jr., as their congressman and John Wimer as their mayor.

"Enemy Inside the Walls," warned the *New Orleans Delta*. After the enemy's "cry of 'Free Kansas,'" their "next shout . . . will be 'Free Missouri.'" The *Richmond South* predicted that the "conquest of Missouri . . . will open the way through Kentucky and Tennessee" to "Maryland and Virginia." If Kansas became free soil, concluded the *Richmond Enquirer*, "the very center of the southern column [would] be pierced."[3]

Southern morale would also be pierced. Yankees decry slavery as too barbarous for Kansas, stormed the *Montgomery Advertiser*. We must meet the insult "like men, or shrink from it like cowards." The South "can not flinch," added the *Richmond Enquirer*, except with "the penalty of everlasting disgrace. . . . Every impulse of pride, every instinct of policy, every calculation of policy" demands our "prompt and effective aid to the slaveholders of Kansas." Otherwise, a "multitudinous horde of barbarians from the North" will pervert "Kansas into a free negro state" and leave Missouri "too exhausted . . . to defend its institutions."[4]

Such pleas invaded private mailboxes as well as public newspapers. Slaveholding migrants to Kansas, Alexander Stephens wrote a prominent Georgia judge in early 1857, will "immediately and without doubt double their property." They will also win a referendum in "favor of their institutions." Let slaveholding entrepreneurs realize that "Kansas is the place they should go."[5]

Instead, planters considered the Southwest the place where they should go. Slaveholding entrepreneurs no longer suffered the impoverished 1840s, when they had urged Texas annexation as a safety valve for excess blacks. Now, cotton boomed. Now, excess Texas and Arkansas bottomlands beckoned. Perhaps, as propagandists fantasized, the Kansas hemp fields also offered rich profits. But southwestern cotton magnates preferred a certain killing at their own business in their own latitudes.

The risks of the Kansas latitudes also deterred southwestern investors. "Capital is proverbially timid," wrote Edmund Ruffin, and "of all capital, that in slaves is (for obvious reasons) the most timid." When an entrepreneur could profitably move hundreds of slaves to Texas, hundreds of miles from the nearest incendiary, he would be "mad" to move ten negroes within ten miles of Bleeding Kansas. Or as the *New Orleans Commercial Bulletin* inquired, who would "take negro property" to "such precarious circumstances," when every available slave was "wanted for more profitable labor further South"?[6]

As that inquiry indicated, slaveholding entrepreneurs' desire for fresh land was *not* much involved in Kansas, *the* territorial controversy of the 1850s. The Kansas controversy had major practical political roots, especially the drive to save Missouri and to secure two more U.S. senators. But a fierce border battleground as a practical spot for investments in slaves—well, almost all slaveholding capitalists preferred secure virgin land in the safer U.S. tropics.

– 2 –

With slavery too risky on cooler and warring plains, slaveholders preferred to send poor men to wage rich men's fight. Let us finance nonslaveholding yeomen's migration to Kansas, went the most viable southern strategy of 1856–57. Then our hired settlers will secure the state and buttress Missouri.

Jefferson Buford of Eufalia, Alabama, led this rescue effort. A gentle scholar when not raising his fists, this combative ex-Whig lawyer displayed no softness when defying either insulting Yankees or compromising Democrats. Similar contempt for the Democracy drove many ex-Whigs in the so-called Eufalia Regency toward disunion. In contrast, Buford's contempt for Democratic Party posturing drew him toward Alabama State's Rights Whigs, to expose Democrats as proslavery phonies.

Like most ex–Deep South Whigs in the crude Southwest but unlike Virginia's refined Thomas Flournoy, Alabama foes of the Democracy relished crass electioneering. The Bufords used coarse oratory to teach rednecks that the Democratic Party offered gaudily wrapped proslavery presents, empty inside. Democrats' supposedly proslavery Kansas-Nebraska Act, urged these ex-Whigs, illustrated the emptiness. Southern Democrats' alleged victory for slave labor could yield only a free labor Kansas. But ex–Southern Whigs, prayed Jefferson Buford, could push southern settlers toward Kansas and reap genuine proslavery coin.

Jefferson Buford put his money where his rhetoric directed his auditors. He sold forty slaves. He pledged three-fourths of the proceeds to take hundreds of nonslaveholders to Kansas. Before departing for the plains in April 1856, he toured the Lower South, begging more rich men to send more poor men to the territory.

Buford called Kansas our "great outpost." He warned that "a people who will not defend their outposts have always succumbed to the invader." Once abolitionist invaders had Missouri "surrounded on three sides, they would begin their assaults on her, and as fast as one State gave way, attack another." So southern patriots would storm Kansas, "unless *public virtue has decayed,* and therefore we have become unequal to the successful defense of our rights."

As befitted a rich white who financed poor whites, Buford claimed to defend not so much property in black men as "the supremacy of the white race." "Rich and poor" whites, he declared, equally dreaded sinking "to the level of the Ethiopian" and clasping "him in the fond embrace of political and social equality and fraternity." Was he "mad for periling my estate," to "transmit conservative institutions to my children?" Or were "you mad," for eagerly gathering "wealth" so "that free negro drones may have . . . it"?[7]

On April 6, 1856, 500 citizens of Montgomery, Alabama, gave Buford's 415 supposed madmen their sendoff.[8] A band of Negro (!) musicians played. Each Bufordite received a Bible. The holy soldiers elected Buford their general. Then they paraded onto the steamship *Messenger*, waving banners conveying Buford's twin messages: "The Supremacy of the White Race" and "Kansas the Outpost." These latest ruffians arrived in Kansas on May 2, 1856, in time for the bloodiest Kansas wars. Buford bought horses for his warriors. They gained renown as members of Buford's Cavalry. Buford here proved a point that the Civil War would reinforce: Southern poor men would kill Yankees to keep blacks ground under.

Still, Buford's poor men had come to farm rather than to kill. Here the cavalier on horseback let the commoners down. Buford offered to pay for half his troops' homesteads but not for their hotels while they searched for land. The homeless poor men knew neither where to search for farms nor how to finance the farming. Buford knew little about the locale of the best land and cared less. Within a few weeks, he dashed off for less grimy adventures in Washington. His dusty cavalrymen mostly milled around, then also left. Buford returned for a few weeks in late 1856, then departed for good in early 1857. He left behind half of his financial stake and few Alabamians.

Buford's debacle showed what the South most lacked, to place an additional 5000 voters in Kansas: not the potential (nonslaveholding) settlers, not the potential (slaveholders') funds, but the remotest equivalent of northern entrepreneurial acumen at settling newcomers, after they arrived. Buford badly played the other section's game. Northern capitalists excelled at buying cheap land, luring free laborers to it, financing yeomen's purchases, and reaping a developer's fortune. Eli Thayer's New England Emigrant Aid Society exuded these northern entrepreneurial skills. Thayerites bought prime Kansas land and guided settlers to the holdings.

In contrast, Buford's southern development skills involved forcing slaves to work virgin acres. Like a cavalier instead of like a free labor capitalist, he brought the soldiers and a pocket full of cash ($5000 of which was promptly stolen). But he possessed no land for the recruits and no patience to find it for them. The verdict on Jefferson Buford (how he would have loathed this one): if only the southern-style knight had been a northern-style materialist.

Yet this misplaced knight still partially triumphed. Buford widened southern perceptions of potential Kansas warriors. Before Buford's Cavalry, Lower South leaders had seen Kansas as Missourians' game to win or lose and slaveholders as the necessary players. After Buford, and after few slaveholders would risk slave laborers in Kansas, southern communities beyond Buford's stepped up, to finance nonslaveholders' migration to the plains.

Mississippi's U.S. Senator Albert Gallatin Brown epitomized the change. "When the Kansas bill passed," Brown correctly recalled, "very few of us expected Kansas to become a slave state, and very few of us cared much whether it did." But in November 1855, after Missourians had made Kansas a slave territory, Brown believed that in twelve months Buford-style migrants could establish "a slave colony in Kansas." Then, "all the abolitionists in the Union could not expel" the heroes. Mississippi should accordingly tax each slaveholder one dollar per slave owned. The state should send 300 slaveless yeomen to Kansas and buy each a slave. If all fifteen southern states adopted the plan, 4500 poor migrants, each given a slave and a ticket to Kansas, would do all "the necessary voting, and if need be, the fighting."[9]

Both Alabama and Mississippi legislators turned down proposals such as Brown's. The lawmakers preferred that private citizens finance private migrants. The decision illustrated a southern-style repugnance for governmental intervention in citizens' affairs. Brown's rejection also avoided a southern-style debacle, for the Mississippi senator's quixoticism outdid Jefferson Buford's. Imagine, 4500 poor whites, each with a gun in the back of one black, all scrounging around for forty acres to farm, with not one dollar to buy one acre heaven knows where in Kansas.

With neither Brown's nor Buford's organized (sort of) scheme working, the task fell to villages' unsynchronized efforts. Itinerant publicists brought Buford's message to many Lower South towns in early 1856. Major Warren D. Wilkes, for example, spoke in twenty South Carolina villages in thirty nights in 1856, urging each spot to send five migrants. The contest, declared Wilkes, marks "the turning point in the destinies of Slavery and Abolitionism. . . . If the North secures Kansas," neighboring slaveholding states "will gradually become abolitionized."[10]

The potential Kansas turning point impelled Lower South and Virginia associations toward fundraising. The results were impressive, not in number of dollars raised (maybe $50,000 in all of the South) but in numbers of fundraisers and contributors (well over a thousand Southrons, including prominent communal leaders). Jefferson Buford received almost $14,000 in contributions, mostly in dribbles of ten dollars here, fifty dollars there. The Charleston Kansas Aid Association's $100 dribbles added up to $9000, financing seventy migrants. Savannah, Georgia, enthusiasts raised $1114 in a day; Aberdeen, Mississippi, patriots $4000 in a week. South Carolina Congressman Robert F. W. Allston sent $100 to Buford and another $100 to a South Carolina migrant, for we must save "our beautiful country" from "the ravages of the black race and amalgamation with the savages."[11] Or as Judge Samuel J. Gholson claimed during his fifteen-day blitz of fifteen northern Mississippi hamlets, "If the abolitionists accomplish their hellish designs, many" whites "will be compelled to take the place of the slaves." The white mudsills will "be found blacking boots, or with long aprons around their necks, waiting on the tables of their superiors."[12]

Having doled out contributions and dispatched poor men to save all white men, communities eagerly consumed their mercenaries' news. Joshua Halbert, for example, reported back to Aberdeen, Mississippi, that "northern fanatics sought to make" Kansas "the grand depot for all their underground railroads." If "emissaries . . . steal" their slaves, Missourians will ship blacks southward by the "thousands, 'till none are left."[13]

While folks back home became vicariously involved in saving the Kansas outpost, uncoordinated communities became as ineffective as Buford's misplaced cavalry. Once in Kansas, poor folk, including Halbert, wondered where to go. Only 500 of them were on the ground. The 500 wonderers did not balloon to 5000, nor did enough twenty-five dollar contributions swell to $2500, nor could the unorganized South organize the migrants. South Carolina's John Townsend lamented a paralyzing "want of *hopefulness* in the cause." People told him that "they would give" more, "but the North is richer than we, and can give more, and drive us from the ground."[14]

There spoke a touchy folk, swift to battle to save interests and reputation but not fully engaged in this uncertain enterprise. By early 1857, Southerners, having failed to settle those extra 5000 voters in Kansas, hunted for a scapegoat for the failure.

– 3 –

The scapegoat arrived in Kansas in the form of President Buchanan's appointed territorial governor, Robert J. Walker. The new governor bore the president's hopes, similar to Buchanan's prayers when intervening in Dred Scott deliberations. The president and his new governor would oust the territorial issue from national contention, this time not by congressional surrender to a Supreme Court decision but by settlers' surrender to the climate.

The weather, thought the borderland Northerner in the White House, would slowly drain slavery southward from Kansas' Border South zone, just as climate had slowly drained the dwindling system from his own Border North zone. Let Kansas voters, in a referendum on their constitution, ratify geography's decree against slavery in their northerly area. Then sweating slaveholders and shivering Yankees could celebrate a Union based on tolerance of weather impelled differences.

By sending Robert Walker to be Kansas territorial governor, Buchanan chose the ideal messenger to spread this isothermal message. Walker, the native Pennsylvanian who had been a U.S. senator from Mississippi, had used his Border North mentality to become a southern hero during the annexation of Texas. Back in the economically depressed 1840s, Southerners had applauded when Walker championed Texas as an escape valve for superfluous black barbarians, who would all supposedly drain from North America down to South America.[15]

On May 27, 1857, Walker's inaugural address as Kansas territorial governor reasserted his previously popular viewpoint. Proslavery voters could afford to reject a proslavery constitution, declared this tiny, sickly agitator, for the healthy location of slavery could "no more be controlled by the legislation of man than any other moral or physical law of the Almighty." God's "isothermal line, . . . regulating climate, labor and productions, and, as a consequence profit and loss," barred slavery from Kansas.[16]

Southerners' instant outrage at this isothermal outburst revealed how profoundly the South had changed, not only since Robert Walker had pronounced the theory in Texas times but also since the first half of the nineteenth century. The slow drain of slavery from cooler to hotter climes had been an American constant longer than Walker's auditors could remember. The institution had crept downward, sinking altogether out of Buchanan's Border North, partly out of the Border South, and someday, Walker prayed, out of America.

In the 1830s, Virginia's Thomas Dew, in a supposed defense of permanent slavery, had called the Old Dominion "too far North" for perpetual servitude. At midcentury, Border South abolitionists, including Cassius Clay and Frank Blair, Jr., had applied Dew's too far North verdict to their states. They had claimed that a cooler climate, with a nudge from the legislature, could emancipate Kentucky and Missouri from slavery (and blacks). Walker in the 1840s, by declaring that an annexed Texas would draw down North American slaves and then send slaves to slavocracies south of the United States, had simply given new voice to an old theory—to a supposedly inevitable isothermal process that had drawn multiple cheers from Jefferson and from the Upper South apologists who perpetuated his tradition.[17]

In the 1850s, Southern Democrats no longer cheered. Robert Walker's latest isothermal eruption represented just the step backward, into the bad old Jeffersonian apologies and acceptance of slavery's doom northward, that the South's Kansas struggle sought to repudiate. The *Charleston Mercury* called Walker "the greatest Abolitionist in Kansas." The *Jackson Mississippian* labeled him a "treacherous appointee." Men angrily recalled, wrote Francis Pickens of South Carolina, that Walker had wished to use Texas annexation to "redeem . . . the South from slavery." Now, the governor would use his isothermal theory to reconcile slaveholders to the surrender of Kansas and of the whole Border South.[18]

Privately, Walker, having surrendered his temporary status as southern resident, conceded that he hoped to reconcile Southerners to the surrender of slavery everywhere. In his inaugural address, he bragged to Buchanan, he had "reintroduced the Negro theory of my old Texas letter, and reopened the true safety valve of abolition"—the diffusion of blacks to areas south of America. He furthermore hoped, Walker whispered, that the diffusion of blacks to Africa "on a large scale" would hasten U.S. abolition.[19]

That private confession confirmed that Walker's public position could no longer be southern orthodoxy. 1857 was not 1844. Now, Southerners prospered. Now, they needed more slaves, not a safety valve for excess slaves. Now, Missourians battled to stop border slaves from draining to the deeper South. By now endorsing the isothermal impossibility of slavery in Kansas (and therefore in the entire Border South), Walker in effect advised Southerners not to come rescue Kansas's (or Missouri's) allegedly unsalvageable slavery. That pronouncement led to a great hue and cry that Walker had caused too few whites to come. The South had found its scapegoat for its own failure to bring the proslavery voters.

– 4 –

Most Southern Democrats protested still more angrily against Robert Walker's version of Popular Sovereignty theory, also announced in his inaugural. All Democrats, North and South, affirmed Popular Sovereignty's basic premise: that local settlers, not far-off congressmen, must decide whether to allow slavery in their territory. Before Walker's speech, Democrats' only Popular Sovereignty division had concerned *when* local voters could decide to abolish slavery. Southerners thought that settlers could not abolish the institution until the moment before the territory became a state. Northerners retorted that local voters could abolish slavery anytime, including when the first settlers entered a territory.

Robert Walker's inaugural address raised another, previously undetected controversial aspect of Popular Sovereignty: not only when but *how*? How must local settlers decide about slavery, when they adopted their constitution? One possibility: After the people selected delegates to a constitutional convention, the people's convention could make the final decision. Another possibility: After the people's convention decided, the people had to reaffirm their representatives' decision in a popular referendum.

Both choices would follow American precedent. When the people of an American state made a constitution, a convention, elected by the people, drafted a fundamental text. Then the state's convention customarily decided whether the populace must reratify the constitution that their convention delegates had ratified.

During the aristocratic Founding Fathers' years, the people's conventions had ratified, without the people reratifying. Of the original thirteen colonies, only the Massachusetts convention had submitted its state constitution to the people for reratification. Moreover, only state conventions had ratified the U.S. Constitution. In the nineteenth century, however, as a more popular, less elitist version of republicanism took hold, the people's delegates to the state conventions customarily decided that the people must reratify, in a popular referendum on the convention's constitution.

Except in the South. As of 1858, the people in all but one of the northern states, but in only seven of the fifteen southern states, had reratified their convention's constitutions. The slave-based section, more prone to denounce direct popular rule as mob rule, more often insisted that the popular will must be filtered through their representatives' decisions, in constitution making no less than in lawmaking. Northern fanatics' Jacobinical notion that the people must reratify their delegates' ratification, declared the *Charleston Courier,* exemplified Yankee infatuation with "wild democracy and mere numerical ascendancy."[20]

Kansas proslavery zealots' last chance to save a proslavery commonwealth depended on scuttling wild democracy, alias the northern theory that the people must reratify their own convention's ratification of a state constitution. In 1855, one-day Kansans had elected proslavery legislators for only a two-year term. In the October 1857 election, Kansas's now more numerous free soilers figured to win the territorial legislature. So in February 1857, the expiring proslavery legislature called a popular convention, charged with writing a constitution for a state before a free laborers' territorial legislature could convene. Popular elections for delegates would take place on June 15 for a mid-September convention. The people's state convention, after writing and ratifying a constitution, would decide whether to submit its handiwork back to the people for reratification. If by some subterfuge, proslavery Kansans won a convention majority but the proslavery convention had to send the proslavery constitution back to primarily antislavery settlers for reratification, the Kansas popular majority would have a (probably fatal) second chance to kill the institution.

The Yankee president had no desire to kill slavery in Kansas. James Buchanan only craved escape from a (probably fatal) national controversy over whether Kansans wished slavery to live or die. He prayed for a Kansas popular referendum that would preclude congressional dispute over Kansans' wishes.

So before Robert Walker left for Kansas and for months thereafter, Buchanan reiterated the northern slant on Popular Sovereignty. He urged any Kansas convention to submit its constitution to the Kansas people for final approval. Robert Walker, in his inaugural address, transcended mere urging. He declared that the convention *must* resubmit the constitution to "all the actual residents of Kansas." Otherwise, "the constitution will be and ought to be rejected by Congress."

Walker's ultimatum inflated the stakes in the Kansas struggle. More was now at issue than continued Kansas bondage for 200 slaves, more even than the southern boon of a sixteenth slave state, more even than antislavery danger to embattled Missouri. By dictating to a sovereign state convention, this federal agent threatened the very core of state's rights ideology and thus slaveholders' final line of defense.

The threatened state's rights principle transcended whether the federal government possessed power over this or that, whether over tariffs or whatever. The issue involved whether any mere government possessed the slightest authority over the supreme American sovereign, a people's state convention, when that absolute authority engaged in the highest American act, writing and consenting to a constitution. The sacred state's rights distinction between all-powerful state constitution makers and potentially powerless federal agents slammed the door against federal antislavery or any other alleged federal tyranny. A state convention could withdraw its consent from any government. Then no governmental inferior could coerce the departing superior.

Walker's ultimatum, coming from a mere government agent, would instead dictate to an almighty sovereign convention, and on the principle of how it could make constitutions! From Walker's proposed enslavement of the Kansas convention could follow future enslavement of secession conventions.

The president, only a mere federal agent just like Walker, could deny a sovereign state convention's right to withdraw its consent to the U.S. Constitution.

The southern politics of loyalty precluded surrender of this ultimate state's rights principle. In the Lower South especially, seething ex-Whigs remained at large, ready to pounce on their Democratic Party tormentors' slightest tendency to ease off southern insistence. Thus any true blue Southerner, screamed ex-Whigs' Lower South newspapers, must affirm the sovereign Kansas convention's sole right to decide how to write and ratify its constitution. Otherwise, the phony prosouthern party would plead guilty of treason to slavery.[21]

A few Lower South and more Middle South Buchanan supporters still dared to stand up for Governor Walker, including the *New Orleans Picayune,* the *Richmond Enquirer,* and Virginia's Governor Henry Wise. But other respected voices worried Buchanan's southern Directory. Howell Cobb had hailed "our friend and kinsman" Lucius Q. C. Lamar's imminent election to Congress, for "I shall have some good friends in the next House."[22] But Lamar, writing Cobb as "a friend whose heart will be true to you till its latest throb," warned that "dear as you are to me, I would have to cling to principles," if Cobb clung to "Walker's shameless abandonment of our right." Lamar could not "entertain the thought that *you* would oppose the admission of a slave state, merely because her constitution was not submitted to the people." The people's sovereign convention, declared Cobb's southern friend, must decide such matters, not a federal agent trespassing on forbidden ground. That opinion "pervades the whole mass of the Democracy here."[23]

Cobb's reply demonstrated how profoundly the slavery and state's rights issues now endangered the Union. The secretary of the treasury was too proud of his immersion in the Lamar clan, thanks to wife Mary Ann, and too entangled in southern postulates, thanks to his huge slaveholding interests, to deny his in-law's assumptions. Lucius Lamar was correct, Howell Cobb conceded, that Robert Walker had no right, as a mere federal agent, to present ultimatums to that imminent absolute sovereign, the coming Kansas people's convention.

But the imminent absolutist might be *persuaded,* added Cobb, to hold a popular referendum on the whole constitution. After a definitive postconvention popular referendum on what the settlers desired, Congress would have to accept the indisputable popular voice. But without a popular referendum, congressional disputes over whether the Kansas convention truly represented the Kansas voters would devastate the administration, the party, and the Union. James Buchanan passionately concurred.[24]

Given the overriding importance the president and the supreme member of the Directory placed on a Kansas popular referendum, why would not Cobb insist, Robert Walker style, that a Kansas constitutional convention must authorize that vote? Because this passionate opponent of the expediency of secession, like the vast majority of Southerners, accepted a state's right to secede. The acceptance precluded any right to *insist* on anything when *advising* that final authority, a sovereign state convention. According to the marrow of southern state's rights assumption, the almighty body could decide everything about anything, and especially about how to write and consent to constitutions. Since Cobb could not deny that southern orthodoxy, he could not join that mere federal agent, Governor Walker, in federal ultimatums to an invincible state convention.

– 5 –

In Kansas, the mere agent still pressed his ultimatum. Governor Walker, although an ex–U.S. senator from Mississippi, now acted more like the native Pennsylvanian who had graduated from the University of Pennsylvania and lately had haunted New York City commercial houses. He would defy the southern gospel of a state convention's absolute sovereignty. He would order the allegedly almighty convention to behave. If the delegates disobeyed his command, he would rally Congress to deny Kansas statehood, with, so he said, the president's blessings.

During the nineteen days between Walker's inaugural and the Kansas populace's June 15 selection of convention delegates, the governor also promised to ensure a fair election. But ever since one-day Kansans had fraudulently won control of the first territorial legislature, northern settlers had shunned that government's elections. Instead, free soilers had elected their own government, a shadow regime that met in Topeka. Since free soilers abstained from the other government's elections, fraud could never again defeat them. Since they participated in the Topeka fraud-free elections, Yankees proved that they had many more voters than did Southerners.

Now, free soilers doubted that Governor Walker could stop Southerners' election fraud or force a fraudulent convention to hold a popular referendum on its constitution. So Yankees again stayed home on Election Day. The abstainers enabled the Kansas minority of Southerners to elect every delegate to the Lecompton Convention (so called because it would deliberate in Lecompton, on the Kansas River some forty miles west of the Missouri border).

The Lecompton Constitutional Convention met for three days in mid-September 1857. Then delegates recessed, to observe the October 5–6 election for Kansas Territory's second legislature. This time, northern voters braved the Kansas polls. But as in the first election of territorial legislators, fraud defeated them. In Oxford, for example, containing only six houses near the Missouri boundary, proslavery legislators received 1628 votes (or 271 voters per residence).

Robert Walker investigated. He found that the Oxford election returns consisted of a fifty-foot-long list of names, copied in one man's handwriting from an 1855 Cincinnati directory. The governor threw out the Oxford and other fraudulent returns, thus awarding free soilers control of Kansas's new territorial legislature.[25]

Proslavery delegates to the Lecompton Convention, now the last gasp of the 1855–57 proslavery territorial regime, thus would lose if they submitted a proslavery constitution to the heavily free soil electorate for reratification, particularly if Robert Walker ensured a fair election. Yet if they refused to hold a popular referendum on the state convention's constitution, the national congressional majority, especially if led by the president, might refuse to admit the state to the Union. Then the newly elected free soil territorial legislature would take over Kansas Territory. After two years of guarding slavery in Kansas and thus in Missouri, the Lecompton crowd had little time and scant options left.

– 6 –

When the Lecompton Convention reconvened on October 19, 1857, Howell Cobb and Jacob Thompson sent a special messenger to plead with the supposed unlimited sovereign one last time for a popular referendum on any Lecompton Constitution. The Directory's emissary, Henry L. Martin of Mississippi, a clerk in Thompson's Department of the Interior, delivered a letter from his superior, conceding the absolute sovereign's sole right to decide whether to submit its constitution for popular reratification.

But Martin also delivered Thompson's appeal and an even stronger appeal from Howell Cobb, advising that a popular referendum would be highly expedient in pushing a constitution through Congress. At first, the convention delegates fastened on Thompson's concession that they could refuse all referendums. Rejecting Cobb's and Thompson's advice, conventioneers narrowly voted to send their whole constitution to Congress, with no popular referendum whatsoever.

But then Henry L. Martin's pleading helped bring off a revote and a subsequent 27-25 victory for a compromise, one that had the Directory's agent's blessings. The barely passed bargain sanctioned a popular referendum, scheduled for December 21, on only Article Seven of the proposed Lecompton Constitution. Among that article's many protections of slavery, one attracted all the controversy: that future slaves could be imported into the state.[26]

If a popular majority rejected Article Seven, declared the convention, "slavery shall no longer exist in the State of Kansas, *except* that the right of property *now* in this Territory, shall in no manner be interfered with" (emphasis mine). If voters rejected Article Seven, in other words, the some 200 slaves then in Kansas, but no additional bondsmen, could labor in the state. To supervise the referendum on whether a future enslaved Kansas could contain more than its present 200 slaves and their descendants, the convention appointed its president (and not Governor Walker!).[27]

When news of this partial referendum appeared in the nation's newspapers, predictably different northern and southern responses exploded. Most Northerners (and all Northern Republicans) denounced the December 21 referendum. They pointed out that Kansans could reject neither nonslavery aspects of the constitution nor slavery's continued presence. Moreover, the president of the Lecompton Convention, as supervisor of the referendum voting, could allow fraudulent voters to force future slave imports on the Kansas majority. In every way, Yankees protested, the Lecompton outcome violated the spirit of Popular Sovereignty.

Southerners responded that the Lecompton decision had followed the letter of Popular Sovereignty procedure. The Lecompton Convention delegates had been legitimately elected. True, Yankee voters had been absent. But according to the letter of democratic procedure, as Robert Walker had pointed out in his inaugural address, "absentees are as much bound . . . by the act of the majority of those who do vote, as if they had participated in the election."

After this legitimate Kansas election, continued the southern position, the people's absolutely sovereign convention had the sole right to decide whether to submit the constitution back to the people. The convention had decided to submit the slave importation essence of the slavery issue for popular decision. If Kansas voters rejected future slave imports, they would render the Peculiar Institution almost extinct.

As for the 200 slaves remaining after voters killed slave imports, continued the southern plea, the trace of slavery would simply repeat the *northern* example. After the 1787 Northwest Ordinance and after northern states' antislavery laws, slaves on the ground before the edicts remained enslaved. The December 21 Kansas referendum on Article Seven thus allowed voters to affirm or reject the Yankee path to eventual abolition.

– 7 –

Buchanan's southern Directory applauded the Article Seven compromise that Cobb's and Thompson's agent, Henry Martin, had with difficulty helped secure. Howell Cobb cheered that the Kansas voters could decide the most important "question at issue," the future expansion of a minuscule amount of slavery. Thus "the material point has been attained." The Directory pled that case to the president. Buchanan swiftly proclaimed the coming December 21 referendum on Article Seven a legitimate test of Popular Sovereignty.[28]

Supposedly, he thereby blundered. Actually, he no longer had a choice. After Buchanan's favorite members of the Directory had sent their own agent to the Kansas convention, and after that agent had triumphantly secured a compromise, and after the Directory had hailed the bargain as an acceptable referendum, the president would have lost most of his cabinet and most of his Lower South supporters if he had rejected his own men's handiwork.

If the president blundered, the mismanagement came before the Directory's agent entered the Lecompton Convention. If Buchanan had insisted, to Robert Walker's delight and Howell Cobb's horror, that any agent of his executive department must *require* the convention to hold a full popular referendum, not *advise* it to do so, he would have intervened before his window of opportunity slammed shut. Why did he instead allow the Directory's agent to restrict intervention to mere advice?

Posterity only definitively knows that in mid-July, six weeks after Robert Walker's late May inaugural but three months before the Directory's mid-October advice to the Lecompton Convention, Buchanan wrote Walker that "on the question of submitting the constitution to the *bona fide* resident settlers, I am willing to stand or fall."[29] But a privately expressed willingness to stand remains a long stride short of a publicly expressed pledge to deliver. After his mid-July letter to Walker, Buchanan neither strode toward insistence nor aborted the Directory's stride toward advice. Again, why?

Speculations must begin with the fact that during the long hot summer of 1857, as before and after, the president practically lived for conversations about politics, particularly with his favorite cronies. Buchanan and Howell Cobb especially loved to exchange the latest political gossip. Thus Buchanan almost surely knew that Cobb went out of his way, and as far as the secretary felt he could go, toward defending Walker's inaugural against southern critics such as Lucius Lamar. The president also almost surely knew that Cobb, like almost all Lower South Democrats, considered a federal ultimatum to a limitless state sovereign absolutely forbidden. So Buchanan almost surely knew that as a mere federal agent dictating to an alleged absolute sovereign, he would alienate (and perhaps lose) Cobb—the vital center of that alliance between Border Northerners and moderate Southerners that the president considered perpetual Union's best prayer. The president furthermore almost surely knew that Cobb and Thompson sent Henry Martin as a merely persuading agent, and Buchanan almost surely (and likely reluctantly and silently) concurred in their strategy of noninsistence.

The president may also have seen insufficient practical reason to defy Cobb. Cutting past theories about state's rights, the practical issue was whether imperious ultimatums or respectful advice would best stir a stubborn Kansas convention. Buchanan, a master at cutting deals in country lawsuits and political crises, may well have found Cobb more strategically plausible. Walker's imperious dictations could force proud Kansans' backs to go straight on up. In contrast, Cobb's respectful persuasions could lure self-respecting frontiersmen toward accommodations. Moreover, if the administration sought to force the convention's hand, Southerners might rise up against the enslavement of the sovereign.

Buchanan had married his Union-saving mission to Cobb, the most amiable, most conscientious, most powerful, most committed unionist among Lower South Democrats. Like all enduring marriages, this political partnership sometimes required accommodations, especially when one partner felt that a holy principle was at stake. So the president, runs the guess here, knowingly acquiesced in his partner's prayer that the Directory's special envoy to the Lecompton Convention would be sufficiently persuasive.

Buchanan thereby surrendered the initiative to a pack of frontier rowdies, free to heed or ignore Washington's preferences. So might history's path have swerved at least temporarily toward sectional peace if the Buchanan administration's word to the Kansas convention had been *Do,* not *Please do*?

The guess here is that proslavery convention desperadoes would have plotted some way around any administration intervention, whether the intrusion involved advice or insistence. The delegates' passion to save slavery in Kansas (and thus, so they thought, slavery in Missouri) seems too consistent, and a fair referendum on slavery seems too obviously a slaveholders' loser, for a convention surrender without a last proslavery hurrah. So too, Lower South Democrats' opposition to federal coercion of the state sovereign seems too intransient for Buchanan's heavily southern coalition to have survived a presidential ultimatum to the Lecompton Convention.

Yet an alternative guess certainly has its plausibility. A Buchanan ultimatum possibly could have precluded the climactic Lecompton disruption, and Lower South Democrats possibly would have begrudgingly acquiesced. If faced with a presidential insistence, Lecompton desperadoes might have decided that a full popular referendum offered their only (slim) hope of securing a sixteenth slave state. So too, Lower South Democrats might have decided that even a soiled Buchanan administration offered their only hope of regaining slaveholders' national control. If this happier outcome can be deemed plausible, Buchanan's retreat from intervening in the Lecompton Convention proceedings damaged the Union as much as did his advance toward intervening in the Supreme Court's so-called Dred Scott proceeding.[30]

The possibility that a Buchanan ultimatum could have yielded a better Kansas finale, plus the probability that Howell Cobb pushed the president away from Walker's ultimatum, makes the Georgian's state's rights religion especially important. That theory, so directly responsible for restraining Cobb from a federal insistence to a state convention, probably thereby restrained Buchanan, too. The state's rights gospel of sovereignty would soon again demonstrate its power to ensnare southern unionists and thereby to decimate the Union.

– 8 –

Whether or not Buchanan blundered before the Lecompton Convention, afterward he saw only the opportunity to stay the course. The president had to announce his support of the partial referendum swiftly, on the chance he could prod Kansans to the polls on December 21. If the Kansas free soil majority shunned the Lecompton polls, the minority of southern voters would save Article Seven. Then Northern Democrats would have to swallow not just 200 slaves but also a slave-importing state. In contrast, if Yankees in Kansas defeated Article Seven and slave importation on December 21, Northern Democrats would only have to stomach a barely enslaved state (containing only one-tenth of the slaves in barely enslaved Delaware).

Northerners in Kansas deplored the Lecompton Constitution, with or without Article Seven, and they doubted that referendum votes on Article

Seven would be fairly counted. So they shunned the Lecompton polls on December 21. Their absence allowed the southern minority, by a vote of 6266–567, to affirm Article Seven and seek admission to the Union, with constitutional protection for future slaves to join the lonely 200.

On January 4, 1858, the Topeka free soiler crowd held its own referendum on the Lecompton Constitution. Topeka voters chose among the constitution with Article Seven, the constitution without Article Seven, and no constitution at all. No constitution at all secured 10,226 votes to 162 for any Lecompton Constitution. Combining the Lecompton and Topeka tallies, 6428 Kansans voted for the Lecompton Constitution and 10,793 against it.[31]

Stephen A. Douglas did not need this mathematical proof to repudiate the Lecompton referendum. A month and a day before the Topeka crowd thumpingly rejected the Lecompton Constitution, he descended on the White House to denounce the sellout of Popular Sovereignty. No witness recorded the curses exchanged, but the final epithets seem clear enough. Buchanan declared that like President Andrew Jackson, he would destroy any Democratic Party senator who dared to oppose a Democrat's administration. "Mr. President," spat back the senator, "General Jackson is dead."[32]

The insult inaugurated a showdown between two irreconcilable northern warriors. Where Buchanan considered Popular Sovereignty a treasured weapon to keep slavery controversy out of Congress, Douglas considered local self-government itself the treasure. Where Buchanan, a narrowly practical lawyer, demanded that the letter of a legal process be legitimate, Douglas, a charismatic seer, insisted that the spirit of democracy be sustained. Where Buchanan had to have his southern support, Douglas had to have his northern constituents. The Illinois senator, up for reelection in 1858, would be finished as a national politician if he lost at home. He could never win in Illinois if he endorsed Lecompton's desecration of the spirit of Popular Sovereignty.

By consistently refusing to trample on Popular Sovereignty, Douglas served as both the midwife of the Kansas-Nebraska Act and a slayer of its Lecompton fruits. In 1854, Southern Democrats had insisted that Douglas would no longer be Douglas unless he authorized Kansas/Nebraska settlers to decide on their local institutions. In 1857–58, Illinois constituents insisted that Douglas would no longer be Douglas if he allowed the Kansas minority to enslave the majority. If the Lecompton Constitution "is to be forced down our throats," Douglas responded, he would "resist . . . to the last."[33]

Considering all that Buchanan had to resist—Douglas's revolt, the Topeka referendum's proof that most Kansans loathed the Lecompton Constitution, the inclusion of the notorious Article Seven in an already iniquitous democratic swindle (so most Northerners considered everything coming out of Lecompton)—considering in short how tainted was his cause in the North, this powerful political infighter swung a remarkable percentage of Northern Democratic members of the House of Representatives, fully 60 percent, behind the Lecompton Constitution. That topped the percentage of Northern Democratic congressmen that Douglas had rallied behind the Kansas-Nebraska Act, barely over 50 percent. This continued Northern Democratic appeasement of the South illuminated again why the minority South had long controlled the majoritarian republic: The Democratic Party was the nation's majority party, and the South was the party's majority section. Buchanan never forgot that reality. Douglas now defied it.

Unfortunately for Buchanan, Yankees had grown obsessed with stopping the Slave Power minority from ruling the northern majority. Stoppage demanded obliterating the appeasing Northern Democrats. Where eighty-one Northern Democrats had served in the Kansas-Nebraska House, only fifty-three Northern Democrats remained in the Lecompton House. Fifty percent of eighty-one Northern Democrats had been enough to pass the Kansas-Nebraska Act by eleven votes, even with thirteen Southern Whigs voting no. In contrast, 60 percent of fifty-three Northern Democrats could approve the Lecompton Constitution only if all but one Southerner voted yes.

Southern congressmen ardently sought this unanimity. They displayed none of the half effort that had crippled attempts to pour nonslaveholders into Kansas. Failures such as Buford's had demonstrated Southerners' scant ability at free labor migrating ventures and at uniting migrants from scattered communities. But when Southerners massed in Washington, D.C., and faced Yankee insulters, they could better forge the necessary united front.

"I am nothing like as well satisfied here, as I was in Richmond," first-term congressman (and future Virginia governor) John Letcher privately wrote. "In Richmond," we were "personally attached to each other, however divided we were politically." But in Congress, we are "thrown into association with people . . . for whom we care not" and who "care as little for us." Worse, "many of them are bitterly prejudiced against us, and our institutions."[34]

As Howell Cobb's brother, Thomas R. R. Cobb, described the bitter prejudices that spawned divided packs of congressional warriors, Southerners' "contempt" for northern maligners bred our "overbearing conduct," which in turn bred "a rancorous hatred of the South. . . . Vast numbers" of Northerners "believe us to be Tyrants. . . . To believe us humane & just would grate not only on their prejudices but on their pride." We must proudly scream back that we will not be treated as inferiors.[35]

In 1856, proud screaming had provoked the Brooks-Sumner mugging. In 1858, a bloodless clash, more comic than tragic, demonstrated that consuming hatreds had become no laughing matter. Near midnight on February 4, 1858, exhausted members of the House of Representatives tensely debated the Lecompton Constitution. Galusha M. Grow, a Pennsylvania free soiler, trenched on the Democratic Party's side of the aisle. Laurence Keitt, the South Carolina ultra who had blocked John Crittenden from stopping Preston Brooks's swings of the gutta cane, lay sprawled over two seats, one shoe off. "Go back to your side of the House, you Black Republican puppy," snarled Keitt. Grow retorted that a white man could stand where he pleased, "and no nigger driver is going to come up from his plantation and crack his whip about my ears."

South Carolina's slave driver responded that we'd see about that, as soon as "I put on my shoe on." Keitt fastened the buckle. He charged. He grasped Grow's throat. Then he strode away (unlike Preston Brooks!).

"You can't come from your slave plantation and expect to apply the lash to me," squealed Grow. Keitt seized the Yankee's throat again. Others dove into the melee. The two dozen combatants included two huge men, Barksdale of Mississippi and Washburne of Illinois. Washburne's awkward blow sent Barksdale's wig flying. The Mississippian's heretofore unsuspected hairpiece disappeared amidst trampling feet. Calmer sorts separated the fighters, with Barksdale's toupee the only casualty and the Mississippian sputtering about his shame.[36]

The shaming felt grievous. The Grow/Keitt comedy epitomized the power of self-respect and self-esteem to cleave lawmakers, whatever the practicalities at stake. The vocabulary of Grow and Keitt—Black Republican puppy, nigger driver, Keep your despotic hands off a white man, I'll go wherever I want in freedom's chamber—all these words bespoke a national schism over more than whether Kansans could enslave 200 blacks and over more than whether slaveholders, to protect slavery, could dictate to white majorities. Two packs of white men fought over who were really republicans, really equals, really Christians. On character assassination, the South could *almost* unite.

Thus did the Lecompton finale illuminate how minuscule minorities' initial concerns ballooned into unmanageable majoritarian crises. The tiny fraction of Missouri slaveholders who lived near the Kansas border, comprising a tinier fraction of the South and a still tinier fraction of the Union, had demanded their chance to protect the southern hinterlands. Southerners in Congress (unlike potential settlers in the countryside) flew to the aid of their fighting outpost, both in the Kansas-Nebraska Act and in the Lecompton proceedings. Both times, Northerners loathed the southern minority for demanding that the white majorities, whether in Kansas or in Congress, kowtow to Slave Power tyrants. Southerners loathed Northerners for calling them tyrants. The mutual loathing had helped doom one national party, imperil the other, and threaten the minority's control over majoritarian Union. That control would snap over Lecompton unless almost every southern House member rose against the Yankee majority.

– 9 –

Enslaved Kansas lost all hope for a saving southern unanimity on March 23, 1858, when the Senate voted 33–25 to admit Kansas to the Union under the Lecompton Constitution.[37] While the South triumphed, two Upper South ex-Whigs, John Bell of Tennessee and John Crittenden of Kentucky, voted against Lecompton. An equivalent percentage of Upper South ex-Whig congressmen, by following these two anti-Lecompton senatorial leaders when the House voted a week hence, would doom slaveholders' proposed sixteenth state.

On April 1, the House in effect rejected the Lecompton Constitution, 120–112.[38] The victors included all Northern Republicans, 40 percent of Northern Democrats, and the pivotal killers, six Upper South ex-Whigs. The South had almost pulled off the necessary unanimity. All Southern Democrats, all Lower South congressmen, and all but one of the Middle South congressmen (an ex-Whig) massed behind Lecompton. But a fatal five of the eight Border South ex-Whig congressmen emulated John Bell's and John Crittenden's anti-Lecompton example.

Southerners had never before lost on a major slavery issue. This time, their Border South Achilles' heel failed them. "None of the" deserters, noted the *Charleston Mercury*, "are from the Cotton-growing states. All represent States where slavery may be gradually and safely abolished without ruin. . . . The unsoundness of these states on the slavery question killed Lecompton."[39]

The John Crittendens and John Bells declared themselves perfectly "sound." They plausibly argued that Southern Democrats damaged slavery and Union by pushing Northern Democrats over the edge. Better to accept inevitable defeat and contain the damage, thought Crittenden, Bell, and the five allegedly disloyal House members. The *Charleston Mercury* correctly saw another reason for the Border South ex-Whigs' uncommon southern disposition: "We believe that . . . between the Union and the institution," these sensibly asouthern Southerners "would not hesitate to choose the former."[40]

That diagnosis of southern disunity discounted the South's remarkable coming together throughout the Lecompton crisis. Southerner after Southerner had swallowed doubts that Kansas was worth the turmoil. Time after time, they had voted the South's way, proving themselves true blue to their own folk. "I stood out to the last against it," Congressmen Guy M. Bryan of Texas wrote his brother, then "said, '*because* the South votes aye, I vote aye.' "[41]

Ninety-four percent of southern U.S. House members voted aye in the Kansas crunch. So too, whatever Davy Atchison's worry about slavery's staying power in Missouri (the concern that had first sparked this four disastrous years of Kansas turmoil), Atchison's supporters overwhelmingly prevailed except in Missouri's cities. And so too, whatever Howell Cobb's wish that proslavery Kansans would compromise a little, such southern unionists accepted disunionists' uncompromising theory of a state convention's absolute sovereignty. That acceptance crippled the administration's best unionist strategy for blocking the Lecompton Convention's disruptions. To like effect, Dred Scott's moderate judges accepted southern extremists' theory of slaveholders' property rights. That acceptance propelled a Union-smashing Supreme Court decision. This culture had a unity problem?!

Yes. True, the minority South long prevailed in the Union and long lasted on Civil War battlefields partly because a proud, touchy culture largely massed against outsiders. But some softness weakened the culture's northern edges; the Kansas turmoil had started as a way to harden the hinterlands; and those very outposts had rallied insufficiently in the climactic House vote on the Lecompton Constitution. Precisely those peripheral areas would put slavery most at risk if Southern Republicans, emboldened by federal patronage, attacked from inside the exposed hinterlands.

Border South ex-Whigs' anti-Lecompton votes, when contrasted with Lower South ex-Whigs' pro-Lecompton pressures, indicated again that the more extreme northern and southern Souths were different worlds, generating different politics. In the Kansas affair, the Lower South's Whiggish political brawlers, including Jefferson Buford and all the politicians who stuck it to the Democrats over Robert Walker's inaugural address, stood for arousing proslavery zealotry. In the Lecompton climax, however, Border South Whiggish compromisers stood for soothing the Union. So a fraction of the peripheral hinterlands had deserted the core of the South in the climactic struggle within the Union. That result would be repeated on Civil War battlefields.

– 10 –

After Lecompton's defeat, the losers sought to place a face-saving mask over their fiasco. Two Democrats, Indiana's William English and Georgia's Alexander Stephens, championed the disguise—the so-called English Bill. The Lecompton Convention had asked for an uncommonly large grant of virgin federal land, upon their slave state's admission into the Union. The English Bill offered Kansas voters admission under the Lecompton Constitution, if they would accept 84 percent less land (approximately the land grant normally given to new states). If voters rejected this normal land grant (and the Lecompton Constitution), Kansas could not enter the Union until the territory possessed a more normal new state population (about three times more people than inhabited Kansas in 1858).

The English Bill allowed Kansas voters to reject the Lecompton Constitution by seeming to reject only the shriveled land grant. Northern Republicans disdained this subterfuge. So did Stephen A. Douglas, the South's newest bête noir. But on April 30, the House and Senate passed the face-saving compromise. On August 30, Kansas voters rejected the shrunken land grant (and the Lecompton Constitution), 11,812–1926. Kansas would remain a territory until after the Lower South seceded.[42]

After the cosmetics came the postmortems. To a huge majority of Northerners, spreading beyond Republicans to anti-Lecompton Douglas Democrats, Congress had barely turned back a gigantic Slave Power Conspiracy to bend white men's majoritarianism to slavemasters' dictatorial needs, first in Kansas and then in Congress. The almost victorious supposed swindle, atop the Dred Scott supposed fraud, showed that white men must put down the southern-dominated Democracy, once and for all. Almost all Yankees still repudiated an antislavery intervention in the South. But a bipartisan Yankee surge meant to sweep over Washington, to ensure that a Slave Power minority never again enslaved white majorities.

When James Buchanan took the oath of office, the ninety-two Northern

Republicans already outnumbered the fifty-three Northern Democrats in the House of Representatives. In the congressional elections of 1858, the fifty-three Northern Democrats shrank to thirty-two, twelve of them anti-Lecompton, anti-Buchanan Democrats. Thus the president's northern House backers sank to twenty of 145 Yankees. Worse, voters flushed away Buchananites in the only northern subsection that the Democracy had saved in 1856—the Border North. New Jersey and Illinois voters returned no supporters of Lecompton among their fourteen congressmen. Indiana voters selected only two of eleven, and Buchanan's fellow Pennsylvania citizens but two of twenty-five.

Northern Democrats' only bright spot looked gloomy to Buchanan. In 1858, the president's hated new opponent, Stephen A. Douglas, defeated the Republicans' Abraham Lincoln in the newly elected Illinois state legislature. So the Little Giant stayed in the U.S. Senate. Yet pro-Douglas legislative candidates garnered only 121,090 popular votes, compared to 125,275 for pro-Lincoln candidates. Douglas's victory thus defied the Illinois popular majority—an ironic triumph for a preacher of Popular Sovereignty. But that irony scarcely comforted the president, who suffered the fact that Douglas's defiance of the southern minority and the Buchanan administration had spread throughout the Border North. How, then, could the Border North's president save the Democratic Party or the Union in 1860?

In the South, Kansas postmortems also could yield dismay. Southerners usually blamed the six Upper South ex-Whigs or Stephen A. Douglas for the loss of Kansas. But they occasionally ate their words about Robert Walker's isothermal predictions. A few of them even declared that Kansas and the entire Border South might indeed be too far north for slavery.

C. C. Woolworth, for example, a southern itinerant book dealer, traversed the Kansas-Nebraska-Missouri area during the 1855–58 years. Kansas, he conceded in May 1857, "may commence her history as a slave state. But the tremendous free state majority," he argued, "will immediately change it." The "immense . . . throng of travelers seeking new homes in the Missouri Valley" have also "virtually" settled Missouri's "question of slavery in favor of Emancipation." In "five years, Missouri will be freed" and "Virginia, Kentucky and Tennessee are likely to follow." Woolworth disliked northern abolitionists "as heartily as any Southron can." But "the law of political economy . . . ultimately will manage" the question, "in spite of politicians," in spite "of justice and humanity."[43]

Woolworth's demographic determinism, like Walker's geographic determinism, may have been correct. Slaveholders may have faced impersonal doom immediately in Kansas, soon in the Border South, and eventually in the whole South, however much they railed against their fate. Since southern *unionists* dominated the Kansas and Dred Scott affairs, and since the likes of Howell Cobb and Roger B. Taney ironically hastened disunion, these slaveholders did bear the aspect of pygmies, defying gigantic forces that they only made more destructive.

The mass of Southerners cheered such defiances. They staged one of America's most colorful histories because they remained aggressive defenders, determined to go out with a splash if they went out at all. After the Kansas failure, only a tiny minority of them whined, in the spirit of Woolworth and Walker, that climate or anything else trapped them. Rather, they sought better escapes from history's traps.

Thus Kansas frustrations encouraged a rising campaign to reopen the African slave trade. Many imported Africans, so southern ultras dreamed, could correct all slaveholder weaknesses. More slaves could be sent to some future Kansas, to seize a slaveholding empire. Fewer slaves would have to be drained from the Border South, to develop the Lower South.

The Kansas debacle also spurred a widening disunion movement. Kansas proslavery warriors had shrewdly scheduled the statehood showdown before northern numbers became overwhelming. In that spirit, disunionists prayed that an early secessionist showdown could barricade the South in a southern nation, before Southern Republicans surged over the borderlands.

A less extreme strategy could turn Walker's isothermics to the South's advantage. Instead of defying the weather northward, the *New Orleans Louisiana Courier* argued, our "finger of destiny" should point southward. If "half the discussion, time and brain-work that have been wasted" on Kansas had been lavished on "southern progressive enterprise" in Caribbean climes, we would have had "acquisitions a thousand fold more important to the South than Kansas."[44] With slavery still seeping downward in the continent, southern expansion still farther down in the tropics looked ever more enticing.

CHAPTER 11

Caribbean Delusions

In antebellum Southerners' most exotic fantasy, proslavery expansionists would land several dozen or several hundred American freedom fighters on Central or South American shores. The tropical targets would include the New World's two largest slaveholding nations beyond the United States (Cuba and Brazil) plus the nations rimming the Caribbean Sea (Mexico, Nicaragua, Guatemala, Honduras, El Salvador, Costa Rica, and New Granada). The freedom fighters would alert submerged natives to rise up against tyrants. The conquering rebels would then add perfect land for slavery to an expanded Union.

If that plot sounds too wild even for an extravagant southern romance, much of it would entice President John F. Kennedy in 1961. A century before Kennedy's Bay of Pigs disaster in Cuba, southern soldiers of fortune achieved a dozen and more Caribbean landings. The impulse behind these escapades exploded disproportionately from racy New Orleans, itself engaged in a perpetual dance of life and death with the nourishing, punishing Gulf of Mexico waters. The resulting Caribbean carnival cast bizarre light on a Southland once again divided, this time along unfamiliar fault lines.

– 1 –

The most prominent early seeker of American Manifest Destiny, Caribbean style, drew his support not from New Orleans, not even from the South, but from the most cosmopolitan Yankee city. John L. O'Sullivan, a New York newspaper editor and Democratic Party publicist, had an Irish name, two American parents, a European education, and a Cuban brother-in-law. In 1851, the effusive New Yorker furnished the ship *Cleopatra* with guns and several hundred Hungarian and German revolutionaries, to sail to Cuba and seize the island. After federal authorities instead seized the *Cleopatra*, O'Sullivan charmed his jury, dotted with Democratic Party expansionists, into

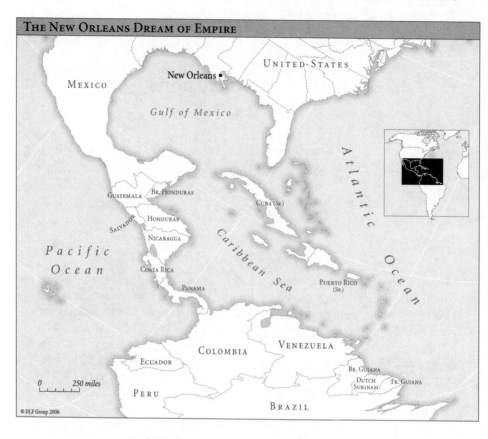

THE NEW ORLEANS DREAM OF EMPIRE

freeing him. As O'Sullivan summed up the nonsectional Manifest Destiny that enabled a Yankee jury to release a New Yorker who schemed for a slave-holding empire, we want "more, more, more!" until "the whole boundless continent is ours."[1]

Yet most Northerners had long since decided that a democratic Manifest Destiny must not mean more, more, more land for undemocratic slavery. No more slaveholder expansion, answered the *New Orleans Commercial Bulletin,* "is almost as senseless as 'No More Sun.' . . . The Negro in a hot clime, where white men can with difficulty labor in the broiling sun, is an agricultural and commercial necessity." So too, Robert Barnwell Rhett urged Northerners to "colonize the colder regions, where the white man can labor advantageously. . . . We, with the African, will possess the rest." Or as Virginia's John Randolph Tucker exclaimed, "When I see the Queen of the Antilles" and "the rich clime of the Amazon valley awaiting the labor of the African under the direction of the intelligent Southerner," I see "a nobler destiny for the South . . . than awaits any other people." No Yankee "shall dictate terms . . . to such a people."[2]

President James Buchanan wished neither North nor South to dictate terms of boundless national acquisitions. This Border Northerner, aspiring to keep Americans above and below Pennsylvania in the same Union, favored American expansion in all directions. As for "the destiny of our race to . . . flow South," President Buchanan told Congress, "nothing can eventually arrest its progress."[3]

Buchanan had furthered American flow southward as James K. Polk's secretary of state in Texas annexation and Mexican War times. Subsequently, as Franklin Pierce's minister to England, Buchanan joined two other American ambassadors in the 1854 Ostend (Belgium) Conference. The trio issued an Ostend Manifesto, calling on the United States to buy Cuba. If Spain would not sell, and if "Cuba in the possession of Spain seriously endanger[s] our internal peace and the existence of our cherished Union," declared the Ostend Manifesto, "every law, human and divine," would justify us "in wresting it from Spain."[4]

President Franklin Pierce favored the purchase but not the threats. Pierce remembered that the Mexican War had aroused Northerners against a war for slaveholders' land. A war with Spain for Cuba's enslaved terrain invited a congressional refusal to appropriate funds. Moreover, an American military takeover of an enslaved island guaranteed a new Wilmot Proviso, reaffirming that new terrain in freedom's nation must be free soil.

The one American territorial acquisition to the south in the 1850s, the Gadsden Purchase of 1854, demonstrated the continued northern repugnance for slaveholder empire. The Gadsden Purchase swallowed only a sliver of Mexico, now part of southern Arizona and New Mexico. Although the fragment could be peacefully acquired, largely for railroad development, the North blocked the purchase until land for slaveholders had been whittled down. The Gadsden Treaty finally squeaked through the Senate only because Southerners reluctantly agreed to reduce the terrain purchased. After his circumscribed Gadsden Purchase, Pierce restricted his quest for Cuba to futile attempts at yet another purchase.

James Buchanan repeated the futility. In 1859, Congress balked at funding even exploratory negotiations for Cuba, much less a purchase. Furthermore, neither Spain nor Cuba would negotiate, much less sell. Imagine the Yankee ambassador to Madrid, scoffed Alexander Stephens, "walking up to the door of the Palace and knocking as a peddler, asking to see the Queen, and upon her coming out, saying in real Yankee style, 'Madame, have you any Islands for sale today?'"[5] Since Yankee presidents could find neither Caribbean sellers nor any northern tolerance for a war for a slaveholder empire, only private adventurers could secure American Manifest Destiny, southern style.

– 2 –

Contemporaries called the adventurers "filibusterers." The word "filibusterer" then connoted not a congressional minority that talked a bill to death but a freebooter who shunned diplomatic talk. The most prominent filibusterers were Narciso López, who organized several private armies to sail toward Cuba in 1849–51; Mississippi's John Quitman, who picked up López's Cuban mantle in 1854–55; Tennessee's William Walker, who briefly captured Nicaragua and legalized slavery there in 1856–57; and George Bickley, the Texas commander of the "Knights of the Golden Circle," who schemed to sic his knights on Mexico in 1860 and instead turned his paramilitary society loose on Texas unionists.[6]

None of these buccaneers hailed from the southern filibuster mecca, New Orleans. López disembarked from New York. Walker's first expedition sailed from San Francisco. All the Caribbean pirates received cash and recruits from these Yankee cities and from sundry southern urban areas. But New Orleans, and especially its merchant community, provided a disproportionate share of these buccaneers' money, recruits, publicity, spirit, and rationale. A visit to Sin City thus offered the best chance to savor the flavor of filibustering's indelicate allure—and to understand why more puritanical southern warriors preferred more refined tastes.[7]

Antebellum New Orleans could be challenging to reach, unless one sped down the Mississippi River. Americans customarily located their port towns on the spot where transportation routes from the interior met ocean routes to the world. New Orleans sprawled over the southernmost point where Mississippi River vessels could land goods from the Ohio, Missouri, and Mississippi river valleys. But this locale, presiding over a great bend in the river (hence the name Crescent City), was still almost a hundred miles above the Gulf. Below the water's curve, where the river turned shallow and meandering, captains of Mississippi's steamboats dared not risk the downstream current. Nor could the Atlantic's sailing brigs profitably depend on the upstream winds.

So to reach New Orleans from the Gulf (and thus from the Atlantic world), the mighty two- or three-masted ocean brigs had to be rendered powerless. At Pilottown down on the Gulf, their sailors had to roll up the sails, hail a tugboat, and trail behind the ugly sea steamer up toward New Orleans. Alternatively, one-masted schooners or small ocean steamers could sail from Mobile, Alabama, through a series of lakes to Lake Pontchartrain, six miles above New Orleans. From the lake, still smaller crafts could crawl through the primitive Old or New Basin canals to New Orleans. But most passengers had to board the Smoky Mary railroad or ride a stagecoach over the Shell Road toward the city.

Tropical vistas compensated for tardy arrivals. Thick groves of orange trees dominated some spots between the lake and New Orleans. Oaks, cottonwoods, and cypresses, drooping with eerie Spanish moss or voluptuous wild vines, often blotted out the sky. But fetid pools of inky water, recalling the deadly jungle around Charleston, mixed a black speck of peril into nature's brighter colors.

Once safely landed in New Orleans, the upriver end of the levee first captured attention. There, belching steamboats and packed flatboats regurgitated their cotton, sugar, and grains. There, blacks and Irishmen struggled to haul bales and hogsheads to warehouses in time for the next vessel to disgorge the next riches.

Downriver from this chaos, dozens of sailless ocean brigs lined the silent end of the levee. There, lifeless hulls awaited their turn to be jammed with exports and towed back to sea, where their sails would be blown back into full might. The informed knew that these ghosts would eventually connect New Orleans to far-off ports. To the uninformed, however, the spooky masts looked like dead trees, barring Mississippi River produce from Atlantic Ocean consumers.

New Orleans advertised more mortal disasters. Human bodies decayed not in invisible graves but in towering mausoleums aboveground. This best-drained urban spot on the lowest Mississippi remained below sea level, too swampy to protect a corpse. The living often remained equally naked of protection. Even if no surging waters filled New Orleans's soup-bowl-like terrain, a visitor too easily became a victim. Fires often blazed out of control. Thugs often roamed over streets strewn with garbage. At night, when faking one way and then diving under the mosquito netting, ahead of the (we now know) yellow-fever-bearing mosquitoes, antebellum visitors (unknowingly) dodged to live another day.

The intersection of gayest life with gravest danger gave New Orleans its decadent frenzy. The most famous uproar transpired at Mardi Gras on Shrove Tuesday, the day before Lent. Crowds of drunken revelers packed the streets, as carnival parades inched toward alcoholic balls. Yet Mardi Gras offered a misleading guide to New Orleans. That celebration came only once a year. Street revelers celebrated every day, including the Lord's Day. New Orleans sensualists paused only briefly on Sunday mornings, to attend churches and hear sin berated. Then sinners hustled toward either the ancient French Quarter or the new American business sector across Canal Street.

The French Quarter (or Vieux Carré) featured a maze of narrow streets, with stucco houses colored in many hues. Many residences displayed a mixture of Spanish and French tastes and exquisite wrought-iron lacy balconies. In contrast, the American sector's short, squat commercial houses bore a sterile sameness, with only an occasional canopy out front.

In either sector, frolic abounded. Slaves in gay turbans shimmied to the beat of congo drums. Sailors in bright costumes eyed fetching quadroons. Natives and tourists could savor the prizefights or the cockfights outside the St. Louis Hotel. Alternatively, open doors beckoned the rowdy off the street, here to gamble, there to whore, everywhere to drink and dance and shoot billiards and roll tenpins.

New Orleans led the South in refined pleasures too. At the Opera House, 150 soldiers sometimes jammed the stage. On a given weekday (or Sunday!), one could catch Edwin Booth playing Shakespeare at the St. Charles, or the piano concert at Odd Fellows Hall, or Jenny Lind singing at the New American Theater. Or one could take dancing lessons from French masters, or watch racehorses skim over the Metairie track, or gape at the six-legged calves and the world's fattest man amidst clowns and elephants at the circus. What city offered more ways to violate the Sabbath?

That question disturbed many southern tourists. The potentially distressed came to New Orleans to see if it was awful. They exclaimed that it was worse. While Georgia's Thomas R. R. Cobb warned Benjamin Palmer's New Orleans Sunday school class that they must resist the "Sodom of our land," martial music blared from the streets, drowning out the naysayer. As Cobb struggled to capture someone's attention, restive youths stared out the window at lads flying kites and at placards announcing a balloon ascension. These "natives," exclaimed Alabama's C. C. Clay, Jr., "are the most unchristian, ungodly, devilish, pleasure-seeking people I have ever seen."[8]

To southern conservatives, the most ungodly aspect of Sin City was not the sinning on the Lord's Day but the desecration of the southern social essence—that society must be a hierarchy, with all sexes, classes, and races fastened in their proper place in proper households. Blacks were supposed to be enslaved. But in New Orleans, 45 percent of blacks were free. Foreign immigrants were supposed to be almost nonexistent. But in the Crescent City, immigrants outnumbered slaves five to one. Irishmen alone outnumbered free and enslaved blacks, taken together.

The Old South's blacks were supposed to monopolize menial labor. But in New Orleans, lower-class whites bottomed out blacks for grunt work. Blacks and whites were not supposed to intermingle sexually. But in Sin City, quadroons were social belles and mulattoes rich tycoons. Whites and blacks were supposed to live in families. But in the Crescent City, much of the population was transient, and many a white enjoyed not a wife but a "placée" (a mulatto or quadroon mistress, for whom he had legally assumed financial responsibility). New Orleans aficionados thought nothing of the spectacle when a married rich man fell to his death from the third floor—of a whorehouse on Sunday.[9]

Crescent City folk became temporary equals in more places than bed. In reception halls of the gigantic (1000 guests each) St. Louis (French Quarter) and St. Charles (American sector) Hotels, millionaires played cards familiarly with plebeians who cared to gamble. In raucous coffeehouses, with mirrors on all four sides and everyone sharing tables with anyone, all glances in all directions connected with strangers.

The promiscuous conglomeration of what other Southerners called opposites dominated New Orleans's most famous place, Jackson Square. Buildings lined three sides of this jewel of the French Quarter. Only the square's southern side, facing the river, was wide open. Opposite the river, on Jackson Square's northern side, the towering St. Louis Cathedral predominated.

Here Creoles, Arcadians, Cajuns, Irishmen, free blacks, slaves, planters, men, women, children—seemingly everyone—kneeled together in what looked to other Southerners very much like promiscuous prayer. As if to contain the disorder, stone government buildings guarded each side of the cathedral.

Down the eastern and western ends of Jackson Square, two long buildings, erected in the 1850s, reestablished unruly mixtures. The buildings, dubbed Madame Pontalba's Apartments after their planner, contained apartments for domestic escape from commercial life, but only on their second floors. Downstairs, the most raucous commercial life in the South exploded from the retail stores onto the streets.

In the center of Jackson Square earthy life, a statute of Andrew Jackson commanded the eye. The hero shone atop a rearing horse, balanced precariously on its rear legs, facing the untamed West and oblivious to lovers embracing below. The whole Jackson Square scene, positioned to look toward the untamable Gulf and exuding relaxed attitudes toward sex, race, class, and liquor, seemed more a Caribbean oasis than anything southern.

Jackson's statue presided over a world mad for Yankee-style consumption. Even the urban high culture of opera and concert was all about consuming. New Orleans led the South in staging spectacles to pay money to experience. But the Crescent City lagged way behind Charleston and other southern centers in producing creative prose or art or colleges. So much money to be spent required fortunes to be made. New Orleans enjoyed a glorious boom in the 1850s. Its population leapt 45 percent in the decade, trailing only Baltimore in the South. The Gulf mecca surpassed the next ten most populated Middle and Lower South urban centers, put together.

Yet despite booming growth, commercial leaders gloomed that the city's economy was poised as precariously as Jackson and his horse. New Orleans titans misunderstood why their boom was fragile. The business community feared that New York, with its new railroads to the West, would soon monopolize the trade of the Upper Mississippi. The worse problem, however, as would be clear by Reconstruction times, was that the connection to the Gulf via towed ocean brigs would soon end, as mounting sandbars turned the river shallower and larger ocean vessels, requiring deeper channels, multiplied. Those antebellum sailless masts, creating an illusion of impassible barriers between city and sea, became not so illusory after all.

But in the 1850s, mercantile leaders, thinking their predicament centered on railroad competition up north, plotted solutions down in the Gulf. Yankees could have the Ohio Valley's trade. New Orleans would seize the Caribbean's commerce. If those Latin nations in and around the Gulf were not quite hierarchically southern, well, neither was half-Caribbean New Orleans. It seemed altogether natural to annex South and Central American New Orleans–style cultures to create New York–style profits—except to those dismissive puritans from other Souths, who found Sin City an antiparadise, even an anti-South.[10]

– 3 –

New Orleans publicists for Caribbean filibusterers celebrated all the southern arguments for an empire to the south. The Crescent City's newspapers urged that the South needed more U.S. senators and representatives, that slaveholders must not be squeezed inside a circle of hostile neighbors, and that a tropical kingdom for the South perfectly served Americans' Manifest Destiny to spread (white men's) democracy. But New Orleans publicists added their special rationale, generating their special filibustering spirit.

The *New Orleans Commercial Bulletin* called "the 'natural advantages' of New Orleans" insufficient. God made the Mississippi River to drain commerce to our city. But man's artifice, the Yankees' railroads, now run from every city on the Atlantic coast to western trading centers on our "great artery," drawing off our "lifeblood commerce."

"New Orleans," added that city's *Delta,* "has approached the crisis of her destiny." Our city, proclaimed the *Courier,* must not become a pathetic metropolis of a "limited and circumscribed" southland. Instead, "the epic march of American nationality" southward must make New Orleans "the great commercial focus for Mexico, Central America, and the western states of South America." Then "the wealth, population, commerce, and importance of this great emporium of the South will be quadrupled."[11]

This main New Orleans case for Caribbean expansion exuded classic urban imperialism. More markets, more trade, more ships, more dominance over a commercial orbit—all this urban boosterism hardly epitomized what most rural planters desired. New Orleans was a sport in the southern world, and so was its mercantile community's infatuation with Gulf imperialism.

The impulse that propelled poor young adventurers to sign up for filibustering excitement also recalled the New Orleans spirit. The followers who sailed with López and Walker (and who pined to sail with Quitman) had as little determination to seize fresh land to farm with slaves as did the city tycoons who financed and publicized their attempted piracies. Filibustering offered the most intoxicating carnival to young urban bloods who ached for exotic flings, before settling down to anything practical.[12]

Beyond New Orleans, southern rage for filibustering most infected the Crescent City's commercial tributaries on the Gulf and lower Mississippi. Mobile, Alabama, and Galveston, Texas, both on the Gulf, as well as Natchez and Memphis, both on the lower Mississippi, joined New Orleans in showering a disproportionate share of rhetoric, cash, and soldiers on Caribbean freebooters. The strip of heavily slaveholding western Tennessee, running from Memphis east to Nashville, also supplied uncommon quantities of adventurers, including William Walker (and Andrew Jackson, who arguably initiated the southwestern filibustering enthusiasm).

But east and north of western Tennessee, and in much of Dixie to the west and south, too, filibustering seemed more like forbidden than nourishing fruit. True, multiple annexations of tropical areas could give Southerners additional senators and representatives. Gulf acquisitions, however, could suck off more southern power than the new land added, economically, morally, or politically.

Economically, sugar lands in a U.S. Caribbean extension could damage the titans of New Orleans's own hinterland, the fabulously successful Louisiana sugar planters. No other American capitalists prospered so outlandishly in the 1850s, thanks not least to a federal protective tariff. That tax on imported sugar protected Louisiana producers from more tropical areas such as Cuba, where more sugar could be cultivated less expensively. If Cuba entered the Union, her sweet staple, no longer taxed as a foreign import, could sweep away the Louisiana sugar land's exquisite white-columned Greek mansions like a Mississippi River flood. The potential "injury to our sugar culture," lamented the *New Orleans Delta,* turned "the minds of many of our planters" toward "gloomy apprehensions."[13]

Morally no less than economically, southerly annexations could make Southerners gloomy. Slaveholders congratulated themselves on maintaining a hierarchical world, with whites and blacks supposedly frozen in their assigned places. But the allegedly semibarbarous Caribbean world, like New Orleans, abounded with freed blacks and racially mixed couples. Many Southerners found the Gulf apples of New Orleans folks' eyes as rotten as Sin City itself. "Let us," intoned Jefferson Davis, "remain unmixed." We must not, warned John Bell, add "twelve million . . . perfectly imbecile" Mexican and Central American citizens.[14]

While many Southerners feared that Caribbean mongrels would poison hierarchical liberty, still more slaveholders worried that tropical acquisitions would emancipate the Upper South. With the exception of Cuba and Brazil, potential Caribbean targets of southern annexation had scant slave populations. To realize their (high) potential to become the Slave South's tropical bastions, annexed countries such as Nicaragua and Mexico would need to draw slaves from somewhere. Most likely, the bondsmen would drain from the less tropical Border and Middle Souths. An accelerated slave drain southward might net the slavocracy counterproductive political arithmetic, with some slave states gained and more lost.

Some famous southern appeals for expansion prayed for just that abolitionizing consequence. In the 1840s, Mississippi's Robert Walker had praised Texas as the safety valve for blacks to flow out of the United States. In the early 1850s, Virginia's Matthew F. Maury hoped that Brazil's Amazon Valley would draw slaves from the American republic. Maury, a renowned naval officer and oceanographer, cheered that American slaves' development of Brazil's "howling wilderness" would be "*the* achievement . . . of the nineteenth century." The triumph would enrich America's commerce and end her slavery and race problems. Brazil would become "the safety valve of this Union."[15]

The oceanographer's beloved cousin, Mary Blackford of Lynchburg, Virginia, blasted Maury for waxing rhapsodic over transferring slavery, the

"greatest of all human wrongs," to a spot where the sin could be better perpetuated. "You call the plan you propose a 'Safety Valve,'" scoffed cousin
Mary. "When was it safety to do wrong?"[16]

Maury answered that already enslaved Brazil, once inside the United
States, would commit fewer wrongs against humanity. United States laws
that barred the overseas slave trade would spare Africans from Brazil's curs-
edly open trade. Nor would a U.S. slave state of Brazil enslave an additional
U.S. black. Instead, my plan will "relieve our blessed Virginia of the curse."
When "the plague comes, my first duty is to get my own family rid of it."
America's first duty required ridding its current terrain of blacks and thus of
"the horrors of that war of races" that is "almost upon us. . . . I may be
wrong," conceded this troubled expansionist. "I may be doing a very wicked
thing by preaching up Amazonia, but I am, dear cousin, as firm in my conviction of right as you are. . . . May God help us both."[17]

Frank Blair, Jr., the South's most politically successful emancipationist,
further publicized Caribbean expansion as a southern antislavery weapon.
Blair, arch enemy of Davy Atchison and a sometimes congressman from St.
Louis, gave a notorious public lecture in Boston in 1858, published as *The
Destiny of the Races.* As Blair explained beforehand to his prominent Maryland father, a fellow detester of the Slave Power, he would illuminate the easy
way to rally nonslaveholders to make America lily-white. "I will take the
ground boldly" that the federal government, by acquiring tropical land, will
"secure the ultimate emancipation of every negro, . . . because the free white
laborers of the South will recognize that the slaves should no longer be allowed to compete with them."[18]

In Boston, Blair explained that racist nonslaveholders, "aroused by the
fact that they have been injured by the competition of slave labor," would
vote for "emancipation when they know that" the blessed reform "includes
[free blacks'] removal." If Central American acquisitions furthered easy removal, the borderland majority would demand deportation of the least tropical South's slaves. Later, the slave drain downward would make the most
tropical South lily-white. Thus would America's southward expansion secure "the inevitable destiny of the races to resume their true zones on this
continent."[19]

In Maryland and Delaware, prominent southern newspapers often sec-
onded Blair's prophecy, while removing the liberator's class-war threats.
Caribbean expansion would indeed whiten and free the Upper South, not because nonslaveholders would vote for lower-class interests but because migrating slaveholders would seek upper-class profits. That very depopulating
prospect made some of slavery's champions chary about Caribbean expansion. The South might have been fortunate to lose California in 1850, conceded the *Richmond Enquirer,* for probably the most northern "slaveholding
states would at once have transferred the bulk of their slave property to the
gold fields of California." So golden California would have extinguished

"slavery in Maryland, Virginia, North Carolina, Tennessee, Kentucky, Missouri and Arkansas. In other words, the South would have gained two senators and lost fourteen."

The Gulf states' demand for Upper South slaves, continued the *Enquirer*, "has already proved a serious drain" to our slave population. If the lush Caribbean augmented the drain, what would be the eventual "political status of Maryland, of Virginia, of the Carolinas, of Tennessee, Kentucky, Missouri, Arkansas—even of the Gulf States themselves?" As the *Jackson Semi-Weekly Mississippian* concluded, slave-exporting states must never "be permitted or induced to rid themselves entirely of slaves."[20]

– 4 –

The most startling reluctance to charge ahead with Caribbean expansion occurred amidst those precipitous chargers, the South Carolinians. Some South Carolina disunionists favored Caribbean expansionism. Laurence Keitt and Robert Barnwell Rhett, for example, advocated southern Manifest Destiny with New Orleans fervor.[21] South Carolina hotheads, however, usually remained cool on Caribbean adventuring, particularly as the Civil War approached.[22] Partly, the disapproval reflected disunionist strategy. Most South Carolina leaders had given up on Union, especially after the Lecompton fiasco. The Democratic Party's Caribbean expansionism fostered false hopes (so South Carolinians thought) for slavery's salvation inside the Union.

More often, the scoffing at Caribbean hopes reflected the state's peculiar identity, isolating South Carolinians from the southern and especially New Orleans crowd, whether the issue was breaking up the Union or breaking out over the Gulf. No other southern area so clung to everything preciously old or so opposed everything suspiciously new. Many South Carolina squires wanted to stay home, perfect eighteenth-century hierarchy, and consolidate the most English culture in the New World. They lamented that instead, mid-nineteenth-century South Carolinians, white and black, left by the ten thousands for new adventures and raw cultures on nouveau frontiers. Cuba and Central America, with their supposedly loose sexual/racial mores and mongrel populations, would allegedly become the most disgusting southern area yet—and the most enticing to entrepreneurs grown tired of wrestling with South Carolina's tired soil. Better to frown down loose New Orleans, avoid promiscuous Cuba, restrain degenerate adventurers, and lead the South backward toward a properly conservative republic.

The very look of Charleston frowned on New Orleans. These two most memorable southern cities both decorated their stucco houses in every color of the rainbow. But Charlestonians lavished ironwork on gates and fences, keeping commoners outside rich men's private spaces. New Orleans residents displayed equally sumptuous ironwork on balconies above the streets, where titans could cheer the intoxicating life down on the avenues.

Austere, genteel Charleston (above), looking more than half a continent removed from earthy, energetic New Orleans (below). Courtesy of the I. N. Phelps Stokes Collection, Miriam and Ira D. Wallach Division of Art, Prints and Photographs, The New York Public Library, Astor, Lenox, and Tilden Foundations (New Orleans) and the South Carolina Historical Society (Charleston).

Again, Charleston's most important public space was the Battery, that outermost tip of the city jutting into the Atlantic, out of sight of ship landings and stores and churches and any but the most lavish houses. Here, declining nonentrepreneurs could gaze toward their imagined (and no longer existent) ideal, stable old eighteenth-century England. New Orleans's wildly different most important public space was Jackson Square, that block of land surrounded by middle-class apartments and hawking shops and government buildings and a cathedral and the din of the levee. Here booming capitalists could gaze toward their cherished hope, raucous Gulf connections.

New Orleans parlors, stuffed with black, heavy Prudent Mallard furniture only yesterday ornately carved, were a world away from Charleston drawing rooms, dotted with brown, delicately carved English Georgian furniture, fifty years or more ancient. So too, nothing published in New Orleans sounded anything like Leonides Spratt's reactionary daily, the *Charleston Standard*. In issue after issue, Spratt broadcast the ideal of standing still. "The strength gained to the institution on the frontier," exclaimed one of Spratt's favorite correspondents, "is lost upon the seaboard. Our districts are becoming depopulated. . . . If we are to fight the great and inevitable contest for slavery upon our present numbers, I want them more compressed. We become weaker by expansion."[23]

John C. Calhoun a decade previously, when opposing the annexation of all of Mexico, had anticipated this foreboding about spreading slavery into polyglot areas. "More than half of the Mexicans are Indians," he had winced, "and the other is composed chiefly of mixed tribes. I protest against such a union as that!" James Gadsden, South Carolina's author of the federal purchase of a slim bit of Mexico, echoed Calhoun's misgivings when protesting against acquiring another inch: "You could not place a more irritating [cancer] on the Body Politic of our Federation than the annexation of Mexico—we have trouble enough with 3 millions of Africans." Or as South Carolina's favorite relic, old Francis Sumter asked, with Cuba annexed, what were we to do with the island's 200,000 free Negroes? "It is not by bread alone that man liveth. We want some stability in our institutions."[24]

The South Carolina case for a stabilizing disunion—and against a destabilizing territorial expansion—echoed in Lewis Ayer's 1855 oration at Whippy Swamp. From that lowcountry platform where so many South Carolina defiances of Yankee-style modernity commenced, Ayer pronounced "a fig" on Northerners, whose "civilization differs so entirely from our own." Any Union-based remedy for defeating northern tyranny resembles "a white-livered surgeon, who continued to apply simple lotions to the gangrene wound," when only "the amputating knife could save life."

The annexation of Cuba, continued Ayer, would be a fetid lotion. Cuban sugar lands and climate, four times more productive than the Louisiana sugar-growing milieu, would force sugar planters on the fertile lower Mississippi to switch to cotton, driving our own cotton cultivators on our *"thin lands . . . from the business."* Furthermore, Cuban tobacco growers, with their superior quality and super abundant yield, would render Upper South tobacco planters obsolete. "Are you ready to give up Virginia, Kentucky, and perhaps Tennessee too, for Cuba? Would that strengthen slavery in the South?" In truth, answered this South Carolina reactionary, the Manifest Destiny chimera has "depraved . . . our true men."[25]

Gulf expansionists answered that superior American Caucasians would end the depravity of Central American mongrels and free blacks. Sometimes New Orleans modernists even called overly raw Central American hustling a good trade for overly refined Virginia sneers. But New Orleans expansionists' contempt for South Carolina's negations overwhelmed their distaste for Upper South naysayers. During the 1850s, South Carolina secessionists and New Orleans imperialists periodically staged memorable newspaper wars. The warfare demonstrated that divisions between the oldest and newest Lower Souths could be as vicious as between the most northern and most southern Souths.

The newspaper war reached its peak in 1856, when the *New Orleans Delta* outdid Charles Sumner in heaping insults on poor Andrew P. Butler. Butler had warned the U.S. Senate against "intermeddling adventurers," alias New Orleans–based filibusterers. The *Delta* shot back that Butler was thankfully "one of a few straggling remnants of the *ancient regime*." It will "be a glad day for the South, and for the century, when the last leaf flutters in the autumnal wind upon that withered and sapless tree." South Carolina's withered extremists had trailed on Texas annexation, trailed on Kansas, trailed on Cuba, and now trailed in the holy fight for "the tropicalization of commerce in . . . Central America." Where "other Southern States were active, practical," and full of "healthy manhood and vigorous chivalry," South Carolina "wrapped itself in the solicitude of its own abstractions."

Witness Andrew Butler, a worthy specimen of these "few dozing pundits," whose "principal political stock in trade appears to be respectability— intense respectability—petrified respectability." To South Carolina's petrified old fogies, New Orleans merchants screamed: Wake up, stop obsessing on disunion, and start working to expand southern territory and markets. Then you will charge ahead with the modern South that you can not lead backward.[26]

This time no Preston Brooks could answer insults aimed at Andrew Butler. Most South Carolina radicals were proud to be petrified fogies, proud of their eighteenth-century respectability, proud to be against the hustle and bustle of America's gross capitalistic expansionism. Their antiexpansionism, together with their suspicion that Caribbean adventuring would damage and deplete the older South, underlines important points about the southern road to disunion. Instead of needing fresh land, southwestern planter capitalists already had too much land to cultivate in the 1850s. The *economic* roots of Caribbean expansionism flourished elsewhere, particularly rankly among the South's most classic capitalists, those New Orleans merchants with the imperialistic dream that gained Caribbean markets would offset lost upper Mississippi markets. Meanwhile, opposition to Gulf expansionism waxed particularly strongly among those old-fashioned South Carolinians, fearful that new fresh land would depopulate tired old acres.

Nor had Kansas adventurism centered on quests for new acres to cultivate with slaves, not with fresh land abundant in the more tropical Southwest, not with border ruffians' most pressing concern being saving Missouri for slaveholders. Nor would secession become any frenzied movement of

southern planters for virgin land to cultivate. The most important secessionists, the South Carolinians, usually thought that nouveau territorial expansionism would weaken their proudly antique state. The most important territorial expansionists, the New Orleans mercantile entrepreneurs, usually
thought that Union would strengthen their ultramodern commercial adventuring. Unfortunately for the filibusterers, such New Orleans mercantile sentiments had too restricted a geographical base in so agrarian a civilization,
with its geographic center far from the Gulf.

– 5 –

The qualms about the Caribbean (and about New Orleans) fed qualms about
the illegality of filibustering. Before U.S. filibusterers could replace foreign
regimes, they had to defy their own nation's Neutrality Laws. Back when the
new American government had striven to be neutral in Europe's Napoleonic
Wars, Congress had passed these laws. The edicts required private individuals to be as neutral as their government. American citizens could not join foreign wars, civil conflicts, or revolutions when the United States remained at
peace with the combatants. Federal officials could seize suspected filibusterers before they sailed from America. If convicted, suspects could be fined up
to $3000 and jailed for up to three years.

In the presecession years, the northern presidents who presided over national laws enforced these edicts enthusiastically. Both Pierce and Buchanan
sought legal purchases in the Caribbean as zealously as they repressed illegal
freebooting from the United States. That even-handed attitude toward expansionism, they believed, best ensured sectional peace. Intolerance for law-
breakers also best preserved a nation worth saving.

Those immune to Gulf fever agreed. Jefferson Davis, for example, expected the United States to control the entire hemisphere "in the remote future." Yet he noted that we had always "obtained territory . . . fairly, honorably, and peaceably." We must be able to "invite the world to scrutinize our
example of representative liberty." Likewise, the *Aberdeen* (Mississippi)
Sunny South demanded that "annexation" be consistent "with a decent respect for the opinions of mankind."[27]

The South's conception of decent national law made the filibusterers'
plight more difficult than the secessionists'. In both cases, the southern majority called extremism inexpedient. But since southern state's rights orthodoxy gave a southern state convention absolute sovereignty, the sovereignty's
secession edict would bring other states to the rescue, if the federal government coerced a seceded state. After legitimate federal enforcement of legitimate neutrality laws, in contrast, filibustering captives enjoyed scant southern
rescuers. Because President Buchanan, according to the Directory, could not
hand ultimatums to Kansas's sovereign Lecompton Convention, the president
could not preclude the Lecompton Constitution. But since the president could

imprison pirates, according to the South's understanding of the law, he could repress Caribbean adventurers.

The president's empowerment became obvious, even the one time that Southerners censored Buchanan for jailing a filibusterer. The Neutrality Laws authorized federal coercion only while a filibusterer remained on U.S. soil or on contiguous ocean areas. In November 1857, William Walker, having slipped out of Mobile and landed his freebooters in Nicaragua, thought he had evaded federal neutrality laws. But U.S. Navy Commodore Hiram Paulding landed in Nicaragua and hauled the freebooters back to America for trial.

President James Buchanan conceded that the arrest on foreign soil was a "grave error." But Buchanan also praised both the Neutrality Laws and Paulding's patriotism. The commodore, after all, had "relieved" the Nicaraguan government from "dreaded invasion."

Lower and Middle South newspapers pounced on Buchanan's qualified apology. Then southern congressmen voted 52–20 in favor of censoring the administration for Paulding's illegal capture of Walker on Nicaraguan soil. But the twenty southern votes for the Buchanan administration's illegal seizure contrasted with the merely six southern votes against the Lecompton Constitution. With 28 percent of southern congressmen favoring even lawless jailing of lawless pirates, Buchanan's several other lawful arrests of buccaneers inspired most Southerners' silent acceptance. Thus did the South pile further difficulties on filibustering extremists.[28]

– 6 –

The Neutrality Laws most deterred John Quitman, the most proslavery of the filibusterers, not least because this native Yankee brought the most pragmatic caution to his southern adventure. Quitman saw scant chance for Caribbean triumph unless he landed a private army of thousands in Cuba. Yet such a massive troop deployment invited federal detection before the soldiers of fortune left U.S. soil.

In contrast, Narciso López's and William Walker's willingness to gamble with smaller bands of invaders allowed them to slip away from the Neutrality Laws' enforcers more easily. Thus Caribbean firing squads, not U.S. judges and presidents, usually presided over their debacles. True, federal officials stopped Narciso López in 1849, before his private armies could pounce on Cuba. But the fiery López tried again in 1850 and yet again in 1851, both times eluding American detention and suffering defeat on Cuban terrain.[29]

López expected that freedom-loving Cubans would rise up against Spanish tyranny the moment some 400 American freedom fighters stepped off the boats. Instead, overwhelming numbers of Spanish soldiers massed, routing López twice and executing him in 1851. As one New Orleans wit summed up such disasters, "I hope we shall send no more missionaries" to the oppressed Cubans, bearing "kettle drums and French horns, to sing to them, in plaintive accents under their drowsy palm-trees,

> Won't you come out tonight,
> *Won't* you come out tonight,
> *Won't* you come out tonight,
> And *fight* by the light of the moon?"[30]

Just as López only once experienced a northern president's enforcement of the Neutrality Laws, so his was only imperfectly a southern crusade. The buccaneer hailed from Venezuela, married a Cuban, and spoke no English. López also little emphasized saving slavery in Cuba, as befit an expedition that raised some of its funds in New York and many of its troops in Ohio.

William Walker, briefly president of Nicaragua in the mid-1850s, can be more easily seen as a planters' partisan and the Neutrality Laws' victim. This native Nashvillian and (sometimes) resident of New Orleans articulated (on occasion) a brilliant slaveholder case for Caribbean expansion. Sounding just like a western Missouri slaveholder, worried that free soil Kansas would imprison the state on a third side, Walker told Georgia planters that the Nicaraguan question involves "whether you will permit yourselves to be hemmed in on the south, as you are already on the north and west." The South must not remain "quiet and idle, while impassable barriers" closed up "the only side left open."[31]

Compared to López, the more southern Walker also suffered the Neutrality Laws more famously, thanks to Hiram Paulding. The U.S. Navy, however, collared Walker only that once, just as it did López. Neither capture discouraged either filibuster. In Walker's most triumphant escape from the Neutrality Laws, he sailed from New Orleans to Nicaragua in 1855 with all of fifty-seven compatriots. But where López, with eight times more soldiers, had crashed against a consolidated Cuban regime, Walker swept through an unconsolidated Nicaragua, torn apart in civil war. By the end of the year, America's "Gray-Eyed Man of Destiny" controlled Nicaragua militarily. In mid-1856, Walker won the Nicaraguan presidential election. By then, some 1200 Americans had joined the conqueror, 600 of them in Walker's army.

They were not enough. Walker swiftly generated enemies after he seized the presidency. In November 1856, his various foes—Costa Ricans, Hondurans, Guatemalans, El Salvadorians, and especially the New York merchant prince Cornelius Vanderbilt—had him on the run. On May 1, 1857, he sailed back to America. The Paulding affair followed six months later. Death by firing squad in Honduras came in another fifteen months.

This latest casualty not of Yankee presidents but of Latin executioners was only occasionally more proslavery than López. William Walker preferred free soil California, his most common American residence in the 1850s, to enslaved New Orleans, where he restively spent the late 1840s. The "Gray-Eyed

Man of Destiny" never held slaves, never farmed, never married, never owned land, never settled in any profession, never stayed in any community.[32]

This anti-type Southerner also looked like an antitype filibusterer. Walker was short, slight, and emaciated, with hands as tiny as a girl's and face as freckled as a boy's. His famous grayish eye had almost an idiot's stare. His long, thin lips, usually sealed shut, occasionally barely parted to emit a drawling southern monotone. One bored visitor, trying to get a rise out of this brawling tyrant, congratulated Walker on his great acquisitions in Central America. "Yeeeees," whispered the "Man of Destiny," "but-----I-----intend-----to-----have-----it-----all-----before-----I-----have-----done." Southern audiences often wondered if this dreamy reclusive would ever have another acre. As one Walker partisan lamented after the hero whispered his plea for support, "He came, he saw, and he got—nothing."[33]

The shy dreamer, always wrapped (even on the battlefield) in an enormous preacher's frock coat, never preached a proslavery syllable in his conquered land or legalized Nicaraguan slavery until his hold on the country had slipped, a year after he seized power. His speeches down south on proslavery Caribbean adventuring came only after his support in New York and San Francisco capitalistic circles had dried up. He first based his filibustering operations in San Francisco, not New Orleans. His first soldiers were failed gold dusters, not enterprising slaveholders. His Nicaraguan army ultimately enrolled as many foreign-born as southern-born troops and more northern-born soldiers. His men were scarcely ever slaveholders, rarely farmers, usually the poor young sports in the cities where capitalistic merchants financed his flings in Nicaragua. When this strange general swore at his enemies, he could sound as fanatical as John Brown of Harpers Ferry fame. But as fanatical on slavery as was John Brown and equally the victim of U.S. capture?! No way, answered most Southerners, who generally considered this curiosity some species from another civilization.

– 7 –

John Quitman, unlike López and Walker, truly was a proslavery partisan and a victim of the Neutrality Laws. Where William Walker wandered from Nashville to Philadelphia to New Orleans to San Francisco during a decade on the move, Quitman migrated from New York to Natchez and stayed there. Where Walker wandered from practicing the law to medicine to journalism to filibustering (and never was a slaveholder), Quitman augmented his lawyer's income with plantations and eventually over 300 slaves. Where Walker never married, Quitman remained wedded to his Mississippi belle, provider of his first plantation. Where Walker was a minor and quasi-antislavery politician in California, Quitman was governor of Mississippi and an early secessionist. Where Walker disdained drinking, gambling, and even talking, Quitman boisterously talked and enthusiastically partied. Where the wispy Walker was less visible than his great frock coat, the imposing Quitman was six feet tall, with flowing curly hair, sweeping mustache, and fancy waistcoats bulging over great girth.[34]

Monmouth, Quitman's famous house in Natchez, epitomized the Mississippi filibusterer's masculine power. To Monmouth's federal brick front, Quitman attached Natchez's prescribed decoration, one of those two-storied white Greek porticoes, emboldened with white columns. But almost uniquely in Natchez, Quitman made Monmouth's columns square, not round. Again almost uniquely in Natchez, Quitman eschewed the lacy decorations that usually softened Georgian bulk. Utterly masculine Monmouth signified that a male colossus here reigned.[35]

Quitman's male charisma came connected to this native Northerner's southern ferocity, a zealotry that exceeded all but a very few native Southerners'. The passion to stop at nothing that would save his adopted paradise made him the South's pivotal secessionist in 1850 and its supreme filibusterer in the mid-1850s. His death in the late 1850s left the ensuing colorful tale of the Southern Confederacy a little paler than it would otherwise have been.

Like all the extremists who ultimately made a revolution, Quitman considered southern moderation the barrier to destiny. He saw southern national party politicians as keepers of slaveholders' prison. In their hunger for national party patronage, politicos dumbed down awareness of the South's dangerous problems and taught the folk to cherish compromised solutions. Like Yancey and all the other ultras, whether they operated inside or outside a national party, Quitman meant to find the issue that would remove the blinders from falsely educated eyes.

Yet what made this charismatic educator so unforgettable was less his success at teaching Southerners to be ultras than his capacity to stay simultaneously northern—to remain a very shrewd and practical operator—even in his highest southern flights. No other southern extremist charged ahead so recklessly—or reconsidered so cautiously. Before his Cuban adventure, this Mississippi governor advocated disunion, in response to the Compromise of 1850. In his typical buccaneering spirit, the governor told South Carolina secessionists to back off for a moment. Then he would lead Mississippi out of the Union first. Skittish South Carolinians gladly obliged. But Quitman, after reconsidering, saw that his pledge had come too soon. So momentum was lost, secession folded, and the chagrined fire-eater learned never to move again until he had the firepower to triumph.[36] By accepting that lesson, Quitman showed he was no Walker, no López, just a shrewd ex-Yankee who sought to make practicality a hallmark of the southern extremist.

The annexation of Cuba, Quitman believed in 1853–55, offered the practical issue to goad moderates toward extremism. The Mississippian considered President Franklin Pierce an unusually dangerous moderate. The president sought to buy enslaved Cuba, thus mollifying the Southerners, even though purchase was impossible—an impossibility that mollified the Northerners.

The severe, masculine lines of John Quitman's Monmouth (above), and especially its blocked columns, contrasting with the lilting, soft lines of Dunleith (below), and especially its circular columns that spread over all four sides of the mansion. The two Natchez gems, both now hotels, brought the Southwest's Greek revival style to climax—a culmination a century removed from Charleston's late eighteenth-century Georgian climax, the Miles Brewton House (see p. 358). Courtesy of the Library of Congress (both Natchez images).

The crisis in Cuba, Quitman conceived in 1853–55, must destroy toleration for mollification—must annihilate the pols' anesthetizing solution of waiting patiently for unattainable purchases. One word summed up Quitman's sense of crisis at his supreme filibustering moment: Africanization. "Spain under advice from England has determined to Africanize Cuba," he warned. One of his prime supporters, John S. Thrasher, privately explained why the warning added a sense of impersonal urgency to that prime personal motive for most filibusterers—a romantic knight's lust for a quixotic escapade. Was not Cuba, Thrasher whispered, "the heart's mecca to everyone whose soul burns with a single spark of nature's fire? . . . What hills and vales! What picturesque men! What soul enhancing women!" And now what a crucial mission, to "save our brothers of the Island of Cuba from social death, under the iniquitous plottings of black European philanthropy. . . . The question is, shall the African or the American Caucassion rule in that lovely island."[37]

As evidence that Africans might rule, the *New Orleans Delta* pointed to Cuba's (Spain-appointed) new captain general, Juan M. de la Pezuela. Shortly after taking over his near dictatorial office in December 1853, Pezuela notified some slaves that they had been freed. Their crass owners had never informed these unfortunates. Pezuela also eased other slaves' purchase of their freedom. He legalized racial intermarriage. He invited blacks into the military. He encouraged the importation of Africans who would be apprenticed for only two years and then freed. Were we disposed "to see a new Hayti, or even a new Jamaica, so near to our shores?" asked the *Delta*. With that question, southern precipitators once again called their fellows to a war to preserve a borderland, even if ninety miles of sea this time separated an edge of the South from a contaminating neighbor.[38]

Apprehension about this alleged Africanization led swiftly to Southwide urgency, even briefly consuming the usually antifilibustering Upper South. "When the barbaric passions of the African are let loose," shuddered the *Richmond Enquirer*, "it will be too late to talk of the annexation of Cuba," just as it became too late to move "against the insurgent negroes of San Domingo." The *Baltimore Republican* wanted "no other negro kingdom— no second Haiti or San Domingo erected upon our borders." As the *New Orleans Courier* explained, "With such a nursery of Abolitionists upon our southern border," slaves "will be carried off every year, and thousands of desperadoes . . . will sow the seeds of servile insurrection throughout the South."[39]

The Southwide shudder at a free black Cuba widened the New Orleans perspective that a Caribbean empire would bring a nourishing Gulf commerce. Racial hysteria also supplemented the hope that a new slave state of Cuba would give the South two more U.S. senators and more members still of the House of Representatives. Above all else, because of the looming specter of an abolitionizing captain general, the Caribbean issue at last pressed on the South's sorest points. The central southern drives for territorial expansion had always started with horror visions of contiguous free soil enclaves, whether in a potentially English abolitionized republic of Texas or in a northern liberated territory of Kansas or now in a Spanish emancipated nation of Cuba.

Quitman's impeccable proslavery message and credentials gave the Mississippian a southern organization far more sweeping than Walker's or López's. Quitman's recruiters and money raisers fanned over the Gulf South and especially over New Orleans, supplementing the Cuba junta's work in New York. Hard workers for Quitman included Lamars in Georgia, Davises in Mississippi, William Walker's brother in Tennessee, James P. Henderson and Rip Ford in Texas, Duncan Kenner, John Slidell, and Pierre Soulé in Louisiana—a veritable who's who of rich southwestern planters, governors, and U.S. senators (but not one a South Carolinian!). The enthusiasts raised hundreds of thousands of dollars and enlisted a thousand men.[40]

Then the federal government struck. In May 1854, President Franklin Pierce announced that be would "prosecute with due energy" any filibustering expedition. A month later, U.S. Supreme Court Justice John Campbell, presiding over the U.S. Circuit Court in New Orleans, handed a grand jury very wide license to indict Quitman and followers for violating the Neutrality Laws. Giving speeches or raising funds, insisted the judge, was as indictable as stepping onto a Cuba-bound vessel. When the grand jury still could not justify indictments, Campbell became juror as well as judge. He insisted that Quitman put up a $3000 bond, to ensure that the filibusterer would suspend operations for nine months.[41]

Campbell exemplified how the South hurt the South when it came to filibustering. A native of Mobile, a center of filibustering second only to New Orleans, the judge had been an issuer of the so-called Dred Scott Decision, that prosouthern event second to none in the Buchanan years. But Campbell, much like Buchanan, stood for law and Union, not John Quitman's highest priorities. The Alabama jurist winced at slavery because his sacred text, the law, did not sufficiently protect bondsmen. Campbell wished that state law would bar slaveholders from breaking up slave families and from putting up slaves as collateral for loans. John Quitman, so John Campbell thought, must not place imperious slaveholders still further beyond the law's restraints.

By demanding a bond for good behavior, Campbell slowed Quitman's momentum. Men now wondered if Quitman would ever leave America, much less conquer Cuba. Fundraising and troop raising almost stopped, as southern partisans questioned whether to risk their dollars, much less their lives, on Monmouth's shackled master. Nor did risks seem as necessary after Spain replaced Captain General Pezuela with José G. de la Concha, a less committed "Africanizationist." Nor did prospects seem auspicious after U.S. officials seized the New York Cuban junta's ship in early 1855.

In one last grasp for hope, Quitman journeyed to Washington. There he sought to persuade President Pierce to suspend the Neutrality Laws. Pierce more persuasively handed Quitman some news about Cuban repressions awaiting freebooters. In April 1855, the most proslavery of filibusterers sur-rendered his command.

– 8 –

Quitman's surrender to the practicalities signified that despite isothermics, a Caribbean empire had become an even more unreachable southern dream than an enslaved state of Kansas. Natchez's favorite ex-Northerner saw that Caribbean purchase would never come off and that a López-like force of only 400 men would never conquer. Quitman also came to see that a filibus-terer army of thousand(s) could never leave these shores, not in the face of a significant southern opposition that both discouraged recruitment and en-couraged a northern president's (and a southern judge's) enforcement of the Neutrality Laws. If all the South had been New Orleans and had demanded no federal insistences to the filibusterers, as almost all the South had de-manded no federal insistences to the Lecompton Convention, presidents might not have been so quick to enforce the Neutrality Laws. But all the South did not sympathize with Caribbean adventuring or filibustering illegalities (or New Orleans!), as John Campbell demonstrated.

For a few months, Walker's Nicaragua invasion proved more invulnerable than Quitman's and López's projected Cuban incursions. But Nicaragua, like the rest of Central America, not only encouraged more filibusterer hopes than Cuba, because of its less consolidated regime, but also discouraged slave-holder hopes, because of its slaveless population. Where would the American slaves come from, even if some William Walker stabilized a proslavery govern-ment for more than a few months? Southwestern planters still saw little to rec-ommend unstable Central America or shaky Kansas, compared to virgin Texas and Arkansas acres. As for Border South and South Carolina slavehold-ers, they shuddered at shaky regimes even more than did nouveau southwest-ern slaveholders. Moreover, would the South strengthen itself by depopulating these states?

That question, asked in the South ever more incessantly as Caribbean adventurers staggered toward their denouncement, showed that the South needed more than isothermically superior land to escape the Kansas futility. To expand over southerly acres without losing northerly hinterlands, the South needed more slaves—many more slaves. As that realization hardened amidst the latest (Caribbean) futility of the Buchanan years, the road to dis-union took a revealing swerve.

CHAPTER 12

Reopening the African Slave Trade

We come now to the startling episode that best connects both ends of the road to disunion. In both Thomas Jefferson's era and William L. Yancey's, the African slave trade issue achieved illuminating (and neglected) importance. The Founding Fathers' closure of the overseas trade represented precisely the damaging step toward emancipation that the Founders supposedly never took.[1]

By seeking to repair the damage, late antebellum proslavery ultras highlighted their view of an imperiled culture. Their extremist movement to reopen the African slave trade defied mainstream moderation. The ultras still brought off a meteoric rise and near triumph in three states. But the reopeners' ultimate frustration matched Kansas and Caribbean disappointments—and fueled the desperation that must underlie a revolution.

– 1 –

Southerners' mid-nineteenth-century campaign to reopen the African slave trade began in—where else—South Carolina. Back at the beginning of the century, only South Carolina had reopened the trade. After the state's 1803–7 importation of approximately 40,000 Africans, the federal government had barred the trade. For almost a half century, few Southerners decried or defied this ban. According to the slaveholders' conventional wisdom, the overseas slave trade had been wrong even though slavery became right.

No important southern figure questioned that position until 1853. Then Leonidas W. Spratt, editor of the *Charleston Standard*, initiated the reopening craze. No South Carolinian better epitomized, in personality, ideology, and accomplishment, why the state's leaders sought to prod less reactionary, more prosperous squires elsewhere out of the Union. Preston Brooks, with his gutta cane, wielded a more savage weapon. James Hammond, with his mudsill terminology, devised a more disruptive phrase. James Henley Thornwell, with his shudder at slaveholder obligations unmet, formulated a more subtle psychology. But Leonidas Spratt exuded South Carolina's high-toned—some would say precious—reactionary desperation.[2]

Spratt, although a native of the South Carolina upcountry, came naturally by his conviction that lowcountry gentlemen supplied the last, best bulwark against American mobocracy. By 1818, when Leonidas was born, the coastal aristocrats' antique mentality had spread to the uplands, where Spratt's wealthy father resided. The uplander gave his youngest son the best training for South Carolina refinement, including a South Carolina College education. But père Spratt's holdings descended to his oldest son. Young Leonidas possessed an aristocrat's mentality but a plebeian's purse.

Like many of South Carolina's penniless rich boys, Spratt sadly deserted his contracting state in order to seek expansive opportunity on unseemly frontiers. Most such exiles ventured to the roaring Southwest. The bookish Spratt preferred the tamer Southeast. Quincy, Florida, became this aspiring lawyer's booming arena to win the dollars to match his cultivation.

Potential Quincy clients, however, resented a snobby lawyer who considered his surroundings beneath his talent. Too refined to ascend where the grubby were the comers, Spratt retreated to the oasis where the cultivated were the heroes. By moving backward to Charleston, Spratt joined the city's impoverished sophisticates, each genteelly competing for a spoonful of the city's declining resources.

Shortly after coming home to mecca, Spratt hit a scarce South Carolina jackpot. By deploying a rich man's manners, he won a rich heiress's heart. The groom secured less funds than James Hammond, another upcountryman who captured his fortune in a Charleston drawing room. Then again, Spratt needed less cash to soar. Hammond, a butcher's boy, married an Irish liquor magnate's daughter and longed to lord it over disdaining squires. Spratt, a squire's offspring, married into a cultivated family and sought to join the admiring Charleston intelligentsia. After he wed Carolina Cooper in 1851, Spratt managed her small town house, her ten slaves, and enough of her cash to buy the floundering *Charleston Standard* in 1853.

The purchase represented a riskier gamble than Spratt's retreat to Charleston. Antebellum American newspapers characteristically served national political parties. The editor broadcast propaganda for the politicians, and the politicians supplied printing contracts for the journalists. But genteel Charleston, with its disdain for partisan electioneering and national parties, scorned crass politicos and demagogic journalists. Instead, Spratt had to formulate ideas that would sell newspapers to worried aristocrats, in a city saturated with unionist ideas in the *Courier* and secessionist ideas in the *Mercury*.

By personality no less than by financial interest, Spratt inclined toward betting on his ideas. Only thirty-five years old when he bought the *Standard*, the editor meant to become the intellectual leader of South Carolina's climactic generation of hotspurs. To transcend their fathers' abortive charges and dispirited retreats, Spratt thought the young turks needed a clearer blueprint of their culture's essence.

Spratt looked like an abstractionist who drew up abstruse blueprints. He was pale, sickly, retiring, with a black beard straggling from a weak chin and black eyes nervously darting under a furrowed brow. Like John C. Calhoun, South Carolina's previous favorite abstractionist, the worrier turned conversations into soliloquies. But where Calhoun had delivered clipped certitudes in compact sentences, Spratt's phrases stretched out and out and out, so that some called L. W. Spratt not Leonidas William Spratt but Long Winded Spratt.[3] Others, complaining that he thought as hard as spare Cassius, wished that the journalist would pause from long-winded repetitions at least long enough to chew a bit of supper.

Spratt's windy editorials offered up a seductive remedy for slipping glory. Spratt considered Charleston wonderfully a nonfrontier. In its drawing rooms, gentlemen met over brandy to deplore American hustle. Where New Orleans, to its ofttimes disapproving visitors, was all about consuming raw entertainment, Charleston, to its proud gentry, was all about producing refined criticism (or, as some would have it, generating effete condemnations of any American who did not live on the Ashley or the Cooper River).

Charleston squires deplored American demagogues as well as the American rabble. They considered an aristocratic republic the best of all governments, cultivated gentlemen the best of all rulers, and the mob's flatterers the worst of all saboteurs. Reactionaries cheered that nineteenth-century South Carolina offered few opportunities for unprincipled demagogues to provoke unpropertied voters. A South-leading 49 percent of South Carolina voters owned at least one slave, compared to the Lower South average of 37 percent. No South Carolina county possessed under 20 percent slaves. No other state could remotely match that universal penetration of slaves. The slaveless toiler in a white belt area, that Southerner most likely to listen to an antislavery demagogue, remained scarce in crusty South Carolina.

South Carolina propertyless whites furthermore lacked other southern citizens' eligibility for the people's offices. In South Carolina, voters elected only legislators, who had to meet property qualifications and selected all other officials, who in turn had to meet higher property qualifications. Moreover, unwritten custom dictated that South Carolina legislative candidates seldom discussed policy with lesser folk and that South Carolina politicians shunned national political parties and demagogic national campaigns. The superior race should elect superior planters to forge superior legislation. Then slavery would remain the cornerstone of aristocratic republicanism.

The North, Spratt exclaimed, lacking the cornerstone, demonstrated that a "pure democracy" sped past "agrarianism to anarchy." Because Yankees possessed no black nonvoting slaves, white voters became the afflicted lower class. Because no customs or constitutional provisions barred demagogues from rousing white mudsills, "the heels rather than the heads of society" would someday dispossess the propertied. "When France shall reel again into the delirium of liberty," shuddered Spratt, and when in the North and in England "all that is low and vile shall have mounted to the surface, . . . when the sexes shall consort without the restraints of marriage and when youths and maidens, drunk at noon day and half naked, shall reel about the market places—the South will stand, secure and erect," for slavery will restrain the mudsills, black nonvoters all.[4]

Yet even in Charleston, gloomed Spratt, modernity eroded the cornerstone. In the 1850s, South Carolina lost slaves faster than any other state. The lowcountry's departure rate exceeded the upcountry's. Charleston's departures exceeded the rural coastal parishes'. Poor white immigrants arrived as ominously as slaves departed. From 1850 to 1860, the city's slave workingmen declined 46 percent, while its foreign-born white workmen increased 25 percent. Irishmen comprised over half the immigrants. Over half the Irishmen competed with blacks for grunt work. These unskilled whites petitioned the legislature, demanding that black slaves be barred from urban menial labor. Before long, Spratt warned, resentful mudsill voters, roused by unscrupulous demagogues, would have at the slaveholders. Thus a class with "no direct and legitimate connections with slavery" might determine "the fortunes of our institution."[5]

Spratt's colleague at the highest level of Charleston drawing room cultivation, William Henry Trescot, also exclaimed that U.S. slavery "has its inexorable requirements." Black slavery's "very first requirement" demands that "the white race must preserve its superiority." We "cannot with justice or safety allow the white man to come into competition with the black simply as a laborer." We must establish "an impassable gulf between the lowest and humblest form of white labor and the highest development of black."[6]

Trescot would create his impassable gulf by educating all whites to pursue mental, not menial, labor. In contrast, Spratt would eliminate white menials by importing 10,000 Africans for city labor. With sufficient black proletarians in Charleston, white proletarians would depart. With all mudsills black, enslaved, and disenfranchised, Charlestonian voters, nonmudsills all, would save aristocratic republicanism from a mudsill mobocracy.

An expanded reopening of the African slave trade would save more of South Carolina than Charleston. As Spratt traversed the lowcountry rural parishes, "ruined mansions" met his "every step." These "moldering ruins," formerly the seat of prosperity, refinement, and the arts, had once commanded plantations that brought fifty dollars an acre. Now, bankrupt owners could scarcely receive five dollars an acre.[7]

Some of our fraying gentlemen, lamented Spratt, conclude that a slave labor society can never match free labor Boston, whether in generating material progress or cultural flowering. Nonsense! We must be "done with the admission, among Southern men, of inferiority to the North." We must realize that a slave labor system best sustains aristocratic superiority. We must remember that no labor system flourishes without new laborers. Massachusetts imports endless European immigrants. We cannot import one African. Massachusetts newcomers fell trees, plough prairies, grade railroad tracks, build canals, erect factories, launch ships. Boston's prosperous intelligentsia thus have "leisure and repose," spawning "cultivation and refinement."[8]

The South Carolina lowcountry needs equally cheap immigrant labor— 10,000 more workers to level forests, another 10,000 to reclaim plantations, 20,000 more to build roads. But more lower-class white workers would poison the racial slave system, and the federal government bars more lower-class blacks from coming. The result: Slave prices spiral, only southwestern frontiersmen can afford them, and South Carolina's men of refinement must send their blacks—and themselves—to Mammon. The solution: Import 100,000 Africans into South Carolina, use the black imports to remake the economy, send the cursed Irishmen back to Boston, and watch Charlestonians build America's intellectual metropolis.[9]

Spratt scorned other solutions. Kansas? The South lacked the excess slaves to populate the plains without depopulating South Carolina. Adopt Jefferson Buford's scheme for dispatching southern white paupers to capture Kansas? The mudsills would undermine slavery in Kansas as surely as Irish proletarians would undermine slavery in Charleston. Annex Cuba? That hardly "very prodigious blessing" would cause even more South Carolina slaves "to be transported to a more profitable laboring field."[10]

The South most needed, Spratt insisted again and again, not expansion of new territories but consolidation of old establishments. Let us see what "slavery can do when its efforts are directed to higher objects than merely extending a frontier." Then southwestern profits would no longer destroy "the integrity of slave society in the center of our strongest state."[11]

There echoed the South Carolina haughtiness that incensed southwestern frontiersmen. If Spratt had pled only to save the elderly South from hemorrhaging to the youthful South, Southwesterners would have ridiculed his reopening essays. But this South Carolina provincial urged that the whole South suffered from predicaments similar to Charleston's. Just as European newcomers pushed Boston ahead of Charleston, so immigration from overseas boosted the North ahead of the South. In 1808, when Congress shuttered the African slave trade, free labor and slave labor states had contained almost the same numbers of peoples. Since then, Spratt pointed out, the North had received over five million more immigrants than the South. The immigrants gave Yankees their huge margin in the House of Representatives, their enormous advantage in populating Kansas, and their colossal lead in industrial development.

Spratt affirmed that slaves could man factories. Crude industrial labor required only repetition of tasks, and "the negro, in his common absence of reflection, is, perhaps, the greatest manipulist in the world." Give the South millions of Africans. Then see who develops the greater industrial colossus, who populates more territories, and who elects more congressmen.[12]

The crippling black exodus from South Carolina, Spratt continued, paralleled the debilitating slave drain from the Border South now and from the Border North earlier. The Border North states of Pennsylvania and New Jersey, together with New York, had been bulwarks of the colonial slavocracy. But since a constricting African slave trade could not provide enough laborers for the more southern North, Europeans filled the vacuum. Northern slaveholders then sold bondsmen to more prosperous planters farther south. The Border South followed that Border North road from slavery. If "interests" dictated that the northern South's masters still "hold their slaves," they would "do so." But when southwestern capitalists paid extravagant prices for blacks, Border South entrepreneurs had "no motive to retain them."

Leonidas Spratt did not consider Upper South nonslaveholders actively antislavery. But they would prefer that blacks be sold away, they "have no interest in the institution," and "they look with complacency on any effort to break it down."[13] Spratt feared that some slaveholders also lacked sufficient commitment. Too many patriarchs still thought that the institution had originated in a sinful trade and remained an evil, however necessary. Such compromised sentiments would inadequately fuel a crusade to save a Christian blessing. But let slaveholders realize that the African slave trade providentially placed savages under Christian paternalists' direction. Then patriarchs would fight for their expanded holy mission.[14]

Spratt saw scant slaveholders with "armor on and braced for battle." Even more than economic strength, political power, and intellectual development, the South needed "the moral strength of an aggressive attitude." The issue must no longer be whether a contracting slavocracy could apologize for a constricted institution. We must no longer watch "men diffident of" slavery's "endurance move away from it" or "its pious people . . . instructed to deplore it." When we become proud of black slavery as the salvation of white aristocratic republicanism, proud of our forebearers for originating a saving flow of Africans, proud of our intention of adding millions more blacks to America's saving institution, we will strike down the African slave trade ban that has broken our power and savaged our spirit.[15]

Charleston's tired gentlemen may have relished Spratt's style even more than his solutions. In this most revolutionary yet most reactionary of cities, in this area eager for a rebellion yet quailing at its own precipitousness, a hero scornful of delay at last demanded action. Spratt was wonderfully unlike previous disunionists, with their blazing starts and embarrassed halts, blissfully unlike Preston Brooks, with his passion to maul Charles Sumner and his tremble to begin the mugging.

The editor was moreover a Charleston-style unconditional charger. Spratt was a retiring bookworm who scorned frontiersmen's bustle. He was a rarified scholar who put his bride's small purse to big work for the intelligentsia. He was a brilliant analyst who cut past politician's superficialities to the core of Charleston's, and the South's, predicament.

A century and a half later, Charleston's admiration still seems well placed. In Spratt's understanding of immigration as Yankees' source of power, he exuded more insight than Southern Know-Nothings, who would take away newcomers' vote but leave foreigners' economic impact untouched. In his understanding of how the 1808 law against the African slave trade had destroyed the equality of North and South, he outshone latter-day historians who think the Founding Fathers did nothing to cripple slavery. In his thesis that the lack of sufficient workers made slavery an untested source of economic development, he rivaled theorists who blamed slavery per se for every aspect of southern backwardness. In his perception that territorial expansion demanded an accompanying population expansion, he cut past politicians who thought expansion of acres would alone save the slavocracy. In his conviction that black proletarians could not govern themselves and that a white proletariat could not govern a republic, he put together the clearest and cleanest plea for an aristocratic slavocracy, with different degrees of direction from above for different degrees of disability below. No wonder that Charlestonians lined up to buy the *Standard*—and shook their fists at the rest of the South, for ignoring South Carolina's latest genius.

– 2 –

For three years, the ingenious editor remained obscure beyond Charleston. Spratt's first, 1853–54 call to arms secured little notice amidst the South's flush of enthusiasm over Kansas-Nebraska. His appeals continued largely unheeded during James Buchanan's early presidential forays. But as Kansas soured, filibusterers failed, and Buchanan's victories looked ever more empty, Southerners sought a way past futility. Then Spratt became, in Lower South circles beyond Charleston, the prophet of the fastest-growing movement in mid-'50s American politics, including the booming Northern Know-Nothing movement.

In its latter day, Lower Southwide form, the reopening argument played down Spratt's South Carolina emphases. Muted were anxieties about South Carolina's depopulation, Charleston's white proletariat, and the city's failure to match Boston's cultural creations. Expanded were apprehensions about nonslaveholder restiveness, slaveholder passiveness, the slave drain from the Border South, and the South's paucity of slaves for expanding acres or industries. Reopening, went the Southwide argument, could alone secure the blacks to make every nonslaveholder a slaveholder, to allow the South to cultivate new areas without depopulating old ones, and to fortify the slaveholders to match the Yankees stride for stride in Congress, in factories, and in the expanding countryside.

Still, reopeners had to transcend the worldwide judgment that whatever U.S. slavery's latter-day blessings, the institution had originated in an horrendous overseas trade. Slave trade advocates regretted that Southerners had ever accepted that condemnation. When Christian slaveholders instead of coarse Yankees scrupulously conducted the traffic, the trade would feature fair transactions in Africa, healthy conditions on ships, and Christian salvation in America. Then it could no longer be even arguably sinful, exclaimed South Carolina's Edward Bryan, "to transfer the African savage from his heathen home, and place him in a sphere of usefulness in a Christian land."[16]

How providential, continued the *New Orleans Delta*, that this "startling charity to hordes of sable savages" also would yield the "only practical measure" for "a balance of power within the Union" and within the South. With a bondsman costing $2000, "only the wealthy class can buy." A tenfold increase of slaves, however, would decrease the price to $200. Then yeomen could become slaveholders. Thus "African Labor Immigration is a movement by the poor people of the South, for the benefit of the poor people of the South, . . . to keep their wives from the washtub, their daughters from the frying pan and scrubbing brush, and their sons from the hoe, curry-comb and muck-rake."[17]

Like Spratt and all the other reopeners, Edward Bryan granted that non-slaveholders would today rally for slaveholders' property. Yet slavery's protection might require monumental future sacrifices. Allow a "slave aristocracy in the very heart of the South" and poor men might someday "recoil from the struggle."[18]

The Border South already recoiled. "Where material interests cease," warned the *New Orleans Delta*, ideological alliances fade. Without "any real pecuniary gain from slavery," Americans are "very apt to become sentimental and free soil." Since no foreign slaves could now be imported and since our "sugar and cotton regions" demand more bondsmen, a "demoralizing drain" of slaves ushered the institution out of our outposts. Now abolitionism "has crossed our border and is squatting in all its hideousness at our hearths." The fanatics show their teeth in Virginia and howl in Missouri. The drainage of slaves will "end in the loss" of these states and North Carolina, Kentucky, Maryland, and Delaware too, unless a reopened African slave trade relieves "the South's undeniable deficiency of slave labor."[19]

The South's new terrain, lamented the reopeners, has worsened our predicament. "The leaders of the free soil movement no doubt smiled in secret to think that in order to overspread Texas, New Mexico, and Kansas, we are preparing to make them a present of Maryland, Virginia, Kentucky, and to illustrate our generosity, to throw Kansas into the bargain." Anyone who watches the "self-elimination of slavery going on in Maryland, Kentucky, and Missouri" knows that "without vigorous measures for the restoration of Slavery to a healthy status, a terrible doom lies before the South."[20]

– 3 –

The most vigorous advocates for reopening the slave trade tended to be dis-unionists. Secessionists hoped the issue would at very least divide the National Democratic Party, the first step toward severing the Union. To split the last national party, secessionists needed an abstraction that would goad Southern Democrats toward an extremism that Northern Democrats found insufferable.

The reopening issue at first seemed calculated to lure southern moderates toward extremism. Wipe out the apology that the system originated in wrong. Then the folk would be more righteous defenders. Persuade citizens that more African savages would benefit from more Christian paternalism. Then voters would wish party compromisers off the holy road. Goad southern voters toward demanding more Africans. Then northern politicians would not abide such compatriots.

The disunionists' problem remained that actually reopening the trade and inundating the South with supposed savages might make this radicalism too bitter for moderates to swallow. By reformulating the issue, Alabama's cunning William L. Yancey sweetened the cure. This strategist said little about whether the South should decide to reopen. He instead stressed that the decision, like every verdict about slavery's morality, must be the South's alone to make. He despised holier-than-thou Yankees who told Southerners that slavery had originated in piracy. He deplored the federal government's ban on the origins of the South's supposed crime. Let the federal government remove the officious condemnation. Then the South could decide whether bringing savages to Christendom was satanic.

Yancey here played his trump card. An extremist could unite the divided South by damming Yankee critics. Then a disunionist could divide the united National Democratic Party by insisting on southern morality. Let the South "simply" insist that the Democracy "wipe out from our statute books the mark of Cain which has been placed upon our institutions." Then our supposed northern friends will be revealed as our enemies, scorning "defense of our rights."[21]

Yet not every reopener shared Yancey's disunionist prayer. Some unionists hailed reopening as the alternative to secession. E. W. Fuller, a Louisiana state legislator, illustrated the type. "I regard the institution of slavery," said Fuller, "as absolutely necessary to Louisiana, and I regard the preservation of the Union and our Constitution as absolutely indispensable for the preservation of slavery" and the importation of African slaves as "absolutely necessary . . . for the preservation of slavery where it now exists." We cannot attain "equality in the Union without new slave states." But we cannot enslave "new territories without abandoning the more northern slave states to the Abolitionists, unless we can procure a supply of slaves from some other source." With the price of slaves soaring, "the dollar is an almighty Abolitionist." In "three fourths of our states," overly expensive slaves means overly unprofitable slave labor.[22]

Fuller's plea answered every question left over from the frustrating Buchanan years. The newer South's economic boom increased slavery's vulnerability in the older South? Then expansive cotton and sugar magnates should drain bondsmen from Africa rather than from Missouri (or from South

Carolina!). The South lacked the slaves to consolidate slavery in Kansas or in Missouri or in William Walker's Nicaragua, no matter the local police protections? Then bring in Africans to populate a protected empire. Because of high slave prices, nonslaveholders could not share the slaveholding dream? Then increase the supply and drive down the price. Northern immigrants dangerously augmented Yankees' territories, factories, and congressmen? Then let the South enjoy an equal number of immigrants. Too many Southerners apologized for slavery and allowed compromised national party politicians to govern? Then teach the folk to glory in the uncompromising African slave trade and watch them oust the compromisers.

The reopeners showed again how profoundly the South had changed since the 1840s. Then amidst an economic depression, Southerners had sought Texas annexation as a safety value for excess blacks. Now amidst an economic bonanza, the slavocracy needed more blacks to work its excess of lands, to seize yet more lands, and to keep slaves from draining downward in the South. By championing an initially seductive solution to a growing southern consensus about exasperating problems, southern extremists had found the issue that could take off like the economic boom itself.

– 4 –

Yet if this panacea seemed to solve every southern problem, opponents quickly found the perfect response: The solution would actually worsen the problems. Where reopeners affirmed that more barbarians should be brought under patriarchal Christians, naysayers answered that barbarians would compel patriarchs toward anti-Christian savagery. "Providence" has guided paternalists to "great improvement," urged South Carolina's J. J. Pettigrew in a particularly brilliant elaboration of the position, because imports from African have been suppressed. But "reopen this floodgate of impurity, and all that we have accomplished in half a century would be lost."

After raw Africans have spent "several generations in a Christian land," explained Pettigrew, "continual terror" becomes "no longer necessary." The Americanized black obeys not because of fear but because of education. But if we belatedly introduce "one hundred thousand idle, slovenly, insubordinate barbarians among our educated, civilized negroes," "brute force" will again become necessary. What did the savage "know of duty? What did he care for a moral rebuke? He must see his blood flow." There is, in short, a "vast difference between a system of civilized and a system of barbarian slavery."[23]

Arguments such as Pettigrew's helped inspire a culture-wide shudder at importing millions of supposed barbarians. For reopening to occur, winced ex-senator Walker Brooke of Mississippi, "every semblance of humanity would have to be blotted out from the statute-books, and the slaveholder would become—instead of the patriarchal friend and master of his slave—a bloody, brutal, and trembling tyrant." South Carolina's Alfred Huger declared that "I would rather see Every Slave that I own emancipated tomorrow" than resurrect "scenes of horror witnessed in my childhood and indispensably connected with the African trade!! Assure yourself that the punishments inflicted on those savages and cannibals to reduce them to subordination would make abolitionists on both sides of the Potomac and *that* speedily."[24]

The barbarous reopening policy, opponents continued, would turn the slaveless into abolitionists, not the nonslaveholders into slaveholders. What nonsense that slicing the price of slaves would transform poor men into masters. Cheaper slave labor would instead slice white men's wages, transform them into poorer men, put even cheaper slaves even more out of reach, and soon enough make them into enemies of rich men.

What nonsense, furthermore, that reopening the African trade would consolidate the slave-selling northern South's interest in slavery! The slave-breeding Upper South thrived on high slave prices. Borderites would sell slaves before the African surplus arrived or give up an unprofitable investment. Some borderites, added the *Baltimore Courier,* wanted "the whole African race now in the United States returned to Africa." They would shun the "horrible barbarity" of "additional importations." No Upper South slave seller, screamed almost all Virginians, wanted lower prices for slaves. David Campbell of Tennessee warned that "utter loathing of the proposition" would drive the Upper South into a third confederacy, if disunion came.[25]

But while opponents of reopening urged that the supposedly unifying panacea would fracture the South more than ever, they usually conceded that troubling divisions existed. "We all know," wrote South Carolina's Robert Goodloe Harper, "that slavery is gradually concentrating in the cotton country. It is receding from Delaware and Maryland, Virginia, Kentucky, and Missouri." Harper, whose antireopening pamphlet rivaled Johnson Pettigrew's as the supreme statement of the position, sadly concluded that "we cannot stay those results; but let us, at least, not precipitate them."[26]

So too, Mississippi's U.S. Senator Henry S. Foote, the leading opponent of reopening in the 1859 Southern Commercial Convention, conceded that in twenty-five years "we shall have, by natural increase, between nine and ten millions" of blacks. "By the expected emancipation of Maryland, Virginia, Kentucky, and Missouri, those slaves will be pent up within ten or eleven extreme Southern States." Would we then want "thousands, and perhaps millions, of Africans to add to our cares?"[27]

In addition to conceding that the Border South was incrementally slipping away, those against reopening often concurred that only new slaves could enable the South to populate new territories. Alexander Stephens so adamantly declared that the limited numbers of slaves made territorial expansion impossible that for months Southerners falsely thought that he advocated reopening. Jefferson Davis so confidently declared that the South's lack of slaves doomed New Mexico Territory to be free soil that he seemed to be urging, again falsely, that the territory import Africans.[28]

As this partial acceptance of the reopeners' logic showed, the Spratts had found the right issue to illuminate the South's angst but the wrong remedy to relieve it. How could reopening boost nonslaveholders' commitment to slavery, asked Mississippi's U.S. Senator Albert Gallatin Brown, when rednecks would not tolerate "an influx of untold millions of wild Africans?"[29] How could boatloads of Africans keep the Upper South loyal, when this slave-selling region loved soaring slave prices? And how could the theoretical glory of bringing cannibals to civilization rout moderate politicians, when voters thought a vomit of blacks would drown the South in savagery? As the reopening issue shot up in the southern political skies, William L. Yancey's gambit seemed to shatter the South, not the National Democracy.

– 5 –

Still, reopeners stuck to their desperate cause in three Lower South legislatures. There, they almost scored incredible victories. As always, South Carolinians first sought precipitous victories—and first retreated from precipitousness. In November 1856, Governor James H. Adams, an upcountry owner of almost 200 slaves, told the legislature that the South needed more slaves to meet the world's demand for more cotton, to match the North's bludgeoning immigrant population, to rescue Southerners' "self-respect" from outsiders' "brand" against slavery, and above all else to preserve the racial "integrity of slave society." Since the South desperately needed more laborers, warned Adams, "we must expect" a white immigrant proletariat to come. That "species of labor," however, "does not suit our latitudes." Fresh Africans better suit our predicament. Leonidas Spratt, delighted to have the governor sound like a *Charleston Standard* editorial, hailed the message as "the most important" American "document . . . since the Revolution."[30]

The legislature delayed decision on the revolutionary document. Under South Carolina's unique aristocratic republicanism, cultivated gentlemen felt compelled to take the time to write state papers, defending enlightened opinions. When the opinions appeared during the next, 1857 session of the legislature, they read like a first-class debate between Supreme Court judges. Edward Bryan's brief, written for the majority of the joint legislative committee that considered Adams's message, superbly explained why reopening would rescue paternalistic mission. J. J. Pettigrew, writing for the minority, skillfully responded that fresh African cannibals would steal the paternalism from paternalistic slavery.[31]

While the legislative joint committee sided with Bryan, the 1857 legislature overturned the verdict. Upcountry supporters of Congressman James L. Orr, seeking to nudge South Carolina into the American mainstream, called reopening the extremists' worst lunacy yet. Robert Barnwell Rhett, who usually considered Orr the worst enemy, this time considered Spratt more dangerous. Reopening, once intriguing to Rhett's *Mercury*, now seemed calculated to isolate South Carolina disunionists from 90 percent of the South. "To agitate" reopening and thus "divide the South . . . is sheer madness. It is worse. It is directly cooperating with the abolitionists in the submission and subjugation of the South."[32]

Even though Orr and Rhett called Spratt a madman from the two extremes of South Carolina's political spectrum, reopening secured powerful support in the 1857 legislature. But the South Carolina Senate indefinitely postponed Spratt's brainchild, 22–14.[33] The panacea now had a legislative future only in Spratt's despised area, the frontier Southwest.

Georgia, more of a New South state than South Carolina, came closer to legislative action for reopening. In November 1858, State Senator Alexander Atkinson moved to repeal Georgia's 1797 law, closing the trade. United States law, Atkinson pointed out, would still bar the trade. No reason, then, for Georgia laws to declare the origins of our positive good an "evil." Georgians who called importing Africans into America a travesty, charged Atchison, traitorously resembled Black Republicans, who called allowing slaves to enter American territories a crime.

Atkinson's opponents resented his "uncharitable and unkind" charge. They saw nothing "Black Republican" about keeping an "immense horde of barbarians" outside Georgia. Still, Atkinson struck home with his insistence that Georgia's laws must not gratuitously contain a "sour reflection upon . . . slavery." Given our "sensitiveness upon the subject," reported a legislative observer, "men are afraid of having it said they are opposed to slavery." This clash, pitting fear of unsoundness on slavery against fear of unsound barbarians, created almost a dead heat on Atkinson's proposal. The Georgia Senate voted 47–46 to table Atchison's proposal.[34]

While the Georgia Senate came within one vote of repealing its law against reopening, the Louisiana legislature came closer to reopening the importation. As with filibustering passions, Louisianans espoused reopening passions with expansionist zests that contracting South Carolinians could not match. In the 1850s, Louisiana's sugar lands offered the South's lushest profits amidst the section's most top-heavy establishment. Slaves grew so expensive in Louisiana that the percentage of white families owning slaves plummeted from 48 percent in 1850 to 32 percent in 1860. During the decade, the number of Louisianans owning five or less slaves dropped 15 percent, while the number owning over twenty slaves increased 29 percent and the number owning over fifty slaves shot up 50 percent. Meanwhile, Louisiana's value per farm, price per acre, and acres per farm all almost doubled. This southwestern wonderland was becoming forbidding for poor yeomen yet sublime for rich planters, especially if booming capitalists could find cheaper slaves to work expensive terrain.

James Bingham, a prominent Louisiana entrepreneur, emphasized the state's uneven economic opportunities when he petitioned the legislature in early 1858. Bingham begged authorization for his Feliciana Company to import blacks. Like Spratt, Bingham affirmed nonslaveholders' present loyalty. Yet since "the enormous prices" of slaves "debarred . . . most of them" from "hope of ever becoming slaveholders," we cannot reasonably expect that "deep . . . willingness to make sacrifices in defense of the institution that may be demanded of its defenders."

Nor can we expect proslavery sacrifices from border Southerners, continued Bingham, if we bleed them of slaves. If "the cotton-growing States . . . continue" to drain our "more northern slave states," we will aid "our enemies, in . . . abolitionizing the South." But we can stay "the dreaded tide of abolitionism" by importing "fresh laborers from Africa." We can also "bring into cultivation the millions of acres of rich southern soil, now laying waste."[35]

Yet how could the state authorize Bingham to import fresh Africans, after the U.S. government had barred the importation? In his cunning answer, Bingham improved on a Mississippi proposal of Henry Hughes, that proslavery writer of "warrantee" notoriety. With his usual linguistic obscuration, Hughes had proposed that his state import not slaves, not free blacks, but "apprentices," with the provision that once their twenty-nine-year apprenticeship ended, the "apprentices" should become "warranties." Bingham erased Hughes's "warrantee" lingo, sliced the apprenticeship term to fifteen years, required Africans to sign supposedly voluntary agreements to become temporary apprentices, and implied that after their service, apprentices might return to their homeland. Here was a clever (perchance too clever) detour around the U.S. prohibition of importing involuntary, perpetual slaves.[36]

On March 3, 1858, fifty-one years to the day after Thomas Jefferson signed the U.S. act closing the African slave trade, the Feliciana Company's proposal entered the Louisiana legislature's proceedings. Two days later, the House, by a whopping 46–21 margin, authorized James Bingham and his associates to import 2500 apprentices per year, each with a fifteen-year labor contract, "voluntarily" signed.[37] Within the week, a unanimous Senate committee, chaired by Edward Delony, cleared the House bill for Senate passage.

We need more laborers, Delony urged, to acquire and populate Cuba, Mexico, and Central America. In addition, because we lack "an adequate supply of suitable labor, millions of acres of the richest soil on which the sun shine lies untouched" in Louisiana. Moreover, with "the price of negroes" booming, "in a few years the purchase of a valuable slave will be unattainable except by the wealthy." This bias against the lower and middle classes collided "with the genius of Republican institutions."

The apprentice idea, Delony continued, would spread American genius to Africa. African barbarians, now living under "the absolute and brutal sway of their chiefs," suffered the most "extreme degradation." The victims' voyage to America would be like "passing out of night into day." Their "temporary apprenticeship on American soil" would train them "to return to their native" continent, prepared to spread "appreciation and enjoyment" of "republican and Christian" virtues.[38]

Throughout the Louisiana bayous, cheers erupted at the revelation that the state House had passed, and a Senate committee had approved, the panacea for a depraved Africa and a shackled South. This most expansive of southern areas had felt in a straitjacket, as filibusterer after filibusterer sailed for glory and returned in irons or as a corpse. Now, with the culture's handcuffs apparently about to be unlocked, exhilarated Louisianans reacted a little like Preston Brooks, when he finally dared swing freely at Charles Sumner (and a lot like Leonidas Spratt's early Charleston readers, when their newest star intellectual seemed to have the remedy for their insufferable paralysis).

Slavery "is daily rising from its ancient and petrified fixedness," breathed the *Houma Ceres,* "to feel the power of illimitable expansion." The glorious proposal, exalted the *New Orleans Courier,* "will double the products of the agricultural districts and thus mightily increase the commerce, prosperity, and wealth of New Orleans." It will be like "the opening of the gold mines of California," soared the *Bastrop Advocate.* "We *must* have" more territory, concluded the *Point Coupee Echo,* and to get that, "we *must* have" more laborers. Once we "have both the land and the negroes, let Abolitionism, with its Southern echoes, howl as it may."[39]

Yet despite joyful howls as the state Senate approached a final decision on the Bingham bill, statesmen had to weigh the value of their state's other expansive weapon. This world, unlike South Carolina's, retained hope for the Union, votes for the National Democratic Party, and expectations that its favorite U.S. senator, John Slidell, would yet push his favorite Yankee, James Buchanan, into a crusade for Cuba. To go for reopening the slave trade was to embarrass Slidell, to wreck the alliance with Northern Democrats, and to go it alone in the Caribbean, in the futile style of isolated South Carolina.

So Louisianans paused and thought, and paused and thought. Then on March 11, 1858, after the state Senate deadlocked 12–12 on the House apprentice bill, the presiding officer, Lieutenant Governor Charles H. Mouton, voted aye. Applause erupted from spectators. The Louisiana legislature had approved reopening.[40]

But only for four days. On March 15, one senator who had voted for reopening, B. B. Simms, changed his mind. Simms declared that he only wished to pause, to consult his constituents.[41] His egalitarian republican logic, requiring that a representative consult the represented, contrasted with the reasons why the South Carolina joint legislative committee tabled reopening for a year. J. J. Pettigrew and Edward Bryan conceived, in the style of aristocratic republicanism, that the best men must write elaborate state papers, before deciding for the plebeians. But in both of these very different states, legislative reopening had become the bombshell that shockingly exploded—and then could not sustain the blaze. After Simms quit the reopening column, Bingham's apprentice idea fizzled and expired.

– 6 –

After the Louisiana fireworks, all was anticlimactic on the reopening front. But two dying embers made the anticlimax interesting. First of all, reopening came up for its only Southwide consideration in the 1855–59 Southern Commercial Conventions. These annual voluntary assemblages of entrepreneurs, aimed at modernizing the South's economy, demonstrated how badly the South split on slave-trade reopening, whether as an economic or as any other kind of panacea.

The angriest convention divisions severed the Upper South from the Lower South. The ugliest linguistic brawl came in 1858, when Alabama's William L. Yancey verbally mugged Virginia's Roger Pryor. Even though Pryor, editor of the *Richmond Whig,* was one of the fieriest Virginians and Yancey was not the fieriest reopener (he only wanted federal insulting hands off the issue), the two went after each other as if Robert Barnwell Rhett and William Lloyd Garrison were warring to the death. Pryor declared that to rest the rights of the South upon the "proposition to kidnap cannibals from Africa" was to "throw the gauntlet in the face of the Christian world." Yancey shot back that Virginia's supposedly Christian opinions were "semi-abolition in tendency."[42]

A year later, the Southern Commercial Convention voted 44–19 against Pryor. The almost two-to-one majority declared that "all laws, State and Federal, prohibiting the African slave trade, ought to be repealed." But the whole South had hardly so resolved. Not a single Border South man was present. The few Middle South representatives voted nay, 12–4. Reopening won because the reopening issue had emptied the Commercial Conventions of the moderate Upper South, leaving Lower South extremists, a minority in even the Cotton South, free to have their way. Yet the Lower South landslide in this unrepresentative convention raised new questions about whether South Carolina, always the first state to scream for action, would ever act rather than talk. South Carolinians split four to four on the decisive vote. The rest of the Lower South delegates voted 36–3 to get on with reopening the trade.[43]

In the second anticlimactic episode, South Carolina again wobbled. To defy the U.S. government on the African slave trade, an extremist could import a shipload of Africans. Then a southern jury might refuse to convict the importer. After that judicial nullification of federal law, more intransigents might import more Africans.

That reopening gambit started auspiciously. On August 21, 1858, the USS *Dolphin* captured the slaver *Echo* off Cuba and brought 314 Africans to the Charleston federal jail, with U.S. Marshal D. H. Hamilton in charge. Three months later, Georgia's young hotspur, Charles Augustus Lafayette Lamar, landed some 170 Africans at Jekyll Island from his ship, the *Wanderer,* and sold them to Savannah River masters. The federal government attempted to bring crew members of both ships to justice in Charleston and Savannah. Southern juries and/or judges then refused to indict and/or convict anyone.[44]

This nationally notorious judicial nullification amounted to a spit in the wind, unless the *Echo/Wanderer* cases inspired an epidemic of lawbreaking importations. But no other case developed, not least because reopeners lost their taste for the adventure. United States Marshal D. H. Hamilton, for example, possessed the pedigree to lead South Carolina. His father, Little Jimmy Hamilton, had been governor of the state and Nullifiers' canniest politician when the state took on Andrew Jackson in 1832–33. D. H. Hamilton had newly come to agree with "intelligent and humane persons," he wrote in 1856, that allowing the North, but not the South, to receive millions of new laborers was "a monstrous inequality and injustice."[45]

Two years later, U.S. Marshal Hamilton's conceptions of the monstrous changed. The jailer's "care of so many unfortunates" from the *Echo* left him "cured . . . forever" of tolerating "the amount of misery and suffering entailed upon those poor creatures by the African slave trade. . . . No one who has witnessed," as "I have been compelled" to observe, "practical, fair evidences of its effects . . . could for one moment advocate a traffic which insures such inhumanity to any family of the human race."[46]

South Carolina's ex-governor James Adams found another reason to recant. This titan who had begged his legislature to reopen the trade now stood appalled at a scene that the *Wanderer* had provoked. A proceeding "among the Baptists of Edgefield," he wrote, indicated that upcountry non-slaveholders, outraged at the *Wanderer* importation, might assault slavery itself. Such a "disastrous and fatal . . . quarrel among ourselves must be the beginning of the end."[47]

Adams's sentiments ended any hope that Charles Lamar, the *Wanderer,* the *Echo*, and jury nullification had begun a widespread overseas trade. South Carolinians such as Hamilton and Adams had lately cheered Long Winded Spratt's dream about how the South could break out of prison. When confronted not with dreams but with the thing itself, however, South Carolina gentlemen reaccepted imprisonment. Spratt had rightly called southern geographic and class bonds potentially fragile. Yet the importation of supposed savages now seemed the best way to snap rather than fortify the social bonds. With that conclusion widespread, Spratt's wild detour around the frustration of the Buchanan years had yielded still more frustration. To add to South Carolina's anxiety, happenings in Charleston and in the Border South reconfirmed Spratt's initial diagnosis. A new uproar over free blacks showed that the cornerstone distinction between black menials and white nonmudsills had been compromised.

CHAPTER 13

Reenslaving Free Blacks

A movement to cleanse the South of free blacks accompanied the campaign to import Africans for cleansing. Both crusades drove the gospel that all blacks needed southern masters to an extreme. Each extremism could be dismissed as lunatic antics, except that portions of the mainstream sought the alleged lunacy. Both extreme proposals appeared as if out of nowhere in the 1850s. Each streaked toward almost capture of some state legislatures on the eve of the Civil War.

Reenslavers of free blacks deployed the more promising strategy. Where reopeners had to blast (or sneak) past federal law, reenslavers only had to convince southern lawmakers. Where reopeners faced the apprehension that African alleged savages would convulse the South, reenslavers wished to rid the South of free blacks' allegedly convulsive presence. Yet despite its advantages, the reenslavement excitement fizzled as swiftly as the reopening craze. Both frustrations left extremists the more on the hunt for a final solution.

– 1 –

A startling statistic: In 1860, slightly more free blacks lived in the enslaved South than in the free North. A less startling statistic: The 250,751 southern free blacks comprised only 6 percent of the South's 1860 blacks. But as always in matters southern, the overall average masked divisive exceptions. Free blacks comprised 2 percent of the Lower South's 1860 black population, 7 percent of the Middle South's, 49 percent of Maryland's, and 91 percent of Delaware's. At the South's Maryland/Delaware northeastern fringe, a North American middle ground between slavery and freedom, supposedly existing only south of the United States, thrived surprisingly.

Whether massed overwhelmingly in Delaware, threateningly in Maryland, or spottily elsewhere, most free blacks endured dismaying economic conditions and racial prejudices. Free blacks' economic opportunities usually remained tenuous, their possessions limited, and their wages low. They could not vote or serve on juries or testify against whites. Often they could be reenslaved if convicted of a petty crime, or if they left their state and returned, or if a white guardian failed to vouch for their good behavior.

Despite these exploitations, southern free blacks sometimes crept ahead. A few climbed miles ahead. Free mulattoes especially soared, boosted by whites' prejudice that blacks needed some white blood to succeed. Lightened blacks even sometimes became that southern anomaly, brown slaveholders. A South Carolina ex-slave mulatto, William Ellison, possessed an important cotton gin as well as 900 acres and sixty-three slaves. This brown master's slaveholdings exceeded 99 percent of white slaveholders'. Six Louisiana free blacks owned still more slaves, including Andrew Dubuclet, a sugar planter worth a quarter million dollars. This heretical evidence cast doubt on the orthodoxies that all blacks must be enslaved, and that only whites could be slaveholders, and that no middle ground of free browns could exist.[1]

The defense of slavery, responded the *Richmond South* in 1858, "stands upon the theory . . . that nature intends" every black "for the *status* of servitude. . . . If one Negro may be free, why not another?" Unless no Negro is capable of self-government, our whole system is "a logical absurdity." Or as a Virginia legislator exclaimed, I "would not own a slave for one moment, . . . if I was convinced that the God of nature who smiles upon this land, intended that freedom should be the lot of that race."[2]

To make slavery last longer than a moment, declared the *Aberdeen* (Mississippi) *Sunny South,* we must "prove the sincerity of our avowed convictions." Have we repudiated the old "maudlin sensibility" that "human servitude" violates "individual liberty"? Do we believe that the "radical inferiority of the Negro" makes a black freedman "incapable of individual culture?" If so, we must demonstrate "our conviction by reducing the free [black] population to bondage."[3]

The reduction of liberated blacks to servitude would eliminate more than defective belief. Maryland's and Delaware's crawl away from slavery would be reversed. Slaves' potentially disruptive interaction with liberated blacks would vanish. White wage earners' free black competitors would disappear. "We can only have a healthy state of society," declared the *Mobile Daily Register,* "with but two classes—white and slave."[4]

But how should that third class of free blacks be eliminated? An uncompromising proslavery mentality would have demanded that all blacks, all supposedly helpless, all must immediately be given the mercy of a master. The compromising democratic mentality, however, intruded, dictating that freedmen retained some choice. Thus reenslavement proposals always included the qualification that black freedmen, to escape slavery, could choose to depart the state.

The departure option paralyzed whites' capacity to remove all free blacks. Economically, a labor-starved culture hardly welcomed the departure of black workers by the tens of thousands. Moreover, free blacks' coerced departure seemed cruel, especially to the paternalists who had freed them, particularly when freedmen had prospered without masters and/or when cherished enslaved family members would have to be left behind.

Thus in 1859–60, some 1193 outraged white Mississippians petitioned their legislature, deploring the fate awaiting eighty-two successful free Americans, if lawmakers passed departure/reenslavement. The black freedmen, declared the petitions, had financed their own freedom, bought their own farms, established their own shops, preserved their own families, and served their white neighbors. These boons to the community, if harried out of the South, would be ripped from enslaved spouses and/or children and deprived of their property.

Mississippi petitioners cited the plight of A. L. Chevis of Hinds County, for thirty-five years a valued barber and bricklayer for whites. This outstanding freedman, who had never made "his residence here objectionable," now faced exile from his slave wife and eight children. Reenslavement/departure's victims would also include Edward Hill of Hinds County, for more than twenty years the owner of a blacksmith shop that whites treasured. Now this successful southern entrepreneur would have to risk his chances among racist Yankees, despite knowing "nothing of the manners, habits, and customs of the people in the Northern States."

Yet another victim would be Jordan Cheeves of Warren County, freed for good military labor in the War of 1812, now infirm. How "cruel and unjust to drive him in his old age from the country he, in his youth, fought to protect."[5] Or as these petitions all indirectly asked, must a paternalistic domestic institution smash blacks' domiciles and consign southern paternalists' family friends to the heartless North? When the question took that form, pitched battles beckoned over a heartbreaking (and labor-draining) plan to obliterate the supposedly impossible middle ground between enslaved blacks and free whites.

– 2 –

Extremists' assault on the middle ground came to one of its two spectacular climaxes in, where else, the capital of southern extremism. In Charleston, South Carolina, impoverished white nonslaveholders led the onslaught on free blacks. Another supposed southern impossibility provoked the assault. According to proslavery dogma, poor white mudsills only existed in the North. Slavery supposedly consigned only black serviles to muddy tasks, elevating all white citizens above grimy toil.

This proslavery fancy aside, dirt-poor rural nonslaveholders usually worked their own few muddy acres. Though they suffered the mud, these petty landowners suffered no confusion with southern chattel slaves, lashed to work masters' fields. Nor could poor rural farmers be confused with Yankee "wage slaves," paid a pittance to sweat in city factories. But southern class problems pressed more painfully on white urban nonslaveholders. These white mudsills received meager pay to perform the same menial labor as blacks.

Urban poor whites' plight especially soured class relations in late antebellum Charleston. During the 1850s, Charleston's masters sold slaves to the more prosperous Southwest at a record pace. White immigrants moved in to fill the unskilled labor vacuum. From 1850 to 1860, some 5623 Charleston slaves departed and 3300 whites arrived, over half of them foreign immigrants. For the first time, Charleston had a white majority.

Impoverished white newcomers especially loathed rich free blacks, almost all of them mulattoes. In 1860, two-thirds of Charleston's free black male freedmen occupied skilled labor positions, compared to only half of the white immigrants. The richest free brown skilled laborers displayed not only whitened black skin but also superior finery, to the fury of white nonskilled laborers, whose race supposedly monopolized whiteness and superiority.

Charleston's brown-skinned irritant remained small in size. In 1860, only 19 percent of Charleston's blacks were free. Only 25 percent of the freedmen owned property. Still, fifty-five free browns owned at least one slave plus at least $2000 worth of real estate. The wealthiest brown commanded fourteen slaves and $40,075 worth of real estate. The brown elite, managing their carpenter, tailor, and millwright shops by day, cherished their exclusive Brown Fellowship Society at night. Snobby browns held unwhitened blacks at a distance and comfortably rubbed shoulders with their white customers as members of the Grace Episcopal Church. Were white mudsills equal to these brown achievers?[6]

Leonidas Spratt feared that the city's white wage slaves would rise against a social system that generated such questions. His solution, reopening the African slave trade, sought to import black mudsills to replace white mudsills. White mudsills had a better idea: Expel uppity browns and elevate downtrodden whites. Bridling at "the degradation, . . . hardship, and injustice of having the entire free Negro population thrust upon us as competitors," white laborers wished to remove "from our body politic this cankerous sore, and stand among our fellow citizens as equals."[7]

Would-be equals at the bottom of the white social ladder found their leadership several rungs higher. The Charleston reenslavement movement's directors included James M. Eason, a mechanic who owned an iron foundry and six slaves, and Harry T. Peake, who supervised the South Carolina Railroad's shop and owned nine slaves. Eason and Peake competed for skilled labor contracts against rich browns. Often, provokingly respectable browns won the jobs. In retaliation, provoked white entrepreneurs coalesced with equally provoked white mudsills, both seeking to oust all free blacks. The coalition posed an ominous challenge to the few free brown entrepreneurs, to the more numerous free black mudsills, and to the much more numerous white squires who patronized the browns' workshops and shared membership in Grace Episcopal.

Many of Charleston's upper-class patrons shielded their favorite mulattoes from the Eason-Peake storm. The protective patriarchs thus added another anomaly to this crazy quilt reenslavement drama, starring folks that this enslaved society supposedly precluded. Just as no black supposedly should have been freed, and no brown should have existed or been rich, and no white should have been a mudsill, so only owners should have felt paternalistically obligated to protect a laborer. According to proslavery gospel, unless a superior owned an inferior as he possessed dogs and horses and wives and children, he would become a cannibalistic capitalist, devouring all those less powerful.

Charleston paternalists' uplift of browns mocked that crabbed theory of paternalism (as did James Buchanan's caring relationship with his paid white house servant, Miss Hetty). Patriarchs sought to protect esteemed mulattoes that they did *not* own (and had sometimes proudly and paternalistically freed). All free people, the Charleston lawyer Christopher Memminger explained to the South Carolina legislature, have "rights . . . to the protection of our laws." Memminger would especially protect his fellow brown worshippers at Grace Episcopal. They possessed a "most estimable character," more so than lower-class whites who "are demoralizing our slaves."[8]

In the spirit of this politically indiscreet preference for cultivated browns over uncultivated citizens, South Carolina paternalists stymied proposals for reenslavement/departure in South Carolina's upper-crust legislature in both 1859 and 1860. But white mudsills mustered the legal ammunition to retaliate. Previously unenforced laws, by being newly enforced, could send brown aristocrats scurrying beyond the state, to the horror of white patriarchs.

According to the state's legal code, blacks remained enslaved unless they possessed both manumission papers and a court-appointed guardian, responsible for their good behavior. Moreover, when city paternalists allowed petted slaves to pick an employer and pocket most of the wages, the not-quite freedmen had to buy expensive slave badges. In previous permissive times, few blacks had bothered to save manumission papers or to secure a court-appointed guardian or to purchase slave badges.

Disgruntled white plebeians had only to locate a politician who would enforce the black codes. They found their enforcer in Charleston's Mayor Charles Macbeth, who wished their political support. In the fall of 1860, as Mayor Macbeth's agents combed Charleston for blacks without proper papers and/or badges, over 1000 of Charleston's 3000 free blacks despairingly left for the North.

Memminger, one of Charleston's greatest lawyers, could do nothing to stem this legal savagery. Savaged evacuees included families that had enjoyed freedom for two generations (but had not the papers to verify their founder's manumission). Those frightened into departure often suffered severance from relatives and friends, in the manner of slaves sold down the river. Those pressured to leave also included some star American Horatio Alger types, lately risen from enslaved beginnings, now removed like a wealthy Cherokee banished down a trail of tears.[9]

A less paternalistic ruling class would have cynically sacrificed a third of the city's free blacks (and would have accepted new laws that would have savaged the other two-thirds). Free blacks had become useful scapegoats, deflecting impoverished whites' fury away from the culture's establishment and toward the brown fringe. At this unprecedented moment when the Charleston riffraff got uppity with the silk stocking crowd, the resentful did not assault the slaveowners or free the slaves. Instead, angry white mudsills insisted that nonowned folk who bore nonwhite skin must be ousted.

By embracing this escape valve for lower-class steam, upper-class patriarchs would have defused trouble. Instead of lording it over poorer whites and uplifting middle-class browns, slaveowners would then have patronized only slaves and allowed all whites to submerge all browns. Then racial prejudice would have united rich and poor whites, all treating each other as equals, all striving to keep nonwhites inferior.

But with genteel patriarchs rejecting this crass solution, the story had reached a precarious juncture. White toilers had not ousted all free browns, and white patriarchs had not reversed departed freedmen's plight. The impasse demonstrated the Lower South establishment's strength, despite its inconsistencies. Although the proletarians' reenslavement shove had been aborted, white menials only had muttered their resentment. Although Charleston patriarchs had lost a third of "their" free browns to a merciless deportation scheme, they had mercifully helped two-thirds of their freed slaves to defy ouster and still had suffered no mudsill attack on slavery itself.

But Leonidas Spratt had his point. A revolt from the lily-white bottom against competition with blacks might ascend from the crusade to deport middle-class browns to a campaign to oust the aristocrats' slaves. With all nonwhites, free or enslaved, driven from the city, white nonmasters would monopolize employment opportunities. This escalated crisis could especially erupt if Northern Republicans handed the loathsome (to the patriarchs) Charles Macbeth a patronage job, to arouse the rabble against the rich.

– 3 –

While Charleston's reenslavement crisis spotlighted Lower South squires' powerful grip, even when (rarely) challenged, Maryland's reenslavement epic illuminated Border South slaveholders' loosening grasp, amidst ceaseless erosion. In Charleston, a small number of unskilled whites confronted a small number of skilled browns inside the urban fringe of an overwhelmingly rural civilization, with slavery's future not even an issue. In Maryland, in contrast, large planters confronted large numbers of both manumitting masters and free blacks inside a fabled plantation area, with rural slavery's future in a pivotal Border South black belt at the crossroads.

When free blacks' numbers rose to equal slaves', one borderland crossroad had already been reached. In Delaware, where around 20 percent of the population was black throughout the 1790–1860 period, that crossroad had been passed by 1800, when 57 percent of blacks were free. In 1860, enslaved Delaware was mostly a dim memory, with the state's free blacks outnumbering slaves twelve to one and the fifteen slave states almost down to fourteen.

In 1860, neighboring Maryland approached Delaware's 1800 crossroads. Maryland's blacks, a quarter of the state's population in 1860, then included 83,942 freedmen and 87,189 slaves. The commingling of equally large masses of enslaved and free blacks could provoke more slaves to sprint for freedom. More slaves' flight toward liberty in neighboring free labor states could provoke more slaveowning capitalists to move their investment toward safe Lower South states. More free blacks, by providing more good labor and good order, also could impel more whites to doubt that only slavery could control large numbers of blacks.

Maryland's legislature initially faced these subversive possibilities three decades before the state's 1859–60 reenslavement showdown. By 1830, Maryland's 1790 ratio of thirteen slaves to one free black had already plunged to two to one. Then in 1832, another southern crossroad in a neighboring state inspired the Maryland legislature's first effort to abort free blacks' increasing presence. After the Nat Turner insurrection, the Virginia legislature staged far from the only and far from the last full-scale southern consideration of abolition.

In an 1832 discussion as searching as the Virginians', Maryland legislators came to a more conclusive verdict: All blacks thereafter freed must be deported. When a master manumitted a slave, lawmakers decreed, the Maryland State Colonization Society must remove the freedman to the state's colony near Liberia, called Maryland in Africa. Only a court could grant the liberated soul a renewable annual permit to stay, and only if "extraordinary conduct and character" had been proved. The legislature pledged over $200,000 to ensure that nonextraordinary freedmen involuntarily departed.[10]

Only voluntary departures ensued. "Not one Negro has been *forced* to leave the State," the Maryland State Colonization Society complained in 1858. On "many" occasions, "we have . . . used every endeavor" to enforce deportation. But "some man of influence" has always secured a court's "permission" for the freed black "to remain."[11] The paternalism of the influential remained alive and well *after* slavery, in Maryland no less than in Charleston.

After 1832, with most free blacks remaining in Maryland, with some enslaved blacks fleeing to the North, with other borderland slaves sold to the Lower South, and with more border masters turning slaves into freedmen, the plurality of slaves over freedmen continued to shrink. By 1860, the shrinkage had almost polished off slavery in North Maryland (meaning the tier of counties closest to free labor Pennsylvania). In North Maryland's metropolis of Baltimore, the ratio of slaves to free blacks plunged from one to three in 1830 to one to twelve by 1860. In North Maryland's rural areas, the ratio dipped from one to one to one to three. North Maryland had been proved too urban, too close to Yankee meddlers, too unsuited for large plantations—in short too far north for much slavery.

South Maryland, meaning the rest of the state, seemed too far south for such trouble, which made slavery's decline here a headline Old South story.[12]

South Maryland had been a bulwark of the institution ever since colonial times. In 1860, 46 percent of South Maryland's population was still black, besting the Lower South average. No other black belt area in the Border South and only eastern Virginia in the Middle South displayed such extensive plantation areas. Not even Virginia's James River planters outdid the dandies who developed South Maryland's lush eastern and western shores of the Chesapeake Bay. Yet South Maryland's ratio of slaves to free blacks dropped from three to one in 1830 to two to one in 1860.

In the three Eastern Shore counties at the southeastern extremity of Maryland, the ratio plunged further. Dorchester, Worcester, and Somerset counties contained a 40 percent black population throughout the antebellum period. Yet the three counties' ratio of slaves to free blacks sank from two to one in 1830 to one to one in 1860. These plantation-dominated counties provoked the climactic crisis over free blacks in 1859–60. Dorchester County initiated the reenslavement movement. Worcester County supplied the great leader. Somerset County came to the most reactionary decision.

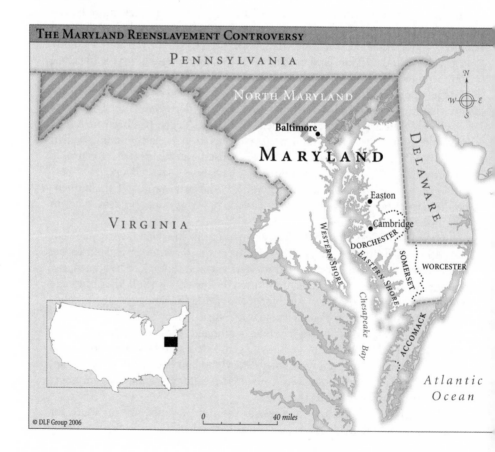

Reactionaries in these three half-emancipated Eastern Shore counties confronted freedom's contagions both outside and inside their area. On the east, barely enslaved Delaware loomed. To the south, Accomack County, Virginia, sported many nonslaveholding fishermen, object of Governor Henry Wise's intense suspicion. To the west sprawled the Chesapeake Bay, one of fugitive slaves' favorite waterways toward the free labor North.

Comparisons with other endangered border areas indicate the Eastern Shore's special predicament. North Maryland, while closer to the free North, contained far lower black concentrations. Western Missouri, while surrounded on three sides in Kansas times, contained only half the Eastern Shore's density of blacks. South Maryland's Western Shore of the Chesapeake Bay, while even blacker in population than the Eastern Shore, suffered no neighbors as deeply infected as Delaware and Accomack County.

Libertarian ideas within the three especially besieged Eastern Shore counties swirled as contagiously as liberty without. Nowhere else in the United States did as dense a concentration of plantation slaves work side by side with as dense a concentration of free blacks. Nowhere else in the South's blackest belts had so many planters freed so many slaves. Nowhere else in the Old South did liberating and reactionary masters stage such a showdown.

On one side of this schism in the Eastern Shore ruling class, manumitting masters cherished pragmatic paternalism. To avoid slavery's premature collapse, they adjusted to free and open conditions. In the manner of North Maryland slaveholders who lived close to the South's northern border, the Eastern Shore's manumitting masters used credible promises no less than savage lashes to keep slaves from daring relatively easy (albeit still risky) flights toward freedom. Emulating a long-standing practice in Baltimore, many Eastern Shore patriarchs promised their slaves freedom after a period of resourceful toil. Sometimes, seven years of hard work would secure the reward. More often, creditable toil during the master's lifetime would earn liberty after the owner's death.

This semienslaved system most resembled American colonials' indentured servitude system. Impoverished seventeenth- and eighteenth-century immigrants had often paid their way to American with seven years of slavish labor in the New World. Then they had been freed. Initially, black labor in the Chesapeake Bay area had evolved from indentured servitude to perpetual slavery. Now, the Eastern Shore evolution crept backward toward freedom, from permanent to temporary servitude.

Paternalists, when acting as temporary masters, envisioned a future as temporary employers. While still owners of slaves, these pragmatists would prepare supposedly depraved blacks for freedom. After emancipation, employers of freed blacks would prepare wards for the final solution. Wholly redeemed blacks would eventually return to Africa, with the returning voyagers carrying American democracy, free labor, and Christianity back to their unredeemed homeland.

Where perpetual slaveholders saw blacks as perpetual children, temporary masters believed that benevolent parents prepare children to grow up.
They meant to teach irresponsible enslaved wards to become responsible free
workers. They saw no reason to tremble that wards who had almost grown
up (their free black workers) would rouse the wards who had half grown up
(their enslaved workers) to run away from a paternalistic regime that would
be benevolent in all its stages. They affirmed that God had put heathens in
America so that paternalists could prepare ex-Africans to redeem Africa.
While Christian providence slowly evolved, evolutionary slavery allowed a
property holder to procure decent work from temporary slaves.

This heady combination of crassness and Christianity brought the flexibility of Latin American slavery to the usually racially inflexible North American slaveholders. The Eastern Shore manumitters rejected a two-class theory
of enslaved blacks and free whites. They affirmed the three-class slave society
rampant in Cuba and Brazil, with a huge middle ground of manumitted
blacks.

In the three Eastern Shore counties, conventional masters stormed at
the heresy. They denied that American blacks' rescue of Africa was a cos-
mic certainty, that paternalism could be saved by manumitting slaves, that
black savages could be trained to be like white employees, and that free
blacks would fail to infect enslaved blacks with visions of liberty. Orthodox slaveholders found themselves trapped in a world with heretics just
outside, free blacks abundant inside, and compromising whites mastering
half the terrain. Their crisis mentality needed only a spark to ignite a
firestorm.

– 4 –

As usual in exposed border areas, fugitive slaves lit the first spark. Especially
in Dorchester County, whites experienced the most provocative border scenario: an ongoing series of gang runaways, allegedly provoked by a northern
Liberty Line that extended inside the South. On the Eastern Shore, freedom's
agitators supposedly included free blacks, who taught by their very presence
that liberty need not be reserved for whites, and white strangers, who helped
slaves flee toward liberty. The *Baltimore Sun* reported two results of Dorchester County's blur of slavery and freedom:

> October 31, 1857. "A Grand Stampede" of Dorchester slaves. 30 escaped, mak-
> ing 44 in two weeks, 15 belonging to one robbed capitalist. He offers a $3100
> reward.
>   July 31, 1858. "SLAVE STAMPEDE—There was another slave stampede in
> Dorchester County, Md. last week." Seven slaves worth $10,000+ absconded.

Such stampedes could impel owners to sell more slaves to safer Lower South
areas. With more slaves fleeing north, more owners selling slaves south, and

more masters offering future freedom to keep slaves toiling, slaveowning capitalism looked to be spinning out of control—and out of Maryland. Seeking to restore equilibrium, the Convention of Slaveholders of the Eastern Shore of Maryland met in Cambridge, Dorchester County's largest town, on November 3–4, 1858. Near the convention site, a white named Haslet languished in prison, having allegedly run off seven slaves, as northern abolitionists' paid agent. Yet another alleged heretic, James L. Bowers, having allegedly also run off slaves, had himself been run off with a festive coat and feathers.[13]

Alas, the allegations could not be legally proved. Only whites could testify against whites in white men's republican courts. Only blacks knew about a supposed abolitionist agent's supposed sabotage. Delegates to the Convention of Slaveholders thus declared that they faced triple peril: paralyzed legal deterrence inside, "the influence of abolition from abroad," and "free-negroism in our midst." In response, the Maryland legislature must "manfully and without hesitation" act up to the principle that "free-negroism and slavery are incompatible with each other." If legislators fail to expel or reenslave free blacks, Marylanders would in effect "acknowledge to the world that they have not the energy and determination to protect their domestic institutions from gradual overthrow."[14]

Agitated Eastern Shore reenslavers needed to arouse serene Maryland areas. Otherwise, too few legislators would favor reenslavement/departure. In hopes of rallying Baltimore, serene about its 25,680 free blacks compared to its 2218 slaves, the Eastern Shore conclave took its cause to the city. The November 1858 Cambridge Convention of Slaveholders called a statewide slaveholders' convention to convene in almost-emancipated Baltimore in June 1859. The Baltimore assemblage, resolved the Eastern Shore convention, must press the next state legislature to make the ultimate decision: Either abolish free blacks immediately or allow slaves to become free blacks gradually.

Baltimoreans considered abolition of the middle ground too fanciful to bother considering. Not one delegate from the host city showed up in early June 1859, when the slaveholders' convention came to town. The spurned delegates gave passing thought to moving to Frederick. They relented after a couple of Baltimoreans tardily appeared. At least all parts of the drifting Maryland establishment now deigned to listen, if some Eastern Shore fossil called the drift away from slavery disastrous.

Curtis W. Jacobs gave the drifters an earful. Jacobs, Worcester County's favorite reactionary, had risen to Eastern Shore prominence as the leader of the 1858 Cambridge convention. He would imminently rise to statewide notoriety as leader of the reenslavers' climactic 1860 legislative effort. In both these impassioned endeavors, sandwiched around his June 1859 agitation at the Baltimore slaveholders' convention, Curtis Jacobs drew on his uniquely broad experience in colliding Souths. With his wife, Jacobs owned not only fifty-six slaves in Maryland (only eighty other Marylanders owned as many or more) but also a few in almost-emancipated Delaware, his native state, and thirty-six in Alabama, his ideological mecca.[15] This champion of Maryland's reenslavement/departure solution epitomized the wider problem. Jacobs could easily become the wholly Lower South planter who threw up his hands at the Border South's irresolute drift.

Jacobs urged instead that the Maryland legislature must "terminate free Negroism at an early date, and on the most advantageous terms to our white population." While "a prudent discrimination should be made in the case of meritorious and aged free negroes," the rest should be forced to choose between leaving the state, selecting a master, and accepting state conscription. The state should sell "said conscript slaves," in small quantities and at a "low" price, payable in "installments," to nonslaveholders or owners of a few slaves. Then we would "enable our citizens of limited means" to become slaveholders. Otherwise, "lazy, degraded, immoral" free blacks, "like the locust clouds of Egypt, shall spread out over our State in all directions, paralyzing our energies, demoralizing our people, and devouring our substance."[16]

Curtis Jacobs's proposition was either genius or madness. The conscript plan was Extremism with a capital *E*. It would triple the number of Maryland slaveholders and double the number of slaves, if free blacks chose conscription over departure. It would obliterate the Latin American–style middle ground of free blacks and reverse eighty years of Maryland's drift away from slavery, whichever option the freedmen chose. It would force the most compromised slave state, save only for Delaware, to swallow the most uncompromising version of reenslavement/departure, flavored with the uncompromising possibility of conscripting some 80,000 free Americans to be largely nonslaveholders' slaves.

In the June 1859 slaveholders' convention, Judge J. Thompson Mason declared Jacobs a genius. "The great question at issue was simply this," urged the judge: "Shall Maryland become a Free State or a Slave State?" Curtis Jacobs realized, cheered Mason, that Maryland's house divided could no longer stand. Marylanders could no longer survive both classes of blacks in the same place, with the one paid "off in cash, whilst the other, with an imploring look, would seem to say, 'shall I get nothing.'"

Of convention delegates who considered Jacobs's genius more like madness, U.S. Senator James Pearce, chairman of the resolutions committee, was the most appalled. Faced with Jacobs's conscription, free blacks would flee the state, warned Pearce, deducting "nearly 50 percent from the household and agricultural labor furnished by people of this color." Rather than our free blacks being "idle, vicious, and unproductive," declared the U.S. senator, "a large portion of our soil could not be tilled without their aid." Nor would "the great body of the people of Maryland" deprive more than 80,000 blacks "of the right to freedom which they have acquired by our laws and the tenderness of their masters, whether wise or unwise."

A state without sufficient "white people to do the work," concluded James Pearce, could not afford to require hardworking free blacks "to remove or go into slavery." That choice was also morally as monstrous as "the highwayman who demands of the traveler his money or his life." Pearce's fellow delegates overwhelmingly agreed. They voted 59–33 against Jacobs's proposition that "free negroism should be abolished."

After slaveholders in the 1859 Baltimore convention had affirmed two to one that a reenslaver was a highwayman, and with Maryland nonslaveholders outnumbering slaveholders seven to one, the 1858 Cambridge convention's plan to ask the 1860 Maryland legislature for reenslavement/departure invited another mauling. Still, eight months after the Baltimore slaveholders' convention had in effect invited the Eastern Shore's favorite spokesman to go live among fellow Alabama spirits, Curtis Jacobs asked compromising Maryland legislators to act like William Lowndes Yancey. In February 1860, as chairman of the Committee on Colored Population of Maryland's House of Delegates, Jacobs reported out a bill that would have reenslaved all blacks freed after 1832, unless they departed the state by May 1.

If Maryland continued to drift toward Delaware's "sickly sentimentalism," Jacobs told legislators, black freedmen "would either destroy the white population . . . or the whites, in self defense, would destroy" the blacks. Divided Marylanders must instead resolve to "have but one mind, one will, one God" and "but two classes—white freemen—negro slaves." Then Maryland, having adopted Alabama's enlightened proslavery faith, and having quarantined itself from Delaware's deplorable antislavery contagion, would "stand or fall with the South."

Jacobs conceded that "some of Maryland's free blacks are industrious." Yet even the "few industrious ones" wreak damage, for they drive "an equal number of our native whites . . . out of the State." Meanwhile, the "vast majority" of free blacks are "so much dead weight upon the State." They labor badly and contaminate dreadfully, turning cheery slaves into desperate runaways. They are "the pabulum on which abolition feeds and lives in our midst." If the legislature votes against "reclaiming our beloved state from the thralldom and blighting influence of free-negroism," Maryland will be ruined by "her own madness."[17]

The state's shocked reaction showed the power of its middle-ground mentality. In the House of Delegates and in the Baltimore newspapers, Jacob's foes called free blacks fine laborers. They praised the humanitarians who freed their slaves for good service. They termed slavery without freedom's incentives a monstrous system, dependent on terror to reduce fellow humans to servility. They continued to pray that hardworking slaves would become hardworking free laborers, then hardworking missionaries to Africa.[18]

Stung by this overwhelming condemnation, Jacobs threatened to resign, certainly from the legislature and perhaps from the state. Compromising legislators then decided that uncompromising anti-Jacobsism, like Jacobsism itself, had gone too far. Seeking a revised middle ground, the legislators barred future manumission. They also authorized any county to hold a local referendum on whether to appoint a Board of Commissioners, charged with insuring that propertyless free blacks hired themselves out for a year.

This diluted version of Jacobsism failed almost as completely as the undiluted conception. In November 1860, most North Maryland counties refused even to vote on the Board of Commissioner proposal. South Maryland voters rejected the scheme by almost a four to one margin. Only the Eastern Shore's Somerset County voted to establish the board, which only had power to ensure that free blacks labored. Even Dorchester County, where reenslavement had started, and Worcester County, Jacobs's own, rejected the diluted clamp on free blacks. Jacobs's rout confirmed that a step beyond the crossroad had been taken. Maryland would continue meandering up Delaware's northward path, with no swerve back Alabama's way.[19]

The different outcomes of the South Carolina and Maryland reenslavement crises showed that the two most dissimilar Souths headed in opposite directions. In Charleston, where free blacks' numbers remained trivial, angry white plebeians ousted a third of the browns. In Maryland, where free blacks almost outnumbered slaves, not a soul had to depart. South Carolina gentlemen were serene enough about slavery's internal strength to balk at reenslavement consolidations. Yet half of the Eastern Shore gentry became so distressed about slavery's waning clout that they desperately sought reenslavement. The other half of the Eastern Shore upper crust remained so content with *free* blacks that they buried Curtis Jacobs's attempt to play William L. Yancey in Maryland. The stage was set for South Carolina disunionists to fear that Abraham Lincoln's Southern Republicans would be an immediate menace inside Maryland unionists' middle ground.

- 5 -

The reenslavement effort, like the reopening attempt, had its revealing anticlimax after its climactic episodes. In the eastern Upper South, where free blacks were omnipresent, the Jacobs panacea largely failed. But in the western Upper South, where fewer free blacks resided, reenslavers slightly succeeded.

The older, seaboard Upper South states had nurtured ancient Jeffersonian qualms about slavery and multiple manumissions. The newer, more frontier Upper South states displayed less apologetics and fewer freed slaves. Thus in 1860, where the eastern Border South's Delaware and Maryland contained over 100,000 free blacks (over half the two states' black population), the western Border South's Kentucky and Missouri contained under 15,000 free blacks (under 4 percent of their black populations). So too, where the eastern Middle South's Virginia and North Carolina contained almost 70,000 free blacks, the western Middle South's Tennessee and Arkansas contained under 3500.

This difference highlighted an important fact. The eastern and western Upper Souths differed from each other as much as the eastern Lower South differed from the western tropics. Just as reactionary South Carolina could never be confused with expansive Louisiana, so western Missouri's nouveau frontiersmen could not be confused with eastern Maryland's aristocratic dandies. But then why should reenslavement have come closer to success out west, where few blacks resided?

Because areas mostly devoid of free blacks remained mostly devoid of practical reason to resist the reenslavers. Where scant free blacks labored, scant labor would be lost if the liberated departed. Furthermore, scant liberating masters would be there to protest against their wards' deportation.

With practical reason to oppose reenslavement slight, the panacea offered proslavery extremists easy rewards. Those who would reenslave free blacks, like those who would reopen the African slave trade, conceived that whites did not believe universally enough or passionately enough (or at all) in the abstraction that all blacks must be enslaved. Sluggish belief bred not only free blacks but also political moderation. Zealous belief would breed not only reenslavement/departure but also intransigent politics. As a tool to shock the sluggards into cheering for slavery's genius, the abstraction that freedom and blacks must be severed was a cheerleader's delight—especially where orthodox amens would cost few free blacks their liberty.

Yet the shock of reenslavement/departure extremism might also goad the silent toward denouncing a travesty. Of those out west who had previously held their tongues, Tennessee's U.S. Supreme Court Justice John Catron became the most prominent protester against the reenslavement/departure shock. Catron, it will be recalled, had secured President-elect James Buchanan's secret intervention in the so-called Dred Scott Decision. He had sought Buchanan's help not to perpetuate slavery but to save the Union. His horror was northern extremists, not least because they empowered southern extremists. If the Supreme Court settled the territorial issue, he hoped, abolitionists and disunionists would vanish, southern calm would return, and his way of easing slavery away might slowly spread. His way: allowing some of his nominally enslaved blacks to live like respected, respectable freemen. And now in 1859, the convulsed South proposed to force perfectly respectable freemen to be slaves or to leave!

This movement in the wrong direction impelled Tennessee's greatest jurist to go public with his outrage. Catron would not "mince words." No "Christian country . . . this side of Africa" could abide the monstrosity that "the strong" could "capture the weak and enslave them." His heart especially went out to folk who had been free for generations, who had only a speck of black blood, who owned prime property, and who worshipped in our best churches. The "great bodies of Christian men and women" will not "quietly stand by and see their humble co-workers sold on the block."[20]

Catron was half right. In southern areas without many free blacks, half of the great body of Christians thrilled to the cheer that providence created all blacks to be slaves. The other half of western Upper South folks considered reenslavers to be outrageous rabble-rousers. With outrage battling cheers to a standstill, state after state fell into deadlock. In 1859–60, reenslavement/departure swept the Tennessee House but lost in the Senate, captured the Missouri and Florida legislatures but fell before both governors' vetoes, secured two victories in the Mississippi legislature but lost on the third reading. Even in Arkansas, where the 1859 legislature decreed that free blacks must depart the state before January 1, 1860, or suffer reenslavement, the threat partially failed. Some 500 free blacks fled Arkansas before the deadline. The next legislature allowed the remaining 144 to retain freedom.[21]

– 6 –

Arkansas's retreat meant that pre–Civil War reenslavers shoved not one free black into bondage, not even where free blacks were few, not even where Charleston's proletariat rallied against brown laborers' competition, not even where Maryland's free blacks' numbers almost overtook slaves'. Of the approximately 250,000 free blacks in the South when the reenslavement campaign commenced, only around 1000 South Carolina and 500 Arkansas free blacks ever traveled up exiles' trail of tears. The skimpy yield recalled African slave trade reopeners' slim catch from their ocean of tears: the almost 200 African unfortunates on the *Wanderer*.

The moral of both losing attempts at purification, to the South's Judge Catron: Southern extremism was counterproductive and moderation safe. The judge's moderation had so far yielded nothing more dangerous to slavery than his verbal diatribes against reenslavement and his own few slaves' loosened chains. That loosening stood counterbalanced by Catron's so-called Dred Scott Decision and by the judge's failure to acknowledge or aid his own mulatto son, except once to give him twenty-five cents![22]

The endlessly defeated reopeners and reenslavers, however, saw moderation's ascendancy as dangerous. Compromised viewpoints like Catron's had made first Delaware's, now Maryland's middle ground unconquerable for proslavery zealots. Moreover, Catron's dictum that slavery equaled "might makes right" would help lead the judge and several hundred thousand Upper South anti-Confederates into the arms of northern moderates, after disunion and war engulfed the Lower South.

Three years before the reenslavement furor, Virginia's Henry Garnett had predicted that compromised opinion would pave the northern South's path toward the North. Maryland, wrote Garnett in 1856, is already "rotten to the core on the subject of slavery. . . . We could only rely on her for a few years longer." In the next few years, as agitators farther south observed Curtis Jacobs's futility, they thought Garnett's prediction prescient. "*Attachment to the institution is weakening on our frontier*, where it ought to be the strongest," wrote the *Montgomery Advertiser*, after hearing about Jacobs's desperation in the Eastern Shore slaveholders' 1858 Cambridge convention. "Are we not hemmed in, cramped, encircled, driven to a corner?"[23]

A year later, after watching Jacobs repudiated in the Baltimore statewide slaveholders' convention, the *New Orleans Crescent* called Maryland "already well-nigh half-abolitionized" and Delaware only nominally enslaved. "Black Republicanism is gradually undermining the outposts of slavery, and will obtain possession of them in a few years."[24] At this uncomfortable moment, with Buchanan's proslavery initiatives coming up empty, slavery's frustrated defenders suffered four shocking lessons in how Yankee meddlers might invade a compromised borderland.

PART IV

JOHN BROWN, AND THREE OTHER MEN COINCIDENTALLY NAMED JOHN

John Brown's raid on Harpers Ferry, Virginia, commencing on October 16, 1859, assuredly helped spawn disunion. But *how* did Brown have that impact? After a few weeks of hysteria, after all, Southerners realized that Brown's tactics had failed to arouse a single slave, much less a general revolt. Nor did many Southerners tremble that a future version of Brown's strategy would awaken Cuffees to seek mass slaughter.

But some very prominent Northerners' enthusiasm for John Brown stretched Southerners' fury. What kind of monsters share our Union, many a Southerner stormed, who thank their Lord for a wild individualist who would demolish our social order and savage us all, helpless women and children included? And what other intruder, with what alternate strategy, will next penetrate the South, bringing Yankees' loathing unspeakably inside? The answers came soon enough, from three other men coincidentally named John.

CHAPTER 14

John Brown and Violent Invasion

John Brown's raid, and especially northern cheers for the raider, would have outraged Southerners anytime before emancipation. In the context of 1859, however, with Northern Republicans apparently about to seize national power, Yankees' applause for a murderous invader assaulted southern eardrums like amplified thunder. Did Brown indicate a horrifying answer to the big question about Northern Republicans: How does the foe secretly plot to pierce our borders and do in slavery?

– 1 –

By 1859, the infant Republican Party had become precociously mature. Only five years earlier, before Davy Atchison pressed Stephen A. Douglas toward repealing part of the Missouri Compromise, a Republican Party had existed only in several thousand free soilers' imaginations. In the early 1850s, an anti-immigrant party had seemed the more likely northern successor to the defunct National Whig Party. But the Kansas-Nebraska Act revitalized Yankee determination to contain the Slave Power. Containment's political appeal swelled when one-day Kansans mauled territorial democracy and Preston Brooks mugged Charles Summer. In 1856, the new Republican Party almost won the White House. Two years later, after the so-called Dred Scott Decision and the Lecompton Crisis, Republicans almost captured a congressional majority.

Throughout their climb toward victory in the 1860 presidential election, Republicans mixed unlimited antislavery ideology with limited antislavery policies. As ideologues, Republicans fulminated against slavery. As policymakers, they conceded that the U.S. Constitution barred federal emancipation inside southern states' jurisdiction. They would only abolish slavery outside southern states' purview—in U.S. territories, in the U.S. capital, and in U.S. forts and naval yards. They would thus contain the Slave Power's breach of white men's republicanism. But the Slave Power's enemy hid any intention to penetrate contained southern areas.

"We understand" their "game," Virginia's Roger Pryor told the House of Representatives in 1859. Republicans' "mailed hand is gloved for the moment," as "the beast sheathes his claws." Camouflaged abolitionists claim to wish only "the restriction and disparagement of slavery." But once in office, Republicans intend to "renew the work of encroachment," until they achieve "the eventual extinction of slavery."[1]

Republican soundbites occasionally hinted that the Slave Power's foe might someday seek more than containment. "A house divided against itself cannot stand," Abraham Lincoln told the state Illinois State Republican Convention on June 16, 1858. "This government cannot endure, permanently half *slave* or half *free*." Lincoln would restrict slavery to half of America. But would he settle for a divided house that could not stand? Lincoln only answered that after Republicans had imprisoned slavery in the South, "the public mind shall rest in the belief that it is in the course of ultimate extinction."[2] Yet what if, public belief to the contrary, containment did not yield extinction? Southerners doubted that Lincoln would then "rest."

Nor did they expect a William H. Seward postcontainment nap. Seward, the New York senator and front-runner for the 1860 Republican Party presidential nomination, announced an "irrepressible conflict" six months after Lincoln deplored a house divided. "Free labor and slave labor," Seward warned, would irrepressibly collide until the United States became "either entirely a slaveholding nation or entirely a free-labor nation." New Yorkers, he promised, would not allow "slave culture" to invade their "rye and wheat fields." Instead, free labor would "soon invade . . . *Delaware, Maryland, Virginia, Missouri, and Texas*."[3] Would a President Seward aid the invaders?

Such questions, and the soundbites' ambiguous answers, hung in the air, turning every northern intruder inside the South into a hint about Seward's and Lincoln's disguised future intentions. The more towering the invader, the more Southerners wondered whether Republicans' postcontainment assault had at last thrown off the mask. So did John Brown reveal how masked Republicans meant to establish an American house undivided?

– 2 –

Other questions better illuminated John Brown. Brown ridiculed Republicans' mainstream tactics. He disparaged even Yankee extremists for deploying too nonviolent a strategy. He shared not a plan but a hatred with other Northerners. He set infuriated Southerners on the hunt for how other Yankees, equally brimming with anti–Slave Power loathing, would pursue better invasive strategies.

This solitary strategist had been born as the century began. John Brown's Connecticut family had antislavery as if in the genes. Brown was reared in

Ohio's Western Reserve, where his father helped found Oberlin College, center of American colorblind higher education.

From that radical atmosphere and that fiery father, John Brown formulated a certitude about divine intervention against sinners, starring himself as God's warrior against slaveholders. Brown could not say how God's antislavery design would unfold. He only knew that Jehovah somehow would use him to wipe slavery from His earth. "Acknowledge *Him* & *He* shall direct thy paths" became Brown's motto; and even "illogical movements" would become "a grand success" in the hands of "an *all good, all wise,* and *all* powerful *Director* & Father."[4]

The restraining hand of churches, political parties, and familial concerns bounded other antislavery warriors. Brown obeyed only his conception of God's unbounded command. Although a zealous Christian, he joined no church. Although a passionate abolitionist, he entered no antislavery organization. Although a devoted father, he would tolerate only sons who would gladly perish to free the slaves. When his son Oliver lay dying at Harpers Ferry, horribly suffering and begging his father to kill him with a merciful bullet, John Brown refused to pull the trigger. "If you must die," proclaimed God's terrorist, "die like a man."[5] No other Yankee better personified one southern monster image: the northern wild individual, serving only infatuated abstractions.

Nor did any other Yankee better exemplify another southern satanic conception: the fanatical New England puritan, declaring holy war against every erring human impulse, including his own. To whip the sin out of the son who bore his name, Brown kept a ledger of John Jr.'s response to flogging. If the offspring disobeyed his mother, the heir received eight lashes; for lying, another eight; for feckless labor, three. When John Jr.'s sins still outnumbered his improvements, John Sr. blamed himself for the spiritual bankruptcy. After laying still more furious stripes on his son, Brown barred his own back. He handed the whip to John Jr. He commanded the sinning offspring to pound lashes into the sinning patriarch. "Harder, harder, harder," cried the fanatic, as the blood poured from his back.[6]

After many merciless self-flagellations, Brown believed that he had become a rarely pure vessel, prepared for Christ's immaculate commands to fill. Before Harpers Ferry, Frederick Douglass warned John Brown that a murderous raid on the federal arsenal would never secure a providential design. Why then, Brown wondered, did God, the master designer, call him to begin at Harpers Ferry? And why dwell on strategy after the beginning when God, the master tactician, would later point the way?

During initial forays, Brown never fretted about follow-up tactics. Pragmatic adjustment of strategy after a first strike, careful calculation of risks and rewards at every subsequent step—Brown always scorned this American formula for calculated success. Scorn for calculation turned Brown into a disastrous capitalist before he became a failed raider. The Connecticut venturer at first succeeded, then failed at farming, at land speculation, at running a tannery, as a wool merchant. He triumphed, then failed in Ohio, in Massachusetts, in New York, in California. He ultimately failed to escape twenty-one lawsuits and more bankruptcies.

Then, after Brown turned fifty, Kansas beckoned. There, a devastating first blow could earn sustained reputation. There, Brown could ambush, kill, and depart, ending the story before poststrike complications spoiled the victory. Thus at midnight on May 24, 1856, Brown and seven compatriots smashed into three cabins in Pottawatomie, Kansas. They slaughtered five slumbering Southerners. They hacked the dead men's skulls, severed a hand from an arm, sliced fingers from another hand, and made off atop the victims' horses. Two years later, Brown burst into Missouri, murdered a slaveholder, seized eleven slaves, and led the new freedmen 1100 miles to Canadian sanctuary.

After the two successful strikes for freedom, Brown heard God's call for the Harpers Ferry strike. The bigger strike required a bigger budget. So Brown, failed financial hustler, resumed his career as money-grubber. He especially begged cash from wealthy northern intellectuals of the Transcendentalist persuasion, baffled about how to turn antislavery ideas into emancipation triumphs. Brown's prime contributors, his so-called secret six, included Theodore Parker, Thomas Wentworth Higginson, George Stearns, Samuel Gridley Howe, Gerrit Smith, and Franklin Sanborn. Most of these Yankee men of mind had been educated at Harvard. One of them had founded the Boston Symphony Orchestra.

All of them despaired that nonviolent ideas might never overturn the slaveholders. Brown preyed on their apprehensions. When they touted their pacific antislavery societies, Brown responded that "your methods are perfectly futile; you would not release five slaves in a century; peaceable emancipation is impossible." When they praised antislavery ballots, antislavery laws, antislavery education, he exploded at "Talk! Talk! Talk! That will never free the slaves." He counseled "action—action," violent action inside the South, to seize the slaveholders' rifles and to arm the slaves.[7]

That was a fiery solution to America's (and Republicans') master antislavery puzzle. Even if hatred of slavery consumed the North, how could that loathing damage slavery in the South? By convincing slaveholders to drop their lashes? Please! By convincing Northerners to vote down slavery? Not if the U.S. Constitution forbade federal intervention in southern states. Not if Northern Republicans drew a line in the sand between opposing slavery in new territories and assaulting slavery in old states. Brown would obliterate that line. He would defy the Constitution. He would turn the secret six's bloodless ideas into killing raids. Powerless eggheads need only finance his firearms.

At first glance, Brown did not look like a frightening gunman. While physically slim and hard, he fell two inches short of six feet. His head seemed too small even for his light frame. But his endlessly long mouth, perpetually frozen in a frown, and his cold gray eyes, endlessly searching for foes, accentuated his usual grim silence, then his occasional outbursts of hate. His boot scarcely concealed the bowie knife jammed between trouser and skin. This "shepherd and herdsman," said Ralph Waldo Emerson, "learned the manners of the animal and knew the secret signals by which animals communicate."[8]

Yankee intellectuals succumbed to Brown's animalistic force. The secret six agreed to help finance the killer, if he would keep their identity secret. With the *very* secret six's financing, Brown prepared to ambush northwestern Virginia.

Initially, he presumed, slaves would lack the training to handle rifles. So he ordered a thousand pikes for a thousand dollars. These modernized spears featured two bowie knives attached to a six-foot-long ash shaft. The knives, each two inches wide and eight inches long, had been honed to a razor-sharp edge.

Then, in a mysterious gambit for a slave rebellion armed with pikes, Brown focused on capturing the federal rifles at Harpers Ferry. Perhaps Brown plotted that southern nonslaveholding mountaineers would come use the rifles. Or perhaps he expected that slaves who initially wielded spears would learn to wield guns. Or perhaps he planned to use violence only to protect runaway slaves as they nonviolently sprinted toward freedom. His postraid statements wove a contradictory path between these scenarios, perhaps because, as usual, his only certain strategy involved the first strike.

Whether the first assault led to an insurrection of black slaves, a rainbow army of black and white lower classes, or a protected runaway stampede, the borderland especially attracted the raider. High up in the South, slaves most often fled their masters, and nonslaveholders most often resented the slavocracy. Inside the borderland's mountains, antislavery guerrilla warriors could easily find hiding places. They also could use a prolonged mountainous tunnel, funneling down to the Lower South and up to the North, to speed runaways toward Canada.

Harpers Ferry, located at the northern end of the Virginia Valley and on the western flank of the mountains, offered an inviting entrance to the tunnel. Firearms packed Harpers Ferry's federal arsenal. The South's largest armory loomed nearby. Slumber disarmed midnight guards. Only frail telegraph wires and railroad tracks connected the isolated town with the outside world. Brown would have to march but six miles from his preparatory Maryland farmhouse, ambush the sleeping, trash the communications, and flee with enough guns for a small army.

This border locale also offered allies to shoulder the guns. Many subsequent critics, including alas this writer, have derided Brown because few slaves lived in Harpers Ferry's immediate neighborhood. But he was wiser than his critics, when it came to the first strike. While the land rimming Harpers Ferry rose too steeply to contain many slaves, the federal arsenal commanded Jefferson County, where almost 4000 slaves comprised over 27 percent of the population. Just south of Jefferson County loomed Clarke

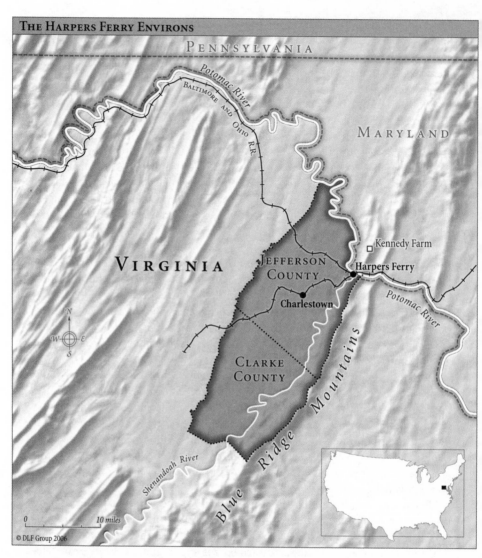

PENNSYLVANIA

Potomac River

BALTIMORE AND OHIO R.R.

MARYLAND

Kennedy Farm

VIRGINIA

JEFFERSON COUNTY

Harpers Ferry

Charlestown

Potomac River

CLARKE COUNTY

Blue Ridge Mountains

Shenandoah River

N
W E
S

0   10 miles

© DLF Group 2006

The map (above) and the contemporary drawing (opposite page) together illuminate Harpers Ferry's epic setting. Here was staged a national trauma that alerted the eyes of Southerners (but has blinded the eyes of posterity) to see the succeeding better answers to the big question: How did Republicans intend to invade the South? Drawing courtesy of Special Collections, the University of Virginia Library, Charlottesville.

County. There another 3400 slaves comprised 47 percent of the population. Such unusually numerous border slaves could quickly hear that a messiah had brought a thousand savage spears, seized 10,000 murderous guns, and summoned blacks to fight for freedom.

In still other ways, Jefferson and Clarke counties were as if God-ordained for a border raid. This rather heavily enslaved hinterland area, scarcely thirty miles from the Pennsylvania border, could be easily reached through scarcely enslaved western Maryland. Partly because hostile Yankees loomed close, both counties' number and percentage of slaves had slowly ebbed. Between 1850 and 1860, Jefferson and Clarke counties lost 8 percent of their 8000 slaves. God's holy terrorist thus understandably spied providential opportunity in a poorly guarded arsenal close to the North, plus mountainous terrain for postraid concealment, plus an incrementally weakening slaveholders' regime, plus a nearby black population.

John Brown's strike started as auspiciously (or if you will, as gruesomely) as the Pottawatomie Massacre. On the evening of October 16, 1859, the liberator led fourteen other whites and four blacks from his rented Kennedy Farm in Maryland to Harpers Ferry, those six miles distant. There the Potomac and Shenandoah rivers unite to heave against a jagged semimountain, before flowing on to the sea. Thomas Jefferson, peering down from the towering bluff above, had called the spectacle "one of the most stupendous scenes in nature."

There transpired one of the most stupendous scenes in American history. In the dark night, Brown's freedom fighters easily captured Harpers Ferry's federal armory, arsenal, and engine house. They sliced the telegraph wires. They halted a train. They dispatched messengers to a nearby plantation, Lewis Washington's (a great-grandnephew of George Washington's), there to alert slaves to spread the invasion. No other first strike has ever been better planned or carried out (which is only to say that John Brown here perfected his lifelong specialty).

No other following tactics have ever been botched so badly (which is only to say that John Brown here succumbed to his lifelong flaw). Where these raiders meant to kill whites, in order to free blacks, they first killed a free black, Shepard Hayward, as he walked harmlessly away from them. Where Brown's warriors meant to bring black fugitives northward, their first slaughtered compatriot paid the ultimate penalty for marching southward. Dangerfield Newby, a Virginia mulatto in his midthirties, enlisted in Brown's army to help his enslaved wife and seven children escape from the Harpers Ferry environs. Newby carried a note from his wife, imploring "oh dear Dangerfield" to "com [sic] this fall without fail. . . . I want to see you so much that is the one bright hope I have before me."

That hope perished when Newby suffered a mortal bullet in the neck while fleeing toward the armory. Posterity cannot tell whether a Maryland journalist's report on his death reflected an actual savage happening or a brutal southern fantasy about slavery, sex, and race. According to the Maryland observer, infuriated whites chopped off the ears and testicles of the corpse. Then they threw Newby's disfigured body into the gutter and watched a roaming hog chew the victim's still-attached member.[9]

After the colorblind raid left a black on each side slaughtered, Brown's ineptitude continued. Since Brown needed to cut off communications with the outside world, his men stopped that first train. They then unaccountably allowed it to puff away, to announce the ambush to unsuspecting whites. Where Lewis Washington's slaves needed to spread the tidings to rebellious slaves, Brown's raiders unaccountably hauled Washington and his bondsmen back to the arsenal. The raiders also brought back a weapon as barren of consequence as the kidnapping: Frederick the Great's sword, a gift to George Washington.

Where Brown and his men needed to transport Harpers Ferry's potentially highly consequential firearms to the nooks and crannies of the mountains in a great big hurry, the raider stayed in Harpers Ferry's death trap. While whites gathered to hurl themselves at the furious old man, their prey jailed himself inside the most innocuous corner of his captured fortress, the engine house. There, the self-imprisoned raider found no food.

The night after Brown struck, U.S. Marines arrived, led by Robert E. Lee. The next day, Lee's assaulters fed Brown's hungry raiders steel for breakfast. The ninety marines stormed the engine house. They killed half of Brown's men, including two of his sons. Lieutenant Israel Green downed the stolid father with devastating but not mortal blows. The lieutenant's ceremonial sword, like Frederick the Great's, lacked a killing edge. That dull instrument gave Brown his saving moment. When confronting Virginia's judges, he could teach Northerners to remember something more than his utter disaster.

– 3 –

It took Southerners a few weeks to discover how totally the raid had been a debacle. In the interim, they staged one of the most savage insurrection panics in southern history. As usual at such hysterical times, paranoid Southerners saw a potential murderer in every Cuffee's every dissimulating movement. They also spied a collaborator in every contact between a white stranger and a slave. They trampled down the color line between their regimes, subjecting white suspects to trial not by courts but by mobs. They assaulted their paternalism toward blacks, replacing genial correction with savage lashings. They turned slavery into not a home but a prison, while shuddering not only at their peril but at their brutal selves.

Their descent into brutality made brief rational sense. At first, they had no idea who the raider was, who sent him, and what Northerners might be massing for his rescue. Another result of Brown's careless tactics spread panic far afield. Brown left three supporters behind in the Kennedy farmhouse when he departed for Harpers Ferry. He failed to instruct his compatriots to remove his incriminating papers if they departed. When they fled, they left behind a swiftly discovered, widely published map of future striking places, some deep in the South. Some of Brown's men at Harpers Ferry also successfully fled, perhaps to join their compatriots at the next target on their maps.

At every spot marked on the discovered map, Southerners shuddered. "The localities marked," claimed the *Norfolk* (Virginia) *Southern Argus,* "had been visited by Abolition emissaries and were found to contain slaves ready for insurrections." But who were the contaminating emissaries? Who were the contaminated slaves?[10]

Letters to Governor Henry Wise of Virginia begged for identification of the culprits. Our neighborhood is marked on the map, noted H. R. Davis of Cold Spring, Mississippi. Should we remove our long-suspected Yankee teacher named Forbers? Might another incendiary be a Yankee named Lacy, living near Kingston in Adams County, another marked spot? What can you tell us about our traitors, inquired the Allenton, Alabama, local postmaster? Our locality is "laid down" on the map among other "favorable points of attack." John Brown could know nothing about Allenton. So he must have received word from secret agents. BUT WHO?[11]

Who indeed? Governor Wise hadn't a clue. Neither did the alarmed citizens of Allenton or Norfolk or Cold Spring. Because anxiety about the unknowable ran wild, every watchman found employment. "You may imagine the state of things here," Andrew Hunter of Charlestown, Virginia, wrote Governor Wise, "when I tell you, that to protect my property from the torch of the incendiary—I have been compelled to place a musket in the hands of my man servant Frank."[12]

With black Frank not the protection most whites had in mind, extralegal committees of inquiry roamed the countryside, tarring, feathering, expelling, and occasionally killing. The inquisition's flimsy evidence led some alarmed democrats to demand proof before punishment. With proof scarce and danger apparently omnipresent, alarmed citizens demanded punishment without evidence.

Near Sparta, Georgia, an impoverished, illiterate nonslaveholder told an overseer that he would paint his face black and join the invader, if John Brown came calling. Blacks hereabouts, explained the future face painter, outnumbered whites. Still, the nonslaveholder "wished there weren't no niggers nohow." Could this foul racist be John Brown's fellow traveler? After some tense moments, the vigilant committee released the terrified fellow.[13]

Again, a Eufaula, Alabama, mob arrested a peddler of ploughs, since the "cut of his coat and his manners" made him seem Yankee. The peddler claimed to be Dr. Malroe of South Carolina, a proslavery zealot who owned two plantations. The committee doubted the plea. Why would a wealthy South Carolina physician sell ploughs in Alabama and dress like a Yankee? The inquisitors asked this alleged South Carolinian to name his parents. The weeping suspect momentarily could not remember. The amnesia aroused new suspicions. But before tar and feathers arrived, a trusted Alabamian rushed in to identify the suspect as indeed Dr. Malroe of South Carolina. Now the vigilant committee did the weeping, for a travesty barely averted. Committee members even bought some ploughs.[14]

The post-Brown fright yielded more travesties than comedies. In Savannah, Georgia, a mob seized a Yankee who allegedly peddled incendiary propaganda. The lynchers carried their victim beyond city limits. They stripped him naked. They clothed him with tar and feathers, decorated with cotton swabs. Then they booted him toward the city. When the culprit displayed his finery near the market, the night watchman "sprang . . . and ran, crying 'the devil—the devil.'"[15]

In southwestern Virginia, a supposed abolitionist had more reason to think that he faced Satan. A kangaroo court sentenced him to be hanged. His illegal judges fixed one end of a rope to his neck, the other end to a tree. He swung in the sky until almost dead. They cut him down. When he caught his breath, they hitched him up again. After he almost expired, they hacked him down again. They repeated his ordeal a third time. A fourth. A fifth. Then they ordered him to run for his life. He galloped away, whooped his lynchers, "like a quarter nag."[16]

Fortunately for further potential victims, neither democratic liberty for whites nor genial paternalism for blacks could be permanently transformed into an ungodly dictatorship over both races. Only evidence that even one more John Brown would invade with even one more pike or that even one slave had volunteered to wield even one spear could perpetuate this mockery of republicanism and paternalism. To paternalistic republicans' relief, not a solitary slave had accepted Brown's invitation. Nor did a solitary Yankee issue another invitation. After those few panicky weeks, Southerners began to believe that Abraham Lincoln, for once, had it right: White men's "attempt . . . to get up a revolt among slaves" had only yielded slaves who "refused to participate."[17]

So southern life eased back toward its edgy mix of democracy for whites, despotism for blacks. Mobs disappeared. Kangaroo courts vanished. Slaveholders resumed their role as patriarchal rulers of loving slaves, albeit a little more charily. Rulers and citizens resumed the open contest of (most!) ideas on the hustings, albeit a little more nervously. With the initially panicky southern reaction fading, only northern enthusiasm for the raider could prolong John Brown's impact.

– 4 –

After his capture, John Brown looked incapable of arousing anyone's applause. The raider lay in a Virginia prison, half deaf, eyes half closed, bleeding profusely from four head wounds and a slash to the kidneys. But the savaged fanatic cared only about the question screaming in his head. Why had God ordered the big strike, then allowed His sinners to smash His servant?

God's warrior soon grasped the answer. Jehovah had wiser uses for a raider than a mere mortal had conceived. God desired an inspiring martyr. A condemned freedom fighter could awaken the slumbering North, alarm the horrendous South, and thus bring on the bloodbath that could alone free the slave. "I can recover all the lost capital," this ever failing capitalist wrote his wife, by "hanging for a few moments by the neck and I feel quite determined to make the utmost possible out of defeat."[18]

A sacrosanct custom empowered the apparently powerless prisoner. Before sentencing, a convict could address his sentencers. Journalists would spread Brown's words throughout the nation. With the gallows looming, no time would remain for succeeding blunders.

A previous change in personal appearance could further Brown's newest first strike. In the months before the raid, John Brown had grown a long, wide white beard, reaching his chest. The growth turned his long grim mouth into a prophet's auspicious hollow. John Brown, the righteous gunslinger who had assaulted Transcendentalists' mere words, had become Saint John, preparing one of America's most holy texts.

On November 2, 1859, in a Charlestown courtroom, the murderous saint rose from his cot to judge his judges, before they judged him. This western Virginia court "acknowledged," he supposed, "the validity of the law of God." In His Golden Rule, God teaches that "I should do" to all men whatever "men should do to me." Those "instructions" make my interference "in behalf of His despised poor . . . no wrong but right." Yet if I had instead "interfered on behalf of the rich and the powerful, . . . this Court would have deemed it an act worthy of reward, not punishment." If their perversion of the Golden Rule demands that "I forfeit my life . . . and mingle my blood further with the blood of my children, and with the blood of the [black] millions," victims of "wicked, cruel, and unjust enactments," I say "let it be done."[19]

Two fanciful, latter-day paintings of John Brown, one (left) showing a gentle idealist, kissing a black baby on his way to the gallows—an image infused with the northern admiration of Brown's spirit—and the other (below) of the violent killer, a rendition saturated with the southern loathing of hateful Yankees. Courtesy of The Metropolitan Museum of Art, Gift of Mr. and Mrs. Carl Stoekel, 1897 (97.5) (Gentle John Brown) and the Kansas State Historical Society (Violent John Brown).

According to the apocryphal legend, on December 2, as John Brown left his jail on his way to the gallows, he stooped to kiss a black babe, nestled in its mother's arms.[20] A few hours later, when the hangman had finished, non-apocryphal bells in northern steeples sang their tribute to the expired martyr. Then weeping thousands cheered Brown's casket as it passed through northern habitats. And then came the evolving song, spreading over the

North, soon to be carried by a hundred thousand chanting soldiers down to the South:

> Old John Brown's body is a-mouldering in the dust,
> Old John Brown's rifle's red with blood-spots turned to rust,
> Old John Brown's pike has made its last, unflinching thrust,
> His soul is marching on![21]

Famous New England intellectuals kept Brown's spirit on the march. Ralph Waldo Emerson declared that Brown "will make the gallows glorious like the cross." Henry David Thoreau breathed that "some eighteen hundred years ago, Christ was crucified." Now, an "angel of light" shone from the gallows. Wendell Phillips shouted that Virginia "is a pirate ship," and "John Brown sails the sea," commissioned "to sink every pirate he meets on God's ocean." The most famous Yankee abolitionist (and, ironically, one of the most famous American pacifists) had the last word. "I am prepared to say: 'success to every slave insurrection at the South and in every slave country,'" intoned William Lloyd Garrison.[22]

– 5 –

That northern applause for a midnight assassin struck Southerners as appalling, insulting, indicative of a more horrifying northern enemy than most Southerners had suspected. Since John Brown became the ultimate wild individualist, his Yankee cheerleaders seemed proponents of unrestrained license, while the South seemed the center of social control. To publicize this alleged difference between northern and southern cultures, a charismatic southern debater rose to share center stage with John Brown.[23]

The two debaters, often conferring during Brown's imprisonment, created an eerie tableau of twins consulting. Both had become notorious as ordinary failures who triumphed at special moments. Just as Brown had fumbled as a capitalist, between his historic thrusts as an ambusher, so Virginia's Governor Henry Wise had floundered as a statesman, between his brilliance at Virginia's epic moments. Throughout almost all of Henry Wise's uneven career, Virginia's most aristocratic squires considered him a perverse symbol of egalitarianism gone astray, a poseur who fudged everything important to please enough plebeians to win elections.

Then the grand pre–Civil War episodes came, and the faltering Wise always rose to the occasion. He had ascended in the midcentury Virginia constitutional convention and in the 1855 Know-Nothing election. He would soar in the secession crisis. He now costarred on John Brown's stage.

Brown and Wise both displayed emaciated frames, unruly hair, and burning eyes. Each dressed in disheveled homespun. Both strutted with the vanity and imperiousness of would-be kings. Each respected the other's sincerity. Wise dismissed some Southerners' notion that Brown was insane. This Yankee's

Two warring titans, John Brown (left) and Henry Wise (right), who tore into each other, despite great mutual respect, over who was the supreme American irresponsible individualist, the fanatical abolitionist or the unchecked slaveholder. Courtesy of the Library of Congress (Brown) and the South Carolina Historical Society (Wise).

alleged lunacy, said Wise, was just the North's conventional antislavery fanaticism.[24] Brown dismissed some Virginians' conviction that Wise was an unprincipled demagogue. The spellbinder's seductive bombast, thought Brown, was just the conventional proslavery fanaticism. Ralph Waldo Emerson exclaimed that these "enemies become affectionate. . . . If circumstances did not keep them apart, they would fly into each other's arms."[25]

Wise reaffirmed his affectionate respect for his enemy in a remarkable postwar incident. In 1865, the prewar governor sought to evict a schoolmarm from his prewar farm. The intruder turned out to be one of John Brown's daughters, come south to educate blacks, including Wise's ex-slaves. When a bystander mocked Wise for falling beneath a contemptible raider's offspring, the defrocked rebel whirled on his tormentor. "John Brown," exclaimed Wise, "John Brown was a great man, sir. John Brown was a great man!"[26]

Wise considered Brown a great man because the Connecticut Yankee shed all northern disguises, stripped away all northern opportunism, leaving only Yankee conviction, straight up and true blue and a shock for all the world to see. Wise had studied Brown very carefully in prison. In his report to the Virginia legislature on his findings, he called the raider's unvarnished hatred of the South a challenge that must be met. "We cannot suffer such insults," warned Henry Wise, "without suffering worse than the death of citizens—without suffering dishonor, the death of a State."[27]

While Wise trembled at undefended honor, he saw nothing to fear in Brown's strategy to rouse the slaves. He wished Virginians would focus on the less conspicuous, more dangerous Yankee raiders, the ones who silently encouraged border slaves to run away. Brown's importance, declared Wise, lay in exuding the mentality that led the secretive conductors of the Liberty Line to steal western Virginia slaveholders' exposed property. John Brown embodied the Yankee "doctrine of absolute individual rights, independent of all relations of man to man in a conventional and social form." To Brown, to his northern cheerleaders, and to the border slave stealers, "each man has the prerogative to set up his conscience, his will, and his judgment over and above all legal enactments and social institutions."

John Brown, like most other Northerners, thought that Southerners suffered mortally from that very disease. This most unbounded of Yankees considered the slaveholder to be America's rank unbounded individualist. The tyrant who flourished beyond social control, Brown raged, could do anything loathsome to his unprotected slave. The despot could lash, smash, mash, slash his people, rape his "wenches," and sell slaves away from their families, with no legislature, no executive, no court to stay his irresponsibly uncontrolled hand. I intervened against *that* unholy individualism, said John Brown. Can the North—can the Lord—call my judges the *Christian* individualists? With that question, the Wise-Brown debate over anti-Christian individualism came to climax.

– 6 –

Brown achieved his climax not with his thousand pikes but with a thousand words. The losing raider's seductive words piled irony atop irony. If Lieutenant Israel Green had grabbed a sharp sword instead of seizing a dull bludgeon as he raced out his door to draw and quarter the insurrectionist, Brown would have been slain and his intensification of the sectional controversy likely stillborn. Lacking Brown's postraid rhetoric to transform a bungler into a martyr, Yankees, always queasy about black violence, would probably have dismissed a wild anarchist as a misguided fanatic. Thus did the accident of Israel Green's nonkilling sword, a random circumstance having nothing to do with the slavery issue, for the first time show how coincidence could help the slavery issue to bring on the Civil War.

To increase the irony, John Brown had secured cash for pikes from abstruse northern wordsmiths because they feared that words would never damage the Slave Power. Yet Brown's savage spears had secured nothing more than a southern pulpit, to fire words back at the North. The most antislavery Northerners' cheers, still more ironically, gave new hope to the secessionists. The disunionists' sleepy southern brethren could now at least see that Yankees' words spat out loathing for the South.

"There has rarely occurred between separate nations," cheered Virginia's Edmund Ruffin, "a more outrageous, and . . . malignant hostility." The arch

Virginia unionist William Cabell Rives, Jr., sadly concurred that not so much "the occurrences at Harper's Ferry" as "their consequences" had done more "to bring about the catastrophe of disunion, than all the other events of our past history put together." Alabama's William H. Tayloe, long a self-styled "obstinate Unionist under the impression that Republicans are not abolitionists," now felt "smothered by the want of sympathy from the North. . . . The time has come at last for war, or the Yankeys [sic] must let us alone."[28]

One well-publicized group of southern nonpoliticians would not wait to see if Yankee insulters let them alone. Over 200 southern scholars, studying at Philadelphia's advanced medical schools, departed the alleged city of brotherly love, to them now a locale of antibrotherly hatred. These seceding Southerners enrolled with southern brethren at their home states' less advanced institutions.[29] Edmund Ruffin worked for more mass departures, the next time from the Union. He sent John Brown's pikes throughout the South for public display, labeling each spear a "Sample of the favors designed for us by our Northern Brethren."[30]

Yet those pikes also epitomized how little northern hatred had yet menaced slavery inside the South. Cuffees' unanimous unwillingness to rise up in group rebellion, even when John Brown offered an array of armaments, indicated (as Southerners had long thought and as Henry Wise had lately emphasized) that dissimulating slaves' only lethal threat lay in individuals' flights or assaults. After the nonexistent group slave revolt, the handful of Yankees who had financed the spears were as invisible as enslaved spear wielders had been. Of John Brown's secret six, only Thomas Wentworth Higginson joined the trifling schemes to rescue Brown on his way to the gallows. (Henry Wise, taking no chances, emptied $250,000 from the Virginia treasury to make the gallows more secure than ever the White House had been.) The other secret sixers scurried into hiding. Gerrit Smith hid out in the appropriate place, from Southerners' perspective—a lunatic asylum.

Republicans convincingly denied any complicity with John Brown's lunatic fringe methods. John Brown "agreed with us in thinking slavery wrong," declared Abraham Lincoln. But that cannot "excuse violence, bloodshed, and treason. It could avail him nothing that he might think himself right." Salmon P. Chase railed at "poor old" John Brown—"How rash—how mad—how criminal." William H. Seward denounced Brown's raid as "an act of sedition and treason." Meeting after meeting in northern cities cheered that condemnation.[31]

A month after John Brown swung from the gallows, the U.S. Senate authorized Virginia's Senator James Mason to chair an investigating committee, charged with discerning whether Republicans had the slightest connection with John Brown. Mason, a fiery Southerner, had been the first provoker of the 1850 Fugitive Slave Law. He had been a relatively rare 1856 advocate of secession if Republicans won the White House. Yet the sometimes hothead conducted one of the coolest, most sensible, most impartial congressional investigations in all of American history. The inquisition ultimately declared Republican hands squeaky clean, at least as aiders of John Brown.[32]

Months before the Mason Committee announced its acquittal, southern congressmen's attention swerved to other ways Republicans might move beyond containment, to invade slavery inside the South. The John Brown trauma left Southerners convinced: Northerners assuredly hate us, insufferably more than we had realized. In turn we despise their puritanism and individualism, far more than we did before Transcendentalist heroes cheered Brown's obscene terrorizing. But how will Republicans' hatred menace more than our pride, if Brown is to be our only invader?

As post-Brown Southerners sought the answer, the Harpers Ferry affair slid into its appropriate niche as but the first exciting act of a surpassing multiact drama. The second act commenced before the curtain ended the first. You wasted your resources on John Brown's anti-Christian violence, a southern visitor to northern pulpits told worshippers during the fall of 1859. But if you will donate peaceable dollars and peaceable teachers, John G. Fee promised northern Christians, I will peaceably spread your and Christ's hatred of slavery inside my southern homeland.

CHAPTER 15

John G. Fee and Religious Invasion

While most Americans recall John Brown, few scholars remember John G. Fee. Yet Fee, more than any other antebellum Southerner, deserves colorblind Americans' admiration. The Kentucky preacher also became Northerners' next hope, immediately after Brown, to assault slavery inside the South.

Fee believed that a Southerner's preaching, aided by northern dollars and teachers, could convert at least the Border South's Kentucky to antislavery. He correctly perceived that Yankees would pour millions into a nonviolent, constitutional assault on slavery, if slaveholders would allow a southern Christian free access to southern souls. For many months, Kentucky, the most enslaved Border South state, allowed Fee, the most extreme racial radical, freedom to agitate in the northern South's most auspicious corner. That antebellum exception made Fee's second act in America's drama of late 1859 and early 1860 as intriguing, in its different way, as Brown's first act.

The acts started with opposite invasive strategies. Brown sought northern spears. Fee recruited northern teachers. Brown meant to savage slaveholders' bodies. Fee meant to seize slaveholders' souls. Brown intended to smash inside an arsenal. Fee intended to hack inside Christian defenses. Both climactically struck, and were struck down, in the last months of 1859. Both defeats showed that antislavery Yankees had not yet found the path inside the South.

– 1 –

Some southern antislavery evangelicals departed to convert the North. Others compromised to persuade the South. But John G. Fee, unlike every other late antebellum southern zealot, sought to rally his native land for uncompromising emancipation. So why did fellow Southerners, however briefly, tolerate his extremism?

In part because Fee was to the manor born. His antislavery ideas were also from the proslavery manor taken. He burrowed inside orthodox southern postulates, turning patriarchs' Christian assumptions into abolitionists' heresy. His pilgrimage offers a tour of the marrow of proslavery divinity, conducted by a brilliant theologian who assaulted James Henley Thornwell's subtlest proslavery assumptions at the highest biblical level.

According to proslavery assumption, erring humans must never loosely interpret Christ's explicit commands. Instead, Christ's unerring Word, strictly constructed, must order every Christian soul and Christian community. John G. Fee's grandfather had transported this orthodoxy and the family's slaves from Maryland to Kentucky before the frontier area became a slaveholding state. The founder dared to own slaves up in Kentucky's Bracken County on the Ohio River, despite Kentucky and Ohio nonslaveholding neighbors. John G. Fee's father continued to work slaves on Kentucky's northern edge. Meanwhile, Fee's mother deplored her fellow Quakers' antislavery bias, cherished her household's thirteen slaves, and wept that her son used the Word to serve the enemy.[1]

Her son met the enemy in 1842, when at the age of twenty-six he crossed the Ohio River and enrolled in Cincinnati's Lane Seminary. Eight years earlier, the seminary had repelled the Lane Rebels. Those students, rebelling against Lane's racist and proslavery teaching, had marched on Oberlin College. There, they had joined hands with such spirits as John Brown's father to forge a biracial antislavery center. Since Fee's father knew that the rebels had moved outside Lane, he assumed that only proslavery zealots remained inside. His son's southern sentiments should be safe enough in antislavery's deserted old arena.

He did not figure on a new generation of rebels. Two of John G. Fee's Lane classmates pressed the slaveholder's son. They insisted that the Word, strictly construed, demanded antislavery. Could Fee deny that Scripture contained the Golden Rule? Could Fee deny that some slaveholders' practices desecrated the Golden Rule? Could any Christian deny that Christ's spirit, explicitly rendered in Scripture, made defining aspects of slavery an abomination?

In the manner of the conversion experience, Fee wrestled down this version of strict construction gospel, time after time. Then he saw the blinding light: "Lord, if need be, make me an abolitionist." Instantly, he "was conscious of an entire surrender—conscious that I had died to the world and risen with Christ."

Fee's father demanded that his son fall no farther from familial grace. "Bundle up your books and come home," steamed the patriarch. "I have spent the last dollar I mean to spend on you in a free state."[2] Fee came home, stayed home, and turned strict construction against the home institution. He ultimately received nothing from his father's estate.

The disinheritance stung. The alleged ingrate cherished his father and fatherland. Yet he remained convinced that Christian patriarchs must repudiate their slave investments. In response, proslavery evangelicals proclaimed investments in slaves biblically safe. The exact words of the sacred text, they reiterated, proved that slavery had existed in biblical times. A precise reading of the Word also proved that Christ and His disciples had never condemned servitude, not even in a syllable.

Fee answered that Christ lacked enough syllables to condemn every human transgression. Instead, His every word condemns all loveless practices and ordains the "supreme love of God and equal love to our neighbors." To achieve a kingdom of love, He commands His creatures to pursue the Bible. But masters decree that *their* creatures shall "scarcely be able to read a sentence of God's holy Word."

Again, the Word "says to the slave, 'Go spend this hour at the house of God in prayer and praise.' But slavery says . . . go and toil in the field." And again, God says to the celebrants of marriage, " 'What I have joined together let no man put asunder.' " But "slavery says" that slaves must "go where . . . the will of the master shall demand," whatever marriage is ripped asunder. And again, "God says to the parent, 'train up your child.' " But slavery says to the enslaved child, go where the master or "his debts . . . shall choose," wherever the parent lives. Above all else, the Word commands that we treat others as we wish to be treated. But masters, never wishing to be sold from kin, sell humans away from loved ones.[3]

Advanced proslavery theologians, including and especially Thornwell, answered that the Golden Rule hardly meant that inferiors must be given the freedom that superiors would deserve, if enslaved. Rather, superiors must bestow the Christian governance that inferiors deserve, in a kingdom of love. The Golden Rule, Fee conceded, required only that superiors govern inferiors lovingly. But slavery's essence, the absolute power of the human owner over the owned human, gave bad masters authority to demolish such necessities of the Christian spirit as blacks' families and their access to the Word.

Worse, good masters could not always preserve the Golden Rule, for slaves could be seized for unpaid debts. After a default, lenders could spray a seized black family in all directions. Heirs could also sever a deceased master's slave families. The impersonal system, in short, blocked even saved Christians from saving the spirit of Christianity.

Harriet Beecher Stowe's *Uncle Tom's Cabin* preached the same message. Slavery smashed Uncle Tom's family, the soul of his merely physical cabin, not because his master was evil but because Tom was property, pledged for Massa's debt. John G. Fee suffered through his own version of *Uncle Tom's Cabin*. His tale of how slavery savaged *his* family's Christian home, this time no fiction, showed why even James Henley Thornwell sometimes despaired. Perhaps the Christian case against absolute power did trump the proslavery version of the Golden Rule.

– 2 –

The star of Fee's true tale played a celebrated southern role: Mammy. The Mammy myth epitomized why slaveholders entitled slavery the *Domestic Institution*. Mammy raised all children in the Big House, her own and the patriarch's. As a nurturer of both blacks and whites, she merged two races into one folk, often holding a black and a white child simultaneously at breast. All "her" children loved her, as did "her" whites. She returned their adoration. Mammy provided the best answer to John G. Fee's heresy that slavery's essence necessarily destroyed Christian love.

The best answer supplied the best retort. Most Big Houses contained several families, white and black. Mammy had to mediate at the center of their jealousies. Envious white children could think she played favorites among them. Her jealous black children could think she favored the patriarch's offspring over them. Her black husband or her owner's white wife could think she favored the patriarch, sexually or otherwise. The Man could think she should give him more favors, sexual or otherwise. If a patriarch resented Mammy's domestic power, he could sell her out of the family circle, with the whites who disliked her cheering, the whites who revered her helpless, and her black children devastated.

The Fee family savaged its Mammy, Julett Miles, in this crossfire.[4] John G. Fee and his mother adored Julett Miles. His father and his younger brother James resented Mammy. In 1848, when John was thirty-one and his younger siblings had also left home, his father resolved to sell the ex-nurse, while keeping her black children as slaves. James encouraged Mammy's eviction. He claimed that the family contained "more women . . . than were needed." His mother responded that she needed "her best help." Mammy wept that she needed to see her black children.

John G. Fee temporarily saved the Christian home. Mortgaging to the losing point the only property he owned, he bought Julett Miles. He freed her, then convinced his father to let her serve his mother, without wages. The liberator could not raise the dollars to fulfill his further ambition: to free Miles's five children and thus remove all Mammy's blacks from all Fees' absolute control.

Fee still felt that his emancipation had lived up to the Golden Rule. He had done to the slave what he would have wanted done, if he had been a slave and able to maintain a Christian family only by serving without pay. Thanks to his hard-earned arrangements, Mammy's wageless service and her black family would continue as before. Slavery had here evolved not into whites' ideal for themselves, egalitarian freedom, but into the only salvation John G. Fee could afford to bestow, an ex-slave's unequal peonage.

Mammy's peonage ultimately saved neither a Christian family nor the Golden Rule. Fee's mother died. Fee's father dispatched Mammy to earn wages in someone else's home. Julett Miles found employment in a neighboring area of Ohio. By coming back across the Ohio River occasionally, the freed mother could visit her enslaved children, who still served in the Fee family's Big House. Inside her Ohio safety from slavery, the ex-Mammy also bore free black children.

Safety ended. In 1859, Fee's father died. With John G. Fee disinherited, his younger brother James, now a cotton merchant in New Orleans, inherited the estate. James Fee, resentful of Julett Miles, had previously wanted her sold. Now he could sell her five enslaved children and *their* children. As an ex-Kentuckian, skilled in New Orleans transactions, James Fee knew the Kentucky property would fetch top dollar downriver, at a Deep South slave auction.

Julett Miles heard that James Fee intended to sell her children forever out of her sight. In desperation, she decided to kidnap her offspring. She would unite her enslaved Kentucky brood with her free Ohio brood inside her free state home.

In this year of John Brown's raid, Mammy's kidnapping scheme was as futile as the Harpers Ferry invasion. The free mother, her enslaved children, and her enslaved grandchildren all suffered easy capture. James Fee sold Mammy's slave family downriver. The river also separated her Kentucky jail from her Ohio free family. The doubly savaged mother languished for a few months in prison (now as the warden's unpaid peon!) before expiring. With this horror, an exasperated John G. Fee had unwittingly proved that you could do onto a slave as you would have done to you only by emancipating *all* servants from the danger of being bought and sold like cattle.

Proslavery evangelicals feared that moral of the story. They shuddered that sinning humans' unrestricted power to sever parents from children, and to bar the heathen from Scripture, did invite biblical abominations, according to the strictest construction of the Word. A decade before Julett's tragedy, evangelicals publicized their best answer: James Henley Thornwell's inspired definition of slavery. The definition claimed slavery's essence to be not ownership of man but obligation to perform service. A master purchased not everything about a human but only the obligation to serve during the workday. All perversions that abolitionists rightly considered Christian monstrosity, whether selling family members from each other or separating blacks from the Word, were incidental to slavery's service essence. Slavery's sinful incidentals must be abolished, while its service essence must continue.

Fee knew as an insider the soft underbelly of his fellow Southerners' most advanced argument. He answered that a slave must be defined not as any Christian server but as a servant "*who, without his consent, is held as property.*" It was not incidental but essential to property in man that "the husband can be torn from the wife, . . . the child from its parents, and the Christian from the chosen service of his God." To end Christian horrors such as Julett Miles's nightmare, evangelists must strip "away the barbarous law that makes man the property of his fellow-man."[5]

Proslavery evangelicals preferred to make slavery biblically right by convincing sinning masters to be Christian paternalists. Fee scorned the illusion that preachers could convert all sinners. Despite all the familial love bolstering his effort, he had failed to convert his father and brother away from their anti-Christian devastation of Mammy. Yet the Christian point transcended James Fee's hard heart. Not the authority of unkind masters but the requirements of impersonal property often tore families asunder. The good master dies, his bad debts must be paid, and his executor must accept *"the liabilities of property."* [6]

Proslavery preachers sometimes conceded that unless they could convert all sinning masters (and executors), the state must intervene. By outlawing masters (and executors) from separating black families and from separating heathen from the Word, southern governments could abolish slavery's supposedly incidental crimes. Then all slaves, not just Julett Miles, would become Christian peons. Otherwise, an angry Jehovah might abolish slavery's service essence as well as its anti-Christian incidentals.

Fee answered that the reformers would never prevail. "The moment you pass a law" forbidding masters to sell property when necessary, "you pass an abolition act—you hurl a death blow at slavery. For, no man will buy a slave under such restrictions." [7]

Fee knew that his strict construction arguments had preachers on the run and running out of biblical places to hide. He believed that in a democracy, where "the free expression of opinion" must prevail, "truth has nothing to fear from error." He concluded that slaveholders had everything to fear from their own Christian assumptions, in the democratic debate that the Lord had called him home to win. [8]

Having arguably bested the South's finest minds in the Christian South's most important intellectual debate, Fee acquired a counterproductive cockiness. If free to argue, he would prevail. No discrete calculation of what to say, when, would be necessary. Just as John Brown scorned planning past the first strike, since God would do the directing, so John G. Fee scorned discretion and trimming, since his strict biblical constructions could conquer all southern Christians, even James Henley Thornwell.

– 3 –

His confidence increased when Cassius Clay, Henry Clay's cousin, called him to an auspicious new Kentucky home. In 1853, Cassius Clay sent Fee quite the invitation. Come build a dwelling on my lands deep in Kentucky, wrote this brawler for Border South free speech. Here I will protect your right to advocate biblical antislavery within hearing distance of friendly nonslaveholders—and antagonistic slaveholders too.

The invitation commenced a weird alliance between one of the Border South's most important compromising antislavery politicians and its most important uncompromising antislavery preacher. From 1849 through 1851, Cassius Clay had been the star of the first full-scale southern debate over abolishing slavery since Virginia's post–Nat Turner legislative discussion of 1831–32. In Kentucky's constitutional convention of 1849, then again in his run for the Kentucky governorship in 1851, Cassius Clay had played the pragmatic moderate, using whites' racism to urge that Kentucky should slowly be swept clean of slavery, and of blacks too. Clay would bar further slaves from entrance into Kentucky. He would enact a so-called post-nati

Two unlikely allies, John G. Fee (left), uncompromising scholar of the Bible that he here clutches, and Cassius Clay (right), brawling deployer of compromised secular reform. Courtesy of the Berea College Archives, Berea, Kentucky (Fee), and Professor Stanley Harrold (Clay).

law, decreeing that several years hence, say in 1860, any slaves born there-after must be freed when they reached adulthood, if they still remained in Kentucky.[9]

Clay claimed that few would remain by the time his law would emanci-pate anyone, an event that would occur no earlier than 1880. Masters would beat the deadline by selling most of their adolescent slaves in Deep South auctions, before the post-nati became free adults. Many years hence, the Kentucky legislature could afford to buy the few remaining slaves and send them to Africa.

Cassius Clay shed few tears over blacks. Under his version of antislavery, most Kentucky slaves figured to become Lower South bondsmen. Cassius Clay instead wept over Kentucky whites' economy, especially nonslavehold-ers'. Clay claimed that slaves' sweating labor made white sweat degraded. He argued that immigrants preferred a free labor society. He asserted that potential newcomers' aversion to slave society left Kentucky with too few workers and thus too few land buyers. By making the state slaveless and lily-white, Cassius Clay would enable fertile Kentucky to compete with Illi-nois and Ohio for white immigrants. The shower of new citizens, eager to toil, would bolster Kentucky's lagging land prices, and her sagging enter-prise too.

Kentucky's slaveholders feared this gradual, racist, crass, and cheap ap-peal to Kentucky's overwhelming majority, the nonslaveholders. Deploying the Slave Power's classic despotic answer to democratic challenge, nonslave-holder mobs with slaveholder leaders dumped Clay's newspapers into the river and threatened to deport him from the state. But "Cash" Clay (one of Cassius's revealing nicknames) would not be silenced. He earned another of his nicknames, the "Lion of White Hall," by defying proslavery mobs. He brandished a bowie knife as chilling as the ones John Brown used for his spears. He killed one proslavery assailant. His supporters warned that if lynchers mobbed Clay, they would mob the lynchers. Thus did Clay's famed bowie knife become symbol of an ominous fact, from a slaveholder's perspective. In this system of democracy and despotism too, a heretic with enough supporters might have to be defeated with votes, not with tar and feathers and rifles and spears.

While Clay won the right for Kentuckians to hear a reactionary version of antislavery, he lost his midcentury elections. He did receive a promising 10 percent of Kentuckians' support in 1849. An agitator could build on that foundation. But his support drooped to 3 percent in 1851. He needed help to turn his antislavery fortunes around. In the emerging Northern Republican Party, Clay thought he saw his helpers.

Clay believed that with a National Republican Party's aid, in the form of seductive patronage, he could be the southern titan of a triumphant ruling coalition. Northern Republicans would then gain what every dominant national party had developed: an important wing in every section. Clay's Southern Republican movement would gain what every successful American reform crusade had secured: an honored and rewarded place inside the national two-party establishment. As for Clay personally, he would no longer be Kentucky's political outsider. Instead he would be at the center of National Republicanism, just as cousin Henry had been at the center of National Whiggery. He would thus be the second Clay to use national patronage to publicize a centrist route to Kentucky whites' prosperity.

But only a truly centrist alliance would suffice. Cassius Clay could not afford identification with a left-wing version of Northern Republicanism. He could abide no talk of a higher law than constitutions, no proposals for making freed blacks equal citizens, no castigation of Southerners as sinners. But a Southern Republican could cherish Northern Republicans who repudiated federal intervention in southern states, who relied on their southern wing to secure southern reform, who scorned making ex-slaves citizens, who preferred that American freedmen be returned to Africa, and who emphasized that barring blacks from national territories would serve white men's economic interests. If Northern Republicans would make Cassius Clay a national titan (maybe even a national presidential or vice presidential candidate) on that moderately antislavery basis, he could give northern antislavery an entrance into the South that John Brown's higher law could never achieve.

The program made Cash Clay almost as different from John G. Fee as from John Brown. Cassius Clay, armed with his bowie knife, had fought and killed for his right to be heard. Fee, armed with the Word, extolled nonviolent resistance (although after mobs violated his person, the preacher would consider carrying a rifle). Clay's delivered the politics of economics, emphasizing slavery's harm to white men's prosperity, especially the nonslaveholders'. Fee espoused the message of Christ, emphasizing slavery's obstacle to sinners' salvation, especially the slaves' and the slaveholders'. Clay, pragmatic politician, sought a mainstream appeal to the Kentucky racist majority. Fee, antipragmatic zealot, aspired to convert racists to colorblind emancipation. Clay would induce masters to sell blacks outside Kentucky. Fee invited blacks inside his colorblind church.

Again, Clay aspired to lead as a Southern Republican from the governor's mansion. He thus allied with moderate Northern Republicans such as Abraham Lincoln. Fee aspired to lead from a college president's house. He thus allied with far-out Northerners such as immigrants from Oberlin College. What did Cash Clay and John G. Fee ever have in common?

They shared, in the beginning, a hope that their separate crusades could find a mutually nourishing meeting ground. They met first on Clay's grounds. Fee supported Clay in 1849, when the Lion of White Hall espoused an antislavery amendment to the Kentucky constitution, then again in 1851, when Clay ran for governor, then again in 1856, when Henry Clay's cousin sought the vice presidential nomination on a National Republican ticket. While the latest Clay could never be Fee's antislavery hero, a compromising antislavery moderate could be the most congenial politician that Kentucky had to offer. Clay the brawler could also offer Fee the boon a democratic agitator most needs and a southern antislavery agitator usually least possessed: free speech.

While Clay, in turn, hardly saw Fee as the ideal pragmatic agitator, the preacher had been a loyal political supporter and could become a valuable religious revivalist. The evangelical extremist might stir the souls. Then the political moderate might harvest the votes. Thus was sealed a precarious Old South bargain. Thus began the ultimate southern test of whether slavery for blacks and wide-open democracy for whites could coexist.

– 4 –

Before Clay invited him to come rouse Kentucky's whites against black slavery, Fee had worked the largely nonslaveholding folk near his ancestral Bracken County, 7 percent enslaved and on the edge of Ohio. Some of Clay's lands lay over a hundred miles deeper south, in Madison County, 35 percent enslaved. Clay's own acres comprised a classic intersection of two border cultures. On the one hand, Clay's so-called glade consisted of a grassy valley, undulating much like the Blue Grass plantation region just to the north. On the other hand, Clay's so-called ridge consisted of a seventy-foot cliff, rising much like the mountainous nonslaveholding region just to the southeast. From the semicircular ridge, Fee could see massively enslaved Blue Grass counties in one direction and scantily enslaved trans-Allegheny mountain counties in the other.

Fee's new Berea habitat was like a funnel, aiming antislavery whispers that wafted over the mountains right at the Blue Grass. Fee aspired for a different mountainous funnel than did John Brown. Brown would use the mountains to pour fugitive slaves toward the free North, hundreds of miles away. Fee would rouse mountain folk to pour the Word at slaveholding areas, only dozens of miles away.

Fee brought to Clay's glade and ridge some apparently curious weapons to triumph as orator. In the pulpit he rarely gestured, rarely screamed, rarely insulted the slaveholders. Nor did his short figure or squarish, balding head announce a charismatic leader. Next to hulking, hard, harsh Cassius Clay, with the weathered face and stubborn chin of a brawler, Fee almost looked effeminate. But the preacher's soft pulpit voice fit his plea for a community of love; and his long, high forehead reemphasized his irrepressible logic on biblical strict construction.[10]

His Christian institutions at first seemed as innocuous as his person. He had scant use for a towering revival tent or a long anxious bench or a boisterous camp meeting of thousands. He favored a few tiny churches, a handful of intimate schools, and a dozen soft-spoken so-called colporteurs. These agents quietly went from dwelling to dwelling, handing out Bibles and antislavery pamphlets and seeking to persuade the homeowners.[11]

Fee and his compatriots reversed the conventional wisdom about how to persuade slaveholders. Masters supposedly would not tolerate outside agitators. Yet imported Yankees comprised over half of Fee's teachers, preachers, and colporteurs. Southern churches supposedly had to admit slaveholders to membership, to convince patriarchs of Christian obligations. Yet Fee barred all slaveholders as unworthy of Christian fellowship. Antislavery Southerners supposedly had to be racists, determined to send freedmen to Africa, or to sell slaves down river, or to segregate blacks in church balconies. Yet Fee invited blacks to his schools and to his dinner tables as equals—and to come on down from the church balconies. A quiet man who embraced blacks, ostracized slaveholders, and recruited Oberlin saints as southern redeemers—this radical could revolutionize a skittish, suspicious culture?!

Not for a second, in the Lower South. But for an hour, in the Border South. No other Southerner ever tried anything so radical. No other Southerner ever spread antislavery so quickly. In the mid-1850s, the Fee movement stirred like the bracing mountain air. One church swiftly became a dozen. Lay schools opened. Colporteurs multiplied.

The Kentucky slaveholders, feeling the slight tremor, deployed the classic dictatorial answer to democratic whispers. In the spring of 1855 at Dripping Springs, a mob seized Fee, dragged him from the church, and escorted him miles away. Fee, beset with a splitting headache, asked the government to jail his savagers.[12]

Receiving no response, he asked his patron to reachieve free speech. Cassius Clay responded at Crab Orchard. Surrounded by armed followers, he insisted that the preacher must be heard. On July 21, 1855, Clay went further. He appeared with Fee, telling the hostile crowd that if they mobbed his colleague, they must lynch him and his supporters first. Few in Border South

Kentucky dared start a war between lynch mobs. No such threat of an anti-slavery mob could have dissolved a Lower South proslavery mob.[13]

A year later, Fee and his protective patron appeared together in public yet again, at a Fourth of July celebration. The cocky preacher, orating first, declared that no proslavery law should be obeyed, for slavery violated God's higher law. Clay, alarmed, answered that all constitutional law must be obeyed. Fee, warming to the conversion of a (he thought) permanent friend, asked if Clay would obey the Fugitive Slave Law. I would not, muttered an increasingly unfriendly Clay, but because the law violated man's Constitution, not because it violated God's law. Fee called this a higher law distinction without a difference. He chuckled that the moderate Mr. Clay had opted for higher law.[14]

Only an arcane abstractionist, brilliant in polemical battle but clueless about practical politics, could have proclaimed so impolitic a theoretical victory. This confrontation involved nothing practical, save the highly practical certainty that Fee would suffer a second disinheritance. Cassius Clay, like Fee's father, disdained the dishonor of a creed dragged through the mud, especially when an insufferably ungrateful dependent issued the insult.

Moreover, Clay, like Fee's father, believed that the ungrateful dependent menaced the assaulted titan's basis of earthly independence. Just as Fee's biblical position threatened his father's base in slaveholding, so the ingrate's higher law position threatened Clay's base in practical politics. No Republican Party nominations or patronage, and few Kentucky votes, would be obtained if Cassius Clay, famous for dulled antislavery no less than for sharp bowie knives, was guilty by association of defying human law.

So Cassius Clay let it be known that he would no longer protect the loose cannon that he had unfortunately installed at the fag end of Madison County. In June 1857, arsonists responded to their new free rein by burning down a Rockcastle County church, full of Fee supporters. A mob then seized Fee from a house, jammed a pistol in his stomach, and forced him to march miles away. Threats and actions culminated in January 1858. An armed mob of thirty ruffians dragged Fee from a church in Estill County along with one of his colporteurs, Robert Jones. The armed marauders forced the two crusaders down to the Kentucky River. They ordered Brother Jones to strip. They lashed his back bloody. Fee, although untouched, thereafter suffered paralyzing headaches.[15]

In the manner of southern lynch mobs, extralegal violence then waned as it had waxed. White democracy remained cherished and free speech essential, unless racial control stood menaced. A frightened preacher might now have been rendered unmenacing. Subsequently, with no mobs striking, Fee's headaches dulled. His energy returned. His oratorical successes increased— and the outside world spied his little earthquake.

In November 1858, Harriet Beecher Stowe urged northern missionaries to journey southward. Northerners fear being "driven out" of the South, Stowe wrote. But "Fee is not driven out of Kentucky." True, he suffers "afflictions."

True, his antislavery churches are "feeble." But every Christian "inch" gained is "mighty in moral force." Northern migrants should extend Fee's Kentucky inches into miles of "every slave territory."[16] Stowe rejoiced that the supposedly closed society had been opened a crack, that a native Southerner had gained a sliver of free speech, that his southern assumptions persuaded, and that northern Christians needed only to aid his preaching. With Fee as guide, Yankee saints might yet convert southern sinners, inside the South.

– 5 –

A half year after Harriet Beecher Stowe urged a Yankee infiltration of at least cash, Fee scored an astonishing success. The centerpiece of Fee's triumph became a private elementary school, called Berea School, located high on the ridge. The school's star teacher became a Connecticut Yankee educated at Oberlin named John Almanza Rowley Rogers, aided by his wife, Lizzie. Rogers's long, thin frame and long, stern rectitude seemed as endless as his name. The teacher, sternest with himself, scoured his own pride, sloth, and idleness. The exasperated would-be saint also scoured his students, damming their complicity in the demon slavery.[17]

For all Rogers's scourings, his genius (unlike John Brown's) was to mix righteous religion with smiling gladness. His little disciples at Fee's Berea School learned to add and subtract by counting the appearing and disappearing squirrels. They sang multiplication tables to the tune of "Yankee Doodle Dandy." They marched to recess chanting "I'm a Pilgrim."

Pilgrims multiplied. Fifteen appeared at Berea School when Rogers began in spring term 1858, forty-five in fall term, over a hundred in spring term 1859. A third of them were slaveholders' children. They learned that their parents sinned against Christ. They took the lesson home, to embarrassed mothers and fathers. Pretty heiresses, dressed in "bewitching little print dresses and white aprons," intermingled with raggedy urchins, dressed in brown mountain homespun, learning together to be Christ's classless warriors.

Almanza Rogers wanted still more egalitarian intermingling at Berea School. He laid down an ultimatum. Black children must be allowed to join the little white pilgrims. Otherwise, he would transfer his call for pilgrims to a more Christian school elsewhere. Under threat of losing the glad puritan, Fee approved Rogers's proposed racial intermingling. But would Madison County, over one-third enslaved, allow this apparent southern monstrosity?

The folks had a chance to kill the monster democratically, with votes instead of mobs. In April 1859, rival boards of trustees of Berea School bid for ballots. One ticket favored a racially integrated school, with Rogers continuing to weave pedagogical magic. The rival ticket favored a school without blacks or the magician. The pro-Rogers slate won by a three to one ratio.

Citizens here hardly endorsed antislavery, much less racial integration. They voted to retain a colorful teacher, where not even a drab school had existed before. Their endorsement still encouraged Fee and Rogers to act as if they had won a colorblind mandate. The two would expand Berea School into Berea College. Berea "shall be to Kentucky" breathed Fee, "what Oberlin . . . is to Ohio."[18] In the fall, Fee marched on the North, seeking more Yankee migrants and more Yankee dollars to make his southern Oberlin the nation's best antislavery vehicle.

His plea for northern funds and invaders was a little like—and vastly unlike—John Brown's late pleadings. The differences could not save Fee from the similarity, not at John Brown's traumatic moment. On October 5, 1859, Fee arrived in the North. On October 16, Brown descended on Harpers Ferry. Fee, undeterred by the Brown uproar, traveled ever farther northward, begging for peaceable northern raiders and dollars.

His pacific plea climaxed on November 13, when he charmed the congregation at Henry Ward Beecher's Brooklyn, New York, church. Beecher, Harriet Beecher Stowe's brother, introduced Fee with the same high praise that his sister had showered on the Berea saints. I "give way tonight," announced Beecher, "to a better man than I am" and "ask you to contribute toward" his magnificent "cause."

Fee begged them to contribute Northerners "like John Brown—of his boldness and honesty—of his self-sacrificing spirit—not to carry the sword, but the Gospel of Love." Beecher's flock sent Fee away with the loving tidings of $217.50. Beecher's parting words cheered the refortified zealot: No contribution would do more "good in the cause of Emancipation."[19]

Brooklyn's contribution instead ended any good Fee could do in Kentucky. Not even Fee's tactical blunder of needlessly taking on Cassius Clay could compare to the blunder of explicitly asking Yankees for more John Browns (albeit peaceful ones), at the peak of the hysteria over Harpers Ferry. Only John Brown's decision to hole up in the engine house could compare as tactical stupidity. Both suicidal strategies drew from the same well: a conviction that the saint who marches with Christ need not plot cautiously about how to step carefully among humans.

Kentucky newspapers summed up Fee's careless outburst with black headlines: "JOHN BROWNS FOR KENTUCKY." In early December, rumors blazed through the state that a crate from the North, addressed to Fee, contained Sharpe's rifles. (It turned out to contain candle molds!) Worse, before Fee could bring dollars for Bibles and Berea School back to his endangered flock, Madison County slaveholders gathered their rifles. Gentlemen claimed that the "right of self-preservation" must supersede state law, especially when "our enemies" seek to administer "a higher law than . . . the Constitution." On December 23, some sixty armed men on horseback besieged Almanza Rogers's house. They demanded that all Feeites leave the state in ten days.

On the anniversary of Christ's birthday, Berea's teachers asked Kentucky's governor for a democrat's rightful protection. Democracy's chief executive offered no such Christmas present. So on December 29, thirty-six stricken crusaders commenced their antipilgrimage toward joining their leader in northern exile. Hearing tidings of exodus, Fee wrote that "my heart almost crushes me." In the remaining prewar months, the crushed Southerner would wander around alien northern acres, his head feeling as if weighed down under lead, his spirit sunk in a paralyzing depression. The Border South, if too unlike the Lower South to stop Fee from planting on Berea's auspicious ledge, had been similar enough to stamp out his fragile plant. He would not be replanting what became Berea College until the Civil War gave way to Reconstruction. In slavery times, republicanism, southern style, had once against shut down unlimited freedom to agitate.[20]

Still, Cassius Clay survived the antidemocratic intransigence. It was one thing to deport a scantily supported extremist who could rally no countermob and whose proposed immediate emancipation could turn racial control upside down. It was quite another to oust a rather popular politician who could raise a countermob and whose gradual antislavery program would leave Kentucky lily-white. While Fee's uncompromising voice had been silenced, Cassius Clay's compromised appeal still echoed in the slightly open spaces that distinguished Border South from Lower South. From his borderland base, Clay could still urge moderate antislavery men, North and northern South, to collaborate in a National Republican Party. After John Brown had proved too violent and John Fee too radical, Fee's ex-patron, having renounced Fee, might yet star in a third act of the drama that had commenced at Harpers Ferry.

CHAPTER 16

John Underwood and Economic Invasion

Virginia's Governor Henry Wise always doubted that John Brown aimed at a slave revolt. So canny a revolutionary, Wise believed, must know that "our border slaves" are already "so liberated . . . that *they*" need "*no . . . arms for their*" complete "*liberation.*" Because "the underground railroad is at their very doors," borderland slaves "can liberate themselves by running away."[1]

Might a shrewd raider, Wise wondered, instead seek to arouse jealous nonslaveholders? The governor winced when slaveless fishermen in his Accomac County home base muttered about grandees' airs. He scoffed that western Virginian plebeians were "coarse and menial and ill-mannered" and "*not Virginians* in their social or political sympathies."[2] He thus understood why southern hotspurs denounced him for allowing some especially suspect Northerners to enter the state.

A Yankee named John C. Underwood directed the suspicious migration from New York City, after Virginians expelled him. Underwood still owned a farm in Clarke County near Harpers Ferry, where his wife and children continued to reside. Several weeks after Brown struck, Wise heard a rumor that Underwood had slipped back into Clarke County. The governor immediately pulled some investigators off John Brown's cold trail to follow the hot new lead.[3]

– 1 –

John Underwood sought northern economic invasion of the South. From his native terrain near New York's Burned-Over District, Underwood gained a devotion to a free labor economy. From his Virginia wife, who was Stonewall Jackson's cousin and Underwood's student when he came down south to tutor, the New Yorker gleaned an understanding of a Southerner's determination to live on southern land, near southern kin.[4]

The Underwoods' marriage, like the union between William L. Yancey's southern mother and abolitionist stepfather, tested whether North and South could live together. With Mrs. Underwood unwilling to tolerate life in the North and Mr. Underwood unwilling to tolerate the South's Peculiar Institution, where could they find a mutually congenial home? Between 1848 and 1856, their answer fastened on that Clarke County farm, bought with her dowry and utilizing his New York experience with free labor dairy farms.

Although my wife and I prefer paid white workers, the dairyman reassured a Virginia friend, she is no "fanatical abolitionist." No member of Virginia's Jackson clan would "rant" in "denunciation of slaveholders" or succumb to "any weak sympathy for the . . . slaves." But after our visits to the North, he reported, my wife believed that men "work better for the cash than the lash. . . . Whenever we fasten one end of the chain upon the ankle of a fellow being, . . . the heavier end becomes inevitably attached to ourselves."[5]

The Underwoods' prosperous free labor dairy operation spread over nineteen Clarke County farms, located beyond slaveholders' favorite valley acres. Slaveholders monopolized the terrain near the Shenandoah River. Underwood preferred the uplands above the valley floor. The rolling terrain reminded him of New York pastureland. Yet the rich turf cost less than equally fertile New York acres. Here an entrepreneurial Yankee could demonstrate that free labor would outperform slave labor in producing an Upper South economic takeoff.

Underwood shared his favorite southern politician's economic vision. Cassius Clay, like Underwood, thought that an enslaved Upper South would always be underpopulated and thus underdeveloped. The northern South would contain ever fewer slaves, because the more prosperous southern South would pull blacks downward. Yet too few white substitutes would come down from the North, because potential migrants preferred free labor terrain. Since insufficient whites would replace dwindling slaves, land prices would remain low. Land speculators' profits would remain trifling. Economic development would remain halting.

Underwood saw economic and antislavery opportunity in this stagnant situation. Northerners' "tide of emigration," he wrote, "will soon take a southern direction and will certainly double the value of all the real estate of the Old Dominion." Only the presence of "colored people" had "prevented it" or "could prevent it much longer."[6]

Cassius Clay would shorten the preventative period with a delayed emancipation law. His proposed edict would impel Upper South masters to sell blacks to the Lower South before an antislavery deadline. Underwood would add economic lures to political compulsion. If publicity about cheap acres attracted more whites, Virginians would sell more blacks out of the state before future antislavery laws forced the exodus.

Suspicious slaveholders despaired of halting Underwood's enterprising movement of Yankee whites, so long as the migrants avoided politics and stuck to the dairy business. In 1856, however, Underwood ventured into the political business. Speaking to the first National Republican Convention in Philadelphia as a Virginia delegate, the adopted Virginian warned that his new state's "blighting curse of slavery" and "the blood of crushed human-ity" must not pollute "the fair plains of the west." The deplorable economic "fate of Virginia" showed "that the curse of Heaven is and ever must be upon human oppression."[7]

After word of that heresy wafted back to Clarke County, a potential lynch mob warned Underwood's wife that her Yankee would be the bleeding hu-man crushed, if the alleged traitor returned to his supposed home. Stonewall Jackson's cousin meant to retain her southern dwelling, but her Yankee must not continually risk residing in her home. "I could not have Jackson blood in my veins," Underwood's wife explained to her husband, without risking "the last drop . . . in defense of life and liberty; but I do not believe in courting mob law or martyrdom." Throughout the later 1850s, Underwood only occa-sionally courted trouble by visiting his mate and their children on the Clarke County farm, where the female Stonewall defiantly remained.[8]

Here again, black slavery hardly perfected white democracy or domestic institutions. This time, the slave system's antidemocratic necessities yielded not slave sales, shattering black families, but threatened lynch mobs, scatter-ing a white family. Back in New York City, the victimized husband became a martyr for free speech, and for Christian marriage too. With that doubled moral capital, Underwood meant to revenge himself on Virginia the entre-preneurial way. He would conduct a more threatening antislavery business than milking cows.

Underwood's new business firm, called the American Emigration Aid and Homestead Society, received its New York state charter in April 1857, with a proposed initial capitalization of $200,000. At this (fleeting) moment of northern prosperity, Underwood offered earthly as well as heavenly prof-its. His company would buy depreciated Upper South land, then sell north-ern settlers cheaper acres than could be found in the free labor Midwest. Yankee newcomers would boost Upper South prosperity and land prices. They would thereby convince Southerners that free labor outperformed slave labor, at least in the South's less tropical areas.

That strategy, duplicating Eli Thayer's Kansas tactics, dissolved when the Panic of 1857 shrank Yankee capital. Underwood, now unable to raise north-ern cash to buy southern land, switched his persuasive tactics. He would convince potential settlers, eager to escape northern misfortune, to move to the Upper South (where the panic ruined fewer enterprises than in the North). For his delivery of land buyers, land sellers would pay him a 5 percent to 20 percent commission.

The strategy exploited another difference between Lower and Upper Souths. Down toward North America's hottest tropics, migrating slaveown-ers sought land speculators' choicest acres. But up toward the cooler North, with slaveholders deserting for profits farther south, land speculators needed alternative customers. By introducing (southern) upper-class land sellers to (northern) middle- and lower-class land buyers, Underwood would develop a classless, nonsectional boost to this American area's economy. My Northerners, he promised a western Virginia entrepreneur, will "double the value of your lands, make your neglected hillsides bloom with cultivation," lead "your hitherto neglected waterpower" to ring "with the music of the wheel, . . . and cause your desert to bloom like the rose." Or as he soared to another Virginian, he could send 50,000 Yankees who would add $2000 per family to Virginia's property values. I wish no further "revenge" from "the indignities heaped upon me by the misguided sons of that state, now cursed by slavery, but before long to be blessed by freedom."[9]

His revenge, he conceded, might free few blacks. His white migrants would mostly push "perhaps inferior" blacks from the redeemed Upper South to the cursed Lower South. But "he loved his own race best" and his Virginia wife most. Because of slavery's "injurious effects to the white race," Virginia should be "deAfricanized & settled by white men with all the energy, love of Freedom, order, & education characterizing the Anglo-Saxon Race."[10]

Between 1857 and 1860, John Underwood sent not 50,000 but maybe 5000 whites from New York City to the sunny South. His land buyers purchased acres in eastern Tennessee, Kentucky, Maryland, North Carolina, and especially northwestern Virginia. His partner, Eli Thayer, dispatched another 500 northern settlers to Ceredo (from the Roman word for the Goddess of Plenty), located high up in northwestern Virginia.[11]

The partners wished to avoid lynch mobs, capable of extinguishing their vision of Upper South plenty. So unlike John Fee, Thayer and Underwood sought not agitators but "Neighbors"—Thayer loved that capital-N word—enterprising Yankee Neighbors who will rain profits on parched Southerners. "Niggers"—Thayer unfortunately loved that terrible alternate capital-N word too—"Niggers did not enter into this . . . speculative money making enterprise, one way or the other." If Southerners shot half of us for seeking "filthy lucre," Thayer added, "the rest would press on toward the shining dollars."[12]

Beneath this shining mask lay the dissimulating Yankee. In private, Underwood and Thayer predicted that dollars, not speeches, would unfanatically show that free laborers, unlike slaves, neither malinger nor intentionally misunderstand, neither "run away" nor "steal ham and chickens." The silent demonstration would bring "the subject of free labor" up for a "full, free, and conciliatory discussion." The Upper South results would "never be doubtful,"[13] not after free labor outperformed slave labor.

Posterity thinks of slavery as the South's leading economic interest. True enough, in the Lower South. But as Thayer and Underwood emphasized, the buying, selling, and working of land, not the buying, selling, and working of slaves, fueled more Upper South materialistic dreams. Again, posterity thinks of the southern nonslaveholder problem as a class threat, since the poor might rise against the rich. But as moneyed economic boosters, Thayer and Underwood saw, more correctly, that southern rich men and poor men alike filled the nonslaveholder ranks, and that all slaveless folk, regardless of class, wished the southern economy to take off.

Again, posterity calls the race problem the South's special predicament. Thayer and Underwood saw, more correctly, that the population problem comprised the Upper South's special drawback. With blacks slowly draining out, whites had to be attracted in or the economy would stagnate. Welcome harmless Yankee Neighbors, they said to the population-starved Upper South, and northern white population will flow southward, not westward. Go south, young man, they said to enterprising Yankees, go to the Upper South, where land is cheap and blacks can be pushed exclusively to the Lower South.

Lower South warriors loathed Upper South moderates for failing to shut off this seductive proposition while the seducers remained few. To proslavery visionaries, the Thayer-Underwood vision seemed obviously full of hatred for slavery under the façade of the good Neighbor. If Upper South trimmers could not see through so transparent a mask—well, no wonder that Underwood thought that half the South could be silently infiltrated.

"The logic of dollars and dimes," warned the *Galveston* (Texas) *News*, could become an irresistibly "strong argument" inside the Upper South's "weak and assailable points." The *Jackson Mississippian* asked "reflecting men" to ponder the "condition of the South, when Virginia, Kentucky, Tennessee, Missouri, and we may add, Maryland, are successfully colonized with free population." The *New Orleans Delta* urged Virginia "to keep her obligations to her sister Slave States" by squelching "a conspiracy to abolitionize the Old Dominion." The *Delta* especially tore into Henry Wise, that self-styled southern hotspur, who did nothing to deter Underwood's invaders.[14]

Governor Wise saw the political risk in doing nothing, but he could not "interfere with peaceable and lawful immigrations." He must welcome all whites, "as long as they will obey our laws." He would "calmly wait" for "*the fact*" of "unlawful" acts.[15]

And then, at the nervous moment of John Brown's raid, Wise believed that the fact might have arrived. As the governor cast about for the raider's real plan, he suspected that Brown's calculations must include hostile nonslaveholders. Then he received secret (and false) word that John Underwood had been spotted at his wife's Clarke County farm, where the Yankee had received crates of Hinton R. Helper's books. The governor rushed detectives in to investigate, for Helper had lately honed a defiantly political edge on Underwood's economic tactics.

– 2 –

John Underwood and the more notorious Hinton R. Helper had linked their slightly different crusades before Wise's detectives descended to explore the linkage. The two heretics both believed that antislavery should rescue primarily whites from primarily economic trouble. Each conceived that relatively low southern land prices exemplified the trouble. Both speculated that in a lily-white, free labor South, land prices and entrepreneurial progress would match the North's booming levels.

Still, the New York entrepreneur and the North Carolina author, having suffered different travails on their paths to the same heresy, mounted initially different crusades. Underwood, eager Yankee hustler, steamed about potential lynchers. He sought classless revenge with a corporation, dedicated to enriching poor and rich, Northerners and Southerners. In contrast Helper, frustrated southern nonslaveholder, steamed about limited economic possibilities. He sought class-infested revenge with a book dedicated to rousing the poor against the powerful. Underwood preferred to begin with economic appeals to potential migrants, hopeful that transplanted Northerners would further southern antislavery. Helper preferred to begin with economic appeals to Upper South nonslaveholders, hopeful that antislavery triumph would lure more migrants.

Hinton R. Helper's preparation for reforming economic visions occurred not in New York's lush dairy country but in North Carolina's hardscrabble Rowan County. Helper's parents never strayed more than twenty miles from their farm in this western piedmont province. Cherishing their (they thought) acres of opportunity, they proudly fastened their county's name inside their son's. The son, although forever stuck with the middle name, shuddered to be stuck inside their (he thought) land of too little opportunity.[16]

With better luck, Hinton R. Helper would have had better Rowan County opportunity. Helper's father was rising beyond the farm, with a flourishing carpentry business and four slaves, when his death canceled his enterprise. Hinton Rowan, then only ten months old, spent his formative years amidst middle-class relatives, afflicted not with lower-class impoverishment but with middling folks' limited endeavors. Hopeful that the precocious Hinton would ascend more quickly than usual in rather stagnant Rowan County, the middle-class clan sent him off to Mocksville Academy, where upper-class heirs more often studied.

We cannot know if Mocksville Academy became the place where Hinton first bitterly resented his supposed betters. But boys will be boys, and richer squires do often mock middling compatriots. We also cannot know if Hinton here first plotted his revenge, although Mocksville clearly gave the imminent author the literary skills to lash back. But we do know that after graduation from Mocksville, wealthy gentlemen went onward to college, while poorer lads sank downward to apprenticeships.

We also know that Hinton Rowan Helper despaired enough to become a thief. Apprenticed to a shopkeeper for three years, the frustrated clerk slowly filched $300 from the till. When discovered, Helper paid back the spoils in full, after the store owner promised to keep the robbery secret. Then Helper, his apprenticeship expired, moved from private humiliation in the backwater to, he hoped, better luck in New York City.

After failing to conquer the big city, Hinton Rowan Helper lit out for another American province, the one that allegedly offered gold for the mere digging. But Helper's scratchings in the California gold fields yielded no more treasure that he could keep than did robbing the North Carolina store. The failed seeker had to trudge back home. In Rowan County, Helper plotted his revenge. He would publish exposés, detailing how rich folk victimized poor folk in the provinces.

In his first book, the poorly selling *Land of Gold: Reality Versus Fiction,* the ex–gold digger castigated the hucksters who lured poor lads like himself to phony El Dorados. Demagogues, with their lies about gold abounding in the dirt, epitomized California's "rottenness and its corruption, its squalor and its misery, its crime and its shame." Helper considered California's crowning shame to be its "complete human menagerie" of "motley and heterogeneous" nonwhites. The North Carolinian lampooned the Chinese ("semi-barbarians"), the Indians and Mexicans ("filthy and abominable"), and the "fawning" Negro who "wept like a child" when emancipated. Some happier day, the "childlike" race would be moved from cooler North America to steaming Mexico and Central America. There they would toil "under the control of new masters, in the fertile wildernesses and savannas nearer the equator." Helper here repeated the Caribbean vision of Missouri's Frank Blair, Jr., the Border South's most popular antislavery politician.[17]

Two years after the California exposé flopped in the bookstores, the frustrated author, now twenty-seven, came back to New York City. He brought along the manuscript of his latest book and his meager share from the sale of his deceased parents' farm. Perhaps unhappiness at the selling price had partly fueled the writing of yet another exposé. At any rate, the manuscript tucked under Helper's arm claimed that a southern economic crisis impended over slaveholders' robbery of nonslaveholders. Helper entitled his diatribe *The Impending Crisis in the South: How to Meet It.*

Not just the mortification of his North Carolina thievery or the disappointment of his California diggings but also resentment of his central piedmont region's slim opportunities drove Helper's pen. In Rowan and the surrounding North Carolina counties, around 20 percent of whites owned slaves. Twice as many whites owned no land. Landless whites slowly trickled out of the area. Helper believed the departing rednecks secretly shared his rage at limited opportunity, at taxation skewed for the benefit of the rich, and at political repression of heretical views. He conceived that "tens of thousands of voters in the Slave States wished" to give their votes "to Republicans." But "the terrors of lynch law . . . put down the pestilent heresy."[18]

In addition to lynch law, slaveholders spread the myth that ownership of slaves comprised the great southern economic interest. But only rich men owned slaves. Poor men owned only acres, if that. Yeomen's small farms would be worth five times more in the free labor North. Get rid of slavery (and blacks), counseled the recently disappointed southern land seller, and northern migrants would boost land prices. But if poor men helped preserve wealthy men's slavery, warned Helper, they would own depreciated terrain, if anything at all. "Nonslaveholding whites!" cried Helper, "look well to your interests."[19]

Helper felt no "special friendliness or sympathy for the blacks." His outrage focused on slavery's economic "curse . . . to those who own" no blacks, and its political curse too. Slaveholders destroyed their own claim that black slavery forms "the very bulwark of white liberties." Instead, "the lords of the lash" made nonslaveholding whites' "freedom . . . merely nominal." If the plebeians dared "to think for themselves" or, worse, expressed "any sentiment at all conflicting with the gospel of slavery," they faced "the terrors of lynch laws," akin to "the meanest and bloodiest despotism of the Old World."[20]

Helper called the New World's despots "more criminal than common murderers." They were worse robbers than thieves, for "thieves steal trifles from rich men," while slaveholders steal free speech from "poor men." Slaveholders formed a "tyrannical" and "inflated oligarchy." They reeked of "arrogance and self-conceit." Their religion stank "in the nostrils of Christendom." Their politics libeled "all the principles" of "Republicanism."[21]

Helper urged fellow nonslaveholders to "wage an exterminating war" against the abomination. Slaveless laborers should never again vote for a "Trafficker in Human Flesh." They should accept "No Co-operation with Slaveholders in Politics—No Fellowship with them in Religion—No Affiliation with them in Society." Helper urged "No Patronage to Slaveholding Merchants, . . . No Fees to Slaveholding Lawyers, . . . No Recognition of Pro-slavery Men, except as Ruffians, Outlaws, and Criminals." The South's impending crisis demanded "Thorough Organization and Independent Action on the part of the Non-Slaveholding whites."[22]

Helper's diatribe, buttressed with fifty-seven statistical tables and still more clever phrases, delighted many New York Republicans. Helper's solution to the supposed U.S. race problem resembled theirs: Send blacks out of the United States. His emphasis on the Slave Power's damage to *whites'* economy and republic also mirrored Republicans' anti–Slave Power appeal. By helping southern ideological compatriots, Northern Republicans could undermine slavery where they could not themselves assault the demon, inside the South. That step beyond containment looked more promising than John Brown's, or John Fee's, or John Underwood's.

New York City Republicans published Helper's *Impending Crisis* on June 26, 1857, only a few weeks after his arrival in the city. Horace Greeley's *New York Tribune* declared that the one-dollar publication at last supplied the southern masses with their fearless, blunt spokesman. Helper relieved his "heavy artillery of numbers" with "rolling volleys and dashing charges of argument and rhetoric."[23]

Despite Greeley's sendoff, Helper soon despaired over another commercial flop. Few Northerners purchased the volume. Few Southerners noticed its insults. When Helper handed his masterpiece to North Carolina's Governor

John W. Ellis, the author suffered a mockery worthy of Mocksville Academy. The proslavery governor lit his pipe with the underling's sheets. When a North Carolina minister, Daniel Worth, was convicted of spreading Helper's words, the populace suspended the required public whipping. The crime was too ineffective to warrant punishment. When Henry Wise's detectives broke into John Underwood's farmhouse, they found no books by Helper and no evidence of John Underwood's recent presence. The intruders discovered only Underwood's irretrievably southern wife. That Stonewall of a lady furiously told them to search elsewhere for John Brown's supposed southern allies.

Henry Wise, hearing that the Helper-Underwood trail had run cold, sought other leads about John Brown's mysterious strategy. Meanwhile, almost every southern congressman ignored Helper and sought investigations of Northern Republicans' relationship with Brown. But Hinton R. Helper would not surrender. He would yet transcend Rowan County's limits.

- 3 -

Helper's recovery from failure partially resembled John Brown's comeback. Just as Brown rescued a smashed raid's impact with a speech to his judges, so Helper rescued a failed publication's importance with a plea for a new edition. Just as the South raged less at Brown's original raid than at subsequent northern cheers for his speech, so the South stormed less at Helper's original book than at Yankees' subsequent publication of his abridged text.

Yet Brown's and Helper's ascent from failure diverged in a crucial way. Republicans scorned a Yankee invader's try for a black insurrection against whites. Republicans, however, embraced a native Southerner's plea for white votes against slaveholders. Helper might propel the Republican Party beyond containing the Slave Power. He might bring Republican appeals inside the South.

Helper, sensing an opening, begged important New York Republicans to publish a cheap edition of the *Impending Crisis*. Other important Border South heretics endorsed the author's appeal. Cassius Clay, Frank Blair, Jr., and John Underwood urged Republican moneymen to finance an inexpensive Helper edition. All the various practitioners of southern heresy, except John G. Fee, here came together to seek an alliance of Northern Republicans and a new Southern Republican faction.[24] The collaboration would start with the dissemination of Helper's appeal for the southern white majority to outvote the slaveholders.

Within a year, southern heretics convinced the Republican establishment to finance 100,000 copies of an abridged *Impending Crisis*. The pamphlet, entitled *The Compendium of the Impending Crisis* and printed in New York in July 1859, was six times slimmer than the original and cost one-sixth as much. The sixteen-cent publication still retained most of Helper's most pungent sentences. The *Compendium*'s producers also augmented Helper's insults by adding provocative headlines. In italicized words, the *Compendium* declared its *"Revolutionary Appeal to Southern Non-Slaveholders."* The pamphlet urged *"The Non-Slaveholders to Strike for Treason."* It proclaimed that a *"Revolution must Free the Slaves."* It praised "Revolution—Peacefully if we can, Violently if we *must.*"

The *Compendium* printed the names of sixty-eight Northern Republican congressmen (62 percent of the party's members of the House of Representatives). All declared that they "cordially endorse the opinion, and approve the enterprise." Cassius Clay and Frank Blair, Jr., helped collect those signatures, while John C. Underwood served on the committee of circulation. The *Compendium* supplied 100,000 proofs that Northern Republicans hoped to enable native Southern Republicans to crack open the South's cordon sanitaire. The evidence portended the fourth and climactic act of the drama that John Brown had initiated, featuring a national crisis over Republicans' most auspicious route past containment.

CHAPTER 17

John Clark and Political Invasion

As southern congressmen journeyed toward Washington, D.C., in early December 1859, eager for the first congressional session after John Brown's raid, Brown swung from the gallows and Yankee church bells saluted the martyr. Incensed Southerners aspired to prove that Northern Republicans had dispatched Brown and might send more insurrectionists. At the beginning of the session, they established that previously mentioned investigatory committee, chaired by U.S. Senator James Mason from western Virginia.

– 1 –

Before Mason's committee reported, southern congressmen pressed their own investigations. With their needling rhetoric on the House floor, southern representatives sought to sting Republicans into admitting that their party had supported John Brown and would fortify future Browns. Republicans' credible denials, however, cooled the prosecutorial ardor. Northern Republicans confessed that they hated slavery. They conceded that they meant to place the institution on the road to ultimate extinction. But they meant to triumph legally and peacefully, without servile insurrections.

Once Republicans' direct support for Brown seemed nonexistent, southern congressmen fell back on Henry Wise's conception of indirect complicity. Yankees' spirit of wild individualism, Southerners charged, nourished Brown's convulsion, even if anarchical spirits disowned this particular anarchist. Republicans "may now disclaim all sympathy with that old traitor," exclaimed Arkansas's Congressman Thomas Hindman. "They may say again and again that they contributed nothing to his enterprise, either in men, money, arms or favorable wishes."

Yet Republicans' "maddening and furious abuse of slavery and slaveholders . . . set on fire the brain of that old fanatic. Had there been no Republican Party, there would have been no invasion of Harper's [sic] Ferry."

246

Because there would continue to be a Republican Party, southern watchmen must be on the alert for the foe's next, more auspicious invader.[1]

– 2 –

One congressman pressed an especially promising inquiry into Republicans' probable next invasion. On December 5, the House of Representatives convened and commenced to elect its Speaker (presiding officer). Immediately, Missouri's Congressman John Clark introduced a resolution, declaring that "the doctrines and sentiments of a certain book, called 'The Impending Crisis of the South—How to Meet It' . . . are insurrectionary and hostile to the domestic peace and tranquility of this country." Therefore, "no member of this House who has endorsed and recommended it, or the compend [*Compendium*] from it, is fit to be Speaker of the House." Clark noted that sixty-eight Republican congressmen had endorsed the *Compendium*, including the party's candidate for Speaker, Ohio's John Sherman (then more famous than his brother, future General William Tecumseh Sherman).[2]

Although the House never passed John Clark's resolution, all Southern Democrats instantly enlisted in the Missourian's surprise war against John Sherman. The resulting unanticipated confrontation paralyzed the House for fifty-eight days. During the forty-four ballots before a Speaker could be elected, Republicans had to switch their Speakership votes from Sherman to a party unknown (and nonendorser of the *Compendium*). Before the Republican retreat, John Brown faded from the limelight, the *Compendium* attracted the spotlight, pistols filled representatives' pockets, and South Carolina's governor conspired to send secessionist troops to Washington if bullets replaced ballots in the House. Thus did an obscure congressman's unexpected motion set off the climactic presecession congressional crisis over slavery.

The road to disunion abounded in surprise crises. These unexpected confrontations always raised two questions. First, why did the initiator spring the destructive surprise on the weakening Union? Second, why did surprised folk turn a momentary shock into a sustained controversy? The answers form patterns that illuminate why a civil war approached.

Initiators started to weave destructive patterns a quarter century before secession. In 1835, U.S. Congressman James Hammond of South Carolina sprang the unexpected issue of gagging congressional discussion of slavery on a Congress that expected to discuss slaveholders' censoring of the U.S. mails. In 1843, Secretary of State Abel P. Upshur of eastern Virginia imposed the unexpected issue of annexing Texas on a presidential campaign that had featured less dangerous discussions. So it went, with increasing frequency in the presecession decade: western Virginia's James Mason in 1850, shoving the draconic Fugitive Slave Law on congressmen who anticipated a more soothing version; the South Carolina lowcountry's Leonidas Spratt in 1853, blasting the closure of the African slave trade, when almost everyone considered the commerce thankfully sealed; western Missouri's Davy Atchison in 1854, insisting that the Kansas and Nebraska territories be opened to slavery, after almost everyone thought that the previous prohibition had been (begrudgingly) accepted (including by Atchison); Atchison again in 1855, leading one-day Kansans to elect a proslavery government for a territory that few thought could be enslaved; tidewater Maryland's Curtis Jacobs in 1857, shocking almost everyone by urging that freed blacks be reenslaved; and now Missouri's John Clark, deflecting surprised southern congressmen from the Republicans and Brown to the Republicans and the *Compendium*.[3]

Two locales spawned these precipitators. Both regions trained the eye to see dangers that other Southerners initially thought came out of nowhere. The oldest, eastern South nurtured one group: Hammond, Upshur, Spratt, and Jacobs (plus, climactically, the leading South Carolina disunionists). All these reactionaries feared that egalitarian mobocracy would shatter aristocratic slavery. All conceived that the newer South's white men's egalitarianism led to myopic vision. All believed that only their ancient elitist viewpoint led to proper perception of such perils as antislavery congressional petitions, British influence in unannexed Texas, a closed overseas slave trade, and multiplying Maryland free blacks (plus, climactically, the immediate menace in Lincoln's election).

The western borderlands nourished the second group of precipitators: Mason, Atchison, and now John Clark. All these noneasterner borderites worried that the relatively unconsolidated northwestern South lay too close to Yankee contaminators. All conceived that slaveholders in the deeper South lived too far away to see the full peril in border slaves' flight, in a free soil Kansas, in John Underwood, in Frank Blair, Jr., and in Hinton R. Helper. The western borderites, like the eastern reactionaries, meant to correct deficiencies in perception.

John Clark lived in the best spot to see the *Compendium*'s menace. This Missouri precipitator much resembled the last one, Davy Atchison. Both Missouri Democrats faced perpetual showdowns with the Thomas Hart Benton/Frank Blair, Jr., sometimes-antislavery wing of their state party. Both proslavery zealots led a rare Missouri cluster of enslaved counties along the Missouri River. Atchison ruled Missouri's western border, across the river from Kansas. Clark flourished in the Missouri River black belt counties in the center part of the state. Counties with few slaves surrounded both Missouri River magnates' slender black belt domains. Both felt the power of white immigrants' rush toward almost lily-white counties to Clark's east (the Benton/Blair, St. Louis terrain) and to Atchison's west (the Kansas terrain).

Both deplored the drooping percentage of Missouri's blacks in the 1850s. Both realized that nonslaveholding newcomers, sharing much of John Underwood's entrepreneurial mentality, helped Frank Blair, Jr., to win two out of three congressional elections in St. Louis District between 1856 and 1861. In their attempts to stymie the only southern antislavery congressman and the most committed, powerful southern antislavery faction, the two western Missourians embodied the most committed, powerful, border proslavery faction.

As befit warriors from the Border South's embattled western frontier, Clark and Atchison ranked among the most blustering, backslapping congressional chauvinists. But similarity bred contempt. Clark fought one of his several duels with Atchison. Thereafter, Atchison reveled in the Senate's spotlight, while Clark fumed in the House of Representatives' shadows. Congressman Clark's square, red face epitomized his mood: lividly jealous of a political colossus whom he considered his inferior.[4]

In some ways, the unknown congressman did outstrip the famous senator. Clark drank more liquor, swore more profanely, slapped more backs, and womanized more undeniably (if in fact Atchison womanized at all; as for Clark, he attempted to seduce the mistress that General Albert Pike had seduced). Clark also owned many more slaves than did Atchison (if in fact Atchison owned any at all; as for Clark, he commanded twenty-seven blacks near Fayette in 1860, putting him in the top 1 percent of Missouri slaveholders.) Clark led the most enslaved Missouri terrain, Howard County in center state, with slaves numbering 37 percent of its population. Atchison led Platte County on Missouri's western edge, only 18 percent enslaved.

Despite Clark's larger stake in slavery, Atchison possessed a larger source of influence among cronies: endearing charm (if Clark could be called charming at all; no one else suffered expulsion from both the U.S. and the Confederate congresses during the Civil War). Since Atchison emerged as the more engaging frontiersman, he sat in the right place, the U.S. Senate, at the right time, the Kansas-Nebraska moment, to become *the* shover of Stephen A. Douglas. Then Atchison resided in the right place, on Missouri's Kansas edge, to become *the* border ruffian.

In the late 1850s, Clark relished his chance to come out from under Atchison's shadow. This time, Atchison could not be found in Congress. Bourbon Dave had become too controversially proslavery to win statewide senatorial election in a Missouri torn between proslavery and antislavery factions, while Clark only had to win election in his own congressional district. This time, the congressman occupied the right observation tower, half a state closer to Frank Blair's spreading base of antislavery support. In the 1850s, while Clark's Howard County grew 25 percent blacker with slaves (and Clark's own slave labor force doubled), whites doubled in population east of Clark's surrounded speck of proslavery counties. Meanwhile, the Missouri antislavery movement crept westward from Blair's St. Louis stronghold to within fifty miles of Clark's plantation, sweeping Jefferson City's municipal elections.

John Clark knew that John Underwood's dream, transporting Northerners to vacant borderlands, had already become a slaveholder's nightmare in eastern Missouri. The embittered congressman noticed that Hinton R. Helper's book sounded like Congressman Frank Blair, Jr.'s speeches. Clark observed that Helper's *Compendium* listed Blair as a collector of northern congressmen's endorsements. Since Blair successfully marshaled Republican support for Helper, he could collect Republican patronage for his Missouri faction. With that added political muscle, St. Louis's congressman might become too powerful for the Atchisons and Clarks to contain.

The underappreciated (so he thought) John Clark now nursed a heightened sense of grievance. All those unjustly more famous southern congressmen, having long mistakenly regarded Davy Atchison as the most important Missouri proslavery Democrat, now erroneously regarded John Brown as the most important emblem of Republican plans to invade the South. The blunderers had obviously not read the *Compendium*. John Clark would train their eyes to see that Northern Republicans meant to empower Southern Republicans. He would thereby save his world and, in the saving, ascend to his proper station, above Atchison and below no proslavery defender. With his motion on the Speakership, John Clark showed again, as Davy Atchison had twice before, why slavery's special vulnerability in its northwestern hinterlands, and especially in Missouri, made bitterly divisive local factional warfare and even more bitterly divisive borderland slavery issues ever more inescapable in national politics.

Location, location, location. In modern times, a mediocre house in a great location sells for millions. A great house in a mediocre location fetches less. So too, in the mid-nineteenth century, an obscure issue or book possessed little consequence, unless infuriating an inflammable spot. Neither the *Compendium* nor a free soil Kansas initially made sense as an angry sore on the national body politic, except high up in Dixie. In that unusual locale, proslavery diehards sounded the first alarms about Kansas free soilers just outside, Southern Republicans creeping inside, and hinterland slavery in danger of ebbing.

– 3 –

Southerners' response to initiators of surprise crises, like the initiators themselves, fell into repetitive, revealing patterns. Over and over again, whatever the unexpected issue, initiators' partial emphasis on northern insult ensured that southern compatriots would enlist, at least for a short term, in a war for slaveholders' honor and pride. By adding hate-streaked headlines to Helper's hate-filled text, the Republicans' *Compendium* raised defamation to nasty heights. Southerners, being Southerners, spitefully screeched back.

John Clark initiated the screeching as well as the controversy. Along with my slaveholding constituents, the wounded Christian protested, I am "equal in intelligence, equal in patriotism, and equal in morals to that of any other gentlemen in this House." Yet "gentlemen have advised" my nonslaveholding constituents "to have no intercourse with me," even to shun any "church where I worship." If I "failed to utter . . . my condemnation" of these slurs, I would be "recreant to my own self respect."[5]

As usual, self-respecting Southerners applauded a compatriot's crusade for equality, honor, and self-esteem. We refuse to be stigmatized, Virginia's Roger Pryor warned, "as outlaws against the moral government of the world." Virginia's Sheldon F. Leake promised that "we will revenge" the "deliberate and intentional insult" involved in "the election to the Speakership of a man who signed that book." Arkansas's Albert Rust added that Republicans' "insulting and dishonoring . . . hatred" in their "infamous" *Compendium* demonstrated not our unpardonable sin but their "groveling, sordid, and very acquisitive natures."[6] Such steaming at insult showed that divided southern whites could temporarily fuse in rage at Yankee struts of superiority—a righteous We against the insufferable They.

Pre–Civil War storms persisted longest when practical danger to slavery accompanied theoretical attack on slaveholders' honor. The *Compendium*'s headlines obviously deprecated slaveholders' Christian credentials. But how would John Sherman's Speakership endanger slavery's survival?

A political scientist might answer that the Speaker held almost monopolistic power over committee assignments and House procedures. A Speaker thus could enhance or cripple Republicans' congressional agenda. The Speaker would also preside over the 1860 decision on the presidency, if no candidate received an Electoral College majority. Then the House would decide an Abraham Lincoln's fate.

Yet that objective peril, so palpable in retrospect, elicited no alarm in the House during the Speakership Crisis. Southerners scarcely mentioned a Republican Speaker's potential procedural power. They instead emphasized that they would (as they ultimately did) accept a Republican Speaker, so long as the presiding officer did not endorse Hinton R. Helper. It was as if the slaveholders shouted at posterity: Read our speeches on the *Compendium*, instead of using your political science models, to discern our intentions. Then you will understand why we considered Republicans' endorsement of Helper dangerous as well as insulting.

John Clark saw the *Compendium* as the smoking gun, demonstrating weapons infinitely more promising than John Brown's pikes. Two days later, Virginia's Representative M.R.H. Garnett demanded to know if Republicans repudiated Helper's dangerous mode of attack. You say that you "do not mean to interfere with slavery in the States," noted Congressman Garnett. But you mean to bar us everywhere outside our states, hemming "us in, as with a wall of fire." You mean "to render the institution valueless upon the borders, by running off the slaves" and supporting a "war between the citizens of the South." We do not mean to stay in the Union, warned Garnett, "until you have converted the border States into free States, and so demoralized and enervated our strength."[7]

Southerners turned the House proceedings into an inquiry. They sought to discover whether Republicans and especially John Sherman would disown or support Helper's assaults inside the Border South. In response, John Sherman disowned neither the *Impending Crisis* nor the *Compendium*. He denied that he had ever "read" either publication. He could not "recollect" signing any endorsement. He presumed that a friend had secured his signature, after promising that the text would be cleansed of Helper's offensive sentences. Even if the published *Compendium* belied his friend's promise, his blind signature counted for less than his highly visible avowal that he opposed "any interference whatever by the people of the free States with the relations of master and slave in the Slave states."[8]

Southerners derided Sherman's avowal. Did the Republicans' candidate for Speaker *now* oppose Republican financing of southern politicians who spoke against slavery? Would he now aid the Helper-Underwood-Blair-Clay strategy of developing a Southern Republican Party, with Northern Republicans' support?

Sherman answered that "I am now willing to have that Helper book read, page by page, and then avow or disavow every sentiment contained in it." But first, John Clark must withdraw his "offensive resolution." Any gentleman with an honorable "sense of manhood," Sherman explained, must have his "lips . . . in a great measure sealed" rather than lower himself to answer the charge of being a dishonorable monster.

Southerners, considering themselves the experts on honor, called Sherman's posture of "insulted honor . . . no escape for a manly man." When Republicans answered that Sherman had "distinctly stated five times on this floor, that he would not interfere with the relations of master and slaves," Southerners reiterated that "there are different ways of operating on slavery." Granted, John Sherman "would not march into the slave States; he would not legislate in regard to that subject." But "does he disclaim the doctrines of the Helper book?" Would he deploy cash and patronage to support Helper and his allies? On that subject, "the gentleman is dumb, . . . dumb as an oyster."[9]

With Sherman's lips sealed, Southerners sought to pry open the attitudes of other Republicans who had signed the *Compendium*. James L. Pugh of Alabama demanded to know whether Republicans intend "to convince the non-slaveholder at the South that his condition as a white laborer would be vastly improved by the absence of slavery? . . . And when you attempt to reeducate him," don't you "hope . . . for an anti-slavery organization in the southern states, which will ultimately strike down slavery?"[10]

Pugh received several answers, all but one of them clipped, all of them hinting at support of the South's own debate over slavery's moral worth. Elijah Babbitt of Pennsylvania, who had not signed the *Compendium*, indicated that he would sign if asked. "I do not know a Republican," declared Babbitt, "who claims the right to interfere with slavery in the States where it now exists. I do not know a Republican who does not repudiate all forcible interference. Not one of them . . . would interfere with it, except by moral suasion."[11]

Except moral suasion! That *except* dominated the remarks of Illinois's Congressman John Farnsworth, the only Republican endorser of the *Compendium* who fully explained his endorsement before the House elected a Speaker. When John Reagan of Texas challenged Farnsworth to "answer, like a man," whether he "endorses or repudiates . . . the doctrines of the Helper book," the Illinois Republican answered that he rejected "any passages" that can "be fairly construed into the advocacy of servile insurrections, or a raid upon the Slave states," or "the use of violence by nonslaveholders against the slaveholders."

But I do "advocate an enlightenment of the nonslaveholders," Farnsworth said. I would "inculcate such doctrines as would lead to a peaceful emancipation." I do "thank God that we have nothing in our part of the country that will not stand free criticism and free discussion and a free press." While "I do not believe that Congress has the constitutional authority to legislate against it," I will support Southerners who advocate "unfriendly legislation" in their own states. In that sense, I endorse the book.[12]

That endorsement vindicated John Clark's accusation. Republicans repudiated Brown's violent methods of arousing the slaves (and they would deliver no pikes to insurrectionists). But they endorsed Helper's nonviolent methods of educating the nonslaveholders (and they would shower patronage on the educators). A climactic exchange between Sherrard Clemens of Tennessee and Thad Stevens of Pennsylvania illuminated the discovery.

Stevens laid out the conventional Republican argument. While "Republicanism is founded in love of universal liberty, and in hostility to slavery," declared the Pennsylvania representative, "the Constitution of the United States gives us no power to interfere . . . with sister states." But where the Constitution throws "the responsibility of government" to Congress, in "the Territories, the District of Columbia, the navy-yards and the arsenals, . . . we do claim the power . . . to abolish slavery." In areas beyond the South, when slavery "can be safely and justly abolished," Republicans will "do so."

Tennessee's Clemens responded with *the* southern question. Did Northern Republicans really think that containing slavery, plus supporting Southern Republicans inside the contained area, would have no impact on slave states? If the gentleman's "policy is carried out," asked Clements, and "if not a single new slave State is admitted" to the Union, and "if slavery is abolished in the District of Columbia, in the Territories, in the arsenals, dockyards, and forts, and if in addition to that, his party grasps the power of the Presidency, with the patronage attached to it," to foster a Southern Republican Party, "wouldn't he have slavery surrounded like a camp in a prairie or a scorpion with fire," and wouldn't it then "sting itself to death?"

Stevens slyly answered that "I do not know, not being" a prophet. The House laughed. When laughter ceased, Stevens thrust in the knife: "The gentleman knows better than I do" whether slavery would endure uninhibited southern debate.[13]

– 4 –

Expanded Border South debates on slavery, southern congressmen emphasized, would enhance the possibility that Frank Blair, Jr.'s swelling wave of
Missouri nonslaveholders would someday outvote John Clark's contracting
crew of slaveholders. Restive slaves also would have enhanced possibilities.
Southern Republicans' agitation might inspire more blacks to flee. More
black Celias might also murder more masters at midnight, even if assassins
again failed to burn the corpse to a crisp. I will not abide a House Speaker,
declared Virginia's Sheldon Leake, who endorses doctrines that will stimulate "my Negroes at home to apply the torch to my dwelling and the knife to
the throats of my wife and helpless children."[14]

Posterity might consider Leake paranoid about Southern Republicans'
(including Helper's) influence on slaves. The *Impending Crisis* hardly advised domestics to brandish knives or torches. Hinton R. Helper solely addressed fellow whites. In the solitary passage that mentioned blacks' attitudes, Helper warned that whites ought to abolish slavery peacefully, lest
blacks less peaceably strike. Had John Sherman's opponents, like Sherman
himself, failed to read the book?

Yes, as Shelton Leake admitted. While the congressional confrontation
might seem to be a curious tiff over a book that few had read, congressmen
actually battled over the sequel to the book. While few southern congressmen had opened the *Impending Crisis,* most witnessed the more incendiary
outbursts in the *Compendium,* for John Clark read the pamphlet's most offensive passages into the congressional record. Clark's quotations featured
not only Helper's words but also the added headlines that Republicans, un-
beknownst to the *Compendium*'s readers, had inserted into Helper's original
text. In the *Congressional Globe* even more than in the *Compendium,* big
black headlines screamed that "REVOLUTION MUST FREE THE SLAVES"
and that we seek "REVOLUTION—PEACEFULLY if we can, VIOLENTLY
if we must."[15]

Some horrifying news, devastating one of their own, helps explain why
southern congressmen trembled at those incendiary words. Politicians, like
all folk, quaver the more at abstract peril when concrete illustrations ravage
their intimate circle. Thus in 1850, during discussions of James Mason's
fugitive slave bill, the Virginian's theories about borderland runaways received a provoking confirmation. Alexander Stephens's and Robert Toombs's
supposedly adoring house servants absconded from the congressmen's Washington, D.C., dwellings.[16] So too, during the Speakership Crisis, agony afflicted a star member of the capital's little community of southern congressmen. A bulletin reduced South Carolina Congressman Laurence Keitt, of all
people, to inert silence. A slave, Keitt heard, had slaughtered his brother in
Florida.[17]

Never before had Laurence Keitt looked shriveled. Keitt had first swelled
into American consciousness when serving as Preston Brooks's bodyguard,

demanding that Charles Sumner's would-be rescuers stand back, lest he savage them. He would depart this life when commanding Kershaw's Brigade of South Carolina Civil War soldiers. He would demand that gentlemen suicidally charge against the suicidally charging Ulysses S. Grant, during Virginia's awful battle of Cold Harbor. Keitt would crash from his beloved iron-gray charger, a musket ball having exploded against his liver.[18]

The assaulter who charged once too often usually exuded a seemingly indestructible virility. In an age when most men observed the clean-shaven niceties, the towering Keitt was among the first to grow a beard (a profusion that he flaunted by pulling at the roughage). In an age when Native American so-called savages displayed most of the pigtails, Keitt swept his hair back, then twisted the braids into a lionesque mane. His warrior's frock coat, with its rich blue lining and its fancy arrow shooting up the sleeve, remains, a century and a half later, a fashion diamond in Richmond's lush Museum of the Confederacy.

This fighting dandy would usually only come to rest on a chair edge, where he reminded observers of a leopard about to spring. When on his feet and verbally assaulting the Yankees, he seemed more akin to a posturing actor. His brow, with its deep scar from an old dueling wound, furled in frown. His feet, one flung before the other, plus his hands, convulsively rubbing together when they were not tugging the beard, plus his arms, shaking as if in spasms, made him seem connected to an electrical apparatus. An enemy, weary of the flamboyant exaggeration, declared that "he has probably long since convinced himself that he was a terrible fellow."

The posture of terrible foe personified Keitt's ambition for South Carolina. The state's warriors had continually only threatened to escape the Union. Keitt, in his midthirties, epitomized youths who meant to carry out their elders' threats. His every movement declared that South Carolina's new knights would be endlessly aggressive, demanding out of a poisonous nation that no manly man could abide.

This was the man, infamous for energy "of the southern polytechnic kind," who slumped as if mortally stricken after reading the awful telegram in early 1860. His ailing brother William, a wealthy Florida state senator, had been murdered in his sickbed at midnight. A slave had slit the convalescent's throat.

Several days later came the better tidings (or more accurately, Laurence Keitt revealed a skittish side of the southern ruling class, by considering the news *better*). I have been "relieved" to hear, Keitt privately wrote, that a recently purchased slave rather than a longtime servant had drawn the blade across the jugular.[19]

Relieved! That whispered word reverberated with deeper meaning than all Keitt's previous and subsequent shouts. "Relieved" connoted that southern masters almost never feared that armies of field hands would rise with guns in hand (much less with John Brown's pikes on their shoulders). "Relieved" declared that the dissimulating Cuffee to be feared was the solitary house servant, living right there in the Big House, with total access to slumbering whites.

Southern patriarchs often conceded that even if almost all their slaves were family friends, a stray black could have a mysterious look. They admitted that even if blacks naturally loved nurturing patriarchs, any impressionable primitive might be corrupted. They knew that one stray servant could savage a household. They believed that one stray sentence could turn one gullible inferior's head. But what could a wary paternalist do about the unspeakable peril, turn a genial home into a despotic dungeon?!

That unacceptable solution yielded a suppression of fear, the more fearful because suppressed. Yet the undercover anxiety burst out in rare, jewel-like expressions. One such gem emerged in 1822, at the time of Denmark Vesey's Conspiracy. The accused slave conspirators' Charleston judges published every supposed finding about dozens of blacks allegedly plotting to seize the public streets. The judges censored only the news that a solitary house servant meant to sneak poison into "his" white family's water![20] No wonder, then, that Laurence Keitt and fellow Southerners, when debating the supposedly insurrectionary *Compendium*, were "relieved" that no ancient family retainer had been the one to slit open William Keitt's jugular.

The dead man's blood still underlined a critical reason why relieved slaveholders wanted no Southern Republican Party. The South's schizophrenic world of democracy and slavery could only genially thrive when white voters could discuss everything except slavery, and black Cuffees could hear nothing except slaveholders' commands. Slaveholders possessed awesome weapons to silence democratic discussion: lynch mobs to expel open heretics, charges of disloyalty to silence secret dissenters.

But an open democracy mitigates against dictatorial closures. Frank Blair, Jr., and Cassius Clay had periodically pried open a little discussion where debate could be most damaging, in the northern hinterlands. The House of Representatives' Speakership Crisis brought potential consequences of increased Southern Republican agitation up close and personal. Even so unrelenting a brawler as Laurence Keitt had sunk to his knees, praying that a family friend had not ambushed inside the home.

The Republicans who signed the *Compendium* pleaded innocent of intending to arouse servants to savage masters. Signees distinguished between Brown the violent raider and Helper the nonviolent persuader. Southerners decried that distinction, for a persuader could produce violence. No more Browns might come South. No slaves might rise in group insurrection. But Republicans intended to encourage internal southern debate, and one impressionable domestic might be listening. Never had the difference over white men's republicanism seemed so naked, so chilling, as when Republicans conceded that they *would* support Southerners' republican discussion inside the South. Never had civil war seemed so close as when congressmen debated whether an advocate of unlimited republican speech, South as well as North, should be (appropriate word!) Speaker.

– 5 –

With their apprehensions about prospective Southern Republicans doubling their fury at insulting Northern Republicans, Southern Democrats took to arriving in the House of Representatives with more than threatening words. Sharpened sabers bulged under their waistcoats. Cocked pistols filled their pockets.[21] Rumors surfaced that that the gunslingers secretly plotted to drive an elected Republican Speaker from the House. The 1859–60 drama had started with an antislavery raider seeking to turn a federal arsenal into a liberating fortress. Would the show now end with slavery's defenders turning liberty's chamber into a shooting gallery?

A fleeting, aborted, almost unbelievable secret plot highlighted that question. The extremists' intrigue involved (who else?) the South Carolinians. In December 1859, William Porcher Miles wished to ensure that if he and South Carolina's other representatives started a disunion revolution in Washington over the Speakership Crisis, folks back home would send the troops. If Sherman is elected Speaker and we forcibly expel the Black Republican from House chambers, Charleston's representative secretly asked South Carolina's Governor William Gist, would you sustain our rebellion?

Miles's impolitic plot came naturally to an antipolitician who had won Charlestonians' hearts an antioperator's way. Where other American congressmen earned their spurs by maneuvering inside national political parties, Miles secured Charleston's adoration by racing to nurse the sick. Upon hearing that smallpox had decimated Norfolk, Virginia, the nonslaveholding mathematics professor at the College of Charleston plunged into the miasmatic city, where he volunteered in a deadly hospital.

Miles survived to secure a Virginia gold medal. Back home, upper-class admirers elevated the medal winner to Charleston's congressional seat, without hearing the new titan's position on anything. For gentlemen who loathed mobocracy, detested the two national parties, and worshiped the disinterested aristoi, a saint without political calculation seemed just the hero for Congress.

Charleston's apolitical hero would represent the city in the U.S. and Confederate congresses. In 1863, this nonslaveholding champion of the slavocracy would win the heart of a Virginia/Alabama heiress. After the war, the once impoverished academic would become president of South Carolina College, then manager of his wife's family's thirteen Louisiana plantations. Thus the impolitic conspirator of 1859, having climbed the most apolitical American ladder, would become one of the Old South's richest surviving politicians.[22]

Miles survived his own 1859 impolitic impulse because, unlike Laurence Keitt at Cold Harbor, he had the postnullification South Carolina instinct to seek assurances before the wild charge. After Miles secretly wrote Governor Gist, asking for assurances that sufficient aid would arrive if the state's delegation forcibly ousted an elected Speaker, South Carolina's governor replied that, if South Carolina congressmen "decide to make the issue" by "ejecting the Speaker-elect by force, . . . write or telegraph me, & I will have a regiment in or near Washington in the shortest possible time." But Gist counseled Miles to take care before risking a "bloody revolution" in Washington. "An act of violence," warned the governor, "might prejudice us in the eyes of the world." In the event that "Sherman is elected Speaker, in consequence of his having endorsed Helper," Gist suggested two more measured secession strategies. The South Carolina delegation should secede from Washington. Or the representatives should urge their constituents to secede from the Union. The governor had "little doubt" that Miles's constituents would sustain either plan, even if "withdrawing alone" would be South Carolina's scary fate.

Gist added a final note of caution. If the House should reject Sherman and then elect a Black Republican who had not committed the "overt act" of endorsing Helper, the governor feared that "our state would hesitate, & you might not be sustained."[23] After Gist's warning, Charleston's apolitical congressman paused. He had better wait to discover whether the new Speaker would be Sherman or a less provocative alternative.

With South Carolinians once again secretly conspiring about (and hesitating about) Separate State Secession, more cautious gentlemen brought the state's long-standing alternative to the fore. In 1859–61 as in 1850–52, the South Carolina question involved not whether but how the state should secede. Separate State Secessionists wished South Carolina to act first and alone. Cooperative State Secessionists urged instead that the state should leave the Union only in cooperation with several states.

Cooperationists feared that Separatists would repeat the nullification trauma of 1832–33, leaving the state alone against all other states. They had sold that qualm to the states' voters in 1852. Now, with a dangerous separate state action again under consideration, cautious Cooperationists devised a plan to prove that this time, they could rally several states to share South Carolina's gamble.

On December 22, 1859, the Cooperationists' Christopher G. Memminger urged the plan on South Carolina secessionists of all persuasions. We all agree, Memminger reminded fellow state legislators, that "this Union" provided "no safety for South Carolina." We also all agree that if our state secedes and no other state follows, South Carolinians would face unacceptable peril. Instead of intolerable Union or unwinnable revolution, South Carolina legislators should unite in favor of a safe rebellion. We should appropriate $100,000 to arm the state. We should call a southern convention, "to concert measures for united action." And we should dispatch a commissioner from sovereign South Carolina to sovereign Virginia, to urge John Brown's victims to join with us in summoning all southern sovereigns to a southern convention.[24]

Separate State Secessionists lost nothing by backing Memminger's cooperative plan. They found their own remedy scary in late 1859. So why not let Cooperationists try (and fail!) to secure theirs? If Separatists dropped back for a moment with Memminger, he might be compelled to step forward with them, after he inadvertently proved that Cooperative State Secession meant a failed southern convention or, worse, a failure to assemble the South in convention.

To avoid a failure that might destroy Cooperationism, Memminger counted on the state's commissioner to persuade Virginians to summon a southern convention. To maximize the persuasiveness of an ambassador from activist South Carolina to laggard Virginia, Governor Gist appointed the ideal commissioner, Memminger himself. If Gist had selected a young hotspur such as Laurence Keitt or William Porcher Miles, he would have widened the gulf between South Carolina and Virginia gentlemen. But no other South Carolina leader more embodied the dependability of a mature old aristocracy than Christopher G. Memminger.[25]

Irony abounded in Memminger's flawless rendition of that hoary part. True, the commissioner to Virginia possessed the necessary age, being twenty years older than Keitt or Miles. Memminger equally projected the right oligarchic appearance, with his ramrod-straight posture, his quiet, clipped manner, and his long, forbidding head. Memminger also assumed the right anti-egalitarian frostiness. He forbade colleagues from dropping by without an invitation. He disdained co-workers who paused from labor to chat. His severity won him few pals but many admirers and ultimately more political power, in snobby South Carolina, than most glad-handers possessed.

Yet no South Carolina patriarch had been farther from the manor born than this future Confederate secretary of the treasury. The *G* in Memminger's middle name stood for Gustavus, perfect for an impoverished lad born in the Duchy of Württemberg. Arriving in America at age three, the destitute ward landed in the Charleston Orphanage a year later. Only one other member of Jefferson Davis's future Confederate cabinet would be foreign born, and none other would be orphanage reared.

Still, the orphan's ascent revealed more about upper-class paternalism than did the well-born Keitt or Miles. Memminger's rise to paternalistic power resembled the trajectory of South Carolina's greatest theorist of proper paternalism, the Reverend James Henley Thornwell. Both Memminger and Thornwell were born in the first decade of the nineteenth century. Both suffered severe impoverishment as youths. Both afflicted adolescents intrigued a benevolent patron.

Both benefited from South Carolina's racially unlimited paternalism. Most Southerners elsewhere thought that paternalism must stop at the door of white adult males, egalitarians all and in no need of a better's uplifting care. The South Carolina upper crust, scorning white men's egalitarianism, thought that the best men in legislature assembled must hand law and ethics to all those lesser. Benevolent stewards must also elevate penniless white youths who gave promise of becoming jewels of the patriarchal class.

Memminger and Thornwell became the most successful white beneficiaries of uplifting paternalism. For both, gratitude to paternalistic saviors swelled into obsession with perfecting paternalism itself. Thornwell's evangelical proslavery theology emphasized that slavery would be biblically sanctioned, *if* patriarchs lived up to their Christian obligations. Memminger's patron, Governor Thomas Bennett, had famously lived up to obligations in the Denmark Vesey Controversy, where he had destroyed his political career by seeking patriarchal justice for perhaps falsely accused slave conspirators.

Bennett, also a leading member of the South Carolina Unionist Party in nullification times, served as a trustee of Memminger's orphanage. When Christopher was a preteen, the patriarch took the precocious youngster into his home, then formally adopted him, then saw him through legal training. From the benefactor, the ward received not only food and shelter but also an education in paternalists' highest obligations.

Because of his Bennett connections and his own talents, Memminger became a star of the Charleston bar. The risen titan accumulated $200,000 worth of property by 1860, including fifteen slaves. But for Thomas Bennett's ex-ward, materialistic success did not alone justify a patriarch's faith. In Bennett's tradition (and Thornwell's too), the ex-orphan outdid the mentor in assaults on imperfect paternalism. As a member of the Episcopal establishment, Memminger sought church curbs on masters whose slave sales split black families. As a state legislator, he sought legal curbs on bankers who spewed out paper money rather than lending gold or silver coin. As a practicing lawyer, he sought court curbs on whites who would oust free blacks from the city. Above all, as a custodian of Bennett's cautious response to South Carolina hotheads, he sought to curb fire-eaters who would throw away South Carolina's ancient traditions in an ill-considered, ill-prepared revolution against the Union, with not one other state pledged to cooperate.

Like most Charleston Cooperationists, Memminger agreed with the hotspurs that divorce from mobocratic Union should be obtained. But in both 1832 and 1852, he urged that a suicidal Separate State Secession would drown the state in democratic excesses. In 1859, as commissioner to Virginia, he meant to prove that Cooperative State Secession would pave gentlemen's cautious path to paternalistic stability in a safe new southern Confederacy.

As he prepared his address to the Virginians, Memminger received colliding suggestions about how to move reluctant Virginians toward responsible disunionism. William Porcher Miles, deploying a young fire-eater's coarse image, instructed his elder to impregnate blushing Virginia with South Carolina's ravishing seed. Memminger should force "a Southern Confederacy . . . to spring from the loins of the Palmetto State!"[26]

From Miles's almost rapist view of how Memminger should jam South Carolina disunionism on Virginia temporizers, the spectrum of state opinion swung toward less heavy-handed domineering. Francis Pickens, imminent governor of the state, hoped that Memminger could coax George Washington's state to call another venerable national constitutional convention. Like the Philadelphia gathering of 1787, the new convention should remake a failed Union. Suppose that "after a full and truthful hearing," Yankees rejected "new securities and guarantees." Subsequently, "Southern States would stand *right before the world and posterity*" if they sought an alternate government.[27]

Where future governor Pickens hoped that a national convention might reconstruct the Union, present governor William Gist prayed that a southern convention might refortify slavery. The governor urged Memminger to inspire Virginia to "save the Union by taking the lead in resistance to this warfare upon our institutions." Then "the South will follow her & an united South can dictate the terms . . . & the North will yield. If however I am mistaken in this, Virginia can unite the South out of the Union."[28]

Congressman William W. Boyce moved still further from Miles's image of South Carolina forcing herself on Virginia. Do not offend "the sensibility of Virginia," Boyce advised Memminger, "by seeming to take the lead. Some people have to be led, by letting them suppose that they are leading." Tell your hosts that we will "receive your directions." If you direct us to "struggle in the Union, we *acquiesce*." If you direct us to seek constitutional guarantees, fine. If, after guarantees fail, you direct us to secure disunion, excellent. "That indeed is our present idea but we are willing to defer to your superior wisdom."[29]

Memminger found Boyce's strategy convincing, despite sharing Miles's conviction that no southern or national convention could save the Union. He would offer cooperation with any Virginia remedy. Then, after South Carolina fell back with the compatriot, and after a southern convention's unionism failed, Virginia laggards would have to catch up with South Carolina sprinters.

Memminger knew that his trap for the Virginians resembled Separate State Secessionists' trap for him. South Carolina fire-eaters fell back with the frosty commissioner because they believed that the Cooperationists' southern convention would fail and then the laggard would have to embrace Separatists' disunion tactics. Memminger gambled the fate of South Carolina Cooperationism on his persuasive powers when he traveled to Virginia at the start of a frightening new year.

– 6 –

Memminger's overnight train from Charleston chugged into Richmond's Union Station on January 12, 1860. In a fine symbolic gesture, South Carolina's commissioner brought his charming daughter along, as if to emphasize, in this male chauvinist age, that his would be the soft tone of the pleader. In another fine gesture, a special committee of the Virginia Assembly met the train and swept the Memmingers toward the city's elegant Ballard House. The procession emphasized that a sovereign state's commissioner must be treated like a prince.

The next day, the minister extraordinaire dispatched his credentials to new Virginia Governor John Letcher. Memminger received in return an invitation to address an historic joint session of the Virginia legislature six days hence, on January 19. In the interim, the debate over John Sherman raged so hot in Washington that Miles dared not come down to confer, lest he miss a physical brawl in Congress.

In Richmond, banquets drove out thoughts of Washington brawling. The visiting potentate enjoyed several state dinners. When it came time for the speaking to replace the feasting, two companies of finely dressed militia escorted Memminger and his daughter from the Ballard House to the state capitol. Flags decorated the streets. Citizens cheered the parade. As the commissioner strode into the legislative hall, applause cascaded from the two galleries, packed with ladies, and from the delegates themselves, almost crowded from their seats by still more ladies. For the next three and a half hours, in this age when historic oratory kept crowds enchanted, Virginia's finest drank in a republican spectacle fit for opera houses.[30]

The commissioner had come, he told his co-sovereigns, to make common cause with Virginia. Even as he spoke, Memminger pointed out, Northerners' antipathy for the South had spilled past the pro-Brown church bells. Now, Republicans demanded a Speaker who endorsed Hinton R. Helper. The travesty climaxed northern outrages that had offended innocent Southerners since Missouri Compromise times. The forty years of outrage (and Memminger exhaustively recalled each insult) had left the South "without any protection from the Constitution," at the mercy "of a sectional party who regard our institutions as sinful" and who consider abolition "only a question of time."

The emergency, urged Memminger, required the South to counsel together. Sovereign South Carolina had called a southern convention. Sovereign Virginia must come and request all other southern sovereigns to join us. The gathering of sovereigns will empower us to save the Union, if we can, and to prepare for disunion, if we must.

My state, admitted Memminger, believes that a southern convention's efforts to save the Union will fail. But "if our [disunion] pace is too fast for some, we are content to walk slower," so "that all may keep together." We will consent to any Southwide decision to move forward. We cannot, however, consent "to stand still."[31]

Virginians' cheers for his effort did not fool Memminger. After days of conversations in Richmond, he knew that his hosts would indeed stand still, even though he thought late events should have pushed them far ahead of South Carolinians.[32] John Brown and John Underwood had invaded the Old Dominion, not South Carolina. Slave runaways had led slaveholders to shrink from Virginia's northern border. The Lower South suffered from no such nearby portal to freedom.

Memminger's Virginia listeners of all persuasions worried about Virginia's vulnerability. Henry Wise declared that "if you allow such helpers of Helper to play incendiaries with torches as flaming as those that were found at Harpers Ferry," antislavery will leave our borderland in ashes. Representative John T. Anderson warned that the Republican Party will deploy "all kinds of machinations to incite our slaves to insurrection, and . . . to unite the non-slaveholders with them in cutting our throats and our children's and in ravishing our wives and daughters."[33] James Barbour concurred that Virginians must no longer submit to "indirect assault" on our border. Already, Yankee aid to fugitives has "struck a fatal blow to us" in western Virginia. There, 200,000 whites owned only 8000 slaves because laws do not stop Yankee forays into our northernmost terrain. We must demand a remedy "or bow down and submit."[34]

But where most South Carolinians called disunion the remedy, most Virginians relished Henry Wise's motto: "Fighting in the Union." Virginians' favorite remedy in the Union, cutting off trade with the North, would strike, in John Anderson's words, at Yankees' "pocket nerve." If all "southern states agree to shut their ports" against northern commerce, explained James Seddon, Yankee materialists will stifle Republican appeals. Economic nonintercourse thus offered "the only way to save the Union."[35]

But where John Anderson and James Seddon wished a southern convention to shutter the ports, James Barbour wished Virginia alone to shut off Yankee commerce. Where Anderson and Seddon feared that separate Virginia action would wreck Virginia's economy, Barbour feared that a southern convention would wreck the Union. The competing visions of wreckage paralyzed the Virginia legislature. Fighting in the Union came to mean no fight at all.

An exasperated Memminger gathered up his daughter and fled home in mid-February 1860. Both the commissioner and South Carolina's equally disappointed governor explained Cooperation's failure with classic South Carolina logic. Virginia, unlike more aristocratic South Carolina, suffered from national parties and mobocratic demagogues. "Distinguished southern men," cried Governor Gist, became "absorbed in the Presidential election, to the neglect of . . . southern rights." Memminger agreed, asking rhetorically, "With three candidates here [in Richmond] in the field for the Presidency, how is it possible to make the people work outside of the Union?"[36]

Memminger knew that he had inadvertently advertised that Virginia would not move forward. The commissioner had meant what he said. He could not tolerate standing still. If only Separatists would push ahead, a Separatist he would reluctantly become. After his failure as Cooperationist, he concluded that his advanced state must make "the issue alone" and take "our chance for the other states to join us." He now even pressed Miles's coercive language on Miles himself: "We further South will be compelled to act and drag after us these divided states."[37]

Memminger's surrender did not spread beyond Charleston's finest drawing rooms. But John Brown's failed raid had indirectly led to Memminger's demoralizing failure and on to an ominous strategic swerve amidst a critical part of the cautious Charleston establishment. Sober gentlemen now plotted not how to reattempt Cooperationism but how to appropriate Separatism from wilder spirits. These unlikely revolutionaries now ached to lead South Carolina soberly and safely out of the Union, at first all by the tiny state's lonely self.

Yet John Brown had also indirectly reared up a new tactical obstacle to Charleston's wealthy fraction of ex-Cooperationists. Before Memminger's humiliating debacle and his faction's conversion to Separatism, he had led his Cooperationist brethren in urging a southern convention on Lower South laggards—all too successfully. The Mississippi legislature had endorsed the Memminger initiative. The legislators had invited the whole South to a mid-April conclave in Atlanta. The state had also dispatched its own commissioner, Peter Starke, to Richmond with the invitation.

This Mississippi venture fizzled. The Atlanta convention never met. Commissioner Starke's appeal fell as flat as Memminger's in Richmond. But Starke never tried a Memminger-style all-or-nothing public spectacle in Virginia. The Mississippian only conferred privately with Virginia sluggards. He thus never suffered Memminger's infuriating loss of face.

Starke came away from Richmond still on South Carolina's (now partially disowned) southern convention bandwagon. Starke wrote Governor John Pettus that despite the temporary setback, Lower South Cooperationists must not "take any step backwards, after the stand they have taken." If a Black Republican wins the presidency, we must reissue our call for all the South to assemble. Otherwise, we must "prepare ourselves for destruction in the Union and the overthrow of our peculiar institutions."

But if South Carolina, Mississippi, and Alabama could convene a post–presidential election southern conference, continued Starke, "I verily believe" that "the patriotic and good people of the North" will "say to their fanatical neighbors, we intend to . . . stop your mad career against our southern brethren." Only if a southern convention fails to secure this "most desirable result" should we "prepare for the last great extremity." With the Mississippi resolution for a southern convention still on the legislative books, Governor John Pettus concurred that the remedy should be tried again, if Republicans won the White House. So too, Alabama's Governor Andrew B. Moore wrote South Carolina's Governor Gist that his state expects "a meeting of the proposed southern convention," if a Black Republican is elected.[38]

Thus where crucial Charleston Cooperationists came away from the Richmond disappointment (and from John Brown) disillusioned with their own southern convention remedy, some pivotal Mississippi and Alabama leaders still clung to the strategy. This potentially paralyzing Lower South disagreement over Separatist versus Cooperationist tactics would lead to a brief interstate conspiratorial correspondence at crunch time for disunion. That old conspirator John Brown would have chuckled at this last indirect consequence of the havoc that his failed raid had spread in the South.

– 7 –

With the commissioner phase over in Richmond, the focus shifted back to Washington for the resolution of the crisis that Hinton R. Helper (and John Clark) had spread in Congress. The first forty-three ballots for Speaker showed that all provocative candidates would lose. Republicans needed five votes from Democrats and/or Southern Oppositionists to win. But not even five non-Republicans would vote for John Sherman or any other endorser of the *Compendium*.

Democrats needed all party members to form a base for a triumphant co-alition. But not even the prospect of party victory could unite all Southern Democrats and all Northern anti-Lecompton (and pro–Stephen A. Douglas) Democrats. Thus was prefigured the split of the party in its national conventions several months later.

Those likely kingmakers in the standoff between Republicans and Democrats, the Southern Oppositionists, almost secured the throne for one of their own, William Smith of North Carolina. But not even the coalition of non-Republicans behind Smith could secure more votes than John Sherman garnered. Only an uncontaminated Republican nonsigner of the *Compendium* could prevail.

On the forty-fourth ballot, transpiring on February 1, 1860, just enough representatives found their uncontaminated Republican. All the voting Republicans, plus nine Northern Democrats, plus one Southern Oppositionist lifted William Pennington, New Jersey's obscure freshman congressman, into the Speaker's chair. The southern lone ranger, Henry Winter Davis of Maryland, sought to resurrect ex–Southern Whigs' failed fusionist strategy of 1856. He would support Pennington, a noncontroversial Republican who had said nothing about this particular slavery issue, in hopes that a new national party against the Democrats, agitating about everything except slavery, would reunite all fragments of grand old Whiggery.[39]

Southern Democrats screamed, in their usual loyalty politics vein, that the latest borderland "traitor" must be soft on slavery. The accusers pointed out that Henry Winter Davis had no idea whether William Pennington would remain safely silent on slavery. The Marylander, like everyone else, only knew that Pennington, only recently a Republican convert, had not yet endorsed or repudiated the *Compendium*. Still, after Pennington secured the most powerful congressional procedural position, this Speaker indirectly proved Henry Winter Davis innocent of treason. The New Jersey congressman neither accelerated nor impeded Republican antislavery legislation. A Georgian captured his blandness in a cruel phrase: "Old Miss Pennington."[40]

Cruelty aside, this controversy had never involved the Speaker's potential antislavery procedural power. Missouri's John Clark and all subsequent Southerners had focused instead on the antislavery potential in Northern Republicans' support for the Blairs, Cassius Clays, Underwoods, and Helpers.

In that sense, John Clark deserved his cry of glee, the day before his (more than Pennington's) triumph: My resolution has "smoked out before the American people the fact that an endorser of the Helper book cannot be Speaker of this House."[41]

Still, the slaveholders' victory over Sherman broke the southern record for empty triumph. The Fugitive Slave Law had yielded at least a few hundred returned slaves. The Kansas-Nebraska Act had come close to yielding the (slightly) enslaved state of Kansas. In contrast, the southern blockage of Sherman yielded only a Republican nonendorser of Helper; and no one could say what Old Miss Pennington might endorse in the future.

Worse, no Northern Republican president would be deterred from building a Southern Republican Party, just because Sherman had lost the Speakership. A Republican president would likely give patronage positions inside the South to his closest southern ideological allies, including Cassius Clay, Frank Blair, Jr., and John Underwood. He could scarcely shower southern posts on Yankees (that would enrage the South) or on Republicans' opponents (that would enrage the president's allies). A Northern Republican president's appointive power explains all by itself why the Republicans' invasive strategy, with its fingerprints all over the *Compendium,* had alarmed the Southerners, even though they discounted the Speaker's procedural power.

The mischief in Congress surrounding "the election of Pennington," Georgia's U.S. Senator Robert M. Toombs wrote Alexander Stephens eight days after the empty victory over Sherman, shows why we cannot permit Black Republicans to wield the presidency. "It would abolitionize Maryland in a year, raise a powerful abolition party in Virginia, Kentucky, and Missouri in two years, and foster and rear up a free labor party in the whole South in four years. Thus the strife will be transferred from the North to our own friends. Then security and peace in our borders is gone forever." Thus did the last congressional presecession crisis point toward a climactic crisis over the presidency.[42]

– 8 –

Toombs's words showed again that a wider drama than John Brown's had greased a slide toward secession. Brown's raid did hand secessionists an infuriating image of loathsome Yankees' sympathy for would-be devastators of slaveholders' homes. But Brown's failed raid supplied no image of how Yankee hatred would effectively be transported south. The *Compendium* controversy, coming after Brown's, Fee's, and Underwood's false starts, finally indicated how Republicans meant to carry the war to the slaveholders. Neither a lone ranger bearing pikes nor an evangelist bearing Christ's spirit nor a developer bringing Yankee laborers but instead a national party bearing patronage would spread northern scorn for slavery inside the South. Not just stray words in the air that had aroused a Keitt slave toward murder but also Southern Republican appeals on southern campaign trails would make slavery and republicanism incompatible.

As the Brown/Helper winter faded into memory, a two-headed image survived. On one side, Brown glowed with Northerners' hatred. On the other side, Helper's *Compendium* glistened with Republicans' tactics. The combination handed disunion propagandists the target of a Republican immediate menace that fused dishonor and danger.

Despite that boon, secessionists faced hard and uncertain work. In February 1860, most southern leaders and followers preferred, in Henry Wise's very popular words, to fight in the Union. Despite Helper, despite Underwood, despite Fee, despite Brown, secessionists had suffered yet another defeat: Memminger's. So too, while John Brown's spirit marched on in northern hearts, his pikes, sent around the South by Edmund Ruffin, lay moldering in southern legislatures' storage bins. Even that momentary symbol of southern withdrawal, the Philadelphia medical schools' empty desks, filled right back up. When courses resumed in the fall of 1860, Southerners formed as high a percentage of the Philadelphia medical students as ever.

First John Brown, then secession? It was not that simple. Rather first John Brown, then Transcendentalists' cheers, then a series of northern alternative invasions during the presecession winter, with the *Compendium* emerging to leaders such as Robert Toombs as the plausible Republican route inside a contained South. Yet most Southerners, as the Virginians had shown, still greeted the springtime with hopes that secessionists could be kept at bay.

In mid-1860, the disunionist lately reduced to shrunken silence best articulated South Carolinians' latest frustration. As he gained some perspective on the congressional winter (and discovered that the spot of his brother's murder appeared on John Brown's map), the chastened Laurence Keitt regained his old roaring self. "Northern men," Keitt warned, must not "get access to our Negroes to advise poison and the torch." Nor could we allow a Republican president to do "irreparable damage" by "sowing division among us." Keitt feared that "a Union party at the South now means an abolition party—not at first it may be but through quick transitions."

Whether in the North or in the South, whether Republicans infected lower-class blacks or whites, Keitt believed that the Yankees who had cheered John Brown's anarchism "will develop the wildest democracy ever seen on this earth—unless it shall have been matched in Paris in 1789. What of conservatism?—What of order?—What of social security or of financial prosperity can withstand Northern Republican license? A drunken and licentious soldier would be hardly as bad."[43]

Alas for Keitt and fellow South Carolina reactionaries, most Southerners continued to think that disunionists were as unreliable as drunkards. Despite congressmen's pistol-laden pockets, ballots rather than bullets still figured to control this democratic nation's future. But if the election of

1860's proceedings smashed the National Democratic Party and elevated a Republican to the White House, South Carolina fire-eaters might push a very reluctant southern majority into revolution, especially if those classy Christopher Memmingers, ominously disillusioned with Cooperationism, added a sober respectability to Separatists' unruly rebelliousness.

PART V

THE ELECTION OF 1860

Unless the presidential election generated two shocks, not even a Keitt-Memminger alliance could push disunionists to triumph in 1860. First, the National Democratic Party had to be severed. Then, a Northern Republican had to be elected.

If the National Democratic Party endured despite a Republican triumph, too many Southerners would consider disunion premature. They would insist that slaveholders could soon again use the Democratic Party to rule the Union. But if the Democracy shattered and Republicans ascended, South Carolina's secession might be unstoppable, particularly in ancient Charleston, mecca of William Porcher Miles, Christopher Memminger, and Union-scorning gentlemen. And where should the Democracy's delegates be headed, to decide the party's fate in its April 1860 convention, but to forbidding old Charleston itself.

On Charleston's eerie stage, one of the strangest, most significant, least understood presecession dramas transpired. The National Democratic Convention's most divisive issue apparently had no immediate practical consequence. The party's triumphant dividers wielded far less than a southern majority of delegates. The most important subsequent disunionists sat out the event in their own hometown. Charleston's passive revolutionary spectators even missed the genius of the puzzling revolutionary hero who most rescued them from their aloofness. These oddities, plus the Union's last major party's crash, earns the tale of William Lowndes Yancey and the demise of the Democracy the most prominent place in the southern story of the 1860 election.

CHAPTER 18

Yancey's Lethal Abstraction

At the National Democracy's convention, opening in Charleston on April 23, 1860, Southerners differed over how totally Stephen A. Douglas had to be destroyed. Would killing the Little Giant's presidential nomination suffice? Most southern delegates, particularly from the Upper South, would settle for that execution. Or must Douglas's position on Popular Sovereignty in national territories also be decimated? The disunionists' William L. Yancey crusaded for that annihilation. When Yancey began his crusade, months before the convention, he had few delegates' support. But the Alabamian wielded a canny position on Popular Sovereignty, capable of summoning at least Lower South Democrats to shatter the Democracy, if the party clung to Douglas's territorial abstractions.

– 1 –

Popular Sovereignty's advocates had always naively proclaimed that their abstraction would prevent national confrontations. If each local territory's voters decided for themselves whether to legalize slavery, the national government supposedly would never need to face the explosive issue. National conflict commenced, however, over *when* the populace could decide. Southerners urged that settlers could abolish slavery only when a territory became a state. Northerners countered that territorial pioneers could always bar the institution.

Then in Lecompton times, disputes over *when* turned into controversies over *how*. Southerners insisted that a settlers' constitutional convention, at the moment of statehood, could make the definitive decision. Northerners exclaimed that only a popular referendum, after the convention's decision, could issue the final decree.

Before this collision over *how* all but destroyed the Buchanan administration, the so-called Dred Scott decision all but destroyed any territorial

271

abolition. The U.S. Supreme Court decree barred Congress from emancipating territorial slaves. Since Congress, the sole source of a territorial legislature's powers, could not delegate unconstitutional authority, the Court's decision also arguably banned territorial governments from abolishing slavery.

At Freeport, Illinois, during the 1858 Lincoln-Douglas Debates, Abraham Lincoln asked Stephen A. Douglas if the Democracy's Popular Sovereignty solution could survive the Court's seeming death sentence. Wouldn't a settlers' decision be a mockery, Lincoln inquired, if a northern majority of settlers could not decide for emancipation? Douglas answered that no territorial majority needed to enact emancipation. A territorial legislature could abolish slavery by doing nothing. Unless such local police laws as fugitive slave edicts protected slaveholders' property, Southerners would take their slaves elsewhere.

This inspired answer, Douglas's so-called Freeport Doctrine, demonstrated the Illinois senator's perception of a pivotal southern social truth. However absolute a master's sway might seem inside his gates, undeterred enemies outside his fence could cripple his dominion. If no territorial fugitive laws prohibited hostile neighbors from urging slaves to escape, slavery could become too risky an investment. Then few slaveholding capitalists would migrate from protected slave states to unprotected national territories.

With the plausibility of his Freeport Doctrine, Douglas helped thrust back (barely) Lincoln's 1858 bid for his U.S. Senate seat. But with his Freeport answer, Douglas also deterred (overwhelmingly) Southern Democrats from backing his 1860 presidential candidacy. During the Lecompton Controversy, Douglas's stand against enslaved Kansas had almost fatally alienated Southern Democrats. His Freeport Doctrine completed the alienation. Since territorial majorities indeed could emancipate by doing nothing to protect slaveholders, Douglas became, in most southern eyes, as much an abolitionist as Lincoln, but more despicably disguised.

Douglas's most detestable hypocrisy, to the southern eye, came in his claim not to care whether a locality voted slavery up or down. Of course the Yankee faker cares, slaveholders exclaimed. Of course he knows that more numerous Northerners will win any race to any territory. So his salesmanship for Popular Sovereignty epitomized Yankee peddlers, selling phony satin as purest silk. Or to use Southerners' favorite image of the faker, Douglas was like Cuffee, only pretending to love his master.

A well-publicized Douglas pose hinted at a charlatan. The Little Giant loved to sprawl in his senatorial chair, with his stubby legs twitching on his desk, his gigantic head bobbing on his massive chest, and his stumpy fingers drumming affectionately on his North Carolina neighbor's knee. I don't have a care in the world, his body language seemed to say, or any ambitions to recline beyond this chamber, or a speck of dislike for you capital southern fellas.[1] All this from a mover and shaker who ached to be president, from an alleged conniver who had supposedly cheated slaveholders out of Kansas, and from a purported neutral who affected not to realize that no police laws to deter fugitives meant no slaveholder expansion.

In December 1859, in retaliation for the supposed hypocrite's Lecompton and Freeport provocations, Southerners stripped Douglas of his chairmanship of the Senate Committee on the Territories. Southern Democrats also vowed to kill at least the Little Giant's presidential candidacy and perhaps his version of Popular Sovereignty at the Democracy's April 1860 national convention in Charleston. Under Douglas's Freeport Doctrine, explained Henry Wise, fanatics could persuade slaves to run away and point out the route to freedom. Then in a single night, all a neighborhood's slaves could disappear. "Talk of underground railroads to run off slaves! Talk of incendiary publications to incite free-soil agitators!—I tell you," Wise emphasized, "no device in all the armory of fanaticism" is "half so subtle, half as effective," and half as "prompt to evil as this same Territorial—Douglasite—Squatter—Sovereignty slave trap."[2]

– 2 –

To escape Douglas's no-protection trap, Southerners insisted that all forms of territorial property must receive specially targeted legal protection. Ownership of land required laws against trespass. Ownership of livestock required laws about fencing. Ownership of humans required laws against inciting slaves or aiding fugitives.

To secure territorial protection equivalent to horse owners' or landowners', if a territorial government refused to pass a protective slave code, slaveholders eyed a congressional slave code. Congress could provide territorial fugitive slave laws, territorial laws deterring antislavery talk, territorial laws that supplied gallows for abolitionists—and before any settlers came. With that previously guaranteed federal protection, slaveholders might risk slave property in new territories, including in genial Caribbean climes.

A U.S. territory way southward in the Caribbean might seem automatically destined to receive a southern majority of settlers. But the most successful proslavery filibusterer in Central America, William Walker, led a majority of northern migrants. Walker's belated proslavery laws never stabilized Nicaragua sufficiently for an American planter to chance a slave in those tropics. Future Caribbean slaveholders would need prompter protection before territorial acquisitions.

If the doctrine of congressional protection should "be abandoned," T. J. Semmes warned a Caribbean-crazed New Orleans mass meeting, we must "bury all hopes" and "stifle all aspirations for expansion." Semmes, Louisiana's attorney general, predicted that, unless Congress enacted a preexistent territorial slave code, "no sooner would Central America or Mexico be annexed than emigrant aid societies" would fill America's new tropical territories with the "more redundant and more mobile population of the North." Migrating Yankees "would incite the mongrel half breeds to exclude slaves."

Then slavery in the surrounded South, "like a 'scorpion encircled by fire, would sting itself to death.' " [3]

At first glance, the congressional protection of territorial slavery seemed, as Semmes phrased it, the South's "only effectual barrier" against a free soil circle of fire. Yet on second thought, Southerners noticed impracticalities in this proposed practicality. Local communities might not allow proslavery laws to be enforced. Furthermore, northern congressional majorities might not write adequate proslavery laws.

"What more could the wildest abolitionist ask," inquired South Carolina's ever quotable William Henry Trescot, than "to be given the legal right to legislate for the negro" in Congress? If hostile Yankees devised national slave codes, blacks might receive "the power to testify" before potentially hostile local juries. Local magistrates might receive authority to determine whether a master clearly owned a slave, before the property could be sold. Blacks might be awarded "certain privileges as to time, food and dress, all perfectly consistent with his slavery" and "utterly" subversive of "the master's authority."

Yet "if I carry my negro into a new territory and I lick him and he knocks me down or walks off," what can I do without a local law? "A congressional slave code for the territories," Trescot conceded, is "a logical consequence of the Dred Scott decision." But when the "circumstances of real life are so multitudinous, so complex," a practical statesman who moves "from theory to theory" commits "scholastic folly." [4]

Trescot's scholasticism ignored the practical impact of bowing the neck before northern theory. If territorial legislatures, per Douglas's invitation, protected every form of property except property in humans, slaveholders would be branded as peculiarly sinful. A surrender to that defamation would make a slaveholder suspect in his own cringing eyes. After the coward submitted, he would never possess the spirit to expand slavery or to stop its Upper South erosion. Then a demoralized Lower South would slowly become an isolated, despised corner of America, loaded with the Upper South's blacks and without an outlet.

The practical threat of ex-Whigs' revenge also barred Lower South Democrats' theoretical surrender to Douglas's Freeport Doctrine abstractions. In 1850–54, Lower South Whigs had been tried and convicted of disloyalty to slavery if they remained in National Whiggery, after Northern Whigs voted against the Fugitive Slave Law. Ever since, these politicians without a national party (and thus without any restraints on their sectional fury) had been scheming to convict Southern Democrats of the same treason to slavery. If Southern Democrats remained allied with Northern Democrats who brandished the potentially abolitionizing Freeport Doctrine, ex-Whigs might be handed their first triumphant campaign theme in almost a decade.

The Democratic Party "has long vaunted itself as the only reliable party for the South," scoffed the ex-Whigs' Benjamin H. Hill, lately almost elected Georgia's governor. "Everybody who refused to act" with the Democracy "has been denounced as untrue and the ally of Abolitionism." But to submit to Douglas is "dangerous, since honest men may be seduced to travel" down his disguised abolitionist path. His doctrine that we have a right to take slaves to a territory "*and hold them there if we can*" packs "the same venom" and antislavery punch as "the doctrine of Seward and the Republicans." A Southern Democrat, if loyal to the South, will see through Douglas's pose. True-blue Southerners will insist that Northern Democrats affirm that the national government has "the *duty* of guarding and protecting the owner in his rights" in the national territories.[5]

That orthodox dogma of any patriotic southern party, conceded the Democrats' *New Orleans Delta,* must be defended. True, "at the present moment," this "abstract question" has "no real value." But what is "not practical today is likely to become practicable tomorrow. To yield the abstract principle now would be to yield its practicable application hereafter."[6] Yet how could Southern Democrats secure their claim at least to future congressional protection (and thus secure political protection right now against ex-Whigs' counterattack) without alienating Northern Democrats?

– 3 –

The problem especially tormented Jefferson Davis, now U.S. senator from Mississippi and lately U.S. secretary of war. No one else in the South's cozy Washington National Democratic establishment took more pride in the Democracy's proslavery laws. None more enjoyed James Buchanan's and Franklin Pierce's chummy White House parties. None more appreciated Douglas's help with the Fugitive Slave Law and the Kansas-Nebraska Act. None more sorrowed that the Illinoisan's late Lecompton and Freeport decisions would preclude a Douglas presidency. None more prayed that the National Democracy, in its post-Douglas phase, would once again cause South and nation to flourish. None better understood that unless the party remained pledged to almost all of Popular Sovereignty, Northern Democrats could be National Democrats no longer.

Davis knew that to save their national political party, his northern friends would have to sacrifice their beloved Douglas. He could not also ask them to sacrifice *all* of their beloved Popular Sovereignty. But his northern friends might qualify the Freeport Doctrine a necessary (in the South) smidgeon, if he reassured them that the South demanded no immediate congressional slave code.

Davis first spread the reassurance in a notorious speech in Portland, Maine, on September 11, 1858, fifteen days after Douglas spoke at Freeport. Davis conceded that an antislavery territorial legislature could abolish slavery by doing nothing. If the inhabitants of any territory refused to pass laws protecting slaveholders, "the insecurity would be so great that . . . slavery would not go in." Douglas could not have said it better.[7]

Angry Mississippi slaveholders swiftly asked whether their senator lay entwined in Douglas's Freeport Doctrine bed. Not at all, Davis protested to the Mississippi legislature in November 1858. "The difference between us is . . . wide," for I only conceded that "all property requires protection," or it can not be "held." Douglas sees no governmental obligation to protect. But I know that a hostile community's power to free a slave generates not "a right to destroy but an obligation to protect."[8]

So who had the obligation to protect, and when? Davis left those questions unanswered in his guarded retreat before Mississippi's suspicious legislature. But he provided an answer in July 1859, when speaking to Mississippi Democrats' state convention. Davis there declared that *courts* could prevent a hostile community from robbing a slaveholder. Thus our "right to protection does not necessarily involve the enactment of additional laws." Maybe someday, if courts fail a slaveholder, we may need congressional protection. We must now claim our right to national protective laws in that possible future contingency. But as for Northern Democrats' fear that we now demand a national slave code, "you know it to be utterly unfounded and . . . absurd."[9]

The absurdity, replied Davis's arch critic among Mississippi Democrats, lies in the senator's reputation as slavery's champion. Albert Gallatin Brown, Mississippi's less prominent U.S. senator, regarded Davis with the outrage of a plebeian who feels that a bluestocking treats him as scum. True, Brown had never been a plebeian. His father had owned eighteen slaves. The son amassed greater riches. But Davis's nemesis came from a relatively scantily enslaved area of frontier Mississippi. Brown could tolerate the big shots, if they did not "play 'big man me and little man you' all the time with me."[10]

Brown thought Davis played the big shot by barely deigning to notice him when they met in Washington. Davis's snobbery led Brown to dwell on pre-Washington days. He never forgot the difference then between Davis "sitting in an easy chair in Washington, getting his 8,000 a year and drinking champagne," and me "riding through the pine woods with the heat at 90° . . . and drinking rot gut."[11] The resentful Brown meant to show those sippers of champagne who really championed slavery. With that kind of enemy, slaveholders could well think, who needs friends? But the hatefully unfriendly Albert Gallatin Brown remained a painful burr under Jefferson Davis's lavish saddle, and never more so than in Davis's tormented 1859–60 period.

In these years, excruciating pain in Davis's eye matched the anguish of trying to be true to the National Democracy, and to the Union, and to slaveholder constituents too. The sufferer's face, an observer noticed, has the look "of a corpse," with its "haggard, sunken, weary eye," its "ghostly white, hollow, bitterly puckered cheek," its "thin, white, wrinkled lips clasped close upon the teeth in anguish," all ending with its graying, wispy attempt at a beard.[12] Albert Gallatin Brown, in contrast, sported a square, tough, unwrinkled face. His eyes glared with hate. His thick beard hinted at an excess of testosterone. It was as if an aging aesthete writhed before an overpowering bully.[13]

Davis's tremulous position on protecting territorial slavery provided the bully's target. Where Davis thought Congress might have to provide future protective laws, if present courts provided inadequate protection, Brown demanded congressional protection "now, do it at once," for slaveholders in Kansas and in all future territories. On January 18, 1860, Brown proposed a senatorial resolution that future bills "for the organization of a new territory" must require "the new Territorial legislature to enact adequate and sufficient laws for the protection of all kinds of property." After a territorial government's "refusal to do so," Congress must "pass such laws."[14]

Against that unconditional call for congressional protection now, unconditionally indigestible for Northern Democrats, Davis called for conditional future protection, hopefully palatable to Yankee allies. In a resolution that he first presented to the Senate on February 2, 1860, then modified on March 1, Davis wrote that "if experience should at any time prove that the judiciary and executive authority do not possess means to ensure adequate protection" for slaveholders, and "if the Territorial government shall fail or refuse to provide the necessary remedies," Congress must "supply such deficiency."[15]

Where Brown demanded immediate relief in a troubled present and said nothing about the intervention of courts, Davis sought only the right to seek relief if future court interventions failed. Where Brown demanded that

Mississippi's two estranged U.S. senators, the suffering Jefferson Davis (left), who outmaneuvered the bullying Albert Gallatin Brown (right) on proslavery territorial abstractions—and thereby ironically put his moderate version of the lethal abstraction into William L. Yancey's revolutionary hands. Courtesy of the National Archives (Davis) and the Library of Congress (Brown).

Northern Democrats now rip Popular Sovereignty to shreds, Davis asked the South's best northern friends to concede that Congress might have to temper local decision someday, if localities defied courts. Chose ye between us, screamed Brown and whispered Davis, to fellow U.S. Senators and to slave-holders throughout the Lower South.

The southern response turned Brown into a powerless bully. Only one senator sided with Brown's demand for an immediate congressional slave code. All other Southern Democrats favored Davis's wish for congressional protection, only if and when later necessary. In late May 1860, the Senate passed Davis's resolutions, while at the same time declaring his abstraction about the future irrelevant to present conditions. Through it all, the South's best disunionist strategist watched, and waited, and saw his way. Yancey would adopt Jefferson Davis's attempts at a party-saving sidestep around the Freeport Doctrine. He would then use the purported moderation to rule or ruin Davis's cherished party at its Charleston national convention.

– 4 –

To other southern extremists in Charleston, and especially to those from South Carolina, Yancey's adoption of Davis's compromised language and dismissal of Brown's uncompromising vocabulary represented the Alabama ultra at his most irresponsible. Posterity thinks of the fire-eaters as a single group, unified in hatred of southern compromising. That homogenization once again decep-tively jams the many Souths into one mold. Yancey's determination to shatter the counterproductively rigid South Carolina mold drove much of the story of the Democracy's collapse in Charleston.

Almost all Americans, North and South, shared South Carolinians' dis-trust of Yancey. The Alabamian seemed such a serene charmer, yet so capa-ble of murderous rages; such a marvelous orator, yet so difficult to hear; such a virile crusader, yet so bent over by neuralgia. Although the champion of uncompromising secessionism, he was such a compromising National Demo-crat. Although an adept party schemer, manipulating toward his own U.S. governmental offices, he was such a disparager of the U.S. government and of its dominant national party. Who was this baffling saboteur, anyway?

South Carolinians found the question especially unanswerable. The state's reactionary aristocratic republicans had had such high hopes for Yancey. He had so often undercut those expectations. The hopes began with this myste-rious extremist's name. Benjamin Yancey, father of the secessionist and the first famous Yancey, had rivaled his officemate, John C. Calhoun, as a South Carolina comer. Then Benjamin Yancey had succumbed to the lowcountry's curse, malaria, at age thirty-four.

The lowcountry's victim had borrowed a famous lowcountry name for his son. William Lowndes, coastal squires' revered congressman after the War of 1812, had personified their incorruptible patriarchal ideal. Lowndes fa-mously stood for undeviating principle. He loathed participation in political parties, especially to seek personal gain. He never asked voters what he could do for them. He always decided what to do for his lessers. Although ruling on the eve of the era of mass party politics, he remained a throwback to the disappearing age when patriarchs presumed that only wealthy gentlemen could guard republican virtue.

As national two-party politics descended on every southern area except South Carolina, that eccentric state's isolated patriarchs saw national party partisanship elsewhere in the South as slavery's executioner. Southern spoilsmen in national parties, hungry for national patronage, would make no demands or empty demands for slavery's protection. They would anesthetize rather than awaken their gullible constituents to slavery's needs. The riffraff instead needed guardians who wished nothing from politics except preservation of their flock. Where a two-party mobocracy would put the section to sleep, antiparty aristocrats would sound a continuous alarm.

During the first half of the nineteenth century, many young South Carolina sports, rich in these attitudes but poor in purse, headed out west to replenish their aristocratic resources. The exodus helped spread South Carolinians' contempt for Yankees and for the Union to the Southwest. But the exiles filled many an empty purse at the expense of much of the aristocratic contempt. Ex–South Carolinians flocked inside mass politics. They courted the voters. They compromised their South Carolina extremism for the moderate good of the National Democracy (and for their own immoderate ambitions).

South Carolinians hoped that William Lowndes Yancey would throw the South Carolina antitype at this disgusting southern type. If Benjamin Yancey's son could replicate the saintly Lowndes out in the brawling Southwest, the exile could make up for all the departing South Carolinians who had deserted their mother state and her contempt for mobocracy. Where other ex–South Carolinians had succumbed to white men's egalitarianism and to the National Democracy, William Lowndes Yancey might rally the newest South for a new southern nation, based on the older South's oligarchic wisdom.

Expectations for a second coming of William Lowndes, out where the moral wilderness most needed a saint, swelled when William Lowndes Yancey starred in two supreme secessionist incidents. In 1848, the ex–South Carolinian helped write (perhaps largely wrote) the Alabama Democratic Party's so-called Alabama Platform. This southwestern document, for once full of South Carolina attitude, demanded that national presidential candidates affirm that neither Congress nor a territorial legislature could abolish slavery in a U.S. territory. When the National Democratic Convention of 1848 rejected this uncompromising ultimatum, Yancey seceded from the conclave. Only one southern delegate followed. No matter, from the South Carolina extremist perspective. Yancey kept the holy flame burning in unholy parts of the South.[16]

Yancey equally starred, ten years later, in a second notorious secessionist moment. In 1858, in partnership with Virginia's greatest secessionist, Edmund

Ruffin, Yancey organized the League of United Southerners. The league, Yancey wrote James S. Slaughter, stood outside all parties, for "no National Party can save us." Only "Committees of Safety all over the cotton States (and it is only in them that we can hope for any effective movement)" could "fire the Southern heart—instruct the Southern mind—[and] give courage to each other." Then, "at the proper moment, by one organized, concerted action, we can precipitate the cotton States into a revolution."[17]

The League of United Southerners, like every other pre-1860 southern revolutionary effort, soon floundered. South Carolinians still admired Yancey's lonely stand. Only those above the National Democracy's corruptions, coastal extremists continued to think, could attain the South's delivery. Only the Lower South and never the Upper South, as the Slaughter Letter proclaimed, could deliver a southern nation.

However, South Carolinians also remembered that Yancey's Lowndes-like purity had leaked even before he deserted to Alabama. In 1834, William Lowndes's namesake had studied law under the upcountry's unionist zealot, Benjamin F. Perry. There had been a laying on of hands, and the hands had not been the extremists'. Before 1834 had half expired, Perry's precocious student had taken over Perry's favorite newspaper, the *Greenville Mountaineer*, dedicated to establishing the Nullifiers' folly. In Yancey's debut as fiery orator, he had derided John C. Calhoun's theory as the "loathsome offspring of failed *Ambition*."[18]

In 1843, in another departure from South Carolina grace angrily noted in that state, Yancey campaigned for a seat in the Alabama State Senate by declaring war against old-fashioned republicanism. The departed South Carolinian denounced a legislative representation based on amounts of wealth rather than on number of voters. The "monstrous inequality" handed "the whole power of the State" to a slaveholding minority—exactly where South Carolina patriarchs believed power should be handed![19]

South Carolinians could discount these declensions from South Carolina orthodoxy as mere youthful indiscretion, after Yancey's mature purism in the 1848 Alabama Platform and in the 1858 Slaughter Letter. But Yancey's return to the Democratic Party in 1855 could not be discounted. Nor could Yancey's hunger for a post in James Buchanan's cabinet or inside the U.S. Senate be admired. Nor could the Alabamian's adoption of Jefferson Davis's compromised position on congressional protection be abided.

But unlike South Carolina reactionaries, Yancey had abandoned the counterproductive politics of uncompromising extremism. Back in 1848, after only one Southern Democrat had joined Yancey's exodus from the party's national convention, the lonely ultra had rejected Dixon H. Lewis's conciliatory advice. Lewis, an Alabama U.S. senator and tight with Calhoun, had warned that "several of the most respectable men in the State . . . are now all Democrats." If you "cut" yourself off from "these gentleman, . . . how powerless" you will become, he said; I doubt if you "could carry a Single County in the State."[20]

When Yancey returned to the Democracy seven years later, he embraced Lewis's strategy for pushing Lower South Democrats in South Carolina's direction. He would become Alabama Democrats' partisan. He would press his extremist views no further than the outer edge of their moderate views. He would then cajole, flatter, and prod moderates toward demanding that Northern Democrats accept this watered-down extremism. His tempered ultimatums would test whether Northern Democrats would provide reasonable slaveholder security. Sooner or later, Northern Democrats would probably flunk the tests. Then enraged Lower South testers would follow Yancey out of the Democracy and later out of the Union.

I now "endeavor to be entirely conciliatory," Yancey wrote in 1856. "While this detracts from the brilliancy and the spice, . . . it gains the ears of the opposition and opens the way to their hearts."[21] Yancey explained his new conciliatory extremism more fully in perhaps his greatest public address, given in Columbia, South Carolina, nine months before the Charleston National Democratic Party convention. "Can we have any hope," Yancey asked folk devoid of hope, of "doing justice to ourselves in the Union?" I have "no such hope, but I am determined to act with those who have such hope, as long, and only as long, as it may be reasonably indulged. Not so much with any expectation that the South will obtain justice in the Union, as with the hope that by thus acting within a reasonable time," we will unify "our people in going out of the Union."[22]

Never again (until Lincoln's election) did Yancey declare the Union hopeless. He would favor disunion, he insisted, only if and when Northern Democrats failed Lower South Democrats' measured tests. He expected that Northerners would eventually refuse to allow national policy to be based on southern tempered ultimatums. But Lower South moderates would see for themselves, after they deployed insistences that Northerners act in a reasonably proslavery manner.

Yancey saw a refusal to issue reasonable proslavery insistences as the root of southern affliction. He denied that any "natural" flow of population and expansion had caused the South to fall behind the North. Instead, Southerners' unnatural acceptance of Yankee abstractions had cursed the South to an unnecessarily small share of American land and people. Early nineteenth-century Northerners had considered slavery wrong. Many Southerners had concurred. Thus the federal government had barred the slaveholders from receiving more Africans and banned them from nine-tenths of the Missouri Controversy terrain. If instead slaveholders, because believing in slavery's permanent good, had demanded that an entering African match every entering European and that every territorial acre be as open to Southerners as to Northerners, slaveholder power would have equaled Yankee power.

The South's acceptance of enfeebling abstractions persisted, Yancey warned. "There is no denying that there is a large emancipating interest in Virginia and Kentucky and Maryland and Missouri."[23] Elsewhere, compromising southern politicians, harboring compromised proslavery beliefs, deployed compromising action against enervating drifts. So the Kansas-Nebraska Act yielded no enslaved state of Kansas, the Fugitive Slave Law yielded few returned fugitives, and Manifest Destiny yielded no Caribbean terrain. Until Southerners insisted that their abstract good demanded real protection against ceaseless trends, they would be silent traitors to their abstraction, to its requirements, and to its staying power.

Yancey saw hope that the Lower South—and only the Lower South—could become conscious of slavery's necessities. Most Lower South citizens already called slavery right. They only had to learn to insist on a moderate version of their rights. Yancey's least favorite southern opponents (and the historians that he would most ridicule) answered that a culture should insist on explosive abstractions only when an important and immediate practical gain would result. In 1860, for the first time in many years, no slaveholder lived in any U.S. territory that lacked protection for slavery. What a time to risk a great party and a great nation, over a "mere" theory about protecting a nonexistent investment in a nonexistent place!

Yancey, like many southwestern Democrats, sometimes answered that today's invisible territorial slaves would be highly visible in tomorrow's territories, if slaveholders in future U.S. Caribbean territories enjoyed prearranged national protection. But Yancey seldom dwelled on future Caribbean practicalities. He instead usually emphasized that allegedly "mere" abstractions determined the course of history.

Personal experience taught this reality, for "mere" abstractions demolished his nuclear family. Yancey's stepfather psychologically brutalized Yancey's mother before sending her packing, after she would not concede her native South's abstract depravity. The abstraction that slavery is wrong had no practical consequences? Tell it to my rejected mother, one can almost hear an outraged son muttering.

Southern outrage about outside critics' insulting abstractions, akin to his own fury against his stepfather, gave Yancey his most practical weapon to reverse southern history. Many citizens, at least in the Lower South, would charge against northern notions that Congress must not protect so depraved an institution, so long as an ultra's demand for protection remained moderate, reasonable. A failure to issue reasonable demands would surrender to the flow of history. That would mean, Yancey believed, the further drain of slavery out of the Border South, further empty national solutions to the problem, and further endless compromises for the sake of the National Democracy (and its southern spoilsmen). But issuance of reasonable demands would force the Northern Democracy to yield real concessions or to suffer a split party (the indispensable step toward a split Union). Either way, insistence on the right abstractions would shove history in the right direction, toward protection of slavery's "merely" abstract blessings.

Abraham Lincoln espoused the same premises about the power of abstractions while seeking exactly the opposite historical direction. In his 1858 debate with Douglas, Lincoln assaulted the Little Giant for refusing to base public policy on the abstraction that slavery was wrong. To teach citizens not to care whether slavery was voted up or down, emphasized Lincoln, was to prepare public opinion for continued national drift toward domination by an expansive Slave Power. Yancey saw an opposite drift of antebellum history, toward a caged and apologetic slavocracy. Both Yancey and Lincoln would reverse their perceived historical drifts by teaching their publics to care—passionately care—about basing all governmental action on the rightness or wrongness of slavery.[24]

To watch Abraham Lincoln's subtle oratorical gambits in his confrontation with Douglas, as to watch William L. Yancey's clever ploys at the Democracy's 1860 conventions, is to observe manipulative genius at the service of profound understandings of how abstruse principles can change a democracy's history. Only extraordinary tacticians could spin historical movements around as if on a dime—a dime's worth "merely" of abstractions. Yancey correctly saw that most Southerners did not want (desperately did not want) to destroy the Union, just as most Southern Democrats did not want (desperately did not want) to savage the party. Their moderation could lead to inertia, compromise, evasion, erosion (and to offices for the moderate). To wrench them toward what they did not want, to put history on a disunionist course they deplored, one had to rally just enough of them, in just enough Lower South spots, to stand and deliver for an abstraction that they did covet, expressed in a temperate, measured way.

As William L. Yancey summed up the philosophy that guided his "merely" abstract strategy, "this government is largely influenced by public opinion." We would suffer from "the height of political folly and weakness" if we "lay silently by and permit public opinion to be formed against us upon any question, however abstract at present." But we reach for glory when we realize that all great "rules for the future conduct and guidance . . . of government or individuals are but abstractions, which in the course of events, become practical." At the Democratic National Convention of 1860, Yancey meant to demand that when Northern Democrats asserted "wrong rules and principles," at least Lower South delegates must insist that slavery is right, that the protection of territorial slavery is right, and that Northern Democrats must pass a reasonable test that slavery's blessing would be protected.[25]

The constant insistence that all tests be reasonable showed how far Yancey had left South Carolina behind. The ex–South Carolinian had learned, during those years in the political wilderness, that on matters of "mere" abstraction no less than on matters of supposed practicality, an extremist had to bend toward the middle in order to lure moderates toward the extreme. He had to find a compromised way to say that Northern Democrats must protect the blessing of slavery. Otherwise, few Lower South Democrats would embrace the vocabulary.

Yancey had tried for the boon of a reasonably extreme demand in the African slave trade controversy. He had not urged the extreme position that the trade must be opened. He had insisted on the (he thought) moderate principle that the federal government must not be the insulting closer. He had found that too many folk found the whole idea of reopening too extremist to credit this stab at moderation.

The territorial issue held more promise. Moderate Southerners did think they had as much right to protection of their property in the territories as did Northerners. They did think that honor required equal protection of everyone's property. An extremist had only to find the moderate way to demand that Southerners be treated as honorable equals.

Before the Charleston convention began, Yancey saw that Jefferson Davis had provided the ideal reasonable vocabulary. Under pressure from both Albert Gallatin Brown and Mississippi ex-Whigs, Davis had concocted his minimal demand for congressional slave codes, only if in the future necessary. But moderate Northern Democrats, Yancey realized, still espoused Popular Sovereignty's dogma of settlers' final power to decide. So they would probably reject the principle of congressional intervention to overturn settlers' decision, now or at any future time. Davis's reasonable abstraction, as the dynamics of centrist Lower South politics defined reasonable, could thus test whether any hope for the Democracy remained reasonable, as the dynamics of centrist northern politics defined reasonable.

The Davis compromised abstraction offered equally reasonable prospects for raising Lower South consciousness toward insisting on a blessing. Albert Gallatin Brown's demand for protection now might seem to have had more teaching value. But only one senator followed Brown. Davis commanded the Lower South congressional establishment. Davis, no less than Brown, defended slaveholders' right to protection of a blessing, some time, some way. If that abstraction eventually became the basis of northern and southern policy, the historical trends against slavery would be reversed. No room would remain for national laws against importing Africans, or against slavery's spread anywhere, or against expansion into potentially slaveholder-friendly Caribbean terrain. But if at any point along this supposedly "merely" abstract proslavery track, Northern Democrats jumped off Lower South Democrats' abstruse train, the road to disunion would be wide open. Now *there* was a practicality! Jefferson Davis's moderation would do Yancey's extremism just fine, even if unreasonable South Carolina extremists could not fathom how.

Davis did fathom how he could be used against himself. He thus urged the National Democratic Convention to pay no heed to his abstraction when writing its platform. Along with Georgia's Robert Toombs and other leaders of the Lower South's Washington establishment, Davis prayed that the Democracy's convention in Charleston would nominate a candidate (anyone but Douglas!) without much fretting about a merely abstract platform.[26]

But Yancey meant to put Davis's moderate abstractions to radical use. He would insist that the national convention base the party's platform on congressional protection of slavery in the territories, *if later necessary*. Otherwise, Alabama Democrats would seek to lead Mississippi's Davis supporters, furious at the uncompromising rejection of *their* man's compromised language, out of the convention. That exodus of a fraction of the Lower South minority of the southern minority of delegates might lead to a more general, lethal southern departure.

The precipitous action of a minority of the minority ranked second only to the precipitating impact of moderately radical abstractions in Yancey's quiver of extremist weapons. Only the Cotton South, he knew, and only the Alabama/Mississippi fraction of that fraction of the South, might first rebel against the party. South Carolina fire-eaters, as Yancey believed stupidly, had taken themselves out of the party where extremist action must first triumph (even when Charleston supplied the physical stage for the Democratic convention). So Alabama must seize the lead in blasting the Democracy away from the milk-toast party platform that the southern (and especially Upper South) majority of delegates favored. If Mississippi followed—well, Yancey could hardly wait to see if the rest of the Lower South might then follow, and if Northern Democrats might then stonewall against departed Lower South delegates, and if Upper South delegates might then be forced out of the Democracy too.

Yancey did not count on immediate victory. He designed his strategy for the long haul. He believed that Northern Democrats, if placed under the gun of a threatened party split, might surrender to Davis-style (and now Yancey-style) abstract reasonableness on the territories issue. Then the Alabama extremist would educate Lower South folks toward their next moderate proslavery ultimatum, and then the next. Eventually, Northern Democrats too would base all national legislation on protecting slavery's blessings—or exasperated Yankees would finally scream "no way." Either endgame would find a very patient William Lowndes Yancey leading Davis's troops beyond the party's previously choking bonds—bonds produced, Yancey passionately believed, by southern failure to issue reasonable ultimatums based on slavery's abstract blessings.

$$- 5 -$$

Yancey also prayed that abstractly reasonable extremism would serve his crassly practical ambitions. The Alabama agitator coveted Benjamin F. Fitzpatrick's seat in the U.S. Senate, especially if the Union survived the 1860 election. In 1859–60, Fitzpatrick opposed any southern ultimatum on protection of territorial slavery, even Davis's diluted demand for possible future protection. If a territorial legislature, wrote Fitzpatrick in August 1859, "should attempt to exclude" slavery, "or fail to pass laws for its protection," then "of course Congress can and ought to intervene, to protect property of every character, slave or otherwise." But since the territorial question would not likely "become a practical issue . . . at an early period," why undermine our northern friends *now* over a presently empty abstraction?[27]

Yancey particularly loathed this nonrecognition that allegedly empty abstractions can control history. He saw in the cursed misunderstanding the opportunity to make Fitzpatrick appear the foe of proslavery abstractions per se and friend only of party victory. Yancey knew that ex-governor John Winston, another Democratic Party aspirant for Fitzpatrick's seat, hovered about, hunting for middle ground between the senator and the fire-eater. If Yancey went for enactment of congressional protection now, against Fitzpatrick's rejection of any opposition to the Freeport Doctrine now, he would hand Winston the middle position: a Davis-like declaration now for future protection later, if necessary. Better to go for center ground and leave Winston nowhere to stand.[28]

South Carolinians disdained such grasps for grubby office. How could a so-called extremist enter the moderate Democratic Party at all, much less adopt Jefferson Davis's moderate abstraction on territorial protection, much less seek the corrupt party's nomination to serve in the foul national government?

Yancey no longer could abide this purism. Of course he had entered the national party where most Lower South folk resided; and he would stay there until they saw the necessity to depart the party behind him. Of course he would deploy the most moderate extremism that they could tolerate. He could then teach them that Northern Democrats would intolerably reject even moderate claims for southern equality. Of course he would seek nomination and election to the highest posts in the foulest American government. He would then attain the loftiest pulpit to preach that the temple must be cleaned or left to molder. At the climactic moment of the slavery expansion issue, a canny extremist contended for mainstream glory by poking Jefferson Davis's precarious moderation a perilous speck toward the precipice.

The almost unbelievable and (on Davis's part) utterly unintended collaboration of Davis and Yancey in a crucial national drama illustrates the historian Michael Holt's wise dictum: national politics is ever grounded in local politics. Before Davis and Yancey could triumph nationally, they had to position themselves perfectly amidst the pressures back home. Yancey had to find an ideal Alabama niche, on the extremist edge—but not far from Benjamin Fitzpatrick's moderation. Davis had to find an equally ideal niche, on the moderate edge—but not far from Albert Gallatin Brown's extremism. In Charleston, Yancey would use Davis's local niche as a foothold, and from there pull Mississippians toward reasonable extremism in national politics.

Yancey even hoped that reasonable extremism might ensure him Fitzpatrick's U.S. Senate seat prematurely. Fitzpatrick's term ended in 1861. But the state legislature, as elector of U.S. senators, could conduct the election earlier. Yancey's supporters would seek his election in mid-November 1859. If they could then elect their man, a formidable senator-elect would espouse Alabama's (and Jefferson Davis's!) reasonable extremism in Charleston.

When the legislature met, however, Yancey supporters found that they had counted poorly. Fitzpatrick had slightly more votes than Yancey, while John Winston controlled about half as many. Since Yancey could not rally a majority, Yanceyites withdrew their plea for an early election.[29]

The sweetest plum in Alabama politics thus remained enticingly available when the Alabama state Democratic convention met in mid-January 1860 to choose delegates to the April national Charleston convention. Yancey ultimately controlled the convention and secured an update of the Alabama Platform of 1848. According to the revised Alabama Platform's command, the state's delegates to Charleston must insist that the Democracy's national platform explicitly endorse congressional protection of slavery in U.S. territories. If the "National Convention should refuse to adopt, *in substance*," our propositions, "our Delegates . . . are hereby positively instructed to withdraw" (emphasis mine).[30]

In substance! With those loaded words, Yancey refuted the persisting myth about his 1860 Alabama Platform: that it demanded an immediate, unconditional congressional slave code, à la Albert Gallatin Brown's resolutions. Instead, Yancey and fellow Alabama delegates demanded in Charleston only a "substantial" retreat from pure Popular Sovereignty. By the time of the Charleston convention, "substantial" meant Davis's resolutions for future congressional protection, if necessary. Sustained by Davis's dance around the Freeport Doctrine, Yancey in Charleston could step beyond Winston and Fitzpatrick in provincial Alabama politics. He could also seek the highest national stakes by canceling Douglas's Freeport dance around the so-called Dred Scott decision.

CHAPTER 19

The Democracy's Charleston Convention

While Yancey traveled over to Charleston, carrying the Alabama ultimatum in his satchel, the National Democracy's southern establishment traveled down from Washington, bearing a fury that heightened Yancey's prospects. Two weeks before the blowup in Charleston, a little-noted congressional brawl had intensified Northerners' and Southerners' contempt for each other. On April 5, 1860, Congressmen Owen Lovejoy of Illinois had provoked the national House of Representatives' version of the U.S. Senate's Brooks-Sumner 1856 confrontation.

– 1 –

The House's and Senate's Yankee protagonists differed. Where Charles Sumner exemplified the impeccably groomed Boston intellectual, Owen Lovejoy personified the shabbily attired midwestern farmer. Where the Harvard University scholar insulted the slaveholders with rehearsed affronts, Lovejoy crucified the Slave Power with uncalculated blasts.

Owen Lovejoy had spontaneously damned the slavocracy for almost a quarter century. Most congressional politicians enjoyed maneuver and compromise. Lovejoy preferred to till midwestern acres and to evangelize fellow farmers. Yet he endured the, to him, unchristian atmosphere of politics throughout the rise of the Liberty Party in the 1840s and the Republican Party in the 1850s. For Lovejoy, enduring political mission had begun at the foot of his brother's coffin. "I shall never forsake the cause that has been sprinkled with my brother's blood," he had there sworn.[1]

Before John Brown addressed his judges, Owen's brother Elijah had been Yankees' favorite antislavery martyr. In the mid-1830s, Elijah provoked southern-style repression in Alton, Illinois, located across the Mississippi River from Missouri. In 1837, a northern mob slaughtered Elijah Lovejoy in the warehouse containing his newspaper press while he aimed rifles as well as Bibles against their curses.[2]

Thereafter, many Northerners plastered abolitionists with more than curses. But Yankees killed no other antislavery agitator. Nor did any other northern zealot fight the Slave Power more unendingly than did the martyr's brother. "Thou invisible demon of slavery," Owen Lovejoy cried in 1859, "*I bid you defiance in the name of my God.*"

Lovejoy's defiances included aid for runaway slaves. The congressional fugitive edict, declared this devotee of the Liberty Line, commands a Yankee to "turn himself into a bloodhound" and to "thrust his canine teeth into the quivering flesh" of the "rifle-scarred and lash-excoriated slave." Then the northern capturer must "hold the captive till the kidnappers come with fetters and handcuffs" and with "a pat on the head . . . and the plaudit, 'Good dog Bose.'

"Sir, I will never do this."[3]

In his April 5, 1860 speech, Lovejoy reaffirmed that he would never have any more "hesitation in helping a fugitive slave than I have in snatching a lamb from the jaws of a wolf." Nor would he credit slaveholders' "right to go with this flesh in your teeth all over our territories." Nor would he fail to support abolitionist campaigns inside the South. Three months ago, he noted, a southern congressman had asked "a man who would endorse the Helper book . . . to stand up, that he might look upon the traitor."

Look then upon this alleged traitor, invited Lovejoy, while I cast my eyes upon Slave Power traitors against republicanism. In endorsing Hinton R. Helper's *Compendium,* declared Elijah's brother, I affirm not his every expression but his right to "address . . . his fellow-citizen in a peaceful way." The Slave Power would hang such dissenters. I say to the hangman that "if you cannot keep slavery and allow free discussion," if you must annihilate "all the rights of free citizens," if you must wield "violence, outrage, tar and feathers, burning, imprisonment, and the gallows," then slavery "must be immolated at the shrine of liberty, free speech, free discussion."

Freedom of discussion, emphasized Lovejoy, empowered Helper or anyone to propose "a Republican party in North Carolina and in all the other slave States. I hope . . . and I expect to see" that "done before very long." Tyrants cannot forever repress a southern antislavery party. You despots may kill Kentucky's "Cassius Clay, as you threaten to do," just as "you shed the blood of my brother on the banks of the Mississippi twenty years ago." But you will again find that "the blood of the martyr" will be "the seed of the church." Just as "I am here today, thank God, to vindicate the principles baptized" in Elijah's blood, so from Cassius Clay's blood "a Republican Party will spring up in Kentucky and all the slave States ere long." Then "more moderate" and "more sensible" Southerners will displace "violent . . . disunionists."

Sensible southern moderates, declared Lovejoy, know that the violent South can not have black slavery and white republicanism too (for slaveholders throttle republican discussion). They know that Southerners cannot be Christians and slaveholders too (for slave sellers gut Christian families). Moderates know that the South cannot have slavery without polygamists too (for no white wife can stop a tyrant from bedding his slaves). They know that slaveholders cannot own humans without being pirates too (for slavery has "the same moral force" as pirates' "division of their spoils"). Moderates know that the South cannot help encouraging slaveholders and robbers too (for a tyrant steals the child "from the bosom of its mother and says 'It is mine; I will sell it like a calf; I will sell it like a pig' ").

The southern pigsty, Lovejoy concluded, summarizes "all villainy." God finds the stench "more offensive" than "the violence of robbery, the . . . cruelty of piracy," and "the brutal lusts of polygamy." Unless we bar you from free territories, we will bar ourselves, for if you sit "there leprous, dripping with . . . disease, no one will go in."[4]

So declared one of Abraham Lincoln's favorite Illinois congressmen. Representative Lovejoy screamed Helper's insults and cheered Helper's remedy while inching close enough to Southern Democrats to spray them with spittle. He emphasized his contempt with swinging fists that barely missed their scornful faces.

Roger Pryor retaliated first. You "*shall not,* sir, come upon this side of the House, shaking your fist in our faces," warned the Virginia congressman. As Pryor lunged forward and Lovejoy held firm, forty-odd congressmen streamed around the orator and the challenger, shoving, screaming, stomping. Georgia's Congressman Martin J. Crawford "cocked my Revolver in my pocket and took my position in the midst of the mob." Assuming that "you want to be in at the end," James Hammond wrote the Virginia secessionist Edmund Ruffin, "come at once" and "see the fun." A "great slaughter . . . may occur any day," Hammond added to another correspondent, for "everybody here has a revolver," and "no two nations on earth are or ever were more . . . hostile."[5]

The hostility coursing through gunmen on the congressional floor, almost a year to the day before cannon blasted Fort Sumter, swelled loathing throughout the nation. Calculating Southerners had rational reasons for wondering if a Southern Republican Party might menace slavery. But enraged slaveholders also had emotional reasons for finding Northern Republicans intolerable. Lovejoy combined it all, the possible practicality of Hinton R. Helper's strategy and the insufferable sting of Charles Sumner's condemnation. A South Carolinian, upon hearing about the southern warriors who swarmed at Owen P. Lovejoy, wondered "how men were able to control themselves and keep *hands* off."[6]

No Preston Brooks laid a hand—or a gutta cane—on the House's version of Charles Sumner. Instead, after Old Miss Pennington futilely pounded his gravel for a tense twenty minutes, Southern Democrats retreated a few steps, back to their seats. Owen Lovejoy also stepped back a few steps, to the House clerk's desk. There, his pounding fists and provoking smears brought

Elijah's revenge to climax. In his wake, and with the Charleston National Democratic Convention only two weeks away, could Northerners and Southerners ever clasp hands again, in any national party or peaceable union?

– 2 –

From a Washington hot with hate, National Democratic Party chieftains struggled toward torrid Charleston, where the rhetoric steamed more than even the temperature. The difficulty of the journey prefigured the ordeal facing America's last mid-nineteenth-century national party, once its politicians reached the South's most eighteenth-century city. To voyage from the capital of the Union to the capital of disunion, travelers had to switch trains six times. At each transfer point, they had to drag body and bags hundreds of yards. Every time they struggled between the termination of one set of tracks and the beginning of another, Charleston seemed more remote from the American center.[7]

Once inside Charleston, party leaders found an even more alien atmosphere. Anticipating a repetition of Washington, D.C.'s early spring chill, politicians brought heavy woolens. They came upon a steam bath. Charleston's heat and humidity peaked at August's inhuman levels.

Not many suffering strangers found comforting hotel rooms. Antebellum Charleston, domain of private hosts, offered few public accommodations. The most fortunate visitors possessed the aristocratic credentials to sleep in a patriarch's exclusive mansion. Less fortunate outsiders had never so flooded this insiders' mecca as when the National Democratic Party convention came to town. Innkeepers, sensing a bonanza, charged staggering prices.

While Charleston's native materialists plagued the strangers, so-called faro bankers descended on the city. These gamblers faintly resembled the turkey buzzards who snatched offal from Charleston's open air market. A faro banker offered a fortune to any sucker who would pay to guess which two cards would next be slapped down. Not even a rare win over the dealers ensured loaded pockets. Itinerant pickpockets, another type not usually seen in Charleston, lightened many a heavy wallet. Yankees' thinning cash forced some delegates and spectators to share a room five ways.

Hard-pressed Northerners boarded less expensively at Stephen A. Douglas's campaign headquarters in Hibernian Hall. There, several hundred cots, arranged by states, had been wedged into a huge second-floor space. The stench of too many bodies, jammed into a boiling upper floor, offset the congeniality of sleeping next to one's own. No victim of Hibernian Hall ever forgot that warm air does rise and hot air does soar.

At high noon on Monday, April 23, when delegates walked down Meeting Street from Hibernian Hall to Institute Hall for the opening of the convention, providence took mercy on Charleston's afflicted strangers. The skies suddenly dropped an icy rain into the muggy air. The natives on Meeting Street cursed rather than cheered. How can cotton planters profit, whined gentlemen, when searing heat draws forth premature blossoms, then frost nips the buds?

When soaked politicians entered Institute Hall, the talk swerved back toward politics, as sweaty conditions returned. High, thin galleries and higher, thinner windows lined all four sides of the convention arena. Even with all windows open, scant rain-cooled air wafted down. For spectators and delegates packed in below, only handheld fans rustled up wisps of moving air.

The rustle, when combined with Institute Hall's poor acoustics, rendered the convention's speeches difficult to hear. The hall's layout, with seats nailed in sixes to a flat floor, made the speakers even more difficult to see. Most delegates glimpsed ahead only dripping necks, drenched suits, and three paintings of femme fatales, high above the stage. All but one of these ladies, portrayed in various stages of undress and inertia, seemed as foreign to this city as the faro bankers. The exotic exception, alone and apart, thrust a bowie knife at a globe.

Steamy April evenings followed by icy spring mornings might be tropical exceptions. Pickpockets and faro fleecers might be alien invaders. Confiscatory hotel prices might be momentary intrusions. But that Lone Rangeress, slashing at strangers the world over—she felt like Charleston's permanent own.

As the Democracy's party savers struggled against northern and southern defiances akin to the lady's, the convention sessions became prolonged, the convention days extended, the conventioneers' dollars scarce, the delegates exasperated. Before the party's fate could be decided, many northern spectators deserted the scene. The South Carolina lowcountry's finest folk filled abandoned seats. From the galleries above the action, squires and their ladies jeered at every attempt to save the party. These coastal folk particularly scorned the upcountrymen on the convention floor, South Carolina's own delegates. The rank antagonism between scornful South Carolinians above and participating South Carolinians below indicated that the state no less than the party faced paralyzing division.

– 3 –

South Carolina's political divisions had been widening ever since the Compromise of 1850. That national settlement discouraged secessionists everywhere except in South Carolina. There, a unique postcompromise debate concerned only *how* to secede. The more reckless Separate State Secessionists, strongest in the lowcountry, wished to depart the Union without waiting for another state. The more cautious Cooperative State Secessionists, strongest in the upcountry, wished to delay disunion until several other states agreed to cooperate.

Lowcountry gentlemen lost in 1852. Thereafter, coastal Separatists could manage only whines about the rest of the South's supposed mobocracy. After Christopher Memminger's debacle in Virginia, many Charleston

Cooperationists could only manage dreams of joining, controlling, and domesticating the Separatists. But upland squires, having apparently won the right to endure the Union's depravity until some other southern states would leave, moved on to enjoy other states' mobocratic politics.

The difference measured lowcountry folks' greater suffering (although oppressions kept the whole state first among secessionists). While South Carolina's upcountry cotton terrain was black with slaves (and with a 57 percent black population, more enslaved than western Lower South states), lowcountry Sea Island cotton and rice habitats were blacker still (70 percent black, and in some parishes 90 percent). While upcountry men started debilitating their soil with the cotton weed two decades before the rest of the Cotton Kingdom, lowcountry culture was a century more aged still, with its terrain still more worn. While South Carolina upcountry cotton producers recovered less completely than southwestern cotton planters from the depression of the 1840s, many lowcountry rice and luxury cotton producers plunged deeper toward economic ruin. While the upcountry lost blacks and whites to the booming Southwest, the lowcountry suffered three times more depopulation. The less afflicted upcountry became ever less ready to gamble on Separate State Secession and ever more willing to lead the National Democratic Party.

South Carolinians' divide over participation in the National Democracy involved a clash over democracy itself. William Lowndes had epitomized the elderly lowcountry's ancient aristocratic conviction. No squires, went the antique creed, could be safe in mobocratic institutions. Republics required the best men to rule, the worst men to follow, and the enlightened to teach uncompromising principle to the depraved. In contrast, political parties required office seekers to pander to voters' compromised preferences.

In the nineteenth century, while the rest of the South's politicians tumbled into mass political parties and massive courting of the (white male) folk, old-fashioned lowcountry gentlemen defied the new-fashioned democratic trends. Slaveholders elsewhere usually cheered that racial slavery required equal white men to command unequal blacks. Instead, the lowcountry slavocracy more often proclaimed that aristocratic republicanism required superiors to command all those lesser, including poorer white males. Again, the rest of the South relished the institutions of white men's egalitarian mobocracy, including national political parties, popular elections for all offices, and no property qualifications for the winners. Instead, South Carolina hung on to almost all her ancient curbs against riffraff rule.

During the first decade of the nineteenth century, South Carolina gentlemen did allow poor white men (except paupers!) to vote for state legislators. But legislators still had to meet a property requirement. Lowcountry parishes also still retained more legislative seats than their white population justified. Inside the gerrymandered legislature, propertied squires still elected all other officials, including governors, judges, U.S. senators, and U.S. presidential electors. Moreover, the gentry still tolerated no sustained parties in the legislature and few popularly contested elections for legislators. Above all else, lowcountry snobs still thought that the National Democratic Party must be shunned.

By the early 1850s, however, most upcountry gentlemen had "had enough," declared Preston Brooks, of the "stupidity" of an aristoi sniffing at the disgusting mobocracy. To exercise power and influence, South Carolina would have to enter the nineteenth century. The state government would have to be democratized. The National Democratic Party would have to be embraced.

I "am disposed to take things as we find them in politics as in real life," explained Brooks. "We know that a President is to be elected." We know that a nominating convention must first select the candidate. Why, then, "throw away our influence in theorizing against practice"? Or as James L. Orr, the leader of the South Carolina National Democrats, exclaimed about his favorite upcountry reactionary, Laurence Keitt, "I have no doubt that his experience in Washington will make him every year more useful to his constituents by teaching him to be more practical"—as practical as Preston Brooks had become.[8]

While the fire-eating Keitt might seem unlikely to become the mild Orr's compatriot, the two merry upcountry foes looked weirdly alike. Both Keitt and Orr had a gargantuan presence: over six feet tall, overly plump in the stomach, overly red in the face. Both had a natty air, with Orr's shiny black hat and shinier gold-headed cane exciting more attention than Keitt's baby blue waistcoat. Both dandies provided charming company at any table groaning with food.

But where Keitt could never sit still, Orr loved to dawdle. Where Keitt jumped from one impractical scheme to another, Orr carefully calculated any shift in position. Where Keitt aspired to lead South Carolina's revolution, Orr schemed to become America's president. Where Keitt forever faulted the Yankees, Orr never found fault, so it was said, save occasionally with his cook. There among South Carolina's aristocratic fossils flourished that supreme American pragmatist, the conniving national party politician, with aspirations to drag Laurence Keitt no less than Preston Brooks into the American two-party system.

The pragmatic Orr wanted South Carolina's voters, not the legislators, to select U.S. presidential electors (by the mid-1850s, commonplace everywhere except in South Carolina). He wanted South Carolinians, not just every other southern state's politicians, to share dominance over the National Democratic Party. The upcountry's favorite politician wished to revoke the lowcountry parishes' privilege of selecting more representatives, despite containing less voters. In 1855, Orr's admirers almost achieved popular election of presidential electors, winning in the State House but losing in the Senate.

In the late 1850s, Orr followers controlled most South Carolina congressional seats. They much influenced both the state's U.S. senators, James Hammond and James Chesnut, Jr., both from the upcountry. On the eve of secession, they raised one of their own, the upcountry's Francis Pickens, to the governorship. Orr himself became a sometimes Speaker of the U.S. House of Representatives. And in 1856, then again in 1860, members of his faction marched into the National Democratic Party as South Carolina's delegation. So many South Carolina folk had not relished such smoke-filled rooms for many years.

To defeat the state's pragmatists, lowcountry reactionaries would have to suffer politicos' haunts. If they could bear to fight the Orrites inside the Democratic Party's state convention, they could win selection as South Carolina's delegates to the party's national convention. Then by agitating down on the convention floor in Charleston's Institute Hall, they could lead a southern secession from the party, the precondition for secession from the Union.

But lowcountry gentlemen scorned a descent from the galleries. In a prescient letter, written three months before the Charleston convention, Robert Barnwell Rhett, South Carolina's prime revolutionary tactician, spelled out a strategy for minority revolution, without the South's most committed revolutionaries. The destruction of the Union, Rhett wrote privately on January 29, 1860, must begin with the "demolition of the party." So long as the Democratic Party, as a " 'National' organization, exists in power at the South, . . . our public men" will "trim their sails." Antiparty patriarchs could never hope for antiparty action from party politicians, or from deluded constituents, or from a united South. "It is useless to talk about checking the North or dissolving the Union with unanimity and without division of the South," and without superior men, possessing "both nerve and self-sacrificing patriotism, . . . controlling and compelling their inferior contemporaries." A "few, bold strong" delegates from "Alabama or Mississippi" would have to wrench their two Lower South states out of the convention. Then other Lower South states would be compelled to depart.[9]

Still, Rhett and his crowd disdained to supply the necessary "few, bold strong" Lower South delegates. If we fight inside the mob's conventions, William Henry Trescot explained, we will suffer mobocracy's pollutions. James L. Orr and his followers "work to contest the spirit and forms of our past life." But "I believe in her as she has been—esto perpetua—I want no change, and least of all such change as they will bring us."

Trescot, like Rhett, conceived that "a revolutionary genius could bring about" the only change desired: "a real crisis" in the Democracy's national party convention and then in the Union. But Trescot "scarcely" hoped that anybody "will arise in the convention and produce his commission to lead us." Among Southern Democrats in or beyond South Carolina, all "public man from the South . . . give out very uncertain sounds." Nor could the Trescots emit their certain sounds inside the party's proceedings without destroying "our independent influence, the result of character rather than positive political strength."[10]

There wrote the revolutionary who barred himself from entering the first arena of revolution. Despite trepidation that Orr would seize their state, despite recognition that a revolution inside the Democratic Party had to precede a revolt against the Union, despite understanding that a revolutionary genius might manipulate a couple of Lower South states to shatter the National Democratic Party's convention, the Rhetts and Trescots imprisoned themselves in the galleries. Some rescuer downstairs would have to save the reactionaries, and not only from the National Democratic Party. A non–South Carolina hero would also have to deliver South Carolina secessionists from their own state, too split to provoke a divided South out of the Union.

– 4 –

William Lowndes Yancey, a special target of Rhett's distrust, had discerned how Alabama and Mississippi could produce Rhett's party-shattering scenario. But when the Democratic Party's national convention convened, few delegates on Institute Hall's floor and fewer South Carolina disunionists in the galleries expected the Alabama Platform to devastate the proceedings. Both the Democracy's precedents and its convention rules encouraged alternate prophesies.

According to the National Democratic Party's rules, a nominee had to win two-thirds of the convention's votes. With Northerners comprising 60 percent of the delegates and Douglas controlling 84 percent of the Yankees, the Illinoisan and his pure Popular Sovereignty program commanded half of the convention's voters. But while the Little Giant's supporters could block anyone else's nomination, the South's 40 percent of the delegates, wielding nineteen votes more than a third of the convention, could block Douglas from that necessary two-thirds majority.

A dozen Southerners each hoped that a deadlocked convention would turn to yours truly. They remembered that the deadlocked 1844 convention had embraced the Tennessee slaveholder, James K. Polk. Various Southerners hoped to become another Polk, for the Democracy could hardly win in 1860 if Southern Democrats left Charleston enraged.

Southern delegates had more leverage over the convention's platform than over its selection of a nominee. Each state had one representative on the 1860 platform committee. The South, with fifteen states to the North's seventeen, controlled 47 percent of the committee (in contrast to 40 percent of the convention). If the fifteen Southerners on the platform committee could cajole only two of the seventeen Yankees to vote the slaveholders' way, a prosouthern Majority Report could repudiate Douglas's Freeport Doctrine.

If Douglas's slight majority on the convention floor rejected such a Majority Report, they would risk a fatal southern exodus. If Douglas delegates then scuttled the two-thirds requirement for a presidential nomination, in order to bypass the South's more than one-third of the delegates, Douglasites would double the risk of a southern departure. If the Democracy's southern power base disappeared, so would the nominee's national election prospects.

The more likely outcome, Southerners thought, would be the highly practical Douglas's surrender. Then one of those dozen aspiring Southrons would win the convention's prize.

Northern Democrats harbored alternate hopes. Douglas's committed convention majority could stop any other candidate. Douglas supporters could also dictate the party platform on the convention floor, whatever the platform committee's Majority Report declared. Moreover, in past conventions, alternate candidates had withdrawn after the leading candidate had achieved a simple majority of votes. Douglas had supplied that courtesy in 1856, so that James Buchanan could be nominated. Douglas supporters expected reciprocal courtesy in 1860. But would Southerners surrender to a simple majority's preference? Or would Douglas surrender to the two-thirds rule? Or would everyone's failure to surrender annihilate the Democracy?

– 5 –

With uncertainty abounding, a tense convention stalled for four days. On the convention's fifth day, April 27, 1860, the platform committee sent both its southern-supported Majority Report and its northern-supported Minority Report to Institute Hall's floor. In the Majority Report, the proposed platform language embodied Jefferson Davis's (and William L. Yancey's) supposedly reasonable extremism. The convention's platform, urged the Majority Report, should declare the "duty" of the federal government "in all its departments, to protect, *when necessary,* the rights of persons and property in the Territories" [emphasis mine]. Or in other words, the Democracy would pledge congressional protection of territorial slavery not now but in the future, if settlers' antislavery decisions needed to be reversed. So much for Stephen A. Douglas's dictum that Popular Sovereignty—the settlers' own decision about slavery—must be final.[11]

The Majority Report's "when necessary" wording fulfilled the Alabama Platform's "in substance" condition for Alabama delegates to remain in the convention. We will settle for protection "whenever and wherever . . . necessary," Yancey told the Charleston convention. We will not press any necessity now, lest we seem to be "dictating to" northern delegates. But they must pledge future congressional redress, if territorial fanatics rob slaveholding settlers. Or as Yancey explained in Alabama later, we asked the convention not for congressional protection now but for "legislation *only* in the event that there exists," in a future territory, "*obstacles* to the full enjoyment" of our property rights (emphasis his).[12]

Southern delegates relished that version of Jefferson Davis's moderation. A unanimous southern minority controlled the platform committee because two Northerners, from California and Oregon, deserted the Douglasites. At midcentury, slaveholders had feared that the two free labor states' entrance into the Union would throw the South into a permanent, helpless minority. Instead, Oregon and California had usually sent Democrats to Congress.

Those Democrats had usually voted with the slaveholders. Unintended consequences did abound on the road to disunion.

The outvoted Northerners on the Charleston convention's platform committee issued a Minority Report, substituting evasive language about Popular Sovereignty, hopefully inoffensive to the slaveholders, for the Majority Report's "when necessary" terminology, irreconcilable with the Douglas position that no necessity could overturn the settler majority's vote. Thus the Douglas partisans' Minority Report affirmed the "duty of the United States . . . to provide ample and complete protection for all its citizens." With their 50 percent of the convention delegates, Douglas supporters had the votes to affirm the Minority Report's soothing words and to reject the Majority Report's insufferable "when necessary" lingo.

In deciding whether to press their advantage, however, Northern Democrats faced a Hobson's choice. On the one hand, if they surrendered to Jefferson Davis's dilution of pure Popular Sovereignty, no Southerner would depart the convention. But then infuriated northern voters would likely depart a party that had become slave of the Slave Power once too often.

On the other hand, if Douglas delegates rejected "when necessary," they would free themselves from the Slave Power. But the rejection would defy Alabama's ultimatum: Repudiate Freeport Doctrine abolitionism "in substance" or our delegates are "positively instructed" to depart. If Alabama delegates left as instructed, Mississippi delegates, bridling at the convention's rejection of Jefferson Davis's compromise, might depart too. If many other Lower South Democrats left with the Alabamians and the Mississippians, not only the party's southern base but the party itself would be crippled.

– 6 –

When politicians dislike their choices, they like to talk. They pray that a discussion will bring one side or the other to see the folly of forcing a Hobson's choice. The platform crisis led the convention to stage that greatest of mid-nineteenth-century American public spectacles, the epic debate.

North Carolina's William Avery initiated the convention's major verbal drama. Avery, chairman of the platform committee, emphasized that congressional protection of slavery, "when necessary," was hardly a "mere" abstraction. Everyone in this convention, Avery pointed out, favors annexing Cuba at the earliest possible date. All Democrats also anticipate that the American flag will someday wave over Central America and Mexico.

Douglas's "principle of Popular Sovereignty," continued William Avery, "will exclude every southern man with his slaves" from any of these territories. The more numerous Northerners can migrate for $200 per settler. The less numerous Southerners must spend $1500 to buy and move each slave. No slaveholding capitalist would risk his investment if the North's more mobile King Numbers could rout King Cotton in a territorial legislature.

Only an assurance of congressional intervention, when necessary, would attract southern investors.

Without congressional proslavery assurance, continued the North Carolinian, Caribbean expansion plus Popular Sovereignty would yield "a cordon of free States on the Gulf." The South would then lie between free soil regimes above and below, with no outlet for redundant blacks. All southern white men would eventually face a racial holocaust, with poor blacks emerging as equal to poor whites. Our Majority Report's "life and death case, for the South," concluded Avery, rests on the master principle that Popular Sovereignty, without a future congressional check *when necessary*, is "as dangerous and subversive" as Black Republicanism.[13]

Northern delegates selected a Southerner to refute Avery. Austin King, governor of Missouri in the late 1840s and early 1850s, begged fellow Southerners not "to contend for a mere punctilio, when it will profit you nothing." King ignored Avery's argument that the punctilio could save slavery in future territories. Instead, he emphasized that no slaveholders now wished to go to any present U.S. territories. So "it is foolish and idle" now to "fuss about abstractions." That "when necessary" abstraction will suicidally "drive the Northern Democrats to the wall, and alienate them, and thereby secure the election of [William H.] Seward to the presidency."[14]

As Northerners applauded and Southerners shrieked "traitor," those who recalled Missouri's recent embattled history knew that Austin King's southern credentials had often been suspect. True, King had always owned slaves (five in 1860). True, he had never denounced the institution. True, when Frank Blair, Jr., had lately started a Missouri wing of the Republican Party (and had given Hinton R. Helper sustenance), King, like Thomas Hart Benton, had broken his longtime ties with Blair.

Yet King still suspiciously espoused the old Blair/Benton slur that Davy Atchison and other proslavery Missourians were but "Nullifiers," always conspiring to break up the Union. In 1849 as governor, Austin King's most controversial action had aroused special suspicions. Six years earlier, the U.S. Supreme Court, in *Prigg v. Pennsylvania*, had declared that state administrators need not enforce federal fugitive slave laws. It was then still a year before the U.S. Congress supplied federal enforcers. Fearing that the vacuum in slaveholder protection would invite slaves to flee, the 1849 Missouri legislature enacted a state fugitive slave law. Governor King reestablished the vacuum. He vetoed the law.

Austin King always had answers to the charges of secret disloyalty. In 1849, he vetoed the state legislature's fugitive slave law, he claimed, not because he opposed police protection of slaveholders. Rather, the U.S. Constitution, as the Supreme Court's *Prigg* decision had emphasized, gave only the federal government power to police fugitives. In 1860, he supported Douglas not because he wished Popular Sovereignty to leave slaveholders unprotected. Rather, no slaveholders now lived or wished to live in U.S.

territories—and slaveholders now needed Douglas to protect the Union against a Black Republican's election.

Slaveholders believed that the gentleman protested suspiciously much. Too many actions precisely like a hostile Yankee's, they thought, hinted at a heart not precisely like a slaveholder's. How could any but a softheart blithely ignore William Avery's case for congressional intervention, when necessary, in future Caribbean territories? Would such a pleader stand with or against us, as slavery's crises intensified?

If such questioners could have glimpsed the future, they would have muttered, *I told you so.* During the secession crisis, Austin King would be all for the Union. During the Civil War, he would be all for Lincoln's Union-saving crusade. In the U.S. Congress in January 1865, he would be all for Lincoln's Thirteenth Amendment, freeing all America's slaves.

But while King would be standing by the Great Emancipator in 1865, his plea for Douglas in 1860 revealed not a northern man in southern clothing but the futility of borderland neutrality amidst Missouri's venomous extremes. Austin King ever cherished Thomas Hart Benton's nonagitation position. He ever denounced Missourians' agitations, for or against slavery, that so constantly shattered the state's and thus the nation's equilibrium, whether Davy Atchison sought Bleeding Kansas or Frank Blair, Jr., sought aid to Hinton R. Helper or John Clark sought repudiation of Helper (and Sherman). King, long allied with Blair and Benton to put down Atchison's proslavery agitations, now could not abide Blair's antislavery agitations. He saw that the agitations that tore apart Missouri would also tear apart the national establishment, starting with the National Democratic Party.

As an elderly statesmen, approaching sixty years of age and witness to state and national turmoil since nullification days, King ached to be for once the Missourian who quieted the nation. This lawyer-farmer's tall, slim, vigorous body, and especially the thick shock of hair that spiked upward from his long, thin face, gave witness to an energy beyond most aging seers' resources. The obscure Missouri ex-governor would become a famous national hero if his plea for sectional nonagitation galvanized enough southern borderites to go for neutrality, prosperity, Union, and Douglas.[15]

– 7 –

Instead, Austin King's convention speech showed again that his angry state, dead center in the nation's North-South axis, could not stop provoking national hatreds, whatever the provoker's intentions. Much of the slaveholders' problem, from the Lower South perspective, involved a Border South that remained too neutral to be sufficiently southern. Austin King in Institute Hall proved that proslavery commitment had not consumed all Southerners— and that neutrality about slavery had consequences. With the pro-Douglas borderite's supposed treachery ringing in Yancey's ears, the Lower South's convention leader rose to his feet, as "the hall rang for several minutes with applause."[16]

This was the moment "for an Alabamian to be heard," William Lowndes Yancey commenced, "after the strange and unnatural speech they had just heard from a son of the South." He asked for an extra half hour, so he could demonstrate what a loyal son must do for the motherland. To more applause, the convention granted his wish. Many delegates now expected to hear the oration of the convention.

Yancey's became indeed a memorable outcry, partly because many auditors had false expectations about the speaker. For a man so prominent to posterity, Yancey had been indistinct to most contemporaries. He had not been in Congress for almost two decades. He had not often corresponded with non-Alabamians. He had almost never spoken outside Alabama. To most delegates, Yancey had been known only as a ferocious orator and an uncompromising extremist—a caricature of a fire-eater.

As he spoke for "whenever necessary" in Charleston, he had all the advantages of a fresh face, different from the ferocious image. His round, jowly visage and perpetual smile seemed that of a mild friend. "The terrible Mr. Yancey is not so terrible after all," remarked a surprised observer. On the podium he looked modest, unassuming, humorous, and, of all things, "a right good fellow." His voice sounded sweet, conversational, mellow, so soft that he had arranged to have the cobblestone streets outside Institute Hall covered with straw. Then convention delegates might hear his hushed call for Jefferson Davis's guarded version of Popular Sovereignty.[17]

Since William Avery had spoken to the practicalities of congressional territorial protection, especially in the Caribbean, Yancey concentrated on his favorite subject: the abstractions at stake. Southern intransigence for principle, he claimed, would reverse forty years of slavery's decline. From now on, he urged, Northern no less than Southern Democrats must base every action on the positive good of slavery. That attitude will purify "the state of public opinion at the North as well as at the South."

Yancey told northern delegates: You must no longer destroy the Union by acting on the principle that slavery is wrong. Instead, you must save the nation by teaching your constituents to protect both section's property. Turning to southern leaders, Yancey warned his fellows: Do not save the party by submitting to Yankee damnation of your inequality. Instead, you must save your institution by demanding northern protection of your equality. You must not "demoralize yourselves" and "demoralize your own people" by renouncing purifying "principle for mere party success." If you "ask the people to vote for a party that ignores their rights," you "ought to be strung upon a political gallows higher than that ever erected for Haman."[18]

As Yancey warned the South's Austin Kings that they deserved a hanging for teaching a shamed people to bow the neck, Charleston's daylight faded, gaslights flickered in the twilight, and enchanted Southerners strained to see the amazingly amiable figure, making even "when necessary" seem congenial. But whatever the Alabamian's mellow body language, Yankee delegates found the Alabama ultimatum to be outrageous blackmail. "Gentlemen of the South," thundered Ohio's George Pugh, "you mistake us—you mistake us—we will not do it," not now, not whenever slaveholders demanded congressional nullification of settler's sovereignty.[19]

– 8 –

After Austin King had failed to rout the Avery-Yancey insistence on "when necessary," and after George Pugh had condemned congressional negation of a settlers' majority, public orations had only hardened both sides' differences. So politicians turned to their next best tactic for softening the uncompromising: private, last-minute, frantic negotiations toward a compromise. With that too failing, men of affairs turned to Christian folks' last recourse: a day of rest and reflection on the Sabbath.

On Monday morning April 30, the convention could not further delay decision. By a vote of 165–138, delegates substituted the North's favorite milk toast, the platform committee's Minority Report, for the South's favorite imperfect substance, the Majority Report. Southern delegates voted for Jefferson Davis's, William Lowndes Yancey's, and the Majority Report's "when necessary," 108–12. Northern delegates voted down possible future congressional negation of settlers' wishes, 153–30.

Southern determination to qualify Douglas's Popular Sovereignty proved 90 percent solid. Northern determination to keep unqualified Popular Sovereignty remained 84 percent strong—too overwhelming for the straying southern 10 percent to matter. Douglas's pure principle would have won, 153–150, even if every southern delegate had voted for the Davis impurity. Of the twelve southern converts to Douglas's purity, ten represented Austin King's Border South. That least southern South still voted 22–10 with the disruptive Yancey (or as borderites saw it, with the soothing Jefferson Davis).

After voting to reject Davis's partial rejection of Popular Sovereignty, delegates and observers held their collective breath. Many Northerners suspected, as they always suspected, that southern threats to secede from party or nation epitomized a bully's bluff. If Yankees called the bluff, the bully would back down. For the first and not the last time in the 1860–61 period, the crisis of the Union had become a poker game. Would the South fold?

The Lower South's answer slowly approached when Leroy Pope Walker, an ailing Alabamian, inched toward the clerk's desk. "A shudder of excitement" coursed through Institute Hall and then, "for the first time during the day, profound silence." The hush lingered when the tall, pale, courtly Walker, looking as little like a southern hothead as Yancey, barely disturbed the silence with a drawl softer than even Yancey's.

To those impatient to know whether Alabama would retreat or revolt, Walker's indistinct reputation offered as insubstantial clues as his murmur.

Although the Alabama stranger was son of a U.S. senator and would be prominent enough to become Jefferson Davis's first Confederate secretary of war, he would have little impact on Confederate councils. He never served in U.S. office. His correspondence rarely transcended Alabama. Inside the state, he seemed too quirky a Yanceyite, being an ex-Whig and a northern Alabamian, to serve as Yancey's puppet. But he had presided over the state convention that had written Yancey's first gospel, the Alabama Platform of 1848. He now presided over the Yancey-led Alabama delegation at the 1860 Democratic National Convention. So his became the duty to indicate whether twelve years' worth of Alabama Platforms had been mere bluster.

Walker went by his middle name, Pope, not by his first name, Leroy. His announcement came off like a papal pronouncement. His auditors first made out the word "retiring." Shunning the battle cry "seceding," Pope Walker murmured that Alabama's delegates were "retiring" from their convention seats. Avoiding also the classic southern whoop that northern hypocrites savaged slaveholders' honor, this gentle cavalier put his complaint passively: "Justice had not been done the South." Never again would "any representation from the State of Alabama" grace "that convention," he whispered.[20]

After tentative cheers trickled down from the still partially uncertain auditors in the galleries, William S. Barry, chairman of the Mississippi delegation, turned the trickle into a torrent. He shouted that his state's representatives were "seceding" too (not "retiring"). Then D. C. Glenn of Mississippi thrust the mood further beyond Pope Walker's understatement. Glenn scrambled atop his chair, flailed his arms, then whipped around to frown down George Pugh's Ohioans. With a face as "pale as ashes" and eyes that "rolled and glared," he declared that the Yankees "must go their ways, and the South must go her ways." Our enemies, spat the Mississippian, might hallucinate that Mississippi and Alabama departed by their lonely selves, "like Hagar in the wilderness." But "in less than sixty days," our foes "would find a united South, standing shoulder to shoulder."[21]

Yet a third verbal tone next proclaimed that the departure was spreading past Pope Walker's quiet retirement and D. C. Glenn's screeching defiance. Alexander Moulton of Louisiana, a thick, graying clump of a man who reminded contemporaries of a surly bulldog, barked out his contempt for party traces in a French accent. As Moulton declared that "the Douglas principles, adopted today by the majority, can never be the principles of the South," his fellow Louisiana delegates announced with their feet that, as Moulton put it, they "will not participate any more in the proceedings of the Convention."[22] Then South Carolina's Orr followers crept reluctantly toward the door, then Florida's delegates rushed toward the exits, then Texas's representatives bounded toward Meeting Street, and finally the Lower South revolt claimed its sole Upper South delegation, that of Arkansas (representing the sole cotton-dominated state north of the Lower South).

– 9 –

By the late afternoon of April 30, Georgia alone, south of Arkansas, remained on the National Democracy's map. Meanwhile, except for Arkansas, every Upper South state remained in the convention. As would be the case immediately after Lincoln's election, Georgia's leaders promptly staged a brilliant debate over whether their most divided of Lower South states should join the precipitous southern South or the antiprecipitous northern South. This time, Georgians displayed their indecision only in secret caucus, several hours after almost all other Cotton South delegates had evacuated Institute Hall. (Except for the Georgians, only two Louisianans, two South Carolinians, and one Arkansan remained in the convention.)

While the Georgia caucus left no records, Georgia orators spoke unreservedly right before and after the secret confrontation. From their comments, the caucus debate can be more or less reconstructed. W. B. Gaulden's blunt words comprised Georgia delegates' most outrageous statements. The Savannah tycoon, loaded with slaves and eager for more, blasted the stupidity of exiting the convention over the wrong issue. The only "remedy for the evils the South complained of . . . was to reopen the African slave trade." Once fortified with millions of fresh Africans to match the North's millions of fresh Europeans, the South could compete equally for territories.

Gaulden urged Georgia's delegates to remain in the convention, drop the distracting "when necessary" issue, and look "to the Northern Democracy to aid them" in the necessary way. If materialists protested that importations of Africans would depress the American economy, Gaulden would remind them that "he could buy a better nigger in Africa for fifty dollars" than "in Virginia" for "one thousand to twelve hundred dollars." If would-be saints trembled that slave-trading profits would degrade American Christianity, he would demonstrate that the "African slave trader" is "the true Christian man," for he "goes to a heathen land and brings the savage here, and Christianizes and moralizes him."

If Northern Democrats still thought that importations of more blacks would mongrelize American Christians, continued Gaulden, he would invite them "down to his plantation" and introduce "Negroes he had purchased in Virginia, in Georgia, in Alabama, in Louisiana, and he would also show them the native African, the noblest Roman of them all." If Georgia's convention quitters wished to laugh at him, "he was in deadly earnest." And after they said that his strategy caused "mortification and disgust to the delegation from Georgia," Gaulden had "as much pity and contempt for them, as they could possibly have for him."[23]

Henry Cleveland, editor of the *Augusta Daily Constitution,* found the convention useful not to import noble Africans but to nominate a sublime presidential candidate. Cleveland claimed that Douglas would eventually concede, knowing that his nomination would capsize his party. Douglas would then support the Augusta hinterland's hero, Alexander Stephens.

President Stephens, Henry Cleveland added, would find better ways to protect the slavocracy than a counterproductive national territorial slave code. Any protection of slavery that a northern majority would accept would protect us "as the lion does the lamb." And, "oh yes, let us have protection, or dismember the party, for *protection* will people with southern planters the sandy wastes of the great American desert, crown with vineyards the earth-bare slopes of the rocky mountains, and be just the thing for the South when Greenland is annexed."[24]

Congressman Martin Crawford piled cynicism atop Henry Cleveland's ridicule. Crawford concurred that Southerners possessed "no" extra Negroes to protect and no territory where protection "is necessary." He presumed that no "good general" would "risk his whole army in a battle" where victory would offer no immediate fruit and where "defeat and disaster awaited him." Yancey surely knew, declared Crawford, that the Alabama ultimatum offered "nothing" except "discord and ruin to our party."

The Alabama Platform, Crawford explained, had only been hatched to elect "its author to the Senate." Upper South delegations resisted Yancey's departure, continued the cynic, only because ambitious Southerners prayed that presidential lightning "might strike" them, after Douglas accepted defeat.[25]

"I am fully aware," answered U.S. Senator Robert Toombs, "that personal hostilities and personal advantages are at the bottom of the strife; but there is a right and a wrong to the controversy for all that." Departure from a pack of disguised abolitionists, added James R. Sneed, was everlastingly right. Sneed, editor of the *Savannah Republican*, prayed that "truth, virtue, and patriotism" would now banish Stephen Douglas's "trickery, fraud, and demagoguism . . . from the land."[26]

Above all else, Georgians reluctantly had to decide who were their true brothers, overly zealous Lower South seceders or overly compromising Upper South stay-at-homes? Because that new basis of decision had become inescapable, some Georgians posted "flaming handbills" that Henry Cleveland was a southern traitor. "If it is treason not to bolt," retorted Cleveland, "I will always be a traitor."[27]

The Georgia caucus finally voted 22–12 to bolt with Lower South patriots, not to stay with Upper South conciliators. Just as Robert Barnwell Rhett had predicted, after Alabama and Mississippi left, other Lower South states felt compelled to follow. The next day, four of the dozen Georgia dissenters announced that the delegation's majority must dictate their departure too. So twenty-six of thirty-four Georgians marched from Institute Hall. By high noon on the first day of May, Charleston's lady folk, determined to decorate every empty delegate seat, rejoiced to place flowers in twenty-six more tombstones of the Democracy.

– 10 –

The afternoon before the Georgia caucus, South Carolina delegates had to decide whether to join the Lower South exodus. James L. Orr's supporters had pledged to stay in the National Democratic Party's convention. But as they wavered about departing their Institute Hall seats, they faced a Charleston political outcry unmatched for a decade. Wherever they stepped, whether in the convention or the hotels or the drawing rooms, scornful South Carolinians pelted them with epithets. "You are a southern traitor." "You are a South Carolina disgrace." "You are a hypocritical deserter." "You said you would embrace a cooperative alliance of several seceding states. Now look at your shame!" "Our patriots have quit the stable, and you prefer to wallow in manure." As the verbal scorn went over the top amidst threats to tar and feather the alleged traitors, Robert Barnwell Rhett claimed that physical lynchings imminently loomed, unless Orrites followed the Lower South out of Institute Hall.[28]

Perhaps Rhett's lately formidable foes quailed at possible physical violence. More likely they quavered at omnipresent verbal violence. Assuredly they reveled in their welcome after the withering social pressure helped shove them outside the convention. Once on Meeting Street, the new exiles became long-lost heroes. Ladies showered them with kisses. Gentlemen flooded them with invitations. In view of their relief at being celebrated as the reborn sons of chivalrous fathers, only some antirevolutionary hero could ever again goad Orr's supporters to stand athwart South Carolina's revolutionary destiny.

The Orrites' surrender offered the first 1860 proof that wicked extralegal pressure could drag along antisecessionist stallers, just as most Georgians' surrender offered the first proof that a secession of part of the Lower South could drag along the rest. South Carolina delegates' capitulation also offered the first (and arguably only) proof that the locale of this convention decisively mattered. While everything else that transpired in the Charleston convention might have happened anywhere, Orr's antirevolutionary roadblock might not have dissolved anywhere else. Without Charleston's merciless hounding of South Carolina's enemies of exodus, Orrites possibly would still have been standing, to fight against the next step in the southern revolution.

Only two South Carolina delegates remained in Institute Hall. Only one of the nonseceders loudly protested. The protestor was, ironically, William Lowndes Yancey's first political mentor. Greenville's Benjamin F. Perry, the upcountry's eternal enemy of South Carolina extremism, dismissed the galleries' hoots and hisses.

Perry pointed out that South Carolina Democrats' state convention had overwhelmingly voted down automatic departure, if the Alabama Platform provoked an exodus. The upcountry's intractable unionist noted that the South, armed with the two-thirds rule and with more than a third of the delegates, could easily stop Douglas. A stalemated convention might eventually select a Southerner such as Virginia's Robert M. T. Hunter as its presidential nominee.

As for the platform, Perry preferred the southern-oriented Majority Report, which articulated his construction of Popular Sovereignty, to the northern-oriented Minority Report, which permitted any construction. But he could hardly blame the South's best northern friends for preferring verbal fudge to a linguistic poison that would kill the Democracy's attempt to defeat Northern Republicans. Southern delegates, concluded Perry, should have stayed and won. They then could have massed with northern delegates to win the White House for yet another Democrat—and probably for a southern slaveholder who would favor future protection of slavery in the territories, if it ever became necessary.[29]

A large majority of southern delegates subscribed to Perry's logic. So did most Georgia and South Carolina delegates, before the Lower South flood swept them adrift from their preferences. After the Lower South exodus, the entire Upper South, with the exception of three of four Arkansans and one of three Delawareites, remained in Institute Hall. In all, fifty southern delegates left and seventy stayed. Since the Georgians and South Carolinians controlled 38 percent of the Lower South's 39 percent of southern convention votes, the decision to depart initially swept up only 25 percent of the Southerners (and only 10 percent of the Democracy's delegates, North and South).

Rhett and Yancey had perfectly anticipated how a minority of the southern minority could escape southern and national majorities. Rhett had written that if a revolutionary genius could maneuver just Alabama and Mississippi out, other Lower South states would have to follow. Yancey had seen that if he based the Alabama ultimatum on Mississippi's Jefferson Davis's minimal insistence on territorial protection, when necessary, he could link Rhett's two crucial states as twins of revolution. Then, Yancey foresaw, Upper South opponents could not stop a spreading revolution to their south, even if they refused to join it. And they might later have to join it.

In May 1860, Yancey would have been delighted to foreknow that after Lincoln's election, the Cotton South, when leaving the Union, would repeat his party-shattering strategy of departure not by some single South but by a fraction of the Lower South's minority of the southern minority. Then once again, the most precipitous Lower South states would drag along the most reluctant tropical states. The only difference, the next time, would be that South Carolina would be first among seceders and Arkansas would lag behind, with the rest of the Upper South.

As architect of a triumphant plan for reconstructing or ruining the Democracy (or the Union), Yancey had accomplished more than improving his chance to whip Benjamin Fitzpatrick. His Alabama ultimatum, based on Mississippi language, had failed to cleanse the National Democracy. But the two states had lifted the Lower South out of the party quagmire. He had thereby fatally crippled the last best institutional hope of the Union savers.

He had taught Lower South patriots to rescue slavery without worrying about whether Upper South foot draggers would join the rescue mission. And he had liberated the titans who would lead the next step of the revolution, Rhett's self-imprisoned lowcountry South Carolinians, from their counterproductive purism and from James L. Orr.

Yancey thus had every right to boast to Charlestonians packed before the courthouse, on the night of the historic departure, that "perhaps even now, the pen of the historian was nibbed to write the story of a new revolution." The crowd had every right to respond with "three cheers for the Independent Southern Republic." Even an optical illusion seemed appropriate. As the first Founding Father of the Southern Confederacy invited his historians to prepare their pens, silvery moonlight gleamed from starry skies, giving the city's multicolored grand mansions the appearance of snow-white marble monuments of a new nation's capital.[30]

CHAPTER 20

The Democracy's Baltimore Convention

On the first day of May, the previous night's moonlight reverie looked premature. In the tropical daylight, Charleston's stuccoed mansions redisplayed their rainbow of colors. Almost all the Upper South's majority of southern delegates resumed their work in Institute Hall. They sought compromises that could lure the Lower South minority of the southern minority back into the Democracy.

The departing minority of southern delegates gathered in Military Hall. Most of the seceders hoped that the party might be reconstructed. Rhett, scorning all parties and their reconstructions, now could despair in his choice of galleries, both hanging over Southerners who remained uncertain whether to finalize the Democracy's ruin.

– 1 –

Yancey derided the shrunken Institute Hall proceedings as the "Rump Convention." Rump or not, a presidential nominee still had to garner two-thirds of the delegates. But two-thirds of what number? Douglas's supporters prayed that two-thirds of the remaining delegates would suffice. Some Douglasites had even cynically hoped that an anti-Douglas surge out of the convention would occur. Departing delegates, according to this fantasy, would lower the two-thirds bar, allowing two-thirds of the remaining delegates to nominate Douglas.

But Caleb Cushing, Massachusetts's southward-leaning chair of the convention, ruled that a presidential nominee still needed two-thirds of the original delegates. New Yorkers joined Southerners in sustaining the chair's ruling.[1] The supportive Yankees may have feared that more Southerners would leave Institute Hall if the convention majority changed procedures in midstream. The New Yorkers assuredly feared that southern voters would reject the convention's nominee if southern citizens considered Douglas's nomination illegitimate. Some may have also thought, as Georgia's Martin Crawford cynically surmised, that after the fullest two-thirds rule stymied both Douglas and the Southerners, presidential lightning would strike one of them.

Lightning could strike no one after the convention sustained Cushing's ruling and the Douglas delegates refused to remove the Little Giant's candidacy. To secure two-thirds of the original delegates, Douglas needed nineteen southern votes, even if every Northerner voted for him. Instead, almost a quarter of the Yankees voted against Douglas, and his southern support peaked at nine and a half votes (compared to the twelve Southerners who had swallowed his platform). Of the South's under 10 percent of delegates who could tolerate Douglas's candidacy, only one represented the world below the Border South and half represented Missouri (whose Austin King placed Douglas in nomination; Yancey must have choked on that supposed recreancy!). The Upper South rejected Douglas's candidacy more solidly than the whole South had rejected his platform.[2]

Southern Democrats' unshakable renouncing of Douglas showed that no merely procedural difficulty caused the party's split. If the Democracy's nomination had required a simple majority rather than two-thirds of the delegates, Douglas would have snuck off with the prize (with a half vote to spare). But he would not have been the nominee of the *National* Democracy. The Lower South, having divided the party over Douglas's dread platform, would surely have also divided the Democracy over the dread man himself. The Upper South, preferring any other candidate to Douglas, would have preferred the Lower South's alternate candidate, who would likely have been an Upper South Democrat (most likely Virginia's Robert M. T. Hunter).

Nor did the decision to select the platform before the candidate cause the convention split. A consistent 90 percent of Southerners considered the opponent of the Lecompton Constitution and proponent of the Freeport Doctrine unelectable in the South (and detestable). An equally consistent 75 percent of Northerners considered only Douglas electable in the North (and sublime). No technical convention rule or tactical convention strategy could dissolve that standoff over the highest priority of national convention delegates: what man can be elected, especially in our own backyard.

Southern delegates' intransigent opposition to Douglas, even after the most intransigent 43 percent of the Southerners quit the convention, left Douglas intransigents with a loathing of all things southern (especially Charleston!) as towering as southern loathing for Owen Lovejoy. South Carolina's Congressman John Ashmore, a soothing Orr admirer, claimed that "moderate men" could have nominated a decent Southerner on a decent platform except for "the obstinate & offensive course of the friends of Douglas," who "damn the South with great fury, saying that they can go to Hell." Northern Democrats' "exasperation and bitterness toward the South," added the convention's most illuminating reporter, Murat Halstead, feeds upon Southerners' "gross repudiation of the only ground upon which they could stand in the North." Yankees fulminate "more uncharitably and rancorously . . . about the South, her institutions, and particularly her politicians" than I have ever "heard Abolitionists talk."[3]

As uncharitable rancor consumed Institute Hall delegates, as their deadlock persisted through fifty-seven roll call votes, as the discomfort on Hibernian Hall's second floor turned horrendous, as Charlestonians' jeers turned nasty, as faro bankers and pickpockets snatched up too many of Yankees' last dollars, Northern Democrats needed a change. So they decided to move the convention to less hateful surroundings and climes, hopefully with less hateful Southerners as delegates. On May 3, the third futile day after the Cotton South's departure, the rump remnant of the National Democratic Convention voted to reconvene in Baltimore on June 18. "The Democratic party of the several States," urged the exit resolution, should fill "all vacancies in their respective delegations to this Convention."[4]

– 2 –

Less than twenty-four hours after departing Institute Hall, the seceding Cotton South delegates convened in Charleston's Military Hall. Charleston disunionists prayed that these political warriors would emulate the building's name. The seceders should declare war on Institute Hall. They should nominate their own candidate. Then they should go home. Their irretrievable exit would bury all hope of party reconstruction.

Yancey at first shared this intransigent strategy. But according to his highest strategic priority, he had to hang back with Lower South troops, so long as they joined him in reasonable tests of Northerners' toleration for a moderate southern ultimatum. Then the testers would charge with him, after Yankees flunked the tests.

In Military Hall, Yancey saw that many hoped for further tests. Almost all seceders from Institute Hall wished to pass a "when necessary" platform plank (which they promptly did) but then pause before nominating their own presidential candidate. They meant to wait and see whether their departure turned the Northern Democracy around.[5] If Douglasites tardily realized that party survival hinged on dropping Douglas, the National Democracy could reunite behind a southern candidate. If Yankees instead insisted on Douglas, Military Hall's patriots would nominate a southern ticket.

The departed delegates' very way of leaving Institute Hall hinted at a hope of coming back. On April 30, as they shuffled toward the exits, some "took position as spectators" briefly. After seeing no white flag waved, they completed their perhaps temporary departure. On the morrow, Military Hall became their observation tower, to see if Institute Hall's remnant would succumb.

By refusing to finalize their retirement, the retirees opened the best window onto why they departed the Democracy—and what they had *not* expected to achieve, at the moment of departure. Most of them did not see themselves as striding toward a southern nation when they strode out of Institute Hall. They did not plot that their departure would automatically shatter the Democracy. They did not scheme in April for a Republican victory in November, much less for a disunionist triumph in December–January. They did not forge a disunionist conspiracy, deploying secret intrigues to savage the last national party. Instead, they worked in the open air to intensify their same old strategy: pressure Northern Democrats to yield proslavery concessions, continuing a quarter century of northern appeasements.

Accusations that departing delegates harbored premeditated disunionism, even conspiratorial disunionism, rang out at the time and reecho still. The Democracy's shattering, after all, led straight to Lincoln's election and on to disunion. The order of events delighted disunionists. Surely, one might assume, they intentionally did something to forge the first chain in a premeditated chain reaction. Surely, some of them even secretly conspired to bring off such a necessary first step.

But a result never proves an intention. Many human actions have unintended consequences—sometimes consequence at war with the intention. To read result backward into intention is to tell a tale that plows ahead of itself, obliterating the swirl of confusion in human attempts to struggle from one historical moment to the next. Hindsight particularly distorts events such as the collapse of the National Democratic Party, where attempts to intensify an old strategy help carry the strategists into a new strategic situation.

Before the Democracy's convention, Yancey came closest to prophesying that Alabama's ultimatum in Charleston would lead straight to disunion. He thought that intensified southern pressure would probably cause Northern Democrats to balk. In that eventuality, he believed that the most intransigent Southerners would depart the convention. But he saw other possible outcomes. Northern Democrats could succumb to the Davis "when necessary" limitation on Popular Sovereignty. Subsequent southern ultimatums could yield subsequent Yankee submissions and eventually, perhaps, even safety for the South in a reconstructed party and Union.

If, as Yancey thought more likely, Northern Democrats rejected southern demands, this time or after some future ultimatum, a Northern Republican might still lose the presidency. According to a plausible scenario, Northern Democrats could win just enough Yankee states, while Southern Democrats or Southern Oppositionists could capture all southern states. Then the election, stalemated in the Electoral College, would be thrust into the House of Representatives. The U.S. Constitution requires the House, when selecting a president, to vote by states. By taking advantage of that voting arrangement, the southern minority had controlled the Charleston convention's platform committee.

Moreover, Northern Democrats in the House of Representatives might side with their former southern allies rather than with their Northern Republican foes. The Lower South delegates' parade out of Institute Hall could thus plausibly end with a Southerner's parade into the White House. From that position of presidential strength (and from Yancey's hoped-for position in the U.S. Senate), more sweeping ultimatums for Yankee surrender could come. Eventually, Northerners would probably snap. If the South had been kept together throughout the ultimatum process, a united southern revolution would ensue.

Yancey sought to produce an age of ceaseless, relentless probing of northern resolve, with an immediate revolution only one possibility. He could accept Military Hall delegates' preference for further probing, before forever leaving the Democracy (or the Union). He would patiently help perhaps temporarily departed folk with any reasonable ultimatum, so that they would help him after failed ultimatums made the need for permanent departure crystal clear. And neither he nor anyone else *conspired* to create the first departure.

The very absence of conspiracy measures the distance, nine months before disunion, between the party politicians who first shattered the Democracy and the South Carolina antiparty politicians who first shattered the Union (and, as we will see, found secret plots briefly helpful). The Lower South political operators who departed Institute Hall had dominated national politics for a quarter century. They had never needed or deployed secret conspiracies. They had always utilized classic nonconspiratorial tactics. Through pressure politics up front and behind the scenes, a determined minority had insisted that a less determined majority must yield concessions. Southern Democrats had squeezed gag rules, Texas annexation, the Fugitive Slave Law, and the Kansas-Nebraska Act out of Northern Democrats.

With the Alabama ultimatum in Institute Hall, Lower South Democrats had again turned up the heat on Northern Democrats. After that ultimatum failed, Lower South Democrats turned the heat still higher by leaving the premises. As their watchful waiting in Military Hall showed, they continued to deploy what turned out to be their last effort, inside the party, to salvage minority control of the Democracy (and thus of the nation) the nonconspiratorial way.

South Carolina leaders of imminent brief conspiracies had no impact on delegates in Institute Hall or Military Hall. All antiparty extremists sat out the event, making themselves powerless up in the galleries. Yancey, in turn, needed no conspiracy to command this season preliminary to disunion (and thus preliminary to fleeting disunion conspiracies). He only needed to give reasonable men reasonable time to discern whether a reasonably compromised ultimatum for "when necessary" would bring Yankees to their knees.

Supposedly (the evidence is sketchy) on the night before the convention voted between the Majority and Minority Platforms, Yancey met with prominent southern seekers of the party's rescue, including U.S. Senator John Slidell of Louisiana. Allegedly, Yancey and fellow conferees sought to hammer out slightly more compromised language than "when necessary." Supposedly, Yancey's last-minute effort explored words that Northern Democrats would be slightly more willing to accept. Allegedly, Yancey tried to persuade his Alabama allies to pause until the final overture succeeded or failed.

A last-minute movement for a slightly less forbidding ultimatum to the North, if it ever existed, failed. Alabama's delegates, if they ever heard of it, would not pause. Yancey, if he was ever involved, furthered just the reputation he desired (and that desire is the best reason to credit the sketchy evidence).[6] The Alabamian always wanted to be seen as one disunion advocate who would give unionists every reasonable opportunity to succeed, so long as they supported tests of whether the Democracy or the Union should survive.

Even if Yancey did contemplate dropping back a trifle, the night before leaving Institute Hall, he assuredly opposed moving ahead even a trifle, once he sensed the mood in Military Hall.[7] Having come so far so fast, he could wait until Military Hall's observers had given up on the Institute Hall convention. Thus did Military Hall's drama without conspiracy become a play without action, featuring a Lower South star passively waiting for Upper South brethren to decide whether to declare war on Northern Democrats. Meanwhile, South Carolina's future disunionist conspirators denounced such foreign antics in their hometown. They especially deplored Yancey, that best ex–South Carolina fire-eater with the best South Carolina name, who stalled when the best South Carolina–style aggression could have (supposedly!) finalized the drama.

When nothing could be finalized about a presidential candidate in Institute Hall, except to try again in Baltimore, nothing beyond the platform plank could be decided on in Military Hall, except to wait and watch once more. Yancey's rump conclave designated Richmond as its next perch for watchful waiting. The Military Hall rebels selected June 11, a week before the Baltimore convention would meet, as their date to reassemble.

As exhausted delegates from both halls limped to Charleston's train station on May 3, they could scarcely bear the thought of struggling in and out of the cars another six times before Washington, D.C., would loom ahead. Amidst bedraggled conventioneers, only two winners had anything to celebrate. The Charleston stalemate had lifted William Lowndes Yancey out of the shadows, giving him an importance that a U.S. Senate post never bestowed on Benjamin Fitzpatrick. Then too, while making Yancey rich in notoriety, the paralyzed proceedings had made faro bankers rich in lucre. One new titan cleared $24,000 from the depleted crowd who had once ridden the Democracy to national power and fortune.

– 3 –

The Institute Hall conclave had asked Lower South states to fill their delegations' vacancies, before the Democracy reconvened in Baltimore. In late May and early June, most Lower South Democratic Party state conventions reassembled to process the request. The Democracy's state conventions had to decide whether to send delegates to the regathering of Institute Hall stalwarts in Baltimore, or to the reassembling of Military Hall rebels in Richmond, or to both new assemblages, or to neither fresh effort.

Robert Barnwell Rhett had scorned all Democratic Party conventions, state or national, for fifteen years. He now came back to one convention in order to keep the wrong South Carolinians out of another and to keep the Lower South out of yet another. Inside his state's reconvened Democratic Party convention, he meant to arrange for only the right delegation (to wit, his own) to journey to only the right reconvened subsequent convention (to wit, Richmond's) to achieve only the right result (to wit, no Lower South participation in Baltimore, least of all to test prospects for party reconstruction).

In the aftermath of the Charleston convention, the lowcountry gaggle of Rhetts, fiery secessionists down to the last cousin, could not fathom how something so rotten as the National Democracy, led by someone so dubious as Yancey, could fashion a road to disunion. Baltimore, itself on the edge of antislavery, could be just the place for the wrong leader to convey the wrong Southerners back into the party morass. Yancey, with his infernal tolerance for test after test of a quagmire already tested to exhaustion, could be just the blunderer to allow one test too many. If southern compromisers secured a party reconstruction in Baltimore, warned Robert Barnwell Rhett, Jr., "the whole movement is likely to prove a failure, the South demoralized, and Seward triumphant."[8]

The Rhetts saw only one way past demoralization. Lower South delegates must nominate their candidate at the Richmond convention, thankfully scheduled to begin seven days before the Baltimore convention. Then the Richmond delegates must go home and give Baltimore nary a thought. To further that tactic, Rhett needed his own South Carolina delegation to replace the Orr supporters in Richmond.

James L. Orr and his followers resented Rhett's attitude.[9] They had, after all, retired from Institute Hall at Rhett's behest. Now the ingrate pronounced them too compromising to serve the state. Worse, at the state Democratic Party convention, Rhett played his undemocratic trump card, the very one that the Orr supporters had long battled against, to bar the suspect uplanders as Richmond delegates. The lowcountry's most famous disunionist claimed as many extra representatives in the Democratic Party's state convention as the lowcountry possessed in the state legislature. With that boon, Rhett's less populated lowcountry parishes dominated Orr's more populated upcountry counties in the state convention. Rhett bullied through resolutions that sent his own slate of delegates (and not Orr's) to Richmond (and not to Baltimore).[10]

Rhett thus hammered a second nail in Orr's political coffin, the pressure to secede from the Institute Hall convention having fashioned the first. When Orrites met this second mugging in a month with only impotent mutterings, they appeared even less likely to stand firm against a subsequent rush to disunion. Rhett seemed to have South Carolina almost unprotest-ingly under his heel. Could he now use the Richmond convention to crush any Lower South (or Yancey) inclination to travel to Baltimore, to make one last stab at party reconstruction?

Rhett would fail if Mississippi's delegates had their way. Mississippi's state Democratic Party convention unanimously sent the same delegates who had followed Alabamians out of Institute Hall first to Richmond (on June 11), then to Baltimore (on June 18). After tolerating Rhett in Richmond, Mississippi's delegates planned to march on Baltimore, to determine finally whether the National Democracy could be reconstructed.

Powhattan Ellis, Sr., an important Mississippi judge, privately explained why Lower South Democrats beyond South Carolina meant to give North-ern Democrats one last chance. If the Baltimore convention "will give us a platform recognizing our own rights and equality," wrote Judge Ellis, "we shall be ready and willing to join them in making a nomination." Douglas is too compromised to receive such a nomination, and Lincoln is too unknown to win the presidency. So if the Northern Democracy will relent, "the politi-cal chessboard presents a favorable aspect."

But if the Northern Democracy throws away its final chance "to join us on fair & equal terms," continued Ellis, and "if the flag of our country can-not protect me and my property wherever it can be rightfully raised," we must "seek safety in our own strong arms." While "many timid and waver-ing men . . . view opposition to the government as dreadful," Judge Ellis en-tertained "no such apprehensions. Even if I did, it is better we should en-counter the struggle now, than postpone it to a future period when our opponents will be comparatively much stronger."[11]

Yancey cherished the Mississippi attitude that Judge Ellis articulated. He found the same attitude in Alabama Democrats' state convention. He had built his Institute Hall strategy on an Alabama ultimatum worded to suit the Mississippians. He could hardly now repudiate a two-state collaboration that was demonstrably pulling both states toward Rhett, just because Rhett distrusted their last attempt to discern whether the National Democracy re-mained unreconstructable. So Yancey helped rally most Alabama Democrats to send their Charleston delegation first to Richmond, then to Baltimore— and to insist again on the Alabama ultimatum in Baltimore before deciding whether to return to Richmond.

Not only Rhett but also the few Alabama Douglasites shuddered at the prospect of Yancey marching on Baltimore. Like all other Lower South Doug-las supporters and like Missouri's Austin King, they saw no present necessity to insist on congressional protection of slavery in the territories, whatever the future necessities. They saw every immediate necessity to rout the North-ern Republican insistence on congressional emancipation in the territories. Only Douglas might defeat the Republicans' presidential candidate in the North. Lower South pragmatists should thus rally behind the best available

Northerner. Southern Douglasites could wait to rally for the best southern principle until it was, to use Jefferson Davis's word, "necessary."

The logic compelled Alabama's Douglas advocates to call their own irregular state Democratic Party convention. While only twenty-eight of fifty-two Alabama counties sent delegates, this sliver of Democrats appointed a pro-Douglas slate of representatives to Baltimore (and not to Richmond). Simultaneously, an equally rump Louisiana state Democratic Party convention, with only twenty of thirty-nine counties represented, dispatched another irregular pro-Douglas delegation to only Baltimore.

In Georgia, Douglas's followers suffered routs by four-to-one and seven-to-one margins in the state Democracy's regular convention. The losers then convened by themselves. This Georgia rump body appointed yet more pro-Douglas delegates to Baltimore alone. So did Arkansas Douglas supporters.

Thus among the eight Cotton South states, only Florida and South Carolina accredited delegates for solely Richmond. The six other regular Democratic Party state conventions sent their old Institute Hall delegations to both Richmond and Baltimore. Only the four irregular state conventions sent new pro-Douglas representatives to Baltimore alone. In Richmond, all the non–South Carolina seceders from Institute Hall would confront Rhett's futile determination to keep them away from Baltimore. In Baltimore, the former Military Hall rebels would face challenges for convention seats from small Douglas minorities of four states' Democrats.

In Richmond, as expected, Rhett begged the Military Hall delegates to forget Baltimore and the Democracy. But after two days of listening to South Carolinians, all the other delegates followed Yancey toward Baltimore and one more effort to reconstruct the National Democracy. Even the Floridians, accredited only to the Richmond convention, preferred observing up in Baltimore to keeping Rhett company down in Virginia.

Rhett and his South Carolina slate suffered grave forebodings that Yancey would be "paralyzed," as Rhett's son put it, up in the neutral borderland. The same "want of nerve" and "want of leadership" that Yancey had supposedly displayed in Military Hall, glowered Rhett Jr., might again abort a permanent party split.[12] To which Yancey would have answered, I will again save you from yourselves.

– 4 –

And so the mellow charmer did, with the ironic help of Douglas's scowling northern supporters. Yancey himself became the special object of Yankee rage. That sweet killer, having murdered Douglas's hopes in Charleston, now dared come back to kill again, with that same charming smile on his face. Northern Democrats could reseat some of the Military Hall crowd. They could especially tolerate the Georgians, who had accepted departure from Institute Hall so hard. *But Yancey!*

As Northern Democrats saw their predicament, their previous willingness to help southern allies had almost annihilated the Northern Democracy. After Republicans' derision about slaves of the Slave Power, Northern Democrats' seats in Congress had dwindled toward zero. In 1852, before the Kansas struggles, Northern Democrats had possessed ninety-two congressional votes, compared to Southern Democrats' sixty-seven. Now, the Kansas turmoil had helped reduce the count to a dismal thirty-two for Northern Democrats, sixty-nine for Southern Democrats.[13]

Stephen A. Douglas's presidential prospects offered Northern Democrats their only apparent escape from this slide into political oblivion. The Little Giant had lately turned back Lincoln in Illinois. In the Lecompton affair, he had demonstrated that Popular Sovereignty could turn back slave expansion, so long as Congress insisted that the true settler majority must prevail. To that possibility of being seen in the North as the candidate who could free the territories (without ever decrying slavery), Douglas added the certainty of being seen as the racist candidate (for he ever decried blacks). If the South would allow him to be the national candidate, with a vaguely Popular Sovereignty platform accepted in all regions, he might defeat Lincoln more thoroughly than in 1858.

While Douglas supporters saw partisan possibilities if the South would accept a milk-toast platform and a Douglas nomination, they foresaw partisan disaster if the Northern Democracy again knuckled under to the Slave Power. Yancey's minority meant to rule the convention or depart. How could democracy function when citizens voted and then the losers seceded from the winners' government? This concern, so similar to Abraham Lincoln's (and James Buchanan's) imminent reaction to disunion, demonstrated how widely Northerners in 1860 conceived that the Slave Power, to protect black slavery from white democracy, had finally encroached too outrageously on white men's majority rule.

Yankees marveled at southern gall in the face of the universal northern cry of enough already. Douglasites ranted that "after all the battles we have fought for the South—to be served in this manner—it is ungrateful and mean!" They only wish "to rule or ruin us!" Indeed, "he would be less than a man who would submit to them." We must not "think of receding" an inch before "Disunion bullying and braggadocio" or "we shall be swept from the entire Midwest." " 'Douglas or nobody' is our motto," and "any other alternative will prove our utter defeat and demoralization."[14]

It felt to Douglas supporters ever so "sweet" at last to demonstrate that they "were not doughfaces," that "the South was never before so well matched in her own game of brag and intolerable arrogance," that Southerners who "had been ruling over niggers so long" could not "rule white men just the same."[15] Reseat William Lowndes Yancey in a white man's democratic convention? The Democracy must instead bar him and his despotic blackmailers from Popular Sovereignty's temple.

Northern Democrats' outrage, together with Lower South Democrats' fury, doomed the Democracy's Baltimore convention before brawls over the platform and the candidate could even resume. First, the convention had to decide whether to admit the old Institute Hall seceders or the new Douglas supporters as delegates from Alabama, Louisiana, Georgia, and Arkansas. Most Northern Democrats turned apoplectic at the vision of Yancey or his lieutenants performing inside the Front Street Theater, site of the national party's resumed deliberations. Most Southern Democrats became stormy at the prospect of southern Douglas partisans, overwhelmingly rejected by Lower South voters, replacing Institute Hall seceders, massively reaffirmed by their constituents.

With a stalemate over which Lower South delegates to seat now adding to the Democracy's paralysis, Stephen A. Douglas wrote two statesmanlike letters to important northern delegates. Douglas offered to withdraw his candidacy if his men in Baltimore thought that another Democrat could better unite the party on pure Popular Sovereignty principles. Douglas's two lieutenants rightly pocketed these conditional letters of resignation. They knew that no other candidate could bring the Lower South around to pure Popular Sovereignty. Or as Yancey expressed southern intransigence, "the friends of Douglas . . . were ostrich-like—their head was in the sand of squatter sovereignty, and they did not know their great, ugly, ragged abolition body was exposed."[16]

Yancey's own ugly image persisted. A savage brawler, Yankee delegates stormed, still remained under the cover of the Alabamian's amiable smile and mellow drawl. While Southerners considered Douglas the great Yankee pretender, Northerners thought that no pretense could beat Yancey's sickening southern sweetness. The great ugly ragged ostriches, alias Northern Democrats, could hardly readmit the great ugly shaming revolutionary (alias Yancey), who, if allowed inside the Front Street Theater, would multiply his insults and ensure that the two-thirds rule would destroy Douglas. Northern Douglasites instead meant to dispatch Yancey and his outrages back to Richmond. Yankees would seat anti-Yancey, pro-Douglas Lower South delegates and nominate the Little Giant, their only potential savior.

Twenty-four hours before Douglas supporters announced their decision, the platform holding the convention's orchestra crashed. After discovering that only a few settees suffered bodily damage, ghoulish jokesters proclaimed that the party suffered from a physically no less than an ideologically shaky platform. The next day, June 21, the fourth day of the Baltimore convention, dark comedy gave way to national tragedy. The convention voted 150-100½ to seat the Alabama and Louisiana Douglasites and to split Arkansas's and Georgia's votes between the former Institute Hall and new Douglas delegations. The convention majority quickly reversed itself on the Georgians' credentials. The old Institute Hall delegation received back all the state's votes in the Front Street Theater. But no reversal could shake

Yankee determination to heave the supposedly bad apples from Alabama and Louisiana back south toward Richmond, where they could harmlessly rot.[17]

After the clerk announced that the former Institute Hall Alabama and Louisiana delegates could not reclaim convention seats, angry Virginians announced that this time the Cotton South would not leave alone. Over half the Border South and almost all the Middle South delegates marched out of the Front Street Theater behind Old Dominion gentlemen. These departing Upper South delegates quit the Yankees not just over the Freeport Doctrine and over Douglas but also over the late vote's supposed trashing of majoritarian rules. The party required that a two-thirds majority of delegates, each representing his state's majority, must concur on a presidential nominee.

Now, Douglas supporters would stuff the ballot box. They would brush aside the two-thirds barrier by seating Alabama and Louisiana delegates, none of them representative of the two states' majority of settlers. Some victory for settler sovereignty *that* Douglas nomination would be! In addition to all other issues that seemed beyond compromise, the Democracy now faced an irrepressible conflict over who gutted white democracy most outrageously. Must the prize be given to Northerners who defied Alabama and Louisiana majorities? Or were Southerners who defied the national convention majority the worse sinners?[18]

– 5 –

The supposed southern sinners' parade out of Baltimore's Front Street Theater would imminently prove to have been yet another rehearsal for disunion. During the breakup of the Union as during the breakup of the Democracy, the Upper South would initially reject departure. On both occasions, the Middle South would eventually join the Lower South, but only after Yankees combated the first departure with a supposed violation of white men's democratic rights. On both occasions, many borderland Southerners would scorn both waves of departures. On both occasions, participants in the first departure would include reconstructionists, hopeful that temporary secession would force a reformed policy. But the next time, Rhett and fellow unconditional disunionists would abort any try for reconstruction.

Although Rhett never saw why, Yancey, by accompanying would-be reconstructionists to Baltimore, proved again that his tactics perfectly fit the April–June presecession situation. Before the Democracy crashed, few Lower South Democrats favored disunion, unless and until their old National Democratic Party lifeline proved to be hopeless. By eternally moving back with reasonable men to perform reasonable tests of the lifeline, Yancey rallied numbers of followers beyond his fondest expectations to move forward with him, when the lifeline proved to be frayed beyond any reconstructive effort. After starting as a largely scorned extremist, he ended up leading not only Lower South Democrats (whom he coveted) but also most Upper South

Democrats (whom he distrusted). Secession itself would ultimately draw a lower percentage of Southerners out of the Union than Yancey's tactics helped draw out of the National Democracy.

– 6 –

Back inside the denationalized National Democracy's depopulated Front Street Theater, Douglas supporters savored their emancipation from the Slave Power. On the second presidential roll call, the freedmen declared Stephen A. Douglas nominated unanimously (even though his vote on the last tally still fell slightly short of two-thirds of the original delegates).[19] Meanwhile, the southern delegates who renounced the Front Street Theater (plus six northern delegates) marched not down to Richmond but over to another Baltimore hall. Their meeting place bore quite the name: Institute Hall!

In this latest Institute Hall (this time Maryland Institute Hall), 105 delegates gathered, all of them once delegates in Charleston's Institute Hall. The congregants totaled over twice as many delegates as had peopled Charleston's Military Hall. On June 23, this expanded rump convention (and not the contracted Richmond convention) first chose U.S. Senator John C. Breckinridge of Kentucky as its presidential nominee on its first ballot, with well over two-thirds of the votes.[20]

During their single-day convention, Maryland Institute Hall's celebrants also endorsed the Charleston platform committee's Majority Report. John C. Breckinridge would seek the presidency under the banner that Congress must protect slavery in U.S. territories, not immediately but only if and when later necessary. This diluted imperative for congressional territorial protection, Jefferson Davis's compromised creation, thus routed Albert Gallatin Brown's uncompromising national congressional slave code for the fourth time in 1860: first in the Yancey-led Alabama state Democratic convention in January, then in Charleston's Institute Hall's platform committee in April, then in the U.S. Senate in May, finally in Maryland Institute Hall in June.

Southern decisions in the latest Institute Hall left poor Rhett the more stranded in Richmond. He remained over 150 miles from southern seceders. His lonely plight had never more resembled the forlornness of Yancey in 1848, with only one seceder from the Democracy trailing behind him, or of Albert Gallatin Brown in early 1860, with only one senator voting for his immediate slave code, or of that Lone Rangeress pictured above the stage in Charleston's Institute Hall, stabbing at everyone with a bowie knife, cutting no one.

Some of Breckinridge's Lower South selectors mercifully stopped off in Richmond on their way home, to help Rhett save what was left of face. Middle South delegates showed Rhett no such mercy, even though he fretted on Virginia terrain. Only one Virginian and one North Carolinian joined forty-six Lower South delegates back in Richmond. On June 26, this most rump of all the 1860 conventions, containing under half of the Maryland Institute Hall delegates, rubber-stamped what the Baltimore seceders had accomplished three days before: John C. Breckinridge's nomination and the "when necessary" territorial platform.[21] It was a fitting finale for a giant step toward disunion that the subsequently crucial South Carolina disunionists had done nothing to accomplish.

CHAPTER 21

Suspicious Southerners
and Lincoln's Election

After the National Democratic Party split, could Republicans reunite the old National Whig Party elements, despite ex-Whigs' failure to fuse in 1856? A Republican Party's southern wing could come from two sources: from Helper-Blair-Clay heretics or from John Bell–John Crittenden–Henry Winter Davis mainstreamers. Either way, Southern Democrats claimed, Southern Republican collaborators, by thrusting free debate inside the South, would make democracy and slavery incompatible.

– 1 –

Every four years after 1836, claims of opponents' disloyalty to slavery had smeared southern presidential campaigns. The slander had most wounded Southern Whigs, allied with northern enemies of the Fugitive Slave Law and the Kansas-Nebraska Act. In the early 1850s, Lower South Whigs had to disown those allies. Seldom again would Whiggish politicians in the most tropical South seek a national opposition to the Democracy.

But Upper South ex-Whigs, lately called Americans or Know-Nothings but now called Oppositionists, remained hopeful of fusing with Northerners who opposed the Democracy. Southern would-be fusionists dreaded any new agitation on slavery, for that issue had poisoned the old National Whig fusion. In 1856, Upper South ex-Whigs had begged former northern colleagues to attack only foreign voters. But ex–Northern Whigs more often assaulted the Slave Power. Fusion with these antisouthern Republicans would convict ex–Southern Whigs, all over again, of softness on slavery.

In early 1860, in hopes of a new fusion, Maryland's Congressman Henry Winter Davis cast the lone southern vote for the Republicans' William Pennington to be Speaker of the national House of Representatives. As 1860 wore on, Davis and other Upper South would-be fusionists begged Northern Republicans to spread Pennington's silence on Hinton R. Helper to all slavery matters. The beseechers prayed for agitation only against Democrats' economic policies. Such a National Opposition Party would stress national expansion of roads, banks, railroads, and canals. By avoiding slavery issues, a National Opposition Party would prove the old adage that sleeping dogs must be kept asleep—or rather the new adage that artificially stimulated dogs must be soothed into taking a nap. Instead of the Democracy's proslavery agitators' "eternal howl on the negro question," argued Henry Winter Davis, let us realize that "the way to settle the . . . question is to be silent on it."[1]

As a motto for a fighting cause, silence had a built-in weakness. Nonagitation usually generated colorless pacifiers. Only the rare agitator who roared for nonagitation could maximize excitement. Understanding this irony, Southern Democrats rushed to the attack when a magnetic champion of nonagitation, Richmond's John Minor Botts, sought a reformulated *National* Republican Party's presidential nomination.

Both worshippers and detesters called Botts "the Bison." Botts possessed the right credentials to charge against the Virginia establishment: a proper father. Benjamin Botts was a famous Virginia lawyer. But John Minor's father and mother perished in the Richmond Theater's famous fire on the day after Christmas, 1811.

The orphan considered himself old enough, at age nine(!), to make his own way. During the nine years after flames consumed his parents, Botts streaked through school, conquering Greek, Latin, French, and mathematics, and then, in a six-week spree, the law. Only Patrick Henry had been admitted to the Virginia bar as swiftly, and Henry, unlike Botts, had served an apprenticeship to a senior lawyer.

In his six subsequent years at the Richmond bar, young Botts secured a golden trail of clients. Then, in his midtwenties, the comer decided that lawyering offered too little reward. On his Henrico County estate, the precocious squire achieved record farm yields and raised famous blooded horses. In 1828, still under thirty, Botts swept into the state legislature as a Whig representative of a usually Democratic district. In the 1840s, he served three terms in Congress from Richmond City.[2]

After all these unlikely triumphs, no one could tell John Minor Botts anything; and he did love to tell off the Democracy. In the Bison's opinion, a land of opportunity deserved loving patriots. Instead, the Democracy harbored reeking traitors. Botts dammed the Democracy's Kansas-Nebraska Act as "the most wanton, the most mischievous, the most suicidal, and the most unpardonable act ever committed." With "utter loathing and contempt," he termed the secessionists "enemies," "insane," "infamous." Such tyrants not only over blacks but also over dissenting whites forget that muzzles are "for dogs, not men. No press and no party can put a muzzle on me."[3]

As befit an unmuzzled insulter, the Bison flaunted a huge frame with a massive chest, a bulging waist, and a thick face. While other squires looked as overbearing, no Virginia titan matched Botts's hint of the savage: his unruly hair. Wayward locks curled crookedly down his stern face and stout neck before brushing his exquisite suit, fashioned from the best English cloth. In appearance as in language, this Virginia squire fused polish and pugnacity.

Botts's pugnacious agitation for nonagitation contrasted revealingly with the other 1860 comer who could be seen as an incongruous combination of opposites. Renowned aristocrats in the oldest South sired Botts and William Lowndes Yancey. Both fathers died tragically early. But where Yancey suffered dependence on a righteous abolitionist stepfather, Botts cherished the independence of an Horatio Alger striver. Where Yancey's experience with a castigator of southern morality provoked hatred of Yankee presumption, Botts's performance of a rags-to-riches saga inspired adoration of a free labor Union. Where the Alabama extremist surprised moderates with his mellow voice and mild appearance, the Virginia moderate unsettled ultras with his fiery insults and unbridled appearance. By acting and looking exactly the opposite of the way that folks expected, both stood out from their own crowd; and opponents considered both eccentrics perilously attractive.

In early 1860, Botts embraced the political peril of fusing with almost anyone—assuredly Republicans and even free blacks—who denounced the Democracy.[4] Botts's only reservation: no one, black or white, could indiscriminately insult all Southerners. A viable National Republican Party must insult only agitators for slavery's unnatural expansion.

Republicans need only halt slavery's unnatural expansion, Botts explained, because natural expansion halted itself. The South lacked the migrants for natural expansion. The Union's remaining territories also lacked the slaveholder-friendly climate for a thinly populated regime to invade without unnatural props. Nor could territories more congenial to slaveholders be added to the Union, unless the federal government unnaturally forced the acquisition. Damn only the artificial forcing, concluded the Bison, and silence all other damnations of Southerners. Then discreet Republicans and uninsulted Southerners could fuse against the Democracy's unnatural slaveholding expansionists—and behind Botts's presidential campaign.

The would-be Republican presidential nominee remained discreetly silent about his belief that without unnatural slavery expansion, the institution would naturally contract to a few Lower South states. To lure Republicans with this disguised antislavery bait, Botts chose Anna Carroll, the wealthy Baltimore lobbyist. Although barred from voting or holding office, rich ladies charmed politicians in Washington drawing rooms. The provoking Botts relied on the winsome Carroll to cajole the cautious Thurlow Weed, New York's Republican titan and a likely mover and shaker in the party's presidential nomination process.[5]

If Southern Democrats had discovered that their Richmond nemesis "unsexed" himself by secretly appointing a lady to sweet-talk him to a Republican presidential nomination, much less that he privately hoped for slavery's Upper South extinction, they would have possessed the smoking gun, demonstrating that this agitating nonagitator masked disloyal principles. But Southern Democrats thought that Botts's thick smoke sufficiently demonstrated a hidden fire. After the Richmonder outdid Republicans in slandering proslavery agitators as immoral and in smearing slaveholder expansionism as unnatural, how could he help but be a secret opponent of slavery? And how could a barely hidden Republican collaborator fail to shuck his camouflage, once his northern friends held power and offered patronage? Then no one would outdo the Bison in selling Republicanism to restive nonslaveholders and (inadvertently) to restive slaves. Thus for a season, John Minor Botts swelled up as the most dangerous of potential Upper South Republicans.

– 2 –

The danger faded not because Botts's foes erred about the Bison but because the Virginian erred about the Republicans. Months before their presidential nominating convention, Republicans dismissed Botts. Unless Republicans taught the public to hate slavery, they believed, the abomination would spread, even if Botts called the expansion unnatural. So a colorless Southerner such as Missouri's Edward Bates, Anna Carroll sadly wrote back to the deflated Virginian, might better muster a Republican fusion by softly calling slavery wrong. In contrast, the colorful Botts's fury at proslavery agitators could impress scant potential northern fusionists, without publicly expressed fury at slavery itself.

With Republicans requiring verbal blasts at slavery as a precondition for fusion, and with such supposedly disloyal verbiage destroying southern election prospects, mainstream Upper South Oppositionists sought alternative political campaigns in 1860, as they had in 1856. Four years earlier, they had supported Millard Fillmore's American Party. In 1860, Southern Oppositionists championed the National Constitutional Union Party.

The new party held its initial presidential nominating convention in Baltimore in early May, five weeks before the second Democratic Party convention disintegrated in the city. Since the National Constitutional Union Party aimed to preclude disintegrations, the peacemakers' platform intoned admiration only for "the Constitution, the Union, and the Laws." For their presidential nominee, these nonagitators paid scant heed to the agitating Botts and focused instead on three older longtime U.S. senators, all aged in the service of Thomas Hart Benton's nonagitating traditions: Tennessee's John Bell, six years older than Botts; Texas's Sam Houston, three years older still; and Kentucky's John Crittenden, seven additional years elderly. On the second ballot, the choice fell upon the youngest of these aging nonagitators, Tennessee's stolid, slow, safe John Bell. If these convention results sounded drowsy, this predominately Upper South movement urged that fanatics above and below most needed to be lulled into silence.[6]

– 3 –

While the Middle South's Bison silently disappeared behind the somnolent John Bell, the Border South's heretics loudly paraded behind Abraham Lincoln. Back in December 1859, at the beginning of the House Speakership controversy, Missouri's John Clark had warned that Northern Republicans' financing of Hinton R. Helper's *Impending Crisis* portended a National Republican Party, with North Carolina's Helper, Virginia's John Underwood, Kentucky's Cassius Clay, and Clark's least favorite Missourian, Frank Blair, Jr., leading the southern wing. During the next year, these Border South Republicans confirmed Clark's warning.

Throughout 1860, the *St. Louis Democrat,* the *Wilmington Delaware Republican,* and northwestern Virginia's *Wellsburg Herald* and *Wheeling Intelligencer* assaulted slavery with Hinton R. Helper's arguments. We care too exclusively about white nonslaveholders, they declared, to be called Black Republicans. Rather, our foes are the Black Democracy. Enslavers forget "that there are other interests . . . than the negro interest."[7]

Slaveholders' interests devastated nonslaveholders' interests, charged Southern Republicans. Only in the South is physical labor derided as "nigger work." Only in the South are poor whites called trash. Only in the South do slaveholders buy up the best land and blacks work the most fertile terrain. Only in the South does slavery repel white migrants, who prefer the free labor North. Only in the South is free public education impoverished or nonexistent. Only in the South do slaveholders repress free speech, a free press, and free discussion. Only in the South does a "dastardly and abominable spy system flourish," ferreting out the supposedly "awfully offending man or woman" who "dares even to *doubt* the holiness and divine right of slavery."[8]

Southern Republicans most aspired to free not blacks from enslavement but themselves from repression—and from blacks. They meant to quicken the Border South's slow drain of slaves toward the Cotton Kingdom. During Kentucky's slavery debate, 1849–51, Cassius Clay had proposed a state law, freeing slaves who remained in the state after a certain date. Then before the deadline, Clay maintained, slaveholders would cash in their blacks at Lower South slave auctions. Almost a decade later, the antebellum South's only antislavery congressman, St. Louis's Frank Blair, Jr., urged Congress to acquire Central American areas, as an outlet for freed blacks.

On January 25, 1860, Blair expanded his message at New York's Cooper Union. The United States, proposed Blair, should acquire tropical areas, open only to slaveholders who signed an emancipation pact. Slaveowners must agree to allow enslaved migrants eventual freedom and land ownership, in reward for hard work. Migrating slaves, enchanted by the goal of liberty, would labor eagerly in torrid tropical areas, yielding their masters "ten-fold" more profits than slaves' slovenly toil in cool borderland climes. In "a few years," the owner's extra profits would "repay . . . the price of manumission" and the price of freedmen's land. With the northern South's slaves' "gradually receding to create tropical wealth," migrants "from the North and from abroad" would replace Upper South slaves' previous "exacted, begrudging toil" with voluntary "self-gratifying labor." Free labor would everywhere triumph in North America, thanks to blacks' salutary departure.[9]

Like Blair's, almost every other southern emancipation scheme, since Thomas Jefferson helped inaugurate the tradition, had included departure of free blacks. Kentucky's John Fee provided the glorious, and doomed, exception. By coupling America's whitening with blacks' liberty, other southern antislavery agitators trumped proslavery agitators' racial argument. Slaveholders claimed that nonslaveholders' racial interests demanded control over blacks in their areas. The South's antislavery men countered that slaveless toilers' economic and political interests compelled removing blacks from their areas.

To triumph in so race-obsessed a democracy, southern emancipators had to demonstrate that the section or the nation could in fact deport blacks. Sometimes, as in the Virginia and Maryland slavery debates of the early 1830s, white emancipators had proposed removal of blacks to Africa. Maryland had developed its own colony for the purpose. Jefferson had suggested cheaper removals, to lands closer to home. Blair adopted Jefferson's position. But no other Southerner, least of all Jefferson, had ever presented a rounded argument for the Jeffersonian panacea so openly on congressional or Cooper Union platforms.

Blair's platform presence made him the more impressive.[10] The Missourian polished his speeches into prose diamonds. Blair looked as polished as his words. In an age when establishment stars displayed swelling midriffs, he was tall, thin, wiry. In an era when titans' beards became more common, he kept clean shaven, save for a perfectly shaped mustache. He also combed his every rebellious wisp of red hair into thick tranquility. This young Southern Republican looked as untroubled as his proposed emancipation idyll.

Appearances deceived, about the planner as much as the plan. The suave public man hid a shaky private soul. His nervous distress came partly from vainly striving to meet a famous father's crushing expectations. Frank Preston Blair, Sr., had been at the center of Andrew Jackson's administration, then at the core of Democratic Party journalism throughout Junior's privileged upbringing. "Preston," as intimates called "Senior," aspired to make "Frank," as friends called "Junior," an even more significant American power broker.

Frank's teachers, however, considered Preston's son of scant significance. Yale College expelled the heir. The University of North Carolina repeated the ouster. Junior then barely graduated from Princeton. Later, Frank fell in and out of western adventuring, into $100,000 of debt (and out again, thanks to Preston's mercies), in and out of a promising law career, in and out of his suffering wife's favor, in and out of his position as Thomas Hart Benton's disciple, in and out of his seat in Congress.

Throughout his chronic ups and downs, excruciating headaches afflicted the junior Blair. Frank also threatened the antebellum records for number of cigars smoked and amount of liquor quaffed. Missouri's antislavery congress-man surprised no one when he drove himself to paralyzing early strokes and a premature demise. But a decade before his demons brought him down, Frank harnessed his inner turmoil enough to become *the* Southern Republi-can. With his national family connections, his education (even if not ex-ploited) at the nation's finest universities, his nervous energy, his debonair appearance, his friendship with Lincoln, and his easy camaraderie, the Mis-souri redhead gave Southern Republicans a vivid leader with a vivid plan to sweep the South's northernmost third clear of slaves, and of blacks too—and thus to fuse with procolonization Northern Republicans.

– 4 –

Fusion came to its first climax when the Blairs swerved to help secure Lin-coln's nomination at the Republican National Convention. The convention, meeting in Chicago's Wigwam from May 16 to 18, 1860, contained ninety Southern Republican delegates, 20 percent of the total. Full delegations rep-resented all four Border South states. Delegates from the most northwestern and most lily-white section of Virginia, along with a few straggling Texans, slightly augmented the Border South force.

Blair Jr. brought to the Wigwam not only southern delegates but also a southern presidential candidate. Frank championed Edward Bates, the color-less St. Louis lawyer who had steamed past John Minor Botts as a fusionist presidential hopeful. Bates's key credential: Unlike Botts, he publicly called slavery an evil.

Blair Jr. secured not only all of Missouri's Republican delegates for Bates but also all of Delaware's and most of Maryland's (controlled by Preston Blair and by Frank's brother, Montgomery). On the convention's first ballot, Bates received 48 votes, almost as many tallies as Pennsylvania's Simon Cameron (50½) and Ohio's Salmon P. Chase (49) but not nearly as many as New York's William H. Seward (173½) or Illinois's Abraham Lincoln (102).[11]

Atop the surprise that a Southerner received 10 percent of the Republi-cans' first-ballot votes came the greater surprise that Seward and Lincoln each received 20 southern votes (a fifth of Lincoln's total). Southern Repub-licans' support for the future Great Emancipator swelled as Lincoln inched toward the nomination. On the second ballot, the Illinoisan secured 29 south-ern votes. On the third ballot, where Lincoln squeaked to victory, Preston and Montgomery Blair switched Maryland's delegation from Bates to Lin-coln, giving the Railsplitter 42 southern votes (almost half of the South's to-tal and 18 percent of Lincoln's tally). Since Lincoln would have been far short (perhaps fatally short) of nomination on the third ballot without this southern support, Southern Republicans helped anoint slaveholders' Civil War nemesis.

After Lincoln's nomination became apparent, B. Gratz Brown, Frank Blair's cousin, punctuated the revealing fact with an outburst: "I am instructed to cast the entire vote of Missouri—eighteen votes—for that gallant son of the West, Abraham Lincoln."[12] Lincoln himself had the last word. Despite Douglas's claim that the Democratic Party was national and the Republican Party sectional, bragged the Republicans' nominee, "I had more votes from the Southern section at Chicago [42] than he had at Baltimore" [28½].[13]

Lincoln's glee was as important as his numbers. The Republicans' choice, an ex-Whig who had loved his former National Whig Party, relished going national again. He already enjoyed a southern wing. Blair Jr. had campaigned for him during the 1858 Lincoln-Douglas Debates. Blair Sr. had swung pivotal votes to his column at the convention's pivotal moment.

A president-elect customarily rewarded such favors with patronage, especially when the chief executive admired his supporters' ideas. Blair's Cooper Union conception of federal colonization of blacks, to ease whites toward gradual antislavery, perfectly fit Lincoln's hopes. As president, Lincoln would help secure over $500,000 for that scheme. So too, Border South Republicans' conception of themselves as Ohio Valley Westerners more than Mississippi Valley Southerners fit Lincoln's conception of himself as a son of the Border West. In another example of supposed southern heretics as actually good midwestern Republicans, Kentucky's Cassius Clay came in second for the Republican Convention's vice presidential nomination, with over a hundred votes on the first ballot.

Any such Border South Republican beginning, John Underwood had predicted in late 1859, would swell when a Republican president handed out federal patronage. "Slaveholding gentlemen will cross the Potomac in swarms," Underwood had gloated, "and clamor at the Capitol for the privilege of serving their country in public office—Slavery or no Slavery." Underwood had in mind just such confidence men as John Minor Botts (who in fact would soon be hinting that he would relish patronage from President-elect Lincoln).[14]

Georgia's J. Henley Smith, himself a Washington, D.C., Treasury Department functionary thanks to James Buchanan's largesse, explained more fully why a southern rush for the loaves and fishes of office could endanger the Peculiar Institution. If a President Lincoln dispensed federal patronage, Smith warned, he would "have adherents and supporters all over the South." Right now, with Southern Republicans condemning slavery only at the fringes of political debate, nonslaveholders "would come up as one man and drive back abolitionism at the point of the bayonet." But not tomorrow, "not after an antislavery party shall get possession of the government" and bring debates about slavery's sins to the respectable center of Border South public life.[15]

– 5 –

After the 1860 presidential nominations, four men competed to direct the nation's public life. Two Illinoisans, the Northern Democrats' Douglas and the Republicans' Lincoln, dominated the northern canvas. Two Upper South U.S. senators, the Southern Democrats' John Breckinridge of Kentucky and the Constitutional Unionists' John Bell of Tennessee, dominated southern votes. While the collapse of the national two-party system muddied the waters, Lincoln could clarify everything by retaining the northern states that Frémont had won in 1856 and adding the Border North states that Buchanan had barely salvaged (and then lost by a landslide in the congressional election of 1858). But while Lincoln needed no southern vote to win, he would need some southern appointments to govern. John Minor Botts and Frank Blair, Jr., could hardly wait to compete for his favors.

The prospect of a mainstream Southern Republican Party, constantly calling slavery wrong in the middle of southern communities, became more alarming during the presidential campaign. A pivotal reason for repression of heretical debate, potential slave unrest, had never seemed so omnipresent. As the long hot summer of 1860 dragged on, panics about supposed black arsonists spread from Texas eastward. The hysteria lasted longer and reached wider than the late fright about Brown's insurrectionary plans, partly because the threat seemed more creditable. John Brown's aim, a mass slave insurrection, had not threatened the regime since Nat Turner's uprising, over a quarter century earlier. Slaves' zero response to Brown confirmed that a successful collective revolt scarcely imperiled this regime.

But another peril swelled. Not the group insurrectionist but the individual black who lived in the Big House and snuck a lethal little something into the pot (or who threw a lighted match into the curtains) became this Domestic Institution's domestic dread. House servants became suspected whenever something went afoul in the household. If a white fell ill, a slave poisoner might have struck. If the Big House went up in smoke, a slave arsonist might have lit the match. If some white stranger inhabited the neighborhood, he might be corrupting the latest gullible Cuffee.

Yet since blacks could not testify in white men's courts, and since blacks' coerced confessions in extralegal courts could be as phony as Cuffee's docility, who would say whether the right culprit had been accused? If domestic disasters multiplied and suspicious whites and blacks abounded, the impossibility of pinning blame nourished ugly waves of extralegal deportations and hangings, amidst a most undomestic Domestic Institution. The Texas Fire Scare of 1860 brought such periodic southern panics about individual slaves to climax, just when apprehensions about Lincoln's boost to Southern Republican agitators mounted.

Individual slaves' most effective resistance had usually featured dashes toward freedom. Runaways had been most successful at the South's edges. The most endangered outposts had been in the Border South, near the northern border.

The scare that individual slaves ignited Texas fires transpired in an intriguingly similar area, albeit this time deep in the South. Northernmost Texas combined a prime Lower South characteristic, a lush tropical river valley, with a prime Border South characteristic, hostile neighbors across the river. The Red River separated northern Texas from the so-called Indian Territory (the state of Oklahoma after 1907). Partly because of nearby Indians, the Texas side of this fertile river valley contained only around 15 percent slaves—a Border South–style pittance, despite lush Cotton Kingdom terrain.

Northern Texas slaveholders also endured an atypically wide-open Lower South culture. In this scarcely inhabited sprawl of land, strangers outnumbered residents whenever cowboys and Indians rode under the big skies. In an even more disturbing Lower South anomaly, the *Northern* Episcopal Church developed northern Texas outposts. Iowa's Reverend Solomon McKinney, for example, migrated to the so-called Cow Country in the late 1850s. The newcomer's sermons to whites stressed a Christian's responsibility to preserve blacks' marriages and to allow the Word to be preached. As for McKinney's sermons to blacks, absent whites could hear only rumors.

On August 17, 1859, the *Dallas Herald* cheered that rumors had at last inspired retaliation.[16] Texans, declared the newspaper, would no longer abide an Iowan's "impertinent and insulting instructions" about "how to manage the servants." Nor would they longer tolerate a Yankee loose in the quarters, "whether his objects be good or evil." Several public meetings had heard "ample evidence" that the supposed fanatic had "preached insurrectionary and inflammatory doctrines" to the slaves. White men's regular courts could not receive the supposedly incriminating evidence, all gathered from blacks. So we must "resort to other means to protect our lives and property."

Undemocratic strategies started with another public meeting, demanding that the preacher take his Yankee opinions back North. The Iowan responded that the Word knew no North, no South. Four "aged and responsible farmers" then went to call on the alleged incendiary. The Yankee confronted his visitors with his rifle. The inquisitors retreated to collect more vigilantes. The refortified mob captured and jailed the outsider and a supposed accomplice, one Parson Blunt.

Another mob ripped the alleged foes from prison. These vigilantes treated the two whites to a black's whipping. Lynchers then followed the humiliated, terrified Yankees to the Texas border, hooting and hollering until the supposed incendiaries fled into Indian Territory.

The two alleged white demons had deserved a black's mortification, bragged the *Herald*, after rousing "a general spirit of insubordination." The preachers had provoked docile slaves to become uppity and thus to be repeatedly flogged. By lashing and expelling the white troublemakers, we have demonstrated "that the 'Cow Country,' as our section of the State is called, is sound on the slavery question."[17]

For the following year, every time a black in Cow Country seemed unsound, blame fastened on Solomon McKinney's late Yankee preaching or on some white's contact with blacks. In February 1860, a black woman belonging to Mr. Collier allegedly thrice attempted to burn down Collier's house. Supposedly, a white foe of Collier's put her up to the arson.[18]

In July, such supposed arsons multiplied, sending shudders across Cow Country, then across the South. A scorching drought afflicted northern Texas. For over six weeks, daytime temperatures, averaging 104 degrees, peaked at 114. Wells dried up. Cornstalks drooped. Cotton plants withered. Mortgage foreclosures blossomed. And then a fierce southwestern wind blew, turning every match into a threat to consume entire frontier towns, dotted with wooden dwellings.[19]

On July 7–8, flames destroyed over half of Dallas, unofficial capital of northern Texas. The following week, blazes lit the skies every day in the countryside beyond Dallas. The next week, Austin, Gainesville, Denton, Pilot Point, Belknap, Black Jack Grove, and Henderson became charred wrecks.[20]

The circumstances invited several explanations. Sober folks knew that any white who disliked another could have won revenge with a match. Any slight accident could have also torched a city. But most communities blamed this world's prime scapegoat. Slaves, went the theory, had seized opportunities ever since Solomon McKinney had planted libertarian Christianity in gullible heads.

The mammoth drought had assuredly given restive domestics unusual opportunity. A Cuffee's single match could consume Massa's entire parched city. A single vial of strychnine could turn a town's shrinking pool of drinking water into a puddle of mass murder.

But blacks faced unprecedented dangers too. The moment any white threw up his dinner or yet another fire lit up the Cow Country, any slave might be blamed. So lynch mobs roved under the big skies. The Rust County Vigilance Committee, bragged a participant, has seized several whites, and "the jail and court house [are] full of negroes." We have [allegedly] uncovered "a deep plot" and "large quantities [of] strychnine." Slaves [supposedly] confess that traveling preachers and peddlers gave them the vials and taught them to poison the wells, torch the houses, and flee across the border. So fifty of us patrol each night, forcing strangers to "show their documents—and prove themselves sound."[21]

In Dallas, kangaroo courts ordered 147 allegedly unsound blacks flogged. In Tyler County, whites mauled four blacks with lashes, killing one. In Chapel Hill, Texas, vigilantes expelled "old man Clock" and his son. Those alleged abolitionists had been seen conversing with slaves. In Anderson County, lynch mobs hung Antney Wyrick and his cousin Alford Cable for [supposedly] "selling liquor to slaves," after "firearms and strychnine were [allegedly] found in possession" of their customers.[22]

Supposedly, Parson McKinney had planned that slaves' domestic demolition would climax while white men voted on the local election day, August 6. Instead, two-thirds of the voters stayed home to patrol their terrified neighborhoods. But vigilantes could find no one to lynch. Then the northern Texas panic collapsed, only to swell up over and over again, as Souths east of Cow Country held their elections.[23]

"These days," reported the *Savannah Republican,* "every passing breeze bears with it rumors of insurrection. . . . Every unusual sound or chance expression is tortured into some secret sign or signal." While the editor considered the "whole matter the veriest humbug" and the lynch mobs more terrifying than the supposed insurrectionists, he urged "officers to be on the alert."[24]

Alabama's Governor Andrew B. Moore kept alert. Two whites, he reported on August 30, had been arrested for slave tampering near Talladega. One had been hanged. Fayetteville citizens, having swept town stores clean of firearms, begged the governor for more; he dispatched fifty pistols. With "these occurrences . . . becoming common throughout the slaveholding states," Moore deplored visiting "Northern fanatics" who aroused "the poor misguided and deluded Negroes."[25]

Panic about allegedly deluded slaves continued to spread as Lincoln's election approached. In early September, the *Baltimore Clipper* claimed that five blacks had attempted rapes of white ladies during the previous three weeks. In early October, vigilantes in Virginia packed the Portsmouth jails with blacks and arrested other supposed incendiaries in Norfolk, Hickory Ground, and Princess Anne County.[26]

In late October in Missouri's Calloway County, an enraged slave assaulted her youthful mistress, Miss Susan Jemina Brown. The black slashed off Miss Susan's lower lip. Then the murderess smashed a fire tong against Brown's head, spewing teeth, brains, and blood all over the house. Civil authorities discovered the slave's bloody clothes while she nonchalantly worked in the field. Then an incensed mob seized the killer from officers and hanged her from the nearest tree.[27]

These Calloway County lynchers possessed, for once, undeniable evidence that a black had harmed a white (although as usual, no undeniable evidence of white provocation). Much more often, indistinct tidbits became evidence aplenty to turn frightened southern communities into paramilitary societies, as the most distressing election these Southerners had ever experienced drew near. "Not one in twenty" Yankee settlers "might tamper with our slaves," conceded George Fitzhugh. "But one man," warned Fitzhugh, "can fire a magazine, and no one can foresee when the match will be applied, or what will be the extent and consequences of the explosion."[28]

Yet distressed Southerners could create a previously nonexistent peril. James Harper Starr, one Texan who believed that few if any slaves' hands had set the horrible fires, warned that "these panics work great mischief." We "magnify" any "actual danger" by showing "the slaves that we are afraid of them." Moreover, hysterias deter needed migrants. No white stranger wants to suffer the "moments of excitement" when "Judge lynch supplants the law (an evil of greater magnitude than all others)." With "panic stricken juries and executioners (the worst as well as the best citizens taking part)," one consequence is all too possible: "innocents killed," white and black. Starr's correspondent, also writhing over undemocratic injustice, concurred that we aid the abolitionist "by exhibiting what they will consider our weakness."[29]

The corrosive weakness threw the South's precarious balance of democracy and despotism into especially dysfunctional disbalance as Lincoln's possible election approached. Five years earlier, James Hitchins, a Northerner, had come South to pursue carriage manufacturing and repairing.[30] Despite his commercial success, the Yankee faced North Carolina mobs in both 1858 and 1859. Each time, vigilantes scoured the artisan's house and found Republican literature. Each time, he told tormentors that he found Republicanism acceptable because the party did *not* urge invasion of the South. Each time, North Carolina mobs tossed the newcomer out of their town.

Hitchins finally landed in the worst state for a Lincoln fancier. In October 1860, South Carolina vigilantes, brandishing bowie knives and hanging ropes, seized him and his carriage-making son, stashed them in prison, threatened his wife, ransacked his house, and confiscated his property. When he pled for a trial under the law, vigilantes informed him that "they were their own law and would try us."

After ten days, inebriated patrolmen opened the jail door and told father and son to get out. The two Hitchinses bolted, with some mob members "threatening our lives" and the "milder ones" aiding their escape. The fugitives took to traveling at "night through woods," to "elude other gangs that were pursuing us." After many nights of terror, they reached the North, but without James's wife, their four other children, and their property. After a month, the two victims had still not heard about their loved ones.

The South's latest well-hunted fugitives, this time prospering white citizens who simply thought Lincoln would be the best president, carried with them a letter from seven "justices" on their kangaroo court. These South Carolinians certified that James Hitchins and his son had "been arrested . . . under suspicion of entertaining feelings unfriendly to the institutions of the South. We have investigated the matter thoroughly and have come to the conclusion that our suspicions were not well founded. They have been honorably discharged with the understanding that they will leave," a decree "deemed prudent from the excitement."

The discomfort of the embarrassed "judges" who found the Hitchinses not guilty, as well as the dismay of the "milder" vigilantes who helped the innocents escape, showed that this dictatorial regime, under this democratic pressure, had turned against itself. A system that separated democracy and despotism at the color line had to preserve democracy for whites and paternalism for blacks. These panics instead produced dictatorial justice for whites, antipaternalistic savaging of blacks, and no way of knowing if a single Texas black ever lit a single match.

The mysterious fires and savage justice underlined tormenting questions about Southern Republicans. What would be the ethical basis of domestic slavery, or its chance for endurance, if Lincoln appointed Southern Republicans to rule inside? What if the appointees incited constant debates over whether slavery was wrong, constant suspicions of blacks, and constant panicky injustice for both races? How indeed could black slavery be defensible in a white republic if the likes of James Hitchins and son were the fugitive slaves? Never, southern ultras such as Yancey exploded, if Republicans' agitation crept inside the South, turning the mix of democracy and slavery intolerable for both races.

– 6 –

In mid-October, William Lowndes Yancey invaded the North, in part to explain why Yankee voters must not impose intolerable conditions on the South. The Alabamian's southern opponents found his mission preposterous. How could the most insufferable disunionist bring Northerners to consider Lincoln disastrous? "If he went North for any other purpose" than offending the Northerners and thus "helping the Republicans," exclaimed northern Alabama's Jere Clemens, he must be "under the influence of a weak & childish vanity."[31]

Yancey's supposedly vain invasion of the North instead deployed his usual tactics. The extremist again went out of his way, this time hundreds of miles out of his way, to convince nonextreme folks that he would fight with them to save a tolerable Union. As always, his listeners, whether southern friends or Yankee foes, found the orator not intolerable but likable. If any southern ultra could charm Northerners out of Lincoln, William Lowndes Yancey was the enchanter.

Around the northern circle the genial extremist swept: New York's Cooper Institute on October eleventh, Boston's Faneuil Hall on the thirteenth, Syracuse on the fifteenth, Cincinnati on the twentieth. Huge crowds packed the great northern temples of liberty, usually the stage for Emerson, Thoreau, Sumner, Lincoln, and lately Frank Blair, Jr., now the arena for a southern disunionist to pray for Union. For three hours each time, Yancey entreated Yankees not to wrap "your arms around the temple of our liberties," thereby bringing "that great temple" down "on your heads as well as ours." Elect anyone except Lincoln and you save the Union. Raise up the Black Republican and you bid farewell to our nation.[32]

Yancey conceded that most Republicans sought only slavery's containment. But "carry out" that aim, "and it will necessarily follow that the institution will die out in . . . many" southern states. "In others, it will be far less valuable than it now is."[33] Moreover, if Lincoln filled southern federal offices with Republican appointees, "abolitionists would be found everywhere through the South, with strychnine to put in their wells as they were now found in Texas. . . . With the offices of the Government in the hands" of our enemy, "property would be deteriorated," with "general desolation" and "universal ruin" following.[34]

Yancey spelled out the ruinous process more completely when he returned to the South. His southern speeches reached their climax in New Orleans on the evening of October 30, a week before the election. New Orleanians loved a parade. Yancey's partisans staged the most colorful march through the Crescent City's streets since Mardi Gras. The Breckinridge Guards, the Yancey Rangers, and the Yancey Guards led the orator toward his pulpit. Bearers of torchlights, ornamental lanterns, and decorated banners pranced behind. Paraders snaked toward a huge reviewing stand, packed with 500 dignitaries, while citizens jammed Canal Street from Camp Street to St. Charles. Yancey treated the crowd to one of his greatest speeches.[35]

"The times are serious" and "the issues . . . grave," declared the orator, and we must emulate "our forefathers . . . in 1776." Some say that Lincoln will be "conservative." They mean that he will reject laws that would interfere with slavery inside southern states. But a president must appoint officers in the South, and "do not suppose that no" Southerners will "take office under Lincoln. Do not suppose that . . . no men among you . . . sympathize with him."

His officers will bring "the irrepressible conflict" seeping "through the Southern States, as water percolates through a rock." His appointees will accomplish "his object . . . without legislation. There will be free speech, as they call it, everywhere for the propagation of Abolition opinions. There will be a free press, as they call it, for the circulation of Abolition documents." There will be a "Black Republican president at Washington, to protect and encourage them." Southern Republican "numbers will soon be doubled, quadrupled,—yea, increased a hundred fold in our midst."

Since slaves torch Texas even before a Republican takes a southern office, continued Yancey, "what mischief may you . . . expect when Lincoln gets into power," even if Republicans "do not legislate at all?" We can expect, answered the Alabamian, that "slave property in Kentucky, and Maryland, and Virginia, and Missouri, would become worthless, by intimidation, by fear, and by other causes." After "the abolition of slavery" in the "border states, . . . the whole South would" become "another St. Domingo or Jamaica." Republicans are already "coming over the border." Look "at John Minor Botts of Virginia, Cassius M. Clay of Kentucky, F. P. Blair of Missouri." Look at the "foundation in the Southern States on which these men stand." Give these heretics "your closest attention, if you wish" to know "the position, power, and aims of the [Republican] party."

As Yancey brought to climax the South's summer of suspicion, torchlights lit up the New Orleans skies, unnervingly like the blazes lately ascending in Cow Country. The South's most fiery disunionists could almost feel, as Albert Gallatin Brown warned in Mississippi, "the stealthy tread" of Black Republicans marching among us.[36]

– 7 –

Lincoln's march to Electoral College victory seems inevitable to posterity. But at the time, the Republican's triumph seemed more uncertain, not least to Yancey and to Robert Barnwell Rhett. Because of disunionists' uncertainty, their secessionist campaign did not begin until mid-October. The resulting short prerevolutionary period provided a crucial atmosphere of rush.

Before the revolutionary haste, revolutionaries wondered whether Lincoln could capture almost every northern state, his only way to procure the required majority of Electoral College votes. If Lincoln fell short in the Electoral College, the House of Representatives, voting by states, would select the president. With just under 50 percent of the states, the South would exert more leverage than in the Electoral College, where the slaveholding states wielded just under 40 percent of the votes.

As if to confirm contemporaries' sense of uncertainty, Lincoln ultimately won an arguably thin Electoral College victory.[37] True, despite losing all southern and three northern electoral votes, the Republican secured 180 Electoral College ballots, a robust twenty-eight more than he needed for his Electoral College majority. Lincoln also gathered a decisive 54 percent of the northern popular vote (although only 40 percent of the nation's voters).

Still, if Lincoln had lost California, Oregon, Illinois, and Indiana, the House of Representatives would have elected the president. The Republican would have fallen short in the Electoral College if 378 Californians, plus 578 Oregonians, plus 5979 Illinoisans, plus 11,763 Indianans had switched their votes from Lincoln to Douglas. Since this 5 percent of Lincoln voters in these four states could have overturned the Lincoln bandwagon, Southerners may well have given Lincoln his decisive momentum. Because Southerners split the National Democracy, Douglas lost the aura of the last national party. The Little Giant thus became less attractive to the few extra Yankee voters that he needed in order to throw the election into the House of Representatives' hands. This southern contribution to Lincoln's victory was fitting, for the South's aggressive defensiveness had precipitated the events (Dred Scott, Lecompton, and proposals for Caribbean expansion and African slave trade opening) that had undermined James Buchanan's slim 1856 victory.

Nothing was slim about the North's 1860 rejection of Slave Power aggressive defensiveness. From many Southerners' perspective, Douglas's Freeport Doctrine, declaring that territorial legislatures could abolish slavery (by doing nothing), was as pernicious as Lincoln's doctrine, affirming that Congress could halt slavery's expansion (by decreeing territorial abolition). Yet the two Illinoisans together received 89.6 percent of northern popular votes, with John C. Breckinridge collecting only 8.2 percent and John Bell only 2.2 percent of the Yankee tally.

For a quarter century, Southerners had shown how minorities dominate majoritarian processes. The overwhelmingly anti–Slave Power North had now shown how an awakened majority routs a minority. Could the minority now show how to secede from the majority?

– 8 –

The presidential election results demonstrated that secessionists faced towering obstacles. Almost all disunionists favored Kentucky's John Breckinridge. Yet the Southern Democrats' presidential candidate secured less than half the Southerners' ballots. Breckinridge's approximately 44 percent of southern popular votes hardly drowned out the around 40 percent for the Constitutional Unionists' (and Tennessee's) John Bell. Meanwhile, circa 16 percent of southern voters preferred Douglas or Lincoln to either Southerner.

The Little Giant, lately the focus of southern rage, won one in seven southern popular votes. Douglas also swept up embattled Missouri's Electoral College votes. How Austin King did love his state's vindication. How William L. Yancey, John Clark, and Davy Atchison did loathe Missouri's statement.

As the Missouri outcome showed, the farther northward in the South, the more Breckinridge's appeal drooped. The Kentucky Democrat won all the Lower South's Electoral College votes and 56 percent of its popular votes (to Bell's 34.7 percent). In the Upper South, however, where two of every three southern whites resided, Bell won thirty-nine Electoral College votes (to Breckinridge's twenty-five) and 43 percent of the popular votes (to Breckinridge's 39.7 percent). Breckinridge barely won the Middle South (where he secured 46.7 percent of the popular votes to Bell's 45.2 percent). The Southern Democrat decisively lost the Border South (where Bell received 40.6 percent of the popular votes to Breckinridge's 31.9 percent).

Nor did Breckinridge's strength in the Lower South necessarily portend imminent secessionist victory in that most enslaved region. In the fall campaign, Breckinridge's positions aimed as little at disunion as Bell's and only a little more at proslavery agitation. Breckinridge campaigned atop not secession but Jefferson Davis's formula that Congress should protect slavery, only if later necessary. Breckinridge trusted "that the time may never come" when the federal government need "interfere for the protection" of our rights.[38] After Lincoln's election, Breckinridge would deny that the time had come for secession. After the Civil War commenced, he would deny for months that the time had come for Kentucky to renounce its neutrality.

Breckinridge could thus attract the many Lower South moderates who always had been Democrats and never had been for secession. He could also attract the extremists who considered Breckinridge's form of southern moderation at least a lesser evil than Bell's. While Breckinridge kept putting the time for agitation into the future, Bell kept insisting that no proslavery agitation had ever been necessary. The Breckinridge vote proved that a large majority of Lower South voters wished to agitate for their rights, not that the majority wished to agitate for disunion. Breckinridge's less than half of southern votes also indicated that no Southwide majority even desired proslavery agitation.

Southern Democrats derided Bell's nonagitation position as a dangerous insistence on saying nothing about the very issue that must be discussed. To Yancey, Bell smacked of the emperor who thought himself "incapable of doing anything for the good of Rome." The hapless fellow "went to his room and picked up a fiddle, and fiddled while Rome burned." Well, not just Texas towns but the Union was now afire, and "Bell would tinkle, tinkle, tinkle. My friends, this is no time for tinkling bells."[39]

Unfortunately for the ridiculer, many southern moderates preferred tinkling bells to crashing alarms. They thought that alarmists had too long been spreading crises rather than saving slavery in such doomed antics as the Kansas caper. They feared that an unnecessary civil war would imminently destroy their beloved Union. They worried that other people's fruitless battles would be fought on their farmlands. Slavery was precisely what they did *not* wish to speak about.

John Bell was their perfect spokesman. If his mind worked ponderously, if his speeches sounded sluggish, if his face and figure looked ordinary, those attributes provided the ideal wet blanket. He had earned the right to tell agitators to cool off with his accurate record of predicting, before every proslavery effort and especially the Kansas hijinks, that hot fury would yield icy disappointment for the South and disaster for the Union. Now, to secessionists' dismay, John Breckinridge's only somewhat warmer attitude toward proslavery agitation had secured only eleven out of every twenty-five southern votes, to ten for tinkle, tinkle, tinkle—and four for the Douglas-Lincoln insistence on no proslavery tinkling at all.

To secessionists' even greater dismay, the election tally showed that Lincoln's forces had established a beachhead inside John Bell's Border South stronghold. None of Lincoln's 26,375 southern votes came from the Lower South and only 1887 from the Middle South (all in extreme northwestern Virginia). But the Republican captured 5.8 percent of Border South popular votes, including 10.3 percent of Missourians' ballots and 23.7 percent of Delawareans' choices. An incrementally swelling Southern Republican Party already existed in these two Border South states, even before the president-elect started handing out that sustenance for party, local patronage offices. The Blair family, having delivered key convention votes for Lincoln's nomination and then one in ten of Missourians' popular ballots, had earned a rich patronage banquet.

Yancey had lately described the consequences of such feasting amidst the flickering New Orleans torchlights. He had instructed his October listeners that now was the time "to show your love for the Union" by preparing your ballots. "After the Lincoln party is elected, . . . you will be called to show your love by preparing your rifles."[40] But after Yankee presidential candidates had secured almost one in six southern votes, and after John Bell had collected two in five votes for nonagitation, and with so many of the South's only 44 percent of Breckinridge voters, including Breckinridge himself, still against disunion, secessionists looked incapable of rallying a Southwide majority for Yancey's riflemen, at least before a civil war commenced.

Then again, secessionists would need no sectionwide majority to commence a departure from the Union, any more than Yancey had needed a majority of southern delegates to commence a departure from the Charleston convention. Back at the time Texas fires had swirled out of control, David Boyd, a professor at the precursor of Louisiana State University, had unhappily prophesied how a minority of the southern minority might begin a revolution. "Disunion might be brought about in many ways," Professor Boyd had warned. "In many places in the South, whoever accepts or holds offices under Lincoln will be lynched." The new president "will of course attempt to enforce the laws; that attempt will be resisted; and once the strife is begun, God only knows where it will stop."[41]

The professor's crystal ball slightly befogged the climactic scenario. But this Virginian turned Louisianan accurately foresaw that a minority of Southerners, provoked by Lincoln's imminent patronage appointments, could start a disruption that the majority could not stop. Still, some one state would have to begin a minority revolution. South Carolina, the most likely beginner, had often shuddered to go first. Would the state this time dare?

PART VI

SOUTH CAROLINA DARES

Just as the Old South's civilization encompassed several different cultures, so the southern secession decision involved several different decisions. The verdicts occurred in sequential order and changed as the sequence unfolded. By far the most important of the evolving disunion decisions, not least because it came first, occurred in South Carolina. Despite the speed and unanimity of that precipitous state's first strike, uncertainty momentarily overcame the necessary daring. South Carolinians' paralyzing nervousness created a suspenseful climactic moment, with some fleeting conspiracy and some perfectly timed luck helping the first rebels to dare the plunge.

CHAPTER 22

The State's Rights Justification

In 1860, a democratic obstacle blocked disunionists' path. Revolution had to be won at the ballot box, not by a coup d'état. Yet most southern voters desired proof that Lincoln's presidency would menace slavery. They doubted that Republicans could secure an overt act against their Peculiar Institution. They realized that the party would lack a congressional or Supreme Court majority. They cheered the *New Orleans Bee*'s one-word response to Lincoln's election: "WAIT."[1]

– 1 –

Many procrastinators wished to wait for years, perhaps forever, until Republicans committed an overt antislavery act. Others would hesitate only for months, until a southern convention met and Republicans rejected its ultimatum. No formal or informal poll demonstrated the size of the initial majority for "WAIT." Nor did any vote demonstrate how many delayers favored only temporary hesitation.

But those in favor of awaiting either a southern convention's failure or a Republican overt act, taken together, had to exceed 70 percent of southern citizens. In the Upper South, where two-thirds of white Southerners resided, secessionists lost prewar ballot tests by an average of four to one (counting Border and Middle South voters together). Disunionists might have even lost an early November Lower South referendum, if all Cotton South states had voted on the same day. Immediately after Lincoln's election, a majority of Georgia, Louisiana, Texas, and Alabama voters possessed grave qualms about immediate disunion.

But in early November, while an overwhelming Southwide majority doubted the expediency of disunion, an even larger majority affirmed a state's right to secede. If secessionists in just one state could secure a majority for the expediency of revolution, and if the federal government coercively

345

denied that one state's supposedly natural right to withdraw its consent to be governed, many southern states might join their coerced brothers. Thus could the secessionists' state's rights justification help swell an initial minority of uneasy rebels into an awesome majority of zealous revolutionaries.

– 2 –

Secessionists' potentially saving state's rights creed started as a legalistic bore. The 1860 secessionists (and their fathers and grandfathers) had grown up listening to endless disquisitions on how the states came before the nation, on how the states had ratified the U.S. Constitution, on how the ratifying bodies retained reserved rights and especially the right to withdraw their ratification, and on how the original parties to a contract can rescind the document if its terms are violated. South Carolina's John C. Calhoun had especially labored (or if you will, lumbered) over a state's legal right to secede. Confederate President Jefferson Davis and Vice President Alexander Stephens would return to such legalistic hairsplitting in their postwar memoirs.

But Calhoun, having died a decade before disunion, could be only partly the father of secession theory. His bloodless legalisms could not wholly overcome the disunity of the South. Daniel Webster's unionist argument that the nation came before the states could be a convincing answer. Worse, tired legalisms dulled attention.

Disunionists needed instead an inspiring justification of a state's holy right to secede, one that aroused cheers even among antisecessionists. In the tradition of 1776—in the (white) people of any single state's natural right to withdraw consent to be governed—disunionists found their stirring state's rights dogma. "Secession is pretty hard to comprehend," wrote a young Virginian. "But we all know the meaning of *Revolution!*"[2]

Some 1860 legalistic disquisitions on a state's right of secession never mentioned any natural right of revolution. More often, secessionists' state's rights justification mixed natural right with legal right. In a classic example, Louisiana's U.S. Senator Judah P. Benjamin told fellow senators that a state held dual rights to secede. "The rights of the states under the Constitution," declared Benjamin the lawyer, resulted "from the nature of their bargain." If "sister states" break "the bargain," the "breach of compact" invites injured states to "consider themselves freed" from the original contract. Yet even "if the bargain be not broken," added this advocate of southern independence, if "wrong and oppression shall become sufficiently aggravated, the revolutionary right—the last inherent right of man to preserve freedom, property, and safety . . . must be exercised."[3]

Unlike Benjamin, most 1860 justifiers of disunion ignored the bore of contracts and stressed the thrill of 1776. In his Inaugural Address as president of the Southern Confederacy, Jefferson Davis insisted that "the sovereign States" had "merely asserted the right which the Declaration of Independence" declared "inalienable."[4] So too, Professor James P. Holcombe reminded Virginia's secession convention of "the right of the people to change their government peacefully, whenever they become dissatisfied."[5]

To deny the people of a state their right of revolution, secessionists claimed, was to repudiate Americans' most original contribution to republican theory. English republican theorists had located the magic power of sovereignty, meaning the uncontestable power to issue the final unchallengeable command, inside the government. In contrast, American late eighteenth-century theorists separated the sovereign from the government. Sovereignty lay in the people, when exercising their authority to make or unmake governments. When the sovereign withdrew its consent to be governed, governance must cease.

The right of the governed to consent to government stemmed from universal natural right, possessed by all peoples at all time. In contrast, the people of a single state's exclusive right to exercise that natural right drew on parochial historical experience, shared only by U.S. citizens since 1776. Here, Calhoun's old legalisms did become newly important. As the South Carolina Nullifier had stressed, the people of each colony had withdrawn their consent from English governance. Then the people of each state had switched their consent to be governed from the Articles of Confederation to the U.S. Constitution. So it had always been, affirmed secessionists. Therefore, so it must always be.

Secessionists here descended from the breathless claim that all mankind could exercise a universal natural right, whatever a parochial culture's experience, to the crabbed plea that only a state could exercise all humans' right, because of America's provincial experience. Disunionists thereby fractured natural rights logic but escaped a quagmire. If all humans could deploy a natural right to change their consent to be governed, wives could withdraw consent from husbands, children from parents, slaves from masters, western Virginians from Virginia. Such multiplying withdrawals could demolish all governance. Abolitionists' fanaticism, Southerners claimed, would produce exactly that anarchistic nightmare.

State's rights precluded the nightmare. By claiming that a state's popular convention (or a state's popular referendum) could alone exercise the right to withdraw consent, the slavocracy handed a sovereign's invincible decree only to the right males of the right race in the right place. In the Lecompton finale of the Kansas crisis, as we have seen, this southern gospel stopped Howell Cobb (and thus James Buchanan) cold. Cobb could merely *suggest* that the almighty Kansas Lecompton Convention should submit its constitution to a popular referendum. A cabinet secretary, even if bearing the wishes of a president on a matter of life or death to the republic, remained a mere governmental agent. The underling could never tell a people's absolutely sovereign state convention what to do. So too, if the sovereign exercised its state's right to tell the federal agency to stop governing, the government must halt.

– 3 –

No believer in republicanism can renounce all claims that a people have a natural right to switch their consent to be governed. The sacrosanct principle justified the American Revolution and continues to justify national severances that Americans applaud. As these words are written, the separation of ethnic groups, each to consent to their own nation, seems an ideal solution in the former Yugoslavia and may become the best solution in Iraq. But the circumstances of the secessionists' claim made their natural rights justification problematic—and overwhelming only to those who experienced the black belt.

Americans usually agree with Lincoln that the right to withdraw consent has to be balanced against election winners' right to rule the losers, unless the winners violate citizens' natural rights. The southern revolution was profoundly a preventative strike, to preclude natural rights violations that had not yet occurred.[6] The largest menace precluded was a perfectly republican debate in the South over slavery. The feared orchestrators of the debate would have been Southern Republicans, assuming office for the perfectly republican reason that the winners have a right to govern with their own governors. The largest reasons Southern Republicans were feared included their perfectly republican right to convince Border South nonslaveholders and the perfectly republican consequence that their democratic agitation might arouse some slaves to seek *their* right to withdraw their consent to be governed. Thus most Americans who lived outside plantation areas, including Northerners and most Border South citizens, challenged a state's right to withdraw consent just because an election had been lost.

Conversely, black belt circumstances made a state's right to withdraw consent overwhelmingly convincing, even to those who wished state secession conventions would WAIT. Southerners' political religion of consent, like all sacred faiths, had its practical side. If all other proslavery defenses failed, a state could withdraw consent from an abolitionist government, and before that government's agents could wreak internal chaos. But practicality aside, the right to consent to be governed held emotional sway over whites in black belts, for no other concept lifted the citizen so irretrievably beyond the slave.

Masters supposedly had every right to coerce black serviles without the underlings' consent. But governments allegedly had no right to dictate to white citizens without equals' consent. To be ruled without consent was to be reduced to a slave. Few white males in black belts could tolerate that humiliation.

Because enslavement without consent troubled slaveholders, they demanded a charade of consent from their slaves. Nowhere else in the Americas did owners persistently require Cuffees to pretend to love their masters, in homecoming or Christmas performances. No master who cherished such charades could tolerate a government that coerced nonconsenting citizens.

Nor could nonslaveholders who lived near slaves abide federal tyrants, clubbing down unconsenting whites as if the coerced were blacks.

Among white males in black belts, the psychological compulsion to defend consent closely resembled the emotional rage to sustain equality. To live in egalitarian America in the neighborhood of coerced slaves was to go wild if Yankees used slurs or pistols to force whites into unequal servility. Slavery as a social system invaded the marrow of southern personality, and never more so than when federal agents coercively violated the (white) people of a state's sovereign right to shift consent to another government.

– 4 –

Defense of *that* state's right *did* help secession to spread past the first seceders, despite much latter-day disparaging of a state's rights explanation of why disunion triumphed.[7] Nothing else so clearly explains why the mass of black belt whites, while initially considering Lincoln's prewar menace to black slavery to be dubious, eventually considered Lincoln's wartime menace to whites' consent to be monstrous. The problem comes when latter-day state's rights enthusiasts confuse a state's right to withdraw its consent to be governed at all, at the moment of disunion, and a state's right to oppose particular acts of national governance, before disunion. Calhoun's Nullifiers of the 1830s, seeking to negate a particular tariff act and yet to remain under the government's sway, tried and failed to obliterate this distinction.

Nullifiers' failure became slaveholders' blessing. According to Calhoun and his Nullifiers, if a state won the right to negate nationalistic tariff legislation, a state would thereby gain the right to void nationalistic slavery decrees. But after the tariff issue faded, Southerners sought not to stop but to gain nationalistic slavery decrees, to secure nationalistic slavery protections. So in the 1850s, Southerners usually became the nationalists and Northerners the state's righters on slavery issues inside the Union.[8] Southerners became rigid state's righters only on a state's right to withdraw consent from all the Union's laws, not on a state's right to hinder particular national laws.

Thus Southerners broke up the National Democratic Party in 1860 over their alleged right to national protection of territorial slavery, if local protection failed. Some Southern Democrats also wanted to use national power to annex the Caribbean, just as national power had annexed Texas (after a very loose constitutional excursion around the necessity to ratify treaties by two-thirds majorities). But the Old South's high nationalism, when it came to using protective national laws inside the Union, reached its apogee, as did the North's use of state's rights, in fugitive slave confrontations.

In their so-called Personal Liberty Laws, Northerners often deployed state governmental decrees to thwart national fugitive slave laws. Almost all the notorious Yankee rescues of fugitive slaves, often employing a northern state's antinational Personal Liberty Laws, occurred in the early 1850s, when the Fugitive Slave Law of 1850 seemed a fresh Slave Power outrage. But the most unforgettable incident, transpiring closer to the secession crisis, destroyed any illusion that the presecession South found anything holy about state's rights, except a state's sacred right to secede.

One of the greatest American novels keeps the incident vivid in American memories. Toni Morrison's *Beloved* transforms into fictional form the real-life story of a fugitive slave murderess.[9] In January 1856, the actual twenty-two-year-old slave, Margaret Garner, fled from Boone County (in northern-most Kentucky) with her four children, her husband, and his parents. The extended family rode over the snow in a large horse-drawn sled, over the eighteen miles from Margaret's master's plantation, Maplewood, to Coving-ton, Kentucky, on the Ohio River. Then three generations of Garners walked across the icy river to Cincinnati and to freedom.

Liberty swiftly perished, as did the intact family. The master, Archibald Gaines, discovered that his vanished property hid in Margaret Garner's cousin's Cincinnati cabin. When deputy U.S. marshals burst into the cabin, Margaret seized a razor-sharp knife, akin to the killing blades on John Brown's pikes. With a sweep of the razor, she slit her three-year-old daugh-ter's throat ear to ear, nearly decapitating the slain child. Better to sever a throat, her defiance screamed, than to allow Massa Gaines to dirty my child back on the plantation. Margaret then went after her other children with a coal shovel, to remove them too from a slave's misery. But the murderess suc-ceeded only in slicing her sons' skin before horrified authorities wrestled her down.

While Margaret Garner languished in jail, Ohio's prosecutors claimed that a state's exclusive right to try a murderess superseded the federal obli-gation to return human property. If Ohio established a state's higher right, the northern state's murder trial would explore whether southern filth had driven a mother to infanticide. According to rumors in Cincinnati, Margaret might claim that her master had raped her, siring the child that she had saved from his clutches. An outraged jury might free the murderess. An outraged community might speed Massa Gaines's freed property to Canada.

Margaret Garner's master did not want her claims aired. His lawyers ar-gued that the national fugitive slave law took precedence over a state's right to try a murderess. In the courts, the master and national power won. The slave and state's rights lost. The federal government conveyed the murderess back to Kentucky, whereupon her master sold her downriver to Lower South slavery.

In Toni Morrison's masterful *Beloved,* Margaret Garner becomes Sethe. Sethe's almost decapitated daughter becomes Beloved, returned as a ghost many years later to haunt the murderess. Beloved also haunts all other blacks in Sethe's community, who shudderingly remember the ghastly act and the Peculiar Institution that yielded such horror. Morrison's ghost story thus carries the message that slavery's legacy lived on past its nineteenth-century times, to prey on latter-day American memories.

Sethe, alias Margaret Garner, must haunt memories of those who think that antebellum Southerners routinely supported state's rights. The image of that defiant fugitive slave, wielding the knife (in her mind) mercifully, epitomizes the runaways who would not be reduced to Cuffees—who belied their powerlessness by forcing their masters to war against routine state's rights. The blood showering Margaret Garner's cousin's cabin, bespattering the latest slave family divided, also epitomized the slaveholders' prewar sense of state's rights gone Yankee and crazy.

Against a northern state's supposed right to defy national fugitive laws, slaveholders had used the National Democratic Party to turn the national state into a nationalistic policeman. Southerners who wielded national power had seized Margaret Garner from northern state's righters' hands, before Archibald Gaines's purse, honor, and reputation had been emptied. So too, the South's use of the national state had for years kept slavery protected in Kansas Territory. By sustaining slavery with the national government, southern moderates had kept disunionists at bay. But now the National Democratic Party lay in ruins; disunionists marched to the fore; and a very different form of state's rights could sustain the ultras.

By raising state's rights to the highest plane, having nothing to do with such lowly matters as tariffs or banks or internal improvements or fugitive slaves or territorial laws, secessionists in any one state could deploy a people's towering elevation over all governmental agents. If the federal agency coerced the people of a single state who had claimed their state's right to remove their consent and never to be enslaved, the state's rights justification could bring other southern states charging to the rescue, whatever they thought of the expediency of the first secession. But an initially lonely southern majority in a single state still had to be highly motivated, to dare rest its fate on the state's rights justification.

CHAPTER 23

The Motivation

South Carolina, always the state most motivated to secede first, always trembled at the danger facing the initiator. Three decades of bad revolutionary memories, atop this oligarchy's long-standing peculiarities, fed these paralyzing apprehensions.

– 1 –

The nullification events of 1832–33 had initiated the sour memories. A South Carolina state convention had declared the federal tariffs of 1828 and 1832 null and void inside the state. If the limited federal agency defied the unlimited sovereign convention, Nullifiers had warned, South Carolina would secede.

The president of the supposed mere federal agency, Andrew Jackson, smothered the threat. Jackson maneuvered so brilliantly that the whole South massed against the Nullifiers. South Carolinians could only stop tariff enforcement with precipitous aggressions, repelling fellow Southerners even more. So South Carolinians backed down from their threatened secession, succumbed to a tariff compromise, and forever folded their nullification tent.[1]

Again and again thereafter, South Carolinians threatened to secede, then remembered the horror of dangling alone, then shrank from their thrust. South Carolina's especially reactionary mentality impelled both the advances and the retreats. Haughty gentlemen, frozen in Anglo-American assumptions a century past, longed to revolt against the new supposed mobocracy and its threat to slavery. At the same time, old-fashioned gentlemen longed to avert revolutionary disorder. Few other ardent revolutionaries have been so terrified of revolution, or so ashamed of their terror, or so aching to seize a destiny that they shuddered to grasp. No other southern squires had charged and retreated so often that they winced at their sputtering selves.[2]

No North American habitat compared with the fertile, fatal South Carolina coast in potential to nourish quaint reactionaries. On South Carolina's edge of the Atlantic Ocean, the tides force dark, dank water some twenty miles into lush, rank wetlands. Colonial South Carolina titans forced large armies of slaves to build dams and sluices, to master nature's pump. The resulting hydraulic achievement helped sustain luxuriously long grains of rice. Simultaneously, huge slave gangs coaxed a luxuriously long cotton fiber, akin to silk, from the fecund Sea Island soil off the coast.

Only coercive slavery could have wrenched tens of thousands of eighteenth-century workers into malarial swamps to raise these unusual products. No other southern region, save for the more confined Georgia coastal swamps, encouraged these crops. No other southern squires owned such expensive acres with such sophisticated improvements or such enormous concentrations of slaves. In 1860, the tiny parishes strung along the South Carolina coast contained a population 80 percent enslaved (compared to an average of 47 percent in the Lower South). Coastal slaveholdings averaged over forty slaves per master (compared to under thirteen in the Lower South). Of southern slaveholders with over 500 slaves, half lived on this sliver of ocean-enriched terrain.

Beyond the state, most nineteenth-century southern titans found coastal South Carolinians' eighteenth-century aristocratic republican viewpoint as odd as the swamp locale. Lowcountry grandees, perhaps the richest late eighteenth-century North Americans, inhaled their proslavery assumptions a half century before the Old South defended slavery. More often than somewhat less wealthy Virginia and Maryland planters, Revolutionary Era lowcountry squires traveled and studied in England. There they savored England's landed elite's noblesse oblige.

English country gentlemen bestowed direction on everyone who lived on their acres, including white tenants. English squires considered their racially unlimited paternalistic ideal to be as cultivated, as civilized, as beautiful as the flowers in their perfectly weeded gardens. By wielding benevolence from above, they sought smiling local communities, weeded of resentments, whether prickly or murderous.

Almost all U.S. Founding Fathers, North and South, admired that English republican ideal. Late eighteenth-century American rulers believed that the best men must govern and lesser men of all colors (and females) must defer. The rich and powerful favored property qualifications for white adult males, whether to vote or to hold office. Wealthy gentlemen sought extra representatives for wealthier districts. They deplored political parties and demagogic electioneering. The Founding Fathers' aristocratic republicanism relied precisely on Fathers—well-born, well-educated, well-heeled patriarchs—to bring good order and good sense to a flock that extended far past their gates.

In contrast, most Civil War–era U.S. slaveholding establishments came to power two decades into the nineteenth century, after the nation's dominant ideology, North and South, had swerved from aristocratic to egalitarian (white) republicanism. Instead of poorer (white) men voting and richer patriarchs deciding, all white males became equal decision makers. The new (white male) egalitarian ideal inspired universal white male suffrage, low if any property qualifications for office, few if any extra representatives for rich districts, two mass national parties, and demagogic appeals to commoners to dictate the nation's policies.

Newcomers plastered this dominant nouveau mentality on all areas of the oldest South except coastal South Carolina. The colonial Upper South world of Delaware, Maryland, Virginia, and North Carolina contained huge geographic areas that planters avoided. Nonslaveholders, including many migrants from the free labor North, relished these widespread slaveless or lightly enslaved Upper South domains. In the early and mid-nineteenth century, alien migrants forced more egalitarian state governments on the elderly aristocracy. But the crusty South Carolina gentry, with practically their whole state a potential plantation region, faced much lighter egalitarian demands; and the aristocracy dominated far larger slave gangs.

Despite their defiance of the new (as they saw it) political barbarism, South Carolina reactionaries made one timely concession to crass populism. In 1810, even before other southern states succumbed to mobocratic suffrage, South Carolinians allowed all white male adults, except paupers, to vote. They then barred all other elements of white male egalitarianism from their elitist republican government. In South Carolina alone, service in the state's nineteenth-century House of Representatives required property worth at least ten slaves plus 500 acres. Tenure in the State Senate required a doubled fortune. Residence in the governor's mansion required another five times more holdings.

In 1860, no other southern legislature remained so malapportioned against one white man, one vote. South Carolina's coastal parishes, with under a tenth of the state's whites, controlled over a third of the House's seats and almost half of the Senate's. The skewed legislature elected the governor (everywhere else elected by the people) as well as the state's U.S. senators (as was true in all other states) and presidential electors (as was true in no other state).

The aristocratic legislature also usually made the policy decisions, without asking voters first (commonplace everywhere else). South Carolina's upperclass republicans usually scuttled popular parties (dominant everywhere else). Lowcountry patriarchs almost always scorned presentation of issues to voters (standard everywhere else). When asked what his constituents thought about an issue, Representative Daniel Huger exclaimed, "Think! They will think nothing about it. They expect me to think for them *here*." Or as James Hamilton, Jr., expressed South Carolina's unique continuing paternalistic prerogative in *white* government, "The people expect that their leaders in whose . . . public spirit they have confidence will think for them—and that they will be prepared to *act* as their leaders *think*."[3]

Such colorblind paternalistic attitudes violated color-exclusive paternalism elsewhere in the mid-nineteenth-century South. Beyond South Carolina, allegedly superior white males only defended the necessity of thinking for supposedly inferior blacks (and white females plus children). Any (white) Tom, Dick, or Harry, soared the wealthy Andrew Jackson, could equally govern. South Carolina elitists retorted that (white men's) egalitarian republicanism erred in its fundamental premise: that all white men were equal. Some white men were more wealthy, more intelligent, more mature, more educated than others. White republics, together with lesser white nonslaveholders and still lesser white women and still lesser white children, continued to need patriarchal guidance, albeit a dominion short of the total paternalistic direction that still lesser black slaves required.

Short of slavery. South Carolina colorblind paternalism did not require George Fitzhugh's politically suicidal path to colorblind slavery. Nor did colorblind paternalism require the Fitzhugh folly that dogs or horses or humans must be owned to elicit benevolent guidance. Instead, wise patriarchs should calibrate the degree of paternalism over inferior folks *not* owned to subjects' degree of inferiority. This calibrated, colorblind, upper-class paternalism helped make South Carolina patriarchs' rage against white men's egalitarian Union peculiarly intense.[4]

To reemphasize that slavery was but the unlimited form of the more limited paternalism that all lessers (and all republics) needed, South Carolina elitist republicans denied that boundless paternalism should even be called slavery. William Gilmore Simms, South Carolina's favorite novelist, urged "that our Institution was not slavery, at all, in the usual" sense "of the term, which implies some wrong done to the party." The Charleston preacher James Warley Miles invented the squires' favorite term for slavery without wrong: "so-called slavery." Under so-called slavery, Simms wrote (and Miles agreed), a black is a "minor, under guardianship." The ward has "forfeited no right." A "representative master" must protect a slave's "rights and privileges," including blacks' rights to keep families intact and to enjoy full access to Christ.[5]

In every aspect of life, lowcountry squires guarded eighteenth-century patriarchal ideals against nineteenth-century egalitarian realities. Paternalistic rulers aimed to squeeze the wrongs out of slavery, leach the demagoguery out of mobocracy, and purge the materialism out of capitalism. Instead of corrupting the making of money, they would perfect the art of living. Like those revered Englishmen a half century before, lowcountry paternalists would make relationships on their estates and in their neighborhoods as lovely as their houses, their furniture, their wines, their paintings, and the poets who celebrated their triumphs over brutalities.

Yet despite their claim to transcend all other Americans, including all other Southerners, in ousting brutishness from their realm, no other Southerners felt savagery to be so uncomfortably close. Few coastal titans could see a neighbor's white face. Pools of water, inked pitch-black by towering cypress, plus forests of live oak, drooping with eerie Spanish moss, severed white specks of lowcountry folk from each other. Nor did anything white seem to dilute slaves' blackness. No other area sustained so few mulattoes or so African a slave culture or so non-American a Gullah dialect. Nowhere else did malarial mosquitoes impel masters to flee their country estates from early spring to late fall.

After patriarchs' flight, their neighborhoods became 90 percent black. On some plantations, the percentage reached 100. Rather than hire inexperienced white overseers, rich white escapees often preferred to allow experienced black slaves, with a lifetime of mastering the intricate dams and sluices, to master the slaves too. In this semiannual upper-class abdication, patriarchs became fugitives from slaves, and (white) runaways depended on supposedly racially inferior black managers to save their civilization from savagery.

After the killing frosts, when the fugitives, alias the planters, returned home to reclaim their paternalistic obligations, their preachers warned them, almost every Sunday, that slavery remained short of so-called slavery. Until they allowed dependents access to the Word and until they protected slave families from separation, they practiced not an unlimited form of colorblind paternalism but an unseemly example of unchristian exploitation. So too, some of their slaves told them, with surly looks and unsettling sabotages, that the lash must replace non-Cuffees' nonexistent consent. Hostile slaves had obviously neither "voted" for "representative masters," nor affirmed that "so-called slavery" had replaced slavery, nor demonstrated that whites had nothing to fear from blacks.

So too, masters' account books told them that slaves in deadly swamps often succumbed to savage fevers (especially the black children). Far-off miasmatic fields (especially far off from absentee planters), and hundreds of slaves (too many sometimes even to know everyone's name) also mocked their claim to personal direction. Above all else, gentlemen uncomfortably imagined how these supposedly impressionistic inferiors might ambush Big House folk if freed or if allowed to hear incendiary propaganda. Would-be paternalists' swamps, source of their supposed power to salvage eighteenth-century civilization, came not just shadowed by giant trees draped with spectral moss but also darkened by specters of nineteenth-century chaos, right around history's corner.

– 2 –

Would-be English country gentlemen felt more comfortable in their favorite city. Their annual evacuation of swamp estates most often led to six-month encampments in barricaded Charleston mansions. Their telltale town fortresses revealingly contrasted with the unshielded houses in another planter town haven: Natchez, Mississippi.

Mississippi River sugar and cotton planters built Natchez's grand houses during the age of the Southwest's economic explosion, 1835–60. Nouveau riche Mississippi gentlemen lavished little extravagance on their mansions' interiors. The mantels, moldings, and furniture looked massive, Victorian, and heavy-handed. Natchez's lilting external façades, in contrast, delicately impressed. The white Greek-columned mansions, usually perfectly balanced and sometimes columned on all four sides, displayed the Old South's most advanced aesthetic sensibility. Few towering stucco walls inhibited the view from the street. This aristocracy wished its Greek extravagance to be admired outside.

Natchez planters seldom lingered inside their newly built displays. They actively managed healthy nearby plantations. These nineteenth-century tycoons remained too enterprising, too prosperous, too optimistic to obsess on racial nightmares, or on secessionist fantasies, or on concealing themselves behind a veneer of eighteenth-century civilization.

Concealment epitomized decaying Charleston. Most of the city's best houses had been built not on the eve of the Civil War but in the wake of the American Revolution. Charleston's best creators, newly rich late eighteenth-century squires, had cherished not ancient Greece but contemporary England. They had lavished cash not on columns that commoners could see from the street but on reception rooms a floor above the avenue, where only fellow aristocrats could be seen. They had filled their second-story drawing rooms with mantels patterned after Robert Adam designs, with plaster-cast moldings, carved interior doors, and papier-mâché ceilings that also graced a midlevel English country gentleman's dwelling. They had imported their eighteenth-century Chippendale furniture from London or commissioned exact copies from craftsmen such as Thomas Elfe, their best (and a superb) carver of imported mahogany.

Out of doors, however, only a fraction of their houses' façades aped Georgian England. This handful of their finest eighteenth-century dwellings, so-called double houses, displayed long brick front façades on the street side. The entrance hall separated two perfectly balanced rooms (hence "double" houses). The front door, centering the street façade, stood atop several stairs. Its rich carving displayed pomp on a public stage. No wall prevented commoners from gaping at this English Georgian extravagance. Instead, elaborate iron fences, with gaps between murderous-looking pikes, attracted strangers' eyes while barring unwelcome feet.[6]

The most sublime Charleston double house, the Miles Brewton House, had been as much built to be seen as Natchez houses would be a half century later. Brewton's double house originally came encased in the red-brick style fashionable in the English late eighteenth century, not in the white Greek style fashionable in mid-nineteenth-century Natchez. Brewton himself, however, anticipated nouveau Natchezites. His fortune came from financing the transportation of Africans to America. Natchezites' fortunes came from exploiting the transfer of Upper South slaves to the Lower South. Both gentries' houses, however different their architecture, displayed the wealth gleaned from wrenching blacks toward North America's lushest tropical spots.[7]

In contrast, Charleston's far more common "single" house hid most of itself from onlookers. A single house's long front façade ran away from the

A typical Charleston "single house" (top
left), displaying only its side and its fake
front door to street observers; the less typical "double house" (top right); and
Charleston's gem, the Miles Brewton
House, with its spiked fence (below right),
the signature of a fortified city. Courtesy of
the Library of Congress (all three images).

thoroughfare. So did its long piazza (porch), also one room deep and attached to the retreating dwelling. Only the house's side, a single room deep
(hence "single" house) endured public scrutiny.[8]

The single house's apparent front door appeared on its narrow street
side. But that door customarily opened only onto the piazza or onto the garden, usually hidden behind high stucco walls that ran over to the adjourning
single house. Entrance to the house usually came through the real front door,
concealed either in the garden or in the piazza. The master often greeted his
guests not down below but high above, where second-floor reception rooms
looked down on urban tumult.

The street walls blockaded not only whites' hidden entrance but also slaves' concealed yard. This little backyard village contained slave dwellings, kitchen, laundry, and other centers of domestic service. The concealment, both of masters and of slaves, made single houses' aesthetic neither English nor southwestern. Charleston's long piazzas, begging for a wisp of breeze, recalled not coolish England but the boiling West Indies and the homes of haughty West Indian slaveholders, from whence the first lowcountry planters came. So too, those high walls, built ever higher, thicker, and more often between single houses as the Civil War approached, epitomized old-fashioned commanders in elevated drawing rooms, on guard against nineteenth-century improvements, alias barbarisms.

Behind the walls and beyond the street, gentlemen won highest esteem not by earning fortunes or by securing offices but by perfecting paternalism. The most admired connoisseurs planned the loveliest gardens and selected the most fragrant wines. The most beloved conversationalists crafted one-line bon mots, whether ridiculing nineteenth-century materialism ("The greatest absurdity in the world is a 'Liverpool gentleman' ") or nineteenth-century mobocracy ("The politics of the immortal Jefferson! Pish!")[9] or even secessionist pretensions ("South Carolina is too small to be a Republic and too large to be an insane asylum").[10] The most esteemed wordsmiths celebrated Charleston's elegance in fastidious essays and poems. William Grayson, "Billy" to the drawing room set, won highest honors for his extended couplets, contrasting exploitations of northern hirelings with protections of southern slaves:

> Where hireling millions toil, in doubt and fear,
> No . . . wants nor sorrows check the Negro's joy . . .
> Why peril then the Negro's humble joys,
> Why make him free if freedom but destroys?[11]

Devoted guardians of lessers won as much drawing room adulation as poetic celebrators of paternalism. By nursing the sick, William Porcher Miles earned a congressional seat. By shielding free blacks from lower-class whites, Christopher Memminger demonstrated caring refinement. By bringing the Word to the slaves and by saving a slave family from an auctioneer, James Warley Miles sought to make so-called slavery a lovely sight.

It was all so precious, so fleeting, so vulnerable to the avenues below and to the world beyond. At night, those towering walls could keep cooks, butlers, and maids isolated from contaminating ideas bruited on the streets. But during the day, Massa's slaves paraded down the thoroughfares, until the 9:00 P.M. curfew bells of St. Michael's warned them to retreat behind the walls. Through such porous barriers, antislavery ideas could seep.

Those ideas threatened far more than fortunes, even far more than lives. The world outside could kill the only existence worth saving. Incendiary propaganda could corrupt the masses of allegedly impressionable blacks, already suspect in those eerie swamps. The resulting uneasiness could abort so-called slavery. Meticulous drawing room dandies could become brutal lashers, omnipresent in really awful slavery. Genial charmers could become red-faced defenders; refined reactionaries could become raw revolutionaries; charming drawing rooms could become empty, hollow, while furious titans swarmed in the streets. So Charleston's edgy reactionaries guarded the elegant veneers that camouflaged their unseemly dangers—veneers only slightly less vulnerable in the walled city than in the miasmatic swamps.

The preemptive strike remained endangered coastal gentlemen's essential defensive strategy, from the days when John C. Calhoun sought to nullify President Andrew Jackson to the days when secessionists sought to escape President Lincoln. The lowcountry gentry continually confronted danger at the threshold, before the enemy could creep inside, indeed before most Southerners could spot a menace outside. In the late 1820s, lowcountry congressmen mystified other Southerners with threats of secession if Congress dared to finance free blacks' transportation back to Africa. In the 1832–33 Nullification Crisis, when other Southerners thought South Carolinians fought only to attain state veto of protective tariffs, lowcountry warriors also fought to secure state power to veto still nonexistent federal antislavery acts.

In 1835, lowcountry Nullifiers, again seeking to preclude the first national glimmerings of antislavery, torched abolitionists' mailings and demanded gag rules against congressional antislavery petitions. As Robert Barnwell Rhett defended the strategy of building barriers against entering wedges, before wedges had entered, "a people owning slaves are mad, or worse than mad, who do not hold their destinies in their own hands."[12] A successful preventative strike would erect high walls against all intrusive hands.

– 3 –

Lowcountry titans' crusades for preventative walls required other white South Carolinians' support. Even in heavily enslaved coastal parishes, nonslaveholders slightly outnumbered slaveholders. Still, slaveless whites throughout the South usually massed behind slaveholders in black belt areas, where racial solidarity and racial safety usually trumped class resentments. "The color of the white man," wrote John Townsend, the most important lowcountry secessionist pamphleteer, is "a title of nobility. . . . Although Cuffy or Sambo may be immensely . . . superior in wealth" and may be "the owner of many slaves, as some of them are, yet the poorest white nonslaveholder, being a white man, is the superior in the eyes of the law."[13]

Lowly whites as black belt political superiors had no qualms about elevating squires to the legislature or about ousting abolitionists from the neighborhood. In the paramilitary societies that patrolled the lowcountry in the fall of 1860, nonslaveholders paraded beside their richer neighbors, proudly keeping blacks ground under. The patriarchal obligation of all white men to guard their wives, gratifying to poor men's chauvinistic egos, included the necessity to keep a 90 percent black majority from murdering white dependents.[14]

Beyond the swamps, white South Carolinians less massively favored preventative strikes against the Union. So-called upcountrymen, comprising the 90 percent of South Carolina whites who lived west of the lowcountry's coastal swamps, sometimes restrained the swamp aristocracy's secessionist escapades. But statewide, planter solidarity usually overwhelmed upcountry restrictions.

The upcountry-lowcountry solidarity emerged early in the nineteenth century, when migrants to the upcountry developed the first sprawling Cotton Kingdom. By 1830, slaves averaged 50 percent of the upcountry's population (compared to the lowcountry's 80 percent). Upcountry agrarians planted the more normal, more coarse, more soil-exhausting short-staple brand of the cotton weed (compared to the Sea Islands' less soil-exhausting long-staple silky fibers).

But the upcountry's more normal version of Lower South black belts early suffered from its own abnormality. As the first Cotton South planters, upcountry pioneers also became the first to wear out their soil. Because of their steep economic decline during the 1820s, the South Carolina upcountry became the only sprawling Lower South area to lose its population by the tens of thousands, as its white people moved themselves and/or their slaves from their depleted soil to the Southwest's virgin terrain.

The upcountry's economic depression and debilitating departures helped unify the first South Carolina defiance. In 1830–33, when less economically afflicted lowcountry squires sought to nullify high protective tariffs, especially to secure a constitutional wall against future abolitionist incursions, more economically afflicted upcountry gentlemen joined the crusade, especially to reduce tax burdens. While the linkage of somewhat different anxieties fueled a common rush toward a preventative strike, another singularity in the South Carolina habitat hampered unionist resistance. South Carolina's scant mountains (really only foothills) and constricted pine barrens (seldom barren of plantations) fostered few clusters of white belts without slaves, the southern condition that elsewhere most encouraged defiance of black belt extremists. In 1860, slavery so saturated South Carolina that only one (of thirty) counties contained under 30 percent slaves (and that one was a hefty 23 percent black). Only five other South Carolina counties remained under 40 percent enslaved.[15] In contrast, 30 percent of Georgia, Florida, and Alabama counties, as well as 53 percent of Texas counties, contained less than 25 percent of their populations enslaved.

Despite almost all South Carolina regions' shared thick quantities of slaves, upcountry and lowcountry aristocracies developed slightly different worldviews. Upcountry squires possessed a somewhat lower percentage of slaves. They also developed their slightly whiter world largely during the more egalitarian (for whites) nineteenth century. These relatively new slave-holding grandees thus harbored some resentment of the antique lowcountry's extra delegates in the legislature. Wealthy uplanders also sometimes participated in allegedly mobocratic national political parties, especially in the 1850s, when James L. Orr asked South Carolina eccentrics to act like normal Americans.

But in this abnormal little state, geographically the smallest Lower South state but ultimately the largest in political impact, rich squires from the oldest and youngest South Carolina sections came to know each other intimately. They mutually attended South Carolina College. They often chose mates from the other section. Every February during race week, upcountry horsemen savored Charleston drawing rooms. Every December during legislative sessions, lowcountry squires relished Columbia drawing rooms.

John C. Calhoun's theory of nullification, like its upcountry author, illustrated the almost complete meeting of minds. Doubters of the nullification logic claimed that if any minority could veto any law, no acts would be passed. Calhoun retorted that if all minorities could nullify any tax, meager revenues would tempt few spoilsmen. With scarce public offices luring scant demagogues, selfless aristocrats would wield public power. Disinterested statecraft would produce compromise, preclude anarchy, and perpetuate chaste republicanism. No lowcountryman could have improved on the arch Nullifier's upcountry logic.

In the wake of nullification, an English visitor marveled at his evening in a South Carolina patriarch's dining room. My wealthy hosts, reported G. W. Featherstonhaugh, "consider themselves . . . *the gentlemen of America*." They look "down upon the trading communities in the Northern States" with an "habitual sense of superiority," with a contempt for "an inferior race of men," and with "a distrust sometimes amounting to hatred. . . . A stranger dropped in amongst them from the clouds would hardly have supposed himself among Americans." Particularly striking "was the total want of caution and reserve" in sneering at the "favorites of the Sovereign People" and in hissing "that there never can be a good government if it is not administered by gentlemen." These reactionaries, predicted Featherstonhaugh, will provide "fine elements for future disunion."[16]

Featherstonhaugh's depiction reads like descriptions of Charleston soirées. Featherstonhaugh instead described an upcountry feast. With the lowcountry's contempt for the Union's mobocracy so rife, so far from the swamps, coastal extremists could rally less rabid uplanders against Yankee entering wedges.

– 4 –

Still, South Carolina's barriers against intrusions proved to be as porous as Charleston's walls. In 1833, nullification failed to be secured. In 1845, gag rules against congressional slavery debate failed to be renewed. Throughout the antebellum period, South Carolina's censoring of U.S. mails failed to keep antislavery whispers off Charleston's streets.

The lowcountry aristocracy's power, wealth, and self-confidence waned at the very time that its multiplying walls failed to exclude. The seemingly perpetual fertility of the Sea Islands and the swamps became, after the first quarter of the nineteenth century, not a bit endless. Rice and long-staple cotton fields wore out slowly, not so precipitously as the short-staple cotton fields west of the swamps but, by the end of the antebellum period, more chokingly. Planters' lavish spending and absentee management came to be less affordable. Lovely Charleston mansions came to be less immaculate. Copies of London extravagant furniture came to involve not expensive reproductions from the Thomas Elfes but cheap imitations from New York, grossly carved and hurriedly slapped together and illuminating the antipatriarchal consequences of the bargain basement. Younger sons, then older sons too, fled aging ancestral fields for the adolescent Southwest. Their late eighteenth-century forbearers had been the richest in cash of North American titans. Instead, mid-nineteenth-century lowcountry gentlemen became the richest in unsustainable pretensions.

As the swamp gentry's debilitating decline progressed, the departure of their peoples matched, then exceeded the upcountry's desertions. By 1860, half of white South Carolinians born since 1800 had departed for the West. In 1830, South Carolina had led Lower South states in both slave and total population. The state had also ranked second (behind only Georgia) in white population. By 1860, the ex–Lower South leader had fallen to sixth (ahead of only Florida) in white population and fourth in both slave and total population. In 1830, the state had possessed nine U.S. congressmen. After 1850, it sported only six.[17]

By spreading across the Lower South, South Carolinians disseminated extremism. The 50,000 ex–South Carolinians in Georgia, 45,000 in Alabama, and 26,000 in Mississippi brought some South Carolina attitude to new frontiers.[18] But Southwesterners diluted South Carolina extremism with egalitarian republican (for whites) compromises. As lowcountry South Carolinians watched their power and people drain toward the Southwest's pale replica of aristocratic hauteur, they despaired, with Charlestonian Hugh Swinton Legaré, that "*we* are . . . the *last* of the race. . . . Why should such a state of things—a society so charming and so accomplished—be doomed to end so soon, and perhaps so terribly! . . . I see nothing before us but decay and downfall."[19]

The lowcountry's decay deepened in the 1850s. Few wealthy Americans have suffered through such a debilitating economic decade, immediately after two decades of such crippling declension. In the presecession decade, the bottom fell out of the long-eroding lowcountry rice economy. Sea Island cotton profits also became as frail as the fiber. To all its other radicalizing "onlys"—the only area with such massive quantities of slaves, the only massive nineteenth century southern fragment clinging to eighteenth-century aristocratic republicanism, the only southern subregion with a City on the Sea so walled against modernity—the lowcountry added its plight as the only southern area plunging toward economic debility during a decade of booming slaveholder profits everywhere else.

Just as Charleston had epitomized the lowcountry's rise, so the walled city reflected its hinterlands' fall. Charleston lost one-fourth of its slaves to the West in the 1850s. Lower-class whites moved in, to take over menial positions. The wrong (white) race's omnipresence in the wrong (menial) roles mocked Billy Grayson's couplets; now Charleston whites were the hirelings. The city's overall population, sixth in the United States in 1830, drooped to twenty-second in 1860.

Economic downturn furthered political extremism. The lowcountry parishes had led the state and the South into the proslavery crusades of the 1830s. In October 1851, after the rest of the South rejected disunion, 61 percent of lowcountry rural voters wished to gamble on Separate State Secession anyway. But with planters back on their estates after the first frost, Charleston voters shrank from recklessness. The town bourgeoisie, merchants and lawyers et al., had vast commercial attachments, transcending the lowcountry. These relative sophisticates considered secession by South Carolina alone to be suicidally provincial. Seventy-one percent of voters in the City on the Sea rejected Separate State Secession, as did 60 percent of upcountry voters.

Amidst this electoral disaster for Separate State Secession, the whole state massed behind Cooperative State Secession—disunion as soon as some other state(s) agreed to cooperate. But would another state ever cooperate, unless South Carolina seceded first and forced some state's concurrence? With that blackmail repudiated in their own state, Separate State Secessionists faced living death, so they feared, in the national sewer. Their reckless star, Robert Barnwell Rhett, after resigning from the U.S. Senate, suffered permanent rejection as the state's leader.

No secessionist lowcountryman rose to take Rhett's place. The most ascendant South Carolina politician after Rhett's plunge became the upcountry's James L. Orr. Orr wanted to lead the state into the stench of the National Democratic Party, its people into the muck of popular elections for presidents, and its majority toward reducing lowcountry parishes' inflated power. Equally dismaying to lowcountry patriarchs, when the state sent Charleston's Christopher Memminger to urge cooperation with Virginians after John Brown's raid, the fellow elderly state sent Memminger home empty-handed. So too, when South Carolina called the South to the Richmond Convention after the Democratic Party's bustup in Charleston, southern delegates instead sped to Baltimore, leaving Robert Barnwell Rhett cooling his heels.

John C. Calhoun had been a dominant Southerner before 1850. But only one South Carolinian counted for much in the national slavery politics of the 1850s. In 1856, that upcountryman, Preston Brooks, gave Charles Sumner the mauling that the New Englander allegedly deserved. In response to this solitary supposed South Carolina heroism of the 1850s, New Englanders brought their contempt for the state to a climax. Brooks, pronounced a Boston newspaper, emitted "but the hissings of a vile serpent . . . whose infectious disgorgings are . . . stench to the nostrils." Let all Northerners "know what sort of being they are dwelling in the Union with."[20]

Such insults increased coastal South Carolinians' determination, as Charles W. Hutson, Jr., declared, to stride "out of reach of the miasma that arises from" that "sink of infamy," the mobocratic Union and its repulsive Yankee majority.[21] "I wish we could leave these swine to wallow in their mire," added Hutson, an important lowcountry heir. In 1860–61, the English visitor Charles Russell heard many lowcountry echoes of Hutson's contempt. It is impossible, marveled Russell, "to give an idea" of how vilely these "courtly, well educated men, who set great store on a nice observance of the usages of society," cursed with "extreme bitterness and anger" at the "'rabble of the North.'"[22]

Russell gave the impossible a try. "Deadly . . . hatred," he reported, "has been swelling for years till it is the very lifeblood of the state." Lowcountry patriarchs have long since decided "to break away from the Union at the very first opportunity," lest they be forever "bound by burning chains" to "the incarnation of moral and political wickedness." They crave divorce from "the birthplace of impurity of mind among men and of unchastity in women—the home of . . . rotten philosophy," of "a corrupt, howling demagogy," of "dishonest commerce," of "Free Love, . . . of Infidelity, of Abolitionism."

But in the late 1850s as in 1852, these incensed reactionaries could only scream haplessly for severance from modernity. The years of screeching for disunion—and the years of impotence to seize the prize—made South Carolinians seem ridiculous, not least to themselves. "Witness" our "blustering bravado" and our "eternally pouring a flood of abuse upon everything that squints of Yankeedom," and our "unceasing ranting about . . . Southern Union." Ours is but an "unremitting and unending cry of wolf, wolf," earning only the laughter of the world.[23]

A people whose futility inspired hilarity, warned Congressman W. W. Boyce in 1859, will be paralyzed by "a hated sense of inferiority and degradation," crushing to "the public spirit." We "will be placed under the ban, provincialized, subordinated," bound "to the stake." We will "suppose that all was lost, because nothing was done." As David Flavel Jamison, the future president of South Carolina's secession convention, added in this year before Armageddon, "We are looking to some sudden turn of fortune, we know not what, to rescue us from the doom we have not the courage to avert."[24]

— 5 —

Lincoln's election elevated gentlemen's courage. The special provocations of the president-elect's supposed immediate menace dovetailed perfectly with the special dreads of these most provoked Southerners. This marriage fit for hell would have seemed less intolerable if lowcountrymen had considered the threat of higher protective tariffs and/or of territorial containment to be Lincoln's supreme menace.

Higher taxes on imports had never been lowcountry Nullifiers' cardinal obsession, not even back when they nullified the tariffs of 1828 and 1832. Federal tax policy slid further down the totem pole of grievances in 1860. True, William Porcher Miles on occasion called new taxes the worst Lincolnian menace. So too, Robert Barnwell Rhett demanded that high tariffs be brought front and center, when the South Carolina secession convention presented its rationale for disunion.

But most lowcountry arguments for secession barely mentioned tariffs. As an economic threat, potentially higher taxes were but a hangnail compared to the potential confiscation of tens of millions of dollars in slave property—comprising more dollars invested per white citizen in the lowcountry than anywhere else in the South. Since the gentry could not imagine rice cultivation without slaves, gentlemen thought emancipation would also lose them more tens of millions of dollars in improved land—again, a more costly investment than planters elsewhere held at risk. So from a narrowly pecuniary viewpoint, secessionists considered the slavery issue far more important than the tariff issue—and slavery involved far more than economics. Without slavery's race control, trembled lowcountrymen, the blackest population in the South would annihilate white society (including its economy).

Lowcountry secessionists also exhibited relatively low interest in territorial expansion. On occasion, lowcountry seers did stress the need to stop Northern Republicans from containing southern expansion. "An all powerful Government," warned William Henry Trescot, desired that "a circle . . . be drawn around the South," so that the region "should stand, like one of its own oaks, rung for slow but certain destruction."[25] John Townsend, in the lowcountry's most widely-read important secessionist pamphlet, popularized Charles Sumner's uglier image. Slavery, said Sumner, would perish in the encircled slave states as "*a poisoned rat dies, of rage in its hole.*"[26]

Furious at this image, Robert Barnwell Rhett and Laurence Keitt did occasionally dream that secession would lead to a vast Caribbean empire, which did beat being holed up like a rat. But territorial bombast remained an exception even in Rhett's and Keitt's oratory. Almost all other important lowcountry secessionist polemicists, including John Townsend, scarcely mentioned territorial containment when emphasizing Lincoln's menace.

During antebellum slavery crises, territorial imperialism had only fitfully been lowcountry folks' passion. Only when slaveholder expansion seemed necessary to safeguard the borders of slave areas, especially amidst Texas and Kansas turmoils, or when Yankees insulted slaveholders as too noisome to grow, had South Carolinians displayed their best extremist style. Even then, the great territorial controversies proceeded with scant South Carolina leadership, a marked contrast with nullification, gag rule, and secession times.

In general, nonmigrating South Carolinians, having decided to stay in-side South Carolina, had the slows about territorial expansion, sometimes, as we have seen, to the fury of southwestern imperialists. Ever since Robert Walker and Texas days, southwestern expansionists had demanded new ter-ritorial outlets, lest they someday be inundated with the Upper South's blacks. Unlike Southwesterners, however, South Carolina already had their (cursed!) outlets for people to depart. All too many South Carolina folk, black and white, deserted Mother South Carolina for the crude, rude South-west. Moreover, the declining South Carolina lowcountry imported scarcely a black from the slave-exporting Upper South. Instead, white mudsills drained toward Charleston, to replace departed black mudsills. Coastal re-actionaries' problem was to keep enough folk, black and white, home from Mammon, so that some power would remain to save the old ways from new contaminations.

The Slave South's most committed disunionists and its most committed expansionists lived in different worlds. South Carolina, cradle of secession, never produced an important filibusterer, while Louisiana, nurturer of ex-pansionists, almost failed to produce a secessionist majority. Where most Louisianans thought that the Union's power could secure the Caribbean, most South Carolinians feared that expansionists' triumphs would delay dis-union. Moreover, should the South expand down to the Amazon, the newest South's tropical enticements would quicken the depopulation of ailing South Carolina.

Fresh tropical terrain would also come pockmarked with the likes of Mex-ican or Cuban peasants, possessing no experience with democracy of any sort, much less a taste for upper-class republicanism. Thus John C. Calhoun had opposed annexing all of Mexico. Nor could dreams of empire propel the South Carolinians of 1860 peculiarly quickly to disunion. As F. F. Warley ex-plained in one of the great secessionist orations, "The safety, yea the very exis-tence! of this institution depends upon its concentration. Expand it—spread over it a vast territory, and we only hold out inducements to Northern emis-saries to come amongst us and stir up sedition in our midst."[27]

Nor could fear of territorial containment answer unionists' best argu-ment against secession. If some future congressional decree against slave-holders' expansion alone imperiled the South, explained disunionists' oppo-nents, we can safely wait for the overt act, which might never come. But South Carolinians could not wait because they focused on a menace that would come: Lincoln's use of presidential patronage to plant a Republican Party inside the South.

Lowcountry secessionists agreed that Republicans would immediately attempt no overt antislavery laws. Such an effort would scare Southerners out of the Union and out of Yankees' clutches. In contrast, Republicans' de-ployment of southern patronage would leave the region enfeebled. John Townsend spread a spooky metaphor for nonovert enfeeblement, as chill-ing as a caged rat: a spider's web. Imagine, wrote Townsend, "some insect, strong in itself, but which has sillily entangled itself in the meshes of a spider. With moderate exertions at first, it could . . . free itself. . . . But it prefers to be *quiescent* for awhile. Fatal hesitation!" The "artful" spider "dashes forth from his hiding place and fastens a cord around the wing," then retreats, pauses, rushes forth, retreats, pauses, assaults, until the prey can barely move.

Republicans will creep southward "stealthily, cautiously at first, lest we break through their meshes, and form a government for ourselves." By appointing southern turncoats to federal stations in the South, including custom houses, post offices, and court houses, Lincoln would spread his meshes inside the South. After we become "unable to resist," we will have to "submit to . . . the mercy of the spider."[28]

Presidential patronage as creepy as a monster spider—and more spooky than the master image for territorial confinement, a rat in a poisoned cage?! Absolutely, for Republican office would supposedly be the poison inside the jailed South. The patronage bait would attract allegedly traitorous southern politicians to make agitation against slavery as democratically normal as arguments against tariffs and banks. It would be as if gag rules had been lifted not only inside Congress but also throughout the South, as if English abolitionists had been allowed to spread their ideology across the Texas Republic, as if Kansas free soilers had been permitted unrestricted access to western Missouri slaves and nonslaveholders, as if Border Northerners had been invited to perfect their Liberty Line inside the Border South—with all of this Jacobinical disruption now contaminating hidebound South Carolina.

The fear of a national party's capacity to purchase southern demagogues, commonplace among all secessionists, especially consumed coastal South Carolinians, with their special contempt for mass democracy. The lowcountry gentry, in contrast to all other Lower South establishments, had long damned all who participated in national parties, Democrats or Whigs, as corrupted Southerners. Supposed party corruption had lately invaded South Carolina itself. Lowcountry reactionaries had fought to blast James L. Orr and his followers out of the National Democracy and its Charleston convention.

That exhausting effort had barely triumphed before Lincoln seemed poised to bribe southern traitors into the most frightful national party yet. Since patronage awaited southern converts to Black Republicanism, John Townsend urged, we must not "wait in the Union a single day" while Lincoln "is organizing his cabinet and distributing his offices," while he is conferring custom house posts throughout the Lower South, while he is entrusting post offices "to Alabama and Mississippi," and while he is using the federal treasury "to bribe traitors amongst us."[29]

An "Abolition Party in the South, of Southern men," warned the *Charleston Mercury*, will make "the contest for slavery . . . no longer . . . between the North and the South. It will be in the South, between the people of the South." United States Marshal Daniel Heyward Hamilton feared that "when we find ourselves fairly embarked in a contest which will shake the world, you will find an element of great weakness in our non-slaveholding population." Hamilton wondered whether "360,000 slave-holders will dictate terms for 3,000,000 of non-slaveholders at the South.— I fear not; I mistrust our own people more than I fear all of the efforts of the Abolitionists."[30]

The "most immediate danger," diagnosed the *Charleston Mercury,* "will be brought to slavery in all the Frontier [Border South] States." First, slaves will be infected. "The *under*ground railroad will become an *over*-ground railroad." Throughout our vulnerable hinterlands, "the tenure of slave property will be felt to be weakened, and the slaves will be sent down to the Cotton States for sale." Subsequently, "the Frontier States" will "enter *on the policy of making themselves Free States.*" Slavery will thus be rolled back into solely the seven Lower South states. The surviving remnant, blackened with ex–Upper South slaves and surrounded by free states, will suffer increasingly dangerous internal debates over their increasingly peculiar U.S. institution.[31]

To detail chapter and verse of this mobocratic process, John Townsend used a quarter of his climactic secessionist pamphlet to reprint the notorious "Python" series of articles in *De Bow's Review.* "Python" (alias Virginia's John Tyler, Jr.) described the future southern states as falling dominoes, tumbling one atop the other. Under the pressure of Southern Republican agitation, Upper South fugitive slaves would multiply, nonslaveholder resentments would rise, slaveholders would sell their people downriver, Kansas would fall upon Missouri, then Missouri upon Arkansas, then Arkansas upon Louisiana, while Kentucky crashed atop Tennessee and then Tennessee atop Mississippi, and while Maryland sank atop Virginia and then Virginia atop North Carolina. Then would South Carolina indeed be like a rat in a poisoned cage.[32]

– 6 –

Peril lay not only in Southern Republicans' pressure on the northerly white belt South but also in Lincoln's capacity to provoke agitation inside the southerly blackest belts. No lowcountryman, not even Daniel Heyward Hamilton, trembled that Southern Republicans could rally nonslaveholders instantly against slaveholders in slave-infested swamps. Patronage for the Hinton R. Helpers would arouse an immediate nonslaveholder party in the white belt Border South. But inside the lowcountry black belt, Southern Republicans' most immediate menace would involve their antislavery agitation, arousing allegedly gullible blacks.

Forebodings about blacks' violence, as usual, little involved expectations of a successful slave revolt or even an unsuccessful general uprising. Instead, lowcountrymen again worried that individual slaves might sabotage or kill. As early as 1822, Charlestonians had most feared that individual slaves would poison water wells. As late as 1859–60, the initial terror, that John

Brown plotted mass insurrection, had swerved into prolonged apprehension that Southern Republicans would incite household assassins. The Texas fire scare had sharpened that focus. Without outside "interference," wrote a wealthy slaveholder on the eve of secession, we have "no apprehension, but if a planter knew his slave were tampered with by incendiaries, the case would be altered."[33]

In the especially densely enslaved lowcountry more than anywhere else, slaveholders' stock images of blacks featured wild gyrations between confidence in genial Cuffees, horror about anti-Cuffees, and apprehension of dissimulating Cuffees. Whites' prayer that Cuffees' bootlicking postures revealed genuinely servile souls explains why gentlemen celebrated with such gusto their almost comic tales of incredible docility. Witness the tale of Frank, the little white boy who scoffed that Sharper (perfect name!), his little black playmate, "warn't worth a hundred dollars." "Me," shot back Sharper (accurately!), "I am worth 500 dollars." Then how much more am I worth, rejoined the imperious little planter-in-waiting? "Lord Marse Frank," said Sharper disdainfully, "you's white! You ain't worth nothing."[34]

Another comforting tale featured the slave who sailed "his little sloop" into Charleston harbor during the secession crisis, under the guns of Robert Anderson's federal soldiers in Fort Sumter. "When asked if he was afraid," the black sailor cast an incredulous look. "If Mass Anderson fire at me *he know* he would hear from Massa *shure*."[35]

More common than such smiling tales of loving Cuffees were bewildering images of Cuffee fakery. Mixed up amidst my "good negroes," lamented a South Carolina slaveholder at the moment of secession, are mysterious others. "I cannot tell whether they have any good feelings for" me. "Sometimes I think they have. Then I think" that they are "as deceitful and lying as any people can well be."[36]

Although blacks "carry" the Cuffee pretense "too far," added Mary Chesnut, we pretend that nothing might be amiss. So "people talk before them as if they were chairs and tables. And they make no sign. Are they stolidly stupid or wiser than we are, silent and strong, biding their time?"[37]

After Laurence Keitt's brother's murder, the congressman implored his "dear Susie," alias his fiancée, Susan Sparks, to "be careful, I beg you, . . . be careful."[38] But how could young Miss Sparks be careful? How could she guard against household Cuffees while she lay fast asleep? To take especial care amongst supposedly trusted family friends would be to give blacks ideas about becoming untrustworthy. To shun unusual care was to lie at the mercy of perchance dissimulating enemies. To split the difference was to turn "be careful" into yet another omnipresent charade, as comic as the black sailor under Fort Sumter's guns.

A memorable incident inside the Chesnut family home exemplified this charade. One "day at dinner," Mary Chesnut reported, her mother-in-law "rushed in" to urge "the family not to taste the soup, it was so bitter. *Some thing* was in it! She meant *poison*." But "the family quietly" ate on, "to keep the negroes from supposing it possible they should suspect such a thing."[39]

Just as news of Lincoln's election swept through South Carolina, a large slaveholder tasted something foul in the coffee. "I felt sick a few seconds since," complained the master in a secret diary, for "the second time—Can it be . . . an attempt to poison—somehow I can't think so." Yet "I have walked through the clearing twice today . . . and cannot think myself safe. . . . So friends," concluded this slaveholder in this intended (and incredible) message from the grave, "if I am suddenly taken off after a meal—remember the coffee."[40]

Laurence Keitt remembered more than the coffee. Since "dear Susie" had no way to be careful, masters must take care for their dependents. Patriarchs must prevent Southern Republican postal officials from controlling the mails' contents. They also must preclude Southern Republican campaigners from spreading words that slaves must not hear. We must "cut loose" from the Union "through fire and blood if necessary," declared Keitt, lest enemies "get access to our negroes to advise poison and the torch."[41]

More even seemed at stake than Sue Sparks's life, if Southern Republicans gained access to Cuffees. Secessionists aimed to secure not only slavery's defense but also an institution worth defending. Here they resembled Dred Scott's southern Supreme Court judges. The jurists had sought to end congressional slavery debates not just as reactionaries, perpetuating a system, but also as reformers, perhaps crafting preconditions for slavery's improvement. So too, lowcountry secessionists were not only reactionaries, bent on preserving black bondage and white aristocratic republicanism, but also paternalists, hoping to perfect so-called slavery. The lowcountry spawned not only James Warley Miles but also the Harvard-educated Edward Pringle, whose elegant pamphlet, published in Cambridge, Massachusetts, spread cultivated hopes for a progressive slavocracy, if only outside agitators such as Harriet Beecher Stowe would hush.

Slavery under noisy siege from Southern Republicans posted *inside,* secessionists shuddered, would instead slide backward. John Townsend winced at the difference between the beneficent glory of so-called slavery without any outside interference, where "the kindliest feeling would grow up between the master and his slave," and the nonbeneficent horror of slavery once "intruded upon by the impertinent self-righteousness" of Yankee would-be saints, "whose ignorance and presumption are only equaled by their vulgarity." With incendiary Southern Republicans loose in the neighborhood, masters would become "moody and irascible" in the face of slaves' "*turbulence and disrespect.*" Increased lashings of blacks and lynchings of whites would turn slavery into an "armed camp," in a brutal *Charleston Mercury* phrase. Profoundly threatened would be not only life, in this most enslaved speck of the South, not only fortunes, in this most expensively developed southern habitat, but also the sacred honor of patriarchs, called by Christ to make so-called slavery into a Christian flower.[42]

More than planters in any other region, lowcountrymen conceived that their honor demanded disunion. They had so often promised to step atop revolutionary barricades. They had equally often failed to deliver on that promise. Now they believed that Lincoln's southern appointees, with potentially unspeakable influence on slaves, made secession more necessary than ever. So what self-respect and honor would they retain if they again cowered?

"South Carolina must either secede," answered Robert Burch, the British consul in Charleston, or expose "herself to the ridicule of the world." From Washington, D.C., William Henry Trescot warned compatriots back home that, oh, "how they laughed at little South Carolina." They said she was like "a child who sulks and won't play." Rather than demonstrate that we have sunk into such infamy, cried Congressman William Porcher Miles, "our pride is enlisted to prove" ourselves "not so poor, weak, and destitute" as to be unable to "hold" our "own in the great community of nations."[43]

They had always fought to keep aristocratic paternalism uncorrupted inside a foul egalitarian nation. Now insufferable egalitarians, aiming to tear down caring paternalism in the name of merciless individualism, would clamber over walls that never seemed high enough to repel mobocratic taints. The invaders would swarm not John Brown's impossible way but Hinton R. Helper's insidious way. Presidential patronage would fuel the corruption of lesser folks, black and white, and thus corrupt paternalism itself. The title of John Townsend's most influential pamphlet summed up why self-respecting patriarchs must this time escape the morass: *The South Alone Should Govern the South.*

As the *Charleston Mercury* pared a complex issue to its explosive essence: "The question now for the South to consider is this—under whose government will the slaves of the South be most quietly kept in subjection and order? . . . If we had a government of our own, the post office, all the avenues of intercourse, the police and the military would be under our exclusive control." Or as the *Mercury* summed up the folly of waiting for an overt act, with Lincoln's nonovert patronage the imminent gunman, "Although you see your enemy load his rifle with the direct purpose of taking your life, you are to wait . . . until he shoots you."[44]

– 7 –

Upcountrymen found Lincoln almost as unsufferable. No coastal aristocrat surpassed the uplands' John Manning's contempt for Lincoln personally or Mrs. Laurence Keitt's scorn for Republicans generally. Instead of nominating their most high-toned leader, cursed Manning, Republicans had selected a "wretched backwoodsman," with "cleverness indeed but no cultivation." Laurence Keitt's new wife, that "dear Susie" who had no way of being careful about domestic ambush, added that "Black Republicans" comprised "a motley throng of Sans culottes and Dame des Halles, Infidels and freelovers, interspersed by Bloomer women, fugitive slaves, and [racial] amalgamationists."[45]

Nor did any lowcountryman outdo either the Reverend J. H. Cornish in mocking Republicans' do-goodism or Augustus Baldwin Longstreet, president of South Carolina College, in deploring do-gooders' consequences. Lincoln's election, intoned the Reverend Mr. Cornish, defied "the scripture rule—'be not busybodies in other men's matters.'" Yankee busybodies, added Longstreet, have alarmed "the tender ones" in "my household" and in "every family in the South, not for a week, or a year, but interminably!" After secession gets "us away from Republican influences," cheered Longstreet, Massa and Cuffee "shall dwell together in peace on earth, and mingle hymns in heaven."[46]

Nor did any lowcountry secessionists surpass Judge T. J. Withers in finding the image to scorn secession's delay, or Mary Chesnut in finding the metaphor for blissfully severed sections. I would much prefer "playing with my Grandson," wrote Judge Withers, to combating New England "fools and knaves," who "resolved that the Earth belonged to the Saints, and that they were the Saints." But Lincoln's party's "deliberate invasion of hearthstone, of good name, of property, of everything valuable" instills "a vehement desire to see this horrid quarrel . . . settled in my lifetime." Or as Mary Chesnut summed up secession, we "divorced, North from South, because we hated each other so."[47]

The upcountry's most systematic argument for divorce, that of State Senator J. Foster Marshall of Abbeville, could just as easily have been a lowcountry gem (not least in barely mentioning that supposedly central concern, the expansion of slave territory). Unionists, scoffed Marshall, would have us wait for the "*overt act*." They would delay even "talk about dissolving this Union" until "Congress passes a law abolishing slavery in the Territories, or in the District of Columbia, or in the Forts and Arsenals of the slave states." For now, southern delayers would prefer to talk Yankees into "a returning sense of justice."

"Ridiculous!" Hateful Yankees consider slaveholders among "the greatest monsters on earth." They wish to possess "this Government . . . to accomplish their hellish work." The foe knows that "direct legislation" would arouse the South "from her supineness and lethargy." Cunning dissimulators will instead creep indirectly inside. They will ply "men in our midst who have 'tender consciences' upon the subject of slavery," with "promises of office and position." These Southerners "of their own stamp," once placed "into our post-offices and post-roads," will form "small parties" in "our every district and county."

Those tiny cells "will increase under the auspices and patronage of the Black Republicans, until district after district, county after county falls into their power." Once we are surrounded with "free states on our North and West" and "with the Atlantic on our East," their agitations will make slavery "'stink in our nostrils.' To save ourselves, our wives, and our children" from the "insolent, and rebellious negro, *we will be made to abolish slavery ourselves.*" Emancipation will be "far preferable than the attempt to hold the negro in slavery, with such influences acting and inciting him to rapine and murder."

Do you protest, roared this upcountry secessionist, that this "is an over-wrought picture of the workings of the Government in the hands of the Black Republicans? Then for proof," look at Frank Blair, Jr.'s victory in Missouri. "Look at the burnings" in Texas. Look at "the poisoning and murdering of her men, women, and children that was contemplated. . . . If the Abolitionists can thus destroy our property and excite our people by merely sending their agents and money in our midst, what can they not do when the Treasury" finances their saboteurs? Lincoln's nonovert threat, answered J. Foster Marshall, "is one of *life or death.*[48]

While a shared sense of life and death impelled both South Carolina sections toward secession, disunion preferences had also been omnipresent in 1850–52. The problem then—South Carolina's problem ever since nullification—had been disagreements over disunion tactics. J. Foster Marshall epitomized the continued strategic barrier. While his fire-eating argument left no room for delay, he saw "everything to encourage us in *deferring yet* to our Southern sisters" and "to exhaust every means to secure united action."[49] With such an ardent immediatist still uneasy about commencing alone, the old tactical debate between Separatists and Cooperationists reached new urgency.

CHAPTER 24

The Tactics and the Tacticians

Civil War risks might seem to explain the first secessionists' hesitation. In less than five wartime years, South Carolinians would lose around half a billion dollars in human property (half of the state's total wealth), plus approximately 60 percent of the state's landed value, plus some 20,000 white men's lives (out of 60,000 white males of military age).[1] The savaged low-country economy would flounder for a century (until those ironic saviors, Yankee vacationers, built seaside resorts and helped turn decaying Charleston into a gleaming shrine of the Lost Cause).

But before they dared secession, South Carolinians seldom wrote about a civil war's potential hazards. Their sparse comments featured not analysis but ridicule. Cowardly Northerners, went a characteristic jeer, would never fill more than a thimble with southern blood. Materialistic Yanks, went another commonplace sneer, would never shun King Cotton's profits. Besides, could northern indoorsmen ride a cavalry horse?

This occasional derision, and the more common silence, conveyed some honest conviction that a civil war would be short or nonexistent, some honorable repression of dishonorable fear of Yankees, and some calculation of the odds. If disunion might bring northern soldiers into the South, Union would bring Southern Republicans into the post offices. Besides, before a Southern Confederacy's military prospects became relevant, a Southern Confederacy had to be formed. By precipitating a revolution that most Southerners considered premature, South Carolinians might isolate themselves against the world, a more shuddering prospect than pitting the South against the North.

– 1 –

In their most isolating imagined disaster, South Carolina precipitators pictured a mob's lawless assault on a federal fort. Such a coup d'état would forfeit the

375

first secessionists' best hope for spreading the revolution: antisecessionsts' belief in a sovereign state's right to withdraw its consent to be governed, so long as the sovereign followed the state's rights legal rules. Yet South Carolinians as prominent as State Senator William Izard Bull pledged that if the South Carolina majority retreated from secession, he would seize "arms, to maintain our honor against" our own "absolute traitors."[2]

Many South Carolina secessionists of 1860 had been college boys during nullification travails. South Carolina had never been the same, the younger generation winced, since their fathers flinched. But could Nullifiers' sons reverse the flinch by permitting a mob's illegal coup d'état or by pitching tiny South Carolina, legally but haplessly, all alone onto that precarious limb once again?

The question hung like a soaking blanket atop South Carolinians' desperation for disunion. The Reverend James H. Thornwell illustrated the smothering effect. To tear down one government, the reactionary had written back in March 1850, and to "attempt to construct" a new guarantor of social order, "in this age of tumults, agitations, and excitement, when socialism, communism, and a rabid mobocracy seem everywhere to be in the ascendant, will lead to the most dangerous experiments, the most disastrous schemes." Amidst "the upheaving of society from its very foundations," what would happen to "schemes of the different churches for the conversion of the world"?

A decade later, while in Europe, Thornwell heard that Separate State Secession gambles again tempted South Carolinians. With revolutionary chaos central in his every imagined scenario, the preacher despaired that his flock's disunion temptation must be an angry God's imposition on sinning Christians, wreaking havoc for His people's defiance of His demand to make slavery truly Christian. So Thornwell "made up his mind to move, immediately upon his return [to South Carolina], for the gradual emancipation of the negro, as the only measure that would bring peace to the country."[3]

Even if Thornwell meant, as he probably did, that only masters' absolute power to split slave families and to bar Christ from the quarters should be abolished, his timing would have wrecked his plea. With disunion turmoil abounding, gentlemen would hardly convulsively experiment with their main social institution. Upon returning to South Carolina, Thornwell wisely repressed his untimely scheme. But the evangelical distress behind his smothered proposal illustrated his state's wary apprehensions.

– 2 –

The question was whether Separatism or Cooperationism portended worse upheaval. Cooperationists claimed that a Southwide decision in a southern convention would avoid the peril of a minority of a minority's revolution. If a southern convention brought off disunion, a southern majority would defy the Yankees.

Separatists, however, did not trust a southern convention's majority to go for disunion. The sectionwide majority, immediately after Lincoln's election, overwhelmingly wished to WAIT. From that majority's preference, in an inevitably unpredictable meeting, many bad decisions for secessionists could flow, including worsening upheavals in a refortified Union.

In contrast, Separatism offered a supreme secessionist advantage. One state's majority could control its decision for revolution. From *that* majority's preference, many good things for disunion could come, including others southern states' decision that they had better back their erring brother. Yet if southern unionists elsewhere could not abide the initial secessionists' error, the lonely state could experience the worst upheavals.

South Carolina's bad choice between the dangers of Cooperationism and of Separatism lent weight to the advice of the state's three most prominent leaders in Washington. Of the trio, only James L. Orr publicly announced his preferences before Lincoln's election. For the congressman as for many other Southerners, the National Democracy's demise had removed the South's best alternative to secession. Meanwhile, Lincoln had "declared war upon our social institutions." If elected, the Republican's threat to our "honor and safety," Orr declared in July, "will require prompt secession."

Yet Orr also declared that secession must be delayed until Alabama, Georgia, and Mississippi agreed to cooperate. In mid-October, Orr publicly added that before calling a state convention, the state legislature must appoint commissioners to other states, to ensure "concert of action." The *Charleston Mercury* retorted that "Mr. Orr may be a capital disunionist, under impracticable conditions." But after his "commissioners have run all around the Southern States," his "recommendation" will yield "postponement, delay, enervation, feebleness, halting, fainting, paralysis, submission— and the downfall of slavery."[4]

The second member of the state's most prominent congressional trio, U.S. Senator James Chesnut, Jr., also appeared to favor delay and cooperation with other states. In the summer of 1860, Chesnut vacationed in the western Virginia mountains at White Sulphur Springs, site of James Buchanan's summer White House. The many southern state's righters who swirled around their favorite Yankee had the "cool impudence," Chesnut privately reported, to suggest that South Carolina should risk everything before they risked anything. Their states would not secede first. But they urged South Carolina "to lead off," and to take her "chances of dragging others." Chesnut answered that their strategy "was not very satisfactory to me." Chesnut also privately told Edmund Ruffin that sufficient Cotton South states must previously agree to join South Carolina to make Separatism viable.[5]

In November 1860, Separatists worried more about what their more prestigious, more unsteady U.S. senator, James H. Hammond, might publicly say. Orr, shrewd pragmatist, would likely bend toward the strongest state wind. Chesnut, well-born son of an establishment upcountry family, likely lacked the originality or the erratic temperament to defy his inherited class. In contrast, the lowly born Hammond dripped originality, especially of the erratic variety. This arguably most brilliant, possibly most neurotic, and assuredly most appalling of mid-nineteenth-century American tycoons had long since earned Separatists' closest attention.

In nullification times, this misfit, son of a half-Yankee and sometimes impoverished meat butcher, had soared into the South Carolina upper class on the wings of a brilliant record at South Carolina College and a forceful courting of a Charleston teenage heiress. With Hammond's shy bride came a huge upcountry plantation, almost 150 slaves, and a purse to match his social betters. The risen son of a mudsill then leapt past smug old wealth. In 1835, as a twenty-eight-year-old freshman congressman, Hammond became a national political star overnight when he initiated the gag rule fight.[6] Subsequently, he sustained his reputation with proslavery polemics, including his famous mudsill terminology.

During his upward flight, the new titan looked like an unstoppable achiever. Hammond's long, narrow head culminated in an extended brow, framed to look even more endless by the thinning hair. The characteristic made him look to be right in affecting to have more brain than his peers. As his face slanted from his unusually extended forehead to his unusually narrow chin, his unusually wide mouth seemed frozen in a sneer. The characteristic made him seem cockier than the white aristocrats he sometimes condescended to charm.

But inside the head fit for a condescending superior, Hammond suffered the neuroses of a squirming inferior. He had had, he privately confessed, "infinite difficulties to overcome, in taking a position to which I had not been bred." He felt himself "no match for the keen worldly-wise boys." No one could "conceive" of the "trial and struggle" involved in rising among gentlemen "who looked *down on me.*"[7] Worried that he would fall, Hammond's psyche gave him honorable ways to quit before his admirers discovered his failings. His psychosomatic stomach agony led to his resignation months before Congress voted against his gag rule motion.

After a sojourn in Europe, Hammond returned to his upcountry estate. There he impatiently waited to be called to his second chance at political fame. He would do nothing to encourage the call. As a disdainer of mobocratic politics and an admirer of South Carolina's aristocratic regime, this nouveau aristocrat looked up to the state's legislators as the purest judges of political virtue. If they elected him governor or U.S. senator, he would happily serve. If the jury of his peers chose someone else, he would remain unhappily isolated on his plantation.

Seven years after Hammond's stomach (and nerves) drove him out of Congress, his peers called him forth, to rule from the governor's mansion. Subsequently, right there in the mansion, his four nieces, daughters of Wade Hampton II and aged fourteen to nineteen, came "rushing on every occasion into my arms and covering me with kisses—lolling in my lap—pressing their bodies almost into mine, . . . and permitting my hand to stray unchecked over every part of them and to rest without the slightest shrinking from it, on the most secret and sacred regions—and all this for a period of more than two years continuously."[8]

Social revenge possibly sweetened the licentious delights. Wade Hampton II, along with many members of Hammond's wife's family, snubbed the fortune hunter ever after he laid siege to his blushing heiress. At any rate, Hammond congratulated himself that he stopped "short of direct sexual intercourse" with Hampton's nonblushing daughters. The governor also bragged that after one of his nieces for the first time objected to an intimacy, he forever turned away from their "loose manners" and "ardent temperaments."

Hammond's own loose manners had cost him dear. One or more of his nieces reported some or all of the escapade to their father. Wade Hampton II punished the governor not by slaying him on the dueling grounds but by savaging his reputation in the legislature. Hampton intimated that Hammond had committed some monstrous (undescribed) indiscretion that required rich men to oust this ex-poor-boy forever from polite society.

For the next twelve years, the shamed ex-governor steamed on his plantation. For years, he suffered alone, except for his two slave mistresses. (His wife departed for half a decade, unable to abide his turning *her* plantation into *his* brothel.) Once again, he continually prayed that the legislature, that trusted jury of his peers, would forgive him his sins by calling him forth to serve. If the legislators continued to judge him a monster, he would accept their verdict (indeed judge them right). The self-condemned monster would then drag himself through his living death, until the grave thankfully beckoned.

Then in December 1857, the jury returned Hammond to fullest life. Although he sent a letter refusing to be a candidate, the South Carolina legislature elevated the ex-congressman who had quit and the ex-governor who had misbehaved to John C. Calhoun's old seat in the U.S. Senate.[9] Hammond came back from the politically dead partly because of his letter of refusal. A superb way to run for office, in antimobocratic South Carolina, was to run away from running. Hammond also profited from Wade Hampton II's occasional dashes off to garner southwestern profits. This state did not relish sons who deserted Mother South Carolina for Mammon. Nor did South Carolinians now fully approve of established aristocrats who drummed ex-commoners into exile without specifying the monster's sins. In the 1850s, James L. Orr instilled some qualms about such antique presumption. But above all else, legislators saluted Hammond as the most brilliant and independent South Carolinian of his time, needed to provide guidance at this most dangerous moment in all their lives.

Hammond's Barnwell Court House speech of October 29, 1858, consolidated his reputation for independent brilliance. The senator thereby gave Separate State Secessionists the sort of shudders that James Chesnut, Jr., never inspired. Before the stunning speech, rumors had circulated that Hammond, upon returning from his first senatorial term, had told his constituents that extremists' panaceas, whether disunion or importing Africans or seizing Mexico, were all like "a railroad to the moon (& everybody knows it)."[10]

Some ultras, not knowing it, demanded fuller explanations. The supersensitive senator, always unable to bear his peers' disapproval, meant to regain awed approval at Barnwell Court House. Trading on his once fabulous reputation, he reminded his auditors that he had last spoken to them twenty years ago. Back in nullification times, we together battled "for the Constitution and our rights, in the Union, if possible—out of it, if need be. And this is our battle now."[11]

He no longer looked like the brash young battler of nullification times. Hammond seemed older, grayer, balder, fatter, more dissolute, more like the chauvinist who had pawed four nieces and slept with two slaves, mother and daughter, and knew that his son shared the bounty. His face, no longer just pale, had become ivory white. His nerves remained the worst in the state. Only halfway through his speech, Hammond became so overwhelmed "with my scalp on fire and every nerve a quiver" that he had to quit the rostrum— just as he had had to vanish to Europe halfway through his gag rule fight.[12]

The whole intended Barnwell Court House speech, when printed, showed that Hammond had become as different as he looked from his younger shade, that South Carolina ultra in nullification times. "For many years of my life," Hammond reminded his old admirers, "I believed that our only safety" lay in disunion. But now I say "not yet." We will be chasing another moonbeam if we attempt revolution when "the great body of the southern people do not seek disunion."

The senator warned that we have lately suffered too much from such folly. The "false and useless" Kansas issue tangled us in "disgusting . . . turmoil over the last four years." We finally could not even secure "a worthless slavery clause," which the flood of free labor immigrants "would have . . . annulled as soon as Kansas was admitted."

We should have known that we lacked the slaves to win that territory. We should now know that we lack the slaves to win other slaveless territories and that the "vast majority" of Southerners do not want the necessary "vast hordes of slaves" to be imported from Africa. If we acquire Cuba, that one new state will drain off "all the slaves" in "Missouri, Kentucky and Maryland." If we seize "Mexico and South America," we will "be contaminated" by "seven or eight millions of hardly semi-civilized Indians and two or three millions of Creole Spaniards and mongrels."

Let us replace such "bootless efforts," Hammond urged, with the realization that "the tide of abolition has begun to ebb everywhere and will never rise again." Let us remember that Yankees' "sense of danger in a civil war" and their love of profits from marketing "cotton and tobacco" will "in every crisis over-ride their love of negroes." Let us recall that "our history proves that no man and no measure has yet been strong enough to stand against the South when united. . . . Let us give to the winds every thought of fear, every feeling of despondency." Let us rejoice "that we can fully sustain ourselves in the Union and control its action in all great affairs."[13]

Two years after this famous outburst, 1860 Separate State Secessionists feared that if Hammond publicly reiterated his newfound unionism, and if Chesnut publicly spread his private distaste for doing non–South Carolina gentlemen's secessionist dirty work, and if Orr reiterated that South Carolina should not secede unless Georgia would too, South Carolina might again shamefully retreat. Then the southern cowardly majority would again rule. If so, Lincoln might be imminently deciding which Southern Republican would control South Carolina's mails.

– 3 –

That perceived potential disaster made South Carolina's Separate State Secessionists desperate. Just as they must not permit Southern Republicans to debate slavery inside South Carolina (or inside Border South states), so they must not permit James H. Hammond to rally a South Carolina majority against Separate State Secession. Nor could other majorities in Lower South states be permitted to call a southern convention. Nor could Upper South majorities in that convention be permitted to set the South's agenda. Deliberately, demonstrably, with no apologies, South Carolina Separatists sought to preclude Southwide or South Carolina popular majorities from defeating or delaying a wiser minority.

Their manipulations against majority decisions, gentlemen felt, required no defense. According to their aristocratic republican gospel, the hoi polloi should never settle public questions, especially not after the bread and circuses of public campaigns. The people should instead pick the wisest patriarchs, and the paternalists should set public policy, in a legislature or in a convention beyond the herd's comprehension. "The true relationship between the constituent and his representative," exclaimed a prominent low-countryman during the December election of secession delegates, "is not 'I select you because you will do my will, but because you will do your own, which I believe to be more enlightened than mine.'" The contrary proposition, that elected convention delegates must follow the electorate's desires, displayed "the concentrated essence of mobbism."[14]

At the peak of the secessionist drama, Alfred Aldrich, one of the Separatists' most important state legislators, called secession the distilled essence of upper-class statesmanship. "I do not believe the common people understand it, in fact, I know they do not understand it; but whoever waited for the common people when a great move was to be made? We must make the move & force them to follow. This is the way," emphasized Aldrich, "of all revolutions & all great achievements." Those who wait "until the mind of everybody is made up will wait forever & never do anything."[15]

South Carolina's recent history proved, from Alfred Aldrich's perspective, that the citizens would never do enough. Three times in three decades, the leaders had asked the voters to defy the Yankees. Twice, in 1830 and in 1851, citizens had voted down nullification or secession conventions. Only once, in 1832, had extremism triumphed at the polls. "I do not want to see another attempt to vote a revolution," Aldrich exclaimed. "The thing is absurd & can't be done." If the "question" of whether South Carolina should secede "must be referred back" to its citizens for decision, "it will be an utter failure." If the secession decision had to be referred back to all the South's citizens, in a southern convention, an even more massive failure would ensue. South Carolinians must alone "dare," added U.S. Congressman William R. Boyce, thereby forcing others to act "with us or our enemies. They cannot take sides with our enemies. They must take sides with us."[16]

As the Robert Barnwell Rhetts, junior and senior, explained how they thought dictation must proceed, "Men having both nerve and self-sacrificing patriotism must lead the movement and shape its course, *controlling and compelling their inferior contemporaries*." Nor need we rally all southern inferiors for secession; that effort would be "as absurd as it is unnecessary." Instead, "all our efforts must be addressed to the cotton states." The noncotton states "can only be managed by the course pursued" at the Democratic National Convention. First wrench the Lower South out, then force the Upper South "to choose between the North and South." Subsequently, folks with fewer slaves "will redeem themselves & not before."

At the Democratic National Party Convention, the Rhetts had hoped Yancey would begin not with the whole Cotton South but with "Alabama and Mississippi, . . . the only states, besides ours," affording "grounds to expect action." But in November 1860, they thought a secessionist could concentrate solely on South Carolina, paying no attention whatsoever to other states. Even if Alabama and Mississippi refuse "to agree beforehand to go out of the Union with us," we should "secede first" and "expect the others to follow." Who could "conceive it possible that the other Slaveholding States, when once the Union is broken," would fail to "rally together to save their institutions, from Abolition rule at Washington"?[17]

Unfortunately for the Rhetts, many fellow secessionists conceived that other southern states would defy so dictatorial a tactic. They preferred Yancey's more accommodating strategy inside the Democratic National Conventions of 1860. They believed that the leader could not arbitrarily leave, too arrogant even to consult those who must follow. Rhett continued to sneer at that tactic. His scornful arrogance, James Hammond reported, made him seem "utterly *odious*" outside South Carolina.[18]

But inside the state, scorn for lesser mortals was gentlemen's signature. Haughty South Carolina patriarchs chafed at Rhett not because of his swagger but because of his recklessness. As Henry Ravenel summed up the common opinion, Rhett is "the most untrustworthy politician in the state. . . . He wants judgment, and can never be relied on for statesmanship."[19]

The master principle of Rhett's statecraft sustained that verdict. This fire-eater always thought that if South Carolina would just do it, even in unpopular or lawless ways, other states would be dragged along. Back in nullification times, he almost alone had counseled that instead of retreating from state veto, the defeated Nullifiers should advance to state secession. In 1851, Rhett had secretly advised the South Carolina governor to seize Fort Moultrie from the federals, so that a military confrontation would drive South Carolinians and other cowards out of the Union.[20] Through all these extreme Separatist proposals, Rhett insisted that he was the true Cooperationist. If I thought we would end up alone, he wrote, I would never advise Separate State Secession. But I am convinced that other states must cooperate after we secede, however we secede, whether they like it or not.

To the many nervous South Carolinians who did not trust such contempt for legal state's rights procedures and other Southerners' opinions, Rhett even looked heedless.[21] His distinguishing characteristic was neither his lanky six-foot frame nor his cool blue eyes nor the perpetual little bandage on his nose. No one, including Rhett, yet knew that the trifling gauze, covering up the apparently trifling pimple, actually hid the precursor of a monster cancer. Someday, the poisonous growth would cause surgeons to slice a progressively more grotesque hole in the ultra's face. Earlier, however, folks most noticed not a carefully bandaged pimple but the wild fringe of graying hair streaming sideward from Rhett's otherwise balding head. The unkempt canopy over his ears seemed to proclaim that uncontrolled frenzy was a South Carolina statesman's highest virtue.

That unruly secessionism made "nothing coming from" Rhett, William Porcher Miles claimed in the fall of 1860, carry "any good" for Separatism.[22] Nor did any other established South Carolina political titan seem a trustworthy guide toward a safe revolution. Miles had erratically contemplated kidnapping John Sherman during the late congressional session. Keitt, always akin to a bucking bronco, had gone wilder since his brother's murder. Memminger had secured no Virginia cooperation after John Brown's raid. To trump a feared Chesnut-Orr-Hammond push toward Cooperative State Secession, or perhaps toward no secession at all, Separatists needed new leaders or at least new tactics, offering not perilous rashness but safe plotting.

– 4 –

In early October, Governor William Gist commenced a secret correspondence, seeking a safe Separatist design. His clandestine communications, together with two simultaneous covert exchanges initiated by other Separatist plotters, briefly fit the dictionary definition of conspiracy: "secret plans . . . by a group intent on overthrowing a government."[23]

During the previous quarter century of southern nonconspiratorial control, extremists deployed only three brief secret plots, all with no consequence or counterproductive impact. In late 1835–36, South Carolina's Congressman James Hammond precipitated the gag rule crisis *before* he received secessionists' undeniably conspiratorial letters, urging him to break up the Union.[24] A quarter century later, during the Hinton R. Helper Speakership Controversy, South Carolina's Congressman William Porcher Miles and Governor William Gist equally undeniably (and abortively) secretly plotted that the governor would rush a state regiment to Washington if South Carolina congressmen bodily threw an elected Republican Speaker out of the House of Representatives.

The only other pre-1860 disunion conspiracy only delayed disunion. In 1850–51, South Carolina's Governor Whitemarsh Seabrook secretly wrote other Lower South governors, seeking an effective disunion scheme. Mississippi's John Quitman secretly responded that he should lead his state out of the Union first. Then South Carolinians should back his initiative. Seabrook bought the Mississippian's plot. But subsequently, Quitman could not deliver his state. Then South Carolinians could not restart their stalled secessionist engines.[25]

With only these meager evidences of conspiracy to cite, posterity has been right to scoff at Northerners' belief that a Great Slave Power Conspiracy dominated slavery politics throughout the road to disunion. In presecession times, the southern minority exerted sway over the national majority through normal, nonconspiratorial, pressure group politics, including and especially using its leverage over the National Democratic Party. Since slavery's defenders long dominated the dominant national party on slavery matters, they needed no conspiracies to prevail.

But in secession times, the National Democratic Party had vanished. (The importance of that disappearance cannot be overemphasized.) Moreover, a southern majority for the expediency of disunion could not be found. (The importance of that absence cannot be overemphasized either). In this new and, to a proslavery extremist, scary revolutionary situation, a brief conspiracy became comforting, indeed indispensable.

The new need in a new era resembled the new relevance of state's rights ideology. Before the secession crisis, mundane state's rights in nonrevolutionary times had been more a northern than a southern need, to transport slave runaways through free labor states. But during revolutionary times, the state's alleged higher right to exercise the American right of revolution became extremist Southerners' necessity, to pressure reluctant Confederates toward joining one state's rebellion.

Revolutionary politics do march to a different drummer. When a scheme may provoke indictment for treason, schemers crave secret understandings before risking the gallows, making clandestine communications newly seductive. To scoff at state's rights and/or conspiratorial influence on the secession crisis, although presecession crises deserve such scoffing, is to forfeit rich understandings. The losses include an insight into South Carolinians' almost losing struggle to master their misgivings, a comprehension of one way Separatists straightened out initially confused (and potentially paralyzing) Lower South secession tactics, and, ironically, a fuller appreciation of why

Great Slave Power Conspiracies failed to control even the revolutionary climax of this history.

– 5 –

The fleeting conspiracy of 1860 initially mirrored the passing plot of 1850, with the South Carolina chief executive again inaugurating the clandestine correspondence. When both Governor Whitemarsh Seabrook in 1850 and Governor William Gist in 1860 commenced their almost identical secret letters to other states' governors, they believed that Nullifiers had erred in 1832 by *not* conspiring with other states. By failing to seek and secure prior promises that South Carolina would not stand alone, the Nullifiers had blindly rushed toward that sorry fate.

Governor Gist meant to avoid not only the blunder of 1832 but also the debacle of 1850–52. Governor Seabrook's plotting with Mississippi's Governor John Quitman had defused South Carolinians' charge. This time, no delay could be tolerated. No foe of disunion could be given time to persuade the whole South to wait for an overt act, or to arrange a southern convention, or to allow South Carolina's disunionist steam to evaporate. Yet if South Carolina instantly decided for Separate State Secession, could the decision makers trust some other Lower South state(s) to follow?

In pursuit of an answer that could soothe worried compatriots, Gist sent identical October 5, 1860, letters to the governors of North Carolina, Georgia, Florida, Alabama, Mississippi, and Louisiana.[26] The geographically selective recipients included all but one Lower South governor (Sam Houston, the notorious Texas unionist, being the glaring omission) and only one Upper South governor (the governor of neighboring North Carolina being the lonely exception). In his private letter, Gist sought a "full and free [and secret] interchange of opinion between especially" the "Cotton States." He wished to hear when other Lower South states' conventions would meet and what "remedy" they would propose. "Confidential" prearrangements on these matters might yield "concert of action, which is so essential to success."

We desire, wrote Gist, "that some other State should take the lead, or at least move simultaneously. . . . If a single State secedes," we "will follow. . . . If no other State takes the lead, South Carolina will secede (in my opinion) alone," but only "if she has any assurance that she will be soon followed by another or other States; otherwise it is doubtful."

Gist should have known that he would receive back scant assurances to relieve the doubtful, after the unsettling response to Christopher Memminger's recent fiasco. In the aftermath of John Brown's raid, it will be recalled, Memminger and the South Carolina legislature had urged southern states to assemble in a southern convention. The Mississippi legislature had set the date and place for the conclave. Mississippi lawmakers had also dispatched a commissioner, Peter Starke, to join Memminger in Richmond, charged with helping to secure Virginia's attendance at the southern convention. But when Virginia had refused to attend a southern convention that anyway never met, Memminger had thrown up his hands at the southern convention remedy. Starke, in contrast, had still favored the southern convention tactic, as had Alabama's Governor Andrew Moore in an April letter to Gist.

The October answers to Gist repeated that unwelcome preference for a southern convention. With the exception of the North Carolina governor's letter (dated October 18) and the Florida chief executive's missive (dated November 9), the governors answered Gist during the last week of October. The letters thus illuminated Lower South chief executives' preferred tactics right before South Carolina's decision altered the tactical landscape.

In only one sense did the governors send Gist his desired Separatist invitation for South Carolina Separatists to plunge alone. If South Carolina alone seceded and Lincoln declared war on the state, Gist's correspondents all pledged that their states would "immediately rally to her rescue." This pledge was auspicious. If war ensued, the state's rights ideology would be a precipitous state's life raft.

But federal coercion might not follow one state's secession. If no other state joined South Carolina outside of the Union, a shrewd president might repeat Andrew Jackson's nullification era strategy. Like Jackson, Lincoln might temporarily forbear to enforce any federal laws, except to collect custom duties far offshore. South Carolina, lacking a navy, could not then pick a fight. The blockaded state would be back in its 1832 predicament.

In hopes of avoiding that forbidding repetition, Gist's October 5 missive invited some other state to secede first. All the governors rejected the offer (the very offer that John Quitman had gummed up secession by accepting in 1850). Even the most secessionist governor beyond Gist in 1860, John Pettus, leading the most secessionist state beyond South Carolina, Mississippi, doubted that his state would "move alone." Nor did Alabama's Governor Moore believe that William Lowndes Yancey's state, although first to secede from the National Democratic Party Convention, would "secede alone."

If South Carolina seceded alone and no war ensued, only Florida's governor, an ex–South Carolinian, pledged that his state would follow. Gist received Governor Madison S. Perry's comforting promise too late, after South Carolina's legislature decided to dare. Governor John Pettus's response, although received in time, offered incomplete assurance. If any "State moves," declared Pettus, "I think Mississippi will go with her." To that inconclusive "think" from Mississippi, the Alabama governor added his "opinion" that, if "two or more States will cooperate with" his state, "she will secede with them."

Between one governor's mere thoughts, and another's opinion that two states' pledges of cooperation must precede his state's departure (and Florida's tardy reply), the Lower South chief executives offered Gist no timely guarantee to support one state's departure, unless federal coercion ensued. Worse, Pettus reported that Mississippians would prefer "a council of the

Southern States." The governors of Georgia, Alabama, and Louisiana reported the same dominant sentiment in their states. All these chief executives implicitly concurred with Georgia's Governor Joseph Brown that their states would appreciate a southern convention's "common action," taken "for the protection of all."

The first wave of 1860 secret letters had yielded no comforting plot for Separate State Secession. Instead, the majority of Lower South governors looked toward Cooperationism in a southern convention, where the Upper South white majority might dominate. These answers to Gist's inquiry brought the secession crisis to its most important tactical turning point. Gist and his state could join, and thereby make irresistible, the Lower South governors' momentum toward a southern convention. Or the South Carolinians could throw Separate State Secession into the teeth of the Lower South's tactical preference (a gamble that Gist had conceded his state might lack the nerve to try).

The very short time for Lower South strategists to think about their response to Lincoln's election made this turning point especially critical. Just here, the uncertainty until deep in the fall about whether Lincoln would win an Electoral College majority became important. If the Republican victory had been certain for months and every Lower South state had had ample time to make its decision before another state moved, a South Carolina lightning-quick strike could not have revolutionized the very context of decision, before decisions had been made.

But with the election long uncertain, emergency thinking and planning did not begin in earnest until late September/early October, even in South Carolina. The first thoughts about the new situation commenced with the last thoughts about the previous emergency: John Brown's raid and Christopher Memminger's failure. Gist's October 5 letter reflected Memminger's judgment that the southern convention strategy had proved forever disastrous. The Lower South governors' responses to Gist's letter, however, reflected Peter Starke's opinion that the tactic deserved another try. If Gist and his state succumbed to that southwestern drift, the Cooperationist preference could swell. But if the South Carolinians instantly, unanimously gave Lower South tacticians only time to respond to an accomplished revolution, a revolutionary history would be on top of other Lower South states before they could wander toward an alternative.

Gist lost scarcely an hour in choosing the Separatist rather than the Cooperationist fork in the road. In a second phase of his own brief conspiracy, the governor secretly asked his cousin to deter the Mississippi governor from a southern convention. As we will see, this clandestine follow-up effort had its impact, but only after the South Carolina legislature made its decision. To lend faltering South Carolina legislators the nerve to press an instant revolution on the Lower South, two earlier waves of South Carolinians' conspiratorial correspondence had more timely consequence.

– 6 –

In late October, three weeks after Gist wrote the Cotton South governors, Robert Barnwell Rhett, Jr., sent Mississippi's U.S. Senator Jefferson Davis and some other Cotton South leaders additional secret inquiries, asking whether an immediate interstate secession could be planned, based on Separatist State Secession. Jefferson Davis, writing what Rhett called "the most discouraging letter received," considered it "doubtful" that Mississippi's legislature would call a state convention. If a Mississippi convention did assemble, secession "would probably fail," unless "neighboring States" adopted the remedy. If South Carolina "alone" seceded, continued Davis, his state's position "would not probably be changed." Especially Georgia might be lost if only South Carolina seceded. Then Separatist State Secessionists would lose Mississippi too.

My state, explained the senator, suffers from "the want of a port." If our neighboring states clung to the Union, we would be commercially isolated after secession. Moreover, if Mississippi and South Carolina alone seceded, our two states would be "geographically unconnected." You need Georgia "to connect you with Alabama and thus to make effectual the cooperation of Missi. . . . If Georgia would be lost by immediate action, but could be gained by delay," Davis climaxed, "it seems clear to me that you should wait." Or as South Carolinians read this (they thought) dismal advice, the most secessionist state should wait for the least secessionist Lower South state to decide.

If South Carolina seceded first, Davis conceded, and if the federal government should "attempt to coerce" Lower South brothers "back into the Union, that act of usurpation folly, and wickedness would enlist every true Southern man for her defense." But instead, Davis predicted, "federal ships would be sent to collect the duties on imports outside" Charleston harbor. "The Southern States would have little power to counteract" that maneuver. For all these reasons, Davis favored "seeking to bring these states into cooperation before asking for a popular decision."[27]

Davis's letter to Rhett Jr., like the Lower South governors' letters to William Gist, demonstrates that just before and immediately after Lincoln's election, the Cotton South instinctively responded to Republican triumph not with one option but with two. Posterity, knowing what happened, thinks that Separate State Secession must have been the master idea. But before South Carolina's legislature struck, many southwestern leaders still considered a southern convention the better alternative. The governors of Mississippi, Alabama, and Georgia themselves prayed for disunion. Each was the reigning expert on his state's likely course. They were biased toward predicting a Separate State Secession destiny. They could make no such prediction unless South Carolina acted. Even then, their predictions wobbled unless war ensued. So did South Carolinians still dare the Separatist tactic, in the face of a conspiracy gone slightly awry?

– 7 –

In response, a tiny group of Christopher Memminger's Charleston compatriots, after suffering with their fellow Cooperationist over his failed Virginia venture, now saw no choice except a reformed Separatist effort, including one more effort at interstate conspiratorial planning. These nervous squires considered a continued Union or a revived southern convention equally suicidal for slavery. Instead, cautious revolutionaries must rally enough support outside South Carolina to make Separatism safe. They then must steer reassured aristocrats down the state's rights' legal path toward a second American Revolution.

The lifelong nonagitators who deployed this sober agitation remained so discreet that they still are invisible in almost all accounts of how these Founding Fathers brought their nervous state to Armageddon.[28] Most history buffs recall Robert Barnwell Rhett. But who remembers Robert Gourdin, or John Townsend, or William Dennison Porter, or Isaac Holmes, or Andrew Magrath, or William Tennent, Jr.?!

All these fresh leaders of the climactic secession movement deserve to come out from history's shadows, for they, not Rhett, became the final guides of South Carolina's presecession world. Their guidance illuminates the steady tone that an uneasy establishment craved, before attempting a perilous gamble. These wealthy and sophisticated possessors of the finest Charleston drawing rooms also illustrate a broader truth about American politics: Far-out extremists cannot usually win popular elections, even in revolutionary situations. Just as the more moderate Abraham Lincolns had to replace the more extreme William Lloyd Garrisons for antislavery men to sweep northern elections, so the more soothing John Townsends had to replace the more frightening Robert Barnwell Rhetts for secessionists to command Lower South voters, even in Charleston, even after Lincoln's election.

Townsend, the greatest pamphleteer of the obscure grandees who seized the revolution, exemplified the safe and sane type. Townsend had put his brilliant polemical skills to work *against* nullification in 1832 and *against* secession in 1851–52. The ex-Cooperationist still shared, he privately whispered to his congressman, his fellows' "undefined dread of terrible consequences which must certainly follow any act of *separate* secession." That attitude "palsies" any state from "taking the first step."

But submission to paralysis and to enemies who intend our "degradation and ruin . . . can only postpone for a few brief years," and "cannot possibly avert," our reduction "to an equality with our slaves." We will never again have "an opportunity so *favorable for decisive action.*" Townsend would conquer the Separatist shakes, including his own, by rallying "a sufficient number of the Southern States to stand by us." Perhaps his massively distributed secessionist appeals would create a Separatism worthy of trust—and at least more trustworthy than Southern Republican officeholders.[29]

Townsend had been born and bred to exemplify the trustworthy patriarch. He entered the world and left it at Bleak Hall, the family's gorgeous country seat on Edisto Island. A graduate of Princeton, he owned 272 slaves and well over half a million dollars' worth of land in 1860. His Bleak Hall cotton won prizes for the longest, finest threads of Sea Island fiber. Belgian and French lacemakers coveted his threads.

At Bleak Hall, Townsend demanded not only immaculate cotton but also impeccable gardens. One of North America's only Chinese gardeners kept the rare plants pristine. Townsend himself bore the look of pruned refinement, crowned with a carefully cultivated heap of profuse hair and featuring reading glasses perched at just the right angle on his nose. Like all Charleston's rising crop of lowcountry Separatist sophisticates, this Beau Brummell wished a revolution as controlled as Bleak Hall, shorn of Rhett's crude plunges.[30]

While Edisto Island's John Townsend thrived as the cultivated leaders' best polemist, Charleston's Robert Gourdin starred as their best organizer. Gourdin had honed organizational skills at his towering capitalistic concern, Gourdin, Mathiesen and Company. The firm specialized in marketing Sea Island cotton, with offices both in Savannah and on Charleston's East Bay. Robert lived with Henry Gourdin, his brother, mercantile partner, and fellow lifelong bachelor, in a grand mansion around the corner on South Battery Street.[31]

Although their business and residential palaces edged on the harbor, neither of the brothers Gourdin evoked hints of crude moneymaking or the turbulent sea. They had been nurtured to be country gentlemen on Buck Hall Plantation in St. John's Parish. Robert, born in 1812, had graduated from South Carolina College the year before nullification and had then briefly practiced law. After deserting the country for the city and the law for merchandizing, he still clung to patriarchal tastes. The Gourdins' wine cellar harbored the best-chosen vintages in the state. Their garden yielded what Mary Chesnut called "the most glorious bunch of roses I have ever beheld," sent over upon her arrival in Charleston—"with a note & compliments."[32]

Robert Gourdin matched his country friend Townsend not only in manners and roses but also in trimmed personal appearance. The East Bay marketing genius sported a solid head, white hair meticulously swept back, a beautifully shaped full beard, and a full set of glasses, giving aid and comfort to the twinkling eyes. Of all mid-nineteenth-century figures, he best anticipated posterity's image of Santa Claus.

In 1860, Robert intended that his Christmas season gift to Charleston's drawing room fanciers would be a revolution that bore no scent of the street. Like Townsend, he aspired to save Separate State Secessionists from wild Rhetts no less than from fanatical Yankees and from the cowardly southern majority. He also meant to improve on Christopher Memminger's first stab at finding some cooperation beyond South Carolina. After Memminger failed in Virginia, the commissioner had concluded that South Carolina "shall finally be brought to the point of making the issue alone and taking our chances for the other States to join us."[33]

But Gourdin had grown rich by avoiding unnecessary chances. The crafty capitalist concluded that Memminger had pitched the correct message to the wrong folk and with the wrong tactics. Lower South patriots, not Upper South compromisers, must be approached. The venture must deploy a sustained barrage of public and private written words, not a single blockbuster oral presentation. The effort must secure enough secret promises of support, if South Carolina acted alone, so that South Carolina gentlemen would and should risk a Separatist destiny.

Charleston's newly organized 1860 Association carried out the assignment. Gourdin and his compatriots' initiative commenced in early September, several weeks before Governor Gist wrote the other Lower South governors. Every Thursday night, fifteen or so wealthy gentlemen met, usually at the Gourdins' house, to decide whether the wine was more fragrant then last week's offering and to discuss how to secure a safe Separatist revolution. Before October commenced, the Thursday night cavorters had settled on an organization and a strategy.

Their 1860 Association featured Robert Gourdin as the chief operating officer (technically the chairman of the executive committee) and as secret correspondent with southern leaders. Henry Gourdin helped with brother Robert's clandestine correspondence. Isaac Hayne directed the committee on publication. John Townsend wrote the great pamphlets. William Dennison Porter served as the titular president. Judge Andrew Magrath offered legal advice. William L. Tennent, Jr., twenty-two years old, became secretary-treasurer.[34]

Young Tennent epitomized the desire, expressed in the 1860 Association's first appeal, "to shake off that lethargy" and that "slow poison called 'Love of the Union' which seems to have stultified" the South's old leaders. "By placing in the hands of the *youth* and *genius* of the South thousands of . . . incendiary pamphlets, by corresponding with all our leading men South, and . . . by putting our gallant little state in a posture of defense," they hoped to produce a viable "resistance of the Cotton States" to "meet the contemplated emergency of Lincoln's election."[35]

The 1860 Association did little to improve gallant South Carolina's armed defenses, except to summon parade companies. The First Regiment of Rifles, the Washington Artillery, the Zoave Cadets, the Palmetto Guards, and the Charleston Riflemen did march around the streets to celebrate, after the association's public propaganda and private correspondents created prospects of Cotton South cooperation. The published propaganda, the very essence of *non*-conspiratorial persuasion, included over 200,000 pamphlets, produced in but sixty days. This little miracle of lightning-fast editing, printing, and distribution showed that the best southern merchants could deploy the capitalist virtues as agilely as a Yankee. Under Robert Gourdin's direction, the association's

This previously unpublished image (opposite page) of the 1860 Association's great pamphleteer, John Townsend, has all the qualities of a supreme American early photograph— perfect clarity, original condition, clever props, ingenious staging, and an important message that transcends its arresting subject. Townsend here exudes the essence of the South Carolinians who first propelled an historic revolution: ultra-refined and ultra-wealthy coastal aristocrats who presented themselves before cameras as well as before deferential followers as old-fashioned republicans, leaning on ancient pillars and ancient texts and determined to achieve a nonrevolutionary revolution, without excesses, egalitarians, rabbles, or mobs. Together with such fastidious patriarchs as Robert Gourdin (this page, upper left), the 1860 Association's skilled organizer, and Andrew Magrath (upper right), the soberly theatrical judge, Townsend ultimately routed the wilder (in appearance as well as tactics) Robert Barnwell Rhett, Sr. (lower right). Courtesy of the South Caroliniana Library, University of South Carolina, Columbia (Townsend and Magrath) and the South Carolina Historical Society (Gourdin and Rhett).

pamphlets flew across the South even faster than John Townsend's Sea Island cotton sped to Belgian and French manufacturers of lace.

Some 165,000 copies of Townsend's *The Doom of Slavery* and *The South Alone Should Govern the South* spread the word that Lincoln's administration would immediately menace slavery by raising up a Southern Republican Party, with no "overt act" needed. Gourdin personally solicited an equally revealing 1860 Association pamphlet. James D. B. De Bow's *The Interest in Slavery of the Southern Non-slaveholder* offered formidable arguments, both economic and racial, for white plebeians to rally behind rich titans. While that proslavery objective had supposedly been clinched thirty years agone, the Robert Gourdins knew that the Solid South was a myth, making Lincoln's imminent Southern Republican Party of potential interest to Border South nonslaveholders.

The 1860 Association's officers prayed that their blizzard of pamphlets would draw forth pledges of cooperation with South Carolina Separatists. Meanwhile, Gourdin's secret correspondence sought assurances that the pamphlets had done their work—that enough Lower South luminaries would now promise to cooperate, once South Carolina Separatists dared secession. This was not the old sort of South Carolina Cooperationism: waiting for everyone else to share the action or someone else to start it. This was an inspired (or if you will, ominous) new sort of Cooperationism: seeking enough clandestine reassurances so that Separatists would dare to act alone.

The Robert Barnwell Rhetts, junior and senior, apparently received quicker answers to their parallel secret inquiries. The Rhetts had come to realize, perhaps because of the Gourdins' efforts, that the state's gentry needed other states' assurances. Rhett still impatiently conceived that South Carolinians should automatically see that Lower South slaveholders automatically would follow any Lower South revolution. But he would give his state's cowards the comforts that they should not need. We wrote "many of the Leading men of the different Southern States," Rhett Jr. later reported, asking questions about their "views and advice as to the course South Carolina should pursue."[36]

Except for Jefferson Davis's "discouraging" message, Rhett claimed that the private answers encouraged South Carolina to strike, certain that other states would follow. With the supposedly sufficient clandestine pledges packed in their bags, the Rhetts sped to Columbia for the early November legislative session. Perhaps their secret mail would brace the state's uneasy establishment to snatch the postelection moment away from Hammond, Orr, and Chesnut, immediately, unanimously, and irrevocably. Then the Rhetts, not such new pretenders as the Gourdins, would become the climactic Founding Fathers of a sublime Southern Confederacy.

CHAPTER 25

The Triumph

South Carolina's aristocratic republicans could all but finalize disunion before other states' egalitarian republicans could even convene a legislature. Only in this state did the legislative elite, not the citizens, continue to select Electoral College representatives. On Monday, November 5, the day before most American white males voted for president, South Carolina's legislative patriarchs met to exercise their archaic prerogative.

After South Carolina's legislators unanimously chose John Breckinridge's electors, Governor William Gist persuaded them to remain in session. If Lincoln won on the morrow and if legislators dispersed until their regular session (scheduled to begin on November 26), compromisers elsewhere would have three weeks to seize the initiative. But since South Carolina's legislators agreed to remain in Columbia, they could produce an instant secessionist fait accompli—if they could summon the nerve to capitalize on their head start.

– 1 –

The legislature could preserve South Carolina's head start by calling an almost immediate state secession convention. According to southern state's rights gospel, only the people of a state, in a state convention or popular referendum, could shift their consent to be governed from one government to another. The South Carolina constitution required a two-thirds legislative majority to summon a state convention. The summons must set dates for delegates to be elected and to convene. Early dates would prevent Cooperationists elsewhere from catching up with South Carolina precipitators.

While early dates came under heavy fire, no South Carolina legislator denied that the Union portended only curses—dishonorable insults, confiscatory taxes, and that Southern Republican Party. In contrast, disunion, *if* successfully achieved, offered only advantages—no insults, no protective tariffs, and no Lincoln party agitating inside the South. But *when* should secession be attempted, to have the best chance of success?

That "when" swelled with the 1850–52 difference between Cooperative State Secessionists and Separate State Secessionists. Cooperationists wished to hesitate long enough to prearrange collaboration with other Lower South states. They would delay a South Carolina state convention until mid-January at the earliest, so other Lower South states' conventions would meet first or simultaneously. Instead, Separate State Secessionists wished to preclude other Lower South states' alternatives to instant secession. Separatists would hurry a South Carolina state convention into session by mid-December at the latest, so other states' conventions would face an accomplished revolution.

A Kentuckian declared that the Separatists' haste "reminds me of the bull that undertook to butt the locomotive off the track—Courage admirable— Discretion small!" An anonymous *Charleston Courier* correspondent, "Festina Lente," cheered by the editor, skillfully developed the Cooperationist case for more discretion. "Festina Lente" would "make haste slowly. . . . Hasty and impatient advisers are bad advisers." Only "ardent and irregular minds" would supply the "calamitous counsels" that one state "should secede singly, under present circumstances." Instead, a southern "Congress of the States proposing to secede . . . should exhaust all honorable efforts to reform and restore the purity of the present Union on a safe basis, before they proceed to destroy it."[1]

Separate State Secessionists retorted that a southern convention would dawdle, or worse. William Porcher Miles emphasized that South Carolina must not delay "for a day. . . . All our best friends in the entire South urge . . . that our delay, under any pretext, would demoralize them at home," while our state's instant secession is "the best step . . . to advance the great cause . . . in all their states."[2]

Delay might also kill the great cause in South Carolina. Only for this one fleeting moment, U.S. Marshal Daniel H. Hamilton wrote, did South Carolina hold "the decision in her own hands." If "she falters, wavers for one moment, . . . 'Union-savers' " will "ask for delay" until "the first overt act on the part of Lincoln's Administration." Then, "the spirit of our people will either be broken, or they will themselves commit an 'overt act' by an attack on the [federal] Forts." That illegal "popular outbreak" would "destroy" South Carolina's "moral effect . . . upon the other Southern States and leave her with but little sympathy from her sisters."[3] Secession's fate thus seemed to hover in the balance, after the South Carolina legislators cast their votes for presidential electors on November 5 and declared war on each other over *when* the South Carolina convention should meet.

– 2 –

The odds on an early date improved that preelection Monday evening, when U.S. Senator James Chesnut, Jr., publicly swallowed his late private funk about fellow White Sulphur Springs vacationers. In the summertime, Chesnut had scorned other Southerners' presumption that South Carolina should suffer all the first risks. But speaking before a thousand cheering secessionists in Columbia on the nation's election eve, Chesnut urged that immediate peril compelled instant disunion, even with no assurances from other southern states.

One question, he declared, covers "all questions" now demanding "immediate solution": Should South "Carolina be governed by Carolinians"? Should outsiders' "blind consciences and crazy brains" govern you? Should you suffer a foe who condemns your folk as "semicivilized barbarians"? Shall you allow a northern enemy to "establish post offices at every crossroads, and fill them with the minions of the Black Republican power"? Should you permit "your cars and your coaches" to "groan beneath the

Certainly South Carolina's supreme power couple (and probably the Old South's too): James Chesnut, Jr., who belatedly came out for Separatism at the most timely moment, and Mary Chesnut, whose lyrical reports on traumatic events bested even William Henry Trescot's bon mots. Courtesy of the Mulberry Plantation, Camden, South Carolina.

weight of [abolitionists'] noxious matter"? If so, when Southerners at last revolt against the incendiaries, they will have "the army and navy" to subject us "to the fate of traitors."[4]

Our greatest danger, Chesnut would add in a December 3 oration, is the "peculiar character of the Puritan mind," at war with "any model save its own pattern." Because of Yankee puritans' invasive mentality, incendiary documents would flood our region. Southern Republicans would fill our offices. Enemies would control our mails. The resulting upheaval would make "Lincoln's election . . . a decree for emancipation. Slavery cannot survive the four years of an administration whose overwhelming influences" will be "brought to bear against it." To submit now is to guarantee that before 1865, we must *"slay the Negro, or ourselves be slain."*[5]

After Chesnut demanded immediate disunion at the Monday evening, November 5, Columbia rally, U.S. Congressman Milledge Bonham concurred. Bonham, previously rather vague about whether South Carolina should go it alone, now warned Columbia's citizens to act before other Southerners decided to hesitate. "If South Carolina goes, the other Southern States will follow." But if South Carolina failed to depart first, the South might wait, allowing Lincoln to put his agents "into the post office. If our own citizens refuse his offered positions, Lincoln will put in some others. . . . It would not be long before they would have a party formed against us." Like Chesnut, Bonham shuddered at the incendiary consequences.[6] With Chesnut and Bonham demanding that the legislature immediately call an early convention, only the dreaded Hammond, among the state's congressional representatives, remained unannounced. That loose cannon, Separatists privately fretted, still might stall the momentum that Chesnut had generated in Columbia, on the eve of Lincoln's election.

– 3 –

On Wednesday, November 7, the day after Lincoln triumphed, just the right sober Charleston revolutionaries staged just the right controlled rebellion. In a minor coincidence that preceded an imminent major coincidence, Robert Gourdin, chairman of the 1860 Association's executive committee, happened to be in the right place at the right time to make the right first move. Some obscure selection process, having nothing to do with secession, had placed the Charleston merchant in the foreman's chair of Charleston's U.S. District Court's grand jury, at the moment when news of Lincoln's election enveloped the city. After Judge Andrew Magrath asked Gourdin to deliver the grand jury's presentments, the foreman balked. A federal grand jury could not "proceed with the presentments," Gourdin announced, for the "ballot-box of yesterday" effectively ended federal jurisdiction in South Carolina.[7]

In his second-floor courtroom of the U.S. Court House building at 23 Chalmers Street, with its red-brick façade plastered over with gray cement,

Judge Magrath wanted the federal grand jury's defiance to be seen as gray and safe, not as red hot and revolutionary. If private citizens on a grand jury could close courts, they might also seize forts. Then disunion would be discredited. Three days later, Andrew Magrath would raspily tell Columbia lawmakers that he became "hoarse in [the] best of causes. I lost my voice in the attempt to say to the people of Charleston, wait the action of the state." The "thousands of men" who "stand on the sea shore with their guns, where three [federal] fortresses bristle with cannon," must allow legitimate authorities to "give the word."[8]

In his courtroom on November 7, after Gourdin gave the word that the people of Charleston would no longer bring indictments in a federal court, Andrew Magrath wished to demonstrate that only a judge could close a court. To emphasize his demonstration, he paused a suspense-filled moment before responding to Gourdin's defiance. Then he slowly rose, declaring that given the probable "action of the state," he must "prepare to obey its wishes." He "must close the Temple of Justice, raised under the Constitution of the United States," before mobocracy had "desecrated . . . its altar."

As he pronounced federal judicial process legally closed, Magrath's fingers crept to the spot where his silken judicial robe was fastened. He slowly undid the garment. He languidly slipped it off. He calmly folded it over his chair. He had, he announced, "for the last time, . . . administered the laws of the United States." Now, "the laws of our State" must become "our duties." Let all South Carolinians remember that "he who acts against the wish, or without the command of his State, usurps" its "inviolate . . . sovereign command."[9]

"There were few dry eyes among the spectators and auditors," reported the *Charleston Courier*, "as Judge Magrath divested himself of the Judicial Robe." Or as a Magrath worshipper marveled, "Here was a great political movement precipitated, not by bloody encounters in the street or upon the field, but by a deliberate and reasoned act in the most unexpected and conservative of all places—the United State courtroom."[10]

Magrath was just the Charlestonian to make the closure of a court seem to conserve law and order. Where Rhett looked like a disheveled revolutionary, Magrath bore the demeanor of a future Wall Street conservative. His hair was impeccably trimmed, precisely parted. His elegant English suit was fastidiously pressed. His head, too large for his body, advertised heavy learning. He had trained at Harvard Law School under Joseph Story, prince of nationalistic jurists, and in the Charleston law offices of James L. Petigru, guru of the scarce lowcountry unionists.[11]

This previous Cooperationist had first earned his reputation as the ultimate non-Rhett (Petigru aside!), in another of those symbolic tableaus in which Magrath seemed born to star. He had gained his U.S. judicial berth by becoming almost the only prominent lowcountryman to assist the upcountry's James L. Orr in achieving Rhett's then-horror, a South Carolina delegation to the 1856 National Democratic Convention. Rhett's *Charleston Mercury* had insulted Magrath as an especially self-serving traitor after Franklin

Pierce, Northern Democrat in the White House, raised the South Carolina "recreant" to the federal bench.

Edward Magrath, Andrew's brother, had thereupon challenged the *Mercury*'s editor (and Rhett's cousin), William Robinson Tabor, to a duel. Mary Chesnut considered Tabor the most beautiful young man in the state. But bullets disfigure beauty on the dueling grounds. Edward Magrath's shot ended Rhett's cousin's life. Andrew Magrath lived on as the man Rhett most loved to hate.[12]

On November 7, Magrath and Gourdin may well have planned their seemingly spontaneous courtroom drama precisely to seize the revolution from Rhett. The two longtime friends, both favorites of Charleston's drawing rooms, had graduated together in South Carolina College's tiny class of 1831. Both squires embodied the high-toned revolutionary—the only kind of rebel that the drawing room set could abide.

But one fact casts doubts on a prearranged scenario. Gourdin, a skilled orchestrator of political drama, had not prearranged a large audience. With only a handful of stragglers watching the foreman, Gourdin may have heard of Lincoln's election and spontaneously seen how a gray courthouse could spotlight a safe revolution. If so, Magrath spontaneously added his own insight into how a judge could advertise a revolution shorn of popular recklessness.

Whether planned or spontaneous, the Gourdin-Magrath spectacle, by hitting the right soothing lowcountry notes, inspired an answering chorus of resignations. Within hours, William F. Colcock, U.S. collector of the port of Charleston's custom duties, James Conner, U.S. district attorney, and Daniel Heyward Hamilton, U.S. marshal, all resigned. Only poor Alfred Huger, postmaster general since nullification times, endured in a Charleston federal post, to face charges of "traitor" and to pray "to God" for His "protection . . . in this Emergency."[13]

Gourdin and Magrath had indeed precipitated an emergency. A democratic government must supply courts. Lincoln could supply court officials only by handing the resigned offices to *someone*, with all the fury that such a potential Southern Republican could arouse. The *Charleston Mercury* had the symbolic and actual importance of the Gourdin-Magrath performance pegged perfectly: "The tea has been thrown overboard. The Revolution of 1860 has been initiated."[14]

Magrath initiated the next cautiously revolutionary scene. At the public celebration of the contagious resignations, the ex-judge, after being introduced, stood on the extreme left of the platform, motioning for cheers to cease. After waiting another of his eternal moments, he barely whispered, in the manner of a cautious nonagitator, that "the time for deliberation has passed." He then paused and crept, with slow, measured steps, to the extreme right of the stage. As he inched along, he passed his large handkerchief, perfectly folded on its diagonal, through his hands, as if pondering what to add. Finally, with no space left to travel, he turned, raised a clenched fist, and screamed that "the time for action has come."[15]

The audience (this time packed!) screeched its glee. This arguably first rebel yell could not be heard in Columbia. But news of the Magrath uproar sped across the telegraph wires. "The telegraphic announcement of the resignations in Charleston," exulted an observer, "was altogether unexpected and produced a thrill of sensation."[16] The revolution seemed to have commenced before legislators could even deliberate on whether to delay it.

– 4 –

Undeterred by the Charleston resignations, Cooperationists in the House and Senate still demanded proof that at least one other state would follow, if South Carolina seceded almost immediately. Other states' leaders could not be summoned to Columbia in time for an immediate legislative decision on an early convention date. Thus Separatists could only assuage Cooperationists' fears by reading encouraging secret letters, previously received from other states. For the moment, the success of immediate disunion would thrive or die on the credibility of a dozen or so clandestine missives.

The first batch of conspiratorial letters, exchanged between Gist and his gubernatorial colleagues, had provided insufficiently comforting assurances. "At first," winced Rhett's longtime ally William F. Colcock, our "correspondence with the leading men . . . of Georgia, Alabama, Florida, and Mississippi" displayed "considerable division of sentiment. But now I believe we have good ground for hope that those States will follow and sustain South Carolina." Colcock, however, also found grounds for "some doubt" that Georgia would cooperate.[17]

James F. Pettigrew, the patriarch who had been most responsible for defeating South Carolina's African slave trade reopening, read Colcock's letters. Pettigrew concluded that ultras again must be deterred. "We receive numerous letters from the Cotton states," noted Pettigrew, "urging us to secede alone" and professing confidence "that that the rest would certainly follow." But Pettigrew, seeing insufficient evidence for that "certainly," saw our "only safety" in "a Union of the Southern States in Convention."[18]

Robert Gourdin's secret letters from Georgians showed why Colcock confessed "some doubt" and why Pettigrew preferred a doubt-free southern convention. "Do not understand me to say that I am entirely without fear of our state," James Mercer Green wrote Gourdin from Macon. But "we all think here" that "the stern march of events will *drag us* out, if the cowards do not go willingly." So too, John M. Richardson of Perry, Georgia, warned Gourdin that cowards here "fear the possible consequences of secession." They forgot the "certainty" that Lincoln's rule "must lead first to the formation of a black republican party in our midst and then to a civil and servile war." Thus your "delay . . . will injure us." But speedy "action will exert a great influence."[19]

Great influence, yes, but an irresistible influence? The Rhetts, fearing this key question about the crucial state of Georgia, believed that their own secret letters would sway doubters. A visitor to Columbia, writing on the day of Lincoln's election, reported that the Rhetts are "in daily communication with various gentlemen from Geo Ala and Fla who say that if South Carolina goes out, those states will follow." The following morning, Wednesday, November 7, at 10:00 A.M. in Kinsler's Hall, the Rhetts put their private letters on public display, at an unofficial caucus of the legislators. To make the unofficial proceeding feel like an official occasion, General W. E. Martin, clerk of the Senate, read aloud the Rhetts' "letters from many of the Leading men of the different Southern States, giving their views and advice as to the course South Carolina should pursue."[20]

After Martin finished reading the letters (and almost at the same moment that Magrath in Charleston removed his robe), the Rhetts strode over to the legislative halls. There Robert Barnwell Rhett, Jr., in the House and Edmund Rhett in the Senate introduced resolutions that called for a South Carolina state convention to meet on December 17, forty days hence and before any other state's convention could assemble. Delegates to the convention would be elected on November 22, fifteen days hence and before South Carolina's outrage at Lincoln's election could cool.

The Rhetts swiftly discovered that their unofficial caucus had left doubters still unconvinced about such early dates. Qualms about immediacy's safety remained strongest in the old Cooperationist areas, the Charleston mercantile centers and the least enslaved, semimountainous upcountry districts. Representatives from these cautious areas preferred two suggested alternatives.

George Trenholm's anti-Rhett alternative, introduced in the Senate, particularly alarmed the Rhetts, not least because Trenholm urged it. This renowned Charleston merchant headed John Fraser and Co., a formidable rival of the Gourdins, with branch offices in Liverpool and New York. A hard-driving capitalist, Trenholm was also a debonair charmer, a favorite of cultivated ladies and of hearty outdoorsman. To this impeccable Charleston persona, Trenholm added impeccable secessionist credentials. He had been one of the few leading Charleston merchants who had favored Separate State Secession in 1850–52. Jefferson Davis would soon choose him to be Confederate secretary of the treasury.

In November 1860, this trusted capitalist considered seceding alone too risky. He especially saw Georgia's support as too uncertain. So Trenholm's Senate resolution called for the legislature to adjourn, with no convention called but a commissioner to Georgia elected. Trenholm hoped that the commissioner would arrange an early joint secession.

South Carolina's ultras despaired that the cursed Georgians would instead force Trenholm's commissioner to arrange joint attendance at a southern convention. Meanwhile Charleston's Henry Lesesne's second alternative to an immediate state convention, presented to the House, would give the governor power to call a convention later, if and when that chief executive had assurances that some other state would secede.

The legislative majority preferred the Rhetts' gamble on immediacy to the Trenholm-Lesesne preference for a later, supposedly surer thing. All those clandestine letters from other states had convinced most legislators that Separate State Secession would be safe enough. But the Trenholm-Lesesne options rallied a Cooperationist minority of indeterminate (and indeterminable) size, still unconvinced by the secret letters.

The South Carolina constitution gave doubters some leverage. Convention bills required a two-thirds majority in each chamber. Even if delayers could not quite scrape up one-third of either Senate or House members, precipitators' need for unanimity would refortify Trenholm and Lesesne. If word went out that South Carolinians disagreed, other states might dodge the state's Separatist force. But if South Carolina legislators unanimously supported immediate action, the epidemic might consume at least some Lower South states.

Sometime on either Wednesday, November 7, or Thursday, November 8, the Charleston delegation met in caucus for five angry hours, seeking a compromise between the Trenholm-Lesesne Cooperationist proposals, with no convention date arranged, and the Rhetts' Separatist proposal, with a December 17 convention assured. Exhausted debaters finally split the difference. They settled on a January 15 date for the South Carolina convention to convene, with delegates elected on January 8. On Friday, November 9, the Senate passed the compromise, 44–1, with Trenholm's blessings. Alfred Aldrich's House Committee on the Territories almost immediately sent the Senate bill to the House floor, with its blessings (and Lesesne's).[21]

The Rhetts found nothing blessed about a delayed state convention. Against their insistence that South Carolina citizens must vote for convention delegates immediately, lest the people's white-hot rage at Lincoln's election would freeze, the legislature's decision for a January 8 election might allow cooler second thoughts to prevail. Against the Rhetts' demand for an early state convention, lest other states' momentum for a southern convention would swell, the legislature's decision for a January 15 convention might allow a southern convention trial balloon to soar. Georgia's resistance could especially become consuming, as it had been in 1850.

Above all else, the Rhetts had exhorted South Carolina to act first, so that the most secessionist state would drag its less secessionist Lower South compatriots out of the Union. Instead, the legislature's timetable might well leave South Carolina deciding last, so that the Lower South majority could drag the most fiery state into a southern convention, where an Upper South majority might rule. Three days after Lincoln's election, Separate State Secession seemed at least temporarily overthrown and Cooperative State Secession in the saddle, by the Senate's 44–1 margin, no less.

– 5 –

Separatists' initial defeat proved that conspiratorial weapons had been too blunt. Secret letters had provided the best source of information on the subject that nervous South Carolinians *had* to see illuminated: Would the state again stand alone? The information had left doubts about Georgia. As Jefferson Davis had emphasized, without Georgia, a gaping geographic hole might preclude any viable Lower South republic.

Worse, the Rhetts had provided the only secret letters available in Columbia, and those agitators faced grave suspicion. While few thought that the Rhetts had cooked the letters, such fanatics might be displaying some missives and hiding others. Worse still, they might not have even written to Lower South correspondents who would discourage disunion. Worst of all, the Lower South leaders who had written the Rhetts back, including Mississippi's Davis and William S. Barry and Alabama's Leroy P. Walker, were Southern National Democrats. Such trimmers were, by Rhett's own standards, suspect dissimulators. Could such wily politicos' secret guarantees be trusted?

Suspicions lingered partly because the letters were secret. No one could watch the pledgers' body language as they pledged. Nor could anyone know whether promises rendered in private would be kept in public. Conspiratorial information, never a republican's favorite, always has the shady feel of the closet. Any democrat who depends solely on pledges shrouded in shadows wishes that promises had been rendered in the glaring sunlight. Here, suspect conspiratorial information stood burdened with suspect South Carolina communicators, plus suspiciously politic Lower South guarantors, plus suspiciously incomplete Georgia guarantees. Conspiratorial letters required supplemental assurances, hopefully proclaimed in the open air.

– 6 –

Instead, the ultras received another secret blow—and an indication that an open-air campaign would further boost the Cooperationists. On November 6, Alfred Aldrich had written U.S. Senator James Henry Hammond on behalf of several legislators, asking Hammond's views on Separate State Secession. Aldrich perhaps had hoped that Chesnut's belated endorsement of instant action would pull along the state's other U.S. senator.[22]

Hammond, anticipating the request, had been drafting his answer since mid-October. On November 8, the senator sent back his thirty-five-page response. The potential bombshell arrived in Columbia that day, or more likely November 9, just as Aldrich's House committee surrendered to the Senate's 44–1 vote for a delayed, mid-January state convention. Richard Yeardon, the Cooperationist editor of the *Charleston Courier* and recent admiring publisher of "Festina Lente," suspected that the author of the Barnwell Court House Address might have again questioned South Carolina's rashness. So Yeardon requested that Aldrich release Hammond's letter for publication.

Aldrich knew that Yeardon's request, if granted, might make the Charleston caucus's compromise, that January 15 convention date, seem recklessly early, not disastrously late. Picking up where the Barnwell Court House Address left off, Hammond's letter declared that "I do not regard our circumstances in the Union as desperate." Like almost all other South Carolina delayers, the U.S. senator conceded that "the South would be better off" in a "properly reorganized" southern republic. The present Union "drains us of our money" and "deprives us . . . of our good name." To "be freed from the antislavery agitation . . . would be a greater blessing to the South even than all the blessings of the Union."[23]

Still, Hammond believed that the Union had its blessings, for "the South . . . can, when united, dictate, as it has always done, the internal and foreign policy of the country." The senator based his optimism on typical South Carolina pessimism about mobocratic politics. "At the North," Hammond declared, "politics is a trade." The spoilsmen "go into it for gain." For that reason, no Yankee has "ever been twice elected President." Mr. Lincoln's administration will also break down "before it can accomplish anything detrimental," for its "antislavery agitation" will "not gain them spoils and power."

Hammond called Lincoln's doomed administration safer than disunion by South Carolina alone. Here again, the senator saw federal politicos through contemptuous aristocratic lenses. He called Southern National Democrats, as he had observed them in depraved Washington, better than Yankees but not by much. They remain so "passionate for" federal "place, for power, and for spoils" that "it would probably require two defeats . . . to bring" them "up to the point of secession." Moreover, southern spoilsmen's "prejudice" against South Carolina's precipitancy has not "abated." For us to "attempt to take the lead" would subject South Carolina "again to the indignities which other states have heaped upon her, by mocking her."

Such insufferable mockery, continued Hammond, forces us to "consider our power before we rush into a contest for our rights." Our state convention must not secede until "one, two, or more other states should, by similar conventions, resolve also to secede." Before we risk secession, all seceding states must also agree to "adopt, without any modification, alteration, or addition, the present Constitution of the United States." Otherwise, the mob's flatterers will "seek notoriety by proposing" popular elections of "judges, Senators, and Representatives annually." Such seducers of the rabble "must be kept from putting their hands upon our Constitution or we shall have the guillotine at work." He feared "our own Demagogues at home more than all enemies abroad." Let us not, James Henry Hammond concluded, risk "utter anarchy" and traitors' "halters around" our "necks" with an "impolitic, unwise, and unsafe . . . attempt" by "one state . . . to dissolve the Union."

Hammond's letter, if rescued from Alfred Aldrich's pocket, could only enhance the senator's reputation for aristocratic brilliance. Where Judge Magrath almost lost his voice in pleading that a revolutionary mob must not close federal courts or seize federal forts, and where James Henley Thornwell preferred the abolition of slavery to the risk of revolutionary chaos, Hammond would shut down the revolutionary process until the masses had been contained. Where disunionists feared that southern demagogues' desire to feed at the public trough would arouse a Southern Republican Party, Hammond answered that southern spoilsmen's appetite at the federal banquet table would dissipate any disunion movement. Where disunionists claimed that Lincoln would perpetuate Yankee tyranny, Hammond answered that no Northerner had ever perpetuated his own presidency. Furthermore, a united South had always dethroned corrupt Yankees.

With delayers in control of the South Carolina legislature, and with James Hammond likely to defuse a popular uprising against legislative delay, the world was closing in on the ultras. Within three days, the bill that delayed a state convention, already approved once by the Senate and by the relevant House committee, would likely pass the required three readings in both the House and Senate. Alfred Aldrich would be fortunate to keep Richard Yeardon's *Charleston Courier* from disseminating James Hammond's letter for even that seventy-two hours.

Only one last ploy seemed possible to stymied legislative Separatists. If a public outburst for instant disunion could be stimulated, before Hammond's letter became public knowledge and before the legislature finalized a delayed state convention, perhaps an early secession convention could be salvaged. Accordingly, Rhett asked others to telegraph William F. Colcock down in Charleston, pleading that an instant public outcry against a delayed convention must be whipped up. Rhett, despairing that his reputation for wildness would poison any such emergency rescue, dared not send the telegraph himself. His, for once, lack of daring again showed that cautious thinking like Hammond's could rule this hour.[24]

– 7 –

But the Separatists' hour was coming, thanks not at all to Rhett's indirect plea to Colcock. Instead, the cautious revolutionaries in Charleston's 1860 Association, the very new leaders who sought to rescue revolution from Rhett, had for days planned a monster public rally in Institute Hall. But no secessionist could have planned the amazing coincidence that allowed this meeting to reverse the legislature's late decision. Because a railroad happened to be completed two weeks before the legislature tentatively voted for a delayed state convention, and because just the right Georgians happened to be in Charleston on the night of the legislature's decision, to celebrate the railroad's opening, the 1860 Association could marshal the perfect speakers in the open air to quiet those qualms about secret letters.[25]

A modern railroad might seem an ironic engine to further a reactionary revolution. But that aspect of the railroad coincidence was not as incongruous as it seems. The Charleston mercantile community had long exuded the capitalistic creativity that its best customers, the absentee lowcountry planters, mocked as overly Yankee. Robert Gourdin's organizational flair with the

1860 Association had been one result of a modern capitalist spirit that thrived among Charleston merchants.

For three decades, Charleston merchants had pursued a challenge worthy of Yankee capitalism: snatching the Savannah River trade from Savannah itself. Charleston's would-be pirates had previously built a railroad from Hamburg to Charleston in the early 1830s. From Hamburg, located up the Savannah River's South Carolina side, produce could be hauled overland the 136 miles to Charleston and then shipped to the outside world.

This then longest railroad in the world deployed the first locomotives built in America for regular steam service. The initial dinosaur, the Best Friend of Charleston, blew up before the railroad line had been finished. Subsequent locomotives, puffing along at ten miles per hour, proved tolerably profitable. But the Best Friend's demise epitomized the initial failure of the city's grand dream to rob Savannah of its river's trade.

As Savannah boomed in the 1850s while Charleston limped, South Carolina capitalists decided that sharing the lush Savannah River trade would be more plausible than stealing it. So the city's merchants determined to build

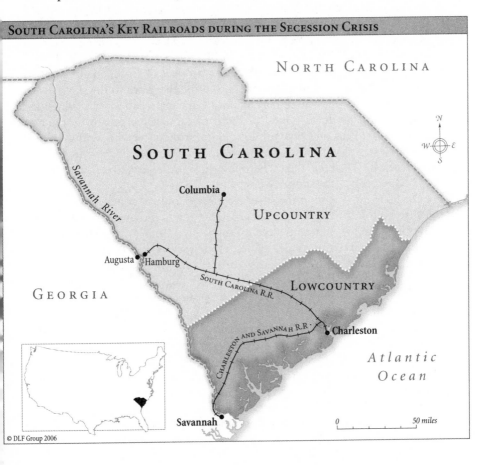

SOUTH CAROLINA'S KEY RAILROADS DURING THE SECESSION CRISIS

NORTH CAROLINA

SOUTH CAROLINA

Savannah River

Columbia

UPCOUNTRY

Augusta Hamburg

SOUTH CAROLINA R.R. LOWCOUNTRY

GEORGIA

CHARLESTON AND SAVANNAH R.R. Charleston

Atlantic Ocean

Savannah

0   50 miles

© DLF Group 2006

another 100-plus-mile railroad, this time running from Charleston to Savannah. Charlestonians dreamed that Savannah's trade with the North would then run through South Carolina's more northerly Atlantic outlet. Alternately, Savannah merchants conceived that Charleston's trade might then run through their more prosperous port.

The Charleston and Savannah Railroad Company, chartered in 1854, had laid down only thirty miles of track from Charleston by 1857. Then the national economic panic forced work to be suspended. On October 28, 1858, construction resumed on tracks over the remaining seventy-three miles of swampy muck to Savannah. Exactly two years later and precisely one week before Lincoln's election, the 300-plus black hands happened to finish their brutal swamp labor. They had lost ten of their number, half to killing fevers and half to brutal accidents.[26]

On November 1, 1860, the first white passengers breezed along the latest fruits of black men's burdens. The next day at 9:00 A.M., eighty prominent Charlestonians boarded their city's (hopefully) new best friend for the six-hour bumpy ride to Savannah. At 3:00 P.M., Savannah's Mayor Charles Colcock Jones, Jr., met the train and began the rendezvous of the two city's elites.[27] The visitors delightedly found that Jones Jr., not yet thirty and Harvard educated, exuded a sophisticate's manners. Savannah's mayor also possessed an ancestry that even Charleston blue bloods could envy. His father, Charles Colcock Jones, Sr., a Presbyterian prophet of so-called slavery, had contributed famously to the movement to bring the Word to the slaves.

The son's contempt resembled a South Carolina reactionary's. When the young Harvard graduate talked of "two races," he meant not blacks and whites but Yankees and Southerners. Jones pronounced the Yanks "a poisonous brood, . . . with hissing tongues and noxious breath," raving amidst their "cold hills" about their "heresies and false conceptions of a 'higher law.'" Obviously, "the sooner we separate, the better."[28]

The young mayor with the silver (to Charlestonians) tongue and the awesome (to high-minded planters) father led his guests through exquisite Savannah, planned in the eighteenth century and lately gloriously enhanced. The old plan had featured twenty-three squares, erected several blocks apart, each a little park lined with mansions. The squares ran in rows from the riverfront to mammoth Forsythe Park. This climactic park's huge 1858 fountain, wrought in iron, charmed as delicately as many European cities' fanciful sprays.

Savannah's far greater prosperity than Charleston's in the 1850s had yielded not higher and thicker walls between older "single" houses but many spectacular new dwellings to accompany the fine new fountain. Many of the new mansions featured a wide-open view, to and from the squares. This opulent city, as open as its profuse parks, could offer a southern republic so wonderfully much, if its fathers would only merge their more public elegance with Charleston's more private brand.

The banquet that November 2 evening at the Pulaski Hotel enhanced the possibility. The main Savannah speaker, Francis Bartow, exuded as much youthful cultivation as Jones Jr. and as congenial visions as Jones Sr. After graduating with highest honors from the University of Georgia, the Savannahian had studied at Yale before coming home as heir apparent to John Berrien. Berrien, Whig Nationalists' longtime U.S. senator from Georgia, laid multiple hands on young Bartow. The heir studied law under the U.S. senator, married his daughter, assumed his partnership in one of Savannah's finest legal firms, and reinvigorated his Lower South nationalistic Whiggery. Meanwhile, Bartow directed eighty-nine slaves, accepted the captaincy of Savannah's elite corps, the Oglethorpe Light Infantry, and traded Harvard-Yale taunts with Harvard's Jones Jr. The Old South did not make cavaliers more at ease than Francis Bartow.

During the Civil War, Savannah's prime ex-American nationalist, now turned into its prime Confederate nationalist, mustered his men into the Confederate, not the Georgia ranks. When Georgia's arch state's righter, Governor Joseph Brown, objected, Bartow wheeled on his state's chief executive, declaring that "I shall never think it necessary to obtain YOUR consent to enter the service of my country." At First Manassas on July 24, 1861, Captain Bartow would not stop changing for his new nation. After a ball killed his horse, he clamored aboard a killed rebel's horse and galloped toward a fatal bullet. As the contemptible Yankee's shot crashed into his heart, he screamed, "They have killed me, but never give up this field." When the coffin containing this first famous Confederate casualty rolled through Charleston, more of its citizens turned out to mourn than ever before.[29]

Back at the November 2, 1860, celebratory dinner at the Pulaski Hotel, Francis Bartow earned Charlestonians' adulation with his "pledge that we will defend South Carolina, rash though we think her, precipitate though we deem her, with all the energy and courage of a brother." A "sovereignty" on your "side of the Savannah River," and a colliding "sovereignty on this side," the ex-Whig nationalist explained, is an "absurdity," as "all history teaches. . . . Are we to play the game now playing in Italy today?" Are we to allow South Carolina to "be a Tuscany" and Georgia to "be a Piedmont," with "one little province . . . under the protection of England, and another tied to France"? If so, "we shall ever be a degraded people."

Bartow conceded that "if you think that the time has come" for disunion, we "differ." But should "you choose to" break up the Union "without consulting us, you have the power of precipitating us into any kind of revolution that you choose. But my counsel to you is not to do it." The balding, mustached patriarch received "tremendous applause" from both coastal Georgia and South Carolina squires.[30]

The next day, the Charlestonians begged their Savannah hosts to let them repay the hospitality, a week hence. Come see us, they urged, and help us celebrate the completion of our mutual railroad, on our terrain next time. On November 3, three days before Lincoln's election (and before South Carolina's ultras had any idea they would be in trouble on November 9), Savannah's finest accepted the invitation to come on over—on November 9! Thus would the chance completion date of a railroad yield the chance presence of just the right Georgians in Charleston on just the right evening.

– 8 –

Chance leads to destiny only when beneficiaries of luck seize advantage of their good fortune. Robert Gourdin, with mercantile offices in both Charleston and Savannah, became one of six members of the committee to welcome the visitors. From this position, Gourdin joined with fellow leaders of the 1860 Association to plan an extravaganza that would still be called the grandest Charleston party a half century later. After the Charleston and Savannah Railroad puffed into its Ashley River station at 3:00 P.M. on November 9, the Charleston city council escorted Savannah's patriarchs onto the steamer *Carolina*. The ensuing tour of Charleston's lovely harbor proceeded up and down the Ashley, up and down the Cooper, with multitudes cheering on all shores. After the *Carolina* landed on Charleston's side of the Ashley, the best Charleston carriages with the finest decorated horses transported the guests to the Mills House. At this hotel, Charleston's plushest, the visitors barely had time to splash their faces before the early evening feast beckoned.

The spread at the Mills House, the *Charleston Mercury* rightly claimed, "would have satisfied the Lord Mayor of London." Seventy-seven Georgians and 123 South Carolinians consumed turtle soup; then turkey, mutton, capon, ham, tongue, lamb chops, and duck with olives; then shrimps, fried oysters, and turtle steak with wine sauce; then pies, pastries, ice cream atop meringue, figs, and coffee; all washed down with sherry, bourbon, scotch, wine, champagne, claret, port, brandy, and Madeira. As the tables groaned less under the weight of the disappearing edibles (and some gourmands secretly groaned more), toasts and speeches came fiery and heavy, first for the wondrous new railroad, then for a collaboration of cavaliers, whether from Charleston or Savannah, to fight to the death for southern honor. Mary Chesnut, trying to sleep in a room above the din, found relief from the "hot, fervid, after supper southern style" only in one sweet voice. She sent down to "ask the name" of the exception. It was old Alfred Huger, still called a traitor for continuing to deliver the U.S. mails, still chanting for Union while other diners ranted for secession.[31]

With the banquet cheers assaulting Mrs. Chesnut's ears, Gourdin and several fellow impresarios escorted several handpicked Georgians over to Institute Hall to speak to the gathering of a thousand and more Charlestonians, less well fed than the Mills House crowd and eager to take in some Georgian oratorical treats.[32] After what they had heard the previous week in Savannah and just now in the Mills House, the 1860 Association leaders figured that Francis Bartow would offer the richest oratorical delights.

Bartow outdid his effort of seven days since. The ex-Whig first reestablished his credentials as a fervent nationalist, still a fancier of the American nation. "I am a Union man," Bartow proclaimed to frowning disunionists, "in every fiber of my heart. I have gloried in its missions of humanity. . . . God has never launched a nation on a more magnificent career. It has been the home of the oppressed and the asylum of the desolate from every land. In it today are wrapped the hopes of universal man."

No other wordsmith in Charleston that word-saturated night, save for Alfred Huger, exuded such spread-eagle American patriotism. At Savannah's Pulaski Hotel a week earlier, Bartow's nationalistic fervor had led him to urge South Carolina not to create an alternate nation. Still, his unionism had made him the more compelling when he conceded that, if his neighboring state did it, their new nationalism must become his too.

In Institute Hall, Bartow reinvented himself as the sincere unionist who had already been yanked away from his adored nation. He now wished South Carolina to tug the South harder toward an inescapable new nation's destiny. After a week of mulling over his personal exposure to these rabid South Carolinians, Bartow declared himself "tired of this endless controversy. I am wearied with seeing this threatening cloud." Since "the storm is to come," as I now know "it must, be its fury ever so great, I court it now, in my day of vigor and strength." He was tonight "ready for it. Put it not off until tomorrow," for "we shall not be stronger by waiting."[33]

This aristocratic soulmate's pledge, presented in person with obvious sincerity, trumped a dozen half-hedging promises, especially about Georgia, in duplicitous politicians' clandestine letters. Gourdin's crowd's other hand-picked main speaker was just the Georgian to complete Separatism's stunning new credibility. Back at the Mills House, Savannah's Henry Rootes Jackson had answered the toast that "Southern Civilization . . . must be maintained at any cost" with a tirade for a southern nation.

Yet the "trumpet-tongued" disunionist also possessed all the old unionist credentials that made Francis Bartow so creditable. Jackson had helped his cousin and political intimate Howell Cobb save the Union in 1850. He had brought to his unionist alliance with his Cobb cousins the same urbane sophistication that Bartow brought to his nationalistic alliance with his Berrien in-laws. Where Bartow had pursued graduate education at Yale, Jackson had there finished first in his undergraduate class. Where Bartow's love of history made him determined not to allow the Georgia–South Carolina environs to repeat Italy's folly, Jackson would be for twenty-five years president of the Georgia Historical Society.[34] To this respect for historical learning, Jackson added the gifts of a minor poet, much like William Grayson in style and substance. Where Grayson's couplets celebrated so-called slavery's superiority to a hireling's bondage, Jackson's *Tallulas* (1850) lamented the elderly South's deserters to the new Southwest:.

> Ye citizens of Georgia!
> Ye have a noble State . . .
> Oh where in South or West,

> Can ye meet a sweeter realm . . .
> Does the exile and the rover
> A true contentment find . . .
> Not in the wild adventure
> Not in the restless mind . . .
> You were born in Georgia . . .
> Could you ask a better home . . .
> She needs but zealous spirits
> Her riches to unfold.[35]

With a gentleman's manners to match an amateur's poetry and with an impeccably carved beard and mustache to advertise his gentility, Henry Jackson delighted the Institute Hall celebrants with another pledge of Georgia's support. His words on that occasion have not survived. But in 1860–61, whenever this hero of Georgia's unionism in 1850 suspected even a "shadow of a doubt" about "going out of the Union *at once*," he roared that "everything may be lost by any sort of delay." We must "cow," as they ought to be cowed, "the cowards." If we retreat "an inch, . . . the *cowardly* . . . will take to their heels" in flight from disunion.

Jackson loved to excoriate not only southern "cowards" but also the "corrupt . . . Yankees, and Yankee gold" that infected North and South too. Anything Yankee, wherever it "skulks," was "impure, inhuman, uncharitable, unchristian and uncivilized." He would add "barbarism and heathen," but those words were "scarcely applicable to demons of hell in the guise of men," who have spawned "all . . . hellishisms, including . . . equalityism and negrophilism."

This Yale man's fighting words were as sweet to the Charlestonians as Jones Jr.'s and Francis Bartow's excoriations had been. The three ex–Ivy Leaguers had lived with those Yankees, knew them intimately, and could not abide the fiends. But equally important, the three wealthy patriarchs were like carbon copies of Charleston's 1860 Association leaders. These Georgians were gentlemen to their heels, fond of elegant morsels for the stomach and for the brain, brethren whose word could absolutely be trusted. Georgia's candid guarantees had come far from the half-guarantees in Rhett's secret letters, written by suspected Southern National Democrats. Now Savannah stood pledged in the open air, and "hurrah" screamed the crowd of Charleston and Savannah dandies, leaping up and down as if in a Baptist revival camp and throwing their hats toward Institute Hall's towering ceiling.[36]

"A wild storm seemed suddenly to sweep over the minds of men," the *Mercury* reported, and "every man" in Institute Hall "instantly recognized . . . that he stood in the presence of the *Genius of Revolution*." Around 10:00 P.M., ecstatic revolutionaries resolved to telegraph the legislature, demanding a state convention "at the earliest possible moment," to "sever our connection with the present Government." The celebrants also resolved to send messengers on "a special train of cars from Charleston to Columbia" on the morrow to repeat the insistence on immediatism in person.

At 10:30 P.M., the telegraph wires conveyed the news to Charleston's startled representatives in Columbia. The telegram declared that "the greatest meeting ever held in this city is now assembled in Institute Hall. . . . Mr. Jackson, Mr. Bartow, and others from Georgia . . . have pledged their state." Charlestonians' demand for a convention "at an early date . . . cannot be restrained." Coming "by train tomorrow" will be further evidence of the "unprecedented and indescribable . . . feeling" here.[37] With Georgia lined up behind South Carolina, how could South Carolina pause?

Early the next morning, three of the four lately resigned federal officials boarded the special train, to carry that question to Columbia. The travelers included ex-judge Andrew Magrath, ex–U.S. attorney general James Conner, and ex–collector of the customs William Colcock. Mary Chesnut rode the train too, beginning her streak of being in the right place at the right time during the Civil War drama. Taking up her pen, she took advantage of her good fortune, giving posterity, in her unrivaled diary, uncanny descriptions of surpassing events. Her literary triumph would follow the formula of the 1860 Association's political exploitation of their railroad coincidence: enjoy incredible good luck, squeeze it for all it is worth, and obscure folk can make—or write—history.

The train riders, wrote Mary Chesnut, "were a deputation from Charleston rising against tyrants," warning representatives in Columbia that "they were too slow, to hurry up, dissolve the Union or it would be worse for them—there was a fire in the rear." As ex-judge Magrath would emphasize in Columbia, Charlestonians came to warn the legislature that the hottest fire, illegal mobs seizure of federal forts, would consume patriarchs who delayed a legal revolution. Ex–U.S. marshal D. H. Hamilton, who remained in Charleston to savor the mood, marveled at "the most impressive sight," a "people rising . . . to hasten the action of the legislature."[38] It was an especially unusual sight in South Carolina, where legislators customarily told citizens when to act. But then again, "the people" who rose up in Charleston were patriarchs such as Gourdin, milking the words of patriarchs such as Bartow, seeking to prevent Charleston's own mob no less than a Yankee president from pitching an upper-class universe into chaos.

– 9 –

Upon arrival in Columbia around 2:00 P.M. on Saturday, November 10, William F. Colcock articulated the new mood in Charleston. "We now stand in the presence of history," cried Colcock, "about to perform the greatest Drama ever enacted." The epic has been delayed because the wrong question has been "asked: 'Do you expect aid in any other quarter.'" The right question must now be asked: "Can we not reasonably expect to have allies from other quarters." After our Institute Hall meeting last night, "I tell you yes! From distinguished sons of Georgians, we have the highest assurance—nay I almost feel at liberty to call it a guarantee—that Georgia will be with us."[39]

Colcock shrewdly here did not overstate his case. One mass meeting with two Georgians did not an unconditional guarantee make. Robert Gourdin and other 1860 Association leaders, after all, had picked and chosen among potential speakers, just as the Rhetts had probably picked and chosen among potential correspondents. But the new filtered information did supplement the old filtered information to create exactly what Colcock claimed: a reasonable expectation that if South Carolina acted, even Georgia would follow.

Henry Ravenel, formerly a Charleston delayer, explained in his diary why reasonable expectation had now turned his head. "I have heretofore always opposed *separate state action*," he affirmed, because "we could do nothing successfully alone—but in joint action we can accomplish our deliverance." Now, "I believe we have assurances" of "co-operation. . . . That contingency now seems so sure, that I approve most heartily [of] the intention of our State to secede first." Ravenel's shift lent truth to William Porcher Miles's whoop of triumph. We "feared" Charleston, wrote the congressman, because "its mercantile interests" might again "hold back and prove lukewarm." Now the city "has led the van in the movement for secession."[40]

The race toward revolution became irresistible because the secret letters and the railroad coincidence eased each other's limitations. Clandestine letters had been too suspect without the railroad meeting. Closed discourse, even in so aristocratic a republic as South Carolina, bore the smell of manipulated distortion. But one public meeting, without all those letters, would have seemed a noisy exception. Taken together, otherwise suspect secret letters and an otherwise suspect open public demonstration had created Charlestonians' reasonable expectation. And if Charleston would finally dare, what legislator could hold back? Or as John Cunningham asked in the state legislature, when Georgians "invoke us to lead, is there a Cooperationist . . . who will ask us to wait?"[41]

– 10 –

Still another coincidence, arriving precisely at this moment of decision, polished off any lingering Cooperationist attempt to wait. Amidst the excitement of the Charleston special train's arrival in Columbia, rumors flew around town that Georgia's U.S. Senator Robert Toombs had resigned, in anticipation of his state's imminent secession. No one in Columbia could be sure that fact lay behind rumor. But Bartow's and Jackson's speeches in Charleston made the apparent news about Toombs seem more creditable, just as the apparent news about Toombs made Bartow and Jackson seem less exceptional. The resignations seemed to be coming as fast as the train and the telegraph could convey them: first Gourdin as foreman, then Judge Magrath, then Colcock and Conner and Dan Hamilton, now Bobby Toombs. With federal officials disappearing, Cooperationists might as well allow Separatists to have their early state convention, rather than hold out for delay and a southern convention.

William F. Colcock, in his November 10 address to the Columbia crowd that met the Charleston train, demanded that all doubters now give way. A "unanimity," he urged, "will have a tremendous effect" in making our reasonable expectation of Lower South secession accurate. Secession's Lower South opponents, explained Colcock, expect "division and discord among ourselves." But if news "goes out to the world that South Carolina, by a unanimous vote," has shucked her doubts, "she will decide the destiny of the South."[42]

Henry Lesesne, along with a few Charleston representatives and a few legislators from South Carolina's least enslaved, partially mountainous districts, still preferred a surer secessionist destiny. They were underwhelmed by two Georgians' after-dinner speeches and by one Georgia U.S. senator's purported resignation. But even to whisper for Cooperation, they had to brave as ferocious an insistence on "traitors'" silence as had ever befouled the Slave South's not-so-republican politics of white republicanism.

The politics of loyalty, with its trademark insistence that disloyalty to the Southland remain undercover, had limited democratic discourse in every presidential election in the South since the 1830s. During the South Carolina secession crisis, intensified social pressure assured dissenters' silence. "In this great turning point in the destiny of the South," wrote John Townsend, "no man can remain neutral. . . . He who is not with her, in the hour of her extremity is, without being conscience of it perhaps, against her . . . and will be an Abolitionist."[43]

With every legislator who still urged delay now called an imminent abolitionist, opponents of a December 17 state convention dove under cover. Henry Lesesne reported that "numbers of men," while "holding the [delaying] views" that he had "expressed," now do "not like to speak openly, so violent is the opposite feeling." With Lesesne already "suspected," any report of "these remarks," warned a friend, must not *"mention his name."*[44]

This smothering atmosphere engulfed Columbia after the transforming news from Charleston arrived. By 4:30 P.M. on Saturday, November 10, almost exactly twenty-four hours after the Senate had voted 44–1 for a January 15 convention (with elections for delegates on January 8), the House voted 117–0 for a December 17 convention (with elections for delegates on December 6). That evening, the Senate concurred 42–0. Two days later, the Rhetts' hasty convention date sailed unanimously through all three readings in both houses.[45]

Only one threat to South Carolina's apparent unanimity remained. James Hammond's letter still smoldered in Alfred Aldrich's pocket. Knowing that Aldrich's censorship would have to end if Hammond objected, William D. Porter wrote the U.S. senator on November 11, a day after the legislature's unanimous vote for a December 17 convention. Porter, president of both the State Senate and the 1860 Association, begged Hammond to forge a "common cause" and "a united front." Because "things have taken a new aspect since you wrote," Porter explained, "I have not shown your letter to a soul." Charleston, the South Carolina site "most exposed" to federal cannon, has become most "clamorous for secession. The advice seems to indicate that Georgia will secede." Since you "are known to have inclined against immediate action," you can "help us with Georgia and with Georgia, we can do everything." Our "ball is in motion." No South Carolinian "can resist the current." I hope "you will not oppose it but help it on. It will at least make them respect us."[46]

William Porter's plea marked another turning point. Just as William Gist's response to southern governors' late October letters could have advanced or precluded a southern convention, so James Hammond's response to the South Carolina legislature could have provoked or canceled a South Carolina public brawl between Separatists and Cooperationists. If Gist had written back encouragement of the budding southern convention movement (and encouraged the South Carolina legislature to set a late date for a South Carolina convention), representatives of the people of all the South, in southern convention assembled, could have made the crucial decision on disunion. If James Hammond had defied the South Carolina legislature by leading a public crusade for cooperation with other states, during the imminent election of delegates to the state convention, the people of South Carolina could have made the crucial decision on Separate State Secession.

But Hammond deplored such mobocratic decisions. Porter's plea that Hammond must not help the world again mock South Carolina counted with the U.S. senator. Still more impelling was Porter's declaration that the aristocracy in legislature assembled had spoken, and all elitist republicans must fall silent. Porter reported "a great desire here that you should follow the example of Toombs" in resigning from the U.S. Senate. "Chesnut has done so."[47]

Chesnut had indeed just done so, even if Toombs had not. On Monday, November 12, thirty minutes after Hammond received Porter's half-false plea, the U.S. senator sent his resignation to the legislature. By quitting, Hammond joined Chesnut in proclaiming to the world that the game was over in their state. The state now had no U.S. senators, no federal judicial officials or federal grand juries in Charleston, no customs collector, no remaining inclination to consult other states before departing the Union, and no chance for public campaigns against Separatism. To be sure that Hammond kept the aristocracy's decision for Separate State Secession unanimous (and kept the public out of the decision-making loop), Aldrich retained the senator's former letter for three more weeks before returning it.[48]

Hammond resented the censorship. He "thought Magrath & all those fellows were great asses for resigning." The "very foolish . . . epidemic" reminded him of the "Japanese who when insulted rip up their own bowels." Why, then, had the one man who might have stalled the epidemic "done it myself"?[49]

Hammond explained that he felt compelled to follow Chesnut's and Toombs's lead. Besides, he claimed, he had always wanted out of the U.S.

The younger Hammond (left), risen bully, and the older Hammond (right), dissolute quitter, both revealing a soul rendered too insecure by ugly personal demons to bring enormous political talent to full flower. Courtesy of the South Caroliniana Library (both images).

Senate. He confessed only half the truth. He had indeed always wanted out—out of the House of Representatives halfway through its gag rule session, out of the Barnwell Court House speech halfway through his presentation—for he had always feared that he was not up to his fellows' visions of his genius. But he had always prayed that the state's legislators, final arbiters in an aristocratic republic, would proclaim him up to the highest mark. Their judgment, to be creditable, had to be an unpressured verdict, with no politicking or whining or begging on his part. So Hammond had never protested their verdict, not even when they ostracized him for twelve years for sexual misbehavior that they lacked the knowledge even to identify (or the imagination even to suspect). But now they asked him to quit, and as ever he would not complain.

Thus did the most talented—and tortured—aristocrat in South Carolina give way before the legislature's aristocratic storm. Ironically and apparently without his realizing the irony, Hammond's surrender actually embraced his best strategic moment. Back in 1850–52, after the state had cowered from seceding, Hammond had suggested that her congressional representatives secede from Washington. South Carolina's U.S. Senate and House resignations, he had suggested, would give other southern states a flag to rally around and an assurance that South Carolina would someday really do it.[50] Now, Hammond's and Chesnut's flag made unmistakably clear that South Carolina had already decided to do it, and fast.

The resignations were symbolically crucial. If the legislature had alone acted and South Carolina luminaries had kept their federal posts, the rest of the Lower South could have wondered if the state's convention might delay the final blow. But with this precipitous state's political giants already gone from the U.S. Senate, and with the Barnwell Court House delayer among the seceders, other Lower South delayers faced a unanimous, accomplished South Carolina decision, a month before the accomplishment became official.

On Tuesday, November 12, the day after Hammond sent his white flag to Columbia, the legislature appropriately celebrated the end of its historic week. As the House and Senate met in joint session to finalize, unanimously, the December state convention, all the events of the last seven days seemed palpably in the air: Chesnut coming out for immediate action, Gourdin and Magrath staging their perhaps spontaneous drama in Charleston's gray U.S. courthouse, the Rhetts' less than successful clandestine caucus, the State Senate's almost unanimous vote to delay secession, the Charleston and Savannah Railroad coincidence, the Mills House and Institute Hall orgies, Francis Bartow and Henry Jackson and William Colcock too, Hammond coming out for Cooperation only to be shoved back into Aldrich's pocket, the legislature's vote to reverse itself, Hammond's move to reverse himself, and now, all South Carolina legislators pronouncing the Union finished. With dissenters stifled and Hammond silenced, the imminent popular election of delegates on December 6 became the nonevent after the epic. To the relief of Alfred Aldrich, the South Carolina public would not have to vote itself a revolution, any more than a southern convention would be given the opportunity to vote itself a continued Union.

– 11 –

During the early December campaign—or rather noncampaign—for South Carolina convention delegates, social pressure prevented any surprise event from developing. When Judge David L. Wardlaw tried to express "his decided wish for Cooperation" at an Abbeville mass meeting, "he was almost *scouted*, told he had nothing to do there." The judge, "greatly moved, . . . came down so far as to endorse their [Separatist] *platform*." The retreat "satisfied in a manner," but not in the "grand" manner of Wardlaw's fellow judge, Andrew Magrath. After Magrath "warmed up" this "community . . . to almost a raving pitch—no one dared dissent."[51]

Or to be accurate, the strongest individualist in the strongest outpost of Cooperationism alone dared to defy the intimidators. Seven months earlier, Benjamin F. Perry had refused to depart from the National Democratic Convention in Charleston, whatever the jeers from the Institute Hall galleries. Perry's home base, semimountainous Greenville County, contained one of South Carolina's rare predominantly yeoman populations. Throughout the nullification confrontations of the 1830s and the secession crises of the early 1850s, Perry's redneck constituents had supported his defiance of South Carolina ultras. Perry's original slate of Cooperationist candidates for the December 6 election included two of the state's most respected men, James Petigru Boyce (president of the Baptist Theological Seminary) and John Belton O'Neall (South Carolina chief justice). Judge O'Neall saw no "cause" for "a Revolution exactly equal to that in '76."[52]

But of the formidable trio who led this promising Cooperationist ticket in this promising district, only Perry outlasted the latest jeers of "traitor." After Boyce and O'Neall quit the canvass, Perry's support shrank to but 225 votes, one-fifth of the winners' total. That beat the tally of any other Cooperationist candidate statewide. Only a dozen of those hapless fellows could be found on December 6 ballots.[53]

The forced unanimity made Separatists, ironically, more nervous than ever. Their intimidation hid what might lie beneath the surface. It was all too reminiscent of forcing slaves to play Cuffee and then wondering who Cuffee really was. Frank De Bow, brother of the *De Bow's Review* editor, meant to "foreswear . . . my native state" if South Carolina failed to secede again, "after all the fuss and furor she has been making." De Bow found intolerable the "storm of ridicule . . . heaped upon South Carolina."

But "I begin to fear" that while "all classes of people in SC" raise secessionist banners, "the state will not secede." He saw "too many flags hung out, too much unnecessary show." I fear that "many of those who hang out flags are afraid their fidelity will be doubted." With Separatists' proscriptions only elevating suspicions, James L. Petigru had it right: "They are afraid to trust the second thoughts of their own people." Or as Howell Cobb added, "It looks as if they were afraid that the blood of the people will cool down."[54]

Leonidas W. Spratt conceded the truth of Petigru's and Cobb's diagnosis. In January, speaking before the Florida secession convention as commissioner from South Carolina, Spratt explained why his state could not delay secession in order to confer with other states. First of all, "other Southern States themselves would have . . . lost the courage necessary," as a result of our "backing down." Worse, *we* would have lost the necessary courage. By appointing "some distant day for future action, to see if other States would join us," we would have "allowed the public feeling to subside." Then our state "would have lost the spirit of adventure, and would have quailed from the shock of this great controversy."[55]

Mary Chesnut was at her best in describing this malaise of the almost triumphant spirit—this relief and disbelief and exaltation and foreboding of a culture that could not quite believe that at last it was meeting its destiny. "I remember feeling a nervous dread and horror of this break," she wrote in February 1861, "but I was ready & willing—SC had been so rampant for years. She was the torment of herself & everybody else." Her ultras "had exasperated & heated themselves into a fever that only bloodletting could ever cure."[56]

– 12 –

The South Carolinian who had worked longest and hardest for the bloodletting thought that this should be his moment. But everywhere, Robert Barnwell Rhett, Sr., found himself discarded. Throughout the state, folks preferred to hear speeches from the coolheads who had supplanted the hothead during that fateful legislative week: Magrath, Gourdin, Memminger, Conner, even Orr. Stung, Rhett tried to force all Charleston candidates for the state convention to pledge for immediate, irrevocable disunion.

The 1860 Association's main leaders denounced Rhett's presumption. They had sought a measured revolution, congenial, fastidious, and safe, with sufficient assurances that others would join and with all legalities observed. Rhett's notion of illegally seizing a fort back in 1851—of doing anything to get out of the Union immediately and irrevocably, on the assumption that other Lower South states would follow *any* exit—that supposed folly had seemed as much an immediate menace as Lincoln's patronage. The fastidious leaders of the 1860 Association, not Rhett, had lately prevailed, especially in taking advantage of the railroad coincidence.

On December 6, Charleston voters officially denied Rhett's claim for paternity of the revolution. The self-proclaimed father of secession squeaked into seventh place as a Charleston delegate to the secession convention, barely ahead of Memminger, a thousand votes behind the leading vote getter, Magrath, and also behind Miles, Townsend, Gourdin, and Conner.[57] Stung once again, Rhett tried to become governor five days later. This time he could muster only third place. The winner was another slap in Rhett's face, Francis Pickens, an old National Democrat, a former Cooperationist, an ally of James L. Orr, and a feeder at the trough of national patronage. Pickens had lately been U.S. minister to Russia. The new governor had also been slow and stolid in coming around to Separatism. He was yet another of the cautious, elegant, law-abiding patriarchs who had finally made revolution seem safe, to reactionaries who trembled at Lincoln—and at Rhett too.

Appropriately, the climactic sermon on secessionists' triumph over recklessness came from the state's most frightened reactionary, James Henley Thornwell. Thornwell had been so nervous that a disunion revolution would topple social order that he had almost called for slavery's abolition. His sigh of relief, published in the *Southern Presbyterian Review*'s January 1861 issue, celebrated America's newest Founding Fathers as patriarchs "unmoved by the waves of popular passion and excitement," not a "collection of demagogues and politicians" or "defeated place-hunters." They were "sober, grave, and venerable men, . . . aloof from the turmoil and ambition of public life, . . . devoting an elegant leisure . . . to the culture of their minds, and to quiet and unobtrusive schemes of Christian philanthropy."

To have "completed a radical revolution," Thornwell breathed, "gravely, soberly, dispassionately, deliberately . . . transcends all the measures of probability."[58] This revolution without excesses—and without Rhett—certainly transcended what Hammond had considered probable. "People are wild," Hammond had shuddered as he resigned from the U.S. Senate. "The scenes of the French Revolution are being enacted already. Law & Constitution are equally and utterly disregarded."[59] But Robert Gourdin, Andrew Magrath, and John Townsend epitomized the nonwild. This scrupulously legal revolution was—had to be—theirs.

– 13 –

On December 17, 1860, when the South Carolina state convention met in Columbia's First Baptist Church, another gentle squire stepped to the fore. Rejecting poor Rhett Sr., who received only 5 of 169 votes, the secession convention elected David Flavel Jamison its president. This cultivated planter lived in Orangeburg County, on the border between upcountry and lowcountry. Jamison's neighbor William Gilmore Simms admired his "great calm of temper," his "thoroughly true" integrity, and his "not brilliant but sensible" mentality. When this balanced patriarch could steal time from directing his people, black and white, he labored on his learned two-volume biography, a decade in the making, of Bertrand Du Guesclin. That early fourteenth-century Frenchman had swept his nation almost clean of English conquerors. Jamison hoped his volumes would illuminate world history at the crossroads, with feudalism and papacy expiring and the modern world dawning. No trace of South Carolina parochialism could be found in this dreamy intellectual's sophisticated oeuvre.[60]

Upon accepting the secession convention's gavel, this exemplar of a gentlemen's revolution struck a scholar's balanced stance. Jamison told his fellows to avoid "too great impatience." No illegal action must tempt them. Yet he also urged them "to dare! And again to dare! And without end to dare."[61] Jamison then presided over a comic version of South Carolina's tortuous daring.

The torture this time involved some cases of smallpox that had arrived in Columbia simultaneously with the delegates. Gentlemen's bravery drooped as the scourge advanced. They wished to cut and run to smallpox-free Charleston, before daring to free themselves from the Union. But that retreat elicited extravagant protest. We must not allow our mockers to say, warned William Porcher Miles, that South Carolinians "are prepared to face a world in arms, but they run away from the smallpox." He would rather risk his life than "budge an inch . . . until we have sundered every tie" with the Union.

Laurence Keitt used humor to pop this nervous fit. We will not invite ridicule, he counseled, by delaying a day. "If we are to go to the tented field tomorrow," declared this irretrievable secessionist, and if "I can sleep in a comfortable bed tonight, I will do it." Delegates tittered. But they would not take the 4:00 A.M. train toward Charleston until they had passed, unanimously, a pledge to secede upon arrival.[62]

One of Benjamin F. Perry's friends still twitted these "sons of sound and fury" who turned tail and evaporated when "the smallpox met them in all its terrors." He mockingly wrote that

Our brave secessionists have met, and
Tarried but a day . . .
Like children scared and terrified . . .
They broke and ran away.[63]

An usually warm December 18–20 period greeted the runaways in Charleston. This time they sped into the history books.[64] After passing secession unanimously, they sought a ceremony as grand as Philadelphia had staged for the signing of the Declaration of Independence. At 6:45 P.M. on December 20, the delegates marched toward the Institute Hall festivities. They were the cream of their world. Ninety percent of them owned at least one slave; over 60 percent owned at least twenty; over 40 percent owned fifty or more; and 16 percent owned a hundred or more. No other southern secession convention would approach this mass of wealth, unknowingly stepping toward class suicide.

At Institute Hall, legislators met the imminent suicides at the foot of the stairs. James Simons, Speaker of the House, and William Porter, president of the Senate, stood decked out in kingly robes of office, puddling on the ground. The delegates followed these patriarchs and Jamison into the hall to thunderous applause from 3000 spectators, with the Senate and House members following.

Jamison carried the Secession Ordinance. The historic document was engrossed on thick linen parchment, twenty-three by twenty-eight inches in size. Jamison spread the latest declaration of independence on a thick table with stubby legs, a weighty platform for a weighty document. The Great Seal of South Carolina, designed by William and Arthur Middleton and executed in silver by George Smithson in 1776, was stamped into the linen. Not since the seal shone on the Nullification Ordinance in 1832–33 had this silver invaded parchment. It has not happened since.

After the Reverend John Bachman prayed for peace, wisdom, and the permanent opportunity "to protect and bless the humble race that has been entrusted to our care," the clerk of the House of Representatives, John T. Sloan, read the delegates' names, alphabetically by election district. As Sloane called each name, the delegate mounted to the great table and affixed his name to the document, with 3000 voices cheering every step.

The procession proceeded uneventfully until Robert Barnwell Rhett, Sr., stepped forth. At the table, Rhett sank to his knees and prayed to his Lord in thanks for thirty years of work triumphant. On so glad an occasion, no one questioned whether the, of late, nonfather of secession deserved to stand out. Rhett, after all, had long kept the fires burning, while such Johnny-come-latelies as John Townsend warned against too hot a flame. After two hours, the Founding Fathers had all signed. At 9:15 P.M. on December 20, 1860, David Flavel Jamison proclaimed the "State of South Carolina an Independent Commonwealth."

After the cheering crowd rushed the stage, a spontaneous tableau crowned the evening. On each side of the table, a palmetto tree, South Carolina's symbol,

David Flavel Jamison (left), solid, stolid, troubled scholar and thus the perfect choice to urge cautious South Carolina gentlemen to dare. Jamison presided over the Institute Hall secession ceremonies with a palmetto tree (famous for its sharp bark and soft core) on each side of his desk—the apt final touch for revolutionaries who had long trembled at revolution. Courtesy of the South Caroliniana Library (Jamison) and Special Collections, University of Virginia Library (palmetto tree).

decorated the stage. The trees, a variety of palm, displayed a bark of sharp profusions, easily stripped away from squishy soft trunks (so soft that during the Revolutionary War, ships built with palmetto logs had harmlessly absorbed the English balls fired into them). As the Institute Hall spectators flooded the stage, they looked like precursors of twenty-first-century football fans who would triumphantly storm the goalposts. The celebrants peeled off the two palmetto trees' sharp profusions. They waved their souvenirs as they paraded into the night, with bands marching down the streets and rifle companies strutting behind.

Back at Institute Hall, the two denuded palmetto trunks remained on each side of the signing table. The Republic of South Carolina had symbolically left its soft core behind. Now the question was whether a broader, rock-hard southern republic would develop, around its daring segment.

CODA: DID THE COINCIDENCE CHANGE HISTORY?

The tales of the fleeting conspiracy and the railroad coincidence throw light on the precise way disunion came—on how South Carolinians mustered the daring to do it and on how close they came again to faltering. But this story of how history actually transpired cannot reveal what might have happened if these short-term occurrences had not crossed the path of the long-term sectional controversy. Or to put the might-have-been question more color-fully, if the Charleston and Savannah Railroad had happened to be com-pleted a month earlier or later, might disunion have come at a different time, and/or in another form, or even not at all?

The guess here is that without the chance occurrence of the railroad's completion date, and thus without the chance presence of the right comfort-ing Georgians at the peak uncomfortable moment, the South Carolina legis-lature would have finalized the delayed date for a state convention. Then the scenario that the 1860 Association most dreaded might well have occurred. An outraged Charleston mob might have illegally nullified the legal delay.

All the conditions for a disreputable coup d'état flourished. The despera-tion was there: Ever after Christopher Memminger's debacle in Virginia, Charlestonians dreaded a southern convention. The fury was there: Low-country grandees found Lincoln's election (and their own faltering) an intol-erable humiliation. The vigilante precedent was there: Lynch mobs had been roving the parishes for months after the Texas fire scare. The opportunity for mob triumph was there: Robert Anderson's exposed federal troops in feeble Fort Moultrie, located in an accessible Charleston suburb, could have been easily annihilated. The leadership was there: In 1851, an exasperated Robert Barnwell Rhett had urged the South Carolina governor to void Sepa-rate State Secessionists' defeat by seizing Fort Moultrie. In mid-November 1860, an even more exasperated (and infuriatingly deposed) ex-father of se-cession would have been even more likely to call forth the troops.

The potential troops were also there. Henry Ravenel reported that "thou-sands of men at the South . . . *will never yield obedience to Black Republi-can rule. . . .* If resistance comes from individuals against the law, it will be met as treason."[65] Treasonous *individuals* would have thrown away that Separate *State* Secessionist trump card—the concession throughout the Lower South of a *state's* right to secede.

The post–1860 election situation augured still another illegal rebellion, if secession was delayed. On November 10, the most important newspaper in Mississippi (not in South Carolina!) promised that anyone who accepted Lincoln's offer of a federal post inside the state would be lynched. The pledge demonstrated that a Southern Republican Party, using normal demo-cratic agitation to criticize slavery within earshot of Lower South slavehold-ers' yards, would have raised the old collision of democratic and despotic re-quirements to new levels of disruption.

If illegal mobs failed to cancel a South Carolina legislature delay, a Mis-sissippi convention might have seized the Separatist initiative, leaving the ini-tial John Pettus–Jefferson Davis preference for a southern convention in the dust. Alternatively, a southern convention might have met and served Sepa-ratists ironically well. Uncompromising Lower South delegates might have stormed out in protest against Upper South compromising. Such an exodus would likely have led to a cooperative Lower South secession. (This time, no clandestine letters needed!) Or the Lower and Upper South might have agreed on demands for northern concessions that Lincoln would have rejected. A northern rejection of a southern convention's ultimatum could have led to disunion as swiftly as did the Charleston and Savannah Railroad's celebration. All in all, the chances for the nation to finish 1861 peacefully intact were very poor.

And yet—and yet against all the probabilities, Union savers just might have hung in there, until the next slavery crisis. That *until* is crucial. The slavery issue would surely have continued to provoke fury between the sections. But even the angriest conflict need not necessarily produce its climactic explosion at any one time or in any one form; and the form or time can yield a hotter or cooler conflagration. Peacemakers can usually accomplish no more than keeping talks open, keeping meetings going, in prayer that some shaky armistice can preserve an uneasy peace until the next crisis explodes.

Delayers in this crisis had some advantages, if South Carolina would allow a pause. Most southern citizens favored WAIT. Those four capitalized letters gave the southern convention strategy viability, including deep in the South. A possibly helpful (and shaky) armistice plan would imminently be in the air. The vast impersonal forces that moved American and southern culture, in short, had not yet progressed so far as to ensure this particular blowup at this particular moment. That is why luck, accident, and coincidence—or the personal strivings and agency of individuals—must usually enter the most impersonal narrative of a disaster.

Thus as South Carolina Separatists feared (and Cooperationists elsewhere hoped), several weeks of delay just might have dulled the first sting of Lincoln's election, even in South Carolina and then in Mississippi too. Subsequently, a southern convention just might have settled for an overt act ultimatum: No secession now but automatic disunion hereafter, if Republicans secured a federal antislavery edict. Or perhaps a southern convention just might have insisted on northern concessions that President-elect Lincoln might have considered negotiable. Or perhaps an unexpected coincidence, akin to the accident of the railroad's timing, might again have deflected history a little off course. All humans know, or should know, that the fortuitous can somewhat deflect apparently remorseless trends at any time or place.[66]

The South Carolina reactionaries who ignited disunion wanted no part of any uncertainties. They aimed to preclude meetings, preclude talk, preclude mobs, preclude further contingencies, preclude southern conventions, preclude the chance that as in 1850 Mississippi would falter, preclude the chance that as in 1833 and 1851 they would falter, preclude riots against Southern Republican appointees. They meant to seize their surest escape route from Lincoln's menace, following the strictest state's rights rules for withdrawing consent. A week after the railroad coincidence threw the best exit door wide open and South Carolina's lawmakers seized the opportunity to barrel through, exultant disunionists had more reason to cheer their good fortune. An historic debate in Georgia's legislative chambers publicized an ultimatum to the North that Lincoln just might have found negotiable and that South Carolinians therefore dreaded—and in their dread had convulsively precluded.

PART VII

LOWER SOUTH LANDSLIDE, UPPER SOUTH STALEMATE

The South Carolina legislature had no sooner moved up the date of the state's secession convention than a second secession crisis erupted, this time inside Georgia's legislative chambers. On this occasion, delay overcame daring. Then, during the third southern confrontation over disunion, sweeping over the Lower South after South Carolina's December 20 secession, extremists overwhelmed moderates. Not just zealots' superior maneuvering but also a failed compromise and a military crisis, both occurring within a week of South Carolina's exodus, crippled Lower South delayers.

In the Upper South, however, where two-thirds of white Southerners lived, disunionists endured another stalemate. Only the mid-April guns of civil war could break the Upper South logjam. Subsequently, during the fourth secession crisis, transpiring in the Middle South from mid-April through May, and during the simultaneous fifth confrontation, consuming the Border South, the Upper South split apart.[1] The Middle South tier of states largely went with their Lower South brothers. The Border South tier of states largely fought with their Yankee brethren. Thus did the South's five secession crises eventually yield a brothers' war, not just between all Northerners and most Southerners but also within the Land of Dixie.

CHAPTER 26

Alexander Stephens's Fleeting Moment

In the Lower South during the second week after Lincoln's triumph, the spotlight swerved from South Carolina to Georgia. The Georgia spectacle featured nightly debates in the state's legislative chambers after the legislature had adjourned. A featured speaker dominated each evening. No multiday southern antebellum forensic clash, and only the Lincoln-Douglas epic in the North, achieved the drama, brilliance, and significance of Georgia's weeklong confrontation.

The dominant Georgia debater looked more like an undernourished boy than an important statesman. Strangers called the skeletal presence "Little Alec." Intimates addressed the aloof sufferer as "Mr. Stephens." In the Georgia debates, this supreme Cooperationist discounted Lincoln's immediate menace to slavery. Alexander Stephens's alternative resistance also threatened to steal the southern agenda from Separate State Secessionists.

– 1 –

In the perspective of the secession crisis of 1850–52, Separatists hardly wished Stephens to establish the 1860–61 southern agenda. With Stephens among the leaders, Georgians had initiated a triumphant unionist response to the Compromise of 1850. In the Georgia Platform of that year, a state convention rejected immediate secession but promised "resistance," if a future Congress menaced slavery.[1]

While South Carolinians had captured the initiative in late 1860, Georgians' geographic position still gave their so-called Empire State special leverage. The state separated the Lower South's Atlantic Ocean and Mississippi River worlds. In late 1860, the prospective void in a southern republic had already dismayed Jefferson Davis and almost delayed South Carolina's Separate State Secessionists.

Georgia's own geographic divisions delayed its decision. Two sprawling Georgia areas contained scant planters and few slaves. Wiregrass/pine barrens in the southeast and mountainous regions in the north comprised Georgia's especially large Lower South white belts. This most geographically divided Lower South state had staged the most divisive debate inside a Lower South state's caucus during the 1860 Charleston National Democratic Convention. But that confrontation had occurred only in secret and only after other Lower South delegations had acted.

In November 1860, Georgia's leaders hoped to hold a public debate before anyone else decided. Georgia's own Francis Bartow and Henry Jackson helped foreclose that aspiration with their speeches in Charleston on November 9. Yet the South Carolina legislative verdict for a speedy state convention, finalized on the day the Georgia debates began, remained largely an unsubstantiated rumor, until Georgia's verbal encounter mounted toward climax. Moreover, Georgia debaters formulated their speeches while South Carolina's legislators still deliberated. Never again could Lower South leaders react to Lincoln's election without also reacting to South Carolina's response.

On Tuesday, November 13, exactly a week after Lincoln's election, a committee of the Georgia House of Representatives invited twenty-four prominent Georgians to hasten to Milledgeville, the state's capital, to give evening counsel to state legislators. The Separate State Secessionists' Thomas R. R. Cobb (Howell's brother) had initiated the evening debates prematurely, the night before the committee issued invitations. His Separatist ally, U.S. Senator Robert Toombs, would dominate the evening after the invitations. Henry Benning, former State Supreme Court justice and an avid Separatist, would climax the debate the following Monday. In between, Separatists' prime Cooperationist opponents, Alexander Stephens and Benjamin Hill, would give formal orations.

The Georgia antagonists called themselves Separatists and Cooperationists, not secessionists and unionists.[2] The revealing names would recur in the five other Lower South states, as they considered their reaction to South Carolina's Separate State Secession. The parties' names signified that not all Lower South Separatists were unconditional secessionists, nor were all Lower South Cooperationists unconditional unionists. Some Separatists wished their state to depart in order to secure a triumphant reunion. They hoped that temporary disunion would pressure Yankees toward making slavery safe in a reconstructed Union.

Meanwhile, almost all Lower South Cooperationists favored disunion if federal authorities coerced a seceded state. Some Cooperationists favored secession even if no coercion occurred, if the cooperative disunion of several states could be prearranged. Many more Lower South Cooperationists pledged disunion if a cooperative southern effort, hammered out in a southern convention, failed to squeeze concessions from the Black Republicans. In Milledgeville, Alexander Stephens brought this dominant form of Cooperationism to climax.

In the evening debates before the Georgia legislature, Stephens shared center stage with only one other Cooperationist (Benjamin Hill), while Separatists enjoyed three main speakers (Thomas R. R. Cobb, Robert Toombs, and Henry Benning). It was still no contest. Stephens's tormented life had prepared him to dominate this moment—and to slide away from dominance a moment later.

- 2 -

Stephens demonstrated that childhood traumas often warp the adult, even if the child struggles past adversity. Stephens suffered a doubled warping, for he painfully lost one struggle and as painfully won another. On the one hand, he could not conquer the misery, both psychological and corporeal, from his savaged physique. On the other hand, he could only triumph over social slurs by occupying a counterproductively isolated perch, beyond wounding mortals.

Some liver disease, deforming from birth, probably caused the Georgian's bodily torment. Stephens's sallow skin drooped over his decently elongated frame, approaching six feet in height. His indecently emaciated body, however, under ninety-five pounds in weight, made his bones disconcertingly visible, protruding at weird angles. A glance at one side of his ashen face, blotched with deep brown caverns, became more unsettling after glimpsing the other side. The two facial angles suggested antithetical skeletons. So too, Stephens's straggly hair tumbled over differently sloped shoulders. His effeminate voice, akin to a scratchy alto's, seemed related to his lack of facial stubble. The beardless invalid usually wrapped himself in a pile of woolens, to combat perpetual shivering.

When Stephens struggled out from under his heap of warmth to give a public address, he would at first stagger light-headedly. Then he would catch his balance and launch into spellbinding speech. As he thundered (or more accurately squeaked) for his vision, he would thump his fist, stomp his foot, and wield his overly long, overly thin finger like a terrible swift sword. Then he would sink back into his chair, creep back under the warmth, and give off the eerie sense of having screamed from the grave.[3]

The perturbing specter of the outer man hinted at what Stephens called "the deep agony" inside. My "torture of body is severe"—toothaches, rheumatism, neuralgia, blinding headaches, nauseous dyspepsia, icy fevers. "But all of them combined are slight ailments" compared to "the pangs of an offended or wounded spirit." His "lifelong pilgrimage through . . . bogs and morasses" had been "beset on all sides" "with brambles and thorns" and "with gnats, flies, mosquitoes, stinging insects and venomous reptiles."[4]

Posterity might speculate that his mother's death, when he was an infant, or his stepmother's demise, a week after his father's, caused some of his gloom. The child's loss of female intimates might also partly explain the adult's apparent disinterest in female companionship. No lady friend appears in Stephens's voluminous surviving correspondence or in contemporaries' recollections of the suffering Georgian.

Stephens, however, blamed his lonely isolation on his beloved father's death, when he was thirteen. "That day above all others of my life," Stephens remembered, "brought the severest pangs of grief and anguish to my heart."[5] The tragedy deprived the adolescent not only of his father but also of his only teacher in the preteen years. He additionally lost his ancestral house, sold away a moment after his paternal soulmate perished. The bereaved teenager and his half brother, Linton, then three years old, became apparently helpless orphans.

Help came, as it did for James H. Thornwell and Christopher Memminger, from wealthy patrons, impressed with an impoverished orphan's intellect. Benefactors enabled Stephens to finish his schooling, ranked first in his class. But after college, the wealthy lads whom he had consigned to the educational dust left him in the social dust. The graduate was "doomed," so he complained, to tutoring the squires' urchins in "the dungeonry confinement of a school room." Engulfed in "intolerable monotony," he longed for "my situation in college and equality there with my wealthy associates."[6]

He also longed for superiority over his patrons. Southern paternalistic society often generated risen orphans who became lofty judges of their patrons' failings. Patronized poor boys, alias egalitarian Americans, relished patriarchs' help but not the patronization. As Linton Stephens described the psychological ache, "Nothing broke my spirit like" that "sense of *dependence* and . . . being pitied." I became so "*humble* in my own" eyes, so "*subdued* within myself and lonely in the world."[7]

The Stephens brothers, Thornwell, Memminger—all these patronized orphans rose to judge their judges. Linton Stephens became a Georgia Supreme Court judge. Thornwell and Memminger became censors of erring slaveholders. Alexander Stephens positioned himself above fellow politicians, looking down "upon the Knaves and fools."[8]

"The secret of my life," Alexander Stephens explained to Linton, "has been *revenge*." I wanted "no foe standing on my rear" and "none to say that I was indebted to him." Instead of wishing "to *crush* or trample on the *vile crew*," he meant "to get above them—to excel them," to force them to "feel . . . my superior virtue." My "*revenge*" could have "nothing low or mean" or "base" about it. "To be successfully *sweet*," my vengeance must be "pure in principle and pure in execution."[9]

But his unworldly aloofness, he conceded, remained vulnerable to the world's judgments. "As *slight a thing as a look*," he winced, goaded him toward "the fury of a lion and the ambition of a Caesar." How he had "suffered from the tone of a remark"! Linton agreed that Alexander's "imperiousness" and love for "show[ing] the vile herd how immeasurably they are your inferiors" proved he cared too much about what others thought. Linton suggested *real* indifference. But the supersensitive elder brother aspired only to transcend his tormentors' alleged wasteland.[10]

Stephens ascended remarkably quickly. After the postcollege miserable months of tutoring, he studied law, flourished, practiced law, flourished, entered politics, and spectacularly flourished. The protégé strode inside the Georgia legislature at age twenty-four and the U.S. Congress at age thirty-one. He became an acclaimed molder of the Compromise of 1850 while still under forty. Meanwhile, he acquired thirty slaves, raised Linton like a prince, and (this was sweet revenge) reacquired the family home that had been sold out from under the brothers when their father died. He called the revered dwelling Liberty Hall.

After Congress adjourned in 1858, Stephens, still under fifty, quit politics cold turkey and came home to Liberty Hall. The oasis stood a merciful twenty miles removed from the convivial, stinging society of Washington, Georgia. Inside Liberty Hall, Stephens communed with his sole constant companion, his great big fluffy elderly blind deaf white dog, Rio. Linton, his only human confidant, occasionally dropped by to make the odd couple a threesome. For the rest, the herd had a standing invitation to take the pilgrimage to Liberty Hall. There, visitors were at liberty to come and go, so long as no guest disturbed Rio and his master during their long retreats to the attached study out back.

From his Liberty Hall isolated haven, Stephens penned contemptuous letters, celebrating his liberty from the fools. Despite the Union's "ominous portents, which the wise and sagacious would do well never to overlook," no other national statesman displayed "the same disinterested motives I had." Had I not been surrounded by demagogues, "I never should have quit my post." Or as Stephens explained more colorfully, "When I am on one of two trains coming in opposite directions on a single track, both engines at high speed, and both engineers drunk, I get off at the first station."[11]

With Lincoln elected and the trains almost crashing, Georgia's supposed demagogues called him back where he had politically begun: to the legislative halls in Milledgeville, to rescue them (as he saw it) from their folly. In Milledgeville, he would not be plunging back into the muck but delivering statesman-like utterances from on high, in the dark night, after daytime legislative antics had shed no light on the nation's problems. So on the evening of Wednesday, November 14, with candles twinkling and tension mounting and Georgia's finest gathered beneath the lectern, the deformed cripple, as usual wrapped up like a mummy, came out from under his cocoon of cloth, staggered once, stretched up to his surprising height, and soared to ascendancy in the greatest weeklong public debate that antebellum Southerners ever witnessed.

– 3 –

No such extravagance would be justified if Stephens had demonstrated only Lincoln's lack of immediate menace. In the Milledgeville debate, Benjamin H. Hill would exceed Stephens in squeezing that argument against Separatists

This 1858 picture of Alexander Stephens (left) shares the rare virtues of the camera's portrait of John Townsend (p. 392): pristine condition, ingenious staging, and an image that burrows beneath its important subject's skin. Stephens's torment, physical and psychological, saturates the image, announcing the agonies that drove this potentially potent Cooperationist into impotent solitude at Liberty Hall (below). Note the attached study, isolated in the rear, where those two ex-orphans, Linton and Alexander, joined Rio in liberation from guests, alias intruders. Courtesy of the National Portrait Gallery, Smithsonian Institution; gift of Roger F. Shultis (Stephens) and the Library of Congress (Liberty Hall).

into a soundbite. "Mr. Lincoln cannot do us damage," Hill would affirm, "cannot get even his salary—not a dime to pay for his breakfast—without the consent of Congress."[12]

Lincoln lacked even a dime's worth of abolitionist menace, Stephens added, because the president of the United States "is no emperor, no dictator,—he is clothed with no absolute power." Without congressional backing, "constitutional checks . . . render him powerless to do any great mischief." Stephens counted a majority of "near thirty" against Republican mischief in the House of Representatives and four in the Senate. (The actual numbers were twenty-one in the House and eight in the Senate.) Stephens did not add, as many Cooperationists would, that Republicans controlled only two of nine U.S. Supreme Court judges. But almost alone among Co-operationists, the Georgian did emphasize that Lincoln could not appoint an officer "without the consent of the Senate." So why "should we disrupt the ties of the Union when his hands are tied"?

The handcuffed president-elect, Stephens pointed out, had been "consti-tutionally chosen." When and "if he violates the Constitution, then will come our time to act. Do not let *us* break" the Constitution because "he may. If *he* does," Stephens repeated, *then* let us "strike."[13]

From this conventional argument against immediate menace, Stephens progressed to an unconventional suggestion for immediate resistance. The Cooperationist advised the legislature to call a state convention. The conven-tion should announce Georgia's "condition" for "remaining in the Union." Northern states must repeal their so-called Personal Liberty Laws. Other-wise, Georgia would secede. To strengthen the ultimatum, the Georgia con-vention should call a prompt "conference . . . of all the Southern States." Stephens predicted that "if this course [should] be pursued," the southern convention would endorse Georgia's fugitive slave ultimatum, the North would repeal its pernicious laws, and the Union would be saved.[14]

Stephens's ridiculed Separatists' accusation that Cooperationists were submissionists—cowards who lacked the manhood to resist northern de-famers. Back in 1850, the Georgia Platform had pledged "resistance," and, "even as a last resort," secession, if *Congress* violated southern rights. Now Stephens raised resistance to a more defiant level. He pledged the "last re-sort" of secession (forget about lesser "resistances") not only if Congress, in the future, violated southern rights but also if northern *states*, right now (forget about the future), failed to repeal their Personal Liberty Laws.

Those northern laws, it will be remembered, had played a crucial role in the Margaret Garner confrontation between national and Ohio officials, af-ter the runaway had slit her daughter's throat. Various Personal Liberty Laws barred state officials from helping to capture fugitive slaves, banned the use of state jails to house alleged runaways, and offered writs of habeas corpus and trial by jury to supposed fugitives. These state laws crippled fed-eral commissioners, charged with returning or releasing alleged runaways. Between 1854 and 1859, the Wisconsin Supreme Court, in defense of Per-sonal Liberty Laws, thrice declared the federal Fugitive Slave Law unconsti-tutional. Thus did a northern state declare its right to nullify a federal edict, in the sprit of John C. Calhoun. In 1859, the U.S. Supreme Court, in the case of *Ableman v. Booth*, struck down the Wisconsin nullification, in the spirit of Andrew Jackson. There matters stood when Alexander Stephens demanded that all Personal Liberty Laws must be repealed or Georgia must secede.

Stephens hoped that his demand would not only rip the delusive "sub-missionist" label from resisting Cooperationists but also shift the deluded nation's focus from obsolete territorial issues to persistent fugitive concerns. Less artful Cooperationists hoped that a southern convention would pledge disunion unless Republicans surrendered Lincoln's main platform: the containment of slavery. That means of avoiding disunion today guaranteed disunion tomorrow. Stephens correctly saw that Lincoln and the Republicans would never renounce their stand against slavery's expansion into the U.S. territories.

But Stephens also saw that the uncompromisable territorial issue could be at least temporarily ignored. In November 1860, no territory inside the Union tempted slaveholders, and no Republican law against slavery's expansion barred them. For the first time since Texas annexation, the United States possessed no territories worthy of dispute between the sections, at the very time that a civil war ostensibly over the territories loomed.

Stephens would replace that, so he thought, idiocy by implicitly pointing the nation's idiots of the 1860s back to the Whigs' wisdom of the 1840s. The Whig motto had proclaimed that to avoid nation-shattering strife over slavery in the territories, "No Territories" should be acquired. Now in November 1860, with no territories in dispute and fugitive slave disputes raging in the *Ableman v. Booth* vein, Stephens made no new demands about territories.

Stephens would revive the spirit of "No Territories" because a national compromise on present fugitive slaves, unlike a compromise on future territorial slavery, just might be achieved. Abraham Lincoln might well favor a fugitive slave compromise. Then enough Republicans might join with all Northern Democrats to form a northern majority for fugitive slave reform. A vast southern majority might also rally for Stephens's fugitive slave ultimatum, including all Upper South states plus Georgia, Louisiana, and Texas. Only four Lower South states would then be odd men out of a massive national majority. Those states might contemplate their isolation, shudder, and pause.

Even if Stephens's plan failed, secession would be delayed. Stephens wanted a year's delay, to see if the ultimatum might work. In that time, the Lower South's first fury at Lincoln's election might subside. Even in South Carolina, Alabama, Mississippi, and Florida, a less fervent majority might find the stymied president not so menacing after all. For that reason, South Carolina secessionists had rejected even a thirty-day pause.

Stephens, in short, sought a changed agenda and schedule, altered for maximum opportunity. He would bypass unsolvable problems (ones that could for now be left unsolved) to solve more malleable problems (ones that for now pressed provocatively). He would replace an (impossible) ultimatum on the territories with a (possible) ultimatum on fugitive slaves. He would replace the fifteen years of post-Texas-annexation territorial strife with the Whigs' pre-Texas-annexation policy of avoiding territorial disputes. He would expand the Georgia 1850 ultimatum about congressional laws with an 1860 ultimatum about state Personal Liberty Laws.

Only a statesman with great mental flexibility could skip nimbly through the decades, picking up past pieces to solve a present crisis. Stephen's isolation, alone with Rio in that Liberty Hall study, lent him the detachment to see his way more quickly, more cleanly than any other Cooperationist. If, very swiftly, Georgia would put Stephens's fugitive slave agenda into play, Separate State Secessionists' rush just might be stalled. Then the scornful Georgian would have brought the fools right, not by plunging into their disgusting politics but by setting them straight in a speech from on high. What pure revenge that would be!

Separatists instantly acknowledged Stephens's potential power. As soon as the invalid dropped back into his seat, Robert Toombs charged the rostrum. Waving his hat, Toombs demanded "three cheers for my honored friend—than whom there is not a brighter intellect or truer heart in Georgia."[15]

Toombs, true to his mercurial self, offered explanations as soon as he descended from the stage. "I always try to behave myself at a funeral," he muttered.[16] But Stephens's old friend had it right the first time. Unless Separatists buried Stephens's reframing of the Cooperationist agenda, disunion might be the corpse, unless and until the president and/or his party deployed an overt act against slavery.

– 4 –

To combat Stephens's Cooperationist logic, Separatists often scorned logic itself. Reason, a Georgia friend wrote Stephens, must give way to "outraged feelings." Our "humiliated South" must renounce "abject" submission to "a vulgar and insulting enemy." Having "waded half across the Rubicon, amidst the taunts and jeers of an insolent foe," we must "cross" rather than "return . . . in disgrace."[17]

Especially Robert Toombs crusaded against disgrace in the Milledgeville evening debates. "Show me the nation," Toombs challenged Georgia's legislators, "that hates, despises, vilifies or plunders" its foes as intolerably as "our abolition 'brethren'" shame us. Toombs, demanding "vindication of our manhood," denounced "base, unmanly" surrender to "degradation and death."[18]

Three nights earlier, Thomas R. R. Cobb had initiated the Milledgeville evening debates with the shout that Southerners faced "the terrible issue of *Disunion,* or *Dishonor.*" Cobb pronounced "the good name a father bequeathed us . . . something more valuable than property, more dear than life." When Yankee insulters called slavery "the greatest of all sins" and the "most horrible of all crimes, . . . every bleeding wound of Georgia's mangled honor" compelled our "cry to Heaven for 'Liberty or Death.'"

Yet Thomas R. R. Cobb conceded that "passion should not rule the hour." Echoing Charleston's Judge Andrew Magrath, Cobb warned that "zealous, warm spirits," preferring "a traitor's gallows" to a slave's "shame," would act illegally, if their state failed to act legally. To make Separate State Secession more viable than a mob's irrational spree, Georgians must summon more than "the quick beating pulsation of hearts burning." We must also invoke all "human wisdom" to decide whether now is the moment to "do or die."[19]

At Milledgeville, Robert Toombs called on the brethren to do or die in part over protective tariffs. The Republican Party, Toombs told Georgia's legislators, combined "thousands of [high-tariff] protectionists . . . who were not abolitionists" with "thousands of abolitionists who were" not protectionists. "The robber and the incendiary struck hands," to "raid . . . the South." In his Separatist speech that ended the Milledgeville debate, Henry Benning estimated Yankee plunder of the South to be four billion dollars over sixty years. "Separation from the North," Benning claimed, would ensure that these "golden waters" would "be retained within" the South.[20]

Despite their golden dream of free trade, Benning and Toombs emphasized the territorial issue far more. The two Georgia Separatists thereby implicitly called South Carolinians' (and Stephens's) relative indifference to territorial expansion overdone. Toombs urged, in the conventional southwestern claustrophobic vein, that "we must expand or perish." Southern blacks, Toombs pointed out, had increased from 800,000 in 1790 to 4,000,000 in 1860. At that "rate of increase, the Africans among us . . . will amount to eleven millions" by 1900. "What shall be done with them?" Toombs answered that we must eventually expand our territories or exterminate our slaves.

Yet Toombs called the possibility of containment "only one of the points of the case." He knew that dwelling on territorial expansion made Separatists vulnerable, for *if* Republicans someday outlawed slavery in a territory, *then* the South could secede. Certain immediate danger, not potential distant menace, best answered Stephens's Cooperationist case for delay.[21]

To illuminate instant menace, Georgia Separatists (like the South Carolinians) emphasized Lincoln's power to exploit southern internal weaknesses, especially in the borderlands. "The fear that slaves will escape to the North by the under-ground railroad, and otherwise," said Henry Benning, "is the chief cause" of "the alarming process by which the [Border South's] slave population is draining off into" the Cotton South. The slave drain has put "some of the slave States . . . in the process of becoming free states." Benning listed Delaware, Maryland, Kentucky, Missouri, and Virginia as becoming "free States," and "in no long time."

Soon, warned Benning, "slavery will be compressed into the eight cotton States." The ensuing combination of southern ex-slave states and northern free states will have the numbers "to amend the Constitution, . . . to emancipate your slaves, and to hang you if you resist." After emancipation, "a war between the whites and the blacks will spontaneously break out." A coalition between the emancipating North and the emancipated slaves "will exterminate . . . or expel" all southern white men. "As for the women, they will call upon the mountains to fall upon them."

By declaring Northern Republicans' aid to fugitive slaves the "chief cause" of a future slave drain to the Cotton South and of a subsequent racial horror, Benning would seem to have played into Alexander Stephens's hands. To remove the "chief cause," why not issue ultimatums on the Personal Liberty Laws? Because, Benning scoffed, repealing those "obnoxious laws" will not remove the "hostility of the *people* of the North to slavery." The North's majority "party *hates* slavery. . . . When a people is universally against a law, you can not execute it." Against Yankee loathing and its consequences, Mr. Stephens's remedy had as puny a value as "a cent does to a dollar."[22]

Where Benning worried that Republicans would intensify the Border South's fugitive slave problem, other Georgia Separatists warned that Republicans would eventually rouse poor whites against slaveholders. Republicans needed no overt act against slavery, declared T.R.R. Cobb, to "bind us hand and foot, and sell us into Slavery, and every Statesman in the country can explain to you the process." As brother Howell explained the process, Lincoln would use federal patronage to organize a band of southern apologists, to wage "insidious warfare upon our family firesides." Governor Joseph Brown added that Lincoln will either bribe "a portion of our citizens . . . into treachery to their own section, by the allurement of office; or a hungry swarm of Abolition emissaries must be imported among us as officeholders," to "insult us" and "corrupt our slaves."[23]

Once "Mr. Lincoln places among us his Judges, District Attorneys, Marshals, Post Masters, Custom House officers, etc., etc.," Governor Brown continued, he will "destroy our moral powers, and prepare us to tolerate . . . a Republican ticket, in most of the States of the South, in 1864." Even if this ticket "only secures five or ten thousand votes in each of the Southern States," Republicans would hold "the balance of power" between other southern "political parties." The leverage "would soon give" Southern Republicans "control of our elections." Without resistance "now, we will never again have the strength to resist." As Georgia's J. Henley Smith privately warned, when "the poor men of the South . . . begin to calculate the value of slavery to them, . . . our government is too democratic" for slavery to endure.[24]

This Georgia diagnosis, like the South Carolina analysis, sensibly called any Lower South flood of nonslaveholders' Republican votes a future problem. (A quicker flood in the Border South was another matter.)[25] In Georgia as in South Carolina, Separatists emphasized that the more immediate Lower South peril would come from blacks, if Southern Republicans, as Governor Brown put it, flooded "the country with inflammatory Abolition doctrines." In a remarkably candid appeal, T.R.R. Cobb urged Georgia legislators to "recur with me to the parting moment when you left your firesides, to attend upon your public duties at the Capitol. Remember the trembling hand of a loved wife, as she whispered her fears from the incendiary and the assassin. Recall the look of indefinable dread" from your "little daughter," as she "inquired when your returning footsteps should be heard. . . . Notice the anxious look when the traveling peddler lingers too long in conversation at the door with the servant who turns the bolt." Notice "the suspicion aroused by a Northern man conversing in private with the most faithful of your negroes."

No white would suffer death, T.R.R. Cobb explained, in a slave revolt. "Mark me, my friends," he emphasized, "I have no fear of servile insurrection." In general, "our slaves are the most happy and contented" as well as "the *most faithful* and least feared" of laborers. But "a discontented few here and there, will become the incendiary or the poisoner, when instigated by the unscrupulous emissaries of Northern Abolitionists." You "can not say" whether "your home or your family may be the first to greet your returning footsteps in ashes or in death."[26]

Cobb here, once again like the South Carolinians, drew on the climactic southern concern after John Brown's raid. Once the initial Brown hysteria passed, Southerners realized that Republicans intended no slave revolt. But the enemy did intend to spread Hinton R. Helper's message inside the South, within household slaves' hearing. Now, Lincoln did intend to give patronage to southern spreaders of Helper's words. With their argument that Lincoln's appointees must not arouse killers of our loved ones, Georgia's Separatist debaters dulled Alexander Stephens's impact.

Alexander Stephens had been least convincing on the patronage danger. To Stephens's antidote that the Senate had to concur in Lincoln's presidential appointments, T.R.R. Cobb retorted that senatorial refusal "to ratify his appointments" would yield no administration, no government. "What is this my friends but revolution and anarchy?" What would best combat individual slaves' disruption: no law enforcers, Southern Republican law enforcers, or true-blue Southerners' governance?[27]

Such questions drove even Stephens's most important supporters to disown his proposal to give a fugitive slave ultimatum a year to work. Republicans must bow to Stephens's ultimatum, they warned, before Lincoln's March 4 inauguration.[28] Otherwise, secession on Inauguration Day must preclude Southern Republicans from manning southern post offices. But while his supporters' attitude shortened Stephens's period of opportunity, his brilliant speech had made his ultimatum plausible for three and a half more months. Within half that time, Georgia's voters would pick state convention delegates. After hearing the evening debates, the legislature scheduled the delegate election for January 2. Unlike the South Carolinians, Georgians would have to vote themselves a revolution—and to outvote Alexander Stephens.

– 5 –

To build a public triumph atop his legislative triumph, Stephens enjoyed one unexpected piece of good fortune. Abraham Lincoln wrote to the Georgian, after reading his old Whig ally's speech before the Georgia legislature. Lincoln told Stephens that "the only substantial difference between us" is that "you think slavery is right and ought to be extended, while we think it is *wrong* and ought to be restricted." Reading between Lincoln's lines, he might consider fugitive slaves, unlike territorial expansion, a negotiable difference. Furthermore, a remade Whig coalition of Lincoln and Stephens might make awesome negotiators.[29]

Lincoln's surprise hint gave Stephens an opportunity, much as the Charleston and Savannah Railroad coincidence gave Robert Gourdin an opportunity. With Stephens as with Gourdin, and as with all humans handed potential good fortune, much now depended on deploying the skill and energy to seize advantage of an unexpected boon. Stephens had to become the Cooperationist equivalent of Gourdin. The Georgian had to move very quickly and shrewdly, in the manner of the 1860 Association, and particularly its party for Savannah celebrants of the railroad, to grasp a fleeting moment.

Stephens could not afford delay. The South Carolina legislature's precipitancy bid fair to drive Lower South deliberations. An effective southern convention movement had to be on the ground and driving before the South Carolina secession convention, meeting on December 18, further seized the initiative. An early date for the southern conclave had to be set. Stephens had to use the mails to agitate for the convention immediately, in the style of Robert Gourdin's massive southern correspondence.

Stephens also had to match the 1860 Association's extraordinary pamphlet campaign. He furthermore had to be out on the Georgia campaign trail every day, supporting the right state convention delegates. His brilliant November 15 speech before the legislature, in short, had to be the prelude to a month and a half of hell—hell for himself, as he ached for the days alone with Rio and Linton at Liberty Hall, but hell even more for Georgia Separatists, who would have to win an election test between a negotiable ultimatum and a scary revolution.

Instead, upon finishing his speech in Milledgeville, the sufferer retreated to Liberty Hall, to Linton, and to that comfortably isolated study. Stephens made only one speech on the Georgia campaign trails. He wrote almost no letters to those outside the state. He did nothing to set a southern convention date. He did nothing to establish an equivalent of Gourdin's campaigning association. If he grasped Lincoln's hint that the two ex-Whigs could form quite the reborn Whig alliance, seeking a fugitive slave compromise that just might save the republic, he paid it no heed. He instead lectured the president-elect about the folly of leading a partisan crowd of fanatics. Alexander Stephens again rose above the battle, looking down on the fools.

Before speaking in Milledgeville, Stephens had written brother Linton that "sometimes I think I will let them do as they please. I fear we are going to destruction anyhow." After his Milledgeville statecraft, he wrote again, doubting that "there is patriotism in the country to save us from anarchy." Linton answered that his brother must not "yet despair of the republic." Get out, speak, write! "If your country is lost in spite of your efforts, . . . your position with posterity" will be "much more noble . . . than if it should perish without an effort on your part." If you attempt no further forays, "*your* despair will be a *cause* of defeat, not an indication of . . . inevitable defeat."[30]

But nothing could goad Alexander Stephens out from under his blankets, out of Liberty Hall, out on the hustings to fight and organize for his ultimatum. With the great man aloof, no lesser Cooperationist, in or out of Georgia, arose to take his place. The leaderless movement stalled, drifted, wandered. Instead of massing behind Stephens's possibly attainable ultimatum on fugitive slaves, Cooperationists meandered toward unattainable ultimatums on the territorial issue or toward making a virtue of meandering itself, in hopes that delay would cool secessionists' ardor.

For this missed opportunity, Stephens's peculiar personality must shoulder part of the blame. The parallel with James Henry Hammond's missed opportunity in South Carolina is intriguing. Where Hammond passively allowed his Cooperationist letter to Alfred Aldrich to be censured, rather than fighting for his remedy on the South Carolina hustings, Stephens passively retreated to Liberty Hall, rather than rallying Georgia and the Lower South behind his panacea. The two leaders' retirements removed major obstacles to Separatists' ability to vote themselves a revolution.

Both retirees resided in the Augusta, Georgia, hinterlands. Both rose from humble origins. Both never recovered from the trauma of the climb. Both lived in proud isolation. Both obsessed over physical ailments. Both sought revenge from insulters. Both benefited from their slaveholding world's openness to the right outsiders. Both impoverished lads enjoyed opportunities to vault into the upper class after college, whether by marriage or lawyering. Both outsiders became insiders who retained the ability to think unconventionally, to find alternatives that escaped more conventional squires. In the secession crisis, both Stephens and Hammond formulated a route beyond Separatism that could have led to a sustained, focused debate during their state's election campaign for secession convention delegates.

Yet during their culture's peak crisis, both eccentrics retreated into their usual crabbed shells. Their neuroses deprived their fellow citizens of what most needed to be forcefully said, at the moment when the saying became most vital. The result: next to no public debate over secession convention delegates in South Carolina, no timely campaign or prompt date for a southern convention in the Lower South, and a far less focused debate before the Georgia public than legislators had enjoyed.

CODA: DID STEPHENS'S AND HAMMOND'S PERSONALITIES CHANGE HISTORY?

The case for emphasizing Hammond's and Stephens's eccentricities, like the case for dwelling on the Charleston and Savannah Railroad coincidence, transcends the possibility (or impossibility) that history could have come out differently without these interventions. Both the coincidence and the personalities make the history more vivid, the forces rushing toward revolution sharper, and the alternatives clearer. Might-have-been history, if not romanticized and if grounded in the evidence, thus adds depth to tales of what did happen.

James Hammond's opportunity to divert historical currents probably exceeded Alexander Stephens's, not least because it came first. Once South Carolina seceded without a dissenting voice, Lower South secessionism possessed a killing momentum. If, however, Hammond had led a vigorous Cooperationist election campaign for South Carolina secession convention delegates, many citizens, in and out of his state, might have rallied to his qualms about Separatism. That is exactly why Alfred Aldrich silenced the U.S. senator. As to whether a rare full-scale, late-1860 public debate in skittish South Carolina could have delayed Separatism—well, Separatists were not disposed to find out, and Hammond was not disposed to defy their censorship.

After Hammond succumbed and after South Carolina unanimously departed, Alexander Stephens would have fought against larger odds if he had waged political war for his fugitive ultimatum. Even if Stephens had been a force on the hustings, South Carolina would probably have faced federal military coercion within ten days of its December 20 secession, with provocative military ramifications throughout an appalled Lower South. So too, Lower South citizens might have clung to their conviction, fifteen years developing, that an ultimatum on the territories, not on fugitive slaves, must be the alternative to disunion.

Nor would a decisive Stephens public campaign for a fugitive slave ultimatum, even if it had swept the South, necessarily have moved the North. Yet even without such a massive southern push, the North had its interest in a fugitive compromise—and its doubts. Lincoln, perfectly catching the guarded possibility, wrote that, while on slavery's expansion "I am inflexible," on "fugitive slaves . . . I care but little," if a compromise can "be comely and not altogether outrageous." Lincoln's proposed comely wording ran "that the fugitive slave clause of the Constitution ought to be enforced by a law of Congress, with efficient provisions for that object," including "punishing all those who resist it," but "with the usual safeguards to liberty, securing free men against being surrendered as slaves."[31]

The advanced Personal Liberty Laws provided those usual safeguards: writs of habeas corpus and trials by jury. A compromise between this Lincolnian conception of liberty and Stephens's conception of fugitive slaves' suppression would have been elusive. But even without the pressure that Stephens might have generated, Northerners discussed fugitive compromises; Congress adopted some vague compromise wording; some promising attempts to split the difference between Northerners and Southerners on jury trials were floated; and the most advanced Personal Liberty Laws came under state scrutiny. This delicate problem, as Stephens hoped, was negotiable, albeit difficult to negotiate; and when negotiations start, as South Carolina Separatists worried, unexpected bargains occasionally develop.[32]

An embattled version of Stephens would have possessed one weapon. Most Northerners and most Southerners preferred a fugitive settlement to disunion. Indeed, in 1860, most Southerners might have agreed, after long and hard argument, that, since no territories were then in dispute, fugitive slaves posed a more clear and present danger, especially in the most northern South. Because of such potential attitudes of a silent southern majority, Lower South Separatists wanted no part of a southern convention. This ferocious southern minority would preclude the majoritarian possibility, unless a charismatic leader rallied his inchoate majority with equally fierce determination. Even then, the last-minute rescue might well have been too little, too late. Witness the fact that the conceivable saviors of a desperate situation had shrunk to such sports as Hammond and Stephens.

The two survivors of the shrinkage illustrated the Lower South slavocracy's awesome safeguard against insiders' deviations. The Hammonds and Stephenses could originate outside the establishment. The eccentrics could think outside the establishment's vision. But they had to be trustworthy conformists when the chips were down. Separatists lined their narrow path to revolution with a spiked fence, precluding the broader paths that uninhibited statesmen might have opened.

Neither Stephens nor Hammond had the personality to defy the establishment's closures. To understand James Henry Hammond is to comprehend why an insecure bully would inevitably stop cold when that jury of his peers, aristocrats in the state legislature, commanded a halt. To fathom Alexander Stephens is to appreciate why a wounded invalid would inevitably crave Liberty Hall's cold comforts, compared to heated agitations against a pack of supposed fools. With these personality types the best hope to thwart a highly focused Separatist minority, the unfocused majority, particularly in dawdling Georgia, could be steamrolled, if Lower South Separatists west of Georgia found the tactics and the message to match South Carolina's roaring haste.[33]

CHAPTER 27

Southwestern Separatists' Tactics and Messages

Southwestern Separatists' tactics and messages differed somewhat from the South Carolina model. But the differences sustained the same objective. A Separatist detour around the southern majority must avoid a southern convention, emphasize immediate menace, lead to a few Lower South states' speedy secession, and thus plaster a fait accompli on delaying states.

– 1 –

South Carolinians' Separatist tactics, it will be recalled, began with Governor William Gist's private letter of October 5 to other Lower South governors (except Texas's Sam Houston). Where Gist urged Separate State Secession, other governors' answers indicated an initial preference, like Sam Houston's, for a southern convention. By encouraging that southern convention preference, Gist could have initiated a very different last mile to disunion (or, as he thought, perhaps encouraged no secession at all).

Instead, at this first and arguably most important strategic turning point during the secession crisis, Gist and other South Carolinians defied Cooperationists' southern convention strategy. Utilizing secret correspondence, they sought to pull the Lower South toward Separatist tactics and to seek reassurances that if South Carolina dared to begin, other states would follow.

This undercover ploy temporarily failed. On November 9, the South Carolina legislature in effect voted that Robert Barnwell Rhett's conspiratorial correspondence revealed too disunited a Lower South for South Carolina to secede first. That evening, in the secession crisis's second strategic turning point, Savannah visitors to Charleston openly promised that Georgia would close ranks behind South Carolina. The next day, the South Carolina legislature dared to act.

Yet another major tactical turning point featured renewed clandestine tactics. On November 8, William Gist's younger cousin, bearing the name

445

(not the nickname!) State's Rights Gist, secretly visited Mississippi Governor John Pettus. The visitor's name could occur only in South Carolina. Nowhere else would a father name his son, born in nullification time, State's Rights.

Governor William Gist urged State's Rights Gist to pull the Mississippi governor away from any intention, communicated in answer to that October 5 letter, to seek a southern convention. State's Rights Gist accordingly warned Governor Pettus that in a southern convention, Upper South compromisers would rout Lower South disunionists. "Do not ask for a Southern Council," reasoned the clandestine visitor, "as the Border and non-acting States would outvote us & thereby defeat action. Let your State immediately assemble in Convention."[1]

From that day forward, the governors of South Carolina and Mississippi, previously differing on separate state versus southern convention action, followed the same Separatist imperative. Within a few days, the governors of Alabama and Georgia, also southern conventionists in their initial reply to Gist, had also swung over to Gist's imperative. Then Lower South Separatists' landslide away from a southern convention became omnipresent.

The developing Separatist consensus dominated Mississippi only two weeks after the John Pettus–State's Rights Gist secret conversation. On November 22, Pettus convened a caucus of Mississippi's congressional delegation. The governor sought advice on what secessionist tactic to press on the imminent Mississippi legislature. Three of Mississippi's men in Washington, including U.S. Senators Jefferson Davis and Albert Gallatin Brown, advised cooperative secession, to take place on March 4.

Pettus had inclined toward some version of that policy in late October. But at his November 22 conclave, three Mississippi congressmen favored separate state secession, to take place immediately. Pettus broke the tie in favor of Separatism and immediacy. The private Gist-Pettus meeting had straightened out the key Separatist tactic for the duration. By the beginning of December, the southern convention gambit, only six weeks earlier Lower South governors' dominant suggestion to Governor Gist, had become wholly a Cooperationist strategy.[2]

– 2 –

While clandestine communication helped rally Lower South Separatists against the southern convention strategy, extremists solved a second interstate strategic problem without secret plotting. The answers to Gist's October 5 letter revealed that other governors planned counterproductively haphazard and delayed dates for state conventions. In hopes of providing a more relentless revolutionary calendar, the South Carolina legislature, acting four days after Lincoln's election, scheduled the state's election for secession convention delegates a mere twenty-six days hence, with the conclave to convene eleven days later.

The tactics of speed proved contagious. Within two weeks of the South Carolina legislature's unanimous decision, all Lower South states, except Texas, scheduled elections for convention delegates. Lower South state conventions would convene within five weeks of the day South Carolina seceded. Tardy Texas would join this hustling crowd within the month.

Lower South states adopted this lethal timetable spontaneously, without prearrangement, with the most secessionist states moving fastest. Where South Carolina allowed only twenty-six days of campaigning for secession convention delegates, Florida matched South Carolina's brevity. Mississippi's campaign was five days briefer still. Thus despite its head start, South Carolina beat Mississippi out of the Union by only twenty days (December 20 to January 9). Florida trailed only a day after Mississippi. These three states, all featuring less competitive Cooperationist factions, thus presented the four other Lower South states, all acting later and initially displaying powerful Cooperationist factions, with a fait accompli.

Modern citizens recognize the leverage of front-loaded schedules. Because such small states as Iowa and New Hampshire hold their presidential primaries earliest in an election season, they disproportionately sway the choice of presidential nominees. So too, in 1860–61, the front-loaded schedule of Lower South state conventions gave Separatists in South Carolina, Mississippi, and Florida clout way beyond the number and typicality of their citizens. These three states, containing the first, second, and fourth *fewest* whites in the Lower South, claimed only 28 percent of the Lower South's citizens and only 9 percent of all southern whites. Yet because these atypical states scheduled the first three decisions on secession, the Separatist minority could start a landslide that threatened to sweep up the South's initial Cooperationist majority.

The most interesting state scheduling decision occurred in the only Lower South state that was long without a schedule. One unique man, Texas's Governor Sam Houston, fashioned the anomaly. Governor Houston's Lower South uniqueness lay not in his opposition to Separatism but in his virtually unconditional unionism. Houston could tolerate neither a Republican overt act against slavery nor federal coercion of a seceded state. But he had no other conditions for staying in the Union.[3]

A comparison with Louisiana's Governor Thomas Moore illustrates the importance of Sam Houston's uniqueness. Moore also harbored qualms about Separatism and preferences for a southern convention. But a virtually unconditional unionist he was not. Moore's Cooperationism demanded that a united South meet quickly and achieve redress before Lincoln's inauguration. So the Louisiana governor called his legislature only a week after Lower South governors called theirs. Moore confessed, without complaining, that his hand had been forced.[4]

Few folks forced Sam Houston's hand. This grizzled veteran of every Texas defiance followed his own lonely star long before he exerted sway over the Lone Star Republic, then over the Lone Star State. Born on the Virginia frontier in 1793, Houston accompanied his family to the Tennessee frontier as a youth. Upon his father's death, Houston ran away from home at an unusually early age, toward an unusual destination. The fugitive spent three years among Tennessee Cherokees. Upon returning to white society, the young adult fought beside his new idol, Andrew Jackson, against Creek Indians. After the War of 1812, with Jackson's blessings, Houston ascended in Tennessee politics, becoming a congressman at age thirty and governor at thirty-four.[5]

After that conventional Jacksonian ascent in Jackson's Tennessee, Houston suffered an unconventional plunge. Governor Houston's new marriage almost instantly fell apart, apparently before being consummated, for reasons still obscure. The rumored cause: The bride shrank from Houston's War of 1812 wounds. Whatever the truth behind the wounding secret, the governor fled his office and his fellows. Returning to the Cherokees, he this time married an Indian princess.

Upon his second reemergence in white society, the disgraced Tennessean pushed deeper into the frontier, to Mexico's colony, Texas. The ex-outcast entered the right place at the right time to become the right insider. After the Texas Revolution, Houston, commanding the Texas Republic's army, captured Mexican General Santa Anna during the Battle of San Jacinto. He thus entitled a city as well as won a fight. His admirers christened the locale of the battlefield Houston.

Houston City's founding son doubled his fame by becoming the Texas Republic's most important Founding Father. As president of the precarious republic, Houston pursued a successfully stealthful road to U.S. annexation. Once in the Union, grateful Texans made Houston a U.S. senator (until 1857) and in 1859 their governor.

The ex-exile shed some early eccentricities. He traded his childless marriage to an Indian princess for a white wife and their son, Sam Houston, Jr. But the white hero who had twice cultivated, then twice rejected an Indian destiny still paraded around Houston City in an Indian chief's fullest regalia. It was like the ultra-sophisticated Benjamin Franklin prancing around European parlors in a frontiersman's coonskin cap. After the Indian headdress outlived its usefulness, the wealthy Houston switched to the huge brimmed straw hat of a western plebian, this time with a rich man's gold-headed cane as accessory.

Houston's odd costumes exemplified his odd stances on slavery. Although no abolitionist (he owned twelve slaves at his death), Houston advocated slavery's (and blacks') possible removal, in the fullness of time. Alone among southern congressmen, he supported every provision of the Compromise of 1850, including the North's favorite bills. Almost alone among Lower South leaders, the Hero of San Jacinto, with his famously blunt rectangular face and stubborn square chin, fought the Kansas-Nebraska Act and defied southern whites to call him disloyal.

So unconventional a southern statesman survived disloyalty smears not only because he had been Texans' most beloved Founding Father but also because he celebrated the Southwest's most beloved warrior president. Houston's supposedly traitorous senatorial votes against proslavery adventurism served Andrew Jackson's patriotic cry: "The Union, it must be Preserved." Houston reserved his most towering hatreds for Andrew Jackson's most hated foes: Calhoun, nullification, and disunion. Houston and Jackson had plotted Texas's entrance into the Union. Jackson's Texas partner would weep over his state's exit from the nation. Governor Houston meant to repulse Calhoun's successors just as he had jailed Santa Anna and just as Old Hickory had cornered the Nullifiers.

On the night after Lincoln's election, Houston wrote his son that "the miserable Demagogues and Traitors," alias "the Demons of anarchy, must be put down."[6] No other Cooperationist possessed such legal power to stymie disunionists. The Texas constitution's explicit grants gave only the governor authority to convene a legislature and only the legislature authority to assemble a convention.

Recent Texas legislative resolutions also gave only Houston power to call elections for southern convention delegates. In early December 1860, the governor designated February 2, 1861, as Election Day for those delegates. Houston simultaneously announced that no special legislative session would be called (and, to repeat, the Texas constitution apparently gave only the legislature power to call a state convention). The governor thus defied the Texas multitudes to storm the gate out of the Union.

Padlocking the gate, not securing a southern convention, became Houston's master passion. True, he wrote other southern governors on November 28, requesting a "consultative" Southwide conclave.[7] But this gesture offered too little, too late. By early December, when Houston's plea arrived in other Lower South governors' mansions, the recipients had raced after South Carolina. If any chance survived to stop Separatism after South Carolina dared, the window of opportunity slammed shut very quickly. Like Alexander Stephens, Houston would have had to send around a blizzard of letters almost immediately after November 6. He would have had to write every powerful Lower South Cooperationist, not just a handful of Separatist governors. He would have had to insist on an early date for a southern convention. Instead, like Alexander Stephens, he sent forth a perhaps promising initiative and then, on the subject of a southern convention, pressed no more.

Like Stephens, Houston counted on delay to calm the overly excited. Unlike Stephens, who proposed a fugitive slave ultimatum, the Texas governor underestimated the Lower South desire for redress of grievances (perhaps because this western frontiersman remained culturally too superficially southern). Houston also overestimated how much his merely legal stall, refusing to call a legislature, could restrain an excited mob (perhaps because he revered Jackson's legalistic taming of Calhoun's Nullifiers).

But Old Hickory he was not; and 1860 more resembled 1776 than 1832. While only the governor could call a state legislature, only the people of a state could withdraw their consent to be governed. As crisp November turned into chilled December, the front-loaded schedule of Lower South decision fanned frustration among Texas voters, barred from deciding anything. The most heated Texas Separatists wanted Houston's head, even if he was Houston, even if a lynching might be necessary.

The threats to have at Houston dismayed Texas Supreme Court Justice Oran Roberts. Like Charleston's Judge Andrew Magrath, Roberts feared for public safety, if a disorderly mob took to the streets. Unless Governor Houston convened a legislature, Justice Roberts wrote around to fellow Texas leaders, the state's establishment must give mass fury a republican outlet. On December 1, in a celebrated public debate in Austin, Roberts established his credentials to steer enraged citizens around the stubborn governor.

The Separatists' Roberts debated James Bell, a fellow Texas Supreme Court justice but an ardent Cooperationist. The high-powered exchange provided the best single-day debate anywhere in the Lower South that fateful December. The debates particularly illuminated one pivotal question: Would Lincoln pose an immediate menace to slavery?

Separatists contended, James Bell pointed out in his December 1 Austin oration, that the president-elect's worst menace centered on a possible Southern Republican Party, with its supposed disloyalty to slavery.[8] That alleged peril, Justice Bell urged, had been exaggerated. Unreasonable fears about disloyalty to slavery had too often transformed southern disagreement into accusations of treason. Today, he would no doubt "be denounced as a free-soiler and an abolitionist, by those who think that the greatest political offense . . . is to differ from them."

The judge pronounced his or any Texan's disloyalty to slavery a "fictitious" concoction. The soft-on-slavery scare, long "manufactured" in Texas, had made the slavery issue "the most sensitive and the most easily inflamed." His cheeks "burned with shame because of the intolerance and proscription."

The shameful exaggeration of supposed treason originated, Bell argued, because Texas newcomers must "ward off all . . . suspicion." They take "great pains to proclaim a most superlative admiration of the [slavery] institution." The preposterous "rivalry, . . . in expressing the ardor of their attachment," only relents when a rival, after proving his loyalty to slavery, "no longer feels it necessary to be continually proclaiming himself its friend." Bell himself illustrated the necessity. He felt it necessary to proclaim himself slavery's partisan.

Judge Bell begged that the destructive necessity cease. Texans must stop founding hysterical policy, much less an irrational revolution, on groundless suspicions of each other. We hear that Lincoln will corrupt "the public mind, . . . that abolition emissaries will be put into all our offices, and that abolition documents will be circulated, and all that. I believe these dangers are imaginary." The U.S. Senate, with its majority against the Republicans, will police Lincoln's appointments. Texans will also scrutinize Lincoln's appointees; and who "will they contaminate? They will contaminate you and me. This argument, fellow-citizens, amounts simply to a declaration that we cannot trust ourselves."

In his countervailing December 1 Austin oration, the Separatists' Judge Roberts implicitly denied that Lincoln's immediate menace involved distrusting you and me.[9] Roberts instead distrusted Border South white belts. There, Southern Republicans already had a constituency.

But even there, Roberts noted, Republicans disclaim "a direct attack upon slavery in the States!" They instead threaten "a protracted siege." By wielding "the executive arm of the government, with all its power, patronage, and influence," the president can protect free press and free speech in the Border South. He can appoint antislavery men to border office. He can refuse to return border fugitive slaves. He can encourage emigrant aid societies to send excess Northerners to southern border states. With "all of these efforts," he can drive "the borders of slavery from State to State, until it shall be hemmed into a small compass upon the Gulf and the Atlantic, where it will destroy itself." Only after we are "shut in on all sides, worn down, dispirited, divided, and not able to resist" will the overt act come. Only then, Roberts implicitly answered James Bell's loaded question, will Texans need to distrust each other.

Oran Roberts's speech, immediately published in Texas newspapers, circulated still more widely as a pamphlet, with over 60,000 copies in print. Lower South 1860 presses produced more copies of only John Townsend's two South Carolina pamphlets. With this December 1 triumph, the Texas Supreme Court justice acquired the majesty to circumvent even the fabled Governor Houston.

With the help of several prominent Texans, also seeking a route around Houston's refusal to call a state legislature, Justice Roberts penned the so-called Austin Call of December 8, 1860.[10] The document summoned the people to summon their own state convention. As befit a Supreme Court justice, Roberts's Call quoted the Texas constitution to justify his summons. The people, declared the highest Texas text, possessed "at all times the inalienable right to alter, reform, or abolish their form of government." Thus Texas citizens, argued Judge Roberts, could transcend the legislature's merely legalistic right to call conventions (and the governor's merely legalistic right to call legislatures).

To exercise Texans' constitutionally sanctioned natural right to abolish their government, Roberts's Austin Call urged Texans to go to the polls on January 8, to elect delegates to a January 28 Texas convention. To preserve the appearance of a convention called by the supreme judiciary, the Call anointed the chief justice of each county as administrator of the popular vote. To preserve the legitimacy of a people's decision to withdraw their consent to be governed, the Austin Call required the convention to refer a decision for secession back to the citizens for their approval. No other Lower South state would require popular ratification of a convention disunion decree.

Roberts's Call swelled still more in judicial force a week later. On December 15, the third and final Texas Supreme Court justice issued his opinion on Separatism.[11] Unexpectedly (and thus the more imposingly), Chief Justice Royall T. Wheeler's long public letter voted emphatically with Roberts and Separatism rather than with Bell and Cooperationism. By an implicit two-to-one majority, the Texas Supreme Court had indirectly affirmed the right of the governed to unlock any governor's padlock.

Sam Houston saw when to relent. Two days after Chief Justice Wheeler wrote his Separatist letter, the governor called the Texas legislature to convene on January 21, a week before the Austin Call's state convention would assemble. When the legislature met, Houston asked lawmakers to repudiate Roberts's summons of a state convention. They should instead endorse the governor's February 2 election of southern convention delegates. The legislature, however, repudiated Houston's election of delegates to the nonexistent southern convention and endorsed the Austin Call's state convention (which elected Oran Roberts its president). With this completion of Lower South convention scheduling, every Lower South state's convention would separately meet in January, to decide whether to join South Carolina's December 20 secession.

Ultimately, Houston's delays, like all Cooperationist stalls, handed Separatists a boon. If the governor had hurried Texas into a state convention, before South Carolina, Mississippi, and Florida struck, the Lone Star State, initially a Cooperationist stronghold, just might have thrown the necessary cold water on the hotheads, at the necessary early date. But after other Lower South states had embraced South Carolina, Texas could only cooperate by joining the new slaveholders' nation.

Houston had failed to appreciate the irony that ever bedeviled the delayers: There was no time for delay. Under the press of such a front-loaded schedule, and with the most Separatist states rushing out of the Union, the most Cooperationist states had to mount an equally rushed countervailing crusade. Otherwise, they would be run over. To delay after the South Carolina legislature's November 10 unanimous decision was to be rendered irrelevant, and in only a few weeks.

Chief Justice Wheeler best articulated the lesson. Writing to a Cooperationist, Wheeler conceded that he would have applauded a swift anti-Separatist plan. But early on, too many Cooperationists "vainly supposed the public mind excited by disunionists and revolutionaries" and delusively believed that delay alone would suffice. Now, everything except Separatism "is plainly out of the question," for "other states" have "taken their course & left us no alternative."[12] Thus did each Lower South state's spontaneous scheduling of its separate state convention, without the slightest interstate planning, speed secession forward, with even Governor Houston ironically helping to clear the way for South Carolina.

– 3 –

While separate states' unplanned spontaneity generated the ideal Separatist schedule of decisions, subsequent interstate planning ensured that the front-loaded schedule delivered relentless secession. This later communication occurred not in the conspiratorial style of Governor Gist's October 5 letters and his early November dispatch of State's Rights Gist to Mississippi but in the open style of Francis Bartow's and Henry Jackson's speeches in Charleston on November 9. Private conspiracy had everywhere given way to public planning, except, as we will see, for a brief, very important military plot at the beginning of 1861.

To pursue interstate cooperation the nonconspiratorial way, Separatists appointed official messengers from one state to another.[13] Five Lower South states together appointed fifty-two of these so-called commissioners, only one of them a Cooperationist. The Separatists' commissioners, many returning as hailed natives to their states of birth, spoke to governors, legislatures, conventions, and public meetings. They emphasized that Republicans' menaces to slavery demanded a new nation, to keep blacks under control.

Thus Judge William Harris, Mississippi's commissioner to Georgia and a native Georgian, told his mother state's legislature that "our fathers made this a government for the white man, rejecting the negro, as an ignorant, inferior, barbarian race." Lincoln's "new administration," Harris erroneously and demagogically claimed, pledges "the universal equality of the black and white races." Well, Mississippi prefers that all white "men, women and children" be "immolated in one common funeral pile, than see them subjected to the degradation of civil, political and social equality with the negro race."[14]

The commissioners not only emphasized racism but also sped the front-loaded schedule forward. Governor Albert B. Moore used his commissioner to South Carolina, John Elmore, to urge full speed ahead in the Palmetto State. Otherwise, Alabama might hesitate. "Tell the [South Carolina secession] Convention," Moore telegraphed Elmore on the day the South Carolinians convened, "to listen to no compromise or delay."[15]

So too, Commissioner Harris, that Mississippi envoy to Georgia, wrote back to Governor Pettus that Georgians wished Mississippians to rush out of the Union immediately after South Carolina, lest Georgia hesitate. Commissioner Harris told Pettus that, despite "differences among her distinguished sons," Georgians assured me that "*her* secession" would be certain if "*Mississippi, Alabama and Florida, shall have taken that step.*" Since "Georgia will never separate herself from . . . the *Gulf States*, nothing but hesitation, indecision or delay, upon their part, will impede her onward march, *with them.*"[16]

The Mississippi secession convention published Commissioner Harris's initially private communication.[17] The publication showed how far Separatists had come from the secret mode of interstate planning that Governor

Gist had initiated on October 5. Clandestine plots to coordinate disunion tactics had ended when State's Rights Gist helped deter Mississippi's Governor John Pettus from the southern convention strategy in their private November 8 conference. Separatists' problem remained the same after conspiratorial solutions ended. Could one state count on the next to follow the leader?

As the broadcasting of Commissioner Harris's private communication revealed, the solution remained the same, after Francis Bartow's November 9 words in Institute Hall: We publicly pledge to follow, if you dare to lead. After the failure of Robert Barnwell Rhett's clandestine letters and the public triumph of the Savannah leaders' visit to Charleston, Separatists never forgot that in republican politics, face-to-face communication in the open air beats closet plotting. To those changed revolutionary tactics, southwestern revolutionaries added variations on South Carolina secessionists' argument for disunion.

– 4 –

As in South Carolina and as in the mid-November Georgia evening debates, southwestern Separatists emphasized the peril of high tariffs a little and the menace of abolition vastly more. "Give me the right to own and . . . protect *my property*," declared a Louisianan, "or give me death." Give us assurance that free blacks will not run riot across the South, urged Alabama's Stephen Hale, or "our wives and our loved ones will be driven from their homes by the light of our dwellings, the dark pall of barbarism must soon gather over our sunny land, and the scenes of West Indian emancipation, with its attendant horror and crimes," will "be re-enacted . . . upon a more gigantic scale." Or as a Texas commoner pornographically described emancipation's supposed horror, white men will be forced to lie "supinely upon our backs" while our "fair daughters" are "reduced to a level with the flat-footed, thick-lipped Negro."[18]

Such nocuous images made disunion seem mandatory, if Lincoln immediately menaced slavery. Like their southeastern predecessors, southwestern Separatists sometimes finessed the immediacy part. They urged that Republicans' containment of slavery's expansion, plus Northerners' surge onto new territories, would yield only new Yankee states. Eventually, a three-fourths northern majority of all states would approve an antislavery constitutional amendment.

Still, as in earlier Separatist arguments, southwestern zealots usually underplayed long-term peril. As before, long-term arguments played into Cooperationists' hands. If possible future overt acts posed the only menace, why not wait until possibilities became realities?

Once again, Separatists parried the long-term query by thrusting at two short-term perils: immediate dishonor and immediate patronage. Lincoln's assault on our honor, declared the *Paulding* (Mississippi) *Eastern Clarion*, includes the claim that slavery "is a disgrace to the country—that the slave-holder is a moral monster," that we are "in league with the devil." A humiliated people cannot accept such "indignity, insult, degradation, and wrong," proclaimed the *New Orleans Delta*, without debilitating "self-abasement and an eternal invitation to continued wrong and insult."[19]

Like the South Carolinians, southwestern Separatists added the peril of Lincoln's patronage, immediately awarded, to the sting of dishonor, instantly imposed. In the beginning, warned Separatists, Republicans would fasten the noose without obvious aggression. "There will be no overt act *until it is too late for the South to resist successfully*," predicted a Southwesterner. Only after we "stand divided" at home will "the overt act . . . come," and at "first only gently."[20]

To illustrate Republicans' strategy of brutal gentleness, southwestern Separatists quoted a *Chicago Journal* editorial, written by a Lincoln partisan. Our "whole policy," proclaimed the editorial, will be infused with "the spirit of liberty." We will exert "the patronage and influence of the Government . . . on the side of freedom." Enslaved states "will be surrounded by a cordon of free states." Slaveholders' "present limits" will be "speedily . . . circumscribed by Delaware and Missouri becoming free." Inside the shrinking circle, Republicans "will no longer permit the sanctity of the mails to be invaded." Nor "will Postmasters of the Southern States . . . be allowed to decide what newspapers the neighbors may read." After Republicans enforce the liberty to disagree "throughout the land, emancipation societies will spring up in all the slave States."[21]

Southern Republicans' most "immediate danger," warned the *Vicksburg Weekly Sun*, will infect "slavery in all the Border States. . . . The underground railroad will become an *overground* railroad." Worried Upper South slaveholders will send their slaves "down to the gulf and cotton states for sale." Then the ever-blacker Lower South will suffer "secret conspiracy and all its horror." If we accept the "humiliating and abject inferiority" of "snug subjection," cringed the Reverend James C. Wilson of Texas, Republicans will squeeze "slavery in on every hand, closing gradually upon it, like the sliding walls of the tyrants' iron prison, which, inch by inch, and hour by hour, closed upon its victim," until hapless folks lay "crushed into a pulpy mass."[22]

A Southern Republican Party, emphasized C. M. Conrad of New Orleans, will become the poison in the contracting cage. "Divide and conquer" will be Republicans' maxim. In the South, antislavery attitudes will become "the sole path to honor and promotion; and every southern traitor would be selected for reward." However great was Conrad's "confidence in the . . . Southern people," he did "not wish to see this tremendous battery of corruption brought to bear upon them." A borderland Republican Party already elevated Cassius Clay in Kentucky, Bates in Missouri, Henry Winter Davis in Maryland. While Lower South voters would for a time shun traitors' demagoguery, "the torch of insurrection," exciting midnight assassinations, would be immediately "brandished in your very faces."[23]

As the *New Orleans Delta* summarized the central warning that had blown west from South Carolina via Georgia, the number of Lower South politicians and voters "who entertain Black Republican principles at this moment . . . must be small." Yet "very many in every community" would succumb "to the allurement of office." Corrupted Southerners, "in a short time after Lincoln's election, . . . would wield all the influence of the Federal Government within the Southern States."

After "this Black Republican party is formed in every Southern State," continued the *Delta,* he who supposes that "it will be without followers . . . has read history to little purpose. . . . Even now, the very arguments of Helper's infamous book have been reproduced in the South." This endeavor "to stimulate the jealousy of one portion of our population against . . . the peculiar rights of a privileged class" will be spread "a thousand times more" after our "submission to Black Republican domination." The South has been fighting the North, the *Delta* concluded, "and we have lost the battle." Now "the struggle shall be transferred to our own soil," and "the armies of our enemies will be recruited from our own forces."[24]

While that view of patronage dangers simply repeated the South Carolina position, Southwesterners found territorial imprisonment more alarming. Back in the Palmetto State, few fears of being trapped with other states' slaves existed. South Carolina was instead losing its slaves. Nor did South Carolinians usually applaud Caribbean expansion. New terrain might draw even more slaves from South Carolina. But in the Southwest, claustrophobic fear of being trapped with blacks, drained downriver from the Upper South, had been omnipresent since Texas times. Caribbean expansion had seemed a merciful safety value. Those southwestern attitudes resurfaced in the secession crisis, giving Lincoln's antiexpansion policy a darker peril than in South Carolina and Caribbean dreams a brighter hope.

"No sane man," declared the *Vicksburg Sun,* "believes that another slave State will ever be admitted in to the Union." But dissolve the Union and the South would "extend her institutions over Mexico, Central America, Cuba, San Domingo, and other West India Islands, and California, and thereby become the most powerful Republic that ever the sun shone upon." That expansive prospect contrasted with constricted images of being trapped with multiplying Upper South blacks. Even the "sad alternative" of "a bloody" civil war, warned Texas's Congressman John Reagan, beats "unconditional submission to Black Republican principles, and ultimately to free negro equality, and a government of mongrels or war of races."[25]

Still, the most important southwestern twist on South Carolina polemics was not the greater interest in Caribbean expansion, not the greater dread of racial claustrophobia, but the demagogic emphasis on a glory word in the western Lower South (and a curse word in lowcountry South Carolina): egalitarianism. South Carolina's antiegalitarianism aristocrats, believing that the best men must dominate lesser whites as well as lowliest blacks, had secured their basic disunion decision in the elitist legislature. Those alleged nonequals, the voters, had but rubber-stamped the decree handed down from above, after an insistently arranged noncampaign for secession convention delegates. Alfred Aldrich caught the paternalistic nature of the triumph in his censorship of James Hammond and in his condescending words that no southwestern egalitarian would utter: The masses could never understand disunion, much less vote themselves a revolution.

Aldrich's upper-class formula for revolution had no resonance west or north of the Palmetto State. In the newest South, white men's egalitarian republicanism dictated that the white masses must vote themselves a revolution, after a sharply contested election campaign for convention delegates. To attain the mass approval that Aldrich called unattainable, southwestern demagogues insisted that Republicans shamed not just the aristoi but all southern white men, all equally humiliated as if they were "niggers."

The modern world wishes that awful word expunged. But no other nineteenth-century word so fully conveyed the filth that southwestern egalitarians felt smeared their skin and their souls, after Republicans humiliated equal southern (white) brothers. The mortification lay in the slur that northern whites morally excelled southern whites, indeed that filthy southern institutions must be caged inside the unequal South.

Separatists called a humiliated egalitarian a "slave." The terrible word, when used about whites, meant not that slaveholders enslaved laborers but that insult enslaved souls. Republican slurs, thundered an outraged Alabamian, would reduce equal white men to the "slavish obsequiousness" of a black slave. Yankees' castigations would force the South "to crouch and cower Spaniel-like at the heels of the loathsome monster," that "imperious and exacting master, the Abolition North."[26]

Black slavery, soared the *Austin* (Texas) *State Gazette*, saves us from "the wretched livery of humiliation and servitude" by guaranteeing "the equality of white men among themselves, and their superiority over the black race." Yet under Republicans' verbal lash, exclaimed Mississippi's *Paulding Eastern Clarion*, white equals "will be subject to orders as the slave is to the master, shut up as if in prison, and threatened with punishment for passing the threshold as the negro is, should he leave the plantation against orders; held under this degrading ban to await a preordained doom at an antislavery master's decree." Only "when the slaves become masters, and masters slaves" will once equal folk "occupy a more abject and meaner position."[27]

Alabama's Congressman David Clopton described his revulsion for verbal enslavement more bluntly: "I would be an equal or a corpse." On the other side of freedom's congressional chamber, Louisiana's U.S. Senator Judas P. Benjamin bid farewell to the Union with an egalitarian's exclamation: Yankees voices will never "degrade" equal whites "to the level of an inferior and servile race—Never! Never!"[28]

Indeed, never, ever, would southwestern egalitarians bow down before linguistic enslavers. They would not be disgraced. They would not be ashamed. They would not be humiliated. They would secede and secure *their* "emancipation" from Yankee verbiage and its trashing of allegedly unequal whites.

– 5 –

Yet despite southwestern demagogues' cry about southern whites "enslaved," they demanded that fellow southern whites be verbally (and sometimes not only verbally) enslaved. Those who thundered against shaming Republican enemies leapt to shame their supposedly equal southern opponents—especially at the moment that Separatists leapt free of Republicans' humiliations. Separatists' drives to make humiliated Cooperationists cower like slaves added the thrill of imposing vicious patriotism to the logic of Lincoln's menace.

Separatists' determination to repress any Southern Republican Party indicated how fully these self-appointed libertarians rejected liberty's requirements. Free speech, a free press, freedom to question institutions—none of these liberties could belong to a southern party that doubted slavery. Nor did Cooperationists merit uninhibited right to persuade and to vote. True-blue Southerners must rally for disunion or suffer the enslaving consequences.[29]

A Mississippi Separatist, privately writing his brother, captured the foul mood that allegedly justified repression of supposedly equal whites. Lincoln's perfectly constitutional nonovert acts, shuddered R. S. Holt of Yazoo City, will produce "panic . . . along the border" and then "slaves forced rapidly southward." Here "in the heart of the planting states," we already suffer "a foretaste of what northern brotherhood means. . . . Almost daily" we face "conflagrations," and "the discovery" of "poison, knives and pistols . . . among slaves. . . . This army of assassins must number thousands," commanding "strychnine and arsenic, in such quantities as show that special factories have been established."

The secession issue, continued Holt, involves "every interest, right, and hope which I have in the world." He must protect "the safety of my roof from the firebrand, and of my wife and children from the poison and the dagger." He had to favor instant secession when he "heard and read of twenty-three of these wretches being hanged in the last three weeks."[30]

Even during these convulsed weeks in the land that staggered to combine democracy and dictatorship, vigilantes usually shamed their supposed equals instead of hanging them. In New Orleans on November 10, a keeper of a horse pen thought he recognized an Arkansas horse thief running down St. Charles Street. Screaming, "Stop Thief," he pursued the fleeing white. The *New Orleans Bee* reported that "the present excited state of the mind of the public" turned "Stop Thief" into "Stop Abolitionist." Men poured into the avenue as their prey tore down Perdito Street, then halfway down Carondelet, where the mob caught him and almost tore him apart, until learning he was but an alleged horse thief.[31]

A day earlier, a mob on Royal Street heard that James Ryback sought to sell a Lincoln campaign button. Crying, "There's the rascally Abolitionist! Let's hang him," the crowd charged after their alleged equal, determined to brutalize him as they would a fleeing slave. Through Exchange Alley fled the accused, down Conti Street to the corner of St. Charles Street, where the exhausted fugitive succumbed gratefully to policemen's protective control.[32]

A month later in Friar's Point, Mississippi, no policemen deterred the rape of white egalitarianism. After two cotton gins and a slave quarters went up in flames, a lynch mob suspected three white carpenters. Lynchers hanged all three, cut down the corpses, and burned them in a public bonfire. A week earlier, Friar's Point vigilantes had captured an alleged abolitionist, hanged him, stuffed his remains into a barrel, and rolled his coffin into the river.[33]

In the electoral showdowns between Cooperationists and Separatists, no voters found themselves jammed into barrels or rolled toward the river. But Cooperationists often suffered ridicule of the sort heaped upon slaves. Secession has been accomplished, claimed one Texas Cooperationist, by the "reign of terror" of a "ferocious *minority*." Thousands of Union men are "overawed by a standing army." Rampant "revolutionary feeling," concurred another Texas secessionist foe, "prevents the freedom of speech": I only dared protest "as strongly as I thought prudent," and "accordingly, I did not *vote*."[34]

I alone in my district voted against the Separatists, remembered a Mississippi citizen, "amidst the frowns, murmurs, and threats of the judges and bystanders. . . . I knew of many . . . who were intimidated by threats." The accompanying "odium" prevented many "from voting at all." An Alabama Separatist, writing a well-loved brother, exemplified the overwrought mood that generated such shaming of supposed equals. "I am in hopes," ran the hot scorn of this humiliator, that "you will vomit up this dirty dirt you have been eating and vote right yet."[35]

In the southern section where black slavery dirtied white liberty, Lower South Separatists demanded liberation from Republicans' "enslaving" scorn. Lower South Cooperationists demanded freedom from Separatists' "enslaving" mobs and demeaning slurs. Meanwhile the only real slaves, those duplicitous Cuffees, remained psychologically free enough to murder on occasion and to flee on more occasions. White men's liberty to speak or write critically could hardly flourish when such black dissimulators could hear or read of freedom. Those who would save a closed society from Southern Republican open agitation instead had to spread intimidation past the slaves, in a cardinal proof that democracy and dictatorship mixed like oil and water.

Southwestern Separatists' passion to sink Cooperationists toward the psychological inequality of dirt-eating slaves, along with their fury to lift themselves from the shameful inequality of Republicans' filthy slurs, threw the full range of egalitarian demagoguery atop South Carolina's elitist case for revolution. In retrospect, the charred pieces of the enflamed rhetorical package can be artificially separated: the rage to save sacred honor, to rescue treasured property, to tighten racial control, to liberate themselves from Republicans' "enslavement," to subject Cooperationists to a slave's humiliation. But at the time, separate travesties fused into a loathsome southwestern vision: of a treasured world's foul imprisonment, of fellow whites as purchased betrayers, of black servants as deluded murderers, of Border South blacks draining toward a Lower South poisoned cage, of obscene repressions mocking liberty for whites.

The very foulness of this egalitarian/antiegalitarian agitation turned many high-minded republicans toward refined dreams of escape from mean-spirited Yankees and the mean-spirited southern reaction. The tension of the Lower South secession campaign turned excruciating, and who wants to exist under such stress? "I am weary of this eternal dingdong on one *subject*," despaired a delegate to the Texas secession convention. We "cannot *live* and remain forever" in such constant "strife on so delicate a subject." Secession is our "last chance for that peace, which alone makes life tolerable."[36]

Secession also provided the best chance to spew out hatred of the intolerable. You seem "to think me bitter, perhaps too bitter, toward the fanatical portion of the North," the editor of the *Montgomery Mail* privately wrote his brother on Christmas night, a day after his Separatist troops had swept to victory at the polls. Well, "I *am* bitter toward them . . . I hate them instinctively. . . . I hate them more than I do anything in this world. . . . They pursue me and mine; if I could, I would visit them with fire, pestilence, famine, and the sword."[37]

– 6 –

Lower South preachers' plea for Separatism turned such unholy malevolence toward holy reform. Evangelicals had long issued soothing justifications of slavery's rectitude, if calm masters lived up to Christ's commands. Preachers had called slavery biblically justified, if slaves' marriages and access to the Word could be guaranteed. They had called on southern Christians to separate themselves from national churches, lest northern abominations further corrupt the slavocracy. Now proslavery divines summoned their congregants to leave the foul Union and then to cleanse their world.[38]

Benjamin Morgan Palmer especially whipped up Christian folk to move beyond antichrist. Palmer, the most famous disciple of the greatest proslavery preacher, South Carolina's James Henley Thornwell, had ministered to Presbyterian flocks in Savannah and Columbia before being called to New Orleans's First Presbyterian Church. The preacher had helped Thornwell found the *Southern Presbyterian Review*. He had been Thornwell's colleague at the Columbia Theological Seminary. He would be Thornwell's biographer and the first moderator of the Confederate States Presbyterian Church. Palmer's towering prestige and his oratorical power put his Thanksgiving Day sermon in New Orleans on November 29 first among preachers in disunionist impact. Among secular pamphlet writers, only South Carolina's John Townsend and Texas's Oran Roberts achieved larger print runs than the 60,000 copies of Palmer's sermon.[39]

When discoursing on disunion's secular appeal, Palmer's oratorical elegance sometimes adorned absurdities. "Any other than a tropical race," the divine claimed, "must faint and wither beneath a tropical sun." The tropical South's millions of nonslaveholding farmers must have frowned (or chuckled) whenever they heard that (amazingly common) proslavery whopper.[40]

When he turned from the secular to the sacred, Palmer served up a more systematic polemic. The gospel of disunion, Palmer claimed in the celebrated November 29 sermon, does not necessarily maintain that "*domestic slavery as now existing* . . . is precisely the best relation" between "employer" and servile, "although this proposition may perhaps be successfully sustained. Still less are we required, dogmatically, to affirm that it will subsist through all time." We claim only "liberty to work out this problem . . . for ourselves," without the "impertinence" of "interference from abroad."[41]

Palmer demanded departure from the "undeniably atheistic" interference of Yankee ministers. Those infatuated divines insist "that every evil shall be corrected" instantly, even if "society becomes a wreck." With a "single and false idea" riding abolitionists "like a nightmare," the fiends are at "furious haste" to deny "that in the imperfect state of human society, it pleases God to allow evils which check others that are greater." Under Republicans' "reign of terror, . . . 'liberty equality, fraternity'" will mean "bondage, confiscation, and massacre."[42]

Palmer contrasted these worst "foes of the black race" with the best of slavery, which protects blacks as "a guardian and a father." Palmer knew that outsiders derided this argument "as the hypocritical cover thrown over our own cupidity and selfishness; but every Southern master knows its truth and feels its power."[43]

After masters save my black "brother and my friend" from a Republican "doom worse than death," Palmer said, our "future generations" will slowly solve "this intricate social problem," with providence providing "the lights." We will move ahead with respect for complexity, for "checks and balances," for the "delicate mechanism of Providence" and the "wheels within wheels, with pivots and balances and springs which the great designer alone can control." Thus will we defend His complex domestic design from simplistic "fierce zealots," who would "blasphemously . . . lay the universe in ruins at His feet."[44]

Palmer's secessionist prayer recalled the Dred Scotts' judges' unionist hope for a reformed slavocracy, after their decree had silenced counterproductive agitation about slavery. In both cases, posterity does not have to believe that insiders, once relived of outside agitation and the resulting internal fury, would have redeemed their world. We just have to understand why such fetching hopes seemed a pilgrim's glory compared to the wicked strife, the lynch mobs, the domestic terror, and the choking hatreds of the south-western secession crisis.

The Reverend J. E. Carnes echoed Palmer in urging that secession might lay a reformed South at His feet. The Galveston, Texas, preacher's sermon of December 12 made disunion part of a universal march toward "judicious separations" in an "epoch of disintegration." Carnes declared that separate cultures, jammed into the same nation, produced angry recriminations, not Christian progress. No nation "without an idea to work out has any excuse for its existence."

North and South faced opposite assignments. "The North has to work out the problem of the hirer and the hired; the South the problem of the owner and the owned." Northerners, instead of solving their own problem, now "join in demonstrations against the South." Meanwhile, Southerners complain that "unjust and ignorant attacks" prevent us from "discharging" our "full duty to the slave." Against northern laughter "at the South for attempting to make anything presentable out of such a system, . . . we are bound to demand" a nation and a government that can make "our social system . . . morally right."[45]

The Reverend William T. Leacock, speaking on the same Thanksgiving Day as Benjamin M. Palmer, gave thanks to God for rousing southern Christians against awful meddling. "Our enemies," declared the Presbyterian minister of New Orleans's Christ Church, have "defamed" our characters, "lacerated" our feelings, "invaded" our rights, "stolen" our property, and let "murderers . . . loose upon us, stimulated by weak or designing or infidel preachers." With "the deepest and blackest malice," they have "proscribed" us "as unworthy members of the . . . society of men and accursed of God." Unless we sink to "craven" begging that they "not disturb us, . . . nothing is now left us but secession."[46] That Christian release, atop the rational case for Lincoln's instant menace, atop the dishonor of his election, atop the emotional case for "emancipating" white equals (and for "enslaving" white traitors) made southwestern Separatists' campaign message a demagogic masterpiece, especially compared to Cooperationists' milk-toast retort.

CHAPTER 28

Compromise Rejected

A double negative defined Lower South Cooperationists. First of all, anti-Separatists always deplored separate states' quick secession, whether because several states' united secession would be more effective or because no secession could yet be justified. Second, Cooperationists usually dismissed unconditional unionism. A few Lower South foes of Separatism opposed disunion under any conditions. Far more pledged to become disunionists if the Union coerced a seceding state. Many also pledged to go for secession unless Northern Republicans granted safeguards for slavery. Those conditions for remaining in the Union doomed Lower South Cooperationists to surrender if federal coercion and/or rejected compromises intervened.

– 1 –

Lower South Cooperationists almost always affirmed southern states' natural right to switch consent to be governed to another government. Former U.S. senator Jeremiah Clemens, Alabama's most important Cooperationist, explained that "some opinions . . . can not be changed." Unless we "withdraw opposition" to the right of revolution, "we shall lose all."[1]

Most Lower South Cooperationists also thought that they would lose all if they favored southern submission without northern concessions. We must secure "redress of grievances, which undoubtedly exist," wrote Clemens. Cooperationists must also obtain "security against other oppressions which we can not fail to see are impending."[2]

Those concessions shrank the distance between Lower South Cooperationists and Separatists. But Cooperationists still cherished the space, especially in order to secure their master panacea: delay. Delayers desired hesitations both before and after a state convention approved secession. Prior to any state's convention, a Southwide convention should convene. After a state convention's disunion decree, the state's voters should approve the convention's decision, in a special referendum.

There Cooperationists' concurrence ended. At one extreme, some Cooperationists hoped the South would suspend resistance unless and until a Republican overt act against slavery demonstrated Lincoln's menace. At the other extreme, some Cooperationists wished for southern conclaves that would arrange an immediate Southwide secession, or at least instant Lower Southwide secession, without even issuing an ultimatum to the North. In between these extremes, many Cooperationists wanted a southern convention to try an ultimatum to the North, before decreeing cooperative secession. Some of the ultimatum crowd favored sweeping demands. Others sought mild concessions. Some ultimatum fanciers expected the North to surrender. Others expected the North to stonewall. Others did not know what to expect.

Whatever a southern convention demanded and however the North responded, weeks would pass, cheered Cooperationists, before state conventions decided. More weeks would thankfully pass before the people of a state endorsed a state convention's secession decree. During both cooling-off periods, resentment at Lincoln's election might abate. Then a more measured southern response might unfold. "*Time* is everything to us," wrote Jeremiah Clemens. "If we fail to gain that we are lost."[3]

But would they gain enraged voters with pleas for delay? Nothing was seductive about the practicality of delay, or, as it turned out, practical. Separatists made Lincoln's Inauguration Day, March 4, 1861, such a dreaded date that Cooperationist campaigns for redress of grievances had to be squeezed into four months. Otherwise, the South would "submit" to Lincoln's control of southern patronage, without northern concessions in place. The need for much to happen in a very short time demanded as relentless a timetable as the Separatists' schedule of state decisions. Cooperationists quickly had to specify deadlines for an early southern convention, for a swift northern response to a southern convention's alternative, for timely southern state conventions to consider the northern response, and for speedy popular referendums to ratify state conventions' decisions—all before March 4.

A practical Lower South Cooperationist alternative had to include not only a rushed calendar but also a plausible escape from Upper South "submissionists." Did Lower South Cooperationists pledge to disown a compromising southern convention, controlled by the Upper South majority of southern whites, if the conclave endorsed an inadequate demand for redress of grievances? And would Lower South Cooperationists pledge to liberate themselves from Upper South snares, if the North rejected an ultimatum and the southern convention still dawdled on secession?

An acceptable ultimatum also had to be quickly defined. Would only northern concessions on territorial slavery be adequate? Or would concessions on fugitive slaves suffice? Or would some combination of these demands and/or others be mandatory? If Cooperationists had supplied plausible details about a hurried calendar, and about Lower South emancipation from Upper South unionism, and about the contents of a satisfactory ultimatum, Lower South voters would have had a clear choice between two campaigns for redress.

Cooperationists might then have piled greater prudence atop equal practicality. Our plan, they could have urged, will produce secession before Lincoln takes office, if ultimatums fail and after southern divisions have been bridged. If Cooperationists had also matched Separatists' dozens of interstate commissioners and thousands of minutemen and millions of pamphlet pages, the Lower South campaign for secession convention delegates might have been a contest. A speedy, well-defined Cooperationist alternative, and especially a swiftly convened southern convention that met by mid-December, might also have delayed the fatal senatorial and military confrontations of late December, until after the Lower South's mid-January secession decisions had transpired.

Those imaginary scenarios required that Cooperationists boldly act during the scant time remaining instead of begging for a time-out. The fantasy never came close to transpiring. Cooperationists never agreed on a date for a southern convention, much less an early date. No consensus on a southern ultimatum ever surfaced. No Lower South promises to defy an appeasing Upper South majority of Southerners, in southern convention assembled, ever won acceptance. No interstate Cooperationist campaign organization ever appeared, to match Charleston's 1860 Association's ocean of pamphlets and rivers of interstate correspondence. No Cooperationist network of interstate commissioners or legions of parading minutemen ever emerged. When Mississippi Cooperationists called a convention for their state's party, all of four counties sent delegates.[4] Ultimately, Alexander Stephens epitomized a crusade without crusaders.

In part, the Cooperationists' weakness followed from their message's strength. Dawdlers who dashed toward provocative alternatives might destroy their cardinal insight: delay's soothing virtues. Their South Carolina antagonists concurred that a delay for second thoughts might devastate Separatism—indeed might undermine South Carolina's shaky nerve. Cooperationists' conviction that time could cure all was not necessarily wrong. But delay was necessarily irrelevant, after South Carolina's rush impelled a swift decision.

To rush toward anti-Separatist alternatives, Cooperationists would also have had to overcome their most prized personality trait: prudence. In the black belts, neither percentages of blacks in the neighborhood nor numbers of slaves on the estate nor quantities of dollars in the wallet but instead character type of the voter established allegiances in the secessionist electoral showdown. Many rich Lower South planters chose to be Cooperationists, as befitted cautious entrepreneurs who feared that a failed revolution could wipe out their holdings. These careful calculators were not the likeliest to rush imprudently forward with alternate crusades.[5]

Nor could prudent Cooperationists match frenzied Separatists rush for rush, speed for speed, detail for detail without risking their unifying umbrella. The very vagueness of Cooperationism—its lack of specific dates and detailed plans and systematic alternatives—enabled it to be all things to all anti-Separatists. Moving beyond the unifying principle of delay might pit Separatists' solidarity against Cooperationists' disarray.

But while Cooperationists' divisions, character traits, and message mitigated against reckless crusaders, Lower South political culture demanded crusading resistance. Because the Lower South was so intolerant of dissent and so quick to conflate disagreement with disloyalty, any massive proslavery movement had to be opposed by an equally massive, equally creditable alternative. Mere delay risked the fatal charge of "submission" to hateful Yankees.

Yet instead of forging a quick alternative to Separatists' frenzy, Cooperationists kept emphasizing delay, time, a pause. But as Sam Houston had discovered in early December, South Carolina's haste created such speed in states where Cooperationists could not compete that delay became irrelevant in states where Cooperationists might triumph. As the December days raced toward Christmas, hasty Separatists' influence on Washington, D.C., showdowns left loitering Cooperationists ever more whipped by the clock.

– 2 –

When congressmen convened on December 2 in Washington's Capitol building, two empty chairs in the U.S. Senate chamber epitomized a history speeding past delayers. South Carolina's James Chesnut, Jr., and James Hammond had lately occupied the now vacant chairs. The two senators' resignations, three weeks before the postelection Congress gathered, announced that their state would depart the Union three weeks after Congress met. Never had missing members so dominated a congressional session. It was as if ghosts sat in those chairs, mocking attempts to resuscitate an expired Union.

A void outside matched vacancies inside. The Capitol's long central entrance hall served as an architectural hyphen. The extended passageway connected the House chamber on one side of the building with the Senate chamber on the other. In December 1860, the hyphen looked like a body missing a head. Above the connecting hall, workers had only begun to erect a giant dome. Sculptors had also only begun to chisel a statue of the Goddess Liberty, to rise atop the dome. Designers meant the doubled crown to epitomize the united Congress of a perpetual republic. But after Lincoln's election, a connecting hall without a top might symbolize a Union without the South— a roofless relic of a ghost house.

Most northern congressmen refused to credit such ghosts. Hammond and Chesnut would be back in the Senate, Yankees scoffed, before other Southerners could leave. After threatening to exit, South Carolinians had always reappeared, to spout off again about departing.

But Lower South men in Washington knew that South Carolina would not automatically return. So Secretary of the Treasury Howell Cobb sought to lure South Carolina with a delayed secession strategy. In early December, he joined fellow southern members of Buchanan's cabinet and some dominant Lower South congressmen in seeking a South Carolina pause, followed by four states' simultaneous secession on February 1. This southern national establishment initiative remains as little known and as revealing as the Charleston and Savannah Railroad coincidence. The obscure story this time illustrated not South Carolina's early jitters but its implacable momentum, once the front-loaded schedule began to crush ineffective delayers.

On December 3, 1860, South Carolina's Congressman Milledge Bonham sent both an emergency telegram and an explanatory letter to Governor William Gist. Howell Cobb came to see me last night, reported Bonham, to ask, on behalf of his brother, Thomas R. R. Cobb, and Robert Toombs, that we should "wait 'till the 1st Feb, & let the four states Geo Ala Miss and So. Ca. go together." Cobb, Jefferson Davis, Virginia's Secretary of War John B. Floyd, Mississippi's Secretary of the Interior Jacob Thompson, and probably Alabama's U.S. Senator Benjamin Fitzpatrick, Bonham reported, "are at the head of the movement to induce" South Carolina to suspend secession for six weeks.

These Washington notables, Bonham continued, had recruited two lowcountry luminaries to urge a pause in South Carolina. Assistant Secretary of State William H. Trescot, the lowcountry's most cultivated historian, essayist, and secessionist, plus Thomas Drayton, the elegant president of *that* Charleston and Savannah Railroad and currently a Washington visitor, had agreed to travel back to South Carolina as Cobb et al.'s advocates. Bonham begged Governor Gist to intercept Trescot and Drayton upon arrival. Alabama's Congressman James E. Pugh warns us, Bonham reported, that "we must let nothing stop our action," for our delay "would be ruinous." Pugh here anticipated Alabama's Governor Andrew Moore's urgent intervention against delay, in his message to the South Carolina secession convention two weeks later. While no one can say whether Alabama would have leapt without South Carolina shoves, some crucial Alabama secessionists had their doubts.

Milledge Bonham worried more about delay's impact on South Carolina. Cobb's February 1 alternative, Bonham warned Gist, would "prevent that unanimity we hope for in our convention. . . . Whilst no human power could" stop secession after our state unanimously dares in mid-December, "an unfortunate division in our own state . . . would ruin the South." The Cobb initiative, as Bonham summed up its alleged disasters, "means, I believe, submission"—submission not only to Northern Republicans but also to the Southwide antisecessionist majority and to South Carolinians' edgy nerves.[6]

Bonham's hyperbole may sound misplaced. Howell Cobb offered to trade, after all, four states' simultaneous secession on February 1 for South

Carolina's lonely secession on December 20. So too, while the secretary of the treasury's version of cooperation projected a six-week delay, he eliminated any need to cooperate with the Upper South southern majority. Only four of the seven Lower South states, under Cobb's plan, would need to cooperate.

Yet the Georgian's scheme, from the South Carolina perspective, allowed Lower South trimmers to wiggle out from under South Carolina's thumb. Especially Cobb's Georgians might not secede by February 1, if South Carolina allowed a free choice. Nor did fiery Alabamians wish to gamble on their state's freedom to ignore South Carolina's insistence. Nor did South Carolina ultras wish to gamble on their edgy state maintaining its nerve, as L. W. Spratt confessed to the Florida secession convention. "Just do it" had become South Carolina extremists' ruling passion and the passionate insistence of Lower South Separatists elsewhere. Then laggards, ran the dominant strategy, will have to follow.

Governor William Gist had given this relentless minority tactic its most important early boosts. He had refused to bow down before other Lower South governors' southern convention preference, in their answers to those October 5 letters, lest the southern majority control the South's response to Lincoln. In early November, he had also ordered State's Rights Gist to warn Mississippi's Governor John Pettus away from southern conventionism. He now would allow no escape from the Separatist express that he had helped put on the fast track. Governor Gist meant to allow Trescot and Drayton only room to surrender to his South Carolina fragment of the southern minority, when they arrived in South Carolina.

I warned Trescot and Drayton, the governor wrote Bonham on December 6, that I will allow no delay. "If the convention postponed the ordinance," I told Howell Cobb's messengers, "I would go to Charleston, make a speech, & advise the taking of the forts at once and I will do it." Join Trescot in telling the Washington delayers, Gist instructed Bonham, that their plan, unless instantly dropped, will "force us to do what we would prefer not doing before the ordinance is passed."[7]

Gist's plausible threat reemphasized that three, not two, alternatives faced the Southerners by this point: not just legal Separatism (as the South's state's rights creed defined legal), not just some form of Cooperationism, but also patently illegal revolution, with swarming vigilantes' illegitimacy routing a state convention's legitimacy. Illegal violence would throw away state's rights' persuasive power. The Lower South's well-nigh unanimous belief in the right of (legal) revolution could no longer trump the culture's divisions over the expediency of revolution. Rebellion by the mob would also toss slavery's fate into exactly the uncontrollable maelstrom that made Cooperationists shudder.

Bonham conveyed Gist's warning back to the South's Washington establishment, as did Trescot upon his return to the capital on December 8. Secretary of the Treasury Howell Cobb still sought delay. Cobb attended the

South Carolina secession convention in mid-December. He bore a note from Governor Joseph Brown, warning South Carolinians to secede immediately or "we are beaten and all is lost." Cobb, however, came to plead against immediacy. He wanted his patron, President James Buchanan, to be spared the necessity to confront secession. He preferred that disunion be approved now but postponed until Lincoln's March 4 Inauguration Day.[8] Jefferson Davis and Albert Gallatin Brown had recommended a similar delay at the November 22 Pettus conference.

South Carolina Separatists loathed the strategy. The be-kind-to-our-pal-Buchanan gambit smacked to them of National Democratic Party compromising, long the source of southern extremists' futility. Imagine, after secessionists had finally smashed the Democracy and dismissed Washington, D.C., antics, Howell Cobb still would base policy on James Buchanan's tender feelings! While Cobb and Davis continued to savor James Buchanan's White House hospitality, conceived South Carolinians, compromisers might try again to patch up the Union, with unreconstructed National Democrats such as Cobb as their Washington point men. Instead, South Carolinians meant to strike while the iron was steaming, lest second thoughts become cooler thoughts (even in South Carolina).

So South Carolina intransigents, in mid-December conferences with Cobb in Columbia, warned the secretary of the treasury to toe their straight and true Separatist line, just as State's Rights Gist had pulled Governor Pettus away from southern convention waverings and William Gist had yanked the Washington establishment away from the February 1 delay. In all cases, Lower South hesitators felt Separatism's relentless momentum and enlisted for the duration. South Carolinians had once again maneuvered all Cotton South Separatists onto the same page—their page.

Or to put their newfound relentlessness in the most revealing context, South Carolinians had become Preston Brooks writ large. Just as Brooks had rushed to the brink, then delayed the assault on Charles Sumner, then finally swung, then could not stop swinging, so South Carolinians had been ashamed of their shrinking after their charging and now would not, could not abort their exhilarating release. They would swing and swing and swing until far more Yankees than Charles Sumner collapsed, and no southern coward could make them pause.

– 3 –

Several days after Howell Cobb saw for himself in Columbia that this convulsive momentum could not be deflected, news of Gist's threats to Trescot and Drayton helped brace a critical mass of Lower South congressmen for Armageddon. Five days after William Henry Trescot's return to Washington, these congressmen publicly declared that "the argument is exhausted" and "all hope of relief in the Union . . . is extinguished." Lower South constituents must not be "deceived," this Southern Manifesto of December 13 urged, by "the pretense of new guarantees." Only "speedy and absolute separation from an unnatural and hostile Union" can insure "the honor, safety, and independence of the Southern people."[9]

The twenty-one signers of this death certificate for the Union swelled their numbers by claiming, in some cases dubiously, that seven more congressmen would have signed. Legend has boosted the twenty-one signers plus seven "would have signers" to thirty. The actual numbers did not require such inflations. Only three signers represented the Upper South. None hailed from South Carolina. The eighteen Lower South signers comprised almost half of the thirty-eight congressmen then in Washington from Florida, Georgia, Mississippi, Alabama, Louisiana, and Texas—the very six states about to decide whether to join South Carolina's imminent exodus.

Kentucky's U.S. Senator John J. Crittenden led the mass of Upper South congressmen who strove to halt further departures. "It is certain, I suppose," Crittenden lamented privately, "that South Carolina will secede." But "conciliatory measures" may prevent "other states . . . from following her bad example."[10]

Crittenden's attempt to isolate the bad example began five days after the Southern Manifesto declared conciliation to be delusive. On December 18, the Senate approved a Committee of Thirteen, to investigate compromise possibilities. Crittenden, although not the chairman, set the agenda. Before the committee's discussions began, the Kentuckian asked the Senate to consider a package of constitutional amendments. The omnibus package strategy emulated Henry Clay's statecraft during Compromise of 1850 deliberations. Crittenden, long Clay's lieutenant, now sat in Clay's senatorial seat. Kentucky's latest "Great Compromiser" arrived in the Senate's Committee of Thirteen with his final test of the Union's viability tucked under his arm.[11]

The other twelve committee members formed a jury of Crittenden's peers, determining whether his omnibus—any compromise—could isolate South Carolina. Three members of the committee hailed from the Upper South, including Crittenden, his Kentucky colleague Lazarus Powell, and Virginia's Robert M. T. Hunter. Two represented the Lower South: Georgia's Robert Toombs and Mississippi's Jefferson Davis. Five Northern Republicans and three Northern Democrats completed the panel.

The senatorial jury sped only one piece of Crittenden's package toward congressional victory. This constitutional amendment declared that the federal government could never abolish slavery in a state and that the amendment could never be amended. On the eve of Lincoln's March 4 inauguration, Congress would pass this unamendable constitutional amendment. The new president would endorse this perpetual barrier to federal emancipation in his Inaugural Address. Three states would ratify the amendment. Three-fourths of the states would have doubtless affirmed this widely popular attempt at peacemaking, if war had not intervened.[12]

Another intriguing "what if" question here arises. If no civil war had ensued, how long would slavery have lasted, with this amendment forever tying federal hands? Some might argue that the institution would have lasted deep into the twentieth century, at least in the Lower South, if only Southerners had had power to emancipate. Some might even argue that slaveholders were fools to trade this safeguard for disunion risks.

So much for Monday morning quarterbacks. The Southerners who sped the contest toward secession saw scant value in a guarantee of no federal action. They feared state action after Lincoln's Southern Republican appointees infiltrated a caged South. They focused on two words in another of Crittenden's proposals, promising escape from a territorial cage.

Crittenden proposed that the Missouri Compromise's 36° 30' line be extended to the Pacific. The Kentucky senator would bar slavery north of the line in the nation's territories but protect the institution south of the line, including in territories *Hereafter Acquired*. Crittenden trembled to include those two words, repulsive to Republicans because enticing to Caribbean expansionists. Later in the congressional session, after the more extremist Lower South had left the Union and Crittenden's attention focused on retaining only the more moderate Upper South, the latest Great Compromiser would scotch the fatal two words.

But in December 1860, Crittenden strove to retain the more fiery Lower South. He knew that countervailing propositions from the Committee of Thirteen's southern members went much further in southern directions than Hereafter Acquired. So he thought that nothing less than the two terrible words could appease the hotheads.

Jefferson Davis told the committee that he would settle for slavery's protection in *all* U.S. territories. Robert M. T. Hunter would settle for Davis's uncompromising "all," *plus* a constitutional amendment prohibiting a federal "local appointment" without "the assent of a majority of the Senators from each section" (that, trumpeted the Virginia senator, would prevent "the abuse of patronage . . . so much feared from Lincoln"), *plus* another amendment that established two presidents, one northern, one southern, each with a veto on all legislation. Robert Toombs would settle for Davis's *all, plus* a constitutional amendment decreeing that a majority of each section's representatives in each hall of Congress must approve all slavery legislation.[13]

Compared to those reincarnations of John C. Calhoun's minority veto of majority decrees, Hereafter Acquired offered slaveholders slim protection. But the two words still proposed considerable relief from many Southwesterners' twin menaces: claustrophobia and insult. Ever since the days of Robert Walker and Texas annexation, Southwesterners had demanded a territorial escape valve for excess slaves, lest whites be imprisoned with multiplying blacks. Ever since the days of David Wilmot and his post-Texasannexation Wilmot Proviso, the men from Dixie had scorned the insult of being declared too morally repulsive to expand beyond their supposedly disgusting domain. Hereafter Acquired would provide an escape valve for any future excess of blacks. By granting slaveholders the theoretical right to sprawl down to the Amazon, Lincoln's party would also take back the slur that migrating slaveholders would pollute an expanding republic.

Crittenden especially hoped that Hereafter Acquired would tempt Robert Toombs. The Georgian loomed as the make-or-break southern committee member partly because the Empire State remained geographically pivotal in any southern republic and partly because Toombs's recent utterances had made him a secessionist who just might compromise. In mid-November 1860, on the day of Stephens's Cooperationist triumph before the Georgia legislature, Toombs had seemed uncompromising. He had demanded that lawmakers "give me the sword; for if you do not give it to me, as God lives, *I will take it.*"[14] William Gist never said it better. Two days later, with inter-state Separatist communication still in its brief conspiratorial phase, the would-be sword seizer had secretly telegraphed South Carolina's Laurence Keitt to "act at once. . . . I will sustain South Carolina in secession."[15] Robert Barnwell Rhett had asked for precisely this clandestine reassurance.

Yet a month later, in Toombs's notorious December 13 Danbury Public Letter, the Georgia senator seemed to counsel possible delay. Toombs suggested that Georgians should "offer in Congress such amendments of the Constitution as will give" their constituents "full and ample security." If "a majority" of "the Black Republican party will vote for the amendments," we should "postpone final action [on secession] until the legislatures of the Northern states could be conveniently called together" (which could be long after March 4).[16]

But if congressional Republicans reject our last offer, concluded Toombs's December 13 Danbury Letter, Georgians "ought not to delay an hour after the fourth of March to secede from the Union." Toombs's Calhoun-like proposals for minority veto offered, in his mind, "full security." But did Hereafter Acquired offer "ample security," at least against the Republican insults that Georgia's favorite knight desired to cut out of foul mouths with the sword?

The Committee of Thirteen's most dramatic confrontation supplied the answer. The face-off featured arguably the two most different southern senatorial titans. John Crittenden, seventy-four years aged, had lived one and a half times longer than Robert Toombs, aged fifty. The Kentuckian had the tall, slim, ramrod-stiff body and the long, pale, rectangular face of a puritan. The Georgian had the portly body and the square red face of an imbiber. Crittenden's snow-white, closely cropped, and meticulously combed hair signaled the cautious conservative. Toombs's black, bushy, and wild locks, with the thick strand curling down his forehead, announced the reckless warrior. Crittenden owned the few slaves and the few hundred acres of a moderately successful borderland lawyer. Toombs possessed the hundreds of slaves and the thousands of acres of a fabulously successful tropical land speculator. Crittenden, long content to recline in Clay's shadow, had won moderate renown as the borderland's favorite post-Clay neutral. Toombs, always the man to cast the shadows, had secured immoderate fame as the slavocracy's favorite political brawler.[17]

Kentucky's latest Great Compromiser, John Crittenden (left), and a secsssionist charger (for Georgia!), Robert Toombs (right), settling for a doomed compromise that would make the unfinished state of the U.S. Capitol building, site of their wary negotiations, all the more appropriate. Courtesy of the Library of Congress (all three images).

When the circumspect mediator faced the flamboyant aggressor across the Committee of Thirteen's conference table, an epic exchange ensued. The reported words may be apocryphal. But the upshot remains indisputable.[18] As the legend describes the language, when Crittenden asked, "Mr. Toombs, will my compromise, as a remedy for all wrongs and apprehensions, be acceptable to you?" Toombs shot back, "Not by a good deal; but my state will accept it, and I will follow my state." Davis and Hunter (and of course Kentucky's Powell) concurred. Crittenden had found the least concession that the southern half of his committee could abide.

The northern half could not bear Hereafter Acquired. Lincoln insisted that if Hereafter Acquired became law, "filibustering and extending slavery" will "immediately" recommence. "On that point, hold firm as with a chain of steel."[19] Republicans on the Committee of Thirteen held firm. They voted down 36° 30' plus Hereafter Acquired, and therefore so did the Lower South senators, Toombs and Davis. In another example of the most basic split in the South, the Upper South senators, Powell, Hunter, and Crittenden, still voted for the compromise.

That December 22 evening, Toombs telegraphed his "Fellow-Citizens of Georgia," reporting the results of the "test" that he had put "fairly and frankly." He had come to Washington, ran the telegram, "to secure your constitutional rights or to demonstrate to you that you can get no guarantees." His "Black Republican" foes had "treated" his "propositions . . . with either derision or contempt." Our "enemies" had also unanimously rejected Crittenden's diluted propositions. The Union has thus been proved "fraught with nothing but ruin to yourself and your posterity. Secession by the fourth of March next should be thundered" by a "unanimous vote" when Georgians elected state convention delegates on January 2.[20]

Perhaps Toombs had always plotted to send this incendiary telegram. Alexander Stephens thought that the senator cynically played the compromiser, both in the Danbury Letter and in Congress, seeking to manipulate Georgians into considering compromise impossible.[21] The senator might have even gulled a reluctant Crittenden to press on with Hereafter Acquired, thereby plotting to make the Kentuckian's compromise unworkable. Toombs had long proved himself wily enough to play such games, both as a crafty land speculator and as a posturing extremist. Yet this southern knight was also wild enough to act the erratic Southron, in the style of such flip-flopping warriors as Mississippi's Henry Foote and Virginia's Henry Wise. But whether a gyrating or a calculating Georgian had helped to dramatize Crittenden's failure, Toombs correctly told his constituents that "if you are deceived . . . with delusive hopes" about compromise before you vote on January 2, "it shall not be my fault."[22]

Nor can Toombs be faulted for spreading delusive hopes when he predicted that Georgia would have accepted Hereafter Acquired. Jefferson Davis, however, would have had less hope of spreading Georgia's possible acceptance to Mississippi. The state's establishment had narrowly rejected

Davis's objection to Separatism at the November 22, 1860, Pettus conference. So too, in early December, Mississippi's Congressman Otho R. Singletary had told South Carolina's Bonham that "we must go ahead" with secession, for "most" of Mississippi's "delegation . . . will not be controlled by Davis."[23] Nor would South Carolina have likely ceased to crash ahead, just because a senatorial committee had allowed slaveholders a shot at Caribbean expansion—a pursuit that the South Carolina establishment often considered distractive or counterproductive. Crittenden had lost not a chance to save the whole Union but a chance to slow secessionists' momentum in Lower South states that still wavered about disunion.

Only a very different Cooperationist campaign might have precluded Crittenden's unintended demonstration, before the Lower South's electorate even voted on Cooperationism, that an ultimatum to the North had already failed. If Lower South anti-Separatists had rushed to convene a mid-December southern convention instead of campaigning against rush itself, Crittenden might have waited to react to a southern convention's imminent ultimatum. Perhaps that ultimatum would have demanded less than Hereafter Acquired, especially if the Upper South had massed behind Alexander Stephens's sole demand that Personal Liberty Laws be repealed. But with no southern convention (or Alexander Stephens) remotely in sight, and with William Gist hurling Howell Cobb's plea for a pause back in the southern Washington establishment's face, Crittenden had felt compelled to appease Robert Toombs. And then before this senatorial disaster was a week old, a military disaster heaped further burdens upon lame Cooperationists.

CHAPTER 29

Military Explosions

Bad news for Cooperationists came in lockstep during the last ten days of December. Six days after South Carolina seceded and four days after Hereafter Acquired failed, federal troops seized Charleston's vacant Fort Sumter. The strike inspired a wide-ranging Lower South military crisis during the next two weeks—the very time when Lower South debate over Separatism came to climax. The almost daily military explosions included seizures of two other empty, monumental federal forts, surrenders of a dozen occupied federal military installations, cannonballs whizzing over a federal relief ship approaching Fort Sumter—all this turmoil over alleged federal military coercion before Lower South conventions could even vote on delaying what had been merely a political crisis.

– 1 –

Once again at this turning point, a stream of occurrences having nothing to do with slavery crossed the stream of slavery incidents. This time, not the completion of a railroad but the development of a military concept coincidentally met disunion events at a pivotal crossroads. This time, the unintended and unanticipated convergence posed a question still absent from the history books: How could federal soldiers have previously failed to occupy the three most formidable Lower South federal forts, thus inviting disruptive seizures at the worst moment?

The answers, as so often in military history, begin with the army's tendency to avoid a past disaster instead of forestalling new dangers. After the War of 1812 had demonstrated the nation's vulnerability to English sea power, the army's Board of Engineers devised the so-called Totten coastal defense system. The name honored the system's most important planner, General Joseph Totten. Totten envisioned a string of massive brick structures with four to seven faces, guarding entrances to the nation's most important Atlantic ports.

The three Lower South pillars of the Totten coastal defense system were Charleston's Fort Sumter, Savannah's Fort Pulaski, and Pensacola's Fort Pickens. All three forts had walls at least two feet thick. All rose atop little islands, surrounded by protective waters. Each was completed or nearly completed by 1860. Each cost almost a million dollars. All featured multiple cannon, ready to be fired.

But none contained troops. Occupation of the three forts seemed unnecessary and thus unnecessarily expensive. Transporting food and supplies to soldiers inside an island fort cost far more in time, dollars, and convenience than sustaining troops in nearby mainland barracks. If invasion seemed imminent, nearby soldiers could be ferried to island fortresses before enemy ships appeared. Thus a trio of empty Lower South military prizes stood ready to be occupied, with only solitary guards or construction workers there to smile or frown at unopposed intruders.

When South Carolina seceded, almost all U.S. soldiers in the state lived not in Fort Sumter but in Fort Moultrie. Charleston's citizens, not harbor waters, surrounded Moultrie. The fort guarded the tip of Sullivan's Island, Charlestonians' favorite suburb. From troops' perch on the northern entrance to Charleston's inner harbor, they could readily bombard foreign ships before the vessels reached Fort Sumter, located on its own tiny island inside the inner harbor.

Hostile South Carolinians could more easily bombard Fort Moultrie than Fort Sumter. Moultrie's new commanding officer in November 1860, Kentucky's Major Robert Anderson, found an impossible military situation. His only sixty men could only briefly defend themselves from sharpshooters on sand hills towering above the fort. Give me orders about how and when to defend this well-nigh indefensible position, Major Robert Anderson implored his Washington superiors.[1]

On December 8, South Carolina's congressmen equally implored President James Buchanan to remove the helpless Kentucky major and his troops. The congressmen came away from the White House, so they thought, with an unwritten gentlemen's agreement. The military situation in Charleston harbor, President Buchanan and South Carolina's congressmen evidently informally agreed, would be temporarily frozen as it stood, with no troop reinforcements, movements, or assaults to transpire.[2]

Buchanan never denied South Carolinians' allegations that he had agreed to a truce in place. But he never ordered Major Robert Anderson to comply. Instead, on December 21, a day after South Carolina departed the Union, Virginia's Secretary of War John B. Floyd wrote Anderson, instructing the major to "exercise a sound military discretion" and to avoid "useless sacrifice of . . . lives."[3]

The soundest "military discretion," Anderson decided, would be to abandon Fort Moultrie and to occupy Fort Sumter, without a life lost. On the night after Christmas, under cover of darkness, the Kentuckian moved his exposed force to the unexposed island fortress. The next morning, while grateful federal soldiers and twice as many construction workers saluted the first raising of the Stars and Stripes over Fort Sumter, enraged Charlestonians found only spiked cannon and incinerated gun carriages in evacuated Fort Moultrie.

Robert Anderson had not only followed orders scrupulously and protected his troops shrewdly but also emulated his Kentucky U.S. senator brilliantly. Like John J. Crittenden, Anderson was a Border South neutral, anxious to avoid war and to save the Union. Anderson's night of sneaking across Charleston's inner harbor, moving soldiers from an easily assaulted fort to a pile harder to dream of conquering, sought to stall off the horrid hour.

The stall provoked immediate confrontation. Between December 27 and January 2, in retaliation for Anderson's shattering of their supposed truce with Buchanan, Charlestonians seized all federal properties in the area except Fort Sumter. The haul included Fort Moultrie, Fort Johnson, and Castle Pinckney, as well as the U.S. Custom House and the U.S. Arsenal. Inside the arsenal lay lush treasure: 20,000-plus badly needed stands of arms.

South Carolinians desired richer bounty. They craved federal acknowledgment that they had formed a legitimate new nation, one that the United States could not legitimately coerce. They thought that Major Anderson's movement to Fort Sumter, in violation of President Buchanan's gentlemen's agreement for a truce in place, gave them a trump card. Buchanan, as an honorable northern friend, would surely redeem his pledge of December 8 by ordering Major Anderson back to disabled Fort Moultrie or, better, out of the nation of South Carolina.

On December 26, the day that Anderson snuck over to Sumter, three of South Carolina's most high-powered patriarchs arrived in Washington as the new nation's new commissioners. The trio included the Harvard-educated Robert Barnwell, as close to a unionist as they came in South Carolina; the Yale-educated James Adams, ex-governor of the state and one of those fiery extremists that Robert Gourdin so distrusted; and James L. Orr, the most successful pragmatic politician in the wonderland of South Carolina extremism. The well-balanced trio visited Buchanan on December 28, as much three gentlemen come to see a fourth as negotiators come to protest a travesty. You must redeem your honor, violated through no fault of yours, exclaimed South Carolina's titans. You must dispatch Major Anderson back to Moultrie or out of South Carolina.[4] The honorable president almost agreed, then asked for time to ponder.

He immediately faced outraged protest from Northern Democratic allies. They thought that this proposed latest submission to the Slave Power would forever destroy their party and their nation. Thus tightened the climactic showdown between ever increasing southern demands and ever increasing northern resistance that had destroyed the National Democratic Party and Buchanan's presidency.

As the president wrung his hands over his latest and worst predicament, a torn nation held its collective breath. Meanwhile Separatists throughout the Lower South, outraged at Buchanan's failure instantly to order Anderson out of Fort Sumter, eyed their states' own federal forts. Most in play were Forts Pulaski and Pickens, those two other empty exemplars of the Totten coastal defense system.

– 2 –

As the post–December 26 military story spread beyond South Carolina, the first hero (or if you will, villain) was neither a state nor a federal official. This loose cannon of a private citizen demonstrated why officials such as Judge Andrew Magrath had worried that an irresponsible individual would inspire a mob to assault the federal government illegitimately, thus discrediting supposedly legitimate disunion. Especially Robert Gourdin had sought to keep sober revolution out of Rhett's wild hands. And then the wildest pair of private hands in the South almost started the Civil War—and (so the outlaw convinced himself) with Gourdin's blessings!

The hands belonged to the only proslavery zany with a more outlandish name than State's Rights Gist. Savannah's Charles Augustus Lafayette Lamar was born in 1824. That year, the marquis de Lafayette, the French hero of the American Revolution, visited England's ex-colonies. During his triumphant tour, the Frenchman attended the baptism and became the godfather of Gazaway Lamar's new son.[5]

Gazaway earned such favors as a capitalist of the Robert Gourdin sort, many times magnified. Although a slaveholder, he amassed wealth largely the Yankee way—in cities, as a merchant and as an industrialist. He not only marketed the crops that came to Savannah but also introduced the first iron steamship into America. Gazaway owned steamboats, railroads, insurance companies, and (this was another first for a southern grandee) a New York bank.

The sober New York banker early turned over his massive Savannah affairs to his wild son. The incongruous pair, along with Gazaway's sister, had been the only Lamar survivors of a horrendous shipwreck in Gazaway's real domain: not the South but the Atlantic Ocean. Having lost his wife and other children to the ocean's fury, Gazaway clung to his remaining offspring with a fellow escapee's passion and a bereaved father's adoration of whatever he had left. Even C.A.L.'s furious southern provincialism never alienated the cautious New York sophisticate, perhaps partly because the son's adventurism usually bolstered the family's bottom line.

Two years before secession, C.A.L. imported Africans for sale, in defiance of the Union's laws. He thereby brought his synthesis of scrounging Yankee and defiant Cavalier to controversial flower. His father thought the flower repulsive. "An expedition to the moon," Gazaway wrote C.A.L., "would have been equally sensible" and as contrary to God's "will and his laws."[6]

If God cheers Georgians who go to Virginia for slaves, answered the son, "what is the difference between going to Africa?" By going to Africa for a boatload of merchandise, C.A.L. would teach fellow Southerners that *everything* was right about slavery, even its African trade origins. He would also amass his rightful profit—$480,000 gained for $300,000 spent.

In December 1858, the thirty-four-year-old tycoon illegally imported Africans in a style that only Gazaway Lamar's heir could deploy. The New York Yacht Club had barred the family's yacht-schooner, the *Wanderer*, from its races because the sleek vessel's sophistication destroyed competition. C.A.L. converted the cosmopolitan craft to provincial moneygrubbing. The *Wanderer* sped Lamar's Africans to their clandestine U.S. landing at Jekyll Island near Savannah (Jekyll, of all places, where Gazaway's fellow New York plutocrats would imminently establish a playground for Yankee millionaires). C.A.L. picked up his merchandise at Jekyll with his steamers, chugged up the Savannah River, and sold choice items at fancy plantations.[7]

The news created a national sensation, as did the government's seizure of the *Wanderer* and arrest of the owner. C.A.L. dealt with the seizure by bidding $4001 against his jailer's $4000, when the classy schooner came up at crass auction. To prevent a higher bid, Lafayette's godson clubbed the jailer to earth and made off with the ship.

When he came back for trial, Lamar negotiated a plea bargain. He paid a $500 fine and served thirty days in confinement—in his own Savannah apartment! "The government has not the power" to "keep me in jail," C.A.L. boasted, "unless they raise a few additional regiments."[8] Thirty days later, the convict strolled out of his apartment, stroking his red mustache with one hand and flaunting his golden cane with the other.

During the secession crisis, the uncontainable redhead clashed with his contained father over a more destructive (and less profitable) venture. Gazaway, true to his New York residence and transatlantic interests, favored unionist compromises. C.A.L., true to his slave trade caper and his loathing of Yankees, supported uncompromising disunionism. "I am about to organize a company," the son wrote his father on the night before Lincoln's election. I have "ordered 100 pistols and 100 sabers this day" from Hartford, Connecticut. "Governor Brown approves of it, and says I can order the Arms and pay for them and he will refund the money out of the 1st appropriation for the purchase of arms." Lamar "would also purchase 4 pieces of cannon" for his troops. He hoped "Lincoln may be elected," for "I want dissolution, & have I think contributed more than any man South for it."[9]

On November 26, C.A.L. wrote Gazaway, again, dismissing his father's prayer for continued Union. "If Georgia don't act promptly," declared this commander of the South's largest, best-equipped private army, "we, the military of Savhn., will throw her in to Revolution. . . . We do not care what the world may approve of—we know we are right and will act regardless of consequences."[10]

After Robert Anderson occupied Fort Sumter, Lamar meant to occupy the Savannah fortress, Fort Pulaski, before federal troops could garrison the empty five-sided brick colossus. Like Fort Sumter, Fort Pulaski loomed over its own island. But Pulaski's Cockspur Island lay not in the middle of an importing city's inner harbor, as did Sumter's little island, but fifteen miles downstream, where the Savannah River enters the Atlantic Ocean.

Lamar dreamed that the very family vessels that had carried his African cargo up the river would now convey his fiery retainers downstream, to swarm inside an empty federal bulwark before another Robert Anderson could reach another strategically placed island fortress. As in his *Wanderer* fling, this rich young sport exuded the combination of private means and illegal bravado that could carry off such a lawless feat. He would thus shove Robert Gourdin's cautious revolution toward a reckless climax.

During the evening of December 29, Lamar sent Gourdin arguably the most astonishing private letter in all the communications leading to disunion. Somehow, the letter revealed, the young hotspur had conceived that the graying Charlestonian had asked him to confiscate thousands of federal guns from Fort Pulaski and bring them to Charleston, to help blast Robert Anderson out of Fort Sumter! Alas, the document that could help explain why Lamar thought such a thing has not been uncovered.

No smoking gun could be more missed, by all who love a psychological puzzle. Perhaps the trauma of Major Anderson's movement had thrown Robert Gourdin, that endless advocate of removing hotheads' hands from revolutionary controls, into uncharacteristically losing his balance. Or perhaps Lamar, that endless advocate of storming balanced elders, had gleefully distorted some ambiguous Gourdin phrase into a summons. But whatever the reason why Lamar felt called to become the Lafayette of the South Carolina revolution, he sadly reported to Gourdin, on the evening of December 29, that this morning, "I had steamboat, men, & mules all ready" to go "to Fort Pulaski," there to seize "the Guns that I promised" you. But "the wind from the N. E., . . . blowing as it was," made it "impossible for a boat to lay alongside of the Northern wharf. . . . I consequently postponed" my seizure until tomorrow morning.[11]

Before Lamar could make good use of the morrow, another Savannah correspondent telegraphed Gourdin about the redhead's planned escapade. The horrified Charlestonian may have reflected on the latest coincidence that had smoothed his alliance with Savannah compatriots. First a railroad commenced at just the right moment! Then a wind howled at just the right instant! At any rate, Gourdin telegraphed Savannah allies, warning them against illegal seizures. Gourdin's Charleston compatriot, the elderly Langdon Cheves, also telegraphed young Lamar "to do nothing without consulting Colonel Lawton."[12]

Alexander Robert Lawton epitomized the cosmopolitan, cautious Savannah businessmen that sophisticates in Charleston's 1860 Association cherished. Born in the South Carolina rice parishes, Lawton had been educated at West Point and at the Harvard Law School. The cultivated lawyer, forty-two years old in 1860, headed the Augusta and Savannah Railroad, served in the State Senate, and commanded the First Volunteer Regiment of Georgia. After the Civil War, Lawton would become a president of the American Bar Association and a United States minister to Austria.[13]

True to a cosmopolitan's worldview, Alexander Lawton had written Robert Gourdin on December 16 to go ahead with revolution, but carefully. A cautiously peaceful disunion would "advance the good cause here." But assaults on U.S. forts would lose us sympathy and be "no holiday's work."[14] On December 29, Gourdin enlisted Lawton to forestall C.A.L. Lamar's holiday in Fort Pulaski.

Upon hearing about Gourdin's intervention, Lamar agreed to await the Charlestonian's further orders. He also agreed to consult Alexander Lawton before assaulting Fort Pulaski. But if Charlestonians decided against his seizing Fort Pulaski's guns, C.A.L. wrote Gourdin, he hoped to go "by steamer to St. Augustine" to seize "larger and superior" federal weapons.[15]

Colonel Lawton feared that private Savannah citizens could not control this desperado. The state's highest public official must contain the hothead. Lawton accordingly telegraphed Governor Joseph Brown in Milledgeville on December 31. "Come to Savannah at once," urged Colonel Lawton. Brown sped over the 170 miles the next day, arriving in the city on January 1 at 9:00 P.M.[16]

With Governor Brown's arrival in Savannah, Lamar's threat to take over the assault on Pulaski (and on Sumter) summarily ended. He would next be seen as a lowly aide-de-camp to southern officials in Fort Moultrie. He would eventually be captured just after the Civil War officially ended and shot fatally in the back, making his demise one of the last (and least necessary) casualties of the war that he had craved. But before the war began, he faded into the shadows with a rebel's high honors. His private irresponsibility brought just the right public official to just the right place, and at just the right time, to preside over a presecession conspiracy to seize all Lower South federal military installations.

– 3 –

While Governor Joseph Brown traveled from Milledgeville to Savannah, the telegraph wires hummed with the news that the wavering Yankee in the White House had made his decision. On December 31, James Buchanan rejected the South Carolina commissioners' demands. Robert Anderson would stay in Fort Sumter, Buchanan wrote.[17] Would the president now take the next step—reinforcing Anderson's sketchy force? Rumors flew around Washington that Buchanan had already ordered up relief ships, bound not only for Fort Sumter but also for the other two empty Totten coastal defense fortresses, Savannah's Pulaski and Pensacola's Pickens, and for a dozen lesser Lower South federal military installations.

South Carolina's three angry commissioners in Washington investigated the rumors. On January 1, they telegraphed their conclusions to the South Carolina secession convention. The convention's president, David F. Jamison, immediately telegraphed Governor Joseph Brown in Milledgeville. Brown's office forwarded the telegram to Savannah, care of Colonel Lawton. The colonel handed the secret missive to the governor upon the chief executive's arrival in town three hours later. "Just rec'd from our commissioners at Washington," ran Jamison's wire, the "following Telegram: War we believe is inevitable" and "reinforcements are now on the way. Prevent their entrance into the harbor at every hazard."[18]

During the late evening of January 1, Governor Brown confronted not only Jamison's secret telegram but also "great popular apprehension," he reported, "that Fort Pulaski would be garrisoned with United States Troops" or with private Georgia armies, unless "occupied by State Troops." Thus on January 2, 1861, the governor confidentially ordered Alexander Lawton, commanding 125 Georgia volunteers, to seize the fort. As Brown explained his justification to Colonel Lawton, "the Government at Washington has, as we are informed upon high policy, decided on the policy of coercing a seceded state back into the Union, and it is believed now has a movement on foot to occupy with Federal Troops, the Southern Forts, including Fort Pulaski." Lawton must thus seize and retain that Savannah fort, until the Georgia state convention "has decided on" secession. In the early morning of January 3, Lawton, unopposed, occupied the empty fort.[19]

Hours after Lawton struck, Governor Brown secretly telegraphed the two Governors Moore (of Alabama and Louisiana), as well as Mississippi's Governor Pettus and Florida's Governor Perry. "In view of . . . the coercive policy understood to be adapted by our Government," ran the missive, "I have ordered Georgia troops to occupy Fort Pulaski at the mouth of the river till our convention assembles." Governor Brown added his "hope" that "you will cooperate and occupy the Forts" in your state.[20]

The Florida, Alabama, and Mississippi governors confidentially telegraphed back that they would swiftly cooperate. So they did. Governor Brown, nervous about Louisiana's missing answer, telegraphed Pettus to alert Louisiana's Governor Moore. Pettus sent the requested telegram, with slightly delayed but ultimately gratifying results.[21]

Alabama's Governor Moore supplied secret gratification more quickly. The day after Brown telegraphed Lawton (and the day Lawton struck), Andrew Moore privately wired Captain John Todd in Mobile. "You are ordered," ran the call to arms, "to occupy Forts Morgan and Gaines and to take possession of the U.S. arsenal immediately and to hold them for the State of Alabama," until I or the Alabama state convention orders otherwise.[22]

I am "advised," continued Moore's order, that "the Federal Government intends to coerce the Seceding States," and thus "that all the Southern forts will be immediately reinforced." To prevent federal reinforcement, Governor Brown "has occupied Fort Pulaski." We must follow suit. But since "Alabama has not yet seceded," we must take "both the forts and the arsenal . . . without bloodshed," lest we begin a shooting war against the government of "which we continue to be an integral part."

Some part! This prerevolutionary plot delivered the simultaneous capture of four states' federal military installations, with the seizures arming imminent rebels and influencing citizens' decision to revolt. As the prearranged military strike evolved, Governor Brown controlled Fort Pulaski two weeks before Georgia's convention acted (and on the very day that his state's voters split their votes almost evenly between Separatist and Cooperationist convention delegates). Alabama's Moore governed Forts Morgan and Gaines, plus the Mt. Vernon Arsenal, four days before his state's badly divided state convention sought to muster a majority for disunion. Florida's Perry occupied Fort Marion and the St. Augustine Arsenal three days before his state's convention authorized disunion. Louisiana's Moore controlled Forts Jackson, St. Phillips, and Pike twelve days before the state seceded. The governor also seized the big Louisiana catch, the Baton Rouge Arsenal, sixteen days before secession.

In the eleven days between Georgia's possession of Fort Pulaski (January 3) and Louisiana's capture of Fort Pike (January 14), the governors of four states, none having yet seceded, had coordinated the ambush of eight forts and three arsenals. No lives had been lost. Almost no shots had been fired. Only one state, Florida, had experienced any trouble carrying out the interstate plot.

The exception involved a serious setback. On January 8, a handful of Governor Perry's Floridians marched on Fort Barrancas in Pensacola Harbor. After U.S. troops fired warning shots, Perry's men retreated. Two days later, with the federal position on the Florida mainland precarious, the U.S. commander at Barrancas, Lieutenant Adam Slemmer, pulled a Robert Anderson. He moved his eighty-two men across Pensacola Bay to empty Fort Pickens on Santa Rosa Island, the Pensacola stronghold of the Totten coastal defense system.[23]

On January 12, Florida militiamen overwhelmed the other U.S. installations in Pensacola, Forts Barrancas and McRee plus the Pensacola Naval Yard. Meanwhile, after an exchange of telegrams that Georgia's Governor Brown initiated, Mississippi dispatched eight companies and Alabama (which still had not seceded!) three companies (and soon another three companies) to Pensacola, to help drive federal Lieutenant Slemmer out of Fort Pickens. Once arrived, this first transstate rebel army, almost a thousand angry Southerners strong, lined the sand beach, eager to have at the island fort but without the ships to reach it (or the orders to invade).[24]

Despite this unfinished business, Governor Joseph Brown correctly bragged that the "responsibility" for state seizure of federal military prizes "was a grave one, but I did not hesitate to take it." Brown was "happy to see" that "other southern governors . . . have followed the example." Or as Georgia's James Mercer Green chortled, Governor Brown heads "a long list of traitors whom the Yankees intend to hang."[25]

A U.S. treason court could indeed have indicted, convicted, and hanged the governors for conspiratorial plotting, if prosecutors had uncovered these still-surviving telegrams. In the case of that previous spree of clandestine disunion plotting, the early October–early November fleeting conspiracy between South Carolinians and Lower South secessionists elsewhere, many of the incriminating letters have disappeared, and nothing happened until planning shifted to the open air. But in the case of the secretly coordinated fort seizures, the smoking guns, that evidence prized by treason courts, are all there (save only for that much lamented lost letter, explaining how C.A.L. Lamar had so misunderstood Robert Gourdin). Furthermore, the undercover plotting directly produced the treasonous activity (as the federal government defined treason).

The military conspiracy, like the political conspiracy before it, showed the strengths and limits of clandestine plotting in an open democratic system. Secret correspondence could not alone build a revolutionary consensus, as Robert Barnwell Rhett had learned in the November South Carolina legislature. Open debate also had to convince the voters, as the Charleston and Savannah Railroad celebration had demonstrated. But clandestine communication could arrange the issues before the public. In October–early November, the Gist-Pettus secret confrontations had arranged a consistent Separatist appeal for serial Lower South decisions on single state secession, not on a southern convention. So too, in early January, the secretly arranged simultaneous assault on all Lower South forts had partially shifted voters' and conventions' decision from whether Lincoln's menace justified immediate secession to whether governors had been justified to defy coercion before the coercive ships arrived.

Or to put the shifting issue slightly differently, the changed context of decision invited citizens to affirm the (uncontested) right to secede before the (highly contested) expediency of secession had been secured. Frustrated Cooperationists even charged, inaccurately, that, in Georgia's Hershel Johnson's words, the fort seizures had been deliberately "designed" at "shaping matters" so "as to render secession a necessity." The simultaneous action of several states showed "concert among the ringleaders," charged Johnson, just as military action before secession is "treason against the U.States."[26]

Alabama's Governor Andrew Moore seems to have especially feared that his participation in secret treason would merit a traitor's gallows. As if filing a preindictment plea before a grand jury, Moore wrote President Buchanan that he had taken "every precautionary step" to maintain the peace. He had been "left" with "little, if any, room to doubt that the Government of the United States . . . was about to reinforce these forts." If I had failed to do "my duty, . . . I would probably have been overruled by an excited and discontent people and popular violence might have accomplished what we did peaceably." I will equally peaceably hand back the forts, arsenals, and guns, if our imminent convention does not secede.[27]

When the four states' conventions did secede, they possessed a treasure of arms at a needy moment. In late December and early January, the four states' governors had urgently been seeking guns to buy all over the South, the North, and Europe. They had succeeded mostly in competing with each other, driving up the prices for excellent guns, and settling for bargain-basement hand-me-downs.[28]

They had especially slim luck with Eli Whitney's famous Connecticut gun factory. That concern accused Mississippi officials of refusing to pay their bills on time.[29] Meanwhile, other Connecticut suppliers of guns gladly served the swiftly paying Charles Augustine Lafayette Lamar. The upshot: While thousands of Lower South volunteers eagerly sought guns, their governors could not find the rifles to spend half their states' appropriations.

The military plot eased the debacle. Some 75,000 stands of arms had been confiscated from U.S. forts and arsenals. The coup highlighted a crucial reason why Separatists demanded that the revolution be completed by March 4. If Lincoln gains "possession of the army and navy—the public treasury and all the patronage," wrote Mississippi's Powhattan Ellis, Sr., on Christmas Day, 1860, "the odds . . . will be against us."[30] The odds against the rebels would indeed have been worse if those circa 75,000 U.S. guns confiscated from federal arsenals and forts in the three weeks after December 26 had not supplied the volunteers.

Still, the governors had not conspired to seize the forts in order to secure the guns for a civil war, any more than they had plotted to take over military installations in order to clinch upcoming secession decisions. Those boons had been unintended consequences of the master intention: to preclude Buchanan's (falsely) expected reinforcements of forts throughout the Lower South. Still, after the unintended consequences fell into Separatists' laps, they took full advantage of the martial excitement, making an electoral victory for secession easier to attain. They also cherished the 75,000-plus rifles, making treason arrests easier to forestall.

- 4 -

On January 5, five days after South Carolina's commissioners correctly surmised that Buchanan meant to reinforce Fort Sumter, the president's reinforcing ship, the *Star of the West*, steamed out of New York City. Hidden under its deck, the otherwise unarmed merchant vessel carried some two hundred soldiers, one hundred rifles, and three months of supplies for Anderson's men, including fresh beef. The *Star* slipped to the edge of Charleston's inner harbor under cover of night on January 8. But the shrouded vessel could not find its way toward Fort Sumter until daybreak on January 9.

Then the provoking ship chugged toward Robert Anderson. Cadets from Charleston's military college, the Citadel, had first crack at the intruders.

The college lads huddled in a battery on Morris Island, across the inner harbor entrance from Fort Moultrie. After the cadets opened fire, the guns of Fort Moultrie remained eerily silent. So did the guns of Fort Sumter. If Moultrie sank the *Star of the West* or if Sumter blasted Moultrie, a civil war would begin.

At this tense moment, Assistant Secretary of State William Trescot, back home again from Washington, "hurried" down to the water's edge, "to hear the proclamation of civil war from Anderson's guns at Fort Sumpter [sic]. . . . The slaughter," Trescot shuddered, would be "dreadful. . . . Every man lost would" leave a "home . . . desolated and a family to mourn."

"The present men in Fort Sumpter," winced Trescot, had been my friends on Sullivan's Island, when they occupied Fort Moultrie. "Almost every summer day after breakfast, I used to light my cigar, walk over to Fort Moultrie, sit down in the piazza, and talk away the long morning." Trescot had also "dined with them" in my own house. "It is mortifying to send a cannon ball into bowels which have digested your hospitality gratefully and thoroughly. To kill them is almost as bad as to be killed ourselves."[31]

The horror of an imminent brothers' war here received affecting expression. The qualms of sophisticated South Carolina precipitators also here received uneasy statement. South Carolina did not make gentlemen more elegant than Trescot, or more sensitive to the contradictions of slavery, or more hopeful that after disunion would come the peace and quiet to reform the culture without outside interference, or more nervous about the abyss that must first be dared. Trescot had carried Howell Cobb's plea to Charleston, to delay secession until February 1. He had reported back to Washington that sterner souls than his had pledged illegal rebellion, if legal revolution should be delayed. Now he watched the *Star of the West* slide past the battery on Morris Island, still unharmed, and approach the guns of Fort Moultrie.

In Fort Sumter, Robert Anderson told his men to aim cannon at Fort Moultrie. They begged to fire. Moultrie fired before Anderson could answer. The ball splashed down half a mile from the *Star*. Moultrie fired again. Another miss. The *Star* seemed to pause. "Hold on; do not fire, I will wait," screamed Anderson.[32] The *Star* turned and steamed back to the open sea.

The myth has arisen that Anderson would have fired, if his orders had arrived before the *Star of the West* appeared. (The orders may have been aboard the *Star*!) But the text of Anderson's orders, subsequently delivered, does not establish that certainty. "Should a fire, likely to prove injurious, be opened upon any vessel bringing reinforcements or supplies," wrote Anderson's superior, "your guns . . . *may be employed* to silence such fire" (emphasis mine).[33]

"*May*," not "must" or "should"! The language left the decision up to the border neutral. The Kentucky major may well have decided to wait, with or without these orders in hand. Perhaps the coincidence of undelivered orders, but more likely the neutrality of this exemplar of the Border South, for one last moment kept Yankees and South Carolinians from pumping iron into each others' bowels.

– 5 –

Subsequently, a truce delayed warfare at Pensacola's Fort Pickens. In early January, President Buchanan dispatched not only the *Star of the West* to Charleston but also the *Brooklyn,* loaded with soldiers and supplies, toward Fort Pickens, where Federal Lieutenant Adam Slemmer and his eighty-two troops still eyed a thousand rebel soldiers on the mainland. Three other U.S. vessels already in Pensacola harbor—the *Sabine,* the *St. Louis,* and the *Macedonian*—awaited orders. All these federal ships ceased and desisted after Florida's ex–U.S. senator Stephen Mallory and President Buchanan arranged a late January truce. Supplies but not soldiers, ran the agreement, could reinforce Lieutenant Slemmer at Fort Pickens, and no shots would be fired. A less formal truce sustained a similar uneasy peace at Fort Sumter. But nothing in either truce would prevent Abraham Lincoln from reasserting Buchanan's reinforcement policy of early January, at Fort Sumter or at Fort Pickens or at both hot spots. No one expected the Republican to do less than the Democrat. The new president, wrote Jefferson Davis, "will have but to continue in the path of his predecessor to inaugurate a civil war."[34]

Davis's prescient comment, correctly conflating our supposedly weakest president's policy on the forts with our arguably greatest chief executive's, must raise questions about the conventional charge that Buchanan's Sumter policy epitomized timorousness. President Lincoln would take thirty-three days to decide to send a relief ship to Fort Sumter, a policy that Buchanan pushed after three days. The revealing difference lay not in the decisive policy but in the speed of decision. James Buchanan's rush to judgment, in sharp contrast to Lincoln's stalling for perspective, illustrated the earlier president's cardinal flaw: his dubious choices of the moment to be decisive. If Buchanan had waited Lincoln's month to send the supposedly coercive ship, no presecession southern plot to seize federal forts would have prematurely occurred. Then the Lower South could have decided on the expediency of secession without yet deciding on the right of secession. Since Buchanan's single reinforcing ship could only spread secession—could never conquer disunionists, much less lead them to quail—Buchanan's decision after but seventy-two hours could only have had counterproductive impact.

The president who boldly threw down his influence against the secessionists, against Stephen A. Douglas, and against an evasive Dred Scott decision hardly vacillated on the sidelines. Rather, Buchanan deployed power imprudently, inside Supreme Court proceedings and later inside Charleston harbor, before six Lower South states decided on the expediency of departure. His nation persistently paid for his errant decisiveness.[35]

– 6 –

The *Star of the West* crisis especially stung the rebels because James Buchanan had initiated it. James Buchanan, for decades the South's most supportive Yankee political friend! James Buchanan, the man who had made the White House a national Camelot for southern cronies! James Buchanan, the one Northerner whose word could be trusted! James Buchanan, the compatriot whose plight led the South's Washington fanciers to wish secession delayed until March 4, so disaster would occur on a less worthy Yankee's watch.

Now look! James Buchanan, the man who broke a gentlemen's agreement with Charleston patriarchs! James Buchanan, the supposedly aboveboard president who sent a hostile ship into Charleston harbor, with 200 coercive soldiers hidden beneath its deck! James Buchanan, who answered southern friends' right of revolution with blood and iron!

Buchanan's supposed betrayal, plus northern cheers for the betrayer, felt like John Brown revisited. How appalling it had been that famous Yankee intellectuals applauded Brown's intention to slay southern whites, so that blacks could be free. How appalling now that Northerners cheered Buchanan, as he sought to sneak soldiers into Charleston harbor to savage southern patriots. If this Yankee had bloody hands, what Northerner could be trusted? Certainly not the Republicans who turned down John Crittenden!

Buchanan's supposed treachery, after Crittenden's hapless compromise, showed again how badly South Carolina's instant disunion had damaged Lower South Cooperationists' election prospects beyond that little state. If South Carolina had waited to decide for secession in conjunction with other southern states, Crittenden would have had no early occasion to try Hereafter Acquired, nor Buchanan to send the *Star of the West,* nor Lower South governors to seize federal forts, all *before* the Lower South electorate decided on the expediency of secession. But South Carolina had rushed to decide *before* that Lower South decision, and the rush had deliberately and successfully changed the issue before the electorate. Crittenden's failure had badly discredited the Cooperationists' argument for the possibility of compromise, and Buchanan's coercion had made expediency irrelevant. The question had become the right of a sovereign state to withdraw its consent to be governed without the federal agency's coercion. As Lower South governors advertised that new issue with their coordinated seizure of Lower South forts, Cooperationists' panaceas had become as hapless as their stalling—and before the electorate had voted on their viability.

CHAPTER 30

Snowball Rolling

Lower South secession resembled a snowball rolling downhill. From east to west, one state and then another and another and another and another and another added to the irresistible momentum. After forty days of serial secessions, the bottom of the old nation had been swept away.

– 1 –

The snowball effect took hold later than its apparent starting date: December 20, 1860. During that day of reckoning, South Carolina's convention seceded and Mississippi's voters elected secession convention delegates. But on December 20, neither Hereafter Acquired's rejection nor Robert Anderson's flight to Sumter nor the *Star of the West* nor the seizure of Lower South forts had yet compounded South Carolina's disruptive departure.

Thus when Mississippians elected secession delegates, no rout occurred. Voters cast 29 percent of their ballots for unpledged candidates, 31 percent for candidates pledged to Cooperation, and only 40 percent for candidates pledged to Separatism. Still more inconclusively, since 40 percent of Mississippi's November voters for president stayed home on December 20, candidates pledged to Separatism collected an anemic 25 percent of the state's recent balloters.[1] In contrast to South Carolina Separatists' uncontested dominance, Mississippi Separatists retained no more than the contested edge that they had previously displayed, both in Governor John Pettus's November 22 conference and in the early December Mississippi congressional contingent.

Then came the transforming aftermath of South Carolina's precipitation. During the eighteen days between Mississippi delegates' election and the state convention, Hereafter Acquired lost, conspiratorial seizures of Lower South forts commenced (with Governor Pettus a cardinal plotter), and the *Star of the West* sailed (with Mississippi's Jacob Thompson, secretary of the

490

interior, wiring that the ship would imminently invade Charleston harbor). After all that provocation, Separatists' contested domination over the December popular election of delegates swelled into uncontested control of the January state convention.

In the Mississippi convention, as in all the post–South Carolina Lower South conventions, preliminary votes on Cooperationist options, not the final vote on a secession ordinance, best measured each party's power. Preliminary votes tested such anti-Separatist propositions as calling a southern convention, trying an ultimatum to the North, delaying secession until three or four or five states concurred, and requiring a popular referendum after a state convention decree. When Cooperationists lost these preliminary tests, some joined with Separatists, thereby inflating the majority for a secession ordinance.

The Mississippi convention's preliminary votes showed how much had changed since the delegates' election. Where Separatists had secured 40 percent of the votes on the day of South Carolina's secession, 75 percent of Mississippi's delegates swarmed against Cooperationist options on the second day after the *Star of the West* approached Fort Sumter. After Mississippi's convention rejected all Cooperationist options, 85 percent of the delegates voted for the secession ordinance.[2]

Mississippi Cooperationists discovered two easy retreats to Separatism. Some surrendering Cooperationists wished to go with their state, which they revealingly prized more than their Union. Others decided that temporary disunion might save state and Union too. These Cooperationists argued that several months outside the Union might bring salutary delay, the Cooperationist objective lost inside the Union. After a cooling-off period had restored Separatists' equilibrium, all Mississippians might demand a full redress of grievances, as the seceded state's ironclad conditions for a reconstructed Union.

Reconstructionists fantasized that Republicans would then concede every demanded protection for slavery. A remade nation, composed of uncompromising Southerners and capitulating Northerners, would anoint the old Cooperationist crowd as the newest heroic Founding Fathers. As the Mississippi Cooperationist leader James L. Alcorn celebrated this fantasy, "I and others agreeing with me determined to seize the wild and maddened steed by the mane and run with him *for a time.*"[3]

Alcorn's attitude comprised a second coming of southern hopes for a reconstruction. Cooperationists' 1861 prayers resembled Yancey's followers' initial aspirations after they seceded from the National Democratic Party's Charleston convention. The Military Hall crowd had hoped for party reunification, as they waited for Institute Hall delegates to surrender. Such waiting had been the bane of Robert Barnwell Rhett, who had feared that the blessed exodus from the party would lead to a cursed reentrance. In 1861, South Carolinians meant to foil the newest reconstructionists, who supplied unwelcome evidence that South Carolina and Mississippi continued to be secession's unidentical twins.

Still, Mississippians remained second only to South Carolinians in determination to fracture the Union. Both states contained the prime prerequisite for widespread secessionism: widespread black belts. In South Carolina and Mississippi, where black belts dominated almost every county, Cooperationists possessed too narrow a geographic base of support. In contrast, Alabama and Georgia contained wide swaths of white belt counties and thus more Cooperationist fervor. But after Mississippi joined South Carolina outside the Union on January 9, the two states with scarcely a white belt had closed the vise on states with more nonslaveholder areas.

On January 10, Florida's convention tightened the squeeze on still unseceded Lower South states. Florida delegates slapped down Cooperationist test proposals by six-to-four margins, then voted to secede, 62–7.[4] With Florida completing the initial secessionist force of Lower South states' frontloaded schedule of secession conventions, and with news of the *Star of the West* and southern fort seizures dominating the telegraph wires, the snowball effect pressed on the four Lower South states still in the Union.

Here once again, secessionists' fracture of the Union resembled Yanceyites' cleavage of the National Democratic Party. In Charleston, Yancey had used Jefferson Davis's compromise language to forge an Alabama-Mississippi alliance. That minority of the Lower South's minority had then pressured reluctant Georgians and South Carolina's Orr supporters to depart the convention. The ensuing almost universal Lower South departures had snowballed in Baltimore, to include Upper South delegates who had shunned secession from the party in Charleston. So too, in early January, the three most secessionist Lower South states pressured the four less secessionist tropical states to depart the Union; and an eventually solid Lower South pressured the Upper South's reluctant potential rebels.

– 2 –

The first closely contested 1861 Lower South state convention, Alabama's, raised the question of whether a close vote legitimated secession. American republican theory distinguishes between a change in sacrosanct constitutional law, customarily requiring more than a simple majority to approve, and a change in lowlier governmental laws, where a majority of one usually suffices. The Alabama constitution did not explicitly require a majority of more than one to affirm constitutional change. But that requirement, according to Alabama Cooperationists, remained sacrosanct American folk wisdom.

The conventional wisdom seemed wisest when a constitutional change lacked even a clear majority of one. In the Alabama popular election for convention delegates, held on December 24, 55 percent of the voters supported a Separatist candidate. But since 20 percent of the state's November presidential voters shunned the December polls, only 45 percent of the state's earlier voters approved disunion.[5]

The problem evaporated in Mississippi. Mississippi Separatists' support in the January state convention leapt to 75, then to 85 percent. That huge majority legitimated the largest changes in the highest law.

No such leap legitimated Alabama Separatism. When that state's convention met on January 7, Cooperationists claimed 48 of the 100 delegates. The minority urged that Separatists' bare margin necessitated a postconvention popular referendum, to ratify constitutional change.

Anti-Separatists encountered instead a hidebound majority, determined to award itself a safer edge. At the beginning of the Alabama convention, Separatists voted to unseat two Cooperationists, on dubious technical grounds. They then seated two Separatists. That maneuver increased Separatists' margin to 54–46.[6]

The heavy-handed gambit opened the oratorical floodgates. Some white belt delegates warned that northern Alabama might withdraw its consent to be governed by Alabama. The threat prefigured white belt Virginians' action during the Civil War, when western Virginians would withdraw their consent to be governed by Virginia. Both the earlier northern Alabama threat and the later western Virginia deed exposed the most dubious part of secessionists' state's rights justification. Since all men possessed a natural right to withdraw their consent to be governed, a portion of a state's population arguably had as much right to withdraw consent from a state government (and for that matter, slaves arguably had as much right to withdraw consent from masters' governance) as the people of a state had to withdraw from the Union's authority. State's rights logicians arbitrarily constricted a universal right into a crabbed right, with only those crabby about the Union allowed to exercise all mankind's sacred prerogative.

After northern Alabamians ridiculed this inconsistency in the secessionists' justification, the most famous disunionist acted as if an abolitionist had flayed an inconsistency in his proslavery argument. William Lowndes Yancey exploded that delegates who "oppose the actions of Alabama will become traitors . . . and will be dealt with as such."[7] The volcanic Yancey had lately been more publicly discreet. He had triumphed in the 1860 National Democratic Convention (and had utterly mystified the indiscreet Robert Barnwell Rhett) by blithely supporting Jefferson Davis's compromised territorial language. Yancey had thus leaned a little away from a fire-eating position, so that moderates would lean a little toward him.

Now the extremist blasted moderates out of the water, and they blasted him out of power. Separatists could not afford their loose cannons, not C.A.L. Lamar, not Rhett, now not Yancey. Calm gentlemen, displaying personas akin to Robert Gourdin's Santa Claus air, had to orchestrate this revolution. Otherwise, wild agitators might repel a folk divided. In December, South Carolinians had repeatedly denied Rhett the offices that he thought the father of secession deserved. Now the Alabama convention denied Yancey a place on the state's imminent delegation to the Confederate nation's planning session, several weeks hence in Montgomery.

A month later in Montgomery, Yancey had to settle for a merely symbolic appearance, comparable to Rhett's cameo role at the signing of the South Carolina Secession Ordinance. Where Rhett halted the Institute Hall proceedings by dropping to his knees in thankful prayer, before signing the historic document, Yancey would introduce Jefferson Davis to the multitudes, before Davis's inauguration as Confederate president. Just as the deposed Rhett deserved the momentary spotlight, for he had kept disunion alive during the dark times, so the deposed Yancey deserved his emblematic linkage with the new president, for he had used Davis's logic to fracture the National Democratic Party. But both South Carolina's and Alabama's supreme extremists suffered the (necessary) embarrassment of losing their power, before their causes could finally triumph.

– 3 –

Yancey's embarrassment did not assuage northern Alabama Cooperationists. After attending a stormy meeting in Huntsville, a prominent northern Alabamian wrote his U.S. senator that "a tempest has been raised that is already beyond control." I fear that "a successful attempt" will be "made to excite the people of N. Ala. to rebellion versus the State and that we will have civil war in our midst."[8]

Separatists' demeaning of such hand-wringers repeated another inconsistency in their case for revolution. Rebels urged that Yankees must not treat southern whites as degraded unequals. But disunionists treated Cooperationists as contemptible inferiors. Again, Separatists urged that national majority tyranny over the southern minority must be scotched. But the southern Alabama majority's tyranny over the northern Alabama minority must be exercised.

As the Alabama convention majority relentlessly proceeded with its rebellion against, and exercise of, majority tyranny, Cooperationists denounced "a prejudging and unrelenting" tyrant. They deplored the news that Alabama troops had just seized Fort Morgan—a fantastic "usurpation," said one, before the convention had made its decision. Troops, Cooperationists complained, also parade our streets. The drum, fife, and tramp of the minutemen disrupt our sleep. We hear that they must take Alabama "straight out" of the Union, "or there will be a hanging." Cooperationists dare not even hint at "any willingness on our part to submit to . . . the black republican party."[9]

Prior to the critical Alabama roll calls, five companies of Alabamians, 500 men in all, departed for Pensacola to help besiege Fort Pickens. Just before the delegates voted to secede, news flashed across the wires that Florida had joined Mississippi and South Carolina outside the Union. Alabama Separatists seized on this momentum. After turning down Cooperationists' preliminary proposals 55–45, the convention voted to secede on January 11, 61–39. An anguished Cooperationist delegate now saw only two alternatives: "either to sway the people of the state, one against the other, in a desperate

Civil War, or to surrender my scruples for the sake of union among ourselves." His "every feeling of patriotism" and his "every sense of good judgment" dictated that "*I* must share the state's destiny."[10]

– 4 –

Georgia's convention, charged with deciding the destiny of the most uncertain Lower South state, met five days after Alabama's convention took the
fourth state out of the Union. On January 2, Georgia's voters for convention
delegates had split almost evenly.[11] But by January 16, the combination of
Hereafter Acquired's defeat, four states' departure, and rebels' fort seizures
weighed on harried Cooperationists. At the state convention, Robert Toombs
demanded an endorsement of Governor Brown's capture of Fort Pulaski, a
denunciation of the *Star of the West*'s coercion, and a repudiation of cowardly submissionists who would not stand to the colors. Defying Toombs's
pressure, Cooperationists proposed a southern convention and an ultimatum
to the North on the territories, as a substitute for immediate secession. The
proposition lost, 164–133.[12]

The rather close vote hardly threatened the Separatists. Back in mid-
November (that seemed like ancient history now), Alexander Stephens's proposals for a more moderate ultimatum had looked like a possible threat to
immediate secession. Stephens had only demanded repeal of Personal Liberty Laws. Lincoln favored concessions on that subject, and congressional
debates hinted that an agreement, while hardly a certainty, possibly could
have been reached. An early southern convention, say in mid-December, held
to demand Stephens's terms, might also have permitted time for northern responses and southern decisions by March 4.

By mid-January, however, two disruptive months of history had left
Stephens's pittance in the dust. Georgia Cooperationists, over Stephens's objections, had to revive an ironclad ultimatum on the territories, not a demand for fugitive slave reform, before reconstructionists in four seceded
states would even think about reunion. It was all reminiscent of John Crittenden's late predicament, wishing to drop Hereafter Acquired but needing
at least that much bait to hook Robert Toombs.

In hopes of pressuring Congress to reverse its Crittenden Compromise
decision, Georgia Cooperationists proposed a southern convention, to meet
on February 16 in Atlanta. A firm Cooperationist date for a southern convention here at last emerged. But what a tardy date. The proposed southern
convention would assemble only sixteen days before the March 4 witching
hour—an impossibly late time to begin impossibly difficult work. If the
Georgia convention had approved this tardy southern convention, called to
seek an already defeated territorial ultimatum, the North's certain rejection
would have turned trapped Cooperationists into zealous Separatists.

The debacle showed yet again that time had been of the essence immediately after Lincoln's election. What just might have been possible, had

Cooperationists hustled in mid-November for a mid-December southern convention, had become impossible by mid-January (much less mid-February). Having conceded that grievances must be redressed and that secession must be allowed, Cooperationists could not recover after Buchanan deployed the *Star*, Crittenden failed to redress territorial grievances, governors seized forts, and four states adopted secession. Georgia Cooperationists' convention defeat comprised the death rattle of an idea. On January 19, the Georgia convention signed the death certificate. Delegates voted 208–89 to secede.[13]

– 5 –

After five states had departed the Union and soldiers marched toward forts, Louisiana's once menacing Cooperationist faction almost disappeared. In the state's popular election for secession delegates on January 7, Separatist candidates received a bare 52 percent majority.[14] But in the state's convention, commencing on January 23, 52 percent for Separatism ballooned to 82 percent against a Cooperationist attempt to secure guarantees inside the Union. On January 26, the convention voted to secede, 113–17.[15] On February 1, the Texas convention followed suit, 166–8. Three weeks later, Texas voters ratified secession, 44,317–13,020.[16]

Texas Separatists' 77 percent of their state's popular referendum and Louisiana Separatists' 82 percent of their state's convention's test votes again accelerated the Lower South snowball effect. These two Lower South states had possessed the least desire for secession after Lincoln's election. Neither state's governor had initially wished to call a legislature or a convention. Many of both states' prominent newspapers had initially screamed WAIT.

But South Carolina had started a secessionist snowball rolling. The momentum multiplied as compromise failed and coercion descended and troops seized, before Lower South voters and delegates could even make decisions on secession's expediency. By the time the expanding movement crashed against the Lower South's western extremities, the only viable Separatist versus Cooperationist issue had become whether to cooperate with the still unionist Upper South or the now departed Lower South. That reformulated issue, in the two Lower South states tardiest to secede, brought a belated rush to join the most tropical South.

– 6 –

Separatists' triumph in Lower South states illuminated both a minority's manipulative leverage and a series of majorities' electoral strength. Immediately after Lincoln's election, no Southwide or probably even Lower Southwide majority desired instant secession. Separatists' primary tactical imperative, to avert a southern convention, aimed at avoiding their likely loss if the southern majority decided on disunion. Separatists would have also lost most of the southern states, and perhaps most of the Lower South states, if all states' voters had decided on secession's expediency on the same early day. In all these important ways, disunion was an undemocratic decision, with the Southwide minority imposing its will on the majority.

Yet the minority's revolution still had to win majorities at each seceding state's polls and conventions. Even a conspiracy to seize forts, the essence of revolution in less democratic nations, here required endorsement after the fact, in democratically elected conventions. But a democratic mandate for secession, in each state, required only a majority in that state.

As in most majoritarian decisions, each Lower South state's voters and conventions faced not a perfect choice of alternatives in an ideal world but impure alternatives at the moment when the decision transpired. Since Separatists scheduled each state's decision on a different day, different decisions involved different impurities. In each Lower South state, Separatists won a mandate to deal with the shifting situation at that state's moment of decision. In this sense, secession *was* a popular revolution that fueled a popular war against a hated foe.

Thus South Carolina's decision reflected its peoples' opinion that the state must charge, once it had reasonable assurances that some other state(s) would follow. Mississippi's decision reflected its citizens' opinion that after South Carolina had seceded, and after Buchanan had sent the *Star,* and after Republicans had rejected Crittenden, any initial preference for a southern convention had become passé. Florida's decision reflected its voters' judgment that with two states departed and military crises exploding, only Separatism remained viable. Alabama's decision reflected its citizens' (close) verdict that, with three states out and the state's own troops marching to Fort Pickens, a delay for a popular referendum could not be tolerated. Georgia's decision reflected its voters' conclusion that, with four states gone, Buchanan's coercion experienced, Crittenden's compromise a loser, and Governor Brown's troops triumphant at Fort Pulaski, Alexander Stephens had become irrelevant. And then the Louisiana and Texas conventions decreed that Cooperationists wanted no separation from already departed Lower South brethren. Texas citizens, in the Lower South's only popular referendum, overwhelmingly endorsed that climactic verdict.

To secure this ongoing, increasingly lopsided achievement of popular consent, Separatists had wisely avoided both provocative illegalities and provoking leaders. The Rhetts, C.A.L. Lamars, and Yanceys had to be replaced, and they were. Mobs had to be deterred from seizing control, and they were. Above all else, South Carolinians had to dare and to persist, and they did. The initial rebels triumphed because they tolerated the risks and because Robert Anderson's Sumter move, plus James Buchanan's coercive *Star of the West,* plus the governors' fort seizures, plus Crittenden's failed compromise, played into their hands. For the many Lower South voters who had initially preferred to delay, the issue quickly became whom they loathed more, Separatists who departed prematurely or Yankees who responded coercively.

After thirty years of escalating sectional hatreds, detestation of Yankees won hands down.

As South Carolina's Congressman William Boyce had prophesied, after we declare independence, "our enemies . . . must let us alone" or "they must attempt to coerce us." If "they attempt to coerce us," Lower South states will be "compelled to make common cause with us." South Carolinians would then "wake up some morning and find the flag of a Southern Confederacy floating over us."[17] As secession rolled ahead, separate Lower South majorities serially voted to raise a passionately embraced flag. Would the Upper South majority now lower the Union's Stars and Stripes?

CHAPTER 31

Upper South Stalemate

After scoring unending Lower South victories during the three months after Lincoln's election, disunionists suffered unending Upper South routs during the next two and a half months. The disparity demonstrated again that the more northern and southern Souths were different worlds, defying efforts to forge a single civilization.

– 1 –

Against any possibility for a united southern revolution stood the facts that almost half of Maryland's blacks were free as well as 90 percent of Delaware's, that Missouri's percentage of enslaved peoples had drooped under 10 percent, and that Virginia, Tennessee, and Kentucky harbored plantation sections that sustained slavery, severed from mountainous sections that considered the institution perhaps disposable and more surely regrettable. A solid South would have had to transcend the social fact that 47 percent of the Lower South's peoples were slaves compared to 32 percent of the Middle South's and 13 percent of the Border South's, the political fact that ex-Whigs (later Americans or Know-Nothings and yet later Oppositionists and still later Constitutional Unionists) had remained very competitive in the Upper South while becoming largely unelectable in the Lower South, and the latest electoral fact that John Breckinridge had received 56 percent of the Lower South's 1860 popular presidential vote compared to 32 percent in the Border South. A will-o'-the-wisp southern monolith would have had to rise above the political fact that the Lower South departed the Charleston Democratic Party National Convention and the Upper South (except Arkansas) stayed, the economic fact that the Border South traded far more with the Border North than with the Lower South, the demographic fact that Upper South slaves were slowly draining down to the Lower South and especially seeping away from the Border South's tier of most northern counties, and the urban fact that cities (and their industries) had a far larger presence and importance in the Upper South lands of grains, livestock, and tobacco than in Lower South domains of cotton, sugar, and rice.

The Upper South surprise was not its majority's initial opposition to a southern confederacy but its minority's initial enthusiasm for a third confederacy. "I fear that our county is destined to be cut up" like "bread," regretted Baltimore's ex-congressman Benjamin C. Howard. If so, "our slice should be" the Upper South plus Pennsylvania.[1]

If the Union sadly fails, declared John P. Kennedy, our slice should more widely include all "the Middle States, on both sides of Mason and Dixon's line." Kennedy, the Maryland novelist, ex-congressman, and ex–secretary of the navy, derided the Lower South as "one vast cotton field," with an eventual "swarm of reinforcements from the shores of Africa" and an "expansive policy of annexation and conquest." The Upper South, in contrast, enjoyed "the most diversified" economy, including grain farms, cities, and mechanical arts. Immigration to the northern South also impelled "the increase of free labor, . . . the gradual diminution of slave labor," and the "final condition—remote but certain—of free labor communities." The Border North, having already made that creeping transition, would be the Upper South's natural partner in a Central Confederacy.[2]

While Maryland's Kennedy led the Border South wing of Central Confederacy fanciers, Virginia's ex-congressman William C. Rives and his family led the Middle South wing. "The great Central States of the Confederacy," wrote Rives's son, must not "be divided from each other." Virginia's "temporary . . . concern with slavery" belies "our permanent . . . interests" with "Maryland & Pennsylvania." If we enter a "Central Confederacy," the more "extreme States, North and South," fearing being *"left out in the cold,"* may yet save the Union. If not, we can thrive in a third nation, peopled exclusively with our own kind. Another Central Confederate fancier, Virginia's Governor John Letcher, added that the border states must "make their own arrangements." Then "the Cotton States are bound to come to them." Cotton snobs "know this, and hence the extraordinary effort to coerce the Border states into their plans."[3]

Resentment of Lower South coercion spread beyond Central Confederacy enthusiasts to most Upper South citizens. Outrage particularly focused on South Carolina, "that crazy state," as the *Wilmington* (North Carolina) *Herald* called it. Those "crack brained fire-eaters," exploded Kentucky's Samuel Smith Nicholas, have "not had a single patriotic sensation for the last thirty years." Because of their "arrogant, dictatorial insolence," they forget that despite "our large interest in slavery," their master interest is not as "transcendently important" as our other "great interests and natural feelings."[4]

The "brunt of" their conflict, regretted a Virginian, "must be borne" by us. Our lands will become their battlefields, while "gentlemen from the cotton states," having driven "us to this catastrophe," will "sit securely in their homes, far from these scenes of turmoil and strife." And why would these tyrants force us out of our beloved Union? Because Lincoln might commit an overt act! Well, "if the Devil himself were President," emphasized a Kentuckian, "I would stand by the Union until he should begin to *play the Devil*."[5]

Upper South folk revered the Union despite potential devils inside, for their American nationalism remained a devout religion. The "inestimable blessings" of Union, wrote Kentucky's Robert I. Breckinridge, combine "the complete possession of freedom" and "irresistible national force, and all directed to the glory of God and the good of man." A native Tennessean would "fight" and "die for my Country—my whole Country, from the Center all round to the sea." Tennessee's Henry Cooper exclaimed that when "my country . . . goes down," so will "all hope of human liberty on earth" and all "hope that man is capable of governing himself."[6]

Cooper added that "a dissolution of this Union is the death knell of African slavery." Disunion will yield civil war. Then "in much blood," our Peculiar Institution will "be swept from the face of the Earth." Even if our "soil should not be drenched with fraternal gore," exclaimed a Baltimore newspaper, slavery in our "midst would be inevitably doomed." Without federal fugitive slave commissioners to police a 2000-mile border, explained a Kentuckian, "the Border States will soon be free states, and so on until there would be no slave states."[7]

Thus a vast Upper South majority considered the folly of disunion boundless. The stupidity would turn Upper South lovers of liberty into Lower South oligarchs' slaves. The tyrants would force the southern majority out of the earth's most glorious republic. The fiends would turn the Upper South into the Lower South's savaged battlefield. The madmen would sweep slavery into the dustbin of history. The blunderers would mutilate the natural economic interests of the great middle of the nation. Against their bungled statecraft, the Upper South's two-thirds of white Southerners must declare holy war.

– 2 –

The ensuing Upper South political warfare diverged from late Lower South battles. The very name of the anti-Separatist movement differed. In the Lower South, Separatists' foes almost always dubbed themselves Cooperationists, not Unionists. They almost always pledged to cooperate in destroying the Union, if Northerners coerced seceded states or rejected major concessions.

In contrast, Upper South opponents of Separatists called themselves Unionists. Many ridiculers of disunion, especially in the Border South, remained unconditional Unionists. Even if civil war ensued, they would support their old nation. Other more conditional Upper South Unionists, especially in the Middle South, often dropped Lower South Cooperationists' condition that Northerners must grant concessions to slaveholders. When Middle

South Unionists did demand concessions, they sought bait to lure Lower South reconstructionists toward reunion. If war could be avoided, these conditional Unionists would delay disunion for months, even for years, in hopes that negotiations would finally restore the grand old Union.

But below the Border South, Lower South Cooperationists' other condition for Union—no coercion of departed brethren—ran wide and deep. Middle South conditional Unionists ever insisted that according to the Declaration of Independence, a state's people's right to withdraw their consent to be governed must never be violated. Here state's rights ideology showed its force, in the making of a viable southern nation. The first secessionists had merely used the ideology to justify their revolution, designed to keep blacks ground under. But if war ensued, the state's rights faith would bring the Middle South (but not the Border South) sprinting to disunionists' rescue, to keep white consent to be governed from being ground under.

Upper South voters, unlike Lower South citizens, could decide on the expediency of revolution before the right of revolution clouded their decision. Lower South states, because blacker with slaves, scheduled secession conventions months sooner than Upper South conclaves. In January, while Lower South voters and convention delegates deliberated on secession's expediency, the *Star of the West* provocation and the fort seizures exploded, changing the issue to secession's legitimacy. Separatists greatly benefited.

Upper South initial decisions on disunion came a month or more later. By then, the first military crisis had dissipated. After Lower South governors seized Buchanan's forts and his *Star of the West* retreated, truces prevented further hostilities. Unless and until Lincoln ended these respites, the Upper South issue could remain the desirability of disunion, not the right of the people of a state to use the remedy.

During the three months between President Buchanan's truces and President Lincoln's coercion, Upper South conditional unionism thrived. Where Separatist lynch mobs often cowed Lower South Cooperationists, scant physical or psychological intimidation afflicted Upper South Unionists. Where Lower South Separatists' pamphlets came in torrents compared to Lower South Cooperationists' trickle of sheets, Upper South Unionists' publications outmatched secessionists' publications.

The Upper South had always more forcefully opposed proslavery extremism. In the less enslaved half of the South, the cry of disloyalty to slavery carried less weight, alliance with suspect Northerners brought less notoriety, and emphasis on nonslavery issues attracted more voters. Lower South Whiggery had thus collapsed sooner than Upper South Whiggery. Southern Whigs' successors—the American, Know-Nothing, Opposition, and Constitutional Union parties—had secured more votes northward in the South than southward, making successive Whiggish parties fully competitive with the Democracy in the Upper South but not in the Lower South.

In the secession crisis, these trends empowered Upper South Unionists. A lesser stake in slavery generated less desperation about Lincoln's supposed immediate menace; and stronger Whiggish parties provided more powerful partisan organizations to sustain unionism.[8] So long as Lincoln honored those Buchanan truces, Unionists' disproportionately Whiggish power base gave Upper South disunionists more than they could handle.

Still, after the Lower South departed, Upper South Unionists faced newly provocative demonstrations of the northern majority's augmented power. Lower South Cooperationists had urged that the Republican Party, lacking a congressional majority, could pass no antislavery acts. But the secession of the seven Lower South states destroyed that argument. With fourteen Lower South senators departed, Republicans for the first time wielded a senatorial majority, to match the North's longtime (and now expanded) House majority.

Congressional Republicans pounced on their opportunity. On January 29, 1861, within days of Lower South senators' exodus from Washington, Republicans admitted Kansas into the Union as a free labor state. The admission gave the North thirty-six senators to the South's sixteen (compared to the northern advantage of but thirty-four to thirty, before the Lower South seceded).

With their new congressional majority, Republicans swiftly reversed the South's favorite U.S. trend, toward lower tariffs. In the so-called Morrill Tariff, passed in early March, Congress doubled the immediate tax rate on imports to 37 percent and scheduled future advances to 47 percent. The routs on both tariffs and Kansas, before Lincoln could even be inaugurated, signaled that southern states now squirmed under the thumb of a permanent northern majority.

Lower South secessionists welcomed these indications of Upper South slavery's doom in an eviscerated Union. Now Upper South dawdlers would surely speed toward disunion! Southern Confederacy stalwarts needed only to demonstrate, so they thought, that they would never rejoin the old republic and that their new republic would serve Upper South no less than Lower South interests.

The demonstrations took center stage when six Lower South states met in Montgomery on February 4, to form a provisional government of the Confederate States of America. (Texas missed the festivities because its popular referendum on disunion remained more than two weeks away.) The Lower South representatives ridiculed reconstruction. They also elevated the two most prominent late stallers on disunion, Jefferson Davis and Alexander Stephens, to be the Confederacy's president and vice president respectively. Furthermore, their provisional constitution, largely a copy of the U.S. Constitution, permanently outlawed the African slave trade. Choose ye between us, Lower South patriots said in effect to Upper South citizens. You can suffer northern tyranny in a lopsided Union. Or you can enjoy southern moderation in a slaveholders' republic.[9]

An angry extremist enhanced the demonstration that moderates controlled the Confederacy. South Carolina's Leondias Spratt called the permanent closure of the African slave trade a slaveholder's disaster. The founding father of that extremist crusade urged South Carolina to reject the Confederacy. "Another revolution *may be painful*," cried Spratt, "but we must make it."[10]

Only a handful of South Carolina ultras fancied Spratt's next revolution.[11] But huge Upper South majorities still rejected the secessionists' first revolution. In Maryland, Kentucky, and Delaware, state legislatures refused even to call a state convention, even to consider secession. These borderland margins against state conventions ranged from two to one up to four to one. Only in Missouri did a Border South legislature summon a state convention. That body turned down secession on March 19, 89–1.[12]

Middle South secessionists suffered a less overwhelming rejection. The Virginia legislature ordered a state convention, and the North Carolina, Tennessee, and Arkansas legislatures let the people decide whether to call such conclaves. In mid-February popular referendums, North Carolina's voters barely defeated a convention (50.3 to 49.7 percent), while Tennessee citizens turned down a convention by a more comfortable margin (59 to 41 percent). In both North Carolina and Tennessee, mid-February electorates also voted for delegates, in case they approved a convention. In both Middle South states, Unionists won over two-thirds of citizens' votes.[13]

Arkansas, the third Middle South state that held a mid-February popular referendum, gave secessionists only slightly more hope. Arkansas, alone in the Upper South, had joined the Lower South's departure from the National Democratic Party's Charleston convention. The state grew Lower South–style crops, including much cotton. Arkansas also contained a Lower South–style percentage of slaves in 1860, 45 percent (compared to 38 percent in Virginia, 34 percent in North Carolina, and 25 percent in Tennessee).

As befit a Cotton South state, the Arkansas electorate called a state convention in mid-February. But in the simultaneous election for delegates, disunionists secured only 43 percent of the popular vote. Arkansas's convention, meeting on March 4, swiftly rejected a proposed May popular referendum on a secession ordinance, 39–35. Secessionists then swore that Arkansas's southeastern black belts would secede from its northwestern white belts and join the Southern Confederacy, unless the convention scheduled some popular referendum on disunion. Compromise ensued. The day after Unionists killed a May popular referendum, they approved an August referendum. The Arkansas convention then disbanded, having apparently stalled off secession for at least five months.[14]

– 3 –

After Arkansas's convention dispersed, only in Virginia did an Upper South convention continue to deliberate. This most historic American convention since the Virginia Dynasty's reign (or so Virginians thought) held the fate of democracy, slavery, and the Union in its hands (or so Virginians conceived). "The eyes of the Country are now resting on Virginia," soared Lexington's

James Davidson. "What a fearful responsibility." The "Old Mother . . . will be heard and heeded when she calls to her surrounding Family—Peace—Be Still!"[15]

Despite Davidson's widely believed (in Virginia) hyperbole, the state long since had ceased to be heard, much less heeded. The nineteenth-century consequences of Virginia's geographically separated cultures had especially caused the declension. In this one state, all three tiers of Souths collided, ultimately leaving an indecisive 1861 state convention at the mercy of decision makers beyond the state.

Once upon a time, a decisive Virginia had commenced east of the Blue Ridge. Since the late eighteenth century, the two parts of eastern Virginia, the piedmont and tidewater, had exuded a Lower South presence, with roughly half of the inhabitants enslaved. But by the middle of the nineteenth century, two parts of western Virginia, the valley and the trans-Allegheny, faced in other directions, both geographically and culturally. The Valley of Virginia, located between the easternmost Blue Ridge and the westernmost trans-Allegheny ranges, had a Middle South air, with one in six of its inhabitants enslaved. The trans-Allegheny region, situated west of both ranges, had a Border South presence, with one in twenty of its peoples a slave.

White-belt western Virginians, like slaveless Yankees, resented slaveholders' imposition on white democracy. In the famous 1829 state convention, egalitarian (for whites) western Virginians demanded that Virginia's

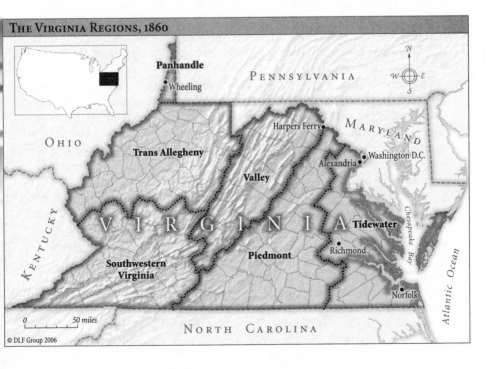

THE VIRGINIA REGIONS, 1860

Panhandle
Wheeling
PENNSYLVANIA
N
W E
S
OHIO
Harpers Ferry
MARYLAND
Trans Allegheny
Alexandria
Washington D.C.
Valley
KENTUCKY
VIRGINIA
Tidewater
Chesapeake Bay
Richmond
Piedmont
Southwestern Virginia
Norfolk
Atlantic Ocean
0   50 miles
NORTH CAROLINA
© DLF Group 2006

legislature be apportioned on a one-white-man, one-vote basis. Eastern reactionaries instead successfully insisted that the rich must retain extra legislative seats, to save aristocratic republicanism (and slavery) from the poor (and the western nonslaveholders).[16]

In the equally famous Virginia legislative slavery debate of 1832, western Virginians warned that unless they could have (white) egalitarianism, eastern Virginians could not have (black) slavery. Easterners in the legislature warded off that threat. Yet restrictions on egalitarian democracy for whites had clearly become a two-edged sword, augmenting slaveholders' protections but swelling nonslaveholders' antagonisms.

At the Virginia state convention of 1851, eastern Virginians agreed to soften slaveholders' protection, in order to dull nonslaveholders' antagonisms. The ensuing state constitution gave western Virginians their treasured one-man, one-vote legislative apportionment. But the settlement, true to Virginia's irresolution, traded one nonslaveholder resentment for another. No tax, decreed the new constitution, could be imposed on human property under twelve years of age. Nor could slaves aged twelve or over be assessed at over $300. With other property assessed at its actual value and with slave prices skyrocketing in the 1850s, yeomen insisted that an iniquitous tax ceiling filled slaveholders' wallets with nonslaveholders' dollars.[17]

Just as the 1832 legislative slavery debate had offered offended nonslaveholders an opportunity to revenge the alleged 1829 thievery, so the 1861 Virginia convention could give yeomen the opportunity to retaliate for the supposed 1851 robbery. Westerners meant to use the state convention to demolish slaveholders' tax breaks and to thwart disunion. Secession, western Virginia nonslaveholders raged, would be the worst example yet of slaveholders' confiscation of white men's egalitarian rights, in order to preserve black men's enslavement.

Inflamed sectional antagonisms dominated Virginia's February 4 election for state convention delegates. The legislature empowered the voters to decide whether the convention could finalize secession, without ratification in a subsequent popular referendum. The citizens voted by a two-to-one margin to require the referendum. Eastern Virginians split evenly on the requirement, while Western Virginians insisted five to one that the popular referendum must be held.[18]

Virginia voters' choices for delegates followed the same divisive pattern. Only around one in six of the elected delegates, around two-thirds of them from eastern Virginia black belts, sought instant disunion. Another one in six of the election winners, around four in five of them from trans-Allegheny white belts, favored unconditional unionism, even if civil war ensued.[19]

Between these two irreconcilable extremes loomed would-be national reconcilers, two-thirds strong at the beginning of the convention. These conditional Unionists sometimes differed on their conditions for a restored Union. But they concurred that if Lincoln coerced any seceded state, Virginia must secede. They also concurred that if no civil war transpired,

Virginia must remain in the Union for many months, patiently seeking a reconstructed Union.

On February 13, impatient secessionist delegates descended on another Institute Hall, this time Richmond's, for the start of the state convention. The ultras meant to abort delays and to preclude any repetition of the 1832 legislative antislavery debate. A priceless private letter from Virginia's ex-governor (and Buchanan's ex–secretary of war) John B. Floyd epitomized the determination to spring free from that past history.

Three decades earlier, John B. Floyd's sire, the first Governor John (without the B.) Floyd, had been Virginia's chief executive during Nat Turner's revolt and the subsequent Virginia slavery debate. When western Virginians menaced the institution, the earlier Governor Floyd had recommended gradual emancipation in at least western Virginia. John B., trained for sterner stuff at South Carolina College, never forgot his father's and his state's lack of (proslavery) backbone. In February 1861, he feared that another slavery debate would overwhelm the latest Virginia apologists for slavery if the state delayed its decision on disunion.

On February 7, Floyd privately wrote that in Virginia's February 4 election, "the southern cause has sustained a fearful defeat. . . . Unless the convention itself shall take high & decided grounds," the previous "symptoms of a coming contest in Va. for the emancipation of the slave" will become "almost irresistible." Because that "temptation . . . in this commonwealth . . . is very strong," we will hear again that emancipation will yield an "increased demand for white labor," an "increased value of land," and increasing "progress of all improvements. . . . Whenever this discussion begins again in Va., slavery will be abolished, and you and I may (if not hung for treason!) live to see it."[20]

The memory of his own father as traitor to Virginia slaveholder interests, when Nat Turner and then western yeomen struck in 1831–33, added intimate forebodings to John B. Floyd's abstract dread of Virginia's persisting apologetics. It was as if a son had to commit patricide to prevent a beloved sire's traditions from dooming the ruling class. That same familial anguish between generations provoked the two best secessionist debaters in the Virginia convention, James Holcombe and George Randolph. The clash between older and younger Virginians would also underlie the convention's final confrontation over Virginia's fate.

George Randolph and James Holcombe shared a common characteristic of eastern Virginia's most determined secessionists: a relatively young age. Both barely forty, Randolph and Holcombe each despaired that older Virginians floundered between Lower South zeal to save slavery and northern abolitionists' frenzy to eliminate the abomination. Drift, not mastery, had resulted from previous Virginia generations' conventional wisdom that slavery was wrong; that emancipation without removal of free blacks was more wrong still; and that the slow drain of Upper South slaves to the Lower South might best secure race removal. Or perhaps the necessary evil could incrementally become unnecessary, after federal or state governments slowly colonized blacks outside the nation.

Two generations before George Randolph, his grandfather, Thomas Jefferson, Founding Father of necessary-evil apologists, had hoped colonization would make the evil unnecessary. But Grandfather Jefferson, ducking any fight for a lily-white America, had instead charged the next and the next generation with the glory of the colonization-emancipation struggle. His son-in-law and grandchildren staggered under the charge and achieved no glory in the struggle. In 1860, George Randolph felt compelled to pick up the pieces.[21]

Randolph, the Founder's youngest grandson, was the last (and eleventh) offspring of the great man's daughter and her husband, Thomas Mann Randolph. George Randolph's austere father, when governor of Virginia, had pressed the legislature (unsuccessfully) to use one-third of the state's revenue to buy and deport Virginia's young female slaves, just before they reached puberty. Grandfather Jefferson protested that older breeding wenches would breed three times faster than potential breeders could be expelled.

Whatever George Randolph thought of this exchange about breeding wenches, the future secessionist eventually felt compelled to spring free from his cherished elder brother no less than from his godlike grandfather and his forbidding father. Thomas Jefferson Randolph, Thomas Jefferson's oldest and favorite grandchild and twenty-seven years older than brother George Randolph, had his own rendezvous with Jeffersonian paralysis after Nat Turner's 1831 revolt.[22] When the black rebel struck, Thomas Jefferson Randolph's terrified wife had urged her husband to carry the family to Cincinnati, away from slavery's horror. But her husband had instead proposed that the state legislature free all slaves born after July 4, 1840, the women at age eighteen and the men at twenty-one. Thus began that 1832 Virginia legislative debate, destined to last two tense weeks and forever in the memories of those who watched, appalled or hopeful.

The Virginia legislature eventually enacted not Thomas Jefferson Randolph's plan but an ambivalent, ineffective colonization experiment. Still, most of the Old Dominion's leading subsequent defenders of the necessary evil (now called a temporary good) continued to expect that African colonization would someday (happily) take Virginia's slaves to the Dark Continent, to spread the light of democracy and Christianity. George Randolph understood why that compromised mentality filled gentlemen like John B. Floyd with forebodings. An 1860 reincarnation of Thomas Jefferson Randolph might be coming, if eastern Virginia stalled again and western Virginia struck again. Still, George Randolph, born and eventually buried at Monticello, could not immediately break from his royal family's drift. Right before Lincoln's election, Randolph privately wrote that "if the states south of us go, . . . we shall not secede but will probably occupy a position of armed neutrality, . . . unless an attempt be made to coerce them."[23]

While George Randolph was not yet ready to assault neutrality, James Holcombe's still more painful familial experience with Jeffersonian apologetics led to quicker impatience with Virginia's drift.[24] At the time of Nat Turner and of the Virginia slavery debate, Holcombe's mother could not tolerate her state's acceptance of slavery. Nor could her husband, Dr. William Holcombe, a prominent Lynchburg physician and preacher, abide masters' resistance to allowing Christ's Word to be heard and read in the quarters.

James Holcombe's parents, with his mother in the lead, ultimately freed their fifteen slaves. They sent some of their freed people to Liberia and others to Ohio. They supplied their ex-slaves with an average of over $500. In defiance of Lynchburg's withering disapproval, remembered one of their younger sons, they also took "open ground in favor of speeding colonization of the whole race in Africa."

Then Mrs. Holcombe heard that her aged, childless uncle had decided to bequeath two plantations and eighty slaves to her children. When James's mother could not dissuade her uncle from the familial step backward, she announced that "the crisis has come." Like Thomas Jefferson Randolph's wife at the time of Nat Turner, she pleaded with her husband to take their children "beyond the reach of . . . evil influences."

Dr. Holcombe, unlike T. J. Randolph, honored his wife's plea. "To the amazement of all his friends," continues his son's remembrance of the familial earthquake, he sold all his cherished Lynchburg possessions, "surrendered all the most sacred ties of his being, sacrificed apparently all his best interests, and took all his family" to Indiana—with one exception.

The exception, Dr. Holcombe's oldest son, James, had recently married a prominent Virginia heiress. The groom hovered between scorn for slaveholders, learned at Yale College, and revulsion for holier-than-thou Yankees, imbibed at the University of Virginia Law School. James Holcombe remained as devoted to his emancipating parents as his new wife was to her slaveholding parents.

The torn young adult was conservative, cautious, studious. Holcombe's tall, lean frame exuded a delicate, fragile air. Deep blue eyes dominated his long, sad, sweet face, the orbs seemingly filled with "mild astonishment" that life was so complicated.[25] It was beyond mildly astonishing to be forced to choose between a darling Virginia wife's family and his own dear tribe of exiles, between a sneering North and a shaky Virginia, between Yankees obnoxiously sure they had every right answer and cousins vulnerably unsure that any answer existed. What was Virginia, anyway? What was he, anyway?

For a time, Holcombe, true to the necessary-evil mentality, split the difference. He commenced his law career in Cincinnati, on the southern edge of the North, south of his parents and north of his in-laws. There he squirmed under Yankee intolerance for any middle way, including his marvelous parents' dearly purchased middle way. Those who would send blacks to Africa, Holcombe heard, were as heartless as those who lashed slaves. Those who brought crumbs of the Word to the quarters, continued the Cincinnati sneer, lent a Christian veneer to an antichristian abomination. A true Christian would help masters' property flee across the Ohio River and help the unliberated rise against the tyrants. "The Northern people," later cried the secessionist who had suffered the Yanks at Yale and in Cincinnati, "have cherished, in the bosom of their society, associations extensive in number and wealth, openly" seeking "to incite and aid the escape of our slaves, and not infrequently expressing sympathy with insurrection, rapine and murder."[26]

Holcombe could not live with these intolerant, humiliating fanatics. He could not fathom how his father could teach Northerners or Southerners to send blacks speedily to Africa. He could only shudder at visions of a South full of free blacks. There was no middle way, no future in balancing on the borderland edge of North and South or on the colonizationist edge of slavery and antislavery. In a manner that resembled another tormented Virginian, Moncure Conway, James Holcombe felt called to live on the other side of the Mason-Dixon line from his beloved parents. But where Conway painfully departed from his righteously proslavery father's ancestral Virginia home, to spread antislavery in the North, Holcombe sadly moved far from his parents' Indiana home, to spread proslavery in the South. At the University of Virginia Law School, he would teach young Virginians to renounce their parents' apologetics and to embrace secession.[27]

The professor, James Holcombe (left), and the grandson, George Randolph (right), decisive young secessionists who had had it with older Virginians' indecisive drift. Courtesy of Special Collections, University of Virginia Library (Holcombe) and the Library of Congress (Randolph).

As the secession winter developed, George Randolph, with his long, dreary, dreamy face, eerily shaped like James Holcombe's, came to see as clearly as Holcombe (and John B. Floyd) that older Virginians' middle way could no longer exist. Virginia's middling choices had been ineffectual enough, and productive of enough declining influence and familial grief, in a Union of seventeen free and fifteen slave states. Now behold a Union with eighteen free states and only eight slave states, with the Border South half of the remaining slave states harboring an even more compromised slaveholding mentality than Virginia's, and with the president-elect poised to develop his own antislavery party in the vulnerable zone. For George Randolph to remain as paralyzed as Grandfather Jefferson, and as ineffective as his father and eldest brother, and as indecisive as the middle-aged majority of the Virginia secession convention delegates would be to ensure that conflicted whites would soon be aswim in a sea of vengeful blacks.

– 4 –

As James Holcombe, George Randolph, and fellow Virginia secessionists began their assault on indecisive Unionists in Richmond, Henry Benning, Georgia's commissioner to Virginia, told the convention that the Upper South's compromised condition had played into his world's uncompromising decision. Since "the Republican party hates slavery," Benning argued, our foes will abolish the institution as soon as they "acquire the power" to "do it." The Georgian warned that "the North is acquiring that power . . . with great rapidity." Kansas shows that "every State that comes into the Union will be a free State." Meanwhile, in "Delaware and Maryland and . . . other States in the same parallel," borderland slaveholders "have a presentiment that it is a doomed institution, and . . . self-interest impels them to get rid of that property." So slavery "will go down lower and lower, until it all gets to the Cotton States—until it gets to the bottom. . . . The weight of a continent" forces "it down."

On the "not distant" day when the bottom of the South contains "the only slave States," climaxed Benning, "the North will have the power to amend the Constitution" and declare "slavery . . . abolished." Then the master who "refuses to yield" will "doubtless be hung." Race "war will break out everywhere, like hidden fire from the earth." Eventually, "our men will be compelled to wander like vagabonds." And "as for our women, the horrors of their state we cannot contemplate."[28]

Virginia convention delegates' long-winded speeches for secession could have been reduced to one pithy affirmation: How right you are, Judge Benning, and especially about our vulnerability in our latitude without your help. Unless cotton states return to the Union, agreed Virginia ultras, we will be "as helpless as a child." Even if eight slave states can block eighteen free states, we will soon lose half our states. Delaware, lamented James Holcombe, is "nominally only" a slave state; "Maryland will soon be a free

State; and so it is with Missouri and Kentucky." These border states, added George Randolph, have "a small and a decreasing interest in . . . slavery, and are not such protectors as we should select."[29]

Even when we had Cotton South protectors, warned Virginia's secession-ist delegates, Virginia's slavery had receded southward. Our counties that border on the Yankees, declared George Richardson, lay "stampeded under the operation of the underground railroad."[30] So exposed masters have slowly moved their slaves southward. Statistics sustained Richardson's claim. Virginia counties bordering on another state lost 4.7 percent of their slaves from 1850 to 1860. Twenty-one of the twenty-five counties suffered losses.

With Yankee slave stealers "driving slavery from those counties," con-tinued Richardson, what "is to prevent . . . the wave of sectionalism" from someday sweeping slavery "away through Virginia . . . and into the far South?" Worse, Lincoln's Southern Republican Party would intensify the wave. President Lincoln, warned ex-congressman Jeremiah Morton, will shower "public patronage upon Virginia and Maryland and Tennessee," and on "Kentucky and Missouri." If we submit to Lincoln's command, we "will find Black Republicans upon every stump, and organizing in every county; and that is the peace that we shall have from this 'glorious Union.' "[31]

That nonpeace, feared secessionists, will foment unrest in the quarters. "Innocent" blacks, winced James Holcombe, can be misled. Slaves' periodic "outbursts of violence . . . will fill the master with continual apprehensions." Slaveholders' "safeguards" will prove so "costly and so burdensome . . . that the institution itself will become intolerable."[32]

Southern Republicans, continued secessionist delegates, would also infect western Virginia yeomen. In the convention itself, secessionists faced alarm-ing evidence of fertile western ground for Hinton R. Helper's economic-based heresy. Especially western Virginia's Waitman T. Willey sought a state con-stitutional amendment, abolishing the 1851 tax breaks for slaveholders. Some time for *this*, eastern Virginians stormed.

This occasion allows us to have at the slaveholders, answered Willey's western admirers. All eastern Virginians' "talk about our rights being stolen from us by the North," Henry Dering of Morgantown privately wrote Willey, "dwindles into nothing compared to our situation in Western Virginia." An "impudent, boastful, and tyrannical" eastern "slavery oligarchy" taxes us un-equally and would divide our "glorious Union." If tyrants "persist," we must renounce our state and thereby "throw of [sic] the Shackles" of "this very *Di-vine Institution,* as they call it."[33]

Henry Dering's representatives in the Virginia convention somewhat toned down this southern version of northern anti–Slave Power outrage. But white belt representatives' edgy insistence on equal taxation, at this (so secessionists thought) scandalous moment, made Southern Republican-ism seem all too plausible. "I now see," wrote Henry Wise privately to his son, that "slavery is doomed in Virginia and we have no hope but in actual

Revolution." Wise was "confident" that "a number" of delegates would "vote for abject submission and abolition of slavery tomorrow."[34]

Because of older Virginians' submissive mentalities, declared George Randolph in a particularly stunning sentence, Republicans "are much more likely to make us wrong than we are to bring them right." Jefferson's grandson noted that proslavery "sentiment with us is recent—it is comparatively a thing of yesterday—it has not been incubated in early life, . . . it has hardly yet had time to be understood and appreciated by our own people. To dash it now against the iron-bound fanaticism of the North, would be the height of folly."[35]

Republicans' "insolent spur of contempt," exclaimed James Holcombe, increases the folly of living among them. The enemy intends "not only to ruin but to degrade" us. Whenever "any people lose that self-respect which is the spring of public virtue," they "must become extinct." George Richardson added that "I will never consent to live . . . with men who claim that I am socially their inferior." Republicans' "insolent pretension," their "bloated arrogance and impudence," their "fanatical, meddlesome, overbearing" insults must be met "with the scorn and defiance" of an aroused "chivalry."[36]

Instead, the Virginia convention majority called the chivalry overly aroused. Rather than fusing with the fanatical Lower South, most delegates wished to use a convention of soothing Upper South states to reconstruct the Union. These reconstructionists rejected the secessionist retort that Union saving had been proven hopeless. Reconstruction required endless attempts, affirmed Unionists, until the right formula tempted the right Lower South reconstructionists to bring their states back.

In a previous rendezvous with reconstruction strategy, the January Virginia legislature had summoned a National Peace Conference to Washington, D.C., on February 4. All states, except the seceded Lower South and the far-off Pacific Ocean states, had sent delegates. These disproportionately elderly gentlemen had elected Virginia's aging ex-president John Tyler as presiding officer.

Tyler's contemporaries had then spent three weeks in search of a reunion bargain, even if no Lower South man was there for the bargaining. The aging titans had finally settled for a version of John Crittenden's tired compromise. Republicans had as little use for this substitute as for the original. Nor did Lower South states bother to reject the irrelevance. Virginia's Washington Peace Conference became derisively known as the Old Gentlemen's last hurrah, before young gentlemen's blood soaked the battlefields.[37]

Nevertheless, on March 9, five days into Lincoln's presidency, the Virginia convention's Committee on Federal Relations recommended the same old route toward peaceable reconciliation, unless and until the Lincoln administration sought to coerce seceded states. "The people of Virginia," declared the Majority Report of the committee, "recognize the American principle that government is founded in the consent of the governed. . . . They concede the right of the people" of a state "to withdraw from . . . the

Federal Government." Our people will never allow "federal power" to sub-
jugate "the people of such States."[38]

Continued peace, however, invited continued negotiations. The convention should formulate constitutional amendments and submit them to the
several states. The convention's proposed constitutional amendments, still
being hammered out when war struck, would have featured yet another version of the Crittenden Compromise. Those measures would have failed again.
The latest failure would have put Virginia on a collision course with Union,
even if peace had persisted.

Yet the Majority Report of the Committee on Federal Relations provided
possible escapes from the collision. The report declared that "Virginia will
await any reasonable time to obtain answers from other States." Citing that
language, future Virginia unionist majorities could deny that "reasonable
time" had passed. The report also urged the eight slave states still in the
Union to meet in convention on May 27 in Frankfort, Kentucky. If that proposed border state conference recommended milder measures than Virginia's
proposed federal constitutional amendments, yet another Virginia Unionist
Party majority might keep negotiating.

Secessionists preferred the Lower South's nonnegotiable stance. "If we
are to be dragged . . . either to the North or the South," declared J. R.
Chambliss, I would rather be dragged "under King Cotton than under King
Abolition." I would rather "be ruled by King Davis than by Autocrat Lincoln." The Unionists' George Baylor answered that Virginia anointed "King
Wheat, King Corn, King Potatoes, King Tobacco, King Flax, King Hemp" as
monarchs. "All these Kings together . . . far over-ride King Cotton."[39]

The issue involved not only which king presided in Virginia but also
whether a choice of monarchs now must be made. Unionists still saw hope of
a middle way, of a Border South conference that could reknit North and
South. Secessionists demanded that conciliators face facts, realize that two
separate kingdoms had been irreconcilably created, understand that no third
choice now existed.

Secessionists further insisted that Lower South leaders had been right to
force the Middle South to choose. Their interests differ from ours, declared
James Holcombe. They must have expanded territory, lest the drain of our
slaves downward leave them trapped in a sea of blacks. Just as they could
not wait for us, we cannot wait for the half-abolitionized Border South. "Are
we prepared to commit the fortunes of Virginia into the keeping of States so
unequally interested in the preservation of this institution?"[40]

Holcombe here reaffirmed the point that came from many secessionist
directions in 1860–61: A committed minority must not turn over its fate to
an uncommitted majority. Lower South Democrats must renounce a compromising National Democratic Party Convention, William L. Yancey had
urged in Charleston, or the party will compromise southern constituents to
death. Lower South secessionists must shun a southern convention dominated by the unionist Upper South, South Carolina's William Gist had told

Mississippi's John Pettus, or the convention's majority will paralyze our resistance. Middle South slaveholders must avoid a border state conference, now urged James Holcombe, or softhearts' decision will soften us. Our minority must decide for itself, Yancey, Gist, and Holcombe all affirmed, and make our own history.

The Virginia convention's majority still preferred to share the history making with Upper South states. On April 4, Lewis Harvie moved that secession be adopted. On this first-month anniversary of Lincoln's inauguration, delegates voted down Harvie, Randolph, Holcombe, and immediate secession by a stunning 88–45.[41] With the cannon that encircled Fort Sumter only a week away from booming, Virginians stood two to one for their fancied middle way—and for the tired illusion that the "Old Mother" could use a border state conference to summon wayward Lower South offspring back to a reconstructed Union.

– 5 –

Younger Virginians could no longer bear the convention's paralyzed conceit. In an impetuousness worthy of Savannah's Charles Augustus Lafayette Lamar, many young sports determined to march on Richmond. They would seize Virginia's destiny from the convention's old fogies.

The young Virginians' leader, George Bagby, was thirty-two years old. The precocious journalist, eight years younger than James Holcombe, had lately become editor of the prestigious *Southern Literary Messenger.* Bagby used his new position, as Holcombe had used his University of Virginia professorship, to deprecate older Virginians' middle way.[42]

Slavery, Bagby insisted in the manner of Holcombe, was either good or evil. Sending blacks away from Virginia was either right or wrong. The Middle South was either northern or southern. Virginia's convention must sustain either the Confederacy or the Union. By insisting that the state immediately choose its southern roots, Bagby became a lightning rod for all younger Virginians who feared, as twenty-seven-year-old George Latham wrote Bagby, "that Virginia was about to disgrace herself."[43]

Latham, editor of the *Lynchburg Express,* saw "no Virginia left in the world now. She was dead long since, when you and I were proud to be her children." While "we did not know then" that "she had gone down into her grave," now "we know." The "craven" submissionists "in the Hall at Richmond . . . disgrace the *memory* of our Old Mother."[44]

Like all the other younger Virginians around Bagby and Holcombe, twenty-two-year-old John Hampden Chamberlayne ached to avert disgrace. In past nonrevolutionary times, Chamberlayne wrote Bagby, "gray heads . . . did very well." But in current revolutionary times, "show me a white head & a boy of twenty, & I will trust the boy." Another comparative boy, thirty-year-old John Esten Cooke, told Bagby that when I hear "*what people think and say of Virginia, . . .* I boil, boil, boil."[45]

In late March, as secessionists' fiery rhetoric failed to ignite the Virginia convention, Bagby summoned young Virginians to a so-called Spontaneous Southern Rights Assembly in Richmond on April 16. "I received your communication this morning [March 26]," wrote back twenty-eight-year-old Henry Gray Latham, "with a thrill of pleasure." Now I have "something to hope for beyond . . . that convention of [Judas] Iscariots. . . . I will be with you in everything," including "dividing the State by a revolution." Or as Latham wrote Bagby a month earlier, "If old Va. don't go out by a vote of the people, . . . we will . . . take the government property, and stand against the whole population of the State & Federal Union."[46]

While Bagby's followers marched on Richmond, determined to force action at last, the state convention remained stuck on nonaction. Despite the storm swirling outside the convention hall—cadets parading in the streets, mobs burning moderates in effigy, young turks massing for their hardly "Spontaneous" assembly—middle-aged convention delegates remained wrapped in their cocoon of self-importance. They would not abandon Mother Virginia. Their delays would summon their Lower South progeny back to the Union's glory.

CHAPTER 32

Stalemate—and the South—Shattered

Lincoln knew as well as Buchanan that any post–*Star of the West* coercive reinforcement of Fort Sumter or Fort Pickens might alienate the Upper South. Within twenty-four hours of his March 4 inauguration, Lincoln responded with ingenious orders to reinforce Fort Pickens without a coercive shot. But throughout most of March, numbing conversations about presidential patronage distracted the inexperienced president from overseeing his military orders. The inattentive hand at the helm allowed Lincoln's subordinates to botch his clever strategy. They botched to perfection.

– 1 –

The comedy of errors trumped Lincoln's best cards, in his poker game with Jefferson Davis. The ostensible jackpot: control of Forts Pickens and Sumter, the Union's only two remaining major Lower South fortresses. The richer winnings: symbolic demonstration that either the Union's majority rule or the Confederacy's consent of the governed would prevail.[1]

The symbolic importance overshadowed the forts' military unimportance. Lincoln could not save Fort Sumter, and the fort could not conquer Charleston. Nor could Davis capture Fort Pickens, any more than that fortress could control the Gulf of Mexico. Yet neither president could relinquish claims to these forts, lest they surrender their republic's legitimacy.

A false first step could be as damaging as a surrender. Each president wished the other side to fire any initiating shot. Then the wavering Upper South might renounce the first destroyer of peace. If all eight Upper South states deserted to the Confederacy, the Union's chances of winning a civil war—and saving majority rule—would be nil. If all Upper South states stayed in the Union, the Confederacy's chances of winning on the battlefield—and establishing its withdrawal of consent to be governed—would approach zero.

517

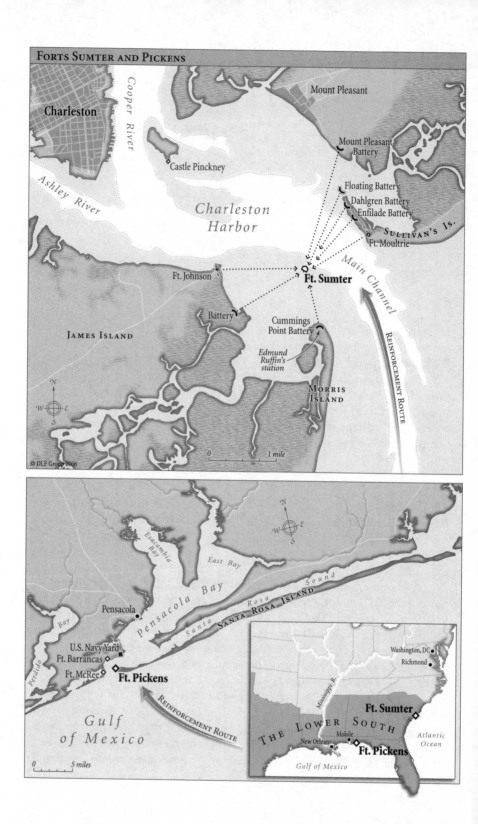

FORTS SUMTER AND PICKENS

Charleston

Cooper River

Mount Pleasant

Mount Pleasant Battery

Castle Pinckney

Ashley River

Charleston Harbor

Floating Battery
Dahlgren Battery
Enfilade Battery

SULLIVAN'S IS.
Ft. Moultrie

Ft. Johnson

Main Channel

Ft. Sumter

Battery

JAMES ISLAND

Cummings Point Battery

Edmund Ruffin's station

MORRIS ISLAND

REINFORCEMENT ROUTE

N
W · E
S

0   1 mile

© DLF Group 2006

Escacambia Bay

East Bay

Pensacola Bay

N
W · E
S

Santa Rosa Sound

Santa Rosa ISLAND

Pensacola

Perdido Bay

U.S. Navy Yard
Ft. Barrancas
Ft. McRee

Ft. Pickens

Gulf of Mexico

REINFORCEMENT ROUTE

0   5 miles

Washington, DC
Richmond

THE LOWER SOUTH

Ft. Sumter

Atlantic Ocean

New Orleans   Mobile

Ft. Pickens

Mississippi R.

Gulf of Mexico

Lincoln had equally scant chance to fortify Fort Sumter peacefully. That fortress, on a tiny island in the middle of Charleston's inner harbor, stood encircled by the South's most determined rebels. Reinforcing ships would have to sail into the inner harbor through a narrow channel. Since slivers of land, infested with cannon, lined the ship channel, federal vessels would be like eyebrows at the mercy of tweezers. At Fort Pickens, in contrast, a federal relief ship could ignore the now 1800 rebel soldiers along the mainland shore, facing the island fort. On the other side of Fort Pickens's long, narrow island coursed the open sea, with its open invitation for ships to approach.

Under Buchanan, a reinforcing ship, loaded with soldiers, had anchored at Pensacola, awaiting the president's order to land troops at Fort Pickens. Because of Buchanan's truce with secessionists, the lame duck president had never issued the orders. Now the new president had only to speed a messenger, bearing the reinforcing order, to the Pensacola environs. Then soldiers could be peacefully landed on Fort Pickens's open ocean side, beyond mainland cannons' range. The Union could thus prove that the majority would rule, without firing a shot.

The ploy, if successful, would hand Lincoln delightful options. He could shun a provocative order to call up more troops, for his current troops could hold the fort. He could evacuate Fort Sumter, for he would have made his symbolic point at Fort Pickens. He could implicitly invite Davis to assault a reinforced Fort Pickens from its landed side, knowing that a massive Confederate bombardment might fail. (The Confederacy would in fact fail to conquer Fort Pickens throughout the Civil War.) With Davis's men (haplessly) shooting all the guns and Lincoln (successfully) spreading all the pacifications, those indecisive Virginians might wonder about Lincoln's supposed coercion.

If Lincoln celebrated these prospects, he rejoiced too soon. His early March order for a decisive reinforcement at Fort Pickens yielded no reinforcement. Instead of immediately sending a messenger to Pensacola, his subordinates dawdled for days. Instead of dispatching the message due south from Washington, they first sent Lincoln's order due north to New York. Instead of speeding the message from New York partly by land and partly by sea (a process that took four days), they sent the command altogether by sea (a process that routinely occupied nine days but this time dragged on a week longer). Instead of ordering the navy to help the army land its troops at Pickens, they dispatched orders only to the army, and the navy balked.[2]

So instead of hearing by March 21 that the gambit had triumphed, Lincoln heard back definitively only on April 6, and only that his troops remained aboard ship. By then, Robert Anderson at Fort Sumter had scarcely a week of provisions left. So Lincoln could only surely demonstrate that the majority would rule with the reinforcement of Fort Sumter—the worst place to begin the Civil War.

Lincoln cannot be blamed for all his subordinates' Fort Pickens errors. He did not send the messenger in the wrong direction to the wrong military branch and partly aboard the wrong conveyance. But he failed to monitor the ongoing misdirections. During early and late March, he apparently never even asked, let alone frantically asked, about what had happened to his order.

Inexperience partly caused Lincoln's error of omission. He had never been an executive. He had not served in Washington for over a decade. He had not commanded a soldier for over twenty years. Furthermore, office seekers swarmed in the White House, diverting his attention at every daytime moment and besetting his sleepless nights with blinding headaches.

One patronage decision deserved his stressed attention. Would the new president use his appointment powers, as secessionists feared, to empower a Southern Republican Party? Lincoln answered in a well-publicized letter to North Carolina's John Gilmer. "As to the use of patronage in the slave states," the president-elect wrote on December 15, 1860, "where there are few or no Republicans, I do not expect to inquire for the politics of the appointee."[3]

Or to translate Lincoln's political doublespeak, he did expect to appoint Southern Republicans where they already agitated, in the Border South. And so he did. Lincoln gave two positions in his cabinet to Southern Republicans: Missouri's Edward Bates (Frank Blair, Jr.'s favorite presidential candidate) and Maryland's Montgomery Blair (Frank Blair, Sr.'s other prominent son and Lincoln's key southern swing man at the Republican National Convention). The Blairs also received some Maryland and Missouri local patronage plums. The president-elect here practiced politics as usual—rewarding the friends who had anointed him, and choosing men who favored his policies to administer his government, in order to bolster the party's fortunes in their area.

Lincoln also here practiced the only antislavery politics he favored beyond containment: empowering Southerners to reform the South. He thereby demonstrated that prescience, not paranoia, characterized his secessionist foes. They understood that he planned no new antislavery laws. They expected that he would boost a southern antislavery party. Most Southerners considered that danger insufficient to justify disunion. But secessionists wanted no part of a wide-open South, with antislavery principles agitated in Border South slaves' and yeomen's hearing. Against that democratic persuasion, the minority meant to consolidate a closed society.[4]

– 2 –

Because disunionists controlled the Lower South and menaced his two forts, President Lincoln eventually had to focus on military instead of patronage predicaments. On March 29, suspecting that his Fort Pickens order had, in his word, "fizzled,"[5] and knowing that Robert Anderson had little food left, Lincoln ordered ships prepared to resupply the Charleston fortress. While he decided whether to send the prepared ships, he developed a shrewd contingency plan. He would inform the rebels that only food would be landed at Sumter, if they allowed that mercy mission to be performed. But if they fired on the ships or on the fort, reinforcing troops would be landed. Whether rebels fired bullets against bread or allowed Fort Sumter troops to be fed (and thus to remain), Lincoln would win this round of the battle for Upper South public opinion. This strategy was less clever than the president's initial Fort Pickens gambit. But he had learned to ensure that clever orders would be carried out. A great president's growth had begun.

A week after Lincoln ordered the Sumter ships prepared (and two weeks after a prompt fulfillment of the president's Fort Pickens order could have widened his Fort Sumter options), Robert Anderson's imminent starvation left no time to wait for better alternatives. On April 6, the president ordered a State Department clerk to speed to Charleston partly by land, faster than the resupplying ships could go by sea, to "notify" South Carolina's Governor Francis Pickens of "an attempt . . . to supply Fort-Sumpter [sic]." Only "provisions" would be landed, continued Lincoln's message, unless "such attempt be . . . resisted." But if rebels resisted, Lincoln threatened, a federal "effort to throw in men, arms, or ammunition will be made." On the evening of April 8, Lincoln's messenger read the communiqué to Governor Pickens, who asked Confederate President Jefferson Davis for instructions.[6]

The next day, Davis and his cabinet debated their response. Rebel leaders could not know that on precisely April 9, exactly four years hence, Robert E. Lee would surrender at Appomattox Courthouse. But Davis's cabinet did know that Lincoln's move left no good countermove. If Confederates allowed the federal ships to sail peacefully into Charleston harbor (assuming, dubiously, that Charlestonians would accept that humiliation), rebels would broadcast their failure to withdraw their consent to be governed. Alternatively, if Davis ordered ships bearing food for hungry men to be sunk, the Confederacy's first shots could appall Upper South fence sitters. Or to put the rebels' choice in the appropriate terms, the U.S. president now sat at the poker table with a pair of aces, waiting for the Confederate president to fold or to raise the ante.

Davis raised the stakes. He ordered the fort reduced before ships arrived (lest the Confederacy have to conquer ships and the fort simultaneously). Davis also decreed that Robert Anderson be given a single peaceful option: evacuate immediately. Instead, Anderson only agreed to evacuate on April 15, and only if federal ships had not reached his fort. Confederates, knowing that reinforcements might soon arrive, informed Anderson that their cannonballs would imminently descend.

The U.S. vessels in fact arrived in the Charleston environs on April 12. On that same day, acting under Lincoln's this time inescapable orders, speedily delivered by land and by sea, the navy conveyed the army's offshore Pensacola troops to Fort Pickens on its safe sea side, without resistance. If that peaceable triumph at Pickens had transpired per Lincoln's original orders, three weeks earlier—well, might-have-beens can be intriguing.

Earlier that April 12, at 4:30 A.M., the first Confederate shot exploded over Fort Sumter. To the Virginia fire-eater Edmund Ruffin went the honor of the second shot, fired from Cummings Point opposite Fort Moultrie. Ruffin

had gone to bed with only shoes and coat removed, in expectation of this moment. As the old warrior ecstatically pulled the lanyard and sent the cannon shell from his sixty-four-pound Columbian smashing into the Totten defense system's prize fort, his glee brought back to mind Rhett kneeling before signing the South Carolina Secession Ordinance and Yancey introducing President-elect Jefferson Davis to the Montgomery multitudes. Each symbolic tableau honored the trio of greatest fire-eaters (and hid their slide into climactic irrelevance).

Virginia's Edmund Ruffin, here literally dressed to kill, had always been the least potent of the three leading fire-eaters (also including Rhett and Yancey). What, after all, could a fiery revolutionary do with indecisive Virginia? Only beg South Carolinians to drive Virginians off the fence, as Ruffin urgently did in the late 1850s. That dangerous strategy ultimately required the provocative fire-eating trio to step unprovocatively back, settling for harmless curtain calls in the climactic moments. Ruffin's cameo role, firing the second shot of the first Civil War bombardment, set off quite the fireworks. A day and a half later, an early Confederate flag, sporting only seven stars, fluttered over a devastated Fort Sumter, as if beckoning Ruffin's Virginia to add its star at last. Courtesy of the National Archives (Ruffin) and the Library of Congress (both Fort Sumter images, opposite).

On April 12, after Ruffin's ball exploded, Confederates' reduction of Fort Sumter began in earnest. First fireworks lit the sky. Then flames licked Fort Sumter. Charlestonians scrambled atop roofs to watch the grandest light show in memory. Forty hours and 5000 artillery shots later, only the sinking sun illuminated Charleston's darkening skies, Sumter's ruins, and Robert Anderson's white flag. But no soldier lay slain. Anderson surrendered his intact corps on condition that the defeated warriors could leave with flags flying and fifty guns firing two shots apiece. The shots killed two Union soldiers and frightfully wounded four others. An awful war had begun.[7]

– 3 –

South Carolina's Governor Francis Pickens immediately telegraphed Virginia's Governor John Letcher that coercion had commenced. Yet Virginia's convention delegates continued their indecisive talk. Not the Fort Sumter fireworks of April 12–13 but Lincoln's proclamation of April 15 shattered the convention's cocoon. The president called on the several states for a combined total of 75,000 troops, to put down the rebellion. Virginians had been summoned to slaughter South Carolinians.[8]

In response, Virginia moderates only changed the terms of their delay. Previously, the Majority Report of the Committee on Federal Relations had championed a border state conference, before any decision on secession. Now, the delayers' leader, Robert Scott, urged a May 23 Virginia popular referendum, charged with deciding (without a convention decision) between "separate and immediate secession" or "cooperation among the slaveholding States yet remaining in the Union." Scott prayed that cooperation would win. Then a border state conference could begin.[9]

Scott had previously hoped that a border conference would secure a reconstructed Union. He now hoped that such a conference would secure unanimous secession. If Virginia seceded without a border conference, he feared, the border states would feel ignored, oppressed, unwilling to follow tyrannical secessionists like slaves. Scott would instead turn Upper South compatriots into masters of their fate, cooperating in an Upper South march toward the Confederacy.

Scott celebrated his proposed delay as "a straight road to secession," for "I cannot doubt that all the Border States will act together . . . with the Southern States." But over half his supporters, unreconstructable Unionists, liked his delay because they did not doubt that border states would act together with northern states. Robert Scott proposes "to get out," scoffed George Randolph, not by seceding but "by getting the States, that everybody knows will not secede, to join with Virginia in a consultation."[10]

Against Scott's latest effort to find a middle way, the disunionists' William B. Preston proposed that at a May 23 popular referendum, the people should be offered only one choice: approve or disapprove of the convention's secession ordinance.[11] Inside the convention, orations swerved to the merits of Preston's immediate decision versus Scott's further delay. Outside Institute Hall, the clamor for instant disunion grew deafening. By a coincidence recalling the Charleston railroad meeting of November 9, 1860, George Bagby's Spontaneous State's Rights Assembly, planned in late March, convened in Richmond's Metropolitan Hall on April 16, just as Preston and Scott crossed oratorical swords in Institute Hall. Wild rumors spilled into Richmond's streets, as young sports inside Metropolitan Hall intoxicated each other with conspiratorial plots. Should we kidnap Governor John Letcher? Should we seize Newport News' federal Gosport Naval Yards? Should we raid the Harpers Ferry federal arsenal?

The proposed version of John Brown's raid, this time featuring Virginia proslavery partisans as raiders, quickly found a formidable champion, himself no stranger to Harpers Ferry.[12] Henry Wise starred as a convention delegate in Institute Hall and as a participant in Metropolitan Hall, where Bagby's "Spontaneous" crowd assembled. The ex-governor preferred younger Virginians' revolutionary fury to older moderates' eternal talking. True, in customary seasons of politics as usual, no other Virginian talked more endlessly (and that said something).

Yet in rare seasons of crisis, no other Virginian acted more decisively. At the Virginia state convention of 1851, Wise had championed the saving compromise between eastern and western Virginia. As candidate for governor during Southern Know-Nothings' key moment, he had pushed the Whiggish alternative back to the Border South. As governor during John Brown's raid, the ultra-thin, ultra-wiry rabble-rouser had brought off the state's calm and secure hanging of the Connecticut killer. Now Henry Wise encouraged George Bagby's young adults in Metropolitan Hall (but not calmly). On April 16, Wise demanded that Harpers Ferry and the Gosport Naval Yards be ambushed, in the name of inescapable revolution.

Acting as if John Letcher had not recently succeeded him as governor, Wise secretly organized an army to march on the morrow, half the troops to stride northwest, to capture Harpers Ferry, the other half to stream southeast, to have at the Gosport Yards. Confronted with this fait accompli, the sitting governor gave the ex-governor's troops official sanction. Possibly, Governor Letcher responded to rumors that the mob would kidnap a resisting chief executive. More likely, Letcher saw, an instant before his moderate friends in the convention, that revolution could no longer be stalled.

On April 17, as his recruits sallied forth for their successful assaults on Harpers Ferry and the Gosport Yards, Wise strode into the convention. Minutes before the ex-governor stole the show, the convention voted down Robert Scott's proposal for a double popular referendum on May 23, 77–64.[13] A switch of only seven delegates would have suspended any secession for thirty-six days. Subsequently, Virginia's electorate would have chosen between the border state conference stall and instant disunion action.

After the vote, Henry Wise ended the stalling. As he started to speak, the ex-governor placed his horse pistol before him. He snapped open his pocket watch. He announced that at this hour, by his command, Virginia was at war with the federal government. If anyone wished to shoot him for treason, they could seek to wrestle away his oversized pistol.[14]

Ten feet in front of Wise, ex-president John Tyler turned his chair around, tears streaming down his worn face, to cheer as the spellbinder ripped into stalling Unionists. To an eyewitness, Wise seemed "supernaturally excited. His features were as sharp and rigid as bronze. His hair stood off from his head, as if charged with electricity." Lincoln's bloodthirsty proclamation, he shouted at his foes, makes waverers into traitors. You must now decide whether to kill your kin, and whether to repudiate your soldiers, and whether to return the murder weapons that your patriotic sons have seized. You must additionally decide whether to repudiate the White House despot or assassinate me.

Henry Wise hardly here saved Virginia's secession. Too many reasons compelled Virginians to fight alongside southern cousins, if a fight commenced. Thanks to Wise's initiative and Letcher's concurrence, Virginia troops already marched toward the fight that warriors north and south of Virginia had irrevocably begun. The convention had already voted down Robert Scott's last bid for Virginia procrastination. But Henry Wise probably forced some reluctant Virginians to accept the unavoidable fact of war days or weeks before these delayers would have otherwise faced this dreaded music. More surely, the image of Wise screaming at the stallers, pocket watch and horse pistol before him, epitomized how reluctantly Virginians chose to become Confederates and how violence alone, as so often, left no room to hide from frightful choice.[15]

Shortly after Wise roared at the reluctant, Virginia's convention voted 88–55 to recommend immediate secession to the state's voters. On May 23, Virginia's citizens voted for disunion more decisively, 125,950–20,373. But would the western Virginia minority accept the Virginia majority's decision?[16]

In the Virginia secession convention, western delegates had denounced slaveholders' tax breaks rather than Lincoln's alleged abolitionism. These delegates voted 26–5 against secession on April 17. Their constituents voted down disunion by a three-to-one margin at Virginia's May 23 popular referendum. These thirty-three Virginia counties contained 33 percent of Virginia's whites but only 3 percent of its slaves. Wheeling, five times closer to Pittsburgh than to Richmond, traded ten times more with nonslaveholding than with slaveholding states.

Between June 11 and 20, 1861, western Virginians met in a Wheeling convention. The convention in effect seceded from Virginia and entered in the Union as the new state of West Virginia. The Virginia stalemate—and Virginia itself—lay shattered.

– 4 –

A comparison of secession in Virginia and in the Lower South throws light on differences between various Souths—and on the developing southern nationalism that overcame many differences. In South Carolina in early December, Governor (about to be ex-governor) William Gist threatened to organize a private posse and seize Fort Moultrie if Lower South congressmen delayed South Carolina's departure. Gist's threats comprised the illegal route to rebellion that Judge Andrew Magrath and Charleston's 1860 Association had been at pains to control. So too, in early January, Robert Gourdin deterred young Charles Augustus Lafayette Lamar's illegal seizure of Fort Pulaski. In South Carolina, the older generation at last brimmed with determination to bring off secession. Seasoned veterans needed to keep younger hotheads from disgracing an orderly rebellion and weakening reactionaries' nerve.

In Virginia, Henry Wise, also lately the governor, organized exactly the sort of military seizures that Gist had threatened. The resulting Virginia coups resembled Lower South secessionists' post-*Star of the West* seizures of federal military installations west of South Carolina. Once again, troops captured federal installations (and thus consummated the revolution) before voters or conventions had voted to rebel. Once again, the supposedly patriotic heroics outmaneuvered moderates, who once again haplessly squealed. But where Lower South Cooperationists' worsened plight became an unintended consequence of their governors' strikes, Henry Wise and his young Virginians fully intended to shove older gentlemen into the maelstrom.

Virginia and the whole Upper South needed to be shoved, albeit far more by Lincoln's military orders than by Wise's, because the president's menace to slavery seemed less threatening where black belts less predominated. Henry Benning brilliantly made his new republic's case that Lincoln posed an instant danger to the institution and to racial order. A third of the Virginia convention delegates concurred, with George Randolph and James Holcombe superbly developing the argument.

The argument did not suffice. Only when Lincoln called up the troops, to destroy the people of a state's alleged right to withdraw their consent, did disunion consume Virginia.[17] William Rives, for example, led the Central Confederacy movement. But after Lincoln summoned the troops, Rives became a Southern Confederate partisan. "Our justification now," soared Rives, lies "in the principles of the Declaration of American Independence"— in the right to throw off a "government, which no longer stands upon the only legitimate foundation, the consent of the governed, but seeks to rule by the sword."[18]

The Middle South's belated wave of revolution, sweeping up even William C. Rives (and Sam Houston), repeated the second stage of the shattering of the National Democratic Party. In Charleston, the Upper South majority of southern delegates rejected the Lower South representatives' case for ripping apart the party over the territorial issue. But in Baltimore, after Northern Democrats threw out some Lower South delegates, most Upper South delegates massed behind the Cotton South. Most Democrats in both southern sections abhorred an imposition of northern will without southern consent. So too, in the secession crisis, the majority of Southerners (and the huge majority of Upper South citizens) rejected Lower South Separatists' case for ripping apart the nation over Lincoln's menace to slavery. But Lincoln's trampling down white men's right to consent was another matter.

Not only a state's abstract right to withdraw consent but also Southerners' visceral loathing of Yankees turned Lincoln's coercion into a summons to disunion. Now Virginians had to decide who they hated enough to kill; and most Southerners loathed Northerners. The Yanks were hypocrites, puritans, holier-than-thous, meddlers, insulters, sanctimonious, insufferable. The swelling of that image had been the single most important southern phenomenon of the 1850s. The emergence of the horrendous Yank had been the reason why the northern response to John Brown (more than Brown's blundering raid itself) had been so provoking, why Owen Lovejoy's tirade in the House of Representatives had been so infuriating, why James Holcombe found Northerners who sneered at his philanthropic parents so appalling, and why William Lowndes Yancey considered his haughty stepfather so outrageous. No true Southerner would murder southern brothers who refused to live with righteous fanatics!

War and the ensuing reconstruction forged a consuming southern nationalism around this prewar kernel of nationalism. Despite their differences over whether slavery should last forever, over whether the African slave trade should be opened, over whether Lincoln's menace to slavery demanded disunion, those who lived in Upper South or Lower South black belts had long agreed that Yankee intrusion without southern consent would intolerably make whites into slaves. Southern nationalism exemplified sociologists' "negative reference group." When black belt Southerners disagreed on what they favored, they agreed on what they despised. They excoriated holier-than-thou outsiders. They would not allow the other section's phony saints to enslave them—and especially not with rifles.

Strikingly often, they coupled visions of emancipating themselves with hints of somewhat freeing blacks, sometime or other. In the spirit of the Reverend Benjamin Palmer, they demanded total control over their own internal arrangements, not always to freeze slavery in place but sometimes to explore whether icy rigidities could be partially thawed. That had been the surprising hope of Dred Scott's judges, even when the Southern Democratic jurists slapped outsiders' hands off territorial slaves. Such occasional surprises do not prove that the South ever would have reformed slavery. But the softer side of southern ferocity demonstrates that Southerners subjected slavery to human prayers for improvement—and that Yankees, in addition to all their other enraging attributes, became infuriating scapegoats for frustrated dreams.

Robert Toombs put this startling side of disunionists' cry for hands off unforgettably, in his farewell oration to the U.S. Senate. You presume that slavery is your infatuated business, declared Toombs on January 7, 1861. But "this is our question. . . . We will tell you when we choose to abolish this thing. It must be done under our direction, and according to our will," in "our native land." If you seek to invade our soil "with the sword in one hand, and the torch in another," we will "meet you upon the border."[19]

That first blush of southern nationalism—that rage to keep meddlers' opinions and especially rifles off our sacred terrain without our consent— would flourish rankly as Yankee soldiers (with blacks' help) battered down slaveholders' defenses. The defeated South's Lost Cause nationalism would ascend the more unconquerably after northern reformers (again with blacks' help) imposed postwar reconstruction. War and postwar occupation, as so often, was midwife of nationalism. But the prewar seed gave enormous leverage to the comparatively few initial secessionists. One more time let posterity remember the wisest sentences on the course of the secession crisis. If our tiny state will alone dare, exclaimed South Carolina's Congressman William Boyce in August 1860, "our enemies . . . must let us alone" or "coerce us." If they "coerce us, then the Southern states are compelled to make common cause with us."

So history transpired in the Lower South, after the *Star of the West* sailed. So history repeated itself in the Middle South, after Abraham Lincoln summoned an army. Then the only choice left, where should I aim my bullets, left divided white Southerners—at least in the black belts—divided no longer.

– 5 –

In Upper South white belts, history moved in the opposite direction. Virginia prefigured both directions. Like most white Virginians, most Middle South citizens stood with southern comrades, after Lincoln called them forth to slay their brothers. In early May, the reconvened Arkansas convention seceded, 65–5. In mid May, the North Carolina convention unanimously concurred. In early June, Tennessee's voters approved disunion in a popular referendum, 104,913–47,238.[20]

But again as in Virginia, most voters in Middle South white belts dissented. Just as western Virginia mountaineers voted three to one against secession, so eastern Tennessee mountaineers cast seven of ten ballots against disunion. Just as western Virginia departed from Virginia, so eastern Tennessee's U.S. Senator Andrew Johnson refused to depart from his senatorial chair. The Democrats' Johnson had the blessings of the ex-Whigs' Parson Brownlow, who had never before blessed anything about Andrew Johnson.

Eastern Tennessee's Brownlow and Johnson overcame their mutual antipathy because both despised southern rebels more. Here as everywhere in America at this terrible moment, men had only one decision: who they hated enough to kill. Johnson, Brownlow, eastern Tennesseans, western Virginians, and northwestern Arkansas nonslaveholders all agreed with the North: The rebels were atrocious. The "overbearing tyrants" of "the Slavery Aristocracy," spat Parson Brownlow, would "drag Tennessee" and all "poor white men . . . to fight their battles" and be "shot down like dogs." The secessionists, concurred Andrew Johnson, mounted "a conspiracy" against "the liberty of the great mass of the people."[21]

At decision-making time over who was the most loathsome American, the Border South largely concurred with Johnson. Some rough patches occurred in saving the most northern South for the Union. For a few days, an April riot in Baltimore, when Lincoln's troops passed through, shook the city. For a few months, Kentucky tried to preserve its neutrality (with John Breckinridge's blessings). For four years, Missouri, repeating its Kansas wars, fell into world-class guerrilla warfare.

But most borderites despised the Southern Confederacy. A barometer of borderland sentiment came in the U.S. congressional elections of mid-June 1861. Unionists won five of six Kentucky seats in the U.S. House of Representatives and amassed more than seventy percent of the vote. Unionists also won all Maryland's seats, by larger landslides than in Kentucky. In August 5 popular elections for state legislators, Kentucky Unionists trumped themselves, winning majorities of three to one in the House and over two to one in the Senate.[22]

Just as the Middle South's whitest belts contained large antisecessionist majorities, so the Border South's blackest belts displayed large secessionist pluralities. Eastern and Western Shore Maryland, western Missouri, and Blue Grass Kentucky sent tens of thousands of troops to the Confederate army. Thus the largest generalization about secession crisis allegiance held firm: the more and the thicker the black belts, the faster and the more enthusiastically a neighborhood massed behind secessionists.

The Border South simply possessed fewer black belts than the Middle South, while the Middle South contained fewer black belts than the Lower South. So the Lower South seceded first (with its blackest states the first out); the Middle South seceded many months later (and only after Lincoln asked for its troops to slay fellow Southrons); and the Border South never seceded (not even after Lincoln's war exclusively for white men's Union belatedly became also a war for black men's freedom). Exactly the borderland region that Lower South ultras had fretted about for decades—and lately feared would be the locale of a swelling, already existing Southern Republican Party—largely saluted the Union's colors, at crunch time for slavery.

During the ensuing road to Appomattox, the South would need all of itself, in order to whip the more numerous, more industrialized Yankees. Instead, too many southern folk, controlling too much southern industry and strategic terrain, would support the Union. These southern anti-Confederates, including at least 100,000 Middle South whites, two-thirds of Border South whites, and some 500,000 fugitive slaves, would help turn the secessionists' panacea into a suicidal gamble. Thus would southern divisions, one of the great causes of the Civil War, become one of the great causes of Confederate defeat.[23]

CODA: *HOW* DID SLAVERY CAUSE THE CIVIL WAR?

That slavery above all else caused this historic war, both within the South and between the Union and the Confederacy, seems indisputable. Contention about slavery shared or transcended the importance of all other contentions at almost every critical pre–Civil War moment. Even in 1832–33, a Nullification Controversy ostensibly about only protective tariffs actually also involved slavery's future.[24] Even in the early 1850s, northern controversy over immigrants swiftly gave way to Yankee blasts against the Slave Power. Even apparently nonslavery causes of the Civil War grew distended because of slavery's omnipresent impact. Southern yeomen's demand for equality swelled because slaves were despised emblems of inequality. State's righters' insistence on a state's right to withdraw consent expanded because only slaves lacked consent. Slaveholders' obsession with preserving honor inflated because Yankees cursed them as dishonorable tyrants and sexual monsters.

Yet *how* slavery caused the Civil War remains elusive despite these puffed-up antagonisms, for heightened resentments often plague human affairs without ending in the blow-up. (Witness, for example, the twentieth-century cold war between the United States and Russia.)[25] Most Northerners, after all, never much liked abolitionists, or voted for Lincoln in 1860 as some Great Emancipator, or disapproved of that unamenable proposed Thirteenth Amendment, keeping federal hands forever off slavery. So too, most Southerners never liked fire-eaters, or saw slavery as a permanent blessing, or disapproved of remaining in the Union, unless and until Lincoln committed an overt antislavery act or coerced departing brothers.

Nor did most white Southerners ever own a slave (or much dream of owning one, after the 1850s inflation in slave prices made the investment forbiddingly expensive). Nor did many fugitive slaves escape to the North in any year, or many slaves ever inhabit Kansas, or many avid disunionists care much about Caribbean expansion, or many avid Caribbean imperialists care much about disunion. Out of such decidedly minority materials, how could the slavery issue have smashed the Union?

Purely abstract answers to that question (to any historical question) must always be partially distrusted, for personality, accidents, timing—in a word, contingency—deflect and condition the most remorseless trends. That is why stories about how trends progressed, step by crooked step, offer crucial information about when and why the most penetrating impersonal abstraction fails to explain enough about personal responses. No abstruse theory can convey the *feel* of the Southron's visceral hatred of the Yank. Nor can any impersonal theory capture the personalities of Alexander Stephens and James

Henry Hammond, or the flash of Margaret Garner's knife across her daughter's jugular, or the Democratic Party local infighting between Mississippi's Jefferson Davis and Albert Gallatin Brown and between Missouri's Davy Atchison and John Clark, or the exaggerated hesitations and then exaggerated spree of Preston Brooks, or the brilliant tactics of William Lowndes Yancey and Robert Gourdin, or the coincidences of the Charleston and Savannah Railroad's celebration, or the winds that deterred Charles Augustus Lafayette Lamar before the 1860 Association could repudiate the loose cannon, or the oddity that John Brown lived to talk because his captor brought the wrong sword, or the errors that wrecked Lincoln's first Fort Pickens strategy. Without, in short, the faces and accidents that partially deflected the impersonal trends, the road to disunion pales toward incomprehensibility.

Still, throughout the nation's movement toward civil war, and especially at the crucial turning points, recurring impersonal forces wrenched the sections apart and made some form of civil war, at some time, highly probable. Embattled minorities' power over sleepy majorities, for example, repeatedly drove the drama. Outnumbered Southerners scored numerous national victories by controlling the National Democratic Party. Outnumbered abolitionists inspired more sympathy for blacks' rights by fanning Yankee outrage at whites' trampled rights. Outnumbered slaves brought an ultimately emancipating civil war closer (and helped win that war and point it toward emancipation) by wielding the leverage of individual massacres and especially of flight. Outnumbered secessionists impelled most of the South toward Armageddon by pressing the leverage of one state's disunion on the next state's decision. And outnumbered slaveholders demagogically used racism to provoke black belt whites to vote for the supposed supremacy of their skin, whatever the inferiority of their purse.

The dialectic between southern division and unity multiplied the destructive sway of minority leverage. On the one hand, many Souths collided. On the other hand, colliding Southerners could usually unite behind indignation at Yankees and defense of white consent to be governed. So multiple southern initiators provoked multiple crises from multiple directions, with the tribe usually massing behind dissimilar first agitators. While most Southerners did not initially covet Kansas, proslavery Missourians did; and the fragment could propel the rest behind rage at Yankee intruders and insulters. While most slaveholders did not find fugitive slaves a menace, slaveholding borderites did; and the fraction could arouse the rest behind wrath at Yankee supposed kidnappers. While most Southerners did not quake at mobocratic democracy, South Carolinians did; and the initial secessionists could inflame most of their tardier brothers against Yankees' coercion.

The collisions between democratic and despotic systems added the killing force to the leverage of minorities and to the dialectic of southern division and unity. A thriving democracy usually must allow dissenting voices. A thriving despotism usually must repress contrary opinions. Thus despotic social systems usually strain democratic political systems, often to the breaking point. Slaveholders' attempts to silence critics, whether by cries of disloyalty to slavery or by lynch mobs or by gag rules or by censoring the mails or by precluding Lincoln's appointees' campaigning—all these dictatorial methods demonstrated the increasing tension between the Old South's colliding governing systems.

Slaveholders particularly dreaded the impact of open debate on duplicitous slaves and suspect nonslaveholders. Usually, the sorest points pockmarked the southern periphery, where slim black belts slowly grew slimmer (as had slowly happened when slavery waned in the Border North). Always, the main controversies' relatively few first precipitators sought to stifle democratic procedures at the section's exposed edges, whether to annex Texas, in order to abort English antislavery agitation, or to enact despotic fugitive slave laws, in order to stop runaways at the South's porous borders, or to buttress Kansas, in order to keep a free soil regime away from vulnerable Missouri, or to secede from Lincoln's menace, in order to prevent Southern Republican discourse.

Always undemocratic closures within or beyond the South's peripheries switched the major northern issue from (rather unpopular) abolitionist crusades, seeking to liberate blacks in far-off states, to (wildly popular) mainstream campaigns, seeking to keep the Slave Power's filthy hands off our white procedures on our terrain (including the western territories that we may enter). Always, northern castigation of southern filth provoked insulted Southerners to line up behind their minority of precipitators.[26]

In the secession crisis, these escalating clashes came to climax. The northern majority would no longer tolerate the southern minority's sway, either in the National Democratic Party or in the nation. South Carolinians would not tolerate the supposedly mobocratic agitation of a Southern Republican Party. James Buchanan would not tolerate the losers' failure to obey the election winners. Lower South states would not tolerate Buchanan's *Star of the West*. Abraham Lincoln would not tolerate southern possession of Forts Pickens and Sumter. The Middle South would not tolerate Lincoln's coercion of seceded states. Once South Carolina's tiny minority of Southerners dared, three decades of mounting intolerance—and hatred—had eaten away too many pillars of majoritarian Union.

The crash of the republic mocked the southern contention that slavery provided the cornerstone of republicanism. Instead, the white minority's protection of black slavery savaged cornerstones of white republican procedure. But while prewar Northerners protected white republicanism from the Slave Power, most of them had hardly been exemplary republicans, demanding despotism's removal from democracy's nation. Even Lincoln's wartime nation would free the slaves and arm the freedmen only after white rebels could be conquered no other way. A redeemed democracy for whites must end despotism over blacks! That colorblind cornerstone of liberty had to be learned the hard way (and incompletely) in the racist North.

Southerners called their cornerstone establishment the Peculiar Institution. The peculiarity lay not in enslavement itself (a most unpeculiar institution in almost every human culture's history). Rather, the oddity lay in the entrenchment of the New World's most powerful slavery system inside the Western World's most egalitarian (for whites) republic.

That signature United States exceptionalism turned despotism into the poison stuck in the democratic body politic. A national creed that led the world in celebration of freedom belatedly inspired some republicans to denounce silent complicity in tyranny. In the 1830s, that small minority of abolitionists thrust the antislavery antidote a little down the nation's throat. The panacea could not be regurgitated, not in liberty's nation. Nor could the cure be readily swallowed, not in a land where racism and property rights were as American as black slavery and white democracy. In the South, Yankee abolitionists inspired nothing except rage to save pride, honor, racial control, property, and our own control over our own problems. In the North, zealots for colorblind freedom scored some conversions but suffered more antagonism and still more indifference, until Yankees' outrage at Slave Power defenses matched slaveholders' wrath at abolitionists' insults.

End slavery peacefully, in democratic deliberations? The road to disunion did not augur peaceable emancipation. Slice out the cancer with the sword? Only after Yankees had overcome some of their indifference to blacks' rights. Celebrate America's new birth of freedom? Only if celebrants remember that 500,000 Civil War corpses did not hallow a democracy's capacity to solve social problems peacefully—or consecrate racism's removal from the flawed republic.

Abbreviations
Used in Notes
(Slightly different than in Volume 1)

AHR	*American Historical Review*
ALA	Manuscripts Division, Alabama Department of Archives and History, Montgomery
BC	Berea College Library, Berea, Kentucky
CC	*Charleston Courier*
CG	*Congressional Globe*
CM	*Charleston Mercury*
CS	*Charleston Standard*
CWH	*Civil War History*
DBR	*De Bow's Review*
DU	Manuscripts Division, Duke University Library, Durham, North Carolina
EU	Manuscripts Division, Emory University Library, Decatur, Georgia
FC	Filson Club, Louisville, Kentucky
GA	Manuscripts Division, University of Georgia Library, Athens
GHQ	*Georgia Historical Quarterly*
HSP	Historical Society of Pennsylvania, Philadelphia
JSH	*Journal of Southern History*
LC	Manuscripts Division, Library of Congress, Washington, D.C.
LSU	Manuscripts Division, Louisiana State University Library, Baton Rouge
MHS	Maryland Historical Society, Baltimore
MISS	Mississippi Department of Archives and History, Jackson
MOHR	*Missouri Historical Review*
MOHS, C	Western Historical Collection, Historical Society of Missouri and the University of Missouri, Columbia
MOHS, SL	Missouri Historical Society, St. Louis
MVHR	*Mississippi Valley Historical Review*
NC	Southern Historical Collection, University of North Carolina at Chapel Hill Library

NOD	*New Orleans Delta*
OR	*War of the Rebellion . . . Official Records of the Union and Confederate Armies,* 128 vols. (Washington, 1880–1901), ser. 1, vol. 1
P., ed., T., S., & C.	Ulrich B. Phillips, ed., *The Correspondence of Robert Toombs, A. H. Stephens, and Howell Cobb* (Washington, 1911; published as vol. 2 of *The AHA Annual Report for 1911*)
PMHB	*Pennsylvania Magazine of History and Biography*
PS	*Plantation Society*
RE	*Richmond Enquirer*
RS	*Richmond South*
SC	South Caroliniana Library, University of South Carolina, Columbia
SCHM	*South Carolina Historical Magazine*
SCHS	South Carolina Historical Society, Charleston
SP, M	Alexander Stephens Papers, Manhattanville College Library, Purchase, New York
SQR	*Southern Quarterly Review*
TN	Tennessee Historical Society, Nashville
TX	Manuscripts Division, University of Texas Library, Austin
VA	Manuscripts Division, University of Virginia Library, Charlottesville
VHS	Virginia Historical Society, Richmond
VMHB	*Virginia Magazine of History and Biography*
VSL	Virginia State Library, Richmond
W&M	Manuscripts Division, College of William and Mary Library, Williamsburg, Virginia
WISC	State Historical Society of Wisconsin, Madison
WVU	Manuscripts Division, West Virginia University Library, Morgantown
YU	Yale University Library, New Haven, Connecticut

Notes

Preface

1. As I emphasized in William W. Freehling, *The Road to Disunion*, vol. 1, *Secessionists at Bay, 1776–1854* (New York, 1990), 659, n. 1, "my" stress on northern rage at the Slave Power's supposed enslavement of *whites* is hardly mine. The central importance of Republican apprehensions about Slave Power intrusions on white democracy is developed brilliantly in Michael F. Holt, *The Political Crisis of the 1850s* (New York, 1978); Leonard L. Richards, *The Slave Power: The Free North and Southern Domination, 1780–1860* (Baton Rouge, 2000); Russel B. Nye, *Fettered Freedom: Civil Liberties and the Slavery Controversy, 1830–1860* (East Lansing, Mich., 1963); Larry Gara, "Slavery and the Slave Power: A Crucial Distinction," *CWH* 15 (1969): 5–18; and William E. Gienapp, "The Republican Party and the Slave Power," in *New Perspectives on Race and Slavery in America*, ed. Robert H. Abzug and Stephen F. Maizlish (Lexington, Ky., 1986), 51–78. If anything is "mine," it is a fresh explanation of how and why key Southerners insisted that key democratic debates must be shuttered, lest free and open processes infect the slaveholders' regime.

As this note indicates, my conversations with fellow historians will occur here, outside a text that I think should emphasize the tale of what happened, not the story of how I differ or agree with other historians about what happened. The intrusion of historiography into historical tales has helped deaden the genre for nonacademics, who these days prefer nonspecialists' often more lively but sometimes more superficial historical renditions. I believe that nonacademics' aesthetic tastes are right and can be squared with specialists' depth if academics restrict the necessary discussion of professional questions to footnotes, endnotes, or appendices.

2. William W. Freehling, *The South vs. The South: How Anti-Confederate Southerners Shaped the Course of the Civil War* (New York, 2001).

3. Since these books were published, Peter Kolchin has skillfully placed this theme in larger context. Kolchin, *A Sphinx on the American Land: The Nineteenth-Century South in Comparative Perspective* (Baton Rouge, 2003). For more excellent comparative perspectives, see David Brion Davis, *Inhuman Bondage: The Rise and Fall of Slavery in the New World* (New York, 2006) and Shearer Davis Bowman, *Masters & Lords: Mid-19th-Century U.S. Planters and Prussian Junkers* (New York, 1993).

4. For a decade, Michael Holt has been asking me how I could have declared, in *Road 1*, that Texas annexation, by provoking destructive territorial issues, was a major turning point in the coming of the Civil War when I meant to declare, in *Road 2*, that

South Carolina's secession had little to do with territorial issues. A good answer is Professor Holt's own, elucidated in his illuminating *The Fate of Their Country: Politicians, Slavery Extension, and the Coming of the Civil War* (New York, 2004): Texas annexation and the subsequent territorial issues boosted northern resentment of Slave Power domineering. Yet another answer is that territorial issues radicalized the more moderate Lower South compatriots that South Carolinians needed to dare secession.

But my best answer is that whether eastern Virginia's frosty oligarch, Secretary of State Abel P. Upshur, shuddered at potential British agitation inside the Texas Republic or whether South Carolina's equally frosty lowcountry aristocrats winced at Lincoln's potential agitation in the Border South, the problem remained whether egalitarian democratic debate could safely be allowed inside or near to a slaveholding regime. The gag rule, fugitive slave, and Kansas issues also came and went—and also fed on the same apprehensions.

Prologue: Yancey's Rage

1. Readers of *Road 1* will know that I am here revisiting the earlier prologue, with the emphasis now shifting from Davis to Yancey. The shift signals that extremists, while long at bay, were moving toward triumph—and in order to triumph, were facing renewed relegation to the shadows.

2. Quoted in William C. Davis's good biography, *Rhett: The Turbulent Life and Times of a Fire-Eater* (Columbia, S.C., 2001), 425.

3. The best biography of Yancey, Eric H. Walther, *William Lowndes Yancey and the Coming of the Civil War* (Chapel Hill, 2006), was published too late for use in this study. See also John Witherspoon DuBose, *Life and Times of William Lowndes Yancey*, 2 vols. (New York, 1942); and Ralph D. Draughon, Jr., "The Young Manhood of William L. Yancey," *Alabama Review* 24 (1966): 28–37.

4. Louisa Cunningham to Benjamin C. Yancey, July 20, August 2, 1833, Benjamin C. Yancey Papers, NC.

5. Theodore Dwight Weld, *American Slavery as It Is: Testimony of a Thousand Witnesses* (New York, 1839), 85, 97, 164, 167.

6. Quoted in Owen Peterson's valuable biography, *A Divine Discontent: The Life of Nathan S. S. Beman* (Macon, Ga., 1986), 123.

7. Beman to Caroline Bird Yancey Beman, February 21, 1835, Yancey Papers, NC.

8. Same to same, February 15, 19, March 15, 1836, April 4, 1837, Yancey Papers, NC.

9. Peterson, *Beman*, 53–55.

10. Nathan Beman to Caroline Beman, March 15, 1836, Yancey Papers, NC.

11. Nathan Beman, *Antagonism in the Moral and Political World* (Troy, N.Y., 1858), esp. 35.

12. Both Yancey speeches can be found in the William L. Yancey Papers, ALA.

Chapter 1. Democracy and Despotism, 1776–1854: *Road,* Volume I, Revisited

1. My professional colleagues will know that I am here taking off on the first sentence of Ulrich B. Phillips's *Life and Labor in the Old South* (Boston, 1929), 3: "Let us begin by discussing the weather, for that has been the chief agency in making the South distinctive." I deploy this device to underline my countervailing conviction that culture trumped geography in making the South distinctive—and that cultural entanglements in the New World's most egalitarian (for whites) democracy explains most about these dictators' sociopolitical peculiarities.

Readers will find full documentation for positions in this chapter by consulting *Road 1* and utilizing the index. Documentation in this chapter thus will be restricted to comments on some especially useful books published since 1990, ones that would have especially eased my way in writing the earlier volume.

The most important recent big syntheses on the antebellum South have almost all been about slavery, not secession, mirroring American historians' current emphasis on social rather than political history. Two splendid exceptions are Michael F. Holt, *The Rise and Fall of the American Whig Party: Jacksonian Politics and the Onset of the Civil War* (New York, 1999), and Don E. Fehrenbacher, *The Slaveholding Republic: An Account of the United States Government's Relations to Slavery* (New York, 2001). Excellent partial exceptions, primarily social histories of slavery but with supplementary political dimensions, include William K. Scarborough, *Masters of the Big House: Elite Slaveholders of the Mid-Nineteenth-Century South* (Baton Rouge, 2003); John Ashworth, *Slavery, Capitalism, and Politics in Antebellum America*, vol, 1, *Commerce and Compromise, 1820–1850* (Cambridge, Eng., 1995); and Steven Hahn, *A Nation Under Our Feet: Black Political Struggles in the Rural South from Slavery to the Great Migration* (Cambridge, Mass., 2003). Among recent more purely social histories of U.S. slavery, pride of place belongs to Ira Berlin for *Many Thousands Gone: The First Two Centuries of Slavery in North America* (Cambridge, Mass., 1998) and *Generations of Captivity: A History of African-American Slaves* (Cambridge, Mass., 2003), fine for replacing what once was a timeless, placeless image of U.S. slavery with a careful attention to evolutions over time and space.

2. Here I need to add a sentence to my previous comments on one of the most important books about antebellum southern politics in the last thirty years, William J. Cooper, *The South and the Politics of Slavery, 1828–1856* (Baton Rouge, 1978). I prefer to call Professor Cooper's phenomenon the politics of loyalty, for his "politics of slavery" continually comes back to loyalty slugfests.

3. This crucial process is newly and expertly detailed from many directions in Steven Deyle, *Carry Me Back: The Domestic Slave Trade in American Life* (New York, 2005); Michael Tadman, *Speculators and Slaves: Masters, Traders, and Slaves in the Old South* (Madison, Wisc., 1996); Walter Johnson, *Soul by Soul: Life Inside the Antebellum Slave Market* (Cambridge, Mass., 1999); Adam Rothman, *Slave Expansion: American Expansion and the Origins of the Deep South* (Cambridge, Mass., 2005); Joan E. Cashin, *A Family Venture: Men and Women on the Southern Frontier* (New York, 1991); and James David Miller, *South by Southwest: Planter Emigration and Identity in the Slave South* (Charlottesville, 2002).

Professor Miller's argument that Old South Southeasterners dropped many of their qualms about New South Southwesterners, thus creating a universal southern celebration of a placeless conservatism based on the (moveable) family, seems very useful for southeastern migrants to the Southwest but somewhat overdone for those who stayed in eastern Virginia and largely overdone for those who stayed in lowcountry South Carolina. Most coastal South Carolinians who rejected migration clung to a reactionary mentality based on the stationary uniqueness of their eighteenth-century elitist viewpoint and culture, including massive distrust of the nouveau South and its egalitarian (white) republicanism (and as we will see, massive distrust of the James L. Orr types that would inject the new disease into South Carolina itself).

4. On the theoretical basis of this powerful abstraction, see the superb introduction by Jack P. Greene and Amy Turner Bushnell in Christine Daniels and Michael V. Kennedy, eds., *Negotiated Empires: Centers and Peripheries in the Americas, 1500–1820* (New York, 2002).

5. On this subject, J. Stephen Whitman's *The Price of Freedom: Slavery and Manumission in Early National Maryland* (Lexington, Ky., 1997) richly adds to our understanding.

Chapter 2. Economic Bonanza, 1850–1860

1. Figures on short-staple cotton prices are taken from U.S. Census Bureau, *Historical Statistics of the United States, Colonial Times to 1970,* 2 parts (Washington, 1975), 1: 209. Figures on short-staple cotton production are taken from Lewis C. Gray, *History of Agriculture in the Southern United States to 1860,* 2 vols. (Washington, 1933), 2: 1026.

2. Figures on sugar, Sea Island cotton, and tobacco are taken from ibid. 2: 1031–33, 1035–36.

3. Cost of living figures are taken from U.S. Census Bureau, *Historical Statistics,* 1: 207–9.

4. Figures on rice prices and production are derived from Gray, *History of Agriculture* 2: 1030. Peter A. Coclanis, *The Shadow of a Dream: Economic Life and Death in the South Carolina Lowcountry, 1670–1820,* is a particularly brilliant and wonderfully written book. Also superb is William Dusinberre, *Them Dark Days: Slavery in the American Rice Swamps* (New York, 1996), showing that careful capitalists could still make a fortune on rice.

5. Figures on agricultural acres and values are derived from Joseph C. G. Kennedy, *Agriculture of the United States in 1860: Compiled from the . . . Eighth Census . . .* (Washington, 1864), 184–88, 222.

6. Joseph C. G. Kennedy, *Preliminary Report on the Eighth Census, 1860* (Washington, 1862), 234–35.

7. [U.S. Census Bureau], *Manufacturers of the United States in 1860 . . .* (Washington, 1865), 729–30.

8. Robert Evans, Jr., "The Economics of American Negro Slavery," in Universities National Bureau Committee for Economic Research, *Aspects of Labor Economics* (Princeton, 1962), 216.

9. James L. Huston, *The Panic of 1857 and the Coming of the Civil War* (Baton Rouge, 1987).

10. The raw statistics for whites, slaves, size of slaveholdings, and free blacks are taken from Kennedy, *Preliminary Report,* 132, and Kennedy, *Agriculture in 1860,* 247–48. Percentages of slaveholding families are calculated by using the ratio of 5.7 whites per family for 1850 given in J. D. B. De Bow, *Statistical View of the United States . . . Being a Compendium of the Seventh Census . . .* (Washington, 1854), 94, and the ratio of 5.3 whites per family for 1860 given in Kenneth M. Stampp, *The Peculiar Institution: Slavery in the Ante-Bellum South* (New York, 1956), 30.

11. Immigrant figures are derived from De Bow, *Statistical View,* 118, and Joseph C. G. Kennedy, *Population of the United States in 1860; Compiled from the . . . Eighth Census . . .* (Washington, 1864), 607.

All further demographic claims and statistics in this volume derive from Francis A. Walker, comp., *The Statistics of the Population of the United States* (Washington, 1872), and from U.S. Census Bureau, *A Century of Population Growth: From the First Census of the United States to the Twelfth, 1790–1900* (Washington, 1909).

12. Ira Berlin and Herbert G. Gutman, "Natives and Immigrants, Free Men and Slaves: Urban Working Men in the Antebellum South," *AHR* 88 (1983): 1175–200.

13. Claudia Dale Goldin, *Urban Slavery in the Antebellum South, 1820–1860: A Quantitative History* (Chicago, 1976).

Chapter 3. James Henry Hammond and the Unsolvable Proslavery Puzzle

1. George Bourne, *Slavery Illustrated in Its Effects upon Women and Domestic Society* (Boston, 1837), 27, 42–43.

2. James Henry Hammond, *Two Letters on Slavery in the United States, Addressed to Thomas Clarkson* (Columbia, S.C., 1845), rpt. in E. N. Elliott, *Cotton is King . . .* (Augusta, 1860), 657, 659.

3. Ibid., 637–39.

4. Ibid., 667–68.

5. Ibid., 649.

6. Ibid., 649–51.

7. Ibid., 643–46.

8. Ibid., 684–85.

9. Quoted in Drew Gilpin Faust, *James Henry Hammond and the Old South: A Design for Mastery* (Baton Rouge, 1982), 102.

10. Quoted in ibid., 73.

11. The incident can be followed in Carol Bleser, ed., *Secret and Sacred: The Diaries of James Henry Hammond, a Southern Slaveholder* (New York, 1988), 17–19, 231–34; Hammond to Harry Hammond, February 19, 1856; Mrs. Hammond to William C. Hammond, July 2, 1851, James Hammond Papers, SC; Hammond to William Gilmore Simms, February 15, 1852, Hammond Papers, LC; Faust, *Hammond*, 86–87, 317–19.

12. Bleser, ed., *Secret and Sacred*, 213.

13. Ibid., 19.

14. Anne Middleton to N. R. Middleton, August 9, 1852, N. R. Middleton Papers, NC.

15. Many German citizens to Hammond, March 20, 1860, Hammond to Alexander H. Stephens, March 31, May 18, 1860, Stephens Papers, LC; Stephens to Hammond, April 8, 14, 1860, Hammond Papers, LC.

16. Hammond to W. M. Wightman, June 7, 1848, Hammond Papers, SCHS. The book in question was Henry B. Bascom's *Methodism and Slavery . . .* (Frankfort, 1845). On Bascom, past president of Kentucky's Transylvania University and future (1850) bishop of the Methodist Episcopal Church, South, see Moses H. Henkle, *The Life of Henry Bidleman Bascom, D.D., LL.D.* (Louisville, 1854).

17. Hammond to Beverley Tucker, November 12, 1847, Tucker-Coleman Papers, W&M. Readers of my discussion of Hammond's distrust of Calhoun during gag rule times, *Road* 1: 317, will find illuminating Hammond's other reason for saying no: He feared that the projected newspaper would become hitched to Calhoun's political ambitions.

18. *DBR* 21 (1856): 92, 132.

19. John Bauskett (of Edgefield, South Carolina) to Iverson Brookes, April 19, 1851, Brookes Papers, NC.

20. John Pattillo (of Emory College) to James H. Thornwell, November 19, 1852, Thornwell Papers, SC.

21. William A. Smith, *Lectures on the Philosophy and Practice of Slavery . . .* (Nashville, 1856), esp. 17–20.

22. Smith to Henry Wise, May 26, 1857, Executive Papers, VSL. I am grateful to Wise's biographer, Professor Craig Simpson, for calling this revealing letter to my attention.

23. George S. Sawyer, *Southern Institutes . . .* (Philadelphia, 1859), esp. 386.

Chapter 4. The Three Imperfect Solutions

1. Harvey Wish, *George Fitzhugh: Protagonist of the Old South* (Baton Rouge, 1943), is still the best biography, albeit on the wooden side. More fun is C. Vann Woodward's introduction to George Fitzhugh, *Cannibals All! or, Slaves Without Masters* (Cambridge, Mass., 1968), vii–xxxix. The best discussion of Fitzhugh's ideas is still Eugene Genovese, *The World the Slaveholders Made: Two Essays in Interpretation* (New York, 1969). In this early phase of his career, Genovese's emphasis on the economic side of the proslavery argument for slavery per se (that is to say, for colorblind slavery, not for *racial* slavery) slighted the religious side of the nonracial argument, a problem that he and his wife have since abundantly corrected. Genovese has, I think, more persistently underemphasized the

racial side of the proslavery argument, which in democratic (for white men) America had to be (and decidedly was) the predominant foundation of the polemics. As will be seen, Fitzhugh was here wonderfully an exception who proves the rule.

2. Quoted in Fitzhugh, *Cannibals All,* xxii.

3. Picture in Wish, *Fitzhugh,* frontispiece.

4. *DBR* 22 (1857): 423.

5. Ibid. 23 (1857): 347. See also *RE,* December 15, 1855.

6. *DBR* 23 (1857): 347; George Fitzhugh, *Sociology for the South, or the Failure of Free Society* (Richmond, 1854), 98.

7. *DBR* 22 (1857): 424 and 25 (1858): 663–64.

8. Ibid. 29 (1860): 153.

9. Ibid. 22 (1857): 421–22.

10. Ibid. 30 (1861): 400–401; Fitzhugh to George Holmes, March 27, 1855, Holmes Papers, DU.

11. *DBR* 22 (1857): 570–71; Fitzhugh, *Sociology,* 46.

12. Fitzhugh, *Sociology,* 246, 298.

13. Ibid., 94; Fitzhugh, *Cannibals All,* 104.

14. Ibid., 40.

15. *DBR* 25 (1858): 655–61; 30 (1861): 404; 23 (1857): 337–49, 449–60.

16. Fitzhugh, *Sociology,* 45.

17. Fitzhugh, *Cannibals All,* 199; *DBR* 22 (1857): 633–44, 23 (1857): 337–49.

18. Fitzhugh, *Sociology,* 84–88, 264.

19. Fitzhugh, *Cannibals All,* 199; *RE,* September 12, 1856.

20. Henry Cleveland, ed., *Alexander Stephens . . . Letters and Speeches . . .* (Philadelphia, 1866), 721–23; *Liberator,* October 26, 1860.

21. James H. Hammond, *Selections from the Letters and Speeches of the Hon. James H. Hammond of South Carolina* (New York, 1866), 317–21.

22. Laurence M. Keitt, *Address on Laying the Cornerstone of the Fire-Proof Building at Columbia, December 15, 1851* (Columbia, S.C., 1851). The secondary literature on proslavery racism is rich. My favorite is George M. Fredrickson, *The Debate on the Afro-American Character and Destiny* (New York, 1971), esp. 43–96. Superb on the colonial background of this overriding aspect of proslavery dialectics is Winthrop D. Jordan's *White over Black: American Attitudes Toward the Negro, 1550–1812* (Chapel Hill, 1968). Although not discussed here, the myth of Ham's curse became an important part of racial proslavery. The pivotal example is Samuel Davies Baldwin, *Dominion . . .* (Nashville, 1858). Good historical analyses can be found in Thomas V. Peterson, *Ham and Japeth in America . . .* (Metuchen, N.J., 1978) and especially in Stephen R. Haynes, *Noah's Curse: The Biblical Justification of American Slavery* (New York, 2002)—a book especially intriguing on Benjamin Morgan Palmer's racism.

23. *Liberator,* October 26, 1860; *DBR* 23 (1857): 116.

24. *DBR* 11 (1851): 65–69; Fredrick Law Olmsted, *A Journey Through the Seaboard States* (New York, 1951), 191–92; James Denny Guillory, "The Pro-Slavery Arguments of Dr. Samuel A. Cartwright," *Louisiana History* 9 (1968): 209–28.

25. The best biography is Reginald Horseman, *Josiah Nott of Mobile: Southerner, Physician, and Racial Theorist* (Chicago, 1960).

26. John Duffy, *Sword of Pestilence: The New Orleans Yellow Fever Epidemic of 1853* (Baton Rouge, 1966).

27. Quoted in Horseman, *Nott,* 147.

28. On the wider movement, see William Stanton's beautifully written *The Leopard's Spots: Scientific Attitudes Toward Race in America, 1815–59* (Chicago, 1960), and Dana D. Nelson's sophisticated *National Manhood: Capitalist Citizenship and the Imagined Fraternity of White Men* (Durham, N.C., 1998).

29. Josiah C. Nott, M.D., *Two Lectures on the Natural History of the Caucasian and Negro Races* (Mobil, 1844), conveniently reprinted in the best modern anthology of

proslavery writings, Drew Gilpin Faust, ed., *The Ideology of Slavery* . . . (Baton Rouge, 1981), 206–38, esp. 232.

30. Nott, *Two Lectures*, 17–18; J. C. Nott and George R. Gliddon, *Types of Mankind* . . . (Philadelphia, 1854), 189.

31. Sawyer, *Southern Institutes*, 196; Daniel R. Hundley, *Social Relations in Our Southern States* (New York, 1860), 221.

32. William Howard Russell, *My Diary North and South* (shortened version of the 1963 edition, New York, 1988), 157.

33. George Fitzhugh to William Lloyd Garrison, December 10, 1856, Garrison Papers, Boston Public Library.

34. John Bachman, *The Doctrine of the Unity of the Human Race, Examined on the Principles of Science* (Charleston, S.C., 1850), 210–11.

35. For a fuller discussion of Thornwell's theology, documentation of his argument, and analysis of the secondary literature on this subject, see my "Defective Paternalism: James Henley Thornwell's Mysterious Anti-Slavery Moment," in Freehling, *The Reintegration of American History: Slavery and the Civil War* (New York, 1994), 59–81 (text) and 281–87 (documentation). Since that book was published, Jack Maddox still has not given us his eagerly awaited volume, but we now have Eugene D. Genovese and Elizabeth Fox-Genovese's long-anticipated *The Mind of the Master Class: History and Faith in the Southern Slaveholders' Worldview* (New York, 2005). While nonprofessionals may find this dense analysis difficult, scholars will find the volume wide-ranging and rich. More accessible for nonscholars and equally important for scholars is Eugene Genovese's pithy, pointed, brilliant *A Consuming Fire: The Fall of the Confederacy in the Mind of the White Christian South* (Athens, Ga., 1998).

As Professor Genovese and I have mutually concluded (see *Consuming Fire*, 32–33, and *Reintegration of American History*, 286–87), despite our once seemingly irreconcilable clash over slaveholders' "guilt," we have come to some common grounds on a central aspect of southern unease: the unchristian practices of some slaveholders. I believe that those common grounds defeat the Genoveses' contention that Southerners "won" the Bible clash over slavery or successfully rendered the abolitionists' stress on the spirit of Christianity irrelevant. Rather, the slaveholders redefined the spirit of Christianity and then trembled that a just God might be consuming them with fire for failing to meet the standards of their own redefinition. For further discussion of this issue, see ch. 15.

One more comment is necessary to square my account with the Genoveses' on the subject of antebellum southern Christianity. They have told me that *Road 1* errs in omitting a crucial event in the breakdown of the Union before 1855—the splintering of national Protestant organizations into southern and northern churches. They are right.

36. Benjamin Morgan Palmer, *The Life and Letters of James Henley Thornwell* . . . (Richmond, 1875), 4.

37. Ibid., 47–48.

38. This and all Thornwell quotes on his theology in the subsequent paragraphs are from the preacher's magnificent "Slavery and the Religious Instruction of the Colored Population," *Southern Presbyterian Review* 4 (1850): 105–41, reprinted as a pamphlet, *The Rights and Duties of Masters* . . . (Charleston, S.C., 1850).

39. Ibid., 108.

Chapter 5. The Puzzling Future and the Infuriating Scapegoats

1. Thomas R. R. Cobb, *An Inquiry into the Law of Negro Slavery* . . . (Philadelphia, 1858), 246.

2. *DBR* 26 (1859): 124–25.

3. Fitzhugh, *Sociology*, 171. See also 95, 211, 250.

4. Fitzhugh to George Holmes, April 4, 1855, Holmes Papers, DU; Fitzhugh to Gerrit Smith, August 14, 1850, February 25, November 29, 1855, Smith Papers, Syracuse University. Or as Fitzhugh privately summed up his publicly camouflaged opinion: "I am no friend of slavery or the slave trade," which are but "necessary evils." Fitzhugh to Jeremiah Black, May 6, 1857, Black Papers, LC.

5. Thornwell, "Slavery and the Religious Instruction," 138–39.

6. Thornwell to R. J. Breckinridge, October 27, 1847, Palmer, *Thornwell*, 301.

7. *DBR* 19 (1855): 130; R. H. Taylor, "Humanizing the Slave Code of North Carolina," *North Carolina Historical Review* 2 (1925): 323–31. Several of the Virginia petitions are in VSL, and a North Carolina petition is in the Harvard University Library.

8. *CC*, May 13–14, 1859.

9. "Falkland" in ibid., May 31, 1859.

10. Quoted in *New Orleans True Delta*, July 22, 1859.

11. *CC*, May 19, 1860.

12. Ibid., May 19, 30, 1860.

13. Diary of Henry Hughes, Typescript in Hughes Papers, MISS, entries for November 16, 1848, February 3, April 13, 1850. For useful overviews, see Stanford M. Lyman's introduction to his edition of the *Selected Writings of Henry Hughes* . . . (Jackson, Miss., 1985), 1–70; and Bertram Wyatt-Brown, *Yankee Saints and Southern Sinners* (Baton Rouge, 1985), 155–82. The best biography is Douglas Ambrose, *Henry Hughes and Proslavery Thought in the Old South* (Baton Rouge, 1996).

14. Henry Hughes, *Treatise on Sociology, Theoretical and Practical* (Philadelphia, 1854), 81, 145.

15. Ibid., 98, 106, 110, 166.

16. Ibid., 166–70, 220.

17. Ibid., 196ff.

18. Ibid., 207, 218–19, 243, 264.

19. Ibid., 239–40.

20. Ibid., 291.

21. Freehling, *Road 1*, part 3.

22. Smith, *Lectures on Slavery*, 14–15, 19–21, 40, 111, 123, 155–56, 182–87, 216, 246–47, 256. The A. W. Magnum Papers, NC, contain excellent notes on Smith's lectures.

23. Richard Fuller, *Domestic Slavery Considered as a Scriptural Institution* . . . (Boston, 1847); Fuller, *Our Duty to the African Race* . . . (Baltimore, 1851), 7, 9, 14.

24. Alfred Taylor Bledsoe, *An Essay on Liberty and Slavery* (Philadelphia, 1857), 54, 139, 292.

25. E. S. Dargan to Robert M. T. Hunter, December 27, 1852, Garnett-Hunter Papers, VA. For some other illuminating examples of Deep South candor *privately*, see Henry McDonald to W. W. McLain, December 14, 1851, Alexander McBryde to McLain, January 30, February 16, 1858, American Colonization Society Papers, LC.

26. Stephen Elliott, *Address to the 39th Annual Convention of the Diocese of Georgia* (Savannah, 1861), esp. 9; Fredrika Bremer, *The Homes of the New World* . . . , 2 vols. (New York, 1853), 1: 328.

27. Charles Colcock Jones, *The Religious Instruction of the Negroes in the United States* (Savannah, 1842), 195; Thomas Smyth, *The Christian Doctrine of Human Rights and Slaves* (Columbia, S.C., 1849), 18–19.

28. Edward J. Pringle, *Slavery in the Southern States* (Cambridge, Mass., 1853), 3–5.

29. Ibid., 17, 32.

30. Ibid., 47.

31. Ibid., 26–27, 43–44.

32. Ibid., 18.

33. Ibid., 38, 44.

34. Ibid., 42, 50, 53.

35. On the important Stringfellow, we fortunately have a masterly essay: Drew Gilpin Faust, "Evangelicalism and the Meaning of the Proslavery Argument: The Reverend Thornton Stringfellow of Virginia," *VMHB* 85 (1977): 3–17.

36. Thornton Stringfellow, *Scriptural and Statistical Views in Favor of Slavery* (Richmond, 1856), 23, 54–56, 146.

37. Faust, "Stringfellow," 17.

Chapter 6. Bleeding Kansas and Bloody Sumner

1. This brief summary of the Kansas-Nebraska Act's origins and passage is extensively discussed and detailed in *Road* 1: 536–60. I have yet to see any dispute of my contention that the law was not "Douglas's." But the myth lives on. Since my account was written, the best essay on an aspect of these matters is Yonotan Etal, "With Eyes Open: Stephen A. Douglas and the Kansas-Nebraska Disaster of 1854," *Journal of the Illinois State Historical Society* 91 (1998): 175–217.

2. Freehling, *Road* 1: 536–37.

3. Ibid., 197–210, 462–67.

4. Ibid., 541–49.

5. See Milton A. McLaurin, *Celia: A Slave* (Athens, Ga., 1991). In addition to McLaurin's fine biography, the best recent histories of the Missouri/Kansas battleground in the 1850s include Nicole Etcheson, *Bleeding Kansas: Contested Liberty in the Civil War Era* (Lawrence, Kans., 2004); Gunja SenGupta, *For God and Mammon: Evangelicals and Entrepreneurs, Masters and Slaves in Territorial Kansas, 1854–1860* (Athens, Ga., 1966); and Christopher Phillips and Jason L. Pendleton, eds., *The Union on Trial: The Political Journals of Judge William Barclay Napton, 1829–1883* (Columbia, Mo., 2005). In addition to coediting the superlative Napton document, Christopher Phillips wrote the penetrating introduction and has also published the best recent biography of a late antebellum Missourian, *Missouri's Confederate: Claiborne Jackson and the Creation of Southern Identity in the Border West* (Columbia, Mo., 2000). I am grateful to Professor Phillips for his advice on many aspects of this book.

6. The following account of the Missouri vigilante uproar is based on the Atchison, Kansas, *Squatter Sovereignty*; on the very important Frederick Starr, Jr., Papers, MOHS, C; and on a trio of good *MOHR* articles: Milton E. Bierbaum, "Frederick Starr, a Missouri Border Abolitionist: The Making of a Martyr," 58 (1964): 309–25; Lester B. Baltimore, "Benjamin F. Stringfellow: The Fight for the Missouri Border," 62 (1968): 14–29; and Roy V. Magers, "The Raid on the Parkville *Industrial Luminary*," 30 (1935): 39–46.

7. The best biography is still William E. Parrish, *David Rice Atchison: Border Politician* (Columbia, Mo., 1961).

8. B. F. Stringfellow, *Negro Slavery, No Evil* . . . (St. Louis, 1854); *Squatter Sovereignty*, February 3, 1855.

9. On this crucial theme, the classic study is Nye, *Fettered Freedom*. Clement Eaton, *The Freedom of Thought Struggle in the Old South* (New York, 1964), is also invaluable.

10. See one of the better Genovese polemical outbursts: Elizabeth Fox-Genovese and Eugene Genovese, *Fruits of Merchant Capital: Slavery and Bourgeois Property in the Rise and Expansion of Capitalism* (New York, 1983), 181, 207.

11. H. Miles Moore Diary, entries for July 20, 23, 1854, YU.

12. Starr vividly reports the incident in letters to his father, October 18, 30, November 29, December 29, 1854, February 20, 1855, Starr Papers, MOHS, C.

13. On the controversy over Stringfellow's speech, see Starr to his father, August 2, 3, 8, 1854, Starr Papers, MOHS, C.

14. *Liberty Tribune,* November 10, 1854.

15. J. F. Grace to Thomas Settle, December 10, 1854, Settle Papers, NC.

16. Louise Berry, "The New England Emigrant Aid Company Parties of 1854" and "The New England Emigrant Aid Parties of 1855," *Kansas Historical Quarterly* 12 (1943): 115–55, 227–68; Samuel A. Johnson, *The Battle Cry of Freedom: The New England Emigrant Aid Company in the Kansas Crusade* (Westport, Conn., 1977).

17. Atchison to Jefferson Davis, September 24, 1854, Davis Papers, DU.

18. Newspaper clipping of Atchison's speech in Starr Papers, MOHS, C. Useful on all aspects of the Kansas affairs are James A. Rawley, *Race and Politics: "Bleeding Kansas" and the Coming of the Civil War* (Philadelphia, 1969), and James Malin, "The Proslavery Background of the Kansas Struggle," *MVHR* 10 (1923): 285–305.

19. F. P. Blair, Jr., *Remarks of F. P. Blair, Jr., . . . Upon . . . the Senatorial Election* (n.p., n.d. [1855]), pamphlet in MOHS, SL.

20. G. W. Goode, *Speech of . . . February 1, 1855* (Jefferson City, Mo., 1855).

21. *St. Louis Democrat*, January 12, 1855.

22. *Jefferson* (Mo.) *Examiner*, February 21, 1855.

23. Quoted in Allan Nevins, *Ordeal of the Union*, 2 vols. (New York, 1947), 2: 385. Nevins's *Ordeal* plus his two-volume *Emergence of Lincoln* remain the best multivolume work on the coming of the Civil War, superseded in places but highly readable and very informative. The best single-volume treatment is still David Potter's magnificent *The Impending Crisis, 1846–1861* (New York, 1976).

24. Atchison to Robert M. T. Hunter, February 4, 1855, in Charles H. Ambler, ed., "Correspondence of Robert M. T. Hunter, 1826–1876," *Annual Report of the American Historical Association for the Year 1916*, 2 vols. (Washington, 1916), 1: 160.

25. Stringfellow quoted in Alice Nichols, *Bleeding Kansas* (New York, 1954), 38–39; Atchison to the editor of the *Atlanta* (Ga.) *Examiner*, December 15, 1855; *CM,* January 12, 1856.

26. Magers, "Raid on Parkville," 40.

27. Moore Diary, entry for May 17, 1855, YU.

28. William Phillips, *The Conquest of Kansas by Missouri and Her Allies* (Boston, 1856), 47–48.

29. *St. Louis Democrat*, January 16, 1857.

30. Norma Lois Peterson, *Freedom and Franchise: The Political Career of B. Gratz Brown* (Columbia, Mo., 1965).

31. B. Gratz Brown, *Speech of . . . February 12, 1857* (Jefferson City, Mo., 1857); James B. Gardenhire, *Speech of . . . October 28, 1857 . . .* (Jefferson City, Mo., 1857).

32. *Jefferson City Examiner,* February 21, 1857.

33. Benton to J. B. Brant, February 13, 1857, in ibid., April 18, 1857.

34. This qualified response was particularly likely in the Upper South. See, for example, *Louisville Journal,* May 28, 1856; *Wilmington* (N.C.) *Herald,* May 26, 1856.

35. For the oration, see Charles Sumner, *Kansas Affairs: Speech . . . in the Senate of the United States, May 19, 1856* (New York, 1856). David Donald, *Charles Sumner and the Coming of the Civil War* (New York, 1960), remains the best biography. Donald may blame Sumner's extended absence too much on psychosomatic illness. But he makes a case for his debatable angle, and his beautifully written portrait will aid even partial critics. Also helpful on the national importance of this incident are William E. Gienapp, "The Crime Against Sumner: The Caning of Charles Sumner and the Rise of the Republican Party," *CWH* 25 (1979): 218–45; Holt, *The Political Crisis of the 1850s,* 194–96; and Michael D. Pierson, "All Southern Society is Assailed by the Foulest Charges: Charles Sumner's 'The Crime Against Kansas' and the Escalation of Republican Antislavery Rhetoric," *New England Quarterly* 68 (1995): 531–57.

36. *CM,* February 12, 1856. The great biography of Brooks has yet to be written; it will demonstrate the more personal reasons why the assailant exuded South Carolina's more general hot-and-cold aggressiveness. The materials for such a biographical foray are rich, for Brooks had a long track record of aborted affairs of honor—and of extremism mixed with extreme (for a South Carolina hotspur) moderation. A start on this assignment

is made in Robert Neil Mathias, "Preston Smith Brooks: The Man and His Image," *SCHM* 79 (1978): 296–310.

On the Southern cult of honor that partially drove Preston Brooks, see Bertram Wyatt-Brown's classic *Southern Honor: Ethics and Behavior in the Old South* (New York, 1982), usefully supplemented by Kenneth S. Greenberg, *Honor and Slavery* (Princeton, 1996). While I find the "honor" concept helpful, I think some of its proponents stretch the usefulness overly far when they ignore the many other aspects of the slavery issue that fueled "the fury of the southern soul" and indeed fueled the honor concept itself. The quoted phrase is Professor Wyatt-Brown's in his latest and most sophisticated articulation of his partially compelling emphasis. Wyatt-Brown, "The Ethic of Honor in National Crises: The Civil War, Vietnam, Iraq, and the Southern Factor," *Journal of the Historical Society* 5 (2005): 431–60.

37. Preston Brooks to Ham (his brother), May 23, 1856, Brooks Family Papers, SC. My account of the caning is drawn from this letter and from *Alleged Assault upon Senator Sumner* (House Report No. 182, 34 Cong., 1 sess.).

38. Emerson and Sumner quoted in Donald, *Sumner,* 297, 311.

Chapter 7. The Scattering of the Ex-Whigs

1. For a full-scale demonstration and discussion of these themes, see Freehling, *Road* 1: 560–63 and passim. For a slightly different slant and a monumental narrative, see Holt, *American Whig Party.*

2. A series of fine books on this temporarily crucial northern activist movement have together been a high point of American political history in recent decades. Among the best are Holt, *Political Crisis;* William E. Gienapp, *Origins of the Republican Party, 1852–1856* (New York, 1987); Ronald P. Formisano, *The Birth of Mass Political Parties: Michigan, 1827–61* (Princeton, 1971) and *The Transformation of Political Culture: Massachusetts Parties, 1790–1840s* (New York, 1983); Joel H. Silbey, *The American Political Nation, 1838–1893* (Stanford, 1991); and John Mulkhearn, *The Know-Nothing Party in Massachusetts: The Rise and Fall of a People's Movement* (Boston, 1990).

3. The best overall study of Southern Know-Nothingism remains W. Darrell Overdyke, *The Know-Nothing Party in the South* (Baton Rouge, 1950). Still, a Southwide update is a pressing assignment for antebellum southern political historians. A preview of the themes and importance of such a book appears in by far the best state study, Jean H. Baker, *Ambivalent Americans: The Know-Nothing Party in Maryland* (Baltimore, 1970). Also perhaps prophetic of enlightened treatments to come are Erik B. Alexander, " 'The Democracy Must Prepare for Battle': Know-Nothingism in Alabama and Southern Politics, 1851–1859," *Southern Historian* 27 (2006): 23–37, and Anthony Gene Carey, *Politics, Slavery, and the Union in Antebellum Georgia* (Athens, Ga., 1997), ch. 7. My own discussion is based on such rich sources as the *Savannah Daily Republican, Mobile Daily Advertiser, New Orleans Commercial Bulletin, Baltimore Clipper,* and *RS.*

4. *Mobile Daily Advertiser,* August 3, 1856.

5. *Savannah Daily Republican,* August 4, 1855.

6. *Baltimore Clipper,* January 2, 1857.

7. Skillfully recounted in Baker, *Ambivalent Americans.*

8. The best account of this turning point is in one of the best biographies of an antebellum Southerner: Craig M. Simpson, *A Good Southerner: The Life of Henry A. Wise of Virginia* (Chapel Hill, 1985), 106–18.

9. Freehling, *Road* 1: 162–77, 511–15.

10. William Kenneth Scarborough, ed., *The Diary of Edmond Ruffin,* 3 vols. (Baton Rouge, 1972–89), 1: 405; Beverley Tucker to James Hammond, February 8, 1850, Hammond Papers, LC. For a more favorable image of Wise on the stump in 1855, see *RE,* February 24, 1855.

11. Flourney's acceptance letter was published in a colorful volume on this campaign: James P. Hambleton, ed., *A Biographical Sketch of Henry A. Wise, with a History of the Political Campaign in Virginia in 1855* (Richmond, 1856), 170.

12. *RE,* April 12, 1855.

13. Wise to his wife, March 14, 23, 1855, Wise Family Papers, VHS.

14. *RE,* April 2, 1855.

15. Ibid., January 17, 1855.

16. Albert Gallatin Brown to J. F. H. Clairborne, March 29, 1855, Clairborne Papers, MISS.

17. Quoted in Gienapp, *Origins of the Republican Party,* 182.

18. Quoted in ibid., 181, 183.

19. Quoted in ibid., 301.

Chapter 8. James Buchanan's Precarious Election

1. Phillip Shriver Klein, *President James Buchanan: A Biography* (University Park, Pa., 1962), 100. Klein's is the best full biography, but a more up-to-date study, sympathetic yet critical, might better capture this crucial figure.

2. Freehling, *Road* 1: 537.

3. Note how often Miss Hetty (Esther Parker) suffuses Klein's biography and sounds like a favorite "darkie." A study of Anglo-American upper-class paternalism is badly needed and would at last put the Old South's nonmonopoly on this class relationship in perspective.

4. Klein, *Buchanan,* 149–50.

5. Freehling, *Road* 1:324–36.

6. For a choice example, see C. C. Clay, Jr., to C. C. Clay, Sr., June 7, 1856, Clay Papers, DU.

7. The finest monograph on Buchanan's election and administration is still Roy Franklin Nichols, *The Disruption of American Democracy* (New York, 1948).

8. Klein, *Buchanan,* 257–58.

9. Wise's call, dated September 15, 1856, survives in the Executive Letterbook, VSL.

10. For an extremist's telling commentary on the (lamented) lack of committees of correspondence, see James A. Nisbet to John B. Lamar, July 27, 1856, Howell Cobb Papers, GA.

11. Gienapp, *Origins of the Republican Party,* is at its best on the coalition in 1856, thus increasing the tragedy that this superlative historian died prematurely, before he could finish his sequel on the 1860 election. Also very fine on Republicanism's varied factions is Eric Foner, *Free Soil, Free Labor, Free Men: The Ideology of the Republican Party Before the Civil War* (New York, 1970).

12. Quoted in Foner, *Free Soil,* 120.

13. Quoted in ibid., 271.

14. William Goode to E. W. Hubard, July 20, 1856, Hubard Papers, NC.

15. *RE,* October 20, 1856.

16. Mrs. Howell Cobb to Lamar Cobb, October 13, 1860, Howell Cobb Papers, DU. A fine biography of Howell Cobb has yet to be written, despite the importance of the man and the voluminous quantities of his surviving letters. For now, the best foray is still John Eddins Simpson, *Howell Cobb: The Politics of Ambition* (Chicago, 1973).

17. Howell Cobb to Mrs. Cobb, June 6, 1857, Cobb Papers, GA.

18. Mary Anne Lamar Cobb to Virginia C. T. Clay, February 5, 1860, Clement C. Clay Papers, DU; Kate Thompson to Howell Cobb, n.d. [late 1850s], Cobb Papers, GA; Varina Davis to James Buchanan, December 25, 1860, Buchanan Papers, HSP.

Chapter 9. The President-Elect as the Dred Scotts' Judge

1. This is the thesis of the best study of the decision, Don E. Fehrenbacher, *The Dred Scott Case: Its Significance in American Law and Politics* (New York, 1978), esp. 3, 5. The partially distorted thesis aside, Fehrenbacher's is a superb volume, especially fine for placing the case in a sweeping chronological perspective.

2. Quoted in a good biography, John P. Frank, *Justice Daniel Dissenting: A Biography of Phillip V. Daniel, 1784–1860* (Cambridge, Mass., 1964), 246.

3. Quoted in Frank Otto Gatell, "John Catron," in *The Justices of the United States Supreme Court, 1789–1869* ..., ed. Leon Friedman and Fred L. Israel, 4 vols. (New York, 1969), 1: 748. With no full-scale biography available, Professor Gatell's excellent short sketch is our best portrait.

4. Quoted in Freehling, *Road* 1: 461.

5. *SQR* 12 (1847): 134. Campbell is the subject of the best biography of any of the associate judges: Robert Saunders, Jr., *John Archibald Campbell, Southern Moderate, 1811–1889* (Tuscaloosa, Ala., 1997).

6. Quoted in the best biography of Taney: Carl Brent Swisher, *Roger B. Taney* (New York, 1935), 517.

7. *SQR* 12 (1847): 134.

8. Quoted in Swisher, *Taney*, 518. I italicize *at the time of* to dispel the important misunderstanding that Taney's manumission of his slaves, because it occurred almost forty years earlier, was irrelevant to his opinion at the time of Dred Scott. "Whatever moral conviction may have inspired" Taney's manumissions, erroneously writes Don Fehrenbacher, "it does not appear again in his ... private correspondence." Fehrenbacher, *Dred Scott,* 560n. The *private* letter to Nott in *1857* belies that sentence. Fehrenbacher's next sentence, that "by 1857" Taney "had become as fanatical in his determination to protect the institution as Garrison was in his determination to destroy it," becomes correct if we add five crucial words—"from northern holier-than-thous": By 1857, Taney had become as fanatical in his determination to protect the institution *from northern holier-than-thous* as Garrison was in his determination to destroy it.

9. *SQR* 12 (1847): 133–35.

10. James M. Wayne, "Address of the Hon. James M. Wayne ... January 17th, 1854," *Thirty-Seventh Annual Report of the American Colonization Society* (Washington, 1854), 33–42. The best biography of Wayne is Alexander A. Lawrence, *James Moore Wayne, Southern Unionist* (Chapel Hill, 1943).

11. On this important point, see Lea VanderVelde and Sandya Subramanian, "Mrs. Dred Scott," *Yale Law Journal* 106 (1997): 1033–120.

12. Fehrenbacher, *Dred Scott,* 323–34, argues that a Court majority could be found against black citizenship. But the strained nature of his argument shows why the Court preferred to choose between the two decisions that could be reached without strain: for the Missouri law or against the Missouri Compromise.

13. The originals of all the judges' letters to Buchanan discussed in the text are in the Buchanan Papers, HSP, and published in Phillip Auchampaugh, "James Buchanan, the Court and the Dred Scott Decision," *Tennessee Historical Magazine* 9 (1926): 231–40. These letters, offering an unusual glimpse inside the Court's private debate on a crucial case, can be usefully supplemented by Benjamin R. Curtis's recollections in *A Memoir of Benjamin Robbins Curtis* ... , 2 vols. (Boston, 1879), 1: 234–35; by Campbell's and Nelson's recollections in Samuel Tyler, *Memoir of Roger B. Taney* (Baltimore, 1872), 382–85; and by Campbell's still later recollections in Campbell to George Curtis, October 30, 1879, Campbell-Colton Papers, NC.

14. This is my best guess at the solution to a minor mystery—why James Buchanan erroneously assumed, in his Inaugural Address, that the Court would rule against emancipation not only by Congress but also by a territorial legislature. According to Don

Fehrenbacher's alternative guess, Buchanan obtained a copy of Taney's written opinion, which as published contained a few sentences on a territorial legislature's power, before the March 4 inaugural. That guess seems to me shaky because Taney was still scribbling right up to his March 6 oral opinion, because he continued to scribble for weeks before filing his written opinion, and because we do not know whether the few sentences in question were in the oral opinion.

I prefer the guess that Buchanan misunderstood the elastic Catron line, "whatever you wish may be accomplished." Until this moment, Buchanan and Catron had perfectly understood each other. Furthermore, Catron, Buchanan's crony, knew exactly what Buchanan wished, and Buchanan knew that he knew. So upon hearing from Catron that "whatever you wish may be accomplished," Buchanan could have thought that his dearest wish, that the Court would sweep away every aspect of the controversy, would be accomplished. Still, this theory can only be a guess, for the surviving evidence is incomplete, lacking especially Buchanan's letters to the justices.

15. The dating of the judges' decisions in my narrative differs from some versions, and the dating is crucial, to establish the possibility that Buchanan's intervention mattered. According to some interpreters, the southern judges surrendered to Nelson on the first day of conference, February 14, and then took back the surrender sometime before February 19. If so, Buchanan's intrusion on Grier's mailbox, which occurred on February 23, would have transpired at least four days too late to matter.

But the notion that the Court decided Nelson's way on February *14* is based entirely on Catron's erroneous prediction, on February *10*, that the matter would on the fourteenth be decided. So too, the notion that the Court decided to repudiate Nelson *before* February *19* is based entirely on Catron's letter to Buchanan of that date. But that letter too contains only a prediction ("a majority of my brethren will be forced up to this point"). Still more important, Grier's letter of February 23 to Buchanan exudes a decision as yet unmade but now, *after* reception of Buchanan's letter, a decision hastily in the process of being made.

Straightening out the dating does not itself establish the importance of Buchanan's intervention. But I am pleased that Roy Nichols and Allan Nevins share my guess that Buchanan's intervention *did* matter. Nevins's subtle account of this case, while shaky on the dates, is especially fine on the uncertainty of whether the five Southerners heard, or only thought they heard, the two northern non-Democrats' threat to issue opinions affirming the constitutionality of congressional territorial emancipation. Nichols, *Disruption of American Democracy*, 78; Nevins, *The Emergence of Lincoln*, 2 vols. (New York, 1950), 1: 90–118, 2: 473–77.

16. Taney's decision and the associate judges' concurring and dissenting opinions can be found in *Dred Scott v. John F. A. Sandford*, 19 Howard 393 (1857).

Chapter 10. The Climactic Kansas Crisis

1. The 1857 Lecompton Convention that wrote a proposed proslavery constitution illustrated the irrelevance of the number of slaveholders. All fifty-two voting delegates sought an enslaved state. Only seven owned slaves. Etcheson, *Bleeding Kansas*, 151.

2. CC, September 5, 1857; RS, July 21, 1857; NOD, July 14, 1854.

3. NOD, March 14, October 20, 1857; RS, May 2, 1857; RE, September 12, 1856.

4. *Montgomery Advertiser*, June 14, 1856; RE, April 14, 1856.

5. Alexander Stephens to Thomas Thomas, January 16, 1857, Stephens Papers, DU.

6. Ruffin in CM, May 13, 1857; *New Orleans Commercial Bulletin*, September 18, 1857.

7. Lower South newspapers often contained this Buford appeal; see, for example, *Montgomery Advertiser*, December 6, 1855; CM, February 4, 1856; DBR 21 (1856): 187–94.

8. *Montgomery Journal,* April 7, 1856; *Washington National Intelligencer,* April 12, 1856; Walter L. Fleming, "The Buford Expedition to Kansas," *AHR* 6 (1900): 38–48.

9. On Brown's expectations when Kansas-Nebraska was passed, see his U.S. Senate speech of December 1856 in M. W. Cluskey, ed., *The Speeches, Messages, and Other Writings of the Hon. Albert G. Brown . . .* (New York, 1859), 498. Brown's initial appeal, dated November 24, 1855, appeared throughout the South; see *St. Louis Democrat,* January 3, 1856; and *Jackson Semi-Weekly Mississippian,* December 11, 1855.

10. *CS,* June 25, 1856.

11. Ibid., June 15, 1856; *Savannah Georgian,* September 4, 1856; Robert F. W. Allston Papers, January–February 1856, SCHS.

12. *Aberdeen Sunny South,* September 18, 1856.

13. Ibid., October 30, 1856.

14. *CS,* July 23, 1856.

15. James P. Shenton, *Robert John Walker: A Politician from Jackson to Lincoln* (New York, 1961); Freehling, *Road* 1: 418–24.

16. Walker's inaugural is in Kansas Historical Society *Transactions* (Topeka, 1890), 5: 328–41.

17. Freehling, *Road* 1: 190–93.

18. *CM,* June 9, 27, 1857; *Jackson Mississippian,* July 1, 1857; Francis Pickens to Buchanan, August 5, 1857, Buchanan Papers, HSP.

19. Walker to Buchanan, October 3, 1856, Buchanan Papers, HSP.

20. *CC,* February 9, 1858.

21. While partisanship had its role in this vicious Lower South ex-Whig attack, the assault also reads to me as sincere conviction that the Democracy was at last showing its hypocritical colors. See in particular the late 1857 files of the *Mobile Daily Advertiser* and its running war with the Democracy's *Mobile Daily Register.*

22. Howell Cobb to John B. Lamar, July 10, 1857, in R. P. Brooks, ed., "Howell Cobb Papers," *GHQ* 6 (1922), 235–36.

23. Lucius Q. C. Lamar to Howell Cobb, July 17, 1857, Cobb Papers, GA, partially printed in P., ed., *T., S., & C.* 2: 405–6. The Cobb Papers contain other Southern Democrats' letters in Lamar's vein.

24. Cobb to Lamar, July 27, 1857, Robert Walker Papers, New York Historical Society.

25. *Lawrence* (Kans.) *Herald of Freedom,* October 10, 24, 31, 1857.

26. On Martin's mission and the Cobb/Thompson letters, see 36 Cong., 1 sess., House Report No. 448, 103, 110–14, 157–71, 314–23.

27. The whole text of the Lecompton Constitution is in *Washington National Intelligencer,* December 7, 1857.

28. 36 Cong., 1 sess., House Report No. 448, 318–19.

29. Buchanan to Walker, July 12, 1857, ibid., 112–13.

30. Kenneth M. Stampp cogently defends the alternative guess about Buchanan's possibilities in the Lecompton Controversy in *America in 1857: A Nation on the Brink* (New York, 1995).

I guess against the probability that Buchanan could have changed history in the Lecompton Convention tale, but for that probability in the so-called Dred Scott Decision, largely because of the difference between private Court deliberations and public political brawls. The Lecompton delegates were frontier ruffians who had been playing a desperate game for Kansas. They seem to me unlikely to have renounced a last wild fling of the dice, whatever a president said. So too, Lower South Democrats such as Cobb seem to me unlikely to insist to an almighty state convention, whatever a president thought, lest their ex-Whig opponents convict them of disloyalty to true-blue southern principle.

The Supreme Court judges in private chambers, on the other hand, had none of the Kansas conventioneers' live-or-die stake in throwing down a particular decree. They also had none of the southern public politicians' peril of being trapped in a demonstration of "disloyalty." They thus seem to me more capable of stepping reluctantly, privately, and silently away from their preferred decision—and more in need of a president-elect's counsel to stride for (they thought) glory.

31. For the Lecompton and Topeka votes, see Rawley, *Race and Politics*, 232–33.

32. Recounted with the dramatic flair I admire in Nevins, *Emergence of Lincoln* 1: 253.

33. Quoted in ibid., 258.

34. John Letcher to Gideon Cameron, February 9, 1859, Cameron Papers, WVU.

35. T.R.R. Cobb to Howell Cobb, March 24, 1858, Howell Cobb Papers, GA.

36. Graphic descriptions are in *CM*, February 8, 1856; Alexander Stephens to Linton Stephens, February 5, 1858, SP, M; J. Holt Merchant, Jr., "Laurence M. Keitt, South Carolina Fire-Eater" (Ph.D. dissertation, University of Virginia, 1976), 167–68.

37. See *CG*, 35 Cong., 1 sess., 1258–65, for the final Senate maneuvering and vote.

38. See ibid., 1435–45, for the climactic House maneuvering and vote.

39. *CM*, April 5, 1858.

40. Ibid.

41. Guy M. Bryan to his brother, May 6, 1858, Bryan Papers, TX.

42. The tale of the English Bill is accurately rendered in Etcheson, *Bleeding Kansas*, 179–84.

43. C. C. Woolworth to Calvin Wiley, May 20, 1857, Wiley Papers, NC.

44. *New Orleans Courier*, August 15, 1857.

Chapter 11. Caribbean Delusions

1. *New York Morning News*, February 7, 1845; Julius Pratt, "John L. O'Sullivan and Manifest Destiny," *New York History* 14 (1933): 213–34. The term "Manifest Destiny" seems to have originated not with O'Sullivan or a southern male but with a lady who wrote for O'Sullivan. See the intriguing detective work in Linda S. Hudson, *Mistress of Manifest Destiny: A Biography of Jane McManus Storm Cazneau, 1807–1878* (Austin, 2001). The best study of the nationalistic origins of what only later became a slaveholders' movement is still Albert K. Weinberg, *Manifest Destiny: A Study of Nationalistic Expansionism in American History* (Baltimore, 1935).

2. *New Orleans Commercial Bulletin*, April 2, 1858; Rhett in *CM*, July 7, 1859; Tucker in *RE*, November 13, 1854.

3. John Bassett Moore, ed., *The Works of James Buchanan*, 12 vols. (Philadelphia, 1908–11), 10: 173–75.

4. *CG*, 33 Cong., 2 sess., House Executive Document No. 93.

5. Alexander Stephens to Linton Stephens, February 28, 1858, SP, M.

6. The best writer on the filibusterers, Robert E. May, has doubled our pleasure with *The Southern Dream of a Caribbean Empire, 1854–1861* (Athens, Ga., 1989) and *Manifest Destiny's Underworld: Filibustering in Antebellum America* (Chapel Hill, 2002). Professor May might have better sorted out the socio-psychological causes of the movement, particularly in New Orleans. But he has found and presented a rich array of data.

7. The first requirement for studying nineteenth-century New Orleans, as for researching Old Charleston, is to visit the twenty-first-century city. Even Katrina has barely touched the rich nineteenth-century remains of the original Crescent City, just as Old Charleston has survived terrible hurricanes. I write about the pleasure and profit of the tourist mode of researching those urban pasts in "Charleston's Battery and New Orleans' Jackson Square," in *American Places . . .* , ed. William E. Leuchtenburg (New York, 2000), 145–56.

Among the many New Orleans literary remains that confirm and add to what the traveler can still see, my favorites include Charles Mackay, *Life and Liberty in America . . .* , 2 vols. (London, 1859), 1: 271; Frederick Law Olmsted, *A Journey in the Seaboard Slave States* (New York, 1856), 587, 594–96; Henry A. Murray, *Lands of the*

Slave and the Free (London, 1855), 248 ff.; Wilham Kingsford, *Impressions of the South and West* . . . (Toronto, 1858), 57ff.; William T. Sherman, *Home Letters* . . . (New York, 1909), letters of February 11, November 4, 1852; Russell, *My Diary North and South*, 227–31; *NOD*, February 15, 1856, September 18, 1858; *Baltimore American*, February 8, 1860; A. R. Reed Diary, entries for December 9–19, 1860, Tulane University Library; John Norris to My Dear Friends, January 13, 1847, Norris Papers, LSU; Memorandum dated June 20, 1848, William S. Cooper Letterbook, TN; William Campbell to David Campbell, December 6, 1853, William Campbell to Mrs. William Campbell, January 7, 1854, David Campbell Papers, DU; James Johnston Pettigrew to James C. Johnston, February 15, 1853, Pettigrew Papers, NC; John Manning to his wife, March 4, 1851, Williams-Chesnut-Manning Papers, SC.

8. Thomas R. R. Cobb to William Mitchell, July 9, 1858, Cobb Papers, GA; C. C. Clay, Jr., to C. C. Clay, Sr., December 11, 1858, Clay Papers, DU.

9. *Baltimore American*, February 8, 1860.

10. To read the New Orleans newspapers of the 1850s, and especially the *Delta*, is to feel the omnipotence of this quest to replace the Mississippi River commerce, partially seized by northern seaboard cities and their railroads, with a Gulf commercial empire, integrated into the United States. This central New Orleans motive for financing and publicizing filibustering is almost as if copied from crude Marxist polemics about commercial imperialism, which makes curious the fact that the several fine Marxist southern historians have largely missed the phenomenon. Excellent (although obscure) exceptions (and perhaps not even Marxists) are Richard Tansey, "Southern Expansionism: Urban Interests in the Cuban Filibusters," *PS* 1 (1979): 227–51; C. Stanley Urban, "The Idea of Progress and Southern Imperialism: New Orleans and the Caribbean, 1845–1861" (Ph.D. dissertation, Northwestern University, 1943); Urban, "The Ideology of Southern Imperialism: New Orleans and the Caribbean, 1845–1860," *Louisiana Historical Quarterly*, 39 (1956): 48–73.

Instead of following the (Marxist-compatible) lead that Stanley Urban exhaustively documented and that Tansey has skillfully elaborated, Marxist historians, led by Eugene Genovese, have seen some alleged rural economic crisis, supposedly caused by the inefficiency of plantation slave labor, as the root of late antebellum southern passion for fresh land. But as Robert May points out, little evidence for any such motive survives in the sources on filibustering (indeed, little evidence that filibusterers had any intention of finding fresh land to farm). Genovese, *The Political Economy of Slavery: Studies in the Economy and Society of the Slave South* (New York, 1965); Robert E. May, "Epilogue to the Missouri Compromise: The South, the Balance of Power, and the Tropics in the 1850s," *PS* 1 (1979): 201–25.

Additionally, I see little reason to think that rural Southerners of the 1850s feared economic crisis, not in the midst of the boom they were experiencing, especially not in the midst of the wildest boom of them all, in the Louisiana delta. The economic compulsion in the rural Southwest during the 1850s was to find the new labor to work the excess of virgin land. Economic despondency only afflicted the South Carolinians (who tended to be against Caribbean expansion, as we will see)—and that real economic proponent of filibustering, the New Orleans mercantile community.

As Robert May again accurately notes, the major slaveholder impulse behind filibustering was nothing directly economic but rather desire to protect slavery politically in the Union. The parallel with the major impulse behind the Kansas fling is obvious. Still, protecting slaves had a major economic aspect, for the pecuniary stake in saving this huge economic system was immense. Here I find myself back where I began. In my first book, *Prelude to Civil War: The Nullification Controversy in South Carolina, 1816–1836* (New York, 1966), I urged that the economic impulse behind nullification was not so much lowering the tariff as sustaining investments in slaves. That same indirect economic concern fortified the primarily political impulses behind the territorial issue, whether in Kansas or the Caribbean.

11. *New Orleans Commercial Bulletin,* May 6, 1850; *NOD,* October 31, 1855; *New Orleans Crescent,* February 18, 1858.

12. My research here confirmed Robert May's masterful analyses in *Underworld,* ch. 4, esp. 104ff.

13. *NOD,* June 14, 1854.

14. Jefferson Davis, *Speeches . . . Summer . . . 1858* (Baltimore, 1859), 27–28; John Bell in *CG,* 35 Cong., 2 sess., Appendix, 1344. Davis, like many Southerners, was dubious not so much about annexing Cuba as about seizing it by filibustering and admitting it to the Union instead of establishing a protectorate over the island.

15. Matthew F. Maury, *The Amazon, and the Atlantic Slopes of South America* (Washington, 1853).

16. Mary B. Blackford to Mathew F. Maury, n.d. [December 1851], Maury Papers, LC.

17. Maury to Bickford, December 24, 1851, Maury Papers, LC.

18. Frank Blair, Jr., to Frank Blair, Sr., October 22, 1858, Blair-Lee Papers, Princeton University.

19. Frank Blair, Jr., *The Destiny of the Races of the Continent* (Washington, 1859).

20. *RE,* March 2, 1859; *Jackson Semi-Weekly Mississippian,* May 24, 1859.

21. Laurence Keitt, *Speech . . . April 16, 1855* (n.p., n.d. [Columbia, S.C., 1855]); Rhett in *CM,* July 7, 1859.

22. May, *Southern Dream,* 203–5. Among the hundreds of examples: James Gadsden to James Hammond, October 25, 1858, Hammond to William Gilmore Simms, April 8, 1860, Hammond Papers, LC; *CM,* March 10, 31, 1859.

23. *CS,* October 12, November 7, 1854.

24. Calhoun quoted in May, *Southern Dream,* 15; James Gadsden to James Hammond, May 20, 1858, Hammond Papers, LC; Francis Sumter to James Chesnut, Jr., February 2, 1859, Chesnut-Manning-Miller Papers, SC.

25. Lewis Ayer, *Southern Rights and the Cuban Question* (Columbia, S.C., 1855).

26. *NOD,* May 10, 1856. See also March 16, 30, 1859.

27. Davis, *Speeches . . . Summer . . . 1858,* 27–28; *Aberdeen Sunny South,* April 16, 1857.

28. Buchanan quoted in May, *Southern Dream,* 114. For the decisive congressional votes, see *CG,* 35 Cong., 2 sess., 318.

29. On López we have a fine book: Tom Chaplin, *Fatal Glory: Narciso López and the First Clandestine War Against Cuba* (Charlottesville, 1996).

30. Henry M. Spofford to Lucy Petway Holcomb Pickens, June 19, 1855, Francis Pickens Papers, DU.

31. Walker to Charles J. Jenkins, September 2, 1857, copy in M. B. Lamar Papers, Texas State Archives and Library.

32. Good on these aspects of Walker is Amy S. Greenberg, *Manifest Manhood and the Antebellum American Empire* (New York, 2005).

33. *RS,* June 23, 1857; *Aberdeen Sunny South,* July 1, 1858. See also *Augusta Constitutionalist,* July 7, 1857, and Albert Z. Carr, *The World and William Walker* (New York, 1963).

34. On this most important, most southern, and, paradoxically, most Yankee of southern filibusterers, we are blessed with the most telling batch of private letters, Quitman Papers, MISS, nicely supplemented by the Quitman Papers, Harvard University, and the best biography, by, no surprise, Robert E. May, *John Quitman: Old South Crusader* (Baton Rouge, 1985).

35. Monmouth is another antebellum Southern phenomenon that is best seen with one's own eyes; fortunately, it is now impeccably restored and a public hotel.

36. Freehling, *Road 1:* 525–28.

37. Quitman to B. F. Dill, n.d [late 1854], Quitman Papers, MISS; John S. Thrasher to J. J. Pettigrew, December 7, 1855, Pettigrew Papers, NC.

38. *NOD,* January 15, May 23, 1854.

39. *RE,* May 26, 1854; *Baltimore Republican,* May 16, 1854; *New Orleans Courier,* November 26, 1854.

40. The many examples of such letters to Quitman in the Quitman Papers, MISS, include missives from H. Forno (February 9, 1855), John S. Ford (June 5, 1854), W. M. Estelle (May 26, 1854), and J. W. Lesesne (June 6, 1854).

41. *New Orleans Crescent,* June 27, July 2, July 4, 1854.

Chapter 12. Reopening the African Slave Trade

1. Freehling, *Road* 1: 135–38.

The movement to reopen the African slave trade almost always receives short shrift in accounts of the coming of the Civil War. The reason: The radicalism never captured anything close to a southern majority and thus allegedly must be considered an antebellum sideshow. But by that reasoning, secessionism, also never commanding a majority until Lincoln "coerced" the disunionists, also must be considered a sideshow. The point is that a disunionist minority ultimately made majoritarian history (as minorities often do). While antisecessionists sometimes wished to reopen the African slave trade, the movement was primarily the secessionists', as was nothing else. (Caribbean expansionism, for example, was most often seen as an alternative to disunion.) Thus the reopening campaign offers the best window into the (minority) mentality that would ultimately make a revolution. Something so analytically valuable deserves central consideration.

The best book on the reopeners' movement remains Ronald Takaki's excellent *A Pro-Slavery Crusade: The Agitation to Reopen the African Slave Trade* (New York, 1971). I believe that Professor Takaki overemphasizes southern "guilt" about slavery. But then again, I believe that the same overemphasis weakens my *Prelude to Civil War.* I also now believe that our inspiring mutual teacher, Charles Sellers, Jr., took this argument somewhat too far in his pathbreaking "The Travail of Slavery," in *The Southerner as American,* ed. Sellers (Chapel Hill, 1960), ch. 3.

That slaveholders' own unease (I now like that word better than "guilt") accounts for part of their mentality and action is now more or less accepted, even by those who once fought the "Sellerites" tooth and nail. This ex-Sellerite, in turn, thinks that the believers somewhat underestimated the Christian sources of unease and somewhat overplayed the republican sources and that divisions between southern races, classes, and regions, more than divisions inside the slaveholder mentality, accounted for the culture's internal turmoil—and for the movement to reopen the African slave trade.

2. The following biographical sketch is gleaned from A. W. Cockrell, Jr., "Descendants of Thomas 'Kanana' Spratt," unpublished ms in SC; *Memphis Daily Appeal,* September 12, 1857; *CC,* January 12, 1861.

3. *NOD,* November 17, 1858.

4. *CS,* August 18, 1855; *DBR* 27 (1859): 210.

5. *CS,* November 21, 1856.

6. *DBR* 20 (1856): 143–56, esp. 150.

7. *CS,* November 25, 1854, September 21, 1856.

8. Ibid., July 25, 1854, September 21, 1856.

9. Ibid., October 10, 1856.

10. Ibid., September 10, 1855.

11. Ibid., April 26, October 21, 1856.

12. *DBR* 24 (1858): 484.

13. *CS,* July 12, 1854.

14. Ibid., August 2, 1855.

15. *CC,* December 22, 1858.

16. Edward Bryan, *Letters . . . in Relation to the African Slave Trade* (Charleston, S.C., 1858), 14.

17. *NOD,* February 17, 1858.

18. Bryan, *Letters,* 35–36.

19. *NOD,* February 14, 1857.

20. Ibid., April 11, 1857.

21. *DBR* 24 (1858): 584–87.

22. *New Orleans Courier,* May 21, 1858.

23. J. Johnston Pettigrew, *Report of the Minority . . . as Relates to Slavery and the Slave Trade* (Charleston, S.C., 1858).

24. Brooke in *DBR* 27 (1859): 361; Alfred Huger to Wade Hampton, December 17, 1856, Huger Papers, DU.

25. *Baltimore Courier,* March 6, 1858; David Campbell to Wilham Campbell, January 30, 1857, Campbell Papers, DU.

26. Robert G. Harper, *An Argument Against . . . Reopening the African Slave Trade* (Atlanta, 1858).

27. *DBR* 27 (1859): 220.

28. Davis in *Jackson Semi-Weekly Mississippian,* July 26, 1859; Linton Stephens to Alexander Stephens, July 3, 1859, and Alexander back to Linton, July 5, 1859, SP, M; J. Henley Smith to Stephens, July 24, 1859, Stephens Papers, LC.

29. Quoted in Takaki, *Pro-Slavery Crusade,* 116.

30. Adams's message was printed first in *CM,* November 26, 1856; Spratt's hurrah was in *CS,* also on November 26, 1856.

31. Edward B. Bryan, *Report of the Special Committee . . . on . . . the Message of his Excellency Gov. Jas. H. Adams . . .* (Columbia, S.C., 1857); Pettigrew, *Report of the Minority.*

32. *CM,* March 9, 1859.

33. *South Carolina Senate Journal, 1857* (Columbia, 1857), 89.

34. *Augusta Daily Constitution,* November 30, 1858; *Milledgeville Triweekly Southern Recorder,* November 27, 1858; John E. Ward to Howell Cobb, November 1, 1858, Cobb Papers, GA; *Journal of the Senate of the State of Georgia, 1858* (Columbus, 1858), 211–12.

35. *New Orleans Crescent,* January 17, 1859; *DBR* 26 (1959): 482.

36. Henry Hughes cleverly defended the proposition (and without obscuration) in *DBR* 25 (1858): 626–53.

37. *Official Journal of the House of Representatives . . . 1858* (Baton Rouge, 1858), 64–65.

38. *New Orleans Crescent,* March 22, 1858.

39. Ibid., April 7, June 6, July 12, 1858.

40. Ibid., April 28, 1858; *Official Journal of the Senate . . . 1858* (Baton Rouge, 1858), 115.

41. *Official Journal of the Senate . . . 1858,* 118.

42. *RE,* May 19, 1858; *Montgomery Advertiser,* August 31, 1859.

43. *DBR* 26 (1859): 713; 27 (1859): 94–99, 205–14.

44. Takaki, *Pro-Slavery Crusade,* ch. 9.

45. D. H. Hamilton to R. J. Cralle, March 1, 1856, Cralle Papers, LC.

46. Hamilton to James Hammond, September 10, 1858, Hammond Papers, LC.

47. James H. Adams to James Chesnut, Jr., January 14, 1859, Chesnut-Miller-Manning Papers, SCHS.

Chapter 13. Reenslaving Free Blacks

1. On southern free blacks, we have Ira Berlin's masterful *Slaves Without Masters: The Free Negro in the Antebellum South* (New York, 1974). Leon Litwack's *North of Slavery: The Negro in the Free States* (Chicago, 1961) provides fine perspective.

More perspectives come from exceptions to the dismal free black norm, including Judith Kelleher Schafer, *Becoming Free, Remaining Free: Manumission and Enslavement in New Orleans, 1846–1862* (Baton Rouge, 2003); William Ransom Hogan and James Edwin Davis, *The Barber of Natchez* (Baton Rouge, 1954); Davis and Hogan, eds., *William Johnson's Natchez: The Antebellum Diary of a Free Negro* (Baton Rouge, 1951); David O. Whitten, *Andrew Durnford: A Black Sugar Planter in Antebellum Louisiana* (Natchitoches, 1981); and especially Michael P. Johnson and James L. Roarke, *Black Masters: A Free Family of Color in the Old South* (New York, 1984) and *No Chariot Let Down: Charleston's Free People of Color on the Eve of the Civil War* (Chapel Hill, 1984).

The latest book on free black exceptions to the normally grim tale, Melvin Ely's *Israel on the Appomattox: A Southern Experiment in Black Freedom from the 1790s Through the Civil War* (New York, 2004), attempts to promote an unusual case into a partial refutation of Professor Berlin's chilling portrait of the awful norm. But the excellent case study is doomed by its very exceptionalness to fall short in this regard.

2. *RS*, February 2, 1858; *RE*, February 10, 1858.

3. *Aberdeen Sunny South*, October 13, 1859.

4. *Mobile Daily Register*, January 8, 1859.

5. Petitions from George Latimer et al., John B. Peyton et al., and Herbert W. Hill et al., Petitions to the Legislature of 1860, Legislative Records, MISS.

6. Ira Berlin and Herbert G. Gutman, "Natives and Immigrants," skillfully puts the Charleston problem in Southwide perspective. For all aspects of the Charleston minicrisis, Professors Johnson and Roarke's two super volumes are indispensable. For the Charleston quantitative data, see *Black Masters*, 177, 185; *No Chariot*, 6, 69.

7. Johnson and Roarke, *No Chariot*, 135.

8. *CC*, December 16, 1859.

9. Johnson and Roarke's *No Chariot* publishes agonized letters on a crisis that tormented the brown aristocrats, even though most of them escaped its ravages.

10. Freehling, *Road* 1: 197–207.

11. *Maryland Colonization Journal* 9 (1958): 273–74.

12. The Maryland reenslavement story, one of the Old South's richest, still awaits a storyteller who can equal Professors Johnson and Roarke's tale of Charleston. But for good perspective, see Barbara Fields, *Slavery and Freedom on the Middle Ground: Maryland During the Nineteenth Century* (New Haven, 1985).

13. Bowers's plight is detailed in *Wilmington Delaware Gazette*, July 30, 1858.

14. *Elkton Cecil Whig*, November 20, 1858.

15. C. W. Jacobs to J.A.J. Cresswell, January 15, 1866, Vertical File, MHS.

16. The Baltimore convention's proceedings, including Jacobs's speeches and delegates' answers, are in *Maryland Colonization Journal* 10 (1859): July issue; *Baltimore Sun*, June 11, 1859.

17. Curtis M. Jacobs, *Speech . . . in the House of Delegates, on the 17th of February, 1860* (Annapolis, 1860). See also Jacobs, *The Free Negro Question in Maryland* (Baltimore, 1859).

18. The best answer to Jacobs was Andrew B. Cross, *To Mr. Jacobs . . . A Few Thoughts on These Most Monstrous Propositions Before the Legislature . . .* (n.p., n.d. [Baltimore, 1860]) The debate on Jacobs's propositions and the ultimate anti-Jacobs resolution can be followed in *Baltimore Republican*, February 7, 8, 11, 15, 25, March 8, 10, 11, 1860; *Baltimore American*, February 14, 15, 21, 27, 1860; Easton *Eastern Star*, February 14, 21, 28, 1860; *Maryland Colonization Journal* 10 (1860): 137–45; *Baltimore Clipper*, February 16, 21, 25, March 3, 1860.

19. *Baltimore American*, November 17, 1860; *Elkton Cecil Whig*, November 17, 1860.

20. *Montgomery Daily Advertiser*, December 21, 1859.

21. Berlin, *Slaves Without Masters*, 372–80.

22. John Hope Franklin and Loren Schweninger, *In Search of the Promised Land: A Slave Family in the Old South* (New York, 2006), 18.

23. Garnett in *RE*, February 19, 1856; *Montgomery Daily Advertiser*, July 24, 1858.
24. *New Orleans Crescent*, June 16, 1859.

Chapter 14. John Brown and Violent Invasion

1. *CG*, 36 Cong., 1 sess., 282.

2. Paul M. Angle, ed., *Created Equal: The Complete Lincoln-Douglas Debates of 1858* (Chicago, 1958), 2.

3. George E. Baker, ed., *The Works of William H. Seward*, 5 vols. (Boston, 1853–84), 4: 289–302.

4. Quoted in Stephen B. Oates, *To Purge This Land with Blood: A Biography of John Brown* (New York, 1970), 249. The following account is drawn from Oates's work and from Richard O. Boyer, *The Legend of John Brown: A Biography and History* (New York, 1973); O. G. Villard, *John Brown, 1800–1859: A Biography Fifty Years After* (Boston, 1910); and David S. Reynolds, *John Brown, Abolitionist . . .* (New York, 2005). Professor Reynolds's book, the latest, is magnificent on Brown's northern intellectual supporters; no one should ever doubt again that American men of ideas can stir epic action. But the book is shaky on the facts and subtleties of the southern response. On the charged Brown subject, even the most skillful historians have trouble getting both sections' stories quite right.

5. Quoted in Reynolds, *John Brown*, 299.

6. Ibid., 26.

7. Quoted in ibid., 272.

8. Quoted in Potter, *Impending Crisis*, 360–61.

9. For the journalist's account and Mrs. Newby's plea, see Reynolds, *John Brown*, 320.

10. *Norfolk Southern Argus*, December 28, 1859.

11. H. R. Davis to Henry Wise, November 16, 1859, J. A. Crook to Wise, December 6, 1859, Wise-Brown Papers, LC.

12. Andrew Hunter to Wise, November 18, 1859, Wise-Brown Papers, LC.

13. Linton Stephens to Alexander Stephens, February 3, 1860, SP, M.

14. *CM*, January 4, 1860.

15. W. D. Duncan to James Hammond, December 2, 1859, Hammond Papers, LC.

16. *New Orleans True Delta*, November 24, 1859.

17. Quoted in Reynolds, *John Brown*, 429.

18. Quoted in Oates, *To Purge This Land*, 338.

19. Edward Stone, ed., *Incident at Harper's Ferry* (Englewood Cliffs, N.J., 1956), 149. Despite the often-made error in its title (it should be Harpers, not Harper's), this is a fine anthology, especially for classroom use.

20. Ibid., 160.

21. Ibid., 218. This is my favorite of several inspiring versions that Yankee troops sang. Evidently all the varieties originated, ironically, in a mocking hymn. See Boyd B. Stutler, "John Brown's Body," *CWH* 4 (1958): 251–60.

22. Emerson quoted in Reynolds, *John Brown*, 366; Thoreau and Phillips in Stone, *Incident*, 186, 188; Garrison in Oates, *To Purge this Land*, 355.

23. The Brown-Wise confrontation is especially skillfully conveyed in Simpson, *Wise*, ch. 11.

24. *RE*, October 21, 1859.

25. Reynolds, *John Brown*, 366.

26. Barton H. Wise, *The Life of Henry A. Wise, 1806–1876* (New York, 1899), 247n.

27. *RE*, December 4, 1859. The following paragraph is based on this same source, comprising Wise's superlative message to the legislature on all aspects of the Brown crisis.

28. Ruffin's newspaper article in *Virginia Index*, January 13, 1860, copy in Ruffin Diary for that date, LC; William Cabell Rives, Jr., to Rives, Sr., November 11, 1859, Rives Papers, LC; William H. Tayloe to B. O. Tayloe, December 17, 1859, Edward D. Tayloe Papers, NC.

29. James O. Breeden, "Rehearsal for Secession? The Return Home of Southern Medical Students from Philadelphia in 1859," in *His Soul Goes Marching On: Responses to the Harpers Ferry Raid,* ed. Paul Finkelman (Charlottesville, 1995), 174–210. This wonderful book of essays wins my vote for the most helpful single volume on the Brown crisis. My favorite essay, Peter Wallenstein's, 149–73, especially shows that the southern side of the crisis involved far more than Brown and far more than fear of Yankee precipitation of slave revolts.

30. Scarborough, ed., *Ruffin Diary,* 1: 361.

31. All quoted in Reynolds, *John Brown,* 361–62, 427.

32. *U.S. Senate Committee Reports, 1859–60* 2: 1–25.

Chapter 15. John G. Fee and Religious Invasion

1. The best biography is Victor B. Howard, *The Evangelical War Against Slavery and Caste: The Life and Times of John G. Fee* (Susquehanna, N.Y., 1993). The best account of the Berea movement, Richard D. Sears, *The Day of Small Things: Abolitionism in the Midst of Slavery, Berea, Kentucky, 1854–1864* (Lanham, Md., 1986), is also full of biographical details on Fee, as is Fee, *Autobiography of John G. Fee* (Chicago, 1891). In addition to these obscure but fine publications, Fee is expertly put in a larger Kentucky perspective in Harold D. Tallant, *Evil Necessity: Slavery and Political Culture in Antebellum Kentucky* (Lexington, Ky., 2003), and in a still larger southern perspective in Stanley Harrold's equally expert *The Abolitionists and the South, 1831–1861* (Lexington, Ky., 1995). About this least well known of the major southern prewar dramas, we also have perhaps the richest mine of manuscripts in the Berea College Library. This irony is likely to be dissolved when Marion B. Lucas's eagerly awaited work on Fee is published. I am indebted to Professor Lucas for his helpful comments on this chapter.

2. Fee, *Autobiography,* 13–17; Howard, *Evangelical War,* 22–23.

3. Fee, *An Anti-Slavery Manual* (Maysville, Ky., 1848), ix, 123, 145. This publication takes pride of place among Fee's teachings, closely followed by *Nonfellowship with Slaveholders: The Duty of Christians* (New York, 1855) and *The Sinfulness of Slaveholding Shown by Appeals to Reason and Scripture* (New York, 1851).

4. This tale, one of the Old South's most riveting and dismaying, can be followed in Fee, *Autobiography,* 61, 65–67; Sears, *Small Things,* 8–10, 98–99, 104–5; I. W. Smith to Fee, Fee Papers, BC; Fee to Lewis Tappan, June 10, 1847, American Missionary Association Papers, Fisk University Library. The Fee family sometimes spelled Julett "Juliet." For a moving use of Julett in Fee's own teaching, see his "Appeal to Kentucky Children," November 1859, Fee Papers, BC.

5. Fee, *Anti-Slavery Manual,* 2, 123, 141.

6. Ibid., 123.

7. Ibid.

8. Ibid., xi.

9. Freehling, *Road* 1: 462–74.

10. Sears, *Small Things,* 36; John White in *Berea Citizen,* September 21, 1922, copy in Fee Papers, BC.

11. Fee's Letter #3 to American Missionary Association, copy in Fee Papers, BC; Sears, *Small Things,* chs. 5–8.

12. Sears, *Small Things,* 38.

13. Ibid., 39–40.

14. Fee described the confrontation in *Berea Evangelist,* March 1, 1885, copy in Fee Papers, BC.

15. Fee described these events in letters to Cassius Clay of July 28, August 3, August 27, September 17, 1857, January 19, 1858, copies in Fee Papers, BC. On Fee's resulting paralyzing headaches, see Fee to Gerrit Smith, March 29, 1862, copy in Fee Papers, BC.

16. Stowe's 1858 article in the *Liberator* is quoted in Sears, *Small Things,* 75.

17. For descriptions of the stern Rogers and the jolly school he ran, with the help of his wife, Lizzie, see Elizabeth Embree Rogers, "Full Forty Years" (1896) and "A Personal History of Berea College" (circa 1910), typescripts in BC; John A. R. Rogers, *Birth of Berea College: A Story of Providence* (Philadelphia, 1904); John A. R. Rogers Journal, Berea College; Sears, *Small Things,* ch. 10.

18. Fee to American Missionary Association, November 9, 1855, December 13, 1856, January 4, 1857, copies in Fee Papers, BC.

19. Quoted in Sears, *Small Things,* 273–74.

20. On the expulsion, see ibid., ch. 12; Rogers, *Berea College,* ch. 10; *Louisville Daily Courier,* January 2, 1860; George Candee to Cassius Clay, December 26, 1859, April 24, 1860, copies in Fee Papers, BC.

Chapter 16. John Underwood and Economic Invasion

1. *RE,* December 6, 1859.

2. Wise to Mary Lyons Wise, March 14, 23, 1855, Wise Family Papers, VHS.

3. Wise to Captain John Scott, November 17, 1859, John Hay Papers, LC; A. R. Boteler to Wise, December 17, 1859, B. H. Ferguson to Wise, December 24, 1859, both in Wise-Brown Papers, LC.

4. A full-scale biography would be an important addition to Civil War history. A start is made in Patricia Hickin, "John C. Underwood and the Antislavery Movement in Virginia, 1847–1860," *VHMB* 73 (1965): 155–68. Dr. Hickin's University of Virginia Ph.D. dissertation, "Antislavery in Virginia, 1831–1861" (1968), and master's thesis, "John C. Underwood and the Antislavery Crusade, 1809–1860" (1961), are packed with useful information. By far the best study of southern antislavery, Harrold, *Abolitionists and the South,* esp. ch. 6, skillfully puts Underwood in perspective. The Underwood Papers, LC, and especially its Underwood Scrapbook, will also ease the way toward fulfilling this promising assignment.

5. Underwood to Gideon Camden, August 8, 1851, Camden Papers, WVU.

6. Same to same, June 19, 1851, Camden Papers, WVU.

7. A newspaper clipping (unidentified) containing the speech is in the Underwood Scrapbook, p. 1, LC.

8. M. G. Underwood to John Underwood, June 23, 1856, Underwood Papers, LC; Underwood to Eli Thayer, March 11, 1857, Thayer Papers, Brown University Library.

9. Hickin, "Antislavery in Virginia," 635–59; Underwood to Gideon Camden, April 4, 1858, Camden Papers, WVU; Underwood to ?, April 20, 1857, clipping of letter in Underwood Scrapbook, p. 37, LC.

10. Undated speech in New York, late 1850s, in Underwood Scrapbook, p. 59, LC; Underwood to Archibald Campbell, March 21, 1859, Campbell Papers, WVU.

11. On the Ceredo episode, Elizabeth K. McClintic, "Ceredo: An Experiment in Colonization and a Dream of Empire," *West Virginia Review* 15 (1938): 168–90, 198–200, 233–54, is a good summary. The Eli Thayer Papers, Brown University Library, 1857, are full of letters from Underwood and from possible purchasers.

12. Clipping in Underwood Scrapbook, p. 58, LC; Harrold, *Abolitionists of the South,* 114–15.

13. Harrold, *Abolitionists of the South,* 114; Underwood to editor of the *New York Evening Post,* November 23, 1858, copy in Underwood Scrapbook, p. 41, LC.

14. *Galveston News,* April 21, 28, 1857; *Jackson Semi-Weekly Mississippian,* September 23, 1859; *NOD,* May 1, 19, 1857.

15. Wise to Albert J. J. Rives, August 24, 1857, Executive Letterbook, VSL.

16. David Brown's "Attacking Slavery from Within: The Making of *The Impending Crisis of the South,*" *JSH* 70 (2004): 541–76, is the most important biographical article about Helper. I predict that his imminent book-length biography will be equally fine. Professor Brown, like Peter Wallenstein, understands that the John Brown crisis swiftly skidded past Brown; while Brown raised infuriated awareness that Republicans meant to press beyond containment, Helper raised acute understanding that Southern Republicans would carry on the invasion. Nothing better illuminates why secessionists considered Lincoln's immediate menace to be his distribution of patronage to the likes of Helper, not any encouragement of the likes of John Brown.

Other useful accounts of Helper, while partially superseded by David Brown, are the fullest (but sometimes inaccurate) biography, Hugh C. Bailey, *Hinton R. Helper: Abolitionist Racist* (University, Ala., 1965); the sharpest assault on Helper's racism, Hugh T. Lefler, *Hinton Rowan Helper: Advocate of White America* (Charlottesville, 1935); and George Frederickson's helpful introduction to the best edition of *The Impending Crisis of the South* (Cambridge, Mass., 1968). All references to the *Impending Crisis* are to the Frederickson edition.

17. Helper, *The Land of Gold: Reality Versus Fiction* (Baltimore, 1855), esp. vi, 221–22, 275–78.

18. *Impending Crisis,* 409–10.

19. Ibid., preface, 44, 327, 330.

20. Ibid., 43–44, 409.

21. Ibid., 28, 140, 411.

22. Ibid., 120, 155–56.

23. Quoted in Bailey, *Helper,* 42.

24. Circular letter from Wilheim H. Anthon and others (including Cassius Clay and Frank P. Blair, Jr.), December 1, 1858, in Benjamin Hedrick Papers, DU; David Brown, "Hinton R. Helper: The Logical Outcome of the Non-Slaveholders' Philosophy," *Historical Journal* 46 (2003): 39–58.

Chapter 17. John Clark and Political Invasion

1. *CG,* 36 Cong., 1 sess., 524. The best account of the Speakership Crisis is still Ollinger Crenshaw, "The Speakership Contest of 1859–1860: John Sherman's Election, a Cause of Disruption?" *MVHR* 29 (1942): 323–38.

2. *CG,* 36 Cong., 1 sess., 1–3.

3. On the initiation of the various pre-1855 crises, see Freehling, *Road* 1: 311–21, 392–407, 500–504, 541–56.

4. Biographical information on Clark comes in bits and pieces, including Richard N. Current, ed., *Encyclopedia of the Confederacy,* 4 vols. (New York, 1993), 1: 342–43; Ezra J. Warner and W. Buck Yearns, *Biographical Register of the Confederate Congress* (Baton Rouge, 1975), 49–50; and Arthur R. Kirkpatrick, "Missouri's Delegation in the Confederate Congress," *CWH* 5 (1959): 188–96. Clark's slaveholdings in 1850 and 1860 are recorded in Howard County Manuscript Census Returns, MOHS, C. I am grateful to Laura Crane for research help with John Clark and Austin King.

5. *CG,* 36 Cong., 1 sess., 3, 17.

6. Ibid., 49, 269, 394.

7. Ibid., 43.

8. Ibid., 21, 427, 547–48.

9. Ibid., 241.

10. Ibid., 407.

11. Ibid., 546.

12. Ibid., 224–27.

13. Ibid., 586.

14. Ibid., 21.

15. Ibid., 16–17.

16. Freehling, *Road* 1: 504.

17. Robert Barnwell Rhett to William Porcher Miles, January 24, 1860, Miles Papers, NC.

18. On Keitt, the best study is still J. Holt Merchant's unpublished Ph.D. dissertation. For contemporary descriptions, see *St. Louis Democrat,* December 31, 1855; *Wilmington Delaware Republican,* December 29, 1859; CC, June 5, 1858; *Savannah Republican,* December 30, 1859; "People We Meet" in *New York Leader,* n.d., copy in Keitt Papers, NC.

19. Laurence Keitt to Sue Keitt, February 29, 1860, Keitt Papers, NC; Caroline W. Keitt to Thomas Waddington, March 22, 1860, Ellison S. Keitt Papers, DU.

20. Freehling, *Reintegration,* 56–57.

21. Martin Crawford to Alexander Stephens, April 8, 1860, Stephens Papers, LC; James Hammond to M.C.M. Hammond, April 22, 1860, Hammond Papers, LC.

22. Current, ed., *Encyclopedia of the Confederacy* 2: 1038. A full-scale biography of Miles, taking advantage of the excellent surviving letters, would be very helpful.

23. William Henry Gist to Miles, December 20, 1859, Miles Papers, NC .

24. *South Carolina Senate Journal, 1859,* 168; Memminger to Miles, December 27, 1859, January 3, 1860 [misdated 1859], Miles Papers, NC.

25. CC, December 29, 1859. On Memminger, there is a good short sketch in Current, ed., *Encyclopedia of the Confederacy* 2: 1022–26, and a decent older biography, Henry Dickson Capers, *The Life and Times of C. G. Memminger* (Richmond, 1893). Once again, a modern biography would be useful, and source materials for it abound.

26. Miles to Memminger, January 10, 1860, Memminger Papers, LC.

27. Pickens to Robert M. T. Hunter, December 10, 1859, in Ambler, ed., "Correspondence of Hunter" 1: 275–77.

28. Gist to Memminger, January 30, 1860, Memminger Papers, NC.

29. W. W. Boyce to Memminger, January 4, 1860, Memminger Papers, NC.

30. Sallie M. Richardson to Ellis, January 26, 1860, Mumford-Ellis Papers, DU; Scarborough, ed., *Ruffin Diary* 1: 394–95.

31. *RE,* February 3, 1860.

32. Memminger to Miles, January 16, 1860, Miles Papers, NC.

33. *RE,* January 31, March 23, 1860; Wise to Fernando Wood, n.d. [early February 1860], Wise Papers, VSL.

34. *RE,* February 25, 1860.

35. Ibid., February 15, 1860.

36. Gist to Memminger, January 30, 1860, Memminger Papers, NC; Memminger to Miles, January 24, 1860, Miles Papers, NC.

37. Memminger to Miles, January 24, 30, 1860, Miles Papers, NC.

38. Peter Starke to John Pettus, July 1860, Governors Records, MISS; A. B. Moore to William Gist, April 2, 1860, Governors Papers, ALA; Ralph Dubay, "Mississippi and the Proposed Atlanta Convention of 1860," *Southern Quarterly* 5 (1967): 347–62. For Pettus's continued Cooperationism, see this volume, 386–87.

39. Gerald S. Henig, "Henry Winter Davis and the Speakership Contest of 1859–1860," *Maryland Historical Magazine* 68 (1973): 1–19.

40. Martin Crawford to Alexander Stephens, March 14, 1960, Stephens Papers, LC.

41. *CG,* 36 Cong., 1 sess., 641.

42. Toombs to Stephens, February 10, 1860, P., ed., *T., S. & C.* 2: 460–62.

43. Keitt to James Hammond, September 10, 1860, Hammond Papers, LC.

Chapter 18. Yancey's Lethal Abstraction

1. William B. Hesseltine, ed., *Three Against Lincoln: Murat Halstead Reports the Caucuses of 1860* (Baton Rouge, 1960), 119.

2. *RE,* October 11, 1860.

3. *NOD,* May 13, 1860.

4. William Henry Trescot to James Hammond, August 19, 1859, Hammond Papers, LC.

5. *Milledgeville Southern Recorder,* January 20, August 9, 1859.

6. *NOD,* July 10, 1859.

7. Davis, *Speeches . . . Summer . . . 1858,* 19.

8. Ibid., 48; Paul Escott, "Jefferson Davis and Slavery in the Territories," *Journal of Mississippi History* 39 (1977): 97–116.

9. *Jackson Semi-Weekly Mississippian,* July 26, 1859.

10. Albert Gallatin Brown to J.F.H. Clairborne, January 4, 1857, Clairborne Papers, MISS.

11. Brown to Clairborne, November 15, 1853, Clairborne Papers, MISS.

12. Quoted in the best biography, and one that gets the Brown-Davis difference on congressional territorial protection right, as few others do: William J. Cooper, Jr., *Jefferson Davis, American* (New York, 2000), 309.

13. The best biography remains James Ranick, *Albert Gallatin Brown, Radical Southern Nationalist* (New York, 1937).

14. *CG,* 36 Cong., 1 sess., 494, 1006.

15. Ibid., 658, 935.

16. Freehling, *Road* 1: 534–35.

17. John Witherspoon DuBose, *The Life and Times of William Lowndes Yancey,* 2 vols. (Birmingham, 1892), 2: 376. The DuBose volumes, while superseded by Eric Walther's new biography, remain valuable for their inclusion of source material.

18. Address in Abbeville District, July 4, 1834, Yancey Papers, ALA.

19. DuBose, *Yancey* 1: 110.

20. Dixon H. Lewis to Yancey, June 18, 1848, Lewis Papers, ALA.

21. William L. Yancey to Benjamin Yancey, July 8, 1856, Benjamin Yancey Papers, NC.

22. *CM,* July 18, 1859. The next two paragraphs are based on the same unrivaled Yancey effort.

23. *DBR* 24 (1858): 586–87.

24. Harry V. Jaffa, *Crisis of the House Divided: An Interpretation of the Issues in the Lincoln-Douglas Debates* (Garden City, N.Y., 1959); William Lee Miller, *Lincoln's Virtues: An Ethical Biography* (New York, 2002). I am indebted to Professor Miller for his encouragement, advice, and friendship throughout the final years of writing this book.

25. *CM,* July 18, 1859.

26. Cooper, *Davis,* 311.

27. Benjamin Fitzpatrick to C. C. Clay, Jr., August 30, 1859, Clay Papers, DU.

28. J. Mills Thornton III, *Politics and Power in a Slave Society: Alabama, 1800–1860* (Baton Rouge, 1978), is brilliant on Yancey's maneuvering amidst Alabama factions (including all Democrats' maneuvering against an ex-Whig comeback and the infighting that culminated in the Alabama state Democratic convention). In contrast, I find Professor Thornton unconvincing in failing to take Yancey seriously, when that Alabamian explained why "impractical" slavery issues were deadly practical. Professor Thornton instead dubiously finds the provoking practicalities in Alabama's newly commercial economy. But the best history books are towering even if one fails to find some central theses convincing.

29. Edward C. Bullock to Clement C. Clay, Jr., December 30, 1859, Clay Papers, DU, is a fine guide not only to Yancey's aborted fling but also to the disunionism of his faction.

30. *Proceedings of the Democratic State Convention* [of Alabama] *Held in . . . Montgomery, Commencing . . . January 11, 1860* (Montgomery, 1860); *Mobile Daily Advertiser,* supplement to January 15, 1860, issue; Thornton, *Politics and Power,* 381–91. Professor Thornton has a particularly acute understanding of "in substance"; see 391.

Chapter 19. The Democracy's Charleston Convention

1. Edward Magdol, *Owen Lovejoy: Abolitionist in Congress* (New Brunswick, N.J., 1967), 24.

2. Merton L. Dillon, *Elijah P. Lovejoy, Abolitionist Editor* (Urbana, Ill., 1961).

3. Magdol, *Lovejoy,* 51.

4. *CG,* 36 Cong., 1 sess., Appendix, 202–7, records Lovejoy's speech.

5. Pryor in ibid., 203; Crawford to Alexander Stephens, April 8, 1860, LC; Hammond to Edmund Ruffin, April 16, 1860, Hammond to M.C.M. Hammond, April 22, 1860, Hammond Papers, LC.

6. W. Duncan to Hammond, April 23, 1860, Hammond Papers, LC.

7. I first found the atmosphere surrounding the Charleston convention enticing in the vivid ch. 15 of Roy Nichols, *The Disruption of American Democracy.* No other historian has done better, although Allan Nevins comes close in *The Emergence of Lincoln.* Professor Nichols derived much of his atmosphere from Hesseltine, ed., *Halstead,* a journalistic masterwork and hereafter cited (extensively!) as *Halstead.*

8. Preston Brooks to James L. Orr, November 10, 1855, Orr to A. D. Banks, August 13, 1857, Orr Papers, NC. On the Orr revolution, we have another fine state study, Lacy K. Ford, Jr., *Origins of Southern Radicalism: The South Carolina Upcountry, 1800–1860* (New York, 1988). For some unbalanced comments on Professor Ford's book, emphasizing problems I still find, see *Road* 1: 541. But that analysis of the volume's problematic aspects needs to be balanced by emphasis on the book's cardinal virtues, and especially its superb understanding that South Carolina's aristocratic republicans faced radical (for South Carolina!) intruders, seeking to turn the old-fashioned remnant of the American eighteenth-century aristocratic republican governance into a new-fashioned American egalitarian republican order. Before the Civil War, the intruders failed, and Professor Ford does not do enough with the failure. But James L. Orr's egalitarian republicans did make a hugely worrisome splash, and any post-Ford account of the worried old guard has to acknowledge the seismic occurrence. A failure to do so makes for polemical strain, as Manisha Sinha's book shows. See below, ch. 23, note 4.

9. Rhett to William Porcher Miles, January 29, 1860, Miles Papers, NC.

10. William Henry Trescot to Miles, March 10, 1860, Miles Papers, NC.

11. For the wording of, and votes on, the Majority and Minority reports, both in the platform committee and on the convention floor, see *Proceedings of the Conventions at Charleston and Baltimore* (Washington, 1860), esp. 37–39, 45, 115–17; *Halstead,* esp. 45–47, 68–70.

12. William L. Yancey, *Speech of the Hon. William L. Yancey Delivered in the National Democratic Convention . . .* (Charleston, S.C., 1860), esp. 8, 16; Yancey's speech at Marion, Alabama, May 19, 1860, copy in Yancey Papers, ALA.

13. *Proceedings,* 48–51.

14. Ibid., 64–66; *Halstead,* 52.

15. *Dictionary of Missouri Biography* (Columbia, Mo., 1999), 459–60; *Messages and Papers of the Governors of Missouri* (Columbia, Mo., 1922), 2: 263–70; *Dictionary of American Biography* (New York, 1933), 10: 382. For the manuscript census of Richmond County, 1860 (listing King's five slaves) and a vivid drawing of the ex-governor in the *Columbia Missouri Herald*'s 1875 historical edition (showing his angular appearance), see MOHS, C.

16. *Halstead,* 52.

17. *New York Herald,* October 15, 1860, clipping in Yancey Papers, ALA.

18. Yancey, *Speech in the Democratic Convention,* esp. 16.

19. *Halstead,* 54.

20. Ibid., 23, 83.

21. Ibid., 76, 84.

22. Ibid., 74, 84.

23. Ibid., 89–90, 246.

24. *Augusta Daily Constitutionalist,* May 5, 1860.

25. Martin Cranford to Alexander Stephens, May 11, 1860, Stephens Papers, LC.

26. Toombs to Stephens, June 9, 1860, in P., ed., *T., S., & C.* 2: 481; *Savannah Republican,* May 8, 1860.

27. Cleveland to Stephens, May 11, 1860, Stephens Papers, LC.

28. Rhett to Miles, May 12, 1860, Miles Papers, NC.

29. CC, May 12, 1860; CM, June 18, 1860; Perry to Benson T. Lossing, September 2, 1866, Perry Papers, SC.

30. *Halstead,* 86.

Chapter 20. The Democracy's Baltimore Convention

1. *Halstead,* 95–8.

2. Ibid., 99; *Proceedings of the Conventions at Charleston and Baltimore* (Washington, 1860), 71–90.

3. John Ashmore to B. F. Perry, July 13, 1860, Perry Papers, ALA; *Halstead,* 101.

4. *Halstead,* 107.

5. Yancey to C. C. Clay, Jr., May 4, 1860, Clay Papers, DU.

6. I would add this speculation to the shrewd speculations about this perhaps happening in Nevins, *Emergence of Lincoln,* 2: 219. The (dubious) source that demands speculation is Richard Taylor's memoirs, published two decades later. Taylor, *Destruction and Reconstruction . . .* (New York, 1879).

7. *Halstead,* 111–17.

8. Robert Barnwell Rhett, Jr. to William Porcher Miles, May 12, 1860, Miles Papers, NC.

9. See B. H. Wilson's speech at the South Carolina Democratic state convention, May 31, 1860, in *CM,* July 8, 1860.

10. CC, May 31, 1860.

11. Powhattan Ellis, Sr., to Charles Ellis, May 26, 1860, Ellis-Mumford Papers, DU.

12. Rhett Jr. to Miles, May 10, 1860, Miles Papers, LC.

13. Potter, *Impending Crisis,* 326.

14. *Halstead,* 263; Democratic National Executive Committee, *To The Democracy of the United States, July 18, 1860* (Washington, 1860), 8; J. L. Foster to Stephen A. Douglas, July 7, 1860, J. Haddock Smith to Douglas, May 4, 1860, Douglas Papers, University of Chicago Library.

15. *Halstead,* 263.

16. Stephen A. Douglas to William Richardson, June 20, 1860, Douglas to Dean Richmond, June 22, 1860, in *The Letters of Stephen A. Douglas,* ed. Robert W. Johannsen (Urbana, Ill., 1961), 492–93; Yancey in *Halstead,* 221.

17. *Proceedings,* 133–70; *Halstead,* 223–25.

18. Among the many statements of Upper South outrage, less at the Douglas platform than at Douglas supporters' trampling on Southerners' democratic convention rights, see *RE,* June 26, 28, 30, 1860; *Kentucky Weekly Yeoman,* June 29, 1860.

19. *Halstead,* 249–50.

20. Ibid., 274.

21. Ibid., 277–78.

Chapter 21. Suspicious Southerners and Lincoln's Election

1. *Baltimore Clipper,* September 29, 1860.

2. For a good contemporary biographical sketch, see *Baltimore Clipper,* May 5, 1860. Unfortunately, no published biography of the Bison exists; the book could be quite the flamboyant read. A start is made in Robert D. Lapidus, "A Southern Enigma: The Unwavering Unionism of John Minor Botts" (M.A. thesis, Ohio University, 1972).

3. Speech at the African Church, August 8, 1856, in John Minor Botts, *The Great Rebellion, Its Secret History, Rise, Progress, and Disastrous Failure* (New York, 1866).

4. *RE,* March 17, 1859.

5. Botts to Anna Carroll, July 31, November 16, 21, December 24, 1859, January 1, 1860, Carroll Family Papers, MHS.

6. *Halstead,* 121–40.

7. F. H. Pierpont to the editors of the *Wheeling Intelligencer,* March 16, 1859, Archibald Campbell Papers, WVU.

8. John Johnson, *A Defense of Republicanism* . . . (n.p., n.d. [1860], copy in LC). This pamphlet, written by the ex-mayor of Kansas City, is the best overall statement of the 1860 Southern Republican position, with the western Virginia newspapers mentioned in the text not far behind.

9. F. P. Blair, Jr., *Speech . . . at Cooper Institute . . . January 25, 1860* (Washington, 1860).

10. This time we have the benefit of an excellent biography, William E. Parrish, *Frank Blair, Lincoln's Conservative* (Columbia, Mo., 1998).

11. *Halstead,* 142–77, expertly reported this convention, too; the presidential roll call votes are on 167–70.

12. Parrish, *Blair,* 84.

13. Lincoln to Anson G. Henry, July 4, 1860, in *The Collected Works of Abraham Lincoln,* ed. Roy P. Basler, 9 vols. (New Brunswick, N.J., 1953–55), 4: 181–82.

14. Underwood in *Wilmington Delaware Republican,* October 17, 1859; Botts to Edward Bates, March 27, 1860, Attorney General's Papers, National Archives.

15. J. Henley Smith to Alexander Stephens, May 7, 1860, Stephens Papers, LC.

16. The *Dallas Herald*'s issues of August 31, 1859, and May 16, 1860, augment the story.

17. Ibid., August 17, 1859.

18. Ibid., February 29, March 7, May 16, 1860.

19. James Harper Starr to Smith & Johnson, July 10, 1860, Starr to E. H. Downing, July 19, 1860, Starr to N. Amory, August 2, 1860, Starr to Francis Von Deer Hoya, August 13, 1860, R. W. Withers to Starr, March 27, 1860, all in Starr Papers, TX.

20. *Clarksville* (Miss.) *Standard,* July 14, 1860; *Austin Texas State Gazette,* July 28, 1860; Enoch J. Withers to Pa, August 16, 1860, Withers-Tavenner Papers, DU.

21. J. M. Fair to E. Fair, August 16, 1860, Hildah Annie Bryant Papers, DU.

22. *Petersburg Express* report from Houston City, August 17, 1860, newspaper clipping inserted in Edmund Ruffin Diary near entry for September 4, 1860, LC; *Austin Texas State Gazette,* July 28, 1860; William L. Man to Thomas Hurling, August 24, 1860, Hurling Papers, TX. For other examples of a terror that momentarily clutched some very cautious conservatives, see Guy M. Bryan to Moses Austin Bryan, July 28, 31, 1860, Guy Bryan Papers, TX; C. G. Forshey to John Liddell, August 18, 1860, Liddell Family Papers, LSU; James M. Cox to Sam Houston, August 2, 25, 1860, Governors Papers, Texas Historical Society, Austin.

23. *Norfolk* (Va.) *Southern Argus,* August 10, 1860; Thomas Affleck to E. H. Cushing, July 13, 1860, Affleck Papers, LSU; *Dallas Herald,* October 10, 1860.

24. *Savannah Republican,* September 20, 1860.

25. A. B. Moore to Walkins Phelan, August 30, 1860, Governors Papers, ALA.

26. *Baltimore Clipper,* September 7, 1860; *Norfolk Southern Argus,* October 6, 10, 12, 1860.

27. *New Orleans Bee,* November 17, 1860.

28. *DBR* 28 (1860): 1–2.

29. James Harper Starr to George W. Smyth, August 17, 1860, Smyth Papers, TX; Smyth to Starr, September 3, 1860, Starr to R. S. Walker, September 1, 1860, Starr Papers, TX.

30. This episode is fully spelled out in James Hitchins to Thurlow Weed, November 10 (or November 16; date is hard to read), 1860, Weed Papers, University of Rochester Library. I am indebted to William Cooper for sending me a copy of this wonderful document. Professor Cooper's generosity exemplifies the best of our profession, for the Hitchins letter, demonstrating secessionists' assault on southern whites' liberty, rubs against the Cooper thesis that secessionists' desire for white liberty especially animated their disunion fling.

Still, Professor Cooper's own countervailing evidence requires only a qualification of his important thesis. As I emphasize elsewhere, southern white egalitarians' passion to protect their own liberty and equality from Yankee insulters and coercers *did* infuse the secessionist mentality, right along with zeal to slap Lincoln's (and his southern appointees') libertarian hands off blacks and to demean (and psychologically enslave) their southern white opponents. The largest point is that the corrosive American mix of slavery, racism, and freedom left liberty both desperately sought and badly besmirched, on both sides of the southern color line and on both sides of the Mason-Dixon line.

31. Jere Clemens to John Bell, October 14, 1860, Bell Papers, LC.

32. Speech at Cincinnati, October 20, 1860, copy (like all Yancey's speeches in this campaign) in Yancey Papers, ALA.

33. Ibid.

34. Speech at Cooper Institute, October 11, 1860.

35. For the parade and the speech, see *NOD,* October 30, 1860.

36. *Jackson Semi-Weekly Mississippian,* September 6, 1860.

37. For 1860 election statistics, see www.data.historycentral.com/elections/1860.

38. Breckinridge's speech of September 5, 1860, is in *Savannah Republican,* September 19–21, 1860. We have two good biographies: William C. Davis, *Breckinridge: Statesman, Soldier, Symbol* (Baton Rouge, 1974), and Franck H. Heck, *Proud Kentuckian: John C. Breckinridge, 1821–1875* (Lexington, Ky., 1976).

39. Yancey's speech at Florence, Kentucky, October 19, 1860, in Yancey Papers, ALA.

40. Ibid.

41. David T. Boyd to William T. Sherman, August 30, 1860, in *General W. T. Sherman as College President . . . ,* ed. Walter Lynwood Fleming, 2 vols. (Arthur M. Clark Co., 1912), 270–73.

Chapter 22. The State's Rights Justification

1. *New Orleans Bee,* November 8, 1860.

2. Francis R. Rives to William C. Rives, Jr., December 24, 1860, Rives Papers, LC.

3. Judah P. Benjamin, "The Right of Secession," in an excellent anthology, *Southern Pamphlets on Secession . . . ,* ed. Jon L. Wakelyn (Chapel Hill, 1996), 101–14, esp. 108. See also Robert M. T. Hunter in *RE,* December 12, 1860.

4. James D. Richardson, ed., *A Compilation of the Messages and Papers of the Confederacy . . . ,* 2 vols. (Nashville, 1905), 1: 32–36.

5. George H. Reese, ed., *Proceedings of the Virginia State Convention of 1861,* 4 vols. (Richmond, 1965), 2: 77.

6. James McPherson has this important point exactly right in *Battle Cry of Freedom: The Civil War Era* (New York, 1988), 861.

7. The disparagers often commit a little error of spelling that stems from a larger error of understanding. The correct spelling is state's rights, not states' rights. The states (plural) arguably have a collective right to oppose nationalistic inflations of power. But only a state (singular) arguably has a right to withdraw consent. Because of that state's rights justification, one seceding state's majority (singular) possessed enormous eventual leverage over all the other southern states' majorities (plural).

8. A point wonderfully made (but irrelevant to a state's right of revolution) in Arthur Bestor, "State Sovereignty and Slavery: A Reinterpretation of Proslavery Constitutional Doctrine," Illinois State Historical Society *Journal* 64 (1961): 117–80.

9. Toni Morrison, *Beloved* (New York, 1987). For the real story, see Steven Weisenburger's superb *Modern Medea: A Family Story of Slavery and Child-Murder from the Old South* (New York, 1998). I am indebted to Professor Weisenburger not only for his acute reading of this chapter but also for his many insights during the decade that we shared on the University of Kentucky's faculty.

Chapter 23. The Motivation

1. Freehling, *Road 1,* chs. 14–15.

2. For an extended cultural analysis, see ibid., chs. 12–13.

3. Quoted in Freehling, *Prelude to Civil War,* 89, 241.

4. Manisha Sinha, *The Counter-Revolution of Slavery: Politics and Ideology in Antebellum South Carolina* (Chapel Hill, 2000), forcefully expands on this aspect of South Carolina secessionism. But Professor Sinha's polemic goes too far in declaring that her South Carolina findings negate the importance of white men's egalitarian republicanism among secessionists elsewhere. The point about South Carolina is precisely its peculiarities; one does not touch Mills Thornton's conception of Alabama by parading South Carolina's eccentricities. Nor is Sinha wise to fulminate against Lacy Ford's conception that egalitarian republicanism invaded South Carolina, in the form of James L. Orr's uplanders. Orr did not capture the state, and Professor Ford too much minimizes that defining fact, but he is right that the nineteenth-century egalitarian enemy had penetrated the state. Ford's invaders made Sinha's elitists even more outraged at modernity.

5. [James Warley Miles], *The Relation Between the Races at the South* (Charleston, S.C., 1861); William Gilmore Simms to William Porcher Miles, March 7, 1861, in *The Letters of William Gilmore Simms,* ed. Mary C. Simms Oliphant et al., 5 vols. (Charleston, S.C., 1952), 4: 343.

6. A fine new book, Maurie D. McInnis, *The Politics of Taste in Antebellum Charleston* (Chapel Hill, 2005), has superseded earlier accounts of nineteenth-century Charleston's socio-aesthetic evolution. But see also the intriguing analysis in Kenneth Severens, *Charleston Antebellum Architecture and Civic Destiny* (Knoxville, Tenn., 1988).

7. John Bivens and J. Thomas Savage, "The Miles Brenton House, Charleston, South Carolina," *Antiques* 143 (1993): 294–307.

8. Bernard L. Herman, "The Embedded Landscapes of the Charleston Single House," in *Exploring Everyday Landscapes . . . ,* ed. Annmarie Adams and Sally McMurry (Knoxville, Tenn., 1997), 41–57.

9. Hugh Legaré quoted in Freehling, *Prelude,* 13, and Freehling, *Road* 1: 217.

10. James L. Petigru quoted in Michael O'Brien and David Moltke-Hanson, eds., *Intellectual Life in Antebellum Charleston* (Knoxville, Tenn., 1986), 221.

11. William J. Grayson, *The Hireling and the Slave . . .* (Charleston, S.C., 1856), 49, 51, 71.

12. *Speeches . . . Delivered in the Convention . . . of South Carolina . . . in March 1833* (Columbia, 1833), 19–27.

13. John Townsend, *The Doom of Slavery in the Union: Its Safety out of It* (Charleston, S.C., 1860), 22. This was the second of Townsend's massively distributed

pamphlets. His sheets and the *Charleston Mercury*'s pages are the most important sources for understanding this pivotal area at this pivotal time.

14. This may be a better (or worse) guess than Stephanie McCurry's speculation that white yeomen massed behind wealthier men's domination over dependent blacks in order to preserve white males' domination over dependent wives. We are all guessing from missing evidence about yeomen's motives; that is usually a difficulty with history from the bottom up. But I've seen no hint that South Carolina white males feared, or had the slightest reason to fear, female domination before the war. In contrast, I've seen much evidence that fear of racial unrest afflicted lowcountry whites—and plenty of reason for that fear. Still, Professor McCurry's gender-based speculation is intriguing; her evidence of poorer whites' full participation in 1860 lowcountry paramilitary pressures is irrefutable; and I applaud her success in making the hitherto invisible lowcountry white nonslaveholders highly visible in the secession story. McCurry, *Masters of Small Worlds: Yeoman Households, Gender Relations, and the Political Culture of the Antebellum Lowcountry* (New York, 1995).

15. The map in Freehling, *Road* 1: 212, illustrates this point.

16. George W. Featherstonhaugh, *Excursions Through the Slave States* (New York, 1844), 155–57.

17. Walter Edgar, *South Carolina: A History* (Columbia 1998), 277. Edgar's is an unusually fine state history.

18. Ford, *Southern Radicalism*, 38–39.

19. Quoted in Freehling, *Prelude*, 5, 15.

20. Quoted in *Sumter Watchman*, February 18, 1857.

21. Hutson to his mother, April 1860, Hutson Papers, SC.

22. William Howard Russell, *Pictures of Southern Life, Social, Political, and Military* (New York, 1961), 4–5.

23. *Pickens Keowee Courier*, July 10, 1858.

24. Boyce in *CM*, September 3, 1859; Jamison in *CC*, November 3, 1859.

25. Quoted in LeR. F. Youmans, *A Sketch of the Life of Governor A. G. Magrath* (Charleston, S.C., 1896), 4.

26. John Townsend, *The South Alone Should Govern the South, and African Slavery Should be Controlled by Those Friendly to It* (Charleston, S.C., 1860), 30. *CM*, November 3, 1860, reported that 30,000 to 40,000 copies of Townsend's polemical masterpiece were already in print.

27. For the origins of the nay-saying that Warley brought to climax, see Ernest M. Lander, Jr., *Reluctant Imperialists: Calhoun, the South Carolinians, and the Mexican War* (Baton Rouge, 1980). For Warley's oration at the Citadel, November 22, 1855, see *CS*, November 23, 1855.

28. Townsend, *South Alone*, 49–50.

29. Ibid., 12.

30. *CM*, October 11, 1860; D. H. Hamilton to William Porcher Miles, January 23, February 2, 1860, Miles Papers, NC.

31. *CM*, October 11, 1860.

32. Townsend, *Doom*, 7–15.

33. Caroline Gilman to her daughter, December 16, 1860, Gilman Papers, SCHS. As the title indicates, Steven A. Channing's *Crisis of Fear: Secession in South Carolina* (New York, 1970) particularly emphasizes terror of black resistance as the cause of the Civil War. This excellent book's value transcends its emphasis on fear, which I think is somewhat overdone and not described in a sufficiently subtle fashion. Dr. Channing does not clearly enough distinguish between terror of general slave revolts, which very infrequently intruded, and the far more frequent fear of dissimulating individual Cuffees. Nor does he clarify enough that fear came related to other apprehensions, especially that so-called slavery could not develop if Cuffees were dangerous fakers. Moreover, slavery could turn intolerable if fears generated wicked lashing of slaves and vicious lynchings of whites. But I

have no right to complain, since my own first try at explaining South Carolina fears, in *Prelude to Civil War* (published five years before *Crisis of Fear*), suffered from the same lack of subtlety.

34. Beth G. Crabtree and James W. Patton, eds., *Journal of a Secesh Lady: The Diary of Catherine Devereau Edmonston, 1860–1866* (Raleigh, N.C., 1979), 45.

35. C. Vann Woodward and Elisabeth Muhlenfeld, eds., *The Private Mary Chesnut: The Unpublished Diaries* (New York, 1984), 78.

36. John Hammond Moore, ed., *A Plantation Mistress on the Eve of the Civil War: The Diary of Keziah Goodwyn Hopkins Brevard, 1860–1861* (Columbia, S.C., 1993), 41–42, 81.

37. C. Vann Woodward, ed., *Mary Chesnut's Civil War* (New Haven, 1981), 48.

38. Laurence Keitt to Sue Sparks Keitt, February 29, 1860, Keitt Papers, DU.

39. Woodward and Muhlenfeld, eds., *Private Mary Chesnut*, 181.

40. Moore, ed., *Plantation Mistress*, 64.

41. Keitt to James Hammond, September 10, 1860, Hammond Papers, LC.

42. Townsend, *South Alone*, 16–17; *CM*, August 8, 1860.

43. Bunch quoted in Laura A. White, *Robert Barnwell Rhett: Father of Secession* (1931; Gloucester, Mass., 1965), 178n.; Trescot quoted in Woodward, ed., *Chesnut's Civil War*, 82; Miles to Howell Cobb, January 14, 1861, in P., ed., *T., S., & C.* 2: 529.

44. *CM*, November 1, 1859, December 3, 1860.

45. John L. Manning to his wife, May 29, 1860, Williams-Chesnut-Manning Papers, LC; Sue Keitt to Mrs. Frederick Brown, March 4, 1861 [Lincoln's Inauguration Day!], Keitt Papers, DU.

46. J. H. Cornish Diary, entry for November 8, 1860, NC; Longstreet quoted in William Barney, *The Road to Secession . . .* (New York, 1972), 199-201. Barney's is an underappreciated short synthesis.

47. T. J. Withers to B. F. Perry, February 10, 1861, Perry Papers, ALA; Woodward, ed., *Chesnut's Civil War*, 25.

48. *CM*, September 11, 1860.

49. See Marshall's climactic sentences in ibid.

Chapter 24. The Tactics and the Tacticians

1. Edgar, *South Carolina*, 358–60.

2. *CM*, September 20, 1860.

3. Quoted and discussed in Freehling, *Reintegration*, 75–76.

4. *CC*, August 4, 1860; *CM*, October 30, 1860.

5. Chesnut to Hammond, October 17, 1860, Hammond Papers, LC; Scarborough, ed., *Ruffin Diary* 1: 448.

6. Faust, *Hammond*, is good on the details of the South Carolinian's rise and fall, except when the narrative arrives at the secession crisis, when it unaccountably skims over the senator's crucial climactic role (or as it turned out, crucial nonrole).

7. Bleser, ed., *Secret and Sacred*, 194; James Hammond to John Hammond, February 10, 1845, Hammond Papers, SC.

8. Bleser, ed., *Secret and Sacred*, 175.

9. Ibid., 270–71; Hammond to editors of *CM*, August 2, 1857, copy in Hammond Papers, SC; A. P. Aldrich to Hammond, December 1, 1857, Hammond Papers, LC.

10. Hammond to William Gilmore Simms, March 13, 1859, Hammond Papers, LC.

11. James H. Hammond, *Speech . . . at Barnwell C.H., October 29th, 1858* (Charleston, S.C., 1858), 3.

12. Hammond to Simms, November 3, 1858, Hammond Papers, LC.

13. Hammond, *Barnwell*, 5–6, 11–12, 14–16, 18, 20, 28.

14. N. R. Middleton in *CC,* December 5, 1860. See also Thomas Middleton Hanckel's superb formulation of South Carolina elitism in *Government and the Right of Revolution* (Charleston, S.C., 1859).

15. Aldrich to Hammond, November 25, 1860, Hammond Papers, LC.

16. Aldrich to Hammond, October 4, 1860, Hammond Papers, LC: Boyce in *CC,* November 7, 1860.

17. Rhett Jr. to Miles, January 29, 1860, Miles Papers, NC; Rhett Jr. to Edmund Ruffin, October 20, 1860, Ruffin Papers, VSL; Rhett [I believe Sr.] to Robert W. Barnwell, October 16, 1860, quoted in White, *Rhett,* 176n.

18. Hammond to William Gilmore Simms, July 10, 1860, Hammond Papers, LC.

19. Arney Robinson Childs, ed., *The Private Journal of Henry William Ravenel, 1859–1887* (Columbia, S.C., 1947), 20.

20. John Means to Rhett, July 30, 1851, Rhett Papers, SCHS.

21. On these matters, Davis, *Rhett,* continues to be a model of balanced judgment.

22. Miles to Hammond, August 5, 1860, Hammond Papers, LC.

23. William Morris, ed., *The American Heritage Dictionary of the English Language* (Boston, 1980), 285.

24. Freehling, *Road* 1: 316–19.

25. Ibid., 520–23.

26. Gist's letters and all the governor's responses can be found in John G. Nicolay and John Hay, *Abraham Lincoln,* 10 vols. (New York, 1909), 2: 306–14. As will be obvious, I agree with Potter, *Impending Crisis,* 488–89, on how to read these letters rather than with the reading in Charles Edward Cauthen, *South Carolina Goes to War* (Chapel Hill, 1950), 52. But this seems to me a rare Cauthen misreading. Although his book is older and academically more staid than the recent, more thesis-ridden accounts of secession in South Carolina, his full and fair narrative is as useful—as older books sometimes are.

27. Davis to Rhett Jr., November 10, 1860, in *Jefferson Davis: The Essential Writings,* ed. William J. Cooper, Jr. (New York, 2003), 182–84.

28. Those inside the University of South Carolina's historical establishment will, however, find this no surprise but exactly what one would expect, after reading Edgar, *South Carolina,* 350, and Robert Nicholas Olsberg's two University of South Carolina theses, "William Henry Trescot: The Crisis of 1860" (M.A., 1967) and "A Government of Class and Race: William Henry Trescot and the South Carolina Chivalry, 1860–1865" (Ph.D., 1972). Nick Olsberg never developed his suggestive hunches beyond a hazy form before he left the profession. But his first steps down the right path live on in his theses and in his helpful research notes, which he kindly deposited in the South Carolina Historical Society.

29. John Townsend to Milledge Bonham, October 16, 1860, Bonham Papers, SC. For Townsend's previous Cooperationist passion, see Freehling, *Road* 1: 530.

30. The best biographical sketch is in John Amasa May and Joan Reynolds Faust, *South Carolina Secedes* (Columbia, S.C., 1960), 220–21.

31. Ibid., 151. The Robert Newman Gourdin Papers, EU, is a treasure chest of information.

32. Woodward and Muhlenfeld, eds., *Private Mary Chesnut,* 48, 56.

33. Memminger to William Porcher Miles, January 24, 1860, Miles Papers, NC.

34. May Spencer Ringold, "Robert Newman Gourdin and the '1860 Association,' " *GHQ* 55 (1971): 501–9.

35. William Tennent, Jr., to M. H. Bonham, October 10, 1860, Bonham Papers, SC.

36. Robert Barnwell Rhett, Jr., to Edward C. Wharton, August 2, 1886, Wharton Papers. Save for Jefferson Davis's answer, the paper trail of Rhett's clandestine correspondence ends here, at least in our current publicly available depositories. But in the late 1920s, Laura White saw early November answers from two key Southwesterners, Alabama's Leroy Pope Walker and Mississippi's William S. Barry, then in the private possession of A. B. Rhett. White, *Rhett,* 176n.

Chapter 25. The Triumph

1. William Nelson to William Porcher Miles, November 17, 1860, Miles Papers, NC; *CC,* November 3, 1860.

2. Miles to Robert Gourdin, December 10, 1860, Gourdin Papers, DU.

3. D. H. Hamilton to Gourdin, November 26, 1860, Gourdin Papers, EU.

4. *CC,* November 6–7, 1860.

5. *Yorkville Enquirer,* December 6, 1860.

6. *CC,* November 7, 1860.

7. Quoted in W. A. Swanberg's older, still useful, vivid narrative *First Blood: The Story of Fort Sumter* (New York, 1957), 17.

8. *CC,* November 12, 1860.

9. William M. Robinson, Jr., *Justices in Gray* (New York, 1941), 4–5.

10. *CC,* November 12, 1860; Robinson, *Justices in Gray,* 6.

11. May and Faust, *South Carolina Secedes,* 175; Youmans, *Magrath.*

12. Youmans, *Magrath;* May and Faust, *South Carolina Secedes,* 175–76; Woodward, ed., *Chesnut's Civil War,* 35, 50.

13. Alfred Huger to Joseph Holt, November 12, 1860, Holt Papers, LC.

14. *CM,* November 8, 1860. This great quote is often rendered as South Carolina's response to Lincoln's election. It was in fact a response to South Carolina's first response: those galvanizing resignations.

15. A. Toomer Palmer, *Led On! Step by Step . . .* (New York, 1899), 119; *CM,* November 8, 1860.

16. *CC,* November 9, 1860.

17. *CM,* November 5, 1860.

18. James S. Pettigrew to William Pettigrew, October 24, 1860, Pettigrew Papers, NC.

19. James Mercer Green to Robert Gourdin, December 21, 1860, John M. Richardson to Gourdin, December 5, 14, 1860, Gourdin Papers, EU. Many other letters in the Gourdin Papers attest to a secret plot to fortify South Carolina's nerve to move first, with reassurances from other states that would not move first. But Gourdin's answers came in December, *after* the South Carolina legislature dared. That fact whets the appetite for the Rhetts' answers in early November, which are almost nonexistent in public archives.

20. R. C. Griffin to D. L. Dalton, November 6, 1860, Milledge Bonham Papers, SC; Rhett Jr. to Edward C. Wharton, August 2, 1886, Wharton Papers, LSU.

21. The legislative deliberations from the Rhetts' November 7 introduction of early convention dates through the Senate's November 9 vote to postpone the dates is accurately described in Cauthen, *South Carolina Goes to War,* 54–57.

22. Aldrich to Hammond, November 6, 1860, Hammond Papers, LC.

23. Hammond to the legislature, November 8, 1860, Hammond Papers, LC. An earlier draft, dated October 15, is in Hammond Papers, SC.

24. Davis, *Rhett,* 398–99, handles this skillfully, until the author's concluding sentence states that "Rhett's last-minute intervention worked perfectly." Not Rhett's intervention through Colcock but the 1860 Association's railroad celebration, planned for a week, and the Institute Hall meeting, planned on November 7 (*CC,* November 8, 1860), worked perfectly.

25. Once again this interpretation may look startlingly new to most readers but will not to the experts. Potter, *Impending Crisis,* 490, and Cauthen, *South Carolina Goes to War,* 58, both see that South Carolina traveled via a railroad coincidence from a 44–1 vote for late dates to a unanimous vote for early dates in a mere twenty-four hours.

I remarked in the preface of my first book, *Prelude to Civil War,* x, that my predecessors in the field had mentioned my "new" interpretation. Generations of good historians are not going to miss an important happening altogether. Originality in history more often consists of adding new context to an old understanding and thus making the obscurely known compelling.

26. *CM*, October 22, November 5, 1860.

27. *CM*, November 5, 1860.

28. Charles Colcock Jones, Jr., to his father, January 28, 1861, and to his parents, March 17, 1861, both in *The Children of Pride*, ed. Robert Manson Myers (New Haven, 1984), 43, 51.

29. For Bartow's short life, his curse at Governor Brown, and his spectacular death, see Lindsey P. Henderson, Jr., *The Oglethorpe Light Infantry* (Savannah, 1961), 1–5.

30. *CM*, November 5, 1860.

31. *CM*, November 10, 1860; Woodward and Muhlenfeld, eds., *Private Mary Chesnut*, 4.

32. *CC*, November 10, 1860.

33. Henderson, *Oglethorpe Light Infantry*, 2.

34. Ezra J. Warner, *Generals in Gray . . .* (Baton Rouge, 1959), 149–50; Wakelyn, ed., *Biographical Dictionary*, 248–49.

35. Henry R. Jackson, *Tallulah and Other Poems* (Savannah, 1850), 91–93.

36. Henry Jackson to Howell Cobb, December 19, 1860, Cobb Papers, GA; Jackson, *The Southern Women of the Second American Revolution* (Atlanta, 1863), vi.

37. *CM*, November 10, 1860; *CC*, November 10, 1860.

38. Woodward and Muhlenfeld, eds., *Private Mary Chesnut*, 5; *CC*, November 12, 1860; D. H. Hamilton to D. H. Hamilton, Jr., November 10, 1860, Ruffin-Roulhac-Hamilton Papers, NC.

39. *CC*, November 12, 1860.

40. Childs, ed., *Ravenel Journal*, 40; Miles to M.R.H. Garnett, November 13, 1860, William Garnett Chisholm Papers, VHS.

41. *CC*, November 12, 1860.

42. Ibid.

43. Townsend, *Doom of Slavery*, 27.

44. Caroline Pettigrew to Charles Pettigrew, November 26, 1860, Pettigrew Papers, NC. See also McCarter's ms Journal, 12–14, LC.

45. Cauthen, *South Carolina Goes to War*, 59–61, wraps up the legislative decision nicely.

46. Porter to Hammond, November 11, 1860, Hammond Papers, LC.

47. Ibid.

48. Aldrich to Hammond, November 25, 1860, James Hammond to M.C.M. Hammond, November 12, 1860, both in Hammond Papers, LC.

49. Hammond to William Gilmore Simms, November 13, 1860, Hammond Papers, SC.

50. Freehling, *Road* 1: 531.

51. Caroline Pettigrew to Charles Pettigrew, November 29, 1860, Pettigrew Papers, NC.

52. O'Neall to Hammond, September 20, 1860, Hammond Papers, LC.

53. Cauthen, *South Carolina Goes to War*, 63–64.

54. Frank De Bow to J.B.D. De Bow, November 19, 1860, De Bow Papers, DU; James Petigru Carson, ed., *Life, Letters, and Speeches of James Louis Petigru . . .* (Washington, 1920), 361; Howell Cobb to "My Judge," November 11, 1860, Cobb Papers, New-York Historical Society.

55. *CM*, January 12, 1861.

56. Woodward and Muhlenfeld, eds., *Private Mary Chesnut*, 4–5.

57. *CM*, December 6–8, 1860; Cauthen, *South Carolina Goes to War*, 66.

58. Wakelyn, ed., *Secession Pamphlets*, 158–59.

59. Hammond to M.C.M. Hammond, November 12, 1860, Hammond Papers, LC.

60. William Gilmore Simms to James Hammond, April 4, 1859, Simms to William Porcher Miles, February 5, 1860, Simms to Miles, December 5, 1860, all in Oliphant et al., eds., *Simms Letters* 4: 140, 193–94, 281 (see also notes at 227, 285, 310); David

Flavel Jamison, *Life and Times of Bertrand Du Guesclin* (Charleston, S.C., 1864), esp. preface; May and Faust, *South Carolina Secedes,* 164–65.

61. May and Faust, *South Carolina Secedes,* 5–6.

62. *CC,* December 18, 1861.

63. Thomas Frian to Benjamin F. Perry, December 18, 1860, Perry Papers, LC.

64. Vivid portraits of the final scene can be enjoyed in *CM* and *CC,* December 21, 1860; Nina Glover to C. J. Bowen, December 21, 1861, Caroline Gilman Papers, DU; R. Hamilton to D. H. Hamilton, Jr., December 21, 1860, Ruffin-Roulhac-Hamilton Papers, NC; Charles H. Lesser, *Relic of the Lost Cause: The Story of South Carolina's Ordinance of Secession* (Columbia, S.C., 1996); May and Faust, *South Carolina Secedes,* 5–72.

65. Childs, ed., *Ravenel Journal,* 40.

66. The point here—the caution that should always condition might-have-been history—is that to think that one contingency will necessarily change all subsequent history, without other surprise occurrences changing things again, is to deny the very nature of contingency. Long-term trends will furthermore likely continue, even if a short-term chance occurrence slightly deflects their path. Thus, I think that historians who rightly see the impact of contingencies must usually restrain themselves to portraying possible short-term deflections rather than naively proclaiming that the long-term outcome would necessarily have been different. When used in this cautious way, the often not-so-cautious parlor game of might-have-been history can illustrate the complexities of history rather than oversimplifying alternate possibilities.

This version of my railroad coincidence thesis bears the marks of superb criticism received after I presented the first version to the BRANCH (British-American Nineteenth-Century Historians) convention in Wales in October 2004. I owe much to the late, much missed Peter Parish (for founding the wonderful organization), to Donald Ratcliffe (for arranging the sessions on my work), to Richard Carwardine (for skillfully presiding), and to Jack Pole, William Dusinberre, and John Ashworth (for particularly shrewd suggestions).

I also presented preliminary versions of this chapter at Randolph-Macon Women's College and the University of Alabama, where the comments of John d'Entremont, George Rable, and Larry Kohl were very helpful. I have furthermore benefited from conversations on this matter with Robert Vaughn (who pressed the necessity to remember that luck only opens an opportunity and becomes irrelevant if opportunists fail to pounce) and with Ron Formisano, Mark Summers, and Calvin Schermerhorn (all joining the BRANCH historians in pressing the necessity to be very clear that my coincidence could only temporarily deflect forces that had built up for many years and would probably continue to upset temporary armistices).

Introduction to Part VII. Lower South Landslide, Upper South Stalemate

1. I first came across the very useful idea that the secession crisis must be seen as a series of crises in William Cooper's work. He initially presented the conception in "The Politics of Slavery Affirmed: The South and the Secession Crisis," in *The Southern Enigma: Essays on Race, Class, and Folk Culture,* ed, Walter J. Fraser, Jr., and Winfred B. Moore, Jr. (Westport, Conn., 1983), 199–215.

Chapter 26. Alexander Stephens's Fleeting Moment

1. Freehling, *Road* 1: 523–24.

2. William W. Freehling and Craig M. Simpson, eds., *Secession Debated: Georgia's Showdown in 1860* (New York, 1992), presents all the Milledgeville speeches,

with introductions and notes. In my introduction, I mishandled the distinction between Cooperationists and Unionists. I am grateful to Anthony Gene Carey for correcting the error in his *Parties, Slavery, and the Union in Antebellum Georgia* (Athens, Ga., 1997), 321.

3. For good contemporary illustrations, see *CC*, June 5, 1858, February 14, 1861; *Milledgeville Southern Recorder*, March 1, 1859; *Baltimore Republican*, March 11, 1854; *Delaware Gazette*, February 15, 1861. The great biography of Stephens still has not been written, despite superb source material, but helpful accounts are in Thomas E. Schott, *Alexander H. Stephens of Georgia: A Biography* (Baton Rouge, 1988); Rudolph von Abele, *Alexander H. Stephens: A Biography* (New York, 1946); and Richard Malcolm Johnston and William Hand Browne, *Life of Alexander Stephens* (Philadelphia, 1878).

4. Alexander to Linton Stephens, February 3, 1851, SP, M.

5. Alexander to Linton Stephens, May 7, 1858, SP, M.

6. James Z. Rabun, ed., "Alexander H. Stephens's Diary, 1834–1837," *GHQ* 36 (1952): 79; Johnston and Browne, *Stephens*, 65–66.

7. Linton to Alexander Stephens, February 9, 1845, SP, M.

8. Alexander to Linton Stephens, February 3, 1851, SP, M.

9. Ibid.

10. Ibid.; Linton to Alexander Stephens, February 27, 1859, SP, M.

11. Alexander Stephens to Dick, July 5, 1860, Stephens Papers, LC; Johnston and Browne, *Stephens*, 353.

12. Freehling and Simpson, eds., *Secession Debated*, 97.

13. Ibid., 55–58.

14. Ibid., 77–78.

15. *Augusta Daily Constitutionalist*, November 17, 1859.

16. Myrta A. Avary, ed., *Recollections of Alexander H. Stephens . . .* (New York, 1910), 81.

17. S. R. Anderson to Alexander Stephens, November 14, 1860, Stephens Papers, LC.

18. Freehling and Simpson, eds., *Secession Debated*, 41, 49.

19. Ibid., 6–7, 13, 29.

20. Ibid., 38, 141–42.

21. Ibid., 39–41.

22. Ibid., 118–21, 129.

23. Ibid., 28; P., ed., *T., S., & C.* 2: 514; *Special Message of Gov. Joseph E. Brown . . . November 7, 1860* (Milledgeville, Ga., 1860), 17.

24. Freehling and Simpson, eds., *Secession Debated*, 148–49; J. Henley Smith to Alexander Stephens, November 16, 1860, Stephens Papers, LC.

25. A distinction so nicely made in Carey, *Parties*, 240, that I have filched some of the phrasing.

26. Freehling and Simpson, eds., *Secession Debated*, 11–12.

27. Ibid., 24.

28. *Augusta Constitutionalist*, November 23, 1860.

29. The complete exchange of letters between Stephens and Lincoln can be found in Alexander H. Stephens, *A Constitutional View of the Late War Between the States . . .* , 2 vols. (Philadelphia, 1870), 2: 266–70.

30. Alexander to Linton Stephens, November 8, 21, 1860, Linton to Alexander Stephens, November 26, December 2, 1860, SP, M.

31. Abraham Lincoln to William H. Seward, February 1, 1861; Resolutions drawn up for Republican members of the Senate Committee of Thirteen, n.d. [February 20, 1861], both in Basler, ed., *Lincoln's Works* 4: 157, 183.

32. Thomas D. Morris, *Free Men All: The Personal Liberty Laws of the North, 1780–1861* (Baltimore, 1974), 202–18, reviews these reconsiderations of the Personal Liberty Laws. Professor Morris sees little chance of a successful compromise in the history as it developed. But he does not consider whether changes would have been enhanced

if a Southwide ultimatum had made it clear that the fate of the Union rode on the negotiations.

33. I first tried out my Hammond-Stephens speculations at an Oberlin College lecture and seminar. The helpfulness of the occasion was no surprise, for this was Oberlin and these were Gary Kornblith's students. Professor Kornblith's "Rethinking the Coming of the Civil War: A Counterfactual Exercise," *JAH* 90 (2003): 76–105, while harboring a larger sense of pre–Civil War alternate possibilities than mine, pushes us all toward deeper thought and more explicit writing about illuminating alternatives—or nonalternatives.

I have also benefited from conversations about Stephens with Craig Simpson and about Hammond with Ann Fuller, Jean Hughes, Carol Lasser, and Lawrence McDonnell.

Chapter 27. Southwestern Separatists' Tactics and Messages

1. S. R. Gist to John Pettus, November 8, 1860, Governors Records, MISS. See also William Gist to Pettus, November 6, 1860, same collection.

2. William L. Barney, *The Secessionist Impulse: Alabama and Mississippi in 1860* (Princeton, 1974), 195. Mississippi and Pettus switched to Separatist tactics so smoothly, so overwhelmingly, and with such passion that it is tempting to see the governor's and Jefferson Davis's late October/early November preference for Cooperationism as a doomed exception, with Mississippi sure to seize the Separatist banner even if South Carolina faltered. That might have happened. But almost all the evidence for an inevitable Mississippi surge came *after* South Carolina's galvanizing action. In the earlier context, before the South Carolina legislature's November 10, 1860, unanimous decision for Separatism, Mississippi opinion was more unformed and still responsive to the December 1859 southern convention call that Christopher Memminger had driven through the South Carolina legislature. If the South Carolina legislature had not changed the context on November 10—if the legislature had invited the southern convention idea to swell as lawmakers did in November 9 votes—the early November Cooperationist leanings of Pettus, Davis, and Mississippi commissioner to Virginia Peter Starke might have seemed more typical of Mississippi opinion. In politics, context is everything, and evidence from the period after the context changed cannot demonstrate certainties before the change.

3. Amelia W. Williams and Eugene Barker, eds., *The Writings of Sam Houston*, 8 vols. (Austin, 1938–43), 8: 192–97.

4. *Alexandria Constitutionalist,* December 15, 1860.

5. The best biographies of Houston are still those listed in Freehling, *Road* 1: 605, n. 25.

6. Williams and Barker, eds., *Writings of Houston* 8: 184–85. My favorite book on Texas during the secession crisis is Walter L. Buenger, *Secession and the Union in Texas* (Austin, 1984). Also full of useful information are Dale Baum, *The Shattering of Texas Unionism . . .* (Baton Rouge, 1998); Edward R. Maher, Jr., "Secession in Texas" (Ph.D. dissertation, Fordham University, 1960); Billy D. Ledbetter, "Slavery, Fear, and Disunion in the Lone Star State . . ." (Ph.D. dissertation, North Texas State University, 1972); and Anna Irene Sandbo, "Beginnings of the Secession Movement in Texas," *Southwestern Historical Quarterly* 18 (1914): 41–73.

7. Williams and Barker, eds., *Writings of Houston* 8: 208. Houston announced his decisions to the Texas populace in a public letter dated December 3, printed in the *LaGrange True Issue,* December 6, 1860.

8. James Hall Bell, *Speech . . . Dec. 1st, 1860* (Austin, 1860), esp. 1–2, 4, 10, 15.

9. Oran Miles Roberts, *Speech . . . 1st December, 1860* (n.p. [Austin], 1860), esp. 24–26.

10. *Austin* (Texas) *State Gazette,* December 8, 1860.

11. Ibid., December 15, 1860.

12. Wheeler to James Harper Starr, January 9, 1861, Starr Papers, TX.

13. Charles B. Dew, *Apostles of Disunion: Southern Commissioners and the Causes of the Civil War* (Charlottesville, 2001).

14. Ibid., 85, 89.

15. *Journal of the Convention of the People of South Carolina, held in 1860* . . . (Columbia, 1862), 11, 26.

16. Harris to Pettus, December 31, 1861, Governors Records, MISS.

17. *Journal of the State Convention* . . . (Jackson, Miss., 1861), 197.

18. *NOD*, November 18, 1860; Dew, *Apostles of Disunion*, 99; *North and South* 7 (2004): 21.

19. *Paulding Eastern Clarion*, November 4, 1860; *NOD*, October 31, 1860.

20. Major Benjamin McCullough to Thomas Duggan, December 22, 1859, in *San Antonio Ledger*, January 12, 1860.

21. *Vicksburg Weekly Sun*, November 19, 1860.

22. Ibid., November 12, 1860; James C. Wilson, *Address . . . November 17, 1860* (Gonzales, Tex., 1860), 6.

23. Conrad to C. W. Allen et al., December 24, 1860, in *NOD*, December 28, 1860.

24. *NOD*, November 1, 1860.

25. *Vicksburg Weekly Sun*, October 29, 1860; Reagan in *Marshall Texas Republican*, February 9, 1861.

26. This marvelous quote is the best evidence in the best of the several recent attempts to explain secession as the determination to save the equality of southern white men from Republicans' enslavement: Thornton, *Politics and Power*, 450. The analytical breakthrough also especially informs William Cooper's fine *Liberty and Slavery: Southern Politics to 1860* (New York, 1983). If it seems strange that masters of unequal slaves should fight a revolution for liberty and equality, the paradox is at the heart of the American Revolution no less than the southern revolution and is the best answer to Samuel Johnson's famous query: "How is it that we hear the loudest yelps for liberty among the drivers of negroes?" American whites' yelp was profoundly a cry to be the reverse of Negroes and slaves, given its stridency by the very presence of despised unequals in the land of supposed egalitarianism.

This new interpretation is a major step forward despite its major limitations—its almost total failure to explain antiegalitarian South Carolina (and thus the very origins of the southern revolution), plus its failure to incorporate southwestern secessionists' ferocious determination to defy egalitarianism, both for blacks and for their white opponents, North and South. For further discussion, see below, n. 29, and above, ch. 21, n. 30.

27. *Austin Texas State Gazette*, March 16, 1861; *Paulding Eastern Clarion*, November 14, 1860.

28. David C. Clopton to C. C. Clay, December 13, 1860, Clay Papers, DU; Wakelyn, ed., *Secession Pamphlets*, 114.

29. This determination not to allow white opponents the democratic rights or social status of equal republicans was one defining contradiction of the southwestern revolution for "equality"—along with the determination to use the liberating revolution to keep blacks ground under. To fail to incorporate this antiegalitarian viciousness in an interpretation of secession (especially one that emphasizes white men's egalitarian salvation) is to miss crucial points not only about disunion but about the Slave South beyond secessionism: the culture's failure to keep white republicanism and black slavery cleanly severed by a color line; its inability to consolidate black slavery without repressing white dissenters; its repugnance for allowing Southern Republicans a republican's right to assume office; and its determination to restrain national white republicanism (for example, free congressional discussion) with antirepublican laws or procedures (for example, the congressional gag rules).

30. R. S. Holt to Joseph Holt, November 9, 1860, Holt Papers, LC.

31. *New Orleans Bee*, November 12, 1860.

32. *New Orleans Courier*, November 10, 1860.

33. Barney, *Road to Secession,* 187–88.

34. Oscar M. Addison Journal, entry for March 6, 1861, Addison Papers, TX; George D. Denison to Sister Eliza, March 29, 1861, Denison Papers, LC.

35. Barney, *Secessionist Impulse,* 269; Joseph Henderson to John Henderson, December 16, 1860, Henderson Papers, ALA.

36. Thomas J. Jennings to James Harper Starr, January 16, 1861, Starr Papers, TX.

37. Johnson J. Hooper to John DeBerniere Hooper, December 25, 1860, John DeB. Hooper Papers, NC.

38. For an excellent account of this vital subject, see Mitchell Snay, *The Gospel of Disunion: Religion and Separatism in the Antebellum South* (New York, 1993).

39. A modern biography of Palmer would be welcome, but Thomas Cary Johnson, *The Life and Letters of Benjamin Morgan Palmer* (Richmond, 1906) remains useful.

40. Wakelyn, ed., *Secession Pamphlets,* reprints this gem, 63–77. For the whopper, see 68.

41. Ibid., 67.

42. Ibid., 70–71.

43. Ibid., 69.

44. Ibid., 69, 71.

45. Rev. J. E. Carnes, *Address on the Duty of the Slave States . . . Dec. 12th, 1860* (Galveston, 1860).

46. B. M. Palmer, D.D., and W. T. Leacock, D.D., *The Rights of the South Defended in the Pulpit* (Mobile, 1860), esp. 15–16.

Chapter 28. Compromise Rejected

1. Clemens to John Crittenden, November 24, 1860, Crittenden Papers, LC—the single most important Cooperationist letter, especially for demonstrating the straitjacket within which Lower South opponents of Separatism struggled.

2. Clemens to William B. Wood, November 26, 1850, Alexander Martin Wood Papers, ALA.

3. Again, Clemens to Crittenden, November 24, 1860, Crittenden Papers, LC, also enclosing the November 19 *Huntsville Circular,* another superb illumination of the edgy Cooperationist spirit. The Cooperationists' limitations enormously aided the Separatists' stampede, which makes the nature of Lower South opposition to Separatism a key cause of disunion. A full-scale study of Cooperationism would fill a surprising hole in pre–Civil War literature.

4. *Jackson Daily Mississippian,* December 1, 1860.

5. One of the best points in William Scarborough's fine study of the South's richest planters, *Masters of the Big House.* The fact that economic motives impelled many an upper-class titan *away* from revolutionary gambles shows that the southern ruling class, like the South itself, lay fractured along geographic and personal lines. A wealthy Louisianan (or Virginian) usually did not emulate a South Carolina tycoon—yet another reason why secession could not come in a Southwide rush but place by place, piece by piece, with *Separatism* an ideal label for disunion achieved by the separated.

6. Milledge Bonham to William Gist, December, 3, 1860, Bonham Papers, SC.

7. Gist to Bonham, December 6, 1860, Bonham Papers, SC.

8. Joseph Brown to Howell Cobb, December 15, 1860, Cobb Papers, GA; John B. Lamar to David F. Barrow, December 13, 1860, Barrow Papers, GA; William Henry Trescot to Cobb, December 14, 1860, in P., ed., *T., S., & C.* 2: 522.

9. Edward McPherson, *The Political History of . . . the Great Rebellion . . .* (New York, 1864), 37. The signers and supposed "would have signed" congressmen are here listed along with the text signed (or not signed!).

10. John J. Crittenden to Orlando Brown, December 6, 1860, Brown Papers, FC.

11. Two fine books trace the Crittenden Compromise from different angles: David Potter, *Lincoln and His Party in the Secession Crisis* (New Haven, 1942); and Kenneth M. Stampp, *And the War Came: The North and the Secession Crisis, 1860–1861* (Baton Rouge, 1950).

12. R. Alton Lee, "The Corwin Amendment in the Secession Crisis," *Ohio Historical Quarterly* 70 (1961): 1–26. I will discuss this illuminating subject extensively in my forthcoming *Lincoln's Room for Growth: A Great President's Early Presidential Stumbles.*

13. McPherson, *Great Rebellion,* 71, 86–88, contains the various senators' suggestions. See also Hunter to James R. Micou, November 24, 1860, in *RE,* December 12, 1860; Hunter to John Randolph Tucker, January 19, 1861, Tucker Papers, NC.

14. Toombs's wording varies in various eyewitness accounts, but I have followed Georgia King to Henry Lord Page King, November 15, 1860, Thomas Butler King Papers, NC.

15. McPherson, *Great Rebellion,* 37.

16. Toombs to E. B. Pullin et al., December 13, 1860, in P., ed., *T., S., & C.* 2: 519–22.

17. The best biographies are Albert D. Kirwan, *John J. Crittenden: the Struggle for the Union* (Lexington, Ky., 1962) and William Y. Thompson, *Robert Toombs of Georgia* (Baton Rouge, 1966).

18. Ulrich B. Phillips handles this matter expertly in *The Life of Robert Toombs* (1913; New York, 1968), 208.

19. Lincoln to Elihu B. Washburne, December 13, 1860, Basler, ed., *Lincoln's Works* 4: 151.

20. McPherson, *Great Rebellion,* 37–38.

21. Phillips, *Toombs,* 204–5.

22. McPherson, *Great Rebellion,* 38.

23. Bonham to William Gist, December 3, 1860, Bonham Papers, SC.

Chapter 29. Military Explosions

1. For Anderson's military estimates and pleas for orders, see *OR,* 74–89.

2. Cauthen, *South Carolina Goes to War,* 94–95.

3. *OR,* 103.

4. Ibid., 109–10.

5. A book on the father and son, or on either eccentric, could be a colorful and informing read, but for now the slim pickings include Takaki, *Pro-Slavery Crusade,* 201–12; and Russell K. Brown, "Charles Augustus Lafayette Lamar," in *Encyclopedia of the American Civil War...*, ed. David Heidler and Jeanne Heidler (New York, 2000), 1137.

6. Takaki, *Pro-Slavery Crusade,* 205, quotes Gazaway's protest and C.A.L.'s response.

7. The story is adequately told in Tom Henderson Wells, *The Slave Ship Wanderer* (Athens, Ga., 1967).

8. Quoted in Brown, "Lamar," 1137.

9. C.A.L. Lamar to Gazaway Lamar, November 5, 1860, C.A.L. Lamar Papers, EU.

10. Same to same, November 26, 1860, C.A.L. Lamar Papers, EU.

11. Charles A. L. Lamar to Robert Gourdin, December 29, 1860, Keith Read Papers, GA.

12. Same to same, same date, Gourdin Papers, EU.

13. Typescript biography in Alexander Lawton Papers, NC. For an indication of Lawton's sober and conservative intentions during the Fort Pulaski seizure, see Sarah (Mrs. Alexander) Lawton to My Dear Friend, January 4, 1861, Lawton Papers.

14. Lawton to Gourdin, December 16, 1860, Gourdin Papers, EU.

15. Lamar to Gourdin, December 29, 1860, Keith Read Papers, GA.

16. So Brown reported in his Executive Minutebook, January 2, 1861, Georgia Department of Archives and History, Atlanta (hereafter cited as Georgia Archives).

17. *OR*, 115–18.

18. Jamison's telegram to Brown, January 1, 1861, is in the Telamon Cuyler Papers, GA.

19. Joseph Brown, Executive Minutebook, January 2, 1861, Georgia Archives.

20. Joseph E. Brown to Governor Moore, January 5, 1861, Samuel Crawford Papers, LC.

21. James Mercer Green to Robert N. Gourdin, January 5, 1861, Keith Read Papers, GA; Joseph Brown, Executive Minutebook, January 2, 1861, Georgia Archives.

22. Moore's orders to Todd, January 3, 1861, were conveyed in two telegrams and a letter of that date, all in John B. Todd Papers, ALA.

23. George F. Pearce, *Pensacola During the Civil War . . .* (Gainesville, Fla., 2000), ch. 1.

24. Ibid., 26–30; Brown to Governor Andrew Moore, January 8, 1861, Samuel Crawford Papers, LC.

25. Joseph Brown to John D. Stell, January 14, 1861, Governor's Letterbook, Georgia Archives; James Mercer Green to Robert Gourdin, January 5, 1861, Keith Read Papers, GA.

26. Hershel Johnson to Alexander Stephens, January 9, 1861, Johnson Papers, DU. Stephens concurred in this (understandable) distortion of wholly unintended consequences into some conspiratorial design: Alexander Stephens to Linton Stephens, January 7, 1861, SP, M.

27. Andrew Moore to James Buchanan, January 4, 1861, Governors Papers, ALA.

28. The Governors Papers in the Mississippi, Alabama, and Georgia state archives, December, 1860, exude the frustrations of chief executives with money to spend on guns that were exasperating to find.

29. See the angry correspondence between Eli Whitney and Jefferson Davis, December 19–29, Governors Papers, MISS.

30. Powhattan Ellis, Sr., to Charles Ellis, December 25, 1860, Mumford-Ellis Papers, DU.

31. William Henry Trescot to Sanford, January 14, 1861, Nicholas Olsberg Papers, SCHS.

32. Quoted in a lively retelling of the *Star of the West* tale, W. A. Swanberg, *First Blood*, 148.

33. *OR*, 132.

34. Jefferson Davis to Franklin Pierce, January 20, 1861, Cooper, ed., *Davis Writings*, 189.

35. For a boldly stated countervailing judgment, see Jean H. Baker, *James Buchanan* (New York, 2004).

Chapter 30. Snowball Rolling

1. Percy L. Rainwater, *Mississippi, Storm Center of Secession, 1856–1861* (Baton Rouge, 1938), 196–200; Potter, *Impending Crisis*, 495, 500. Recent illuminating books on Mississippi politics include Bradley G. Bond, *Political Culture in . . . Mississippi, 1830–1900* (Baton Rouge, 1995); Christopher Morris, *Becoming Southern: The Evolution of . . . Mississippi, 1770–1860* (New York, 1995); and Christopher Olsen, *Political Culture and Secession in Mississippi . . .* (New York, 2000). But pride of place still belongs to William Barney's *Secessionist Impulse*.

2. Ralph A. Wooster, *The Secession Conventions of the South* (Princeton, 1962), 36–37.

3. Quoted in Barney, *Secessionist Impulse,* 309.

4. Wooster, *Secession Conventions,* 73; Dorothy Dodd, "The Secession Movement in Florida, 1850–1861," *Florida Historical Quarterly* 13 (1933–34): 3–24, 45–66.

5. Clarence P. Denman, *The Secession Movement in Alabama* (Montgomery, 1933), 93–116; Potter, *Impending Crisis,* 500.

6. Barney, *Secessionist Impulse,* 298.

7. Ibid., 301; William R. Smith, *The History and Debates of the Convention of . . . Alabama* (Atlanta, 1861), 69–74. Smith's is the best account of convention speeches and debates in any Lower South state; it is particularly valuable for illustrating the clash between northern and southern Alabamians. Barney, *Secessionist Impulse,* is almost as good on Alabama as on Mississippi. Still, Mills Thornton's *Politics and Power,* despite the disagreements with its central interpretations that I record elsewhere in these notes, is the best guide to local politics in any Lower South state.

8. Hugh Lawson Clay to C. C. Clay, Jr., January 11, 1861, Clay Papers, DU.

9. Thomas J. McClellan to his wife, January 6, 7, 8, 13, 14, McClellan Papers, ALA; McClellan to John, January 7, 1861, Buchanan-McClellan Papers, NC; William A. Smith to wife, January 12, 1861, Easley-Smith Family Papers, LC.

10. Wooster, *Secession Conventions,* 59; Smith to wife, January 12, 1861, Easley-Smith Family Papers, LC.

11. See Michael P. Johnson's fine "A New Look at the Popular Vote for Delegates to the Georgia Secession Convention," *GHQ* 56 (1972): 259–75. While I think that Professor Johnson's *Toward a Patriarchal Republic: The Secession of Georgia* (Baton Rouge, 1977) properly stresses fears of a southern internal crisis as central to the secessionist movement, his evidence for the proposition seems based too narrowly on slight changes in the Georgia constitution, and his conception seems too narrowly focused on white Georgians' fear of each other. Still, Johnson's book ranks with Anthony Carey's *Parties, Slavery, and the Union in Antebellum Georgia* as the best guide to that state, especially if supplemented by J. William Harris's superb local study *Plain Folk and Gentry in a Slave Society: White Liberty and Black Slavery in Augusta's Hinterlands* (Middletown, Conn., 1985).

12. Wooster, *Secession Conventions,* 90–91.

13. Ibid., 91.

14. See Charles B. Dew's two seminal essays, "The Long Lost Returns: The Candidates and Their Totals in Louisiana's Secession Election," *Louisiana History* 10 (1969): 353–69, and "Who Won the Secession Election in Louisiana?" *JSH* 36 (1970): 18–32.

15. John M. Sachar, *A Perfect War of Politics: Parties, Politicians, and Democracy in Louisiana, 1824–1861* (Baton Rouge, 2003), esp. 296.

16. Wooster, *Secession Conventions,* 130.

17. CC, August 8, 1860.

Chapter 31. Upper South Stalemate

1. Benjamin C. Howard to John P. Kennedy, December 26, 1860, Kennedy Papers, Enoch Pratt Library, Baltimore.

2. John P. Kennedy to George S. Bryan, December 27, 1860, Kennedy Papers, Pratt Library; Kennedy, *The Border States: Their Power and Duty in the Present Disordered Condition of the Country* (Philadelphia, 1861), esp. 17, 25–27, 30–31.

3. William Rives, Jr., to Rives Sr., December 21, 1860, Rives Papers, LC; John Letcher to James D. Davidson, March 9, 1861, Davidson Papers, WISC.

4. *Wilmington Herald,* November 9, 1861; Samuel Smith Nicholas, *South Carolina, Disunion, and a Mississippi Valley Confederacy* (n.p., n.d. [probably Louisville, 1860 or 1861]).

5. RE, July 13, 1860; J. O. Harrison to Joseph Holt, January 1, 1859, Holt Papers, LC.

6. Robert J. Breckinridge, "Discourse Delivered on . . . January 4, 1861 . . . ," in Wakelyn, ed., *Secession Pamphlets*, 247–61, esp. 249; Thomas M. Peters to James Buchanan, December 6, 1860, Buchanan Papers, HSP; Henry Cooper to M. D. Cooper, April 27, 1861, William F. Cooper Papers, TN.

7. Cooper's same April 27 letter; *Baltimore Courier*, February 2, 1861; R. W. Bush to Linton Stephens, January 27, 1861, SP, M.

8. This point is made especially well in Holt, *Political Crisis of the 1850s*, and in Daniel W. Crofts, *Reluctant Confederates: Upper South Unionists in the Secession Crisis* (Chapel Hill, 1989). Professor Crofts's seminal study illuminates every point in this chapter and has few if any equals among monographs on an aspect of antebellum southern politics.

9. William C. Davis, *"A Government of Our Own": The Making of the Confederacy* (New York, 1994) is the best monograph. The wonderful series of Thomas R. R. Cobb letters from Montgomery to his wife, Marion, in February 1861, Cobb Papers, GA, illustrates the dread of reconstruction, also fearfully expressed in Jefferson L. Pugh to William Porcher Miles, January 24, 1861, Miles Papers, NC.

10. *CM*, February 13, 1861.

11. *CC*, April 6, 11, 1861, reports that Spratt mustered only sixteen reopening diehards, including James H. Adams, with 146 South Carolina convention delegates voting against the far-out extremists, in another indication that moderates (South Carolina style!) controlled the revolution.

12. Wooster, *Secession Conventions*, 207–55, esp. 232.

13. Ibid., 173–203, esp. 180, 193.

14. Ibid., 163–64; James M. Wood, *Rebellion and Realignment: Arkansas' Road to Secession* (Fayetteville, 1987).

15. James Davidson to George Yerber, February 3, 1861, Davidson to A. T. Caperton, February 6, 1861, Davidson Papers, WISC.

16. On the 1829–32 crises, see my *Road* 1: 162–69, and Alison G. Freehling, *Drift Toward Dissolution: The Virginia Slavery Debates of 1831–1832* (Baton Rouge, 1982).

17. Freehling, *Road* 1: 511–15.

18. Skillfully analyzed in Crofts, *Reluctant Confederates*, 140–42.

19. Well analyzed in Wooster, *Secession Conventions*, 142, 152. Two older studies also remain useful here: Henry T. Shanks, *The Secession Movement in Virginia, 1847–1861* (Richmond, 1934), and James C. McGregor, *The Disruption of Virginia* (New York, 1922).

20. John B. Floyd to William R. Burwell, February 7, 1861, Burwell Papers, VA.

21. On George Randolph's father's and grandfather's compromised colonization/ abolition efforts, see *Road* 1: 123–30, 155–57.

22. On John B. Floyd's father's and Thomas Jefferson Randolph's role in the 1831–32 trauma, see ibid., 181–83.

23. George Randolph to Cornelia Randolph, November 3, 1860, Nicholas Trist Papers, NC. See also same to Septima Randolph, October 14, 1860, Randolph-Meikleham Family Papers, VA.

24. Unless otherwise noted, the tone and quotes in this and the next five paragraphs come from the William H. Holcombe Autobiography, typed copy in NC, 36ff. William H. was James P. Holcombe's younger brother.

25. The quote in this sentence is from the *Wellsburg Herald*, March 29, 1861.

26. Speech in the Virginia secession convention, March 20, 1861, Reese, ed., *Proceedings of the Virginia State Convention* 2: 79. I analyze this superb source in *Reintegration of American History*, 3–11.

27. On Conway, see *Road* 1: 102–3; John d'Entremont, *Southern Emancipator: Moncure Conway, The American Years, 1832–1865* (New York, 1987).

28. Reese, ed., *Proceedings* 1: 62–66.

29. Ibid. 1: 759, 2: 99, 3: 89.

30. Ibid. 3: 105.

31. Ibid. 1: 256–57, 3: 106.

32. Ibid. 2: 86. Especially fine on how blacks' resistance helped radicalize secessionists such as Holcombe is William A. Link, *Roots of Secession: Slavery and Politics in Antebellum Virginia* (Chapel Hill, 2003).

33. Henry Dering to Waitman Willey, March 19, 1861, Willey Papers, WVU.

34. Henry Wise to Richard A. Wise, February 18, 1861, in Wise, *Wise,* 270.

35. Reese, ed., *Proceedings* 1: 757–58.

36. Ibid., 2: 93–94, 3: 108.

37. Robert G. Gunderson, *Old Gentlemen's Convention: The Washington Peace Conference of 1861* (Madison, Wisc., 1961).

38. Reese, ed., *Proceedings* 1: 523–28.

39. Ibid., 116, 289. The flamboyant contest of images illuminates Virginians' excruciating plight: at the mercy of outside forces that they could not control and aching to stop from being torn one way or the other. The distress of a folk that had once been king of American political processes and now was pawn is captured with fine depth of feeling at the local level in Edward L. Ayers, *In the Presence of Mine Enemies: War in the Heart of America, 1859–1863* (New York, 2003).

40. Reese, ed., *Proceedings* 2: 103.

41. Ibid. 3: 163.

42. Shanks, *Secession Movement in Virginia,* 79; Joseph Leonard King, Jr., *Dr. George William Bagby: A Study of Virginian Literature, 1850–1880* (New York, 1927). Too late for the researching and drafting of this book, Peter S. Carmichael published his fine *The Last Generation: Young Virginians in Peace, War, and Reunion* (Chapel Hill, 2005). I admire Professor Carmichael's parallel "young Virginia" argument in his ch. 5, although I think that he has not pushed his formidable thesis quite far enough in his secession section.

43. George Latham to George Bagby, December 30, 1860, Bagby Family Papers, VHS.

44. Same to same, March 9, 1861, Bagby Family Papers, VHS.

45. John Hampden Chamberlayne to George Bagby, December 5, 1860, John Esten Cooke to Bagby, January 30, 1861, Bagby Family Papers, VHS.

46. Henry Gray Latham to Bagby, n.d. [February 1861] and March 26, 1861, Bagby Family papers, VHS. See also Edwin R. Page to Bagby, March 3, 1861, R. H. Walkins to Bagby, March 16, 1861, same collection.

Chapter 32. Stalemate—and the South—Shattered

1. The tale of the forts is spun from slightly different directions in Stampp, *And The War Came;* in Potter, *Lincoln and His Party;* and in Richard N. Current, *Lincoln and the First Shot* (Philadelphia, 1963).

2. I look forward to detailing this important story in my forthcoming *Lincoln's Room for Growth: A Great President's Early Presidential Stumbles.* Anyone who wants to trace the tale sooner should begin with *OR,* ch. 4, with an eye out for Winfield Scott's blunders.

3. Lincoln to Gilmer, December 15, 1860, in Basler, ed., *Lincoln's Works* 4: 152.

4. The fact that Lincoln did have a (very moderate) plan to weaken slavery inside the (Border) South and that disunionists partly seceded over that very plan undercuts the old "revisionist" theory that slavery issues were meaningless in the secession crisis and the Civil War a needless blunder (as well as Mills Thornton's neorevisionism, in *Politics and Power,* that no menace can be found in slavery politics—only an imagined monster, stemming from economic politics). The secessionists' and Republicans' meeting of minds on

Lincoln's antislavery menace also partly sustains the theory that Northerners and Southerners irretrievably clashed over slavery's morality.

But that partially viable moral theory of Civil War causation can only take posterity so far—and not far enough to explain why northern and southern masses came to the battlefields. The facts remain that the northern masses did not elect Lincoln primarily to pursue his antislavery plan (a strategy that he barely even hinted at in the 1850s), any more than the Middle South masses fled the Union primarily to escape Lincoln's antislavery strategy. In the racist North, the protection of white men's liberties against the Slave Power had to bolster moral concern about blacks' liberty, just as the protection of white men's state's right to withdraw consent had to bolster concern about Lincoln's immediate menace to slavery in the Upper South. The masses in both regions came to fight passionately for a morally tainted version of their own liberty: Northerners for their freedom from Slave Power assaults on whites' democratic processes (with much less concern until 1863 for blacks' freedom), and Southerners for their freedom to defy federal coercion of unconsenting whites (with every intention to coerce both unconsenting blacks and southern whites who contested slavery or secession). In the land where black slavery everywhere intertwined with white democracy, redemption could only come amidst a morally dubious fog.

On the minority of Republicans who steered atypically free of the fog, Richard H. Sewell, *Ballots for Freedom: Antislavery Politics in the United States, 1837–1860* (New York, 1976) is particularly fine.

5. Montgomery Meigs Diary, entry for March 29–April 8, 1861, in *AHR* 26 (1921): 300.

6. Lincoln to Robert S. Chew, April 6, 1861, and Chew to Lincoln, April 8, 1861, both in Basler, ed., *Lincoln's Works* 4: 323–24.

7. David Detzer, *Allegiance: Fort Sumter, Charleston, and the Beginning of the Civil War* (New York, 2001), 308–9.

8. For Lincoln's fateful proclamation, see Basler, ed., *Lincoln's Works,* 4: 331–32.

9. Reese, ed., *Proceedings* 4: 46.

10. Ibid., 43–49.

11. Ibid., 24–25.

12. This part of the Virginia story is nicely narrated in Simpson, *Wise,* 248–51.

13. Reese, ed., *Proceedings* 4: 122.

14. Eyewitness account of Judge John Critcher, delegate from Richmond, quoted in Wise, *Wise,* 280–81.

15. I have benefited from many talks with Roberta Culbertson about the stark clarification that the onset of violence begets, forcing stallers and fudgers off the fence to decide whether to kill us or them.

16. Reese, ed., *Proceedings* 4: 144; Wooster, *Secession Conventions,* 149.

17. An intriguing historiographical tale throws additional light on this aspect of the text's historical tale. In his latest impressive book, *Apostles of Disunion,* Charles Dew writes that he had imbibed from his southern schools the neo-Confederate position that state's rights as a shield against Big Brother Washington's tariff and other economic intrusions (and not slavery!) caused the Civil War. But Professor Dew found instead that Lower South commissioners to other states emphasized menace to slavery (and especially menace to control over blacks), not menace to state's rights or to economic issues, in their pleas to as-yet-unseceded states to join the revolution. So slavery, he concluded, not state's rights, brought rebels to the battlefield.

His own story, however, makes that generalization only partly true. Lower South commissioners' emphasis on the menace to slavery helps show that the first (Lower South) wave of revolution *did* rise from that apprehension. But the commissioners' arguments on slavery did not sufficiently sweep the Upper South. Rather, for the northern South to join the southern South's revolution, Lincoln's menace to a state's alleged right to withdraw consent had to intrude.

Three qualifications are necessary, before the climactic impact of state's rights becomes plausible. First of all, the state's rights impact on revolution had nothing to do with the neo-Confederates' fancy that Professor Dew learned in southern schools: limitations on ordinary government on such mundane matters as tariffs. As I emphasize in chapter 22, prewar Southerners sought a bigger national government to protect slavery, while Northerners pitched to the state's rights side, on the most contested ordinary matters of governance. The higher state's rights principle that helped spread disunion from Lower to Upper South was the very different alleged right of the people of a state to end a government entirely.

Second, the state's rights boost to Middle South revolution would have been irrelevant if the slavery issue had not already brought something like a third of the region's citizens up to the mark. Third, any attempt to differentiate between slavery and a state's right to withdraw consent is iffy, because *this* state's right and slavery cannot be cleanly severed. Black belt whites who observed slaves daily had a special obsession with protecting a free citizen's right to consent to be governed—exactly the precious right that slaves lacked, precisely the lack that most made a person a slave.

Comprehending a world's revolution partially demands understanding how the very marrow of a social order made certain political abstractions lethal. One could write much of the climactic history of the southern rebellion on a pinhead heralding two explosive ideas: that a self-respecting slaveholder must demand national protection of his (slave) property, as circumstances make protection necessary, and that an unenslaved citizen must righteously guard his consent to be governed, as the people of his state define consent.

18. William C. Rives, Sr., to Rives Jr., May 6, 1861, Rives Papers, LC.

19. Stephens, *Constitutional View* 2: 121.

20. Wooster, *Secession Conventions,* 165, 188, 203.

21. Quoted in Crofts, *Reluctant Confederates,* 158–59.

22. McPherson, *Battle Cry of Freedom,* 295; Michael J. Dubin, *United States Congressional Elections, 1788–1997* (Jefferson, N.C., 1998), 189. I am grateful to Michael Holt for suggesting that these votes marked the termination of the road to disunion—and for helping to make these last three years in Charlottesville a fine climax of my writing life.

23. For full development of the story summarized in this paragraph, see my *South vs. The South* (New York, 2002).

24. See my *Prelude to Civil War,* passim.

25. Jack Pole brought this important comparison powerfully to my attention at the BRANCH discussion of my ideas.

26. Abolitionists' inability to capture the North solely by wielding antislavery ideas hardly means that their role in Civil War causation was minor. Dozens of historians, led by David B. Davis, have made abolitionist scholarship a triumph of slavery studies in late years. These scholars have demonstrated antislavery zealots' central role in awakening a dozing nation to the fact that slavery *was* a problem, in arousing tens of thousands of Northerners to solve the problem, and in provoking the bitter southern reaction against outsiders' problem solving. I have built upon this scholarship by seeking to explain why the nation went all the way to Civil War, even though abolitionists could go only part of the way toward persuading the prewar North.

As I said in *Road* 1: 626, the final words, in notes written primarily for fellow professionals, should be reserved for the pros who eased the final problems of publication. A fossil who still writes on long yellow sheets (and who finds nineteenth-century politics far more comprehensible than twenty-first-century word processors) could not have survived the prepublication rush without his longtime, long-suffering administrative assistant, Lynn Hiler, aided recently by Ann White Spencer. Nor could the manuscript have emerged unscathed through the Oxford University Press labyrinth had not my old friend Susan Ferber stepped in as the new facilitator, after Sheldon Meyer retired and Peter Ginna moved to another press. Nor could Susan have prevailed without the help of two members of Sheldon's old team: India Cooper, incomparable copyeditor (and so much more than a copyeditor), and Joellyn Ausanka, expert production manager. All these compatriots have reminded me (as if I needed a reminder) that while historical scholarship is a lonely pursuit, no professional succeeds alone.

And now, just as this last (I thought) word has been corrected, news arrives that Sheldon Meyer has died. Thus this will be the final Oxford book that he edited. For the last fifty years, Sheldon has been among the best friends of all who love American history. For the last twenty years, he and my wife have been the best friends of this project. So at this sad moment, these two remarkable people must stand together on my dedication page.

Index

Prepared by Peter Brigaitis and Marie S. Nuchols

Note: Page numbers in *italics* indicate photographs and illustrations.

Aberdeen Sunny South, 159, 186
Ableman v. Booth, 435–36
Accomack County, Virginia, 236
Adams, James H., 179, 184, 478
Adams, John Quincy, 89
African colonization. *See* colonization of blacks
African slave trade: and C.A.L., 480; and the Confederate Constitution, 503; and elections, 338; and Leonidas Spratt, 168–74, 503–4; reopening efforts, 144, 177–84, 284, 304, 555n. 1; and secessionism, 175–77, 503–4
Agassiz, Louis, 42
agriculture: and the Kansas conflict, 71, 123–25; and slave labor, 2, 11, 13, 20–21, 293, 353, 361, 363, 366, 390; South Carolina, 11, 13, 19–21; and southern economics, 19–22
Alabama: agriculture, 2, 13, 20; and the Baltimore Convention, 313–14, 316–17, 319, 320; and the Charleston Convention, 285, 287, 296–98, 302–3, 305, 307; and delayed secession plan, 467; and the Democratic Party, 279; demographics, 361; and federal fort seizures, 284, 483; and filibustering, 152; and the Kansas conflict, 127; and Lincoln's election, 345; and maritime trade, 148; and Mississippi secession, 453; mob violence in, 214; and presidential patronage, 382; reaction to Lincoln's election, 436; and the secession debate, 382, 385–88, 401, 446, 453–54, 459, 492–95; and South Carolina immigrants, 363; and southern convention efforts, 264; and the Southern Manifesto, 470; and vigilante violence, 334; and white belts, 16; and yellow fever, 41, 47
Alabama Platform, 279–80, 286–87, 303, 305, 306, 313, 316

Alcorn, James L., 491
Aldrich, Alfred: and class divisions, 381–82; and Hammond's suppressed letter, 405, 415–16, 418, 442; and paternalism, 457; and the secession debate, 403–4, 443
Allston, Robert F. W., 127
American Antislavery Society, 4
American Colonization Society, 112
American Emigration Aid and Homestead Society, 238
American Party (Know-Nothings): decline of, 95; and elections, 104; and nativism, 87, 89–96; and the Oppositionist Party, 326; origin of, 499; and Spratt, 174; and Whiggery, 323, 502; and Wise, 217
American Revolution, 9, 348, 423, 577n. 26
American Slavery as It Is, Testimony of a Thousand Witnesses (American Antislavery Society), 3–4
Anderson, John T., 263
Anderson, Robert, 370, 424, 477–79, 481, 487–88, 497, 519–20
antiegalitarianism, 259, 456, 460, 577n. 26, 577n. 29
Appomattox Courthouse, 521
apprenticeship, 181–82
architecture, *164,* 356–59, 363, 408–9, 466, *473,* 552–53n. 7
aristocratic republicanism: and Aldrich, 381; and Flournoy, 91; and the Founding Fathers, 130; and Hammond, 417; and paternalism, 371–72; and Simms, 182; and South Carolina, xvii, 11, 170–71, 179, 278–79, 293–94, 353–54, 363–64, 378; and Spratt, 171, 173; and Virginia, 263, 506
Arizona, 147

Arkansas: agriculture, 13, 20, 124; and the
Baltimore Convention, 319; and the
Charleston Convention, 303, 307;
demographics, 3; and expansionism, 155,
167; and pioneers, 38; and reenslavement
efforts, 200; and the secession debate, 504,
529–30; and the territorial slavery conflict, 75
arson, 331–37, 341, 370, 424
Articles of Confederation, 347
Ashmore, John, 310
Atchison, David R., 63; and causes of the Civil
War, 532; and the Charleston Convention,
299, 300; and expansionism, 154; and John
Brown's Raid, 205; and the Kansas
controversy, 17, 62, 63, 65, 67–68, 70–79;
and Lincoln's election, 339; and political
invasion of the South, 248–49, 250
Atkinson, Alexander, 180
Atlanta, Georgia, 264
Augusta Daily Constitution, 304–5
Austin Call, 451–52
Austin State Gazette, 457
Avery, William, 298–300, 301
Ayer, Lewis, 157

Babbitt, Elijah, 252
Bachman, John, 44–47, 422
Bagby, George, 515–16, 525
Baltimore, Maryland, 88, 191–92, 195, 309–
11, 326
Baltimore Clipper, 88, 334
Baltimore Convention, 309–22
Baltimore Courier, 178
Baltimore Republican, 165
Baltimore Sun, 194
Barbour, James, 263
Barksdale, William, 140
Barnwell, Robert, 478
Barnwell Court House Speech (Hammond),
379–80, 404
Barry, William S., 303, 404
Bartow, Francis: background, 408–9; in
Columbia, 413; and the 1860 Association,
410; and Jackson, 412; military service, 409;
and the secession debate, 418, 430, 453–54;
and Toombs's resignation, 414
Bastrop Advocate, 182
Bates, Edward, 326, 329, 455, 520
Baton Rouge Arsenal, 484
the Battery, 156
Bay of Pigs invasion, 145
Bayliss, G. W., 69
Baylor, George, 514
Beecher, Henry Ward, 234
Bell, James, 450–51
Bell, John: and the Baltimore Convention, 327;
and elections, 323, 331; and expansionism,
153; and the Kansas controversy, 140–41;
and Lincoln's election, 338–40; and the
Republican nominating convention, 326

Beloved (Morrison), 350–51
Beman, Nathan, 4–6, 5
Benjamin, Judah P., 346, 457
Bennett, Thomas, 260
Benning, Henry, 430–31, 438–39, 511, 527
Benton, Thomas Hart: and Blair, 299; and the
Kansas controversy, 65, 66, 68, 71, 73–74,
77–78; and King, 300; and political invasion
of the South, 248; and the Republican
nominating convention, 326, 328; and Senate
elections, 73
Berea School (Berea College), 233–35
Berrien, John, 409
Best Friend of Charleston (locomotive), 407
Bible, 29, 45–47, 55
Bickley, George, 148
Bingham, James, 180–81
black belts: in Arkansas, 504; Cooperationists in,
465; defined, 15–16; fear of slave rebellion in,
369; and the Missouri River, 248; and
nativism, 90; and paternalism, 57–58; and
racial solidarity, 360; and reenslavement
efforts, 193; secessionism in, 528; and social
order, 584–85n. 17; and state's rights, 348–
49; and territorial slavery, 66; in Virginia,
506
Black Republicanism: Avery on, 299; Blair on,
336; and class divisions, 327; and the
Committee of Thirteen, 472, 474; and
elections, 336–37; Keitt on, 372–73; King on,
300; Moore on, 264; Morton on, 512; and
presidential patronage, 368, 373–74; Ravenel
on, 424; and reenslavement efforts, 201; and
the secession debate, 397; and the slave trade
issue, 180; and the Speakership Crisis, 266;
Stephens on, 430; as threat to slavery, 456
Blackford, Mary, 153–54
Blair, Frank, Jr.: and Benton, 299; and elections,
323, 331; and expansionism, 154; and
Helper, 242, 244–45, 299–300; and the
isothermal theory of slavery, 129; and the
Kansas controversy, 73–74, 77–79, 124; and
Lincoln's election, 340; Marshall on, 374;
and patronage, 340; and political invasion of
the South, 248–50, 254, 256, 266; and
presidential patronage, 520; and the
Republican nominating convention, 327–30
Blair, Frank, Sr., 328, 330, 337, 520
Blair, Montgomery, 329, 520
Blair, Preston, 329
Bleak Hall, 390
Bledsoe, Albert Taylor, 53–54
Bleeding Kansas, 63, 75, 124. *See also* Kansas-
Nebraska Act
Bonham, Milledge, 398, 467–68, 475
Booth, Edwin, 150
Botts, Benjamin, 324
Botts, John Minor, 324–26, 329–31, 337
Bourne, George, 27–28
Bowers, James L., 195

Boyce, James Petigru, 418
Boyce, William R., 382, 499, 529
Boyce, William W., 261, 365
Boyd, David, 341
Bracken County, Kentucky, 230
Brazil, 15, 145, 153–54, 194
Breckinridge, John C.: and elections, 331, 338–40, 395, 499; and Kentucky neutrality, 530; and the Richmond Convention, 321–22
Bright, Jesse, 98
Brooke, Walker, 177
Brooks, Iverson, 33
Brooks, Preston, 83; and the African slave trade, 168, 173; attack on Sumner, 61, 79–84, 83, 95, 139, 173, 205, 254–55, 364–65; and the Charleston Convention, 294; and compromise efforts, 469; and expansionism, 158; and the southern cult of honor, 546–47n. 36
Brown, Aaron, 106
Brown, Albert Gallatin, 277; and the Baltimore Convention, 321; and causes of the Civil War, 532; and the Charleston Convention, 286, 287; and compromise efforts, 469; and the Kansas controversy, 126–27; and Lincoln's election, 337; and the secession debate, 446; and the slave trade issue, 179; and territorial slavery, 276–78, 284; on Wise, 93
Brown, B. Gratz, 77–78, 329–30
Brown, John, 216, 218; background, 206–9; capture and execution, 215–17, 246; and causes of the Civil War, 532; fear of, 369–70; and federal fort seizures, 489; and Fee, 231; hanged, 215–17; Harpers Ferry raid, 209–21; impact on disunionism, 203; Memminger contrasted with, 262; northern support for, 246; and political invasion of the South, 258, 263–64, 266–67; Pottawatomie Massacre, 79, 208, 211; and Southern Republicanism, 561n. 16
Brown, John, Jr., 207
Brown, Joseph: and Bartow, 409; and compromise efforts, 469; and federal fort seizures, 480, 482–85; on Lincoln's threat, 439; and the secession debate, 387, 497
Brown, Oliver, 207
Brown, Susan Jemina, 334
Brown Fellowship Society, 188
Brownlow, William Ganaway "Parson," 529–30
Brummel, Beau, 390
Bryan, Edward, 175, 179, 182
Bryan, Guy M., 141
Buchanan, James, 106; and the African slave trade, 174, 182; and the Charleston Convention, 297; and compromise efforts, 467, 469; and Dred Scott v. Sandford, 109–13, 115–19, 122, 271–72, 550n. 15; and elections, 97–108, 142–43; and expansionism, 146–47, 159–60; and federal fort seizures, 477–79, 482–83, 485–89, 496–

97, 519; and the Kansas controversy, 128, 130, 135–40, 551–52n. 30; and Lincoln's election, 503; and paternalism, 189; and reenslavement efforts, 199, 201; and the Republican nominating convention, 330; and southern minority power, 533; and state's rights, 136–37, 347; and territorial emancipation, 549–50n. 14
Buford, Jefferson, 125–27, 139, 142, 172
Buford's Cavalry, 126
Bull, William Izard, 376
Burch, Robert, 372
Butler, Andrew P., 80, 82, 158

Cable, Alford, 333
Calhoun, John C.: and Brooks, 364; and compromise efforts, 471; and expansionism, 157, 367; and the Gag Rule Controversy, 99–100; and Houston, 449; and nullification, 360, 362, 435; and state's rights, 346–47, 349; and Yancey, 278, 280
California, 105, 242, 297, 338, 456
Cambridge Convention of Slaveholders, 195, 200–201
Cameron, Simon, 329
Campbell, David, 178
Campbell, John A., 110–13, 117, 166–67
Cannibals All! or, Slaves Without Masters (Fitzhugh), 36, 38–39
capitalism: and colorblind slavery, 39; compared to slavery, 28, 55–57, 195; and economic invasion of the South, 239; and expansionism, 158, 162; Fitzhugh on, 36; and Kansas emigration, 126; and paternalism, 99; postmodern traits, 52; and reenslavement efforts, 189
Capitol Building, 466
Caribbean expansionism. *See also* filibustering: and causes of the Civil War, 531; and the Charleston Convention, 298–99, 301; and compromise efforts, 475; critics of, 155–60; and Crittenden, 471; and elections, 338; and the Freeport Doctrine, 273–75; and New Orleans, 152; and South Carolina, 366–67, 456; and state's rights, 349; support for, 152–55; and Yancey, 282, 284
Carnes, J. E., 462
Carolina (steamship), 410
Carroll, Anna, 325–26
Cartwright, Samuel, 40, 57
Cass, Lewis, 105
Castle Pinckney, 478, 518
Catholic Church, 86, 88
Catron, John: and *Dred Scott v. Sandford*, 110–11, 115–17, 549–50n. 14, 550n. 15; and reenslavement efforts, 199, 200
Central America, 155, 273, 298, 327, 456
Central Confederacy movement, 500, 527
Chamberlayne, John Hampden, 515
Chambliss, J. R., 514

Charleston, South Carolina, *156*; and the African slave trade, 170–71; architecture, 356–59, *358*, 363–64, 552–53n. 7; aristocratic society, 362; climate, 291–92, 422; demographics, 171; and filibustering, 155–59; mercantile community, 406–7; and Miles, 257–58; and railroads, 406–10, *407*; and reenslavement efforts, 187–88

Charleston and Savannah Railroad Company, 408, 410, 425, 532

Charleston Courier: and the African slave trade, 169; and Hammond's suppressed letter, 406; on Kansas agriculture, 123; on Memminger, 50; on ratification process, 130; on resignations, 399; on the secession debate, 396

Charleston Democratic Convention, 430

Charleston Harbor, *518, 519*

Charleston Kansas Aid Association, 127

Charleston Mercury: on Georgia secession, 412; on the Lecompton Constitution, 141; on the Mills House meeting, 410; on Orr, 377; on resignations, 400; on secessionism, 372; and the slave trade, 169, 179; on Southern abolitionism, 368–69, 371; on Walker, 129

Charleston Standard, 50, 157, 168–70, 179

Chase, Salmon P., 103, 220, 329

Cheeves, Jordan, 187

Chesapeake Bay, 192, *192,* 193

Chesnut, James, Jr., *397*; and compromise efforts, 466; and Hammond, 379, 416; and Orr, 294; and the secession debate, 377–78, 381, 394, 396–98, 404, 418

Chesnut, Mary, *397*; in Columbia, 413; and fear of slave violence, 370–71; on Gourdin, 390; on Huger, 410; on secession sentiment, 373, 419; on Tabor, 400

Cheves, Langdon, 481

Chevis, A. L., 187

Chicago, Illinois, 329–30

Chicago Journal, 455

Christianity: and moral objections to slavery, 174–75, 510, 543n. 35; orthodoxy, 223; and paternalism, 28, 173, 177, 461; and polygenesis, 42–43; and reenslavement efforts, 194, 199–200; and religious invasion of the South, 222–35; and secessionism, 460–62; and support for slavery, 181

the Citadel, 486–87

Civil War, 47, 57, 67, 79, 375, 409

Clark, John: and the Baltimore Convention, 327; and causes of the Civil War, 532; and King, 300; and Lincoln's election, 339; and political invasion of the South, 247–54, 265–66

Clarke County, Virginia, 209–11, *210,* 236–37

Clarkson, Thomas, 28

class divisions: Aldrich on, 381–82; aristocratic republicanism, 171–72; and causes of the Civil War, 531–32; and the Charleston

Convention, 293–94; and class warfare, 69–70; and colorblind slavery, 28–29, 35–39; and economic invasion of the South, 236–40, 578n. 5; and expansionism, 154; and free vs. slave labor, 327; Hammond on, 34, 378–79; Helper on, 241; and ideology, 25–26; and land ownership, 242–43; in New Orleans, 150; and proslavery ideology, xvi; and racial tension, 569n. 14; and reenslavement efforts, 188; and the secession debate, 381, 390, 456–58; and slave labor, 187–90; in South Carolina, 354–55, 362; and voting requirements, 293–94

Clay, C. C., Jr., 150

Clay, Cassius, *228*; and antislavery sentiment, 103; and B. Gratz Brown, 77; and the Charleston Convention, 289; and elections, 323; and Fee, 227–33; and Helper, 244–45; and the isothermal theory of slavery, 129; and political invasion of the South, 256, 266; and the Republican nominating convention, 327, 330; support for, 235; and threats to slavery, 455; and Underwood, 237; Yancey on, 337

Clay, Clement C., Jr., 107

Clay, Henry, 53, 229, 470

Clemens, Jeremiah, 336, 463–64

Clemens, Sharrard, 253

Cleopatra (ship), 145–46

Cleveland, Henry, 304–5

climate. *See* weather and climate

Clopton, David, 457

Cobb, Howell, *106*; and compromise efforts, 467–69, 475; and elections, 98, 105–7; and federal fort seizures, 487; and Jackson, 411; and the Kansas controversy, 132, 135–37, 141, 143; and the Lecompton Convention, 551–52n. 30; on presidential patronage, 439; and the secession debate, 419, 467; and state's rights, 347

Cobb, Mary Ann Lamar, 107

Cobb, Thomas R. R.: and delayed secession plan, 467; and expansionism, 150; and legal restrictions on slaveholders, 48; on party loyalties, 139; and the secession debate, 430–31, 437–38; on threats to slavery, 439–40

Cockspur Island, 481

Colcock, William F.: in Columbia, 413; and the 1860 Association, 572n. 24; resignation, 401, 414; and the secession debate, 406, 418

Cold Harbor, battle of, 255

Colfax, Schuler, 94

colonization of blacks. *See also* removal of blacks: and Blair, 330; Bledsoe on, 53–54; funding for, 53, 112–13; Hammond on, 32; and post-nati laws, 228; and reenslavement efforts, 191; Republican support for, 103; and the territorial slavery conflict, 69, 70; and Virginia, 508–10

colorblind slavery: and Atchison, 78; and attacks on capitalism, 57; and the economics of slavery, 35–39; and Fitzhugh, 47; and paternalism, 51–52, 355–56

Columbia, South Carolina, 415, 421

Columbia Theological Seminary, 45

Committee of Thirteen, 470–74

Committee on Colored Populations, 197

Committee on Federal Relations, 513, 524

The Compendium of the Impending Crisis (Helper): and Blair, 249–50; and Clark, 250–53; and Lovejoy, 289; published, 244–45; and the Speakership Crisis, 247–56, 265–68

Compromise of 1850: and Brooks, 81; and the Charleston Convention, 292; and Georgia's secession, 429, 433; and Houston, 448; as model, 470; and Quitman, 163

Concha, José G. de la, 166

Confederate Constitution, 503

Congress, 12, 58, 246. *See also* U.S. House of Representatives; U.S. Senate

Congressional Globe, 254

Conner, James, 400, 413, 414, 420

Conrad, C. M., 455

Constitutional Unionists, 499, 502

contingency, 219, 423–26, 531–32, 574n. 66

Convention of Slaveholders of the Eastern Shore of Maryland, 195

Conway, Moncure, 510

Cooke, John Esten, 515

Cooper, Carolina, 169

Cooper, Henry, 501

Cooperative State Secessionists: and Aldrich, 404; arguments supporting, 376; defeat of, 414–15; and the Democratic National Convention, 292–93; and the 1860 Association, 394; and Magrath, 399; and Memminger, 260–61, 263–64, 268, 364, 389; and Rhett, 383; and southern convention efforts, 387, 395–96; and the Speakership Crisis, 258–59; tactics, 396; and Townsend, 389–90; and the Trenholm-Lesesne proposals, 403

Copperheads, 97

Cornish, J. H., 373

Costa Rica, 145

cotton: in Arkansas, 504; and coastal lands, 11; and filibustering, 157; and Kansas agriculture, 124; Sea Island cotton, 11, 13, 20–21, 293, 353, 361, 363, 390; and secessionist states, 2–3; and slave labor, 13, 176, 293, 353; and soil quality, 363; and South Carolina economy, 19–21

counterfactuals. *See* contingency

Crania Americana (Morton), 42

Crawford, Martin J., 290, 305, 310

"The Crime Against Kansas" (Sumner), 80

Crittenden, John J.: and the Brooks-Sumner affair, 82, 84, 139; and compromise efforts, 470–75, 473, 489, 495–97, 514; and elections, 323; and Fort Sumter, 478; and the Kansas controversy, 140, 141; and the

Republican nominating convention, 326; and Virginia secession, 513

Crittenden Compromise, 495–96, 514

Cuba: "Africanization" of, xvii, 165–66; annexation plans, 298; class structure in, 194; and expansionism, 155; and filibustering, 145, 147–48, 153, 157, 160–61, 163–65; Hammond on, 380; and the Ostend Manifesto, 147; and secessionism, 456

Cummings Point, 521–22

Cunningham, John, 414

Cushing, Caleb, 309

Dallas, Texas, 333

Dallas Herald, 332

Danbury Public Letter (Toombs), 472, 474

Daniel, Peter, 110, 111, 117, 121

Dargan, E. S., 54

Davidson, James, 505

Davis, H. R., 213

Davis, Henry Winter, 265, 323–24, 455

Davis, Jefferson, 277; and the African slave trade, 178; and the Baltimore Convention, 312, 317, 321; cabinet, 259; and causes of the Civil War, 532; and the Charleston Convention, 286, 297–98, 302, 307; and compromise efforts, 470–71, 474–75, 493–94; as Confederate president, 1, 503; and delayed secession, 467, 469; and elections, 107, 339; and expansionism, 153, 159, 166; and federal fort seizures, 488, 517, 519, 521; and the Kansas controversy, 72–73; and the secession debate, 388, 394, 404, 424; and Separatist tactics, 576n. 2; and southern divisions, 429; and Southwest secession, 446; and state's rights, 346–47; and territorial slavery, 275–85; and Trenholm, 402; and Yancey, 2–3, 6, 492

De Bow, Frank, 419

De Bow, James, 40, 394

De Bow's Review, 38, 49, 369, 419

Declaration of Independence, 10–12, 18, 346–47, 502, 527

Delaware: abolitionism in, 175; agriculture, 13; and anti-immigrant sentiment, 88; demographics, 3, 71; and expansionism, 154; free blacks in, 499; and immigration, 206, 354; and the Kansas conflict, 123; and manumission, 14; and nativism, 89; and paternalism, 57–58; and reenslavement efforts, 185–86, 193, 201; rejection of secession, 504; and the Republican Party, 329; and territorial slavery, 64; threats to slavery in, 438; and Virginia secession, 511

Delony, Edward, 181

Democratic Party. *See also* Northern Democratic Party; Southern Democratic Party: and Arkansas, 504; and the Baltimore Convention, 310–12, 315–17, 320–21; and Buchanan's election, 97; and Buford, 125; and

Democratic Party *(continued)*
  causes of the Civil War, 532–33; and the
  Charleston Convention, 288, 293–96, 304,
  306–7, 491–92, 527; competition with, 96;
  convention efforts, 514; and delayed
  secession, 469; and *Dred Scott v. Sandford,*
  121–22; and elections, 14, 101, 104, 268–69,
  271, 275–76, 278–82, 338; and ex-Whigs,
  323; and federal fort seizures, 478; and
  immigrants, 87–88, 93–95; and nativism, 86;
  and Orr, 364, 377; and party corruption,
  368; and proslavery laws, 17; protection of
  slavery, 24; and the secession debate, 384,
  386, 399, 404, 405, 412, 418, 420; and the
  slave trade issue, 176, 179, 182; and state's
  rights, 349, 351; and Stephens, 430; and the
  Supreme Court, 110; and the territorial
  slavery conflict, 85; and Wise, 90, 91; and
  Yancey, 1–2, 284, 493–94
demographics: and the African slave trade, 170;
  Arkansas, 504; and economic attacks on
  slavery, 240; and expansionism, 174; Lower
  South, 64–65; Mississippi, 492; Missouri, 66;
  population growth among blacks, 438; and
  reenslavement efforts, 185, 188, 190–93, 198;
  and runaway slaves, 22–23; and secessionism,
  529–30; and slave ownership, 180; slave
  population, 66, 66–71; South Carolina, 171,
  293, 353, 361, 363; and the territorial slavery
  conflict, 66–71, 77; Upper South, 499–500; of
  Virginia, 505; Woolworth on, 143
Denmark Vesey's Conspiracy, 256
deportation of blacks: Blair on, 328; and
  extralegal justice, 331; and filibustering, 154;
  funding for, 360; and gradual emancipation,
  508; Helper on, 243; and Houston, 448;
  northern support for, 12; and reenslavement
  efforts, 190–91, 199
Dering, Henry, 512
despotism, 9–18
The Destiny of the Races (Blair, Jr.), 154
diseases, 41–42, 149, 257, 278, 356, 421
District of Columbia, 253
Dixon, Archibald, 62
Doniphan, A. W., 73–74
The Doom of Slavery (Townsend), 394
Dorchester County, Maryland, 192, *192,* 194, 198
double houses, 357–58, *358*
Douglas, Stephen A., *63;* and the Baltimore
  Convention, 309–11, 316–21; and the
  Brooks-Sumner affair, 80; and Buchanan,
  488; and the Charleston Convention, 291,
  296–97, 304–5, 307; and elections, 100; and
  the English Bill, 142; and the Freeport
  Doctrine, 272–74; and John Brown's Raid,
  205; and the Kansas controversy, 61–62, 103,
  138, 143, 545n. 1; and Lincoln's election,
  338–39; and moral issues of slavery, 282–83;
  opposition to, 309–10; and political invasion
  of the South, 249, 265

Douglass, Frederick, 207
Drayton, Thomas, 467, 469
Dred Scott v. Sandford: and Buchanan, 137,
  199, 488, 549n. 8, 551n. 30; and Campbell,
  166; and Catron, 115–17, 199–200; and
  gradual emancipation, 111–13; implications
  of, 109–11, 141, 271–72; reaction to, 118–
  19, 142; and the Republican Party, 205; and
  state's rights, 113–15; and Taney, 119–22,
  549n. 8, 551–52n. 30; and Trescot, 274; and
  Yancey, 287
Dubulcet, Andrew, 186
Dunleith mansion, *164*

Eason, James M., 188
Echo (slave ship), 183–84
economics: and agriculture, 19–22; Civil War's
  impact, 375; and class divisions, 578n. 5;
  Clay on, 229–30; and demographic shifts,
  23–24; and economic invasion of the South,
  236–45; and expansionism, 147–50, 153,
  364, 553n. 10; Fitzhugh on, 35–39; and
  immigrant labor, 171–72; and land values,
  171; and maritime trade, 148, 151; and the
  Oppositionist Party, 324; Panic of 1857, 238;
  proslavery arguments, 541–42n. 1; and
  railroads, 406–10; and reenslavement efforts,
  186; and the secession debate, 438; and slave
  prices, 22, 172, 175–77, 181, 531; and
  southern divisions, 7, 18; and threats to
  slavery, 236–40, 584–85n. 17; and wage
  pressures, 178, 186
education: and the Berea School, 233–35; of
  Blair, 328; of Fee, 223, 231; and paternalism,
  177; of slaves, 29, 55
egalitarianism republicanism: attacks on, 395; in
  black belt areas, 16; and Orr, 564n. 8; and
  Simms, 182; in South Carolina, 568n. 4; in
  the Southwest, 363, 457; vs. elitism, 354–55
1860 Association: and causes of the Civil War,
  532; control of extremists, 527; and
  Cooperationists, 465; pamphlet campaign,
  441; and the railroad celebration, 572n. 24;
  and the secession debate, 391–94, 398, 406,
  410, 412–13, 420, 424
El Salvador, 145
Electoral College, 14–15, 312, 338, 387, 395
Elfe, Thomas, 357, 363
elitism, 354–55, 456–57. *See also* aristocratic
  republicanism; class divisions
Elliott, Stephen, 54
Ellis, John W., 244
Ellis, Powhattan, Sr., 316, 486
Ellison, William, 186
Elmore, John, 453
emancipation, 77–78, 113–15, 118, 237, 328
Emerson, Ralph Waldo, 84, 209, 217
emigration. *See* expansionism; migrants and
  migration
English, William, 142

English Bill, 142–44
English republicanism, 353
Eufalia Regency, 125
Europe, 38, 64, 86, 173
evangelicals, 44, 223, 226–27, 460–62
expansionism, *146. See also* filibustering; Blair on, 327–28; Caribbean, 153–59; and causes of the Civil War, 531; and the Charleston Convention, 286, 298–300; and compromise efforts, 471; and elections, 338; and the Freeport Doctrine, 273–75; and the isothermal theory of slavery, 144; and López, 160–61; and New Orleans, 148–51, 553n. 10; and O'Sullivan, 145–47; and Quitman, 162–67; and the slave trade issue, 180; and South Carolina, 366–67, 456; and state's rights, 349; and Toombs, 438; and Virginia secession, 514; and Walker, 161–62; and Yancey, 282
extralegal justice. *See* lynch law; mob violence

F Street Mess, 103, 104
families, impact of slavery on: and Fee, 224–27; and gradual emancipation, 112–13; Hammond on, 31; Hughes on, 51–52; and manumission, 111–12; and paternalism, 46, 49, 55, 356; and reenslavement efforts, 187
Farnsworth, John, 253
faro bankers, 291–92, 314
Featherstonhaugh, G. W., 362
Fee, James, 225
Fee, John G., *228*; background, 222–24; and the Berea School, 233–35; and Cassius Clay, 227–33; and the Mammy myth, 224–27; and the Republican nominating convention, 328; support from northerners, 221; and Underwood, 244
Feliciana Company, 180–81
Fifth Amendment, 121
filibustering: critics of, 155–60; and López, 148, 152, 160–61; and New Orleans, 147–52, 553n. 10; and Quitman, 162–67; and the slave trade issue, 182; and Walker, 148, 152, 160–62, 166–67, 177, 273
Fillmore, Millard, 94–95, 326
fire-eaters, 1–2, 6, 260, 531
First Manassas, battle of, 409
Fitzhugh, George: and colorblind slavery, 541–42n. 1; and fear of slave violence, 334; and hierarchical social structure, 44; and the isothermic theory of slavery, 40; and the Kansas controversy, 70, 78; and legal restrictions on slaveholders, 48–50; and paternalism, 355; and polygenesis, 43; and proslavery, 33, 35–36, 55, 57
Fitzpatrick, Benjamin F., 285–87, 307, 314, 467
Florida: agriculture, 13; and the Baltimore Convention, 317; and the Charleston Convention, 303; demographics, 361; and federal fort seizures, 284, 483; purchase of,

12–13; reaction to Lincoln's election, 436; and reenslavement efforts, 200; and the secession debate, 385–87, 401, 419, 447, 492, 497; and the Southern Manifesto, 470
Flournoy, Thomas, 91–93, 125
Floyd, John, 105–6, 507
Floyd, John B., 467, 477, 507, 508, 511
Foote, Henry S., 178, 474
Ford, Rip, 166
Fort Barrancas, 484
Fort Gaines, 284, 483
Fort Jackson, 484
Fort Johnson, 478
Fort Marion, 484
Fort Morgan, 284, 483
Fort Moultrie, 383, 424, 477–78, 482, 487, *518, 527*
Fort Pickens, *518*; attempts to seize, 479; and causes of the Civil War, 532; described, 477; resupply efforts, 483–84, 517, 519–21; siege, 494; truce, 488
Fort Pike, 484
Fort Pulaski, 477, 479, 481, 483–84, 497, 527
Fort St. Phillips, 484
Fort Sumter, *518, 522*; attack on, 520–24; and causes of the Civil War, 533; described, 477; and Lamar, 479–82; resupply efforts, 486–89, 491, 517–19; seized by Anderson, 476–79
Founding Fathers, 168, 174, 353
free blacks, 57–58, 188–90, 193, 195–99
free labor society: and African colonization, 193; economic benefits, 73; and exploitation, 27–28; Hughes on, 51–52; and immigration, 500; and individualism, 57; Pringle on, 55; Seward on, 206; Stringfellow on, 69; Underwood on, 236–40; vs. colorblind slavery, 35–38
free speech and press: and abolitionism, 337; and Botts, 324–25; and causes of the Civil War, 533; and elections, 337; and Fee, 230, 232; and Lovejoy, 289–90; and mail censorship, 363; and postal officials, 371; and racial divisions, 9; and the secession debate, 442; and Southern Republicans, 327, 330; and the Speakership Crisis, 253, 256; and state's rights, 348; as threat to slavery, 455, 458; and Wise, 92
Freeport Doctrine: and the Baltimore Convention, 310, 320; and the Charleston Convention, 287, 296, 298; and Douglas, 272–75; and elections, 275–76, 338
Frémont, John C., 101–5, 110
fugitive slave laws. *See also* runaway slaves: and the Brooks-Sumner affair, 80, 83; and Buchanan, 98–99, 103; and causes of the Civil War, 530–31; and Clay, 232; and compromise efforts, 441–44, 495, 501; and *Dred Scott v. Sandford*, 121; effect of, 266, 282, 533; and elections, 323; and the Freeport Doctrine, 272–75; and Houston, 449; and the Kansas conflict, 63, 67–68, 75,

fugitive slave laws *(continued)*
78; and Lovejoy, 289; and Mason, 17, 220,
247; and Personal Liberty Laws, 349–51,
435–40; and *Prigg v. Pennsylvania,* 299; and
Southern Democrats, 313; and Texas
annexation, 537–38n. 4; and Whigs, 85
Fuller, E. W., 176
Fuller, Richard, 53

Gadsden, James, 157
Gadsden Purchase, 147, 157
gag rules: and the Baltimore Convention, 313;
and Buchanan, 99; and causes of the Civil
War, 533, 537–38n. 4; described, 17; and
Dred Scott v. Sandford, 116; and Hammond,
378; and South Carolina, xvii, 362–63
Gaines, Archibald, 350–51
Galbraith, John Kenneth, 52
Galveston, Texas, 152
Galveston News, 240
Gardenhire, James, 78
Garner, Margaret, 350–51, 435, 532
Garnett, Henry, 200
Garnett, M. R. H., 251
Garrison, William Lloyd: and the African slave
trade, 183; extremism of, 389; and Fitzhugh,
43; and John Brown's Raid, 217; and the
Liberator, 12, 27; and northern abolitionism,
12; and Taney, 549n. 8
Gaulden, W. B., 304
gender discrimination, 90–91, 569n. 14
General Assembly of the Presbyterian Church, 4
Georgia: and the African slave trade, 180;
agriculture, 11, 13; and the Baltimore
Convention, 317, 319; and the Charleston
Convention, 304; and compromise efforts,
470, 472, 474; and delayed secession plan,
467; demographics, 361; and Fort Sumter,
480; and the fugitive slave issue, 436;
geographic divisions, 430; legislature, 427;
and Mississippi secession, 453; and the
secession debate, 385, 387–88, 401–3, 411–
14, 429–31, 433–42, 445–46, 492, 495–97;
South Carolinian immigrants, 363; and the
Southern Manifesto, 470; and the timing of
secession, 345; and white belts, 16
Georgia Platform, 429, 435
Gholson, Samuel J., 127
Gilman, Caroline, 569–70n. 33
Gilmer, John, 520
Gist, State's Rights, 446, 453, 469
Gist, William: and compromise efforts, 475; and
delayed secession plan, 467; and the 1860
Association, 391; and federal fort seizures,
485; and Hammond's suppressed letter, 416;
and Lincoln's election, 395; and Mississippi
separatism, 453–54; and political invasion of
the South, 257–59, 261, 263–64; and the
secession debate, 383, 385–88, 401, 416,
445–46; and South Carolina secession, 527;

and the Speakership Controversy, 384; and
Virginia secession, 514–15
Glenn, D. C., 303
Gliddon, George, 42
gold rush, 242
Goode, G. W., 73–74
Goode, William O., 103, 104
Gorsuch, Edward, 98
Gosport Yards, 525
Gourdin, Henry, 391, 394, 418–20, 441
Gourdin, Mathiesen and Company, 390
Gourdin, Robert, *393;* and causes of the Civil
War, 532; in Columbia, 414; and the 1860
Association, 390–94, 406–7, 410; and federal
fort seizures, 479, 481, 482; and Jackson,
411; and Lincoln's election, 398–400;
resignation, 414; and the secession debate,
389, 401, 420, 493, 527; and secret secession
plots, 572n. 19
Grace Episcopal Church, 188
gradual emancipation: and Brown, 77; and
Buchanan, 98–99; and the Convention of
Slaveholders, 195; and Fitzhugh, 33; and
Floyd, 507; and Fuller, 53; and Taney, 111–
13; and Thornwell, 376; and Wilkes, 127
Grant, Ulysses S., 255
Grayson, William, 359, 411
Greeley, Horace, 243
Green, Israel, 212, 219
Green, James Mercer, 76, 401, 485
Greenville County, South Carolina, 418
Greenville Mountaineer, 280
Grier, Robert, 114–18
Grow, Galusha M., 139–40
Guatemala, 145
Guesclin, Bertrand Du, 421

habeas corpus writs, 443
Halbert, Joshua, 127–28
Hale, Stephen, 454
Halstead, Murat, 310–11
Hamilton, Daniel Hayward, 183–84, 368–69,
396, 400, 413–14
Hamilton, James, Jr., 184, 354
Hammond, Harry, 31
Hammond, James Henry, *417;* and the African
slave trade, 168–69; and causes of the Civil
War, 531–32; and compromise efforts, 466;
on fights in the Senate, 290; and the Gag Rule
Controversy, 247–48, 383–84; and legal
restrictions on slaveholders, 49; "mudsill"
argument, 39–40; and Orr, 294; and
paternalism, 457; and proslavery, 27–34; and
Rhett, 382; and the secession debate, 377–81,
394, 404–5, 415–18, 420; and Stephens,
442–44
Hampton, Wade, II, 378–79
Harper, Robert Goodloe, 178
Harpers Ferry, Virginia, 203, 209, *210, 211,*
234, *525*

Harris, William, 453–54
Harvie, Lewis, 515
Hayne, Isaac, 389, 391
Hayward, Shepard, 212
Helper, Hinton R.: and the Baltimore Convention, 327; and Blair, 299; and elections, 323; and fear of slave violence, 372; and King, 300; and Lovejoy, 289–90; and Pennington, 323–24; and political invasion of the South, 248–49, 251, 254, 262, 265, 267; and presidential patronage, 369; and Southern Republicanism, 561n. 16; and the Speakership Controversy, 384; and threats to slavery, 440; and Underwood, 240–44; and Virginia secession, 512
Henderson, James P., 166
Henry, Patrick, 324
Herald of Freedom, 79
Hibernian Hall, 291, 311
Hicks, Thomas, 89
hierarchical power, 37, 44–45, 57, 150, 153, 155. See also aristocratic republicanism; paternalism
Higginson, Thomas Wentworth, 208, 220
Hill, Benjamin H., 274, 430–31, 433–34
Hindman, Thomas, 246
Hinks, Samuel, 89
Hitchens, James, 335–36
Holcombe, James P., *510*; and the African slave trade, 509–10; background, 509; and the secession debate, 507–8, 511–12, 514–15, 527; and southern nationalism, 528; and state's rights, 347
Holcombe, William, 509
Holmes, George Frederick, 33
Holt, Michael, 286
Holt, R. S., 458
Honduras, 145
honor, 437, 454–55, 531, 533, 546–47n. 36
Houma Ceres, 182
House Committee on the Territories, 403
Houston, Sam, 326, 445, 447–52, 466, 527
Houston, Sam, Jr., 448
Howard, Benjamin C., 500
Howe, Samuel Gridley, 208
Huger, Alfred, 177, 400, 410–11
Huger, Daniel, 354
Hughes, Henry, 51–52, 181
Hundley, Daniel R., 43
Hunter, Andrew, 213
Hunter, Robert M. T., 54, 307, 310, 470–71, 474
Hutson, Charles W., Jr., 365

Illinois, 12, 97, 143, 338
immigrants. See migrants and migration
The Impending Crisis in the South: How to Meet It (Helper), 242–44, 252, 254, 327
Inaugural Addresses: Buchanan, 108–10, 115,

117, 119, 149n. 14; Davis, 346; Lincoln, 470; Walker, 128–30, 135–36, 142
indentured servitude, 193
Indian Territory, 332
Indiana, 97, 143, 338
Indigenous Races of Earth (Nott), 42
Institute Hall, *423*; National Democratic Convention of 1860, 291–92, 295–97, 304–7, 309, 311, 313–15, 317, 319–22; November 9, 1860 secession rally in, 410, 418; South Carolina Secession Convention in, 423
The Interest in Slavery of the Southern Non-slaveholder (De Bow), 394
Iowa, 97
isothermal theory of slavery: Cartwright on, 40–41; and efforts to reopen the slave trade, 179; and expansionism, 144; and filibustering, 154; Helper on, 242; and Kansas, 128–29; Palmer on, 461

Jackson, Andrew: and the African slave trade, 184; and Blair, 328; and *Dred Scott v. Sandford,* 110–11; and elitism, 355; and expansionism, 152; and Houston, 448–49; and the Kansas controversy, 65; and New Orleans, 151; and nullification, 352, 360, 386, 435; and party loyalty, 138; and Wise, 90
Jackson, Henry Rootes, 411–12, 414, 418, 430, 453
Jackson Mississippian, 129, 240
Jackson Semi-Weekly Mississippian, 155
Jackson Square, 150–51, 156
Jacobs, Curtis W., 195–96, 200–201, 248
Jamison, David Flavel, 365, 421–22, *423,* 483
Jefferson, Thomas: and the African slave trade, 168, 181, 508; and colonization of freed slaves, 53, 70, 328; and the isothermal theory of slavery, 129; and the Louisiana Purchase, 12; on slavery, 25; and tobacco, 19–20
Jefferson City, 249
Jefferson County, Virginia, 209–11, *210*
Jekyll Island, 480
John Brown's Raid: background of, 205–12; Brown's capture and execution, 215–17, 246; Cobb on, 440; effect of, 266–67; impact of, 219–21; and Memminger, 262–64; and the secession debate, 385, 387; southern reaction to, 213–15; and Underwood, 244; and Wise, 217–19, 236, 240
John Fraser and Co., 402
Johnson, Andrew, 529–30
Johnson, Henderson, 32
Johnson, Hershel, 485
Johnson, Louisa, 31–32
Johnson, Sally, 30–31
Johnson, Samuel, 577n. 26
Jones, Charles Colcock, Jr., 408, 412
Jones, Charles Colcock, Sr., 54, 408

Jones, J. Glancy, 98
Jones, Robert, 232
jury nullification. *See* nullification

Kansas, 66; abolitionism in, 175; admitted to the Union, 503; agriculture, 123–25; and causes of the Civil War, 531–33, 537–38n. 4; constitutional convention, 130–33; and *Dred Scott v. Sandford,* 110; and elections, 133–34, 277, 340; and the English Bill, 142–44; and European immigration, 172; and expansionism, 158; and filibustering, 553n. 10; Hammond on, 380; and the isothermal theory of slavery, 128–29; and the Lecompton Convention, 133–42; Pottawatomie Massacre, 208, 211; and South Carolina extremism, 366; and southern extremism, xvii; Spratt on, 172; and state's rights, 347, 351; and the territorial slavery conflict, 61–79, 125–28, 248; and Virginia secession, 511
Kansas-Nebraska Act: and Atchison, 17; and Buchanan, 100; and Douglas, 103, 138–39, 275, 545n. 1; and elections, 323–24; and emigrant aid societies, 72–73; and the Fugitive Slave Law, 63–66; and Houston, 448; introduced, 61–63; and the Lecompton Convention, 138–40; national implications, 79, 94, 98, 266, 282, 313; and northern containment tactics, 205; passage of, 59, 61; reaction to, 67–68; and Whig Party divisions, 85–86, 125
Keitt, Laurence: and the Brooks-Sumner affair, 82, 139–40; and compromise efforts, 472; and elections, 269; and expansionism, 155, 366; and fear of slave violence, 370–71; and the isothermic theory of slavery, 40; Orr on, 294; and political invasion of the South, 254–55, 259, 267; on Republicans, 372; and the secession debate, 383, 421
Keitt, William, 255
Kennedy, John F., 145
Kennedy, John P., 500
Kenner, Duncan, 166
Kentucky: abolitionism in, 175, 281; attempted neutrality, 530; and the Brooks-Sumner affair, 82; climate and slavery, 129; and compromise efforts, 470; declining slave population, 71; demographics, 3; and expansionism, 155; and filibustering, 157; free blacks in, 499; and the House Speakership, 266; and the Kansas conflict, 123; and Lincoln presidency, 337; and manumission, 14; and nativism, 89; and northern colonization, 239–40; and post-nati laws, 227–30; rejection of secession, 504; and the Southern Manifesto, 470; and the territorial slavery conflict, 64; threats to slavery in, 438; Unionists in, 530
King, Austin, 299–300, 302, 310, 316, 339
King, William R., 98–99

"Knights of the Golden Circle," 148
Know-Nothing Party. *See* American Party (Know-Nothings)

labor unions, 52
Lamar, Charles Augustus Lafayette: and the African slave trade, 183, 184; and causes of the Civil War, 532; and federal fort seizures, 479–82, 486; and the secession debate, 493, 497, 527
Lamar, Lucius Q. C., 132, 136, 166
Lamar, Mary Ann, 132
Lamer, Gazaway, 479–80
land grants, 142
Land of Gold, Reality versus Fiction (Helper), 242
land values, 171, 236–40, 242–43
Lane, Harriet, 107
Lane Rebels, 223
Latham, George, 515
Latham, Henry Gray, 516
Latin America, 194
Lawrence, Kansas, 94
Lawton, Alexander Robert, 481–83
Leacock, William T., 462
League of United Southerners, 279–80
Leake, Sheldon F., 251, 254
Lecompton Constitutional Convention: and the Baltimore Convention, 310, 318; and Buchanan, 135–40, 551–52n. 30; and compromises, 134–35; and elections, 205, 275, 338; and filibustering, 159–60; and the Freeport Doctrine, 272–73; and the Neutrality Laws, 167; passage of, 140–42; and state's rights, 347; and Walker, 133–34
Lectures on the Philosophy and Practice of Slavery (Smith), 33
Lee, Robert E., 212, 521
legal restrictions on slave owners, 48–52, 350–51
Legaré, Hugh Swinton, 363
legislative emancipation, 77–78, 118
Lesesne, Henry, 402, 415
Letcher, John, 139, 261–62, 500, 524–26
Letters to Clarkson (Hammond), 28, 30–31, 33–34
Lewis, Dixon H., 280
Liberator, 12, 27
Liberty and Slavery (Bledsoe), 53
Liberty Hall, 433, *434,* 441–42
Liberty Line, 194, 219, 289, 368
Liberty Party, 288
Liberty Tribune, 70
Lincoln, Abraham: and antislavery, xvi–xvii, 101–2, 198, 282–83, 345, 369, 405, 435, 438, 528, 533, 583–84n. 4, 584–85n. 17; and the Baltimore Convention, 312, 327; call for troops, 528–29, 530; and compromise efforts, 425, 440–41, 443, 465, 471, 474, 495; and conditional Unionists, 506; and Cooperationists,

464; and court appointments, 400; critics of, 372, 377; and *Dred Scott v. Sandford,* 110; election, 331, 338–41, 365–66, 372–73, 387–88, 395, 398, 424, 496; and federal fort seizures, 488, 517–19, 532–33; and Fee, 230; and Georgian secession, 433; Harris on, 453; inauguration, 440; and John Brown's Raid, 206, 214, 220; and the Kansas controversy, 78, 143; and Lovejoy, 290; as moderate, 389; nomination, 329–30; and nullification, 360; and Popular Sovereignty, 272; and presidential patronage, 367, 369, 372, 381, 398, 450–51, 454–55; and the Republican Party, xvii, 329, 394; and the secession debate, 396; and Sherman, 251; and state's rights, 348–49; and the Upper South, 502–3; and Virginia secession, 512; and Yancey, 281, 336

Lincoln-Douglas Debates, 272, 330
Lind, Jenny, 150
local politics, 286
Longstreet, Augustus Baldwin, 373
López, Narciso, 148, 152, 160–61
Lost Cause, 529
Louisiana: and the African slave trade, 180–81; agriculture, 13, 20; and anti-immigrant sentiment, 88; and the Baltimore Convention, 319–20; and the Charleston Convention, 303; and federal fort seizures, 483–84; and the fugitive slave issue, 436; mob violence in, 458–59; and the secession debate, 385, 387, 447, 454, 496–97; and the Southern Manifesto, 470; sugar planters, 153; and the timing of secession, 345
Louisiana Purchase, 12, 113
Lovejoy, Elijah, 288–89
Lovejoy, Owen, 288–91, 306, 310, 528
Lowndes, William, 278–79, 293
loyalty politics, 77, 85, 87, 132, 265, 415, 444, 533
lynch law: and causes of the Civil War, 533; and the Charleston Convention, 306; and elections, 331–36, 341; and fear of slave rebellion, 569–70n. 33; and Fee, 231–32; Helper on, 242; and John Brown's Raid, 214; and loyalty politics, 85; in Mississippi, 459; and the secession debate, 424; and social control, 24; and Underwood, 238–39; in the Upper South, 502
Lynchburg Express, 515

Macbeth, Charles, 189–90
Madison, James, 19
Madison County, Kentucky, 230
Magrath, Andrew, 393; in Columbia, 413; and the 1860 Association, 391; and federal fort seizures, 479; and Hammond, 416; and Lincoln's election, 398–401; on mob violence, 450; resignation, 414; and the secession debate, 389, 405, 418–20, 437–38, 527
Magrath, Edward, 400

malaria, 278, 356
Mallory, Stephen, 488
Mammy myth, 224–27
Manifest Destiny, 146, 152, 155, 282
Manning, John, 372
manumission: and *Dred Scott v. Sandford,* 549n. 8; and expansionism, 327–28; and Gorsuch, 98–99; and public reforms, 111; and reenslavement efforts, 189, 193–94, 197; and "semislavery," 14; and Taney, 119, 121; and the territorial slavery conflict, 67, 69
Mardi Gras, 149
maritime trade, 148, 151
Marshall, J. Foster, 373–74
Marshall, John, 119
Martin, Henry L., 134–36
Martin, W. E., 402
Marxist theory, 553n. 10
Maryland, *192*; abolitionism in, 175, 281; and African colonization, 53; agriculture, 11; and anti-immigrant sentiment, 88; and the Baltimore Convention, 329; colonization of free blacks, 328; demographics, 3, 23, 71; and elections, 101; and expansionism, 154–55; Fillmore election, 95; free blacks in, 499; and the House Speakership, 266; and immigration, 206, 354; and the Kansas conflict, 123; and Lincoln presidency, 337; and manumission, 14; and northern colonization, 239–40; and paternalism, 57–58; and reenslavement efforts, 185–86, 190–91, 194–98, 200–201; and the secession debate, 500, 504; and the territorial slavery conflict, 64; threats to slavery in, 438; Unionists in, 530; and Virginia secession, 511–12
Maryland House of Delegates, 197
Maryland State Colonization Society, 191
Mason, James: and the Brooks-Sumner affair, 80; and elections, 104; and the Fugitive Slave Law, 17, 220, 247; and John Brown's Raid, 220–21, 246; and the Speakership Crisis, 254; and the territorial slavery conflict, 63, 248
Mason Committee, 220–21
Massachusetts, 12, 82
Massachusetts Emigrant Aid Society, 72
Maury, Matthew F., 153–54
McKinney, Solomon, 332–34
medicine, 10, 40–42, 220
Memminger, Christopher G.: background, 432; and the Charleston Convention, 292; and Cooperative State secession, 364; and the 1860 Association, 390; and the elections of 1860, 269; and legal restrictions on slaveholders, 50; and paternalism, 259–60, 359; and political invasion of the South, 258–61, 261–64, 267–68; and reenslavement efforts, 189; and the secession debate, 383, 385, 387, 389, 420, 424; and Separatist tactics, 576n. 2
Memphis, Tennessee, 152

Messenger (steamship), 126
Mexican War, 147
Mexico, 145, 298, 367, 456
Middleton, Arthur, 422
Middleton, William, 422
migrants and migration. *See also* expansionism: Blair on, 327–28; and causes of the Civil War, 531; and colorblind slavery, 37–38; competition with slave labor, 23; and Davis, 259; and economic invasion of the South, 237–38; and electoral issue, 86–88; English immigrants, 10; and the Freeport Doctrine, 273; Hammond on, 380; immigrant vs. slave populations, 281; and Kansas, 79, 123, 126–27, 205; and the Know-Nothing Party, 95–96; and mob violence, 334; and nativism, 88–89, 93–94; and post-nati laws, 228; and reenslavement efforts, 188, 193; and South Carolina, 363, 367; to the Southwest, 538n. 3; and Spratt, 171–73; and the territorial slavery conflict, 64
Miles, James Warley, 263, 355, 359, 371
Miles, Julett, 225–27
Miles, William Porcher: on Charleston's secessionism, 414; and elections, 269; and paternalism, 359, 372; and political invasion of the South, 257–61; and the secession debate, 383, 396, 420–21; and the Speakership Controversy, 384; on taxation, 366
Miles Brewton House, 357, *358*
Military Hall, 311, 313–14
military plots, 453
Milledgeville debate, 433–38, 441–42
Miller, Robert H., 70
Mills House, 410
Minnesota, 113
Mississippi: agriculture, 13, 20; and the Baltimore Convention, 316; and the Charleston Convention, 285, 296–98, 303, 305, 307; and compromise efforts, 465, 470, 475; and delayed secession plan, 467; and federal fort seizures, 483; mob violence in, 459; and pioneers, 38; reaction to Lincoln's election, 436; and reenslavement efforts, 200; and the secession debate, 382, 385–88, 401, 404, 446–54, 458–59, 490–92, 497; and Separatist tactics, 576n. 2; South Carolinian immigrants, 363; and southern convention efforts, 264; and the Southern Manifesto, 470
Mississippi River, 151, 158, 553n. 10
Missouri: abolitionism in, 175, 281; agriculture, 13; anti-immigrant sentiment, 88; antislavery in, 249–50; and causes of the Civil War, 532–33; and the Charleston Convention, 299; climate and slavery, 129; declining slave population, 71; demographics, 3, 23; and *Dred Scott v. Sandford,* 114–15; and elections, 73–75, 339; and expansionism, 155, 158; free blacks in, 499; and free labor

immigration, 206; guerilla warfare, 530; and the House Speakership, 266; and the Kansas conflict, 123, 136; Kansas-Nebraska Act, 77–79; and Lincoln presidency, 337; and manumission, 14; and nativism, 89; and northern colonization, 240; and the Pottawatomie Massacre, 208; and reenslavement efforts, 200; rejection of secession, 504; slave population, 66; and the territorial slavery conflict, 61–77, 125; threats to slavery in, 438; and vigilante violence, 334
Missouri Compromise: and Crittenden, 471; and *Dred Scott v. Sandford,* 109–10, 115–17; and elections, 102; and John Brown's Raid, 205; repeal, 80; and the territorial slavery conflict, 61–63
Missouri River, 71
mob violence. *See also* lynch law: in Baltimore, 530; and causes of the Civil War, 533; deterring, 497; and elections, 331–36; and fear of slave rebellion, 569–70n. 33; and Fee, 232; in Louisiana, 458–59; and the secession debate, 424; in Texas, 450; and Underwood, 238–39; in the Upper South, 502
Mobile, Alabama, 41, 152
Mobile Daily Register, 186
Mocksville Academy, 241
Monmouth mansion, 163, *164*
Monroe, James, 12, 19
Montgomery, Alabama, 126
Montgomery Advertiser, 124, 200
Montgomery Mail, 460
Moore, Andrew B.: and delayed secession, 453, 467; and federal fort seizures, 483, 485; and mob violence, 334; and the secession debate, 386; and southern convention efforts, 264
Moore, Thomas Overton, 447, 483–84
Morrill Tariff, 503
Morris Island, 487, *518*
Morrison, Toni, 350–51
Morton, Jeremiah, 512
Morton, Samuel G., 42
Moulton, Alexander, 303
Mouton, Charles H., 182
Mt. Vernon Arsenal, 284
"The Mulatto a Hybrid" (Nott), 42
mulattos: and colorblind slavery, 36; Hammond on, 29–30; Hughes on, 52; and John Brown's Raid, 212; in New Orleans, 150; and race-based slavery, 42–43; and reenslavement efforts, 186–89, 200; and sexual exploitation of slaves, 31–32; in South Carolina, 355–56

Napoleonic Wars, 159
Nat Turner's Rebellion, 10, 89, 507–9
Natchez, Mississippi, 152, 356–57
National Constitutional Union Party, 326
National Peace Conference, 513
nationalism, 501, 528–29
Native Americans, 112

nativism, 86–95

Nebraska, 62–63, 110, 248

Negro Slavery, No-Evil (Stringfellow), 69

Nelson, Samuel, 114–18, 550n. 15

Neutrality Laws, 159–62, 166–67

New England Emigrant Aid Society, 72, 79, 126

New Granada, 145

New Jersey, 11, 97, 143, 173

New Mexico, 147, 175, 178

New Orleans, Louisiana, *146, 156*; and the African slave trade, 170; architecture, *552–53n. 7*; and elections, 337; and expansionism, xvii, 145–59, 273, 553n. 10; and the slave trade issue, 182; social structure, 150–51; and yellow fever, 41

New Orleans Bee, 458

New Orleans Commercial Bulletin, 124, 146, 152

New Orleans Courier, 165, 182

New Orleans Crescent, 201

New Orleans Delta: on Butler, 158; on Cuba, 153, 165; and expansionism, 153, 165, 553n. 10; on honor, 455; on the Kansas conflict, 123–24; on patronage, 456; on protection of slavery, 275; on slave prices, 175; on Wise, 240

New Orleans Louisiana Courier, 143–44, 152

New Orleans Picayune, 132

New Testament, 29

New York, 11–14, 173

New York Evening Post, 94

New York Tribune, 243

Newby, Dangerfield, 212

Nicaragua, 145, 167, 273

Nicholas, Samuel Smith, 500–501

Norfolk Southern Argus, 213

North Carolina: abolitionism in, 175; and the Baltimore Convention, 321–22; demographics, 3; and expansionism, 155; and Helper, 241; and immigration, 354; and northern colonization, 239; and the secession debate, 385–86, 504, 529

Northern Democratic Party: and the Baltimore Convention, 310–11, 314, 316–19; and the Charleston Convention, 297–99, 304, 528; and the Committee of Thirteen, 470; concessions to the South, 95; and *Dred Scott v. Sandford,* 109–10, 114–15, 118; and elections, 99–100, 104, 143, 275–78, 281–85, 330; and federal fort seizures, 478; and the Freeport Doctrine, 274–75; and the Lecompton Convention, 137–39, 141; and nativism, 86; and republicanism, 17–18; and the secession debate, 400; and the slave trade issue, 176, 182; and southern power, 14; and the Speakership Crisis, 265; and the territorial slavery conflict, 61–62; and Yancey, 286

Northern Episcopal Church, 332

Northern Republican Party, 94, 229

Northwest Ordinance, 12, 135

Nott, Abraham, 41

Nott, Josiah, 35, 41–44, 47, 52, 54, 57

nullification: and Brooks, 81; and causes of the Civil War, 531; and the Charleston Convention, 302; economic causes, 553n. 10; and Houston, 449; and Jackson, 352; and the secession debate, 383, 386, 389; and the slave trade issue, 183–84; and South Carolina, 360, 362–63; and southern extremism, xvii; and state's rights, 349; and Stephens, 435; and taxes, 366

Oberlin College, 207, 223

Oglethorpe Light Infantry, 409

Ohio, 97, 105, 435

Oklahoma, 332

Old Testament, 29, 45

O'Neall, John Belton, 418

Oppositionists, 323–24, 499, 502

Oregon, 297, 338

orphans, 44–45, 259–60, 432

Orr, James L.: and the African slave trade, 179–80; and the Baltimore Convention, 308; and the Charleston Convention, 294–96, 306; and class divisions, 362; and egalitarian republicanism, 564n. 8, 568n. 4; and federal fort seizures, 478; and Hammond, 379; and Magrath, 399; and party corruption, 368; and Rhett, 364; and the Richmond Convention, 315–16; and the secession debate, 377, 420, 492

Ostend Manifesto, 147

O'Sullivan, John, 145–47

Palmer, Benjamin, 150, 460–61, 528

Panic of 1857, 238

paramilitary groups, 360–61, 569n. 14. *See also* lynch law; mob violence

Park, George, 76, 79

Parker, Theodore, 208

Parkville Luminary, 76

paternalism: and the African slave trade, 177; and Aldrich, 457; and Christianity, 44–47, 52–57, 173, 224, 226–27; and class divisions, 16; and colorblind slavery, 28–29; and "Cuffee" term, 10; English model, 353; and geographic tensions, 57–58; and Hammond, 31–32; and legal restrictions on slave owners, 48–50; and Memminger, 259–60; and Palmer, 461; and proslavery writing, 27; and reenslavement efforts, 187–89, 191, 193–94; and republicanism, 214; and Separate State secession, 381; and the slave trade issue, 177, 179; slavery vs. capitalism, 99; and South Carolina, 353–55, 359; and the Speakership Crisis, 255–56; and Stephens, 432; and Thornwell, 259–60; and vigilante violence, 335

patriarchy: and colorblind slavery, 28–29, 36; and the Mammy myth, 225; and nativism, 91; and the secession debate, 390; and the slave trade issue, 177; and South Carolina, 353–54, 361; and the Speakership Crisis, 256

patronage: and Bell, 450–51; and Blair, 330, 340; and Clay, 229, 232; and Cobb, 439–40; and compromise efforts, 471; and elections, 100, 102–3, 340–41; and Fitzhugh, 36; and Lincoln, 454–55, 464, 517, 520; and Pickens, 420; and the secession debate, 394, 398; and secessionism, 372–73; and South Carolina, 456; and Southern Republicans, 369; and the Speakership Crisis, 266–67; and Townsend, 367–68; and Virginia secession, 512
Paulding, Hiram, 160, 161
Paulding Eastern Clarion, 454–55, 457
Peake, Harry T., 188
Pearce, James, 196–97
Pennington, William, 265, 290, 323–24
Pennsylvania, *192*; agriculture, 11, 13; and Central Confederacy plans, 500; and elections, 97, 101, 105, 143; and immigrant labor, 173; and nativism, 90
Pensacola, Florida, *518*
Pensacola Harbor, 484
Perry, Benjamin F., 280, 306–7, 418, 421
Perry, Madison S., 386, 483–84
Personal Liberty Laws: and compromise efforts, 475, 495; and state's rights, 349; and Stephens, 435–36, 439, 443
Petigru, James L., 399, 419
Pettigrew, J. J., 177, 179, 182
Pettigrew, James F., 401
Pettus, John: and compromise efforts, 469; and federal fort seizures, 483, 485; and political invasion of the South, 264; and the secession debate, 386–87, 424, 446, 453–54, 490; and Virginia secession, 515
Pezuela, Juan M. de la, 165
Phillip, Wendell, 217
Phillips, John, 50
Phillips, William, 76, 85
Pickens, Francis, 129, 260–61, 294–95, 420, 521, 524
Pierce, Franklin, 100, 147, 159, 163, 166–67, 399–400
Pike, Albert, 249
Platte County Rifles, 79
Platte County Self-Defensive Association, 67–68, 70, 74, 76
Point Coupee Echo, 182
Polk, James K., 147, 296
Polk, Tristam, 76
polygamy, 290
polygenesis, 42–43, 44
Popular Sovereignty: advocates of, 271; and the Charleston Convention, 287, 296, 298–300, 302, 307; and Douglas, 143; and elections, 278; and the Freeport Doctrine, 272–73, 275; and the Kansas conflict, 130–33; and the Lecompton Convention, 135, 138; and the Missouri Compromise, 62; and Yancey, 284
population, 22, 174, 239–40. *See also* demographics

populism, 354
Porter, William Dennison, 389, 391, 415–16, 422
postmodern capitalism, 52
post-nati laws, 227–30
Pottawatomie Massacre, 79, 208, 211
poverty, 178, 187–88
Powell, Lazarus, 470, 474
Presbyterian Church, 4, 49
presidential powers, 434–35. *See also* patronage
Preston, William B., 524
Prigg v. Pennsylvania, 299
Pringle, Edward, 54–56, 371
propaganda, 391–94, 441, 451
Protestantism, 543n. 35
Pryor, Roger, 183, 206, 251, 290
Pugh, George, 302, 303
Pugh, James L., 252, 467
Puritanism, 207

quadroons, 149–50
Quakers, 223
Quitman, John: and expansionism, 148, 152, 160–62, 167; and the secession debate, 384–86

racism and racial division: and African colonization, 53; and causes of the Civil War, 534; and the Charleston Convention, 299; and class divisions, 569n. 14; and colonization plans, 103; and colorblind slavery, 28–29, 36; and expansionism, 165; and Fee, 231; and filibustering, 154; and Hammond, 30; and Hughes, 52; and justifications for slavery, 30; and Mississippi separatism, 453; and nativism, 89–93; in the North, 102, 583–84n. 4; and paternalism, 52–57; and proslavery ideology, xvi, 25–26, 39–44, 541–42n. 1; and reenslavement efforts, 186, 190; and republicanism, 12; and the territorial slavery conflict, 72, 125–26; and Townsend, 360; and Underwood, 239; and vigilante violence, 335; and Virginia secession, 511; and wage pressures, 178; and Yancey, 39–40
Radical Republicans, 102
railroads, *407*; and New Orleans, 151–52, 553n. 10; and the secession debate, 406–10, 412–14, 420, 423–26, 532, 572n. 25, 574n. 66
Randolph, George, 507–13, *510, 524,* 527
Randolph, Thomas Jefferson, 508
Randolph, Thomas Mann, 508
rape. *See* sexual exploitation
ratifying conventions, 130–33
Ravenel, Henry, 382, 414, 424
Reagan, John, 253, 456
Reconstruction, 151
Red River, 332
reenslavement, 185–94, 198–201
regulation of slavery, 51–57, 111–12

religion: and anti-Catholicism, 86, 88; and antislavery, 29–30, 207, 223–24, 230, 332, 541–42n. 1, 543n. 35; colporteurs, 231; and disunionism, 376; evangelicals, 44, 223, 226–27, 460–62; and ideology, 25–26; and nativism, 92; and paternalism, 45–47, 461; and polygenesis, 42–43; and regulation of slavery, 54, 56–57; religious invasion of the South, 222–35; revivalism, 47; and secessionism, 460–62; and support for slavery, 226–27

removal of blacks. *See also* colonization of blacks: Blair on, 328; and filibustering, 154; and gradual emancipation, 112–13, 507–8; and Houston, 448; and Jefferson, 25; and reenslavement efforts, 186, 191, 196–97; Starr on, 69

Republican Party. *See also* Northern Republican Party; Southern Republican Party: Anderson on, 263; and Blair, 299; and Botts, 324–25, 327; and Clark, 247; and Clay, 229–30, 235; Douglas on, 330; and *Dred Scott v. Sandford,* 118; and elections, 97, 100, 102, 205; and Helper, 244; and Lovejoy, 288–89; and presidential patronage, 232; Pryor on, 206; threats to the South, xvi; and Toombs, 438; and the Upper South, 503

republicanism, xv–xvi, 12, 14, 18, 28. *See also* aristocratic republicanism; egalitarianism republicanism

revivalism, 47

Revolutionary War, 422

Rhett, Edmund, 402

Rhett, Robert Barnwell, Jr.: and convention proposals, 415; on Hammond, 382; and the Richmond Convention, 315–17; and the secession debate, 388, 394, 401–3, 418

Rhett, Robert Barnwell, Sr., *393*; and the African slave trade, 179–80, 183; and the Baltimore Convention, 320–21; and the Charleston Convention, 295, 305–8; and compromise efforts, 472; and convention proposals, 415; declining power of, 364; and the 1860 Association, 572n. 24; and expansionism, 146, 155; and federal fort seizures, 485; and fire-eaters, 1; and Gourdin, 479; and Lincoln's election, 338; and Magrath, 399; and nullification, 360; and the secession debate, 382–83, 389, 394, 401–2, 404, 406, 418–22, 424, 445, 454, 491, 493–94; on tariffs, 366

rice, 20, 21, 353, 363, 366

Richardson, George, 513

Richardson, John M., 401

Richmond Convention, 314–17, 321–22, 364

Richmond Enquirer, 124, 132, 154, 165

Richmond South, 123–24, 186

Richmond Whig, 183

Rives, William C., 500, 527

Rives, William Cabell, Jr., 220

Robbins, William H., 45

Roberts, Oran, 450–51, 461

Rogers, John Almanza Rowley, 233

Roosevelt, Franklin D., 52

Rowan County, North Carolina, 241

Ruffin, Edmund, *523*; and federal fort seizures, 521–22; Hammond's correspondence to, 290; and John Brown's Raid, 219–20; and the Kansas controversy, 124; and political invasion of the South, 267; and the secession debate, 377; on Wise, 91; and Yancey, 279–80

runaway slaves. *See also* fugitive slave laws: and causes of the Civil War, 533; economic impact, 14, 22; and the Freeport Doctrine, 273; frequency of, 10; and Hammond, 32; and Lovejoy, 289; and manumission, 98–99; political impact of, 58; and reenslavement efforts, 194–95; and the Speakership Crisis, 254; and the territorial slavery conflict, 63–69

Russell, Charles, 365

Rust, Albert, 251

Rust County Vigilance Committee, 333

Ryback, James, 459

San Domingo, 165, 456

San Jacinto, battle of, 448

Sanborn, Franklin, 208

Santa Anna, Antonio López de, 448

Santa Rose Island, 484

Savannah, Georgia, 214, 406–12, 477, 479–83

Savannah Daily Republican, 88, 305, 334

Savannah River, 407, 480

Sawyer, George, 33, 43

Scott, Dred, *120*

Scott, Harriet, 113, *120*

Scott, Robert, 524–26

Sea Island cotton, 11, 13, 20–21, 293, 353, 361, 363, 390

Seabrook, Whitemarsh, 384, 385

Secession Ordinance, 422

secret secession plots, 385, 445–46, 454, 572n. 19

Seddon, James, 263

segregation, 68, 231

semislavery, 193

Semmes, T. J., 273

Senate Committee on the Territories, 273

Separate State Secessionists: and Alabama, 492–95; and compromise efforts, 463–66; and convention efforts, 376–77; and the Democratic National Convention, 292–93; and Georgia, 430, 437–38, 443–44, 495–96; and Hammond's suppressed letter, 416; and Memminger, 260–61; and Mississippi, 446, 491; and secret secession plots, 385; social pressure on, 459; and South Carolina, 364; and the Speakership Crisis, 258; and Stephens, 429; tactics, 320–21, 381–83, 387–88, 390, 396, 402–4, 424, 445, 496–97, 576n. 2; and Texas, 449

Seward, William H., 206, 220, 299, 329
sexual exploitation: and abolitionism, 3–4;
    abolitionist claims of, 99, 102; and causes of
    the Civil War, 531; and Hammond, 27–32,
    378–79, 417; John Brown on, 219; and the
    territorial slavery conflict, 67
Shenandoah River, 237
Sherman, John, 247, 251–52, 258, 262, 265–
    66, 383
Sherman, William Tecumseh, 247
Simms, B. B., 182
Simms, William Gilmore, 355, 421
Simons, James, 422
single houses, 356–59, *358*
Singletary, Otho R., 475
Slaughter, James S., 280
slave codes, 273–74
slave rebellion. *See also* John Brown's Raid:
    Denmark Vesey's Conspiracy, 256; fear of,
    369–71, 569–70n. 33; Marshall on, 374; Nat
    Turner's Rebellion, 10, 89, 507–9
slave trade. *See* African slave trade
Slavery in the Southern States (Pringle), 54–55
Slemmer, Adam Jacoby, 484, 488
Slidell, John, 98, 107, 166, 182, 313
Sloan, John T., 422
smallpox, 257, 421
Smith, Gerrit, 208
Smith, J. Henley, 330, 439
Smith, William A., 33, 53, 265
Smithson, George, 422
Smyth, Thomas, 54
Sneed, James R., 305
social control: and causes of the Civil War,
    532–33; and the Charleston Convention, 306;
    and loyalty politics, 415, 444; and lynching,
    24; and the secession debate, 415, 418, 424;
    Thornwell on, 420
socialism, 37
*Sociology for the South, or the Failure of Free
    Society* (Fitzhugh), 36, 38–39
Somerset County, Maryland, 192, *192,* 198
Soulé, Pierre, 166
The South Alone Should Govern the South
    (Townsend), 372, 394
South Carolina: and the African slave trade,
    168–74, 179–80, 183–84; agriculture, 11, 13,
    19–21, 353, 361; antiegalitarianism, 577n.
    26; architecture, 356–60; aristocratic
    republicanism, 564n. 8; and the Baltimore
    Convention, 313–16; and the Brooks-Sumner
    affair, 61, 81–82; and the Charleston
    Convention, 278–86, 292, 303, 306–7; and
    Christian paternalism, 45; Civil War losses,
    375; critics of, 500; and delayed secession,
    467; demographics, 23–24; economics, 7, 35–
    39; egalitarian republicanism, 568n. 4; and
    elections, 269, 341, 418–19; emigration
    from, 363, 367; and expansionism, 155–59,
    167; extremism in, xvii; and fire-eaters, 1–2;

and legal restrictions on slave owners, 49–50;
    legislature, 354, 395–96, 416–18; and
    manumission, 189; and Mississippi secession,
    453; motivations for secession, 352–56, 360–
    62; and the Nullification Controversy, 81;
    reaction to Lincoln's election, 436; and
    regulation of slavery, 53–54; and the
    secession debate, 376–94, 446–47, 489–90,
    492, 496–97, 527; selection of electors, 395;
    and southern convention efforts, 264; state
    constitution, 403; state convention, 421; and
    state's rights, 346; and territorial slavery,
    537–38n. 4; Unionist Party, 260; and
    vigilante violence, 335; and Yancey, 278–79
South Carolina College, 45, 362
South Carolina Episcopalian Convention, 50
South Carolina House of Representatives,
    354
South Carolina Presbyterian Synod, 49
Southern Commercial Convention, 183
Southern Confederacy Senate, 3
Southern Democratic Party: and the Baltimore
    Convention, 310, 312–13, 318–19; and the
    Charleston Convention, 296, 301, 528; and
    the Democratic National Convention, 295;
    and *Dred Scott v. Sandford,* 109–10, 113–15,
    117–18; and elections, 100, 278, 280, 331,
    339–40; and free speech, 323–26; and the
    Freeport Doctrine, 272–75; and John Clark,
    247; and the Lecompton Convention, 138,
    141; and Lovejoy, 290; and nativism, 87;
    political power, 14; and Popular Sovereignty,
    130; and the secession debate, 405; and the
    slave trade issue, 176; and the Speakership
    Crisis, 257, 265; and state's rights, 349; and
    the territorial slavery conflict, 62, 85, 125,
    129; and Yancey, 283
Southern Institutes (Sawyer), 33
Southern Literary Messenger, 515
Southern Manifesto, 469–70
Southern Presbyterian Review, 420, 460
Southern Quarterly Review, 111
Southern Republican Party: and
    antiegalitarianism, 577n. 29; and Atchison,
    78; Bell on, 450–51; and Blair, 328; and the
    Border South, 530; and causes of the Civil
    War, 533; and the Charleston Convention,
    308; and Clark, 250; and Clay, 229–30; and
    the Committee of Thirteen, 471; and
    elections, 104, 106, 331, 336–37, 340; and
    ex-Whigs, 323; and fears of slave rebellion,
    369–71; and free speech, 327; and Helper,
    244–45, 561n. 16; and the Kansas crisis, 144;
    and Keitt, 267; and the Lecompton
    Convention, 142; and Lincoln, xvii, 520; and
    presidential patronage, 103, 253, 375, 394,
    512; and reenslavement efforts, 198; and the
    secession debate, 381, 389, 395, 398, 400,
    406, 424–25, 439–40; and Sherman, 252;
    and the Speakership Crisis, 254–57, 266; and

state's rights, 348; threat to the South, 290, 455, 458–59

sovereignty, 62, 130–33, 136–37, 159, 347. *See also* Popular Sovereignty; state's rights

Spain, xvii, 166

Sparks, Susan, 370, 371

Speakership Crisis, 247–62, 265–68, 384

Spontaneous Southern Rights Assembly, 516, 525

Spratt, Leonidas W.: and the African slave trade, 168–75, 178–80, 184, 503–4; and political invasion of the South, 247–48; and reenslavement efforts, 188, 190; and the secession debate, 419

Squire, E. G., 42

St. Augustine Arsenal, 484

St. Louis City, 65, 79, 124

St. Louis Democrat, 77, 327

Star of the West (resupply ship), 486–88, 489–92, 495–97, 502, 517, 529, 533

Starke, Peter, 264, 385–87, 576n. 2

Starr, Frederick, 68–69, 71, 76, 79

Starr, James Harper, 334–35

state's rights: and Alabama secession, 493; and causes of the Civil War, 531, 584–85n. 17; and *Dred Scott v. Sandford,* 113–15; and expansionism, 159; and jurisdiction over slavery, 112; and the Kansas conflict, 130–33; and the Lecompton Convention, 136–37; and military draft, 528; and the secession debate, 345–51, 384–86, 425–26, 502; State's Rights Whigs, 125; term, 568n. 7

Stearns, George, 208

Stephens, Alexander, *434*; and the African slave trade, 178; background, 431–33; and causes of the Civil War, 531–32; and the Charleston Convention, 305; and compromise efforts, 465, 472, 474–75; as Confederate vice president, 503; and elections, 105; and the English Bill, 142; and expansionism, 147; and the Georgia secession debate, 433–37, 440–44; and Houston, 449; and the Kansas controversy, 124; and political invasion of the South, 254, 266; on presidential patronage, 440; and the secession debate, 430–31, 495, 497; and state's rights, 346; and white supremacy, 39–44

Stephens, Linton, 432–33, 441

Stevens, Thad, 253

Story, Joseph, 399

Stowe, Harriet Beecher, 49, 224, 232–35, 371

Stringfellow, Benjamin Franklin, 67–69, 70, 75

Stringfellow, Thornton, 56–57

sugar, 11, 21, 153, 157, 176

Sullivan's Island, 477

Sumner, Charles, *83*; absence from Congress, 546n. 35; Brooks' attack on, 61, 79–84, *83*, 95, 139, 173, 205, 254–55, 364–65, 546–47n. 36; and elections, 107; and

expansionism, 158; Lovejoy contrasted with, 288; and southern propaganda, 366

Sumter, Francis, 157

Syracuse, New York, 6

Tabor, William Robinson, 400

Tallulas (Jackson), 411–12

Taney, Roger B., *120*; and *Dred Scott v. Sandford,* 109–11, 113, 116–17, 119, 549–50n. 14; and the Kansas controversy, 143; manumission of slaves, 549n. 8

tariffs and taxes: and causes of the Civil War, 531; and class divisions, 512, 526; Morrill Tariff, 503; and nullification, 81, 352, 553n. 10; and South Carolina, 366; and state's rights, 349; as threat to slavery, 89–90, 584–85n. 17; and Virginia, 506, 512

Tayloe, William H., 220

Tennent, William, Jr., 389, 391

Tennessee: agriculture, 13; demographics, 3; and expansionism, 155; and filibustering, 152, 157; free blacks in, 499; and Kansas agriculture, 123; and nativism, 89; and northern colonization, 239–40; and reenslavement efforts, 200; and the secession debate, 504, 529–30; and the white belt, 16

territorial slavery. *See* Kansas-Nebraska Act; Missouri Compromise

Texas: abolitionism in, 175; agriculture, 13, 20, 124; annexation, 15, 17, 21, 128, 177, 247, 313, 349, 448, 533, 537–38n. 4; and anti-immigrant sentiment, 88; and British antislavery, xvii; and the Charleston Convention, 303; climate, 129; demographics, 361; and elections, 337; and expansionism, 147–48, 167; and filibustering, 153; and free labor immigration, 206; and the fugitive slave issue, 436; and pioneers, 38; Revolution, 448; and the secession debate, 345, 385, 447–52, 459–60, 496–97; and South Carolina extremism, 366; and the Southern Manifesto, 470; state constitution, 449, 451–52; and the territorial slavery conflict, 75; Texas Fire Scare (1860), 331–33, 337, 341, 370, 374

Thayer, Eli, 72, 126, 238–40

Thirteenth Amendment, 300

Thirteenth Amendment (proposed), 531

Thompson, Jacob, 106, 134, 196, 467, 490–91

Thompson, Kate, 106–7

Thoreau, Henry David, 217

Thornwell, James Henley: and the African slave trade, 168–69; background, 432; on Christian morality, 35; and Fee, 223–24, 226–27; and hierarchical social structure, 44–47; and legal restrictions on slaveholders, 49; and paternalism, 259–60; and proslavery, 33, 57; and the religious debate on slavery, 460; and the secession debate, 376, 405, 420

Thrasher, John S., 165

three-fifths clause, 14

tobacco, 11, 19–21, 157
Todd, John, 483
Toombs, Robert, *473*; and the Brooks-Sumner
    affair, 82; and the Charleston Convention,
    305; and compromise efforts, 470, 472–75;
    and delayed secession plan, 467; and
    elections, 105; and Georgia secession, 495;
    and political invasion of the South, 254, 266–
    67; Porter on, 416; resignation rumors, 414,
    416; and the secession debate, 430–31, 437;
    and southern nationalism, 529; on tariffs,
    438; and territorial slavery, 284
Topeka, Kansas, 133
Totten, Joseph, 476
Totten coastal defense system, 476–79, 483–84
Townsend, John, *392*; and fear of slave violence,
    371; and the Kansas controversy, 128; and
    loyalty politics, 415; pamphlets published,
    451, 461; and paternalism, 372; and the
    secession debate, 389–94, 421; on Sumner,
    366; on threats to slavery, 367–69; on white
    supremacy, 360
Transcendentalism, 208
treason, 384, 424, 450, 485
Treatise on Sociology (Hughes), 51
Trenholm, George, 402–3
Trescot, William Henry: and the African slave
    trade, 171; and the Charleston Convention,
    295; and compromise efforts, 467, 469; and
    federal fort seizures, 487; and paternalism,
    372; and territorial slavery, 274; on threats to
    slavery, 366
Tucker, Beverly, 91
Tucker, John Randolph, 146
Turner, Nat, 89, 191, 331, 507–9
two-party system, 96, 278–79, 294, 331
two-thirds rules, 320
Tyler, John, 513, 526
Tyler, John, Jr., 369
Tyler, Robert, 98
Tyler County, Texas, 333
Types of Mankind (Nott), 42

Uncle Tom's Cabin (Stowe), 4, 49, 224
underground railroad, 236, 369, 438, 455, 512
Underwood, John C.: background, 236–40; and
    Helper, 240–45; Memminger contrasted with,
    262; and political invasion of the South, 248,
    266; and the Republican nominating
    convention, 327, 330
Unionists, 96, 260, 501, 506
The Unity of the Human Race (Bachman), 44
Upshur, Abel P., 17, 91, 247–48
U.S. Congress: and the Alabama Platform, 279;
    and colonization of blacks, 360; and
    compromise efforts, 495; and *Dred Scott v.
    Sandford*, 117, 119–21; and elections, 103–4;
    and European immigration, 172; and fugitive
    slaves, 443; and the gag rule debates, 17; and
    the Lecompton Convention, 138–39; and

minority power, 17; and *Prigg v.
    Pennsylvania*, 299; and the territorial slavery
    conflict, 65, 73
U.S. Constitution: and amendments, 15, 514;
    assaults on slavery, 222; and the Confederate
    Constitution, 503; and *Dred Scott v.
    Sandford*, 121; and due process, 121; and
    elections, 312, 435; and fugitive slaves, 443;
    and gradual emancipation, 113; and
    jurisdictional issues, 205; Magrath on, 399;
    and nonintervention, 208; and ratifying
    conventions, 130–33; and the secession
    debate, 405; and the Speakership Crisis, 253;
    and state's rights, 346–47; three-fifths clause,
    14
U.S. District Court (Charleston), 399
U.S. House of Representatives: and elections,
    312; and the English Bill, 142; and European
    immigration, 172; and John Clark, 247–50;
    and the Lecompton Convention, 138, 140–
    42; and Lovejoy, 528; and nativism, 87; and
    Orr, 295; and the secession debate, 401, 417;
    Speakership Crisis, 250–54, 257–61, 265–66;
    and Stephens, 434–35; and the territorial
    slavery conflict, 65; and the three-fifths
    clause, 14; Unionists in, 530; violence in,
    257–61
U.S. Senate: and the Brooks-Sumner affair, 61,
    79–84, *83*, *95*, 139, 173, 364–65; and
    elections, 107, 205; and the English Bill, 142;
    and the Kansas conflict, 73–74, 124;
    resignations from, 466; and the secession
    debate, 401, 417; and Stephens, 434–35; and
    the territorial slavery conflict, 65, 73; and
    Texas separatism, 451; and Toombs, 529
U.S. Supreme Court: and *Ableman v. Booth*,
    435–36; and *Dred Scott v. Sandford*, 109–22,
    141, 371, 549–50n. 14, 550n. 15; and the
    Freeport Doctrine, 272; southern control of,
    15; and Stephens, 435
USS *Brooklyn*, 488
USS *Dolphin*, 183
USS *Macedonian*, 488
USS *Sabine*, 488
USS *St. Louis*, 488

Valley of Virginia, 505
Van Buren, Martin, 99
Vanderbilt, Cornelius, 161
Vesey, Denmark, 256
Vicksburg Weekly Sun, 455, 456
vigilantes, 67, 70–71, 331–36, 424, 458–59.
    See also lynch law; mob violence
Vineyard, John, 68–69
Virginia: and African colonization, 53;
    agriculture, 11, 13; antislavery in, 25; and the
    Baltimore Convention, 320–22; climate, 129;
    and compromise efforts, 470; demographics,
    3; and the economics of slavery, 35; and
    emigration to Kansas, 127; and expansionism,

155; and filibustering, 157; free blacks in, 499; and the House Speakership, 266; and immigration, 354; and Kansas agriculture, 123; and Lincoln presidency, 337; and Memminger, 261–64; and nativism, 89; and northern colonization, 239–40; and reenslavement efforts, 191, 193; and the secession debate, 385–86, 389–90, 467, 504–16, 524–25; and the Speakership Crisis, 262; state constitution, 506; threats to slavery in, 175, 281, 438; and vigilante violence, 334; and the white belt, 16
Virginia Valley, 209
voting, 35, 40, 170, 293–94, 353–54

Walker, Leroy Pope, 302–3, 404
Walker, Robert J.: and elections, 98, 106, 133–34; and expansionism, 153, 367; and the isothermal theory of slavery, 128–29; and the Kansas controversy, 130–32, 142–44; and the Lecompton Convention, 134–36; and Texas annexation, 21
Walker, William, 148, 152, 160–62, 166–67, 177, 273
Wanderer (slave ship), 183–84, 200, 480
War of 1812, 187, 448, 476
Wardlaw, David L., 418
Warley, F. F., 367
Washburne, Elihu, 140
Washington, George, 19, 260
Washington, Lewis, 211–12
Washington D.C., 17
Washington Peace Conference, 513
Wayne, James, 110–13, 116–17
weather and climate: Charleston, South Carolina, 291–92, 421–22; isothermal theory of slavery, 40, 128–29, 143–44, 154, 179, 242, 461; and southern agriculture, 355–56
Webster, Daniel, 346
Weed, Thurlow, 325
Wellsburg Herald, 327
West Indies, 456
West Virginia, 526, 529–30
western expansionism, 248, 363–64
Wheeler, Royall T., 452
Wheeling Intelligencer, 327
Whigs: and Berrien, 409; and Botts, 324; collapse of, 84–86; and Democratic Party split, 323; and the Eufalia Regency, 125; and Henry Clay, 229; and immigration issues, 86–95, 205; and the Kansas Nebraska Act, 62, 73–74; and Lincoln, 330, 441; and loyalty politics, 85–86; and party corruption, 368; and proslavery positions, 17, 142, 265; regional divisions, 95–96, 502–3; and the Republican Party, 100, 102; and Stephens,

436, 441; and the territorial slavery conflict, 139; and Wise, 525
white belts: in Arkansas, 504; defined, 16; in the Middle South, 530; and paternalism, 57–58; in South Carolina, 361; and Southern Republicans, 369; and the territorial slavery conflict, 64, 66; in Texas, 451; in the Upper South, 529; in Virginia, 512
white supremacy. *See* racism and racial division
Whitney, Eli, 13, 486
Wilkes, Warren D., 127
Willey, Waitman T., 512
Wilmington Delaware Republican, 327
Wilmington Herald, 500
Wilmot, David, 471
Wilmot Proviso, 147, 471
Wilson, Henry, 92–94
Wilson, James C., 455
Wimer, John, 78
Winston, John, 286–87
Wisconsin, 113
Wisconsin Supreme Court, 435
Wise, Henry A., *218;* background, 90–93; and compromise efforts, 474; and demographic shifts, 240; and elections, 101, 105; and John Brown's Raid, 213, 217–20, 236, 246; and the Kansas controversy, 132; and the Lecompton controversy, 273; and political invasion of the South, 262–63, 267; and reenslavement efforts, 193; and Underwood, 244; and Virginia secession, 512–13, 525–27
Withers, T. J., 373
Woolworth, C. C., 143–44
Worcester County, Maryland, 192, *192,* 198
Worth, Daniel, 244
Wyrick, Antney, 333

Yancey, Benjamin, 278–87, 307–8
Yancey, William Lowndes, 5; and the African slave trade, 168, 176, 179, 183; and Alabama secession, 493–94; and Atchison, 77; background, 1–6; and the Baltimore Convention, 311–14, 316–21; and Botts, 325; and the Brooks-Sumner affair, 84; and causes of the Civil War, 532; and the Charleston Convention, 296–97, 301–2, 306; critics of, 7; and elections, 269, 271–87; and the Freeport Doctrine, 278; and Lincoln, 336–40; and reenslavement efforts, 197–98; and the secession debate, 386, 491–92, 497; and southern nationalism, 528; and territorial slavery, 278–85; and Underwood, 237; and Virginia secession, 514; and white supremacy, 39–40
Yeardon, Richard, 404–5
yellow fever, 41–42, 149